Time Out

Florence & Tuscany

Penguin Books

PENGUIN BOOKS

Published by the Penguin Group
Penguin Books Ltd, 27 Wrights Lane, London W8 5TZ, England
Penguin Books USA Inc., 375 Hudson Street, New York, New York 10014, USA
Penguin Books Australia Ltd, Ringwood, Victoria, Australia
Penguin Books Canada Ltd, 10 Alcorn Avenue, Toronto, Ontario, Canada M4V 3B2
Penguin Books (NZ) Ltd, 182-190 Wairau Road, Auckland 10, New Zealand

Penguin Books Ltd, Registered Offices: Harmondsworth, Middlesex, England

First published 1997
10 9 8 7 6 5 4 3 2 1

Copyright © Time Out Group Ltd., 1997
All rights reserved

Colour reprographics by Precise Litho, 34–35 Great Sutton Street, London EC1
Mono reprographics, printed and bound by William Clowes Ltd, Beccles, Suffolk NR34 9QE

Edited and designed by

Time Out Magazine Limited
Universal House
251 Tottenham Court Road
London W1P OAB
Tel + 44 (0)171 813 3000
Fax+ 44 (0)171 813 6001
Email net@timeout.co.uk
http://www.timeout.co.uk

Editorial

Managing Editor Peter Fiennes
Editor Ros Belford
Deputy Editor Jonathan Cox
Consultant Editor Nicky Swallow
Researchers Paola Cimmino, Ben McAlister
Indexer Jackie Brind

Design

Art Director Warren Beeby
Associate Art Director John Oakey
Art Editor Paul Tansley
Designer Mandy Martin
Design Assistant Wayne Davies
Picture Editor Catherine Hardcastle
Picture Researcher Michaela Freeman

Advertising

Group Advertisement Director Lesley Gill
Sales Director Mark Phillips
Advertisment Sales (Florence) Nancy Civetta

Administration

Publisher Tony Elliott
Managing Director Mike Hardwick
Financial Director Kevin Ellis
Marketing Director Gillian Auld
Production Manager Mark Lamond
Accountant Catherine Bowen

Features in this guide were written and researched by:

Introduction Matthew Spender. **History** Jonathan Cox, Matthew Spender. **Florence & Tuscany Today** Matthew Spender. **By Season** Nicky Swallow. **The Tuscans** William Ward. **Expats & Eccentrics** Lee Marshall. **Tuscan Wines** Gillian Arthur. **Food in Tuscany** Kate Singleton. **Essential Information** Nicky Swallow. **Getting Around** Nicky Swallow. **Accommodation** Nicky Swallow. **Florence by Area** Ros Belford. **Museums & Galleries** Ros Belford. **Restaurants** Ros Belford, Nicky Swallow. **Cafés & Bars** Danielle Caplan, Crimson Boner, April Rinne, Alessio Olivieri. **Shopping** Ros Belford, Nicky Swallow, April Rinne. **Services** Nicky Swallow. **Dance & Theatre** Nicky Swallow. **Film** Elena Brizio, Lee Marshall, Alexandra Solomon. **Music: Classical & Opera** Nicky Swallow. **Music: Rock, Roots & Jazz** Crimson Boner, Danielle Caplan. **Nightlife** Crimson Boner, Danielle Caplan, Alessio Olivieri. **Sport** April Rinne, Paul Blanchard. **Business** April Rinne, Paul Blanchard. **Children** Elena Brizzio. **Gay** Davide di Cosimo. **Media** Elena Brizio. **Students** Claudia Clemente. **Women** Alexandra Solomon. **Introduction to Tuscany** Ros Belford. **Loving it, Hating it** Jonathan Cox. **A Tuscan Restaurant Tour** Ros Belford. **Specialist Holidays** Gillian Arthur, Ben McAlister. **Around Florence & Pisa** Kate Singleton. **Pisa** Claudia Clemente. **Chianti & Siena Province** Lee Marshall. **Siena** Kate Singleton, Cosima Spender. **Massa Carrara & Lucca Provinces** Ros Belford, Lee Marshall. **Lucca** Jonathan Cox. **Arezzo Province** Kate Singleton. **Arezzo** Kate Singleton. **Livorno, Grosseto & the Coast** Lee Marshall.

The Editor would like to thank the following:

Flaminia Allvin, Alberto Bongi, Charles Carey, Corney and Barrow, Sam Cole, Selena Chalk, Giuseppe Grappolini, Holiday Autos, Luca Moggi, and Nicky Swallow for contributions way beyond the call of duty.

Photography by **Mark Read** except for: pages 17, 250 **AKG**; 41 **Camera Press**; 11, 31, 234, 236, 238, 242 **Jonathan Cox**; 25, 26, 150, 152, 161 **Lucia di Lammamoa**; 185, 217 **Frank Ormond**. Pictures on pages 132, 111, 192 were supplied by the featured establishments.
Illustrations on pages 18, 19, 20, 21 **Carl Flint**.

Contents

About the Guide

This first edition of the *Time Out Florence & Tuscany Guide* has been written by a team of Tuscany-based writers. It is one in a series of 16 city guides that includes Rome, London, Berlin, New York, Madrid, Paris, Prague, Los Angeles, San Francisco, Budapest, Sydney and Amsterdam. The *Time Out Florence & Tuscany Guide* gives you a complete picture of the region and its major cities, from Etruscan ruins, through medieval and Renaissance architectural and artistic glories to Tuscany's finest restaurants and Florence's hippest bars. You'll also get the lowdown on Tuscan eccentrics and Tuscan day trips, the murky world of olive oil and the murky workings of Machiavelli's mind, medieval warlords and modern-day media moguls, hot springs and hot clubs. Tuscany may have an extraordinary past, but it also has a thriving, and constantly surprising, present.

Checked & correct

As far as possible, all the information in this guide was checked and correct at time of writing. However, Tuscan owners and managers can be highly erratic in their answers to questions about opening times, the dates of exhibitions, admission fees and even their address and telephone number: you have been warned. It's always best to phone before visiting, and even then, the information you receive is not always wholly reliable.

In particular, we have tried to include information on access for the disabled, but once again, it's wise to phone first to check your needs can be met.

Prices

The prices listed throughout the guide should be used as guidelines. Fluctuating exchange rates and inflation can cause prices, in shops and restaurants especially, to change rapidly. If prices or services somewhere vary greatly from those we have quoted, ask if there's a good reason. If not, go elsewhere and then please let us know. We try to give the best and most up-to-date advice, so we always want to hear if you've been overcharged or badly treated.

Credit cards

Throughout the guide, the following abbreviations have been used for credit cards: **AmEx** American Express; **DC** Diners' Club; **EC** Eurocheque card; **JCB** Japanese credit card; **MC** Mastercard/Access; **V** Visa/Barclaycard.

Bold

Within any chapter we may mention people, places or events that are listed elsewhere in the guide. In these cases we have highlighted the person, place or event by printing it in **bold**. This means you can find it in the index and locate its full listing.

Right to reply

It should be stressed that in all cases the information we give is impartial. No organisation or enterprise has been included in this guide because its owner or manager has advertised in our publications. We hope you enjoy the *Time Out Florence & Tuscany Guide*, but if you disagree with any of our reviews, let us know. Your comments on places you have visited are always welcome and will be taken into account when compiling the future editions of the guide. For this purpose, you will find a reader's reply card at the back of the book.

There are on-line versions of most *Time Out* guides, as well as weekly events listings for many international cities at:
http://www.timeout.co.uk

Introduction

Familiarity breeds content.

The stereotypical Tuscan film opening: the cypress on the perfectly formed hill backlit by the setting sun; the half-filled wineglass against the remote vineyard, where tendrils droop in soft focus over fatly burgeoning grapes; the crumbling clay hillside that suddenly pans forward into a detail from a painting, where the erosion of the gesso surface by bad cleaning echoes the worn gullies of the real thing. They are all verifiable, these images. The clichés have become clichés because they are true. The problem is to break through to something more spontaneous and fresh.

Some years ago a neuro-biologist interested in genetic archaeology examined the genes of the inhabitants of a little village south of Siena and found they corresponded remarkably closely to the genes of the Etruscan locals who lived here two thousand years previously. The villagers were amused. "O Etruscan," I once heard one of them call out to a friend across a crowded bar, "won't you offer me a cup of coffee?" Tuscans like to tease one another – though it's considered polite after delivering the blow to say that it was only a joke. (*'Stò scherzando'.*)

So are they friendly, the Tuscans? Do they take strangers to their collective bosom? They do, but the rules have to be observed. Always preface an encounter by saying good morning or good afternoon. It's *'buon giorno'* up to midday, after which it becomes *'buona sera'*, even though the evening hour is still far off. Always apologise for an intrusion. Courtesy is vital, for however long you live in the country, you will always be a guest. Even if you stay, as I have, for 30 years, and the children are born and raised here.

Soon after we first arrived, a peculiar incident took place. A neighbouring farmer, fat and not much liked by his neighbours, decided we were using too much water on our flower-beds every day. He began sabotaging our pump. Every so often we'd find mud in the fuel tank or the carburettor and Dino the mechanic would sigh and say "Piccione!" The farmer's nickname was Pigeon, on account of his intestinal pout. Our house was miles from the village, the spring was ours and there was no question of stealing water. Everyone was very sympathetic and shook their heads. We should be patient, we were told. Mr Pigeon had difficulty with his kidneys and anything to do with the passing of water had become an obsession for him. For some reason this explanation made everything all right. We grinned. They grinned back. The situation was comprehensible in human terms! Being thus solved, we did nothing more about the problem. Eventually, a few pumps later, Mr Pigeon died.

In retrospect it strikes me as odd that we didn't make more of a fuss, but the Tuscan attitude towards strangers simultaneously welcomes them and keeps them at a distance. We were in the right and Mr Pigeon was wrong, there was no doubt about that. But all the same he belonged and we didn't.

From time to time some local politician tries to create in Tuscany the kind of xenophobia which the Lombard League is stirring up in northern Italy. A 'problem of foreigners' is raised. Why should a certain part of Tuscany between Florence and Siena be called 'Chiantishire'? It's our Chianti, they say. Somehow, this kind of demagogy fails to grip. The English population of 'Chiantishire' is tiny and the expression is kept alive by Italian journalists, who love the fantasy of Brits wearing jhodpurs pouring each other sundowners and chatting about the decline of the Raj. In fact there are more German than British residents, and pretty soon the Albanian element – cheap labour for Tuscany's wine- and olive-growers – will outnumber both. Meanwhile, unlike the proposed state of 'Padania', Tuscany once possessed its own national frontiers. Except it was an Austrian Grand Duchy, and nobody wants to revive all that.

In Italy, the intensity of small local feelings gets stronger almost daily. These have always been what the visitor notices most in Tuscany – the difference between, say, Pistoia and Prato, two towns 20 miles apart. As EM Forster put it 80 years ago, "the traveller who has gone to Italy to study the tactile values of Giotto, or the corruption of the Papacy, may return remembering nothing but the blue sky and the men and women who live under it". That's not such a bad thing. Bringing the scale of values back to the simply human.
Matthew Spender.

Florence & Tuscany
in Context

Key Events

59BC Foundation of Florentia by Julius Caesar.
56BC Caesar, Crassus and Pompey form first triumvirate at Lucca.
406AD Stilicho holds Florence against the rampaging Ostrogoths.
541 Florence held during campaigns of Totila and Belisarius.
552 Florence falls to the Goths under Totila.
568 Invasion of the Lombards.
778 Charlemagne defeats last of the Lombard kings.
c800 New walls erected around Florence.

10th-11th centuries

Pisa growing in importance as one of Italy's wealthiest ports; Lucca, seat of the Margraves of Tuscany, is the region's most important city; Florence is still only a small trading city.

978 Badia established in Florence by Willa, widow of the Margrave Uberto.
1027 Canossa family become Margraves but take title Counts of Tuscany.
1076 Matilda, daughter of the Canossa Margrave, becomes Countess of Tuscany.
1078 New defences for Florence constructed.

12th century

Siena booming, but Florence becoming increasingly dominant in Tuscany.

1115 Matilda grants Florence status of independent city; on her death she bequeaths all her lands to the Pope except Florence, Lucca and Siena.
1125 Florence captures Fiesole.
1173-5 More new walls for Florence.

13th century

Growing self-dependence and wealth of Tuscan cities causes increased inter-city conflict; the era of Guelph/Ghibelline rivalry.

1207 Florence's governing council is replaced by the Podestà.
1216 Murder of Buondelmonte dei Buondelmonti on the Ponte Vecchio in Florence ignites the simmering Guelph/Ghibelline conflict.
1248 Ghibellines oust Guelphs from Florence.
1250 Guelphs boot Ghibellines out of Florence.
1252 First gold florin minted.
1260 Siena beats Florence at Montaperti; Guelphs again displaced from Florence.
1261 Invasion of Italy by Charles of Anjou.
1266 Charles of Anjou conquers Naples, and in following year becomes Florence's overlord.
1280s Guelphs back in control of Florence.
1289 Florence defeats Arezzo at Campaldino.
1293 Secondo Populo passes reforms including the Ordinances of Justice which exclude the nobility from government and create the Signoria, drawn from the *arti maggiori* (major guilds).
1296 Foundation stone laid for the new Florence cathedral.

14th century

Early years marked by struggle between virulently anti-imperial 'black' Guelphs and conciliatory 'white' Guelphs; increasing Florentine muscle flexing.

1302 Many 'white' Guelphs, including Dante, exiled from Florence.
1325 Lucchese army, under Castruccio Castracani defeats Florence at Altopascio, and goes on to besiege Florence.
1328 Castruccio Castracani dies, saving Florence.
1329 Florence takes over Pistoia.
1333 Severe floods in Florence.
1339 The Bardi and Peruzzi banks, the biggest in Florence, collapse after English king Edward III defaults on his debts.
1348 Black Death ravages Tuscany.
1351 Florence buys Prato from the Queen of Naples.
1375-8 War of the Eight Saints frees Florence from the influence of the Papacy and causes the Guelphs to join up with the *popolo grasso* (wealthiest merchants) to exclude the guilds from power for four decades.
The Ciompi, the lowest class of woollen workers, rebel successfully against their starvation wages and exclusion from guilds, but their new privileges are shortlived.

15th century

Flowering of the Florentine Renaissance and apogee of Florentine power.

1400 Florence threatened by Gian Galeazzo Visconti of Milan.
1406 Florence captures Pisa.
1411 Florence gains Cortona.
1421 Florence buys Livorno from Genova.
1428 Start of war between Florence and Lucca.
1432 Rout of San Romano – Florence beats Siena in a skirmish immortalized by the artist Uccello.
1433 Cosimo imprisoned and exiled by the Albizzi during unpopular Lucchese war.
1434 Return of Cosimo from exile; overthrow and exile of the Albizzi.
1436 Brunelleschi's dome of Florence cathedral finished.
1437 Florence defeats Milan at Barga.
1439 Church Council moves to Florence and succeeds in bringing a shortlived reconciliation between Eastern and Western churches.
1440 Florentines rout Milanese at Anghiari.
1452 Florence abandons traditional alliance with Venice to join with Milan. Naples and Venice declare war on Milan and Florence.
1453 Fall of Constantinople to the Turks.
1454 Threat of the Turks brings Pope, Venice, Florence and Milan together in Holy League.
1464 Cosimo dies; his son Piero takes over control of Florence.
1466 Piero quashes conspiracy to overthrow the Medici.
1467 Florence, Naples and Milan defeat Venice at Imola.
1469 Piero dies; his son Lorenzo 'il Magnifico' takes over in Florence.
1472 Sack of Volterra – Lorenzo held responsible.
1478 Pazzi conspiracy, with contrivance of Pope, kills Giuliano de' Medici but his brother Lorenzo escapes; conspirators and supporters executed. The plot's failure

leads Papacy and Naples to declare war on Florence.
1479 Lorenzo goes alone to Naples to negotiate peace treaty with King Ferrante.
1492 Death of Lorenzo; his son Piero takes over.
1494 Wars of Italy begin – Charles VIII invades Italy. Inept Piero, son of Lorenzo, surrenders Florence on his own authority and then flees.
Piero Capponi leads the government, but this is era of the friar Savonarola's greatest influence.
He persuades Charles VIII to leave Florence, but meanwhile Pisa successfully revolts, leading to a long war with Florence.
Charles VIII dallies in Naples; meanwhile Pope Alexander VI, forms a Holy League, including the Empire and Spain, against the French.
1495 French beat the Holy League at Fornovo on the banks of the Taro, but then withdraw from Italy.
1497 'Bonfire of the Vanities' in Florence.
Savonarola's criticisms of clerical corruption alienate the Pope, who raises a league against Florence.
1498 Florentines burn Savonarola.

16th century

Florence slowly declines, economically and culturally; Pisa subjugated; Siena crushed.

1502 Piero Soderini elected *gonfaloniere* for life; advised by Macchiavelli.
1509 Pope Julius II forms the League of Cambrai with the Empire, Spain and France to pick off the richest bits of the Venetian territories; League beats Venice at Agnadello. On defeat of Venetians allies, Pisa finally sues Florence for peace.
1512 Bloody battle of Ronco between Papacy/Spain and France.
Papal and Spanish armies sack Prato and force Florentines to kick out Soderini and allow the return of the Medici.
Giuliano de' Medici abolishes Grand Council and imposes his own rule, backed by soldiers.
1513 Giovanni de' Medici elected as Pope Leo X.
1516 Giuliano dies; his nephew the unpopular Lorenzo, Duke of Urbino, takes over, but real boss is the Medici Pope.
1519 Lorenzo dies; in name, Giulio, bastard son of Lorenzo il Magnifico's murdered brother Giuliano, is in charge, but Leo X continues to pull Florence's strings from Rome.
Death of Emporer Maximilian; accession of Charles V opposed by both Francis I of France and Pope.
Pope abandons French to ally with Charles V, allowing him to attack France's Italian possessions in return for help against Luther.
1521 Leo dies of a 'violent chill'; little known ascetic Adrian VI elected.
1522 Death of Adrian VI; Giulio becomes Pope Clement VII; continues to run Florence from Rome. Nominal leaders in Florence are bastards Ippolito and Alessandro de' Medici and Cardinal Passerini.
1525 Charles V and Duke of Milan defeat the French at Pavia; Francis I taken prisoner.
1526 Giovanni della Bande Nere, father of future Cosimo I, dies trying to halt the German army on the Po.
1527 Horrific sack of Rome by Charles V's largely Lutheran army.
Passerini and the bastards expelled by the Florentines; new republic declared.
1529 Charles V, now allied with Clement VII, besieges Florence.
1530 Florence falls; end of the Republic.
1531 Alessandro de' Medici is installed as head of government by Charles V; the next year Charles creates him Duke and makes succession permanent; Spanish troops ensure obedience.

1537 Alessandro murdered by jealous cousin Lorenzaccio de' Medici.
Obscure Cosimo de' Medici chosen to succeed; Cosimo defeats Florentine rebels at Montemurlo.
1555 With Imperial help, Cosimo crushes Siena after a devastating war that permanently destroys Sienese power.
1564 Increasingly ill, Cosimo abdicates much responsibility to son Francesco.
1569 Cosimo buys the title Grand Duke of Tuscany from Pope Paul V.
1574 Death of Cosimo I; his son Francesco I accedes.
1587 Death of Francesco; brother Ferdinando I accedes.

17th century

Wool trade finally collapses completely in the 1630s; Tuscany becoming more and more of a European backwater.

1609 Death of Ferdinando; Cosimo II takes over.
1621 Death of Cosimo II; Ferdinando II accedes.
1670 Death of Ferdinando II; Cosimo III inherits.

18th century

Peaceful obscurity; the House of Lorraine establishes an enlightened regime in Tuscany.

1723 Death of Cosimo III; Gian Gastone, last of the Medici rulers, accedes.
1735 Treaty of Aix-la-Chapelle gives Grand Duchy of Tuscany to Francis Stephen, Duke of Lorraine.
1737 Death of Gian Gastone.
1743 Death of Gian Gastone's sister, Anna Maria, the last surviving Medici, who leaves all the Medici art and treasures to Florence in perpetuity.
1765 Death of Francis Stephen; succeeded by son Peter Leopold.
1790 Grand Duke Peter Leopold becomes Emperor of Austria; his son becomes Grand Duke Ferdinando III.
1799 French troops enter Florence.

19th century

Revival of interest in Tuscany; it becomes a major stop for Grand Tourists.

1801-7 Grand Duchy absorbed into Kingdom of Etruria.
1808 Napoleon installs his sister, Elisa Bacciochi, as Grand Duchess of Tuscany.
1815 Grand Duke Ferdinando III returns to Tuscany on defeat of Napoleon.
1824 Genial Leopold II succeeds on the death of his father.
1859 Leopold allows himself to be overthrown in the Risorgimento.
1860 Tuscans vote for unification with Vittorio Emanuele's Kingdom of Piedmont.
1865-70 Florence becomes first capital of the united Italy until the fall of Rome.

20th century

Development of Tuscany as a major tourist destination.

1943 Germans enter Florence; they establish Gothic Line on the Arno.
1944 Germans blow up all of Pisa's bridges and all but the Ponte Vecchio (thanks to Hitler's personal intervention) in Florence. Allies liberate Florence.
1966 The Arno floods to a height of 6.5m, causing huge damage.
1993 Bomb destroys Gregoriophilus library opposite the Uffizi and damages the Vasari corridor.

History

From Etruscans to Renaissance to Risorgimento: blood, sweat, tears and some damn fine art.

DH Lawrence & The Etruscans

"The Etruscans, as everyone knows, were the people who occupied the middle of Italy in early Roman days and whom the Romans, in their usual neighbourly fashion, wiped out entirely in order to make room for Rome with a very big R."

So said DH Lawrence, who loved the Etruscans as much as he hated the Romans. As he grew older, Lawrence became convinced that 'civilization' destroys the human spirit and so he looked back nostalgically to what he saw as the purer cultures of the past.

The Etruscans are ideal material for mythologising. Tantalizingly little evidence remains of their history and culture before they were romantically clobbered out of existence by the Romans, allowing interpreters to make of them what they will.

For Lawrence, they were the perfect symbol for the destruction of rural Albions he saw wrought by the 19th-century industrial societies. Here was a lively, creative, independent people, crushed by a fearsome, brutal, blind machine whose only purpose was conquest and subjugation.

The Etruscans were certainly a highly spiritual people, but they were also partial to a good war, either against other tribes or rival Etruscan cities. This martial proclivity didn't bother Lawrence:

"...if the Etruscans were vicious, I'm glad they were. To the Puritan all things are impure... and those naughty neighbours of the Romans at least escaped being Puritans."

Almost everything the Etruscans built was in wood – except their tombs – and thus their tombs, and the objects recovered therefrom, provide most of the extant evidence on their civilization.

These plain, rather stolid tombs Lawrence sees as having, "...those easy, natural proportions whose beauty one hardly notices, they come so naturally, physically. It is the natural beauty of proportion of the phallic consciousness, contrasted with the more studied or ecstatic proportion of the mental and spiritual conciousness we are accustomed to."

From the frescoes of feasts, festivals, dancing and hunting that adorn many of the tombs Lawrence concludes that, "...death to the Etruscan was a pleasant continuance of life." Other commentators have viewed this in exactly the opposite way – the Etruscans were terrified of, and morbidly fixated with, death and the seemingly carefree paintings were a desperate plea for the gods to go easy on the other side.

The penis-fixated Lawrence gets even more excited by the preponderance in and around the tombs of what he sees as "phallic stones... unmistakeable and everywhere". He even puts the hatred of Roman for Etruscan down to a form of embarrassment at the sight and symbolism of hundreds of primitive willies rising from the earth in such shameless profusion.

The historical bones of what we know about the Etruscans is as follows. The height of their civilization was the 7th and 6th centuries BC, when their loose federation of individually distinctive cities dominated much of what is now southern Tuscany and northern Lazio. Cities like Veii and Caere (Cerveteri) were close to Rome, while northern Etruscan cities (lying in what is now southern Tuscany) included Clusium (Chiusi) and Populonia.

Women played an unusually prominent role in these booming Etruscan settlements, having as much fun as the lads. As Theopompos, writing in the 4th century BC, says,

"Etruscan women take particular care of their bodies and exercise often, sometimes along with the men, and sometimes by themselves. It is not a disgrace for them to be seen naked. They do not share their couches with their husbands but with other men who happen to be present.... They are expert drinkers and very attractive."

The Etruscan cities grew wealthy on the proceeds of trading and mining in copper and iron. Their art and superbly worked gold jewellery displays distinctive oriental influences, adding credence to the theory that the Etruscans migrated to Italy from the east, possibly Asia Minor. Equally, such influences could have been due to extensive trading in the eastern Mediterranean – a general orientalizing trend is observable in most Mediterranean art of the period. The impenetrability of their language adds a further veil of mystery. The problem of Etruscan origins is probably intractable. In all likelihood they emerged from a huge number of mini-migrations within Italy itself.

Opposite: *Penis-free Etruscan tomb, Sovano*

Dante Alighieri

Towering Inferno

Dante Alighieri was born in 1265 into a noble family that had fallen on hard times. In common with most other minor nobles and merchants, the Alighieris were affiliated to the Guelphs and their fortunes during the 13th century were thus dictated by the ups and downs of their party.

Most of Dante's early life coincided with a period of Guelph domination of Florence. The young Dante did his bit to preserve the peace, fighting for the city in the victory against Ghibelline Arezzo at Campaldino in 1289, and later taking part in the siege of the Pisan fortress of Caprona.

His expulsion from Florence with the other White Guelphs in 1302 was a bitter blow and, despite repeated attempts to return, he never saw the city again, dying in Ravenna in 1321.

It was while he was in exile that Dante wrote his greatest work, the *Commedia*, known to posterity as the *Divine Comedy*. This multi-levelled poetic epic is the story of Dante the Pilgrim's journey through Hell, Purgatory and Paradise to God. On the way, Dante the Poet incorporates countless references to the tumultuous events of the preceding century, railing against the injustices of the Ghibellines and lamenting the plight of Florence.

In Canto VI of *Inferno*, a hell-bound soul says to the pilgim,

"Your own city... so filled with envy its cup already overflows the brim."

And Dante agrees:

"Are there any honest men among them? And tell me, why is it so plagued with strife?"

He was a firm believer that temporal and spiritual power should be kept separate. He viewed the Pope's increasing domination of Italian politics as an ominous sign. In Canto XVI of *Purgatorio* he warns that,

"The sword is now one with the crook – and fused together thus, must bring about misrule."

Dante was, however, deeply religious, and particularly outraged by clerical corruption (outspoken criticism of such was one of the chief causes of the split between 'Black' and 'White' Guelphs). In Canto XIX of *Inferno* he condemns the simonists – those who obtained or dispensed religious offices for money – to be shoved down tubes and have flames flicker across the soles of their feet. Popes Nicholas III and Benedict VIII (the latter was instrumental in bringing about Dante's exile) are found ·here, lambasted by Dante the Pilgrim:

"Those things of God that rightly should be wed to holiness, you, rapacious creatures, for the price of silver and gold prostitute."

The *Inferno* is packed with personalities and incidents that would have been familiar to Dante's contemporaries. In Canto X the pilgrim has a slanging match with the haughty Ghibelline Florentine Farinata degli Uberti. Dante upbraids Uberti for siding with the Ghibelline Sienese in their defeat of the Florentine Guelphs at Montaperti in 1260. Famously, as the Sienese prepared to burn Florence, the Florentine exiles declared they would never destroy their own city, and the Sienese backed off. Uberti claims all the credit for this timely intervention.

"I alone stood up when all of them were ready to have Florence razed. It was I who openly stood up in her defence."

Dante also can't resist poking jibes at the rival Tuscan cities.

"Have you ever known people as silly as the Sienese? Even the French cannot compare with them!" he bitches in Canto XXIX.

In Canto XXI, it's the Lucchese who come in for stick.

"You can change a 'no' to 'yes' for cash in Lucca."

Sir John Hawkwood

Medieval Mercenary

John **Hawkwood** was an Essex man and a tanner by trade. As a younger son, job prospects at home were not bright so he became a soldier. In the mid-14th century there was no shortage of employment for fighting men, particularly in France, extending or defending English territory in the southwest. Hawkwood was good at his chosen profession, and when peace came to France he moved on to Italy, where he joined a band of itinerant mercenaries from Brittany, Hungary, Germany, Bosnia and Transylvania.

The general game-plan of the time was confused. The Pope in exile at Avignon wanted to reimpose his authority in central Italy. The Visconti family in Milan was slowly attempting to dominate the Pò valley. In between lay Tuscany, where, then as now, each little city defended its identity against its nearest neighbour. The countryside was all but empty, denuded of more than half its population by the Black Death during the late 1340s, and a soldier commanding 800 men could do very much as he liked. Which is what John Hawkwood did.

He fought with the Florentines against the Pisans, with the Sienese against the Florentines, with the Pisans against the Livornese, and the same again, only in reverse. For a while he campaigned north of the Apennines, fighting sometimes on behalf of Bernabò Visconti, sometimes against. The rival mercenary commanders, the *condottieri*, men like Heinrich Bär, Ambrogio Visconti, Johann Hapsburg, Annechin Bongarten, knew each other well and would earn extra cash by capturing and ransoming each other. Their men fought dismounted, "with their lances pointed low – as though hunting wild boar – and with slow steps, they marched up to the enemy with terrible cries". Nobody got hurt, except peasants. The soldiers were followed everywhere by a team of dedicated arsonists and almost any property in their way, of friend or foe, was liable to be torched.

Allied or separate, none of these bands was ever strong enough to take even the smallest town, nor were the citizens even of the Tuscan cities (without militias of their own) able to defeat

them in the field. So a town would hire a *condottiere* to ward off another city's mercenaries, and hope to be in a position to pay them according to contract when the time came. The consequences if they failed were dire. Hired to protect Faenza in Emilia Romagna, Hawkwood disarmed the men and sent them out of the city, then plundered the place. He used the young women, including the nuns, "*a guisa di meretrici e di schiave*," like whores and slaves. Sacking a town was a way of advertising one's talents, a warning to future clients to pay on time. The same thing happened at Cesena – "an outburst of unspeakable barbarity," says Hawkwood's biographer. At one point the anguished Pope published an encyclical beginning with the words, "the blood of innocents cries out to us from the earth on which it has been spilled." It was no exaggeration. Hawkwood was the inspiration for the local motto: '*un Inglese Toscanizzato è il Diavolo incarnato*' (a Tuscanized Englishman is the Devil incarnate).

The difficulty for the mercenary bands lay in where to stash the profits from their lucrative protection rackets. The contents of Faenza could be sold in Pisa, and Cesena's in Faenza, but where could a land-pirate like Hawkwood keep his savings? Answer: in a bank. The bankers could then, in turn, lend the money to the City Councillors to pay the mercenaries. Nevertheless, Hawkwood was constantly in debt. In 1362, a fund was set up in Florence to loan the soldiers money so that they could retrieve from the pawnshops the arms with which they were supposed to fight on behalf of the city.

In his old age Hawkwood retired to live in Florence, a highly respected soldier despite being responsible for the murder of hundreds of Florentines. The Signoria promised to honour the *condottiere* they knew of as Giovanni Acuto (John the Acute, Sharp or Crafty) with an equestrian monument. It took until 1436 for them to get around to it, and then it was something of a cop out, for instead of a statue, they commissioned Paolo Uccello to *paint* a statue of Hawkwood on horseback. It can still be seen on the north wall of the Duomo.

Leon Battista Alberti

A Renaissance Man

In no respect was the Renaissance's break with the Middle Ages more dramatic than in how man viewed himself. For centuries learning had been in the hands of ascetic clerics, who told people they were nothing but insignificant, impotent sinners, subject to the will and whims of God, their souls trapped within unhealthy, lustful bodies.

However, as the 15th century progressed, educated Florentines started to question this passive, fatalistic, pessimistic view of the human race. The renewal of interest in classical Greece and Rome at this time brought to light texts emphasising a very different view of man. The Greeks and Romans had celebrated the body and exalted human achievement; they believed in fulfilment through action rather than contemplation, of the importance of contributing to civic affairs as well as private virtue. This struck the go-getting, wealthy, public-spirited, well-travelled Florentines as far more in tune with their own inclinations.

They loved to think of themselves as 'new Romans' and evolved the concept of *virtù* to express the qualities and aspirations of the 'complete man', "capable of scaling and possessing every sublime and excellent peak" yet working for the glory of God and the city as much as the individual. Although Dante and Petrarch had been all-rounders, never had there been a concentration of such excellence to match that of 15th-century Florence. Examples include Marsilio Ficino who trained as a physician before becoming a priest, philosopher and translator of Plato into Latin; Gianozzo Manetti, a wealthy property owner, Hebrew scholar and ambassador; Lorenzo 'il Magnifico' de' Medici himself combined considerable skill in politics and diplomacy with an intense interest in philosophy, patronage of the arts and a considerable talent for poetry.

Perhaps the archetypal Renaissance Man, however, was **Leon Battista Alberti**. He was born in 1407, the illegitimate son of a wealthy Florentine banker. As a sickly child he systematically trained and toughened his body by riding, jousting, rock climbing and archery, becoming a noted athlete. Alberti went on to study Latin in Padua and Greek in Bologna, where he took a degree in law, while devouring every classical text he could find. While still a student he wrote a comedy in Latin, *Philodoxus*, that he successfully passed off as a lost Roman text for several years.

Devious cousins swindled Alberti out of his inheritance and he took a job as a writer of briefs for the papacy, coming to Florence with Pope Eugenius IV in 1434. The creative energies of the city, "equalling and exceeding" those of the ancients, were the catalyst for an astonishing outpouring of works.

Alberti taught himself music, wrote songs and sonnets for his lovers, and mastered the organ, being described by a contemporary as "considered one of those most highly skilled in that art". In 1435, fired by the exciting developments in Florentine painting, he wrote the first, highly influential treatise on the art of painting, *Della Pittura*. Along with Brunelleschi and Michelozzo, he was one of the leading architects of his day, putting the

---

At the end of the 7th century BC, the Etruscans captured the small town of Rome and ruled there for a century before being expelled.

The next few centuries witnessed city against city and tribe against tribe all over central Italy until the emerging Roman Republic finally overwhelmed allcomers by the 3rd century BC. Many aspects of Etruscan society were absorbed by the Romans, such as Etruscan gods and divination by entrails, but a distinct Etruscan civilization ceased to exist.

Lawrence, however, fancies that some spark of Etruscan joyousness lives on in the faces of contemporary Tuscans, "...warm faces still jovial with Etruscan vitality, beautiful with the mystery of the unrifled ark, ripe with the phallic knowledge and the Etruscan carelessness!"

Tuscany in the Middle Ages

Unravelling medieval Italian history is not for the faint-hearted. The seemingly interminable progression of petty squabbles, alliances and counter-alliances, scraps and skirmishes between the bewildering number of petty statelets leaves the head spinning.

In the 5th century, the Western Empire finally crumbled before the pagan hordes (some, incidently, considerably more cultured than the clapped-out, dissolute Romans they displaced). Italian unity collapsed as Ostrogoths, Visigoths, Huns and Lombards successively rampaged at will through the peninsula.

In the 8th century, Charlemagne crushed the last of the Lombard kings of Italy and much of the

rediscovered principles of classical architecture, such as pilasters, half columns and scroll buttresses, into practice. The Palazzo Rucellai and the joyful façade of Santa Maria Novella in Florence (*see above*) are perhaps his most celebrated works. "Tell me, is there anything this man doesn't know?" wrote an incredulous contemporary.

Seemingly not. Alberti hung out with blacksmiths and shipbuilders to learn the secrets of their trades; he made a diorama of Rome that doubled as a planetarium; he invented machinery to raise sunken Roman galleys from Lake Nemi. His numerous books included works on horsebreeding, oratory, orthographics, ciphers, sculpture, mathematical puzzles, fables, the

secrets of a lady's toilet and a far-sighted manual for judges which urged that criminals should be reformed rather than punished.

Alberti epitomises one of the most significant changes wrought by the Renaissance: the reawakening of man's interest in himself and belief in his own potential (women, alas, still had several centuries to wait). It is a view that has been fundamental to our thinking, and actions, ever since. As Alberti himself wrote,

"Man is born not to mourn in idleness, but to work at magnificent and large scale tasks, thereby pleasing and honouring God, and manifesting in himself perfect *virtù*, that is, the fruit of happiness."

country came under (at least nominal) control of the Holy Roman Emperors. In practice, however local warlords carved out feudal fiefs for themselves and threw their weight around much as they pleased.

Under the Canossa family, the imperial Margravate of Tuscany began to emerge as a region of some promise during the 10th and 11th centuries. Initially, Lucca was the richest city, but it was Pisa's increasingly profitable maritime trade that provided the biggest impetus of ideas and wealth into the region.

As a merchant class developed in cities all over Tuscany, it sought to throw off the constraints and demands of its feudal overlords. By 1200, the majority had succeeded and Tuscany had become a patchwork of tiny but increasingly self-confident

and ambitious city states. The potential for conflict was huge, and by the 13th century it crystallised into the notorious and intractable struggle between Guelph and Ghibelline.

Guelph v Ghibelline

In the beginning the names Guelph and Ghibelline actually meant something. The words are italianised forms of Welf (the family name of the German Emperor Otto IV) and Waiblingen (a castle of their rivals, the Hohenstaufen). By the time the appellations crossed the Alps into Italy (probably in the 12th century) their meanings had changed.

The name Guelph became attached primarily to the increasingly influential merchant classes. In their continuing desire to be free from imperi-

Girolamo Savonarola

It's the end of the world as we know it

On Shrove Tuesday, 1497, the Florentines erected a 60-feet-high pile of wood in the Piazza della Signoria. On it they placed rich tapestries, wigs, perfumes in exquisite bottles, beautifully-tailored clothes, ivory chessboards, books of poems, works by Boccaccio and Petrarch, paintings by Botticelli and Fra Bartolomeo (willingly donated by the artists) and, on the top, a hastily-made effigy of a Venetian merchant who had offered to buy the lot for a huge sum. The 'Bonfire of the Vanities' was then set alight and the people cheered and danced as some of the finest achievements of the Renaissance burned to ashes.

The man responsible for this extraordinary conflagration was an unprepossessing friar from Padua: **Girolamo Savonarola**. He was born 45 years earlier into a medical family; his grandfather and father had been court physicians for the Duke of Ferrara, but little Girolamo had no interest in court life. Miserable and insular, he spent most of his depressed youth reading the scriptures and composing dreary tunes for the lute; his innate gloominess reinforced when his amorous advances to the daughter of a Florentine exile were bluntly rejected.

In 1475, the spurned Savonarola left home and joined the monastery of San Domenico in Bologna, staying for seven years and living a life of punishing austerity. He refused to speak to women, avoided drink, ate like a bird, wore plain, threadbare clothes and slept on a straw mattress on a wooden board.

Savonarola was sent out to preach all over Italy, finally ending up in Florence where he settled at the Monastery of San Marco (*see picture opposite*). By his own admission, he was a useless preacher at first – without the power "to move a hen" – and seriously considered giving up. He was not helped by a grating voice and startlingly unappealing appearance – short, skinny and ugly, with a large hooked nose and pudgy lips. It is a tribute less to his delivery than to the explosive content of his sermons that he slowly built up a large and devoted following.

He believed that the world was going down the pan. Church and society were corrupt and immoral and in need of a good scourging. Simplicity, austerity and purity were the goals, and could only be achieved by casting aside worldly goods and pleasures. He railed against the new trend in painting that made "the Virgin Mary look like a harlot", he railed against prostitutes ("pieces of meat with eyes"); and, as for sodomites, it was straight into the fire with them.

That Savonarola should have exerted such a powerful grip in what was probably the most liberal and enlightened city in Europe of the time seems paradoxical. For it wasn't just the uneducated masses who flocked to hear him preach. Among his most passionate supporters were members of Lorenzo de' Medici's closest circle of humanist thinkers and artists, such as Pico della Mirandola and Sandro Botticelli. Savonarola's success underlined the (often ignored) deep religiosity behind many of the greatest achievements of the Renaissance, while at the same time capturing a general end-of-the-century public mood of unease and foreboding.

After the death of Lorenzo in 1494, Savonarola's prophecies of doom became ever more intense. He told of his visions of the "Sword of the Lord" hanging over Florence, threatening to wreak revenge, pestilence and disaster on the evil city. When the French king Charles VIII invaded Italy later in the year, the prophecy seemed to have been fulfilled.

Savonarola welcomed the invaders, and during the following three years, he became *de facto* ruler of Florence. He sent out into the streets bands of sinister child supergrasses, clad as angels, to snitch on those wearing fancy clothes or make-up, playing games, boozing or whoring. The people fasted, the people prayed.

al control, they looked around for a powerful backer. The only viable candidate was the Emperor's old enemy, the Pope, who believed that the 4th-century Roman Emperor Constantine had assigned not just spiritual but also temporal power in Italy to the Papacy. The Guelphs, therefore, were able to add a patriotic and religious sheen to their own self-interest. Anyone keen to uphold imperial power and opposed to Papal designs and the rising commercial interests (mainly the old nobility) became known as Ghibellines. That was the theory.

Although the conflict had been simmering for decades, the murder of a Florentine noble in 1215 – the ponderously named Buondelmonte dei Buondelmonti – is traditionally seen as the spark that ignited flames across Tuscany. It soon became clear that self-interest and local rivalries were of far greater importance than theoretical allegiances to Emperor or Pope.

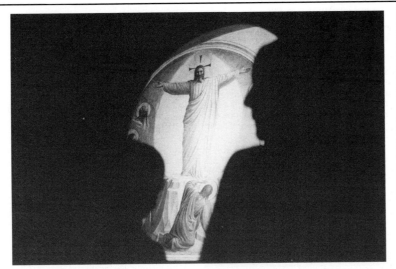

However, the tide was slowly turning against the fiery friar. The Borgia Pope, Alexander VI, became increasingly alarmed by Savonarola's growing independence and criticism of clerical corruption. After trying to buy him off with a cardinal's hat, the Pope was finally driven to excommunicate him. Meanwhile, a protracted and unsuccessful war against Pisa, plague and famine were leaving the Florentines looking for a scapegoat.

The Franciscans challenged the Dominican Savonarola to prove his divine favour and, in an extraordinary throwback to the Middle Ages, an ordeal by fire was agreed upon. On 7 April 1498, lines of oiled sticks were laid out in the Piazza della Signoria in readiness. However, the whole thing descended into farce when it became clear that no-one knew the correct procedure, and eventually heavy rain brought an end to the squabbling.

The mob saw red. They wanted blood, and rioting broke out the next day. The ruling council, bowing to public pressure, arrested Savon-arola, tortured a confession out of him, and sentenced him to death for heresy and schism.

On 23 May 1498, the Florentines piled wood in the same spot in the Piazza della Signoria that, only just over a year previously, had witnessed the Bonfire of the Vanities. Savonarola was hung by an iron collar and then burned, along with two of his followers, "...their legs and arms gradually dropping off", according to one bystander. It was a martyrdom, and one with clear biblical overtones. The authorities were perfectly aware of the possibility of devotees salvaging relics and ensured that everything was burned to ashes, and the ashes scattered in the Arno.

A year later, Botticelli, still tormented by the disgrace of his hero, asked one of Savonarola's examiners what the friar had done to be brought down so ignominiously. "We never found any sin in him, either mortal or venial... if the prophet and his colleagues hadn't been put to death... the people would have rushed on us and cut us to pieces. It was either their lives or ours."

Florence and Lucca were usually Guelph dominated cities, while Siena and Pisa tended to favour the Ghibellines, but this had as much to do with mutual antagonisms as deeply held beliefs. Siena started off Guelph, but couldn't bear the thought of having to be nice to its traditional enemy, Florence, and so swapped to the Ghibelline cause. Similarly, the Guelph/Ghibelline splits within cities were more often class and grudge based than ideological.

Throughout the 14th century, power ebbed and flowed between the two (very loosely knit) parties across Tuscany and from city to city. When one party was in the ascendent its supporters would tear down its opponents' fortified towers (the Guelphs' with characteristic square crenellations, the Ghibellines with swallow-tail ones), only to have its own towers levelled in turn as soon as the pendulum swung back again. In Florence, the Guelphs finally triumphed decisively in 1267 but, as if to prove the essential meaninglessness of the labels, the party soon started squabbling internally. Around 1300, open conflict broke out between the virulently anti-Imperial 'Blacks' and the more conciliatory 'Whites'. After various to-ings and fro-ings, the Blacks booted the Whites out for good. Among those sent into exile was Dante Alighieri (*see box* **Dante Alighieri**).

Eventually, the Guelph/Ghibelline conflict ran out of steam, or, rather, everyone admitted that the names meant nothing anymore and invented new ones to slap on their enemies. It says much for the energy, innovation, graft and skill of the Tuscans (or perhaps much about the relative harmlessness of much medieval warfare in Italy, *see box* **Sir John Hawkwood**) that throughout this tempestuous period, the region was booming economically. The stage was being set for the explosion of curiosity, creativity and achievement that was to characterise 15th-century Tuscany.

Renaissance Tuscany

What wasn't the Renaissance?

1. Solely an artistic revolution

Although the (literally) most visible manifestation of the Renaissance was the astonishing outpouring of art emanating from 15th-century Florence, the spark that lit the Renaissance fire was undoubtedly literary. The word 'Renaissance', meaning rebirth, is most properly applied to the rediscovery of ancient Greek and Roman texts and the new view of the world and mankind they revealed (*see also box* **Leon Battista Alberti**). A few classical works had never been lost, but those that were known were usually only available in corrupted versions and these, anyway, were in the hands of clerics who forbade their dissemination or discussion.

It was the inquisitive Florentines who first decided to take matters into their own hands. Their wealth paid for dedicated manuscript detectives like Poggio Bracciolini to start determinedly digging in neglected monastery libraries throughout Europe. The volume of unknown works discovered was astonishing – and their effect was intellectual dynamite, causing the Florentines to reassess the way they thought about almost every field of human endeavour. Within the first few decades of the 15th century, there came to light Quintilian's *The Training of an Orator* which detailed the Roman education system, Columella's *De re Rustica* on agriculture, works by Vitruvius and Frontinus' *On Aqueducts* (key texts on Roman architecture), Cicero's *Brutus* (a justification of republicanism). Very few Greek works were known in Western Europe; suddenly, discovered almost simultaneously, was most of Plato, Homer, the plays of Sophocles, Aeschylus, Euripides, Aristophanes, histories by Herodotus, Xenophon, Thucydides, the speeches of Demosthenes and many more classic Classics.

2. Synonymous with 15th-century Florence

The Renaissance didn't just happen. Much groundwork had already been laid by the turn of the 15th century (and some historians argue there was a mini-Renaissance as early as the 12th century). Giotto, for instance, had made a decisive break from Byzantine formality in art towards naturalism as early as the late 13th century; Petrarch, Boccaccio and Dante had all collected latin manuscripts. However, such men as these were isolated exceptions, and it was undoubtedly in the city on the Arno in the 15th century that the intellectual ideas of the Renaissance first took hold. Magnificent while it lasted, Florence's pre-eminence was, nevertheless, abruptly snuffed out on the death of Lorenzo il Magnifico and the invasion of Italy by Charles VIII of France in the 1490s. The city would never again achieve such a central position in the European cultural mainstream.

The cutting edge switched to Rome in the early 16th century, where Michelangelo, Bramante and Raphael were creating their finest works; and thence to Venice later in the century – after the Emperor Charles V's sack of Rome in 1527 – where masters such as Palladio and Titian practised their arts. Meanwhile, Gutenberg's invention of moveable type and the widespread introduction of the printing press across Europe in the mid 15th century meant that the new learning reached into the farthest corners of the continent, inspiring the people of cities as distant as Lisbon and Krakow to create distinctive 'Renaissances' of their own.

3. An anti-religious or anti-Catholic movement

Unlike the 18th-century Enlightenment, God was in no danger from the Renaissance. Although scholars started to look for explanations beyond the scriptures, these were seen as complementary to accepted religion rather than a challenge. Much effort was made to present the wisdom of the ancients – in a pre-Christian age – as a hitherto forgotten precursor to the ultimate wisdom of God. Many of the foremost figures of the time – Lorenzo il Magnifico, Michelangelo, Pico della Mirandola – were deeply religious and saw no conflict between

Opposite: Michelangelo's *David*.

God and Plato. Even Lorenzo Valla's exposure of the document known as the Donation of Constantine (on which the Pope's claim for temporal power in Italy was based) as a fake was intended to focus the church on spiritual matters rather than discredit the institution itself.

The Renaissance should also not be confused with the Reformation of the early 16th century, which heartily disapproved of many of the (as the Germans saw it) flowery, frivolous and indecent Italian fripperies of Renaissance artists, writers and architects.

4. The end of Medieval ignorance and superstition
The rarified world of the educated and wealthy might have been electrified by the new learning and exciting achievements in the arts, but the lives of the vast majority of people didn't change at all.

Pretty paintings and handsome buildings were one thing, but real practical advances that would alter and improve their lives, in fields such as sanitation and understanding of disease, were still centuries away. Even among the privileged, it was very clear that the Renaissance was a pre-scientific age. Science – as a process of deduction based on observation and experimentation – didn't really get going until the 17th century. The 15th century was an era where ideas were still paramount. Leonardo may have produced marvellous anatomical drawings but the ancient (and, for practical purposes, useless) medical theory of the four humours was still widely accepted; astronomy and astrology were all but synonymous; mathematics was seen in a Pythagorean way as almost a mystical art; alchemy, the attempted transformation of base metals into gold, was flourishing.

Niccolò Machiavelli

How to make enemies and execute people

"The whole man seems to be an enigma, a grotesque assemblage of incongruous qualities, selfishness and generosity, cruelty and benevolence, craft and simplicity, abject villainy and romantic heroism." (Macaulay)

If Savonarola's fundamentalist crusade was one response to the perceived decadence of Renaissance Florence, then Niccolò Machiavelli's cynicism was another. Machiavelli was a complex, confusing character. When young he was a fervent patriot and idealist and, in many ways, this largely self-educated lawyer's son of a respected Tuscan family was a product of, and beneficiary from, the rebirth of classical learning. He had grown up in Lorenzo il Magnifico's Florence and, as an adult, would dress up in his finest clothes every evening and retire to his study to commune with the ancients, losing himself in the world of the great Greek and Roman writers.

Machiavelli may have venerated the Classical world, but he had little esteem or affection for most of his contemporaries. Shrewd, sarcastic, arrogant and aloof, he thought the achievements of the Renaissance worth nothing if they were not backed by force. He had been in Florence in 1494 when Charles VIII's troops had marched in unopposed and had been horrified by the abject inablity of the city to oppose the invaders. The theory of the pursuit and maintenance of

power became his obsession. Force of arms meant all; weakness was beyond contempt.

On the fall of Savonarola, Machiavelli took up a relatively minor post in the Florentine government. However, he gained considerable influence when his friend Piero Soderini was appointed *Gonfaloniere* (the most powerful position in the administration) for life in 1502 in an attempt to strengthen the Republic. One of Machiavelli's responsiblities was war. The old system of hiring mercenaries to do the dirty work was expensive and unreliable, and put Florence at the mercy of the notoriously untrustworthy *condottieri* (*see box* **Sir John Hawkwood**). So Machiavelli took the revolutionary step of forming the republic's first national militia, the first bands of which paraded in the Piazza della Signoria in 1506. The militia's first test came in 1512.

The Medici had fled Florence in 1494, but Lorenzo's brother, Cardinal Giovanni de' Medici (the future Pope Leo X), was determined to re-establish his family's former power base. With the help of Spanish troops he advanced on the city. The Tuscan militia was called to arms and garrisoned Prato, 12 miles northwest of Florence. Yet as soon as the Spanish attacked, the militia lost its nerve and fled, leaving the hapless inhabitants to be massacred. Florence capitulated without a fight; Machiavelli's cynicism deepened ever further.

He would have been happy to serve the incoming Medici, but was forced into exile at his country villa at Sant'Andrea in Percussina (visitors to the village can still eat in the tav-

Renaissance to 18th century
Medici Who's Who

Medici is a name all but synonymous with Florence and Tuscany from the 15th to the early 18th centuries. The family's origins probably lie in the medical profession – doctors or apothecaries – as the name suggests, although their later wealth was built on banking. The Medici had risen to some prominence in Florence by the end of the 13th century but declined in wealth and influence thereafter before their fortunes revived again towards the end of the 14th century. From then on, it was movin' on up....

Giovanni di Bicci

(1360-1429).
So this was the first Medici bigshot?

In a sense. Giovanni quietly built up a fortune through his banking business (boosted immensely by handling the papal account) that was to be the foundation of the Medici's prominence in the 15th century.
Banking? Wasn't moneylending a no-no for Christians?
Strictly speaking, yes. But all manner of ruses were dreamt up to get around so inconvenient a ruling and Florence by this time was famed for its banks.
So Giovanni concentrated on making cash and keeping out of the public eye?
Exactly. He always acted with the utmost discretion and impartiality, wary of the Florentines' habit of picking on those who got above themselves. It was his son who really shot the Medici into the bigtime.

ern where he drunk away his sorrows, *see chapter* **Restaurants**), where the following year he wrote his most celebrated book, *The Prince*. In his first major political book, *Discourses on Livy*, Machiavelli's praise of early Rome's republican principles was conspicuous. By the time he wrote *The Prince*, however, he had become convinced that the best form of government was that provided by a strong leader, and maintained by armed force. Sometimes citizens must be compelled to obey their ruler for their own good, even if unscrupulous methods are called for – "It is better to be feared than loved if you cannot be both". This was nothing new – rulers had been bullying and brutalizing their subjects, battering and betraying their rivals for centuries. The new thing was spelling it out so shamelessly. Tellingly, Machiavelli chose as his ideal prince one of the most feared and heinous figures of the time, the ruthless, duplicitous and depraved Cesare Borgia.

While Machiavelli's reaction to Florence's military weakness and loss of prestige at the end of the century is understandable, he failed to see that the city's achievements grew out of the very principles he derides as weak: republicanism, civic responsibility, democracy (of a sort) and toleration. Machiavelli's ideal state might be strong, but what is the value of strength without freedom, without intellectual vigour, without compassion?

Ironically, despite many attempts to regain a position of power for himself, Machiavelli never managed to practice what he preached and died in 1527, bitter and unappreciated. He had no inkling of the notoriety his work would one day attract; indeed, in his own time he was far more successful playwright than politician.

NICOLAI
MACHIAVELLI
PRINCEPS.

EX
SYLVESTRI TELII
FVLGINATIS TRADVCTIONE
diligenter emendata.

Adiecta sunt eiusdem argumenti, Aliorum quorundam contra Machiauellum scripta de potestate & officio Principum, & contra tyrannos.

BASILEAE
Ex officina Petri Pernæ.
M D XXC.

His satirical and irreverent plays, such as *Mandragola*, were big hits in his own time (Pope Leo X, perhaps surprisingly, was a fan) and are still well regarded today.

Cosimo 'il Vecchio'

(1389-1464, ran Florence informally from 1434)
Son of Giovanni di Bicci.

'Il Vecchio'? Live to a ripe old age did he?
Yes, but the name is more a mark of respect for
Cosimo's central role in mid-15th-century Florence.
When he died the Florentines inscribed on his
tomb the words *Pater Patriae*, a distinction once
accorded to Cicero.

What did he do that was so great?
Cosimo presided over one of Florence's most prosperous and prestigious eras. He was even more
astute and ambitious a banker than his father (and
far more ambitious) and expanded his fortune to a
level that would have made Croesus envious. At
the same time Cosimo pacified opponents and his
conscience by lavishly endowing charities and
public building projects, introducing a progressive
income tax system and balancing the interests of
the volatile Florentine classes relatively successfully. He also brought much prestige to the city by
persuading the General Council of the Roman and
Greek churches to meet in Florence, where they
achieved a (short-lived) reconciliation.

Did no-one resent him?
Some of the other powerful families certainly did.
The Albizzi had Cosimo banished in 1433 on
trumped up charges (and would have executed
him if they could), but he returned by popular con-
sent the following year and meted out a similar
punishment to his enemies. Cosimo may have kept
the outward pretence of being an ordinary citizen,
but no-one was under any illusion about who was
pulling the strings. As one contemporary commented, he was "king in all but name".

A megalomaniac?
He certainly had his scheming side, but the most
admirable feature of Cosimo's rule was his enthusiasm for, and active support of, the new humanist learning and exciting developments in art that
were sweeping Florence. He built up a magnificent
library, encouraged and financed the activities of
scholars and artists, gave architectural commissions and founded an academy of learning based
on Plato's Academy.

Piero 'il Gottoso'

(1416-69, ran Florence from 1664).
Son of Cosimo 'il Vecchio'.

'Il Gottoso'?
The Gouty. All the Medici suffered from it, but
poor Piero's joints gave him such gyp that he had
to be carried around for half his life. He wasn't
expected to survive his father.

So a bit of a runt?
Well, he didn't last long after Cosimo died, but Piero
was a surprisingly able ruler. He crushed an anti-
Medici conspiracy, maintained the success of the
Medici bank and continued to generously patron-
ise Florence's best artists, sculptors and architects.

Lorenzo 'il Magnifico'

Lorenzo 'il Magnifico'

Son of Piero 'il Gottoso'.
(1449-92, ruled from 1469)

*'Magnificent', eh? An improvement on 'old' and
'gouty'.*
Indeed. This was the big Medici, famous in his
own time and legendary in later centuries.

What did he do that was so magnificent?
Lorenzo's rule marked the peak of the Florentine
Renaissance, with artists such as Botticelli and the
young Michelangelo producing superlative works.
Although much of Lorenzo's glory was reflected,
he did all he could to foster talent and reward
achievement. Indeed, he was an accomplished poet
himself, and gathered round him a supremely talented collection of scholars and artists (*see also box*
Leon Battista Alberti).

It was also a period of relative peace, particularly when compared to the disasters that were to
befall Florence in the decades following Lorenzo's
death. His diplomatic skills were vital in keeping
relations between the perpetually squabbling
Italian states on a relatively even keel.

So he didn't put a foot wrong?
Not exactly. In truth, he was not a patch on his
predecessors as a businessman and the Medici
bank suffered a severe decline during his lifetime
(although this was also related to a general slump
in Florence's economic fortunes). Lorenzo maintained a façade of being no more than *primus inter
pares* but he made sure he always got his way,
and could be ruthless with his enemies (such as in
the aftermath of the Pazzi plot of 1478 which killed
his brother, Giuliano, when anyone even remotely connected to the conspiracy was merciless-
ly punished). However, the ordinary citizens of
Florence always remained loyal and affectionate
towards Lorenzo and the general climate of toleration and intellectual freedom that he supported
was a major factor in some of the greatest achievements of the Renaissance.

Piero di Lorenzo

(1471-1503, ruled Florence 1492-94).
First son of Lorenzo il Magnifico.
As magnifico as his dad?
Alas, no. Sturdy, healthy and a decent looker he
may have been, but he was also ruthless, charm-
less and tactless with a violent temper, no sense of
loyalty and an unpopular haughty wife. Even his
own father described him as 'foolish'.
*It can't have been easy being the son of such a
superstar...*
Perhaps not, but you're not helping yourself if you
abjectly surrender your city to a foreign invader
(Charles VIII of France in 1494) and then flee when
you realise you've cocked up. Piero spent the rest
of his life sulking his way around Italy, trying to
persuade unenthusiastic states to help him regain
power in a Florence that had no wish to see his
duplicitous mug again. Eventually he mercifully
drowned while fighting for France against Spain.

Giuliano, Duke of Nemours

(1478-1516, ruled from 1512).
Third son of Lorenzo il Magnifico.
Surely this son was a better egg?
Only in the sense that he was more nonentity than
swine. After the restoration of the Republic,
Savonarola's ascetic rule followed by a spell under
Piero Soderini (aided and abetted by Machiavelli),
the Medici were restored in 1512. But Giuliano, tit-
ular boss of Florence, was nothing more than a
puppet of his older brother Cardinal Giovanni,
later Pope Leo X.

Lorenzo, Duke of Urbino

(1492-1519, ruled from 1516).
Son of Piero di Lorenzo.
Was this Lorenzo less of a pushover?
Yes, but again, not in any likeable way. Puny, arrogant, high-handed and corrupt, no-one was anything but relieved when he succumbed to TB,
aggravated by syphilis, in 1519.

Giovanni (Pope Leo X)

(1475-1521, ruled indirectly from 1512).
Second son of Lorenzo il Magnifico.
Pope!? This one can't have been such a loser.
Indeed not. The night before his birth his mother
dreamed she gave birth not to a baby but a huge
lion. Lorenzo decided early on that Giovanni was
destined for a glittering ecclesiastical career.
Serious hot-housing and papal earbending saw
Giovanni enter the monkhood at the age of eight,
become the youngest ever cardinal when he was
16, and elbow his way into the papacy in 1513.
*Not bad going! He must have been quite an
operator.*
Not really, Pope Leo (spot the lion reference) was
a remarkably likeable, jolly, open character, and

Giovanni (Pope Leo X)

although portly, lazy and fond of the good life
("God has given us the Papacy so let us enjoy it",
as he is famously reported to have said), he was a
generous host and politically conciliatory.
So an all round success?
Not entirely. His shameless exploitation of the sale
of indulgences to ease his permanent debts added
further fuel to the fires of critics of papal corruption, including Martin Luther. Oh, and a chronic
anal fistula made him not entirely the most fragrant company.

Giulio (Pope Clement VII)

(1478-1534, ruled from 1519).
Illegitimate son of Giuliano, Lorenzo il Magnifico's
brother.
Another Pope? It's good to keep it in the family.
Too right. Nepotism is an ancient Italian tradition,
and Leo heaped honours on his cousin, much to the
chagrin of the other cardinals.
Can't have made him many friends...
It didn't, and his "rather morose and disagreeable"
personality didn't help much either. However, his
management of Florence was astute and he managed to swing the Papacy in 1524.
So at least he knew what he was doing...
Initially, perhaps, but Clement became notorious
for his indecision, irresolution and disloyalty. He
abandoned his alliance with France only to immediately regret it when the Emperor Charles V
invaded Italy and sacked Rome in 1527 (the Pope's
um-ing and ah-ing delayed the city's defensive
works for weeks). In the meantime, the Republic
was re-established in Florence and Clement agreed
to crown Charles in return for his help in retaking
the city for the Medici. Florence fell in 1530.
A triumph eventually then?
For his family, maybe, but when Clement died in
1534 Rome celebrated. The words 'Clemens
Pontifex Maximus' was obliterated on his tomb, to
be replaced by 'Inclemens Pontifex Minimus'.

Alessandro

(1511-37, ruled Florence from 1530).
Probably bastard son of Pope Clement VII.
So things were looking down for the Medici?
You ain't seen nothing yet. When Clement installed the frizzy haired Alessandro in power in Florence in 1530, and Charles V made him hereditary Duke, the city entered one of its darkest and most desperate periods.
Can he really have been that bad?
Oh, yes. Bastard in name and nature, Alessandro abandoned all pretence of respecting the Florentines' treasured institutions and freedoms. He became increasingly authoritarian, tortured and executed his opponents, and outraged the good Florentine burghers by his apalling rudeness and sexual antics.
Oh, yes? Like what?
He had a penchant for dressing in women's clothing, riding about town with his bosom buddy (and sometime bed partner), the equally alarming Lorenzaccio (a distant cousin), screeching insults at the populace.
Couldn't the Florentines do anything about him?
They tried. A deputation of senior figures officially complained to Charles V, but to no avail. It was left to the warped Lorenzaccio to put everyone out of their misery by luring Alessandro into bed in anticipation of a seduction and then stabbing him to death in 1537.

Cosimo I

(1519-74, ruled 1537-64).
Grandson of Lorenzo il Magnifico's daughter, Lucrezia.
Surely the Florentines thought twice about another Medici?
They certainly did. There were no surviving heirs from the direct Medici line, so they chose an obscure 18-year-old Medici who they thought they could manipulate.
And could they?
Far from it. Cosimo was the classic dark horse. Cold, secretive, cunning but effective, he knew exactly how he wanted to rule Florence and set about it with calculated, merciless efficiency – Machiavelli would have loved him.
Doesn't sound like that much of an improvement on Alessandro?
Cosimo may have been deeply unloveable, but he did restore stability within Florence and respect for the city internationally. He built up a Florentine navy (which proved its worth against the Turks at Lepanto in 1571), threw off the dependence on Spanish troops to maintain order and, after relentless lobbying, was made Grand Duke of Tuscany by Pope Paul V in 1569.
So things were back on the right track for Tuscany?

Only up to a point. He could do nothing to halt Florence's continuing economic decline (due in large part to the drying up of raw materials for the city's core cloth trade) and he involved Florence in a protracted and devastating war with Siena that destroyed Sienese power forever, and left half its population dead and the city fit for nothing.

Francesco I

(1541-87, ruled Tuscany from 1564).
Son of Cosimo I.

Francesco I

A chip off the old block?
Not at all – an unpredictable lot, these Medici. Short, skinny, graceless and sulky, Francesco had little in common with his father. He nevertheless kept Florence out of trouble, and liked nothing better than retreating into his own little world, playing with his pet reindeer and dabbling in alchemy. Francesco was not without talents – he became an expert in making vases from metal and crystal, and invented a new process for making porcelain.
Doesn't sound such a bad sort?
He wasn't, particularly when compared to his younger brother Pietro, an unbalanced sponger who strangled his wife for grieving for the lover who Pietro had had executed.

Ferdinando I

(1549-1609, ruled from 1587).
Son of Cosimo I.
Surely this one was an improvement?
Indeed he was. Ferdinando was far more gregarious than his brother and ruled Tuscany efficiently and responsibly. He reduced corruption, improved trade and farming, encouraged learning, and further developed the navy and the port of Livorno. By acts such as staging lavish popular entertainments and giving dowries to poor girls, Ferdinando became the most loved Medici since Lorenzo il Magnifico.

Cosimo II

(1590-1621, ruled from 1609).
Son of Ferdinando I.
Wasn't Galileo doing the rounds about this time?
He was, and the new Cosimo's protection of the
astronomer from a hostile Italy was about the
Grand Duke's only worthwhile act.

Ferdinando II

(1610-70, ruled from 1621).
Son of Cosimo II.
*Did these later Medici want nothing more than
an easy life?*
Not a lot more. Tuscany had lost all pretence of
being anything more than an Italian backwater.
Florence was described by a contemporary visitor as a sad place "much sunk from what it was...
one cannot but wonder to find a country that has
been a scene of so much action now so forsaken
and so poor". Porky, laidback, moustachioed
Ferdinando II did nothing to arrest the trend. He
loved to hunt, eye-up the boys and collect bits of
bric-a-brac. A lightweight when compared to his
learned brother Leopoldo, he was at least not as
bad as another brother, Gian Carlo, a prodigious
glutton and lover who had at least one of his
rivals murdered.

Cosimo III

(1642-1723, ruled from 1670).
Son of Ferdinando II.
*There can't have been much life left in the
Medici line...*
There wasn't. Things were rapidly going down
the pan for the Medici and Tuscany, now seemingly in terminal decline with trade all but completely dried up and plague and famine stalking
the land.
Didn't Cosimo III try to do anything about it?
No, he never even made the pretence of trying to
improve Tuscany's lot. Cosimo was a joyless, glut-
tonous loner who preferred hanging around with
monks to girls (although his unbelievably unoblig-
ing and sulky wife, Marguerite-Louise, must take
some responsibility for this). He was not uneducated but as he got older he grew more and more
prudish and anti-semitic. Intellectual freedom took
a nosedive, taxes soared, public executions were a
daily occurrence.

Gian Gastone

(1671-1737, ruled from 1723).
Son of Cosimo III.
*So we reach the last of the Medici rulers. Was it
out with a bang or a whimper?*
A combination of both. Gian Gastone was a magnificent disaster of a man. Neglected, lonely and
miserable, he was forcibly married to a spectacularly offensive woman, Anna Maria Francesca,

Gian Gastone

daughter of the Duke of Saxe-Lauenberg, who
dragged him off to her gloomy castle near
Prague. He drowned his sorrows in the taverns
of Prague, whoring about with stable boys and
students before escaping back to Florence in
1708. Shocked to find himself Grand Duke in
1723, he started his rule surprisingly coherently,
trying to relieve the burden of taxation, increasing tolerance, and reinstating citizens rights, but
he soon lapsed into chronic apathy and dissolu-
tion.
Was there no way back for poor sod?
None at all. Perpetually pissed, he could hardly
balance on a horse. When his relations tried to get
him back on the straight and narrow he disgraced
himself by, for instance, vomiting into his napkin
at a respectable dinner, then taking off his wig and
wiping his mouth with it. Eventually he couldn't
even be bothered to get out of bed, and had troops
of rowdy boys known as *ruspanti* entertain him
by cavorting about and shouting obscenities. He
only ever came out of his bedroom to prove to his
subjects that he wasn't dead. The poor bugger
was so derided that the Treaty of Aix-la-Chapelle
in 1735 gave the Grand Duchy over to Francis
Stephen of Lorraine without even consulting
Gian Gastone.

Anna Maria

(died 1743).
Gian Gastone's sister.
Not quite the end of the story?
Not quite. The very last surviving Medici was as
much a contrast to her brother as can be imagined.
Every visitor to Florence since the mid-18th century has reason to be grateful to the strait-laced,
solemn and pious Anna Maria. In her will she
bequeathed all Medici property and treasures to
the Grand Duchy in perpetuity – on the one condition that they never leave Florence.

Tuscany in the Risorgimento

Florence never wanted to be capital of Italy. Vittorio Emanuele II, King of Sardinia-Piedmont and leader of the movement to unify the country, the Risorgimento, never wanted to reign from Florence. The Piedmontese people were outraged by the idea. When, in 1865, with Rome still holding out against the nationalists, the 'Convention of September' declared Florence the capital, the people of Turin rioted, and were only subdued after 200 had been killed. It was the culmination of an extraordinary few decades for Florence and Italy.

Tuscany in the 1820s and '30s had been a generally agreeable, benign place. Under the laidback, if not overly bright, Grand Duke Leopold II, the region enjoyed a climate of toleration that attracted intellectuals, dissidents, artists and writers from all over Italy and Europe. They would meet in the Gabinetto Scientifico-Letterario in the Palazzo Buondelmonti in Piazza Santa Trinità, frequently welcoming distinguished foreigners such as Heine, Byron and Châteaubriand.

For a time, Leopold and his ministers successfully kept the reactionary influence of the Grand Duke's uncle, Emperor Francis II of Austria, at arm's length, while simultaneously playing down the growing populist cry for unification. By the 1840s, however, it was becoming clear that the two-pronged nationalist movement, represented by the Piedmontese monarchy and Giuseppe Mazzini's republican *Giovane Italia* movement, had become a serious threat to the status quo. Even relaxed Florence found itself swept up in nationalist enthusiasm, causing Leopold to clamp down on reformers and impose some censorship.

In the tumultuous year of revolutions, 1848, insurrections in Livorno and Pisa forced Leopold to grant concessions to the reformers, including a Tuscan constitution. When news reached Florence that the Milanese had driven the Austrians out of their city, and Charles Albert, King of Sardinia-Piedmont, had determined to push them out of Italy altogether, thousands of Tuscans joined the cause (including Carlo Lorenzini, later better known as Carlo Collodi, author of *The Adventures of Pinocchio*). However, the better trained Austrians beat the Tuscans at Montanara and the Piedmontese at Novara in 1849.

The pendulum seemed to be swinging back Austria's way, but the radicals in Florence dug their heels in and bullied the Grand Duke into appointing the activist reformer Giuseppe Montanelli, a professor of law at Pisa University, to head a new government, and he asked the extremist Francesco Guerazzi to join him. They went to Rome to attend a constituent assembly, but the alarmed Pope Pius IX threatened to excommunicate anyone attending such an assembly.

Leopold panicked, and fled Florence in disguise for Naples. Montanelli, Guerazzi and Mazzini set up a provisional government but, in the absence of armed support, it collapsed. Preferring the devil they knew to the Austrians, the Florentines invited Leopold back; he returned in July 1849, but brought with him Austrian troops to keep order. Grim times followed for a city just recovering from one of its worst ever floods. Seemingly now content to be an Austrian puppet, clamping down on the press and dissent, Leopold's one-time popularity dissipated.

However, the fight continued elsewhere in Italy, with the Piedmontese Count Camillo Cavour persuading Napoleon III's France to join with him in expelling the Austrians. Eventually they goaded the Emperor into action, and war was declared in April 1859.

The French and Piedmontese swept the Imperial armies before them while, in Florence, nationalist demonstrations organised by the *Società Nazionale*, forced the government to resign. Leopold refused to formally abdicate but, on 27 April, he left Florence for the last time with his family, while his former subjects watched in silence. The following year, the minister of justice announced that the Tuscan people had voted for unification with Vittorio Emanuele's Kingdom of Piedmont.

The Florentines greeted their new king with enthusiasm when he arrived in February 1865 to take up residence in the Pitti Palace. The influx of northerners, though, was met with mixed feelings. Business boomed but the Florentines didn't take much to Piedmontese flashiness.

Huge changes were wrought in the city. Ring roads encircled the old centre, new avenues and squares (such as Piazza della Repubblica) were built, residential suburbs were constructed, parks were laid out (for example, the Giardino dei Semplici). Intellectuals and socialites crowded the salons and cafés. In Via Cavour, the Caffè Michelangelo was the favoured hangout of the painters known as the *Macchiaioli*, the Italian version of the Impressionists.

When war with Prussia forced the French (who had swapped sides) to withdraw their troops from Italy in 1870, Rome finally fell to Vittorio Emanuele's troops and Italy was united for the first time since the fall of the Roman Empire.

Florence's brief reign as capital ended, but the Florentines remained phlegmatic. As a popular epigram of the time declared:

Turin sheds tears when the King departs
And Rome's exultant when the King arrives.
Florence, fount of poetry and the arts,
Cares not one whit in either case – and thrives.

Florence Today

The Florentine archipelago.

EM Forster noticed two types of English-speaking visitor to Tuscany a century ago: those clutching Baedekers and "the coupons of Cook", meaning the guidebooks and travellers' cheques of the time; and the permanent residents, who stayed in villas below Fiesole writing pieces with names like "Medieval Byways". Both tribes seemed to him to disapprove of the native Tuscans, on the grounds that they did not understand or appreciate the beauties that surrounded them. This arrogance did not go unnoticed. Some Florentines called them *'scarafaggi'*, meaning cockroaches, as they waved umbrellas and shouted in bad Italian, scuttling round the edges of the buildings dressed in black.

Today, Florence is under pressure from far more interesting migrations than tourists: Chinese, Albanians, North Africans, Polish, Nigerians, Brazilians. Mere tourists can be treated as a peculiar visitation from the insect world; they come, and then they go away again. But these others must sooner or later become integrated.

The black prostitutes, which at the moment seem such an unusual addition to the city, come from Nigeria. A corrupt Italian official in Lagos arranged their passports, though apparently this has now been stopped. Their lives are doubly secluded, as the rest of the small black community of Florence, still struggling to establish a respectable identity, does not want to become associated with criminal activity of any kind.

By chance, the first generation of African immigrants which came to Florence ten years ago originated from Mali or Senegal, two countries whose people are traditionally easy-going. The *vucumprà*, as the street-vendors are called, usually come from these two countries. Florentines have come to think of them as gentle people, and generally they extend this tolerance to the more extrovert and assertive Ghanaians and Nigerians. Not many Florentines could distinguish at a glance a Nigerian from a Malian.

A Nigerian businessman in Novoli is attempting to set up an African Social Club in the outskirts of the city. It is not easy to establish a social centre as rents are high, numbers are few, and a collective identity does not as yet exist. The best that has happened so far is a club, called Sahara Desert, which acts as a meeting point.

Old meets new.

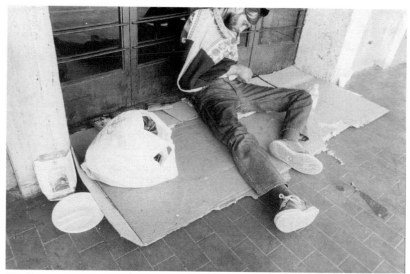

The flip side of Florence.

The *Nord-Africani* are immigrants from the Mahgreb, the arid north edge of the Sahara which can no longer support its local population. Though called generically *Marocchini*, they include Tunisians and Algerians as well. Whereas the Somalians, for instance, form a compact social group, with official spokesmen and a good relationship with the local institutions, the *Marocchini* are disunited. While some work quietly in the building trades, others are suspected of being used as runners in the local hash distribution. Naturally, the Florentine crims are happy to fill Italian jails with *Nord-Africani* rather than Tuscans.

Near Prato, lies a small Chinatown of between eight and ten thousand immigrants. Strange stories used to circulate about them. It was said that nobody ever died in Chinatown. The documents of the deceased were recirculated among the illegal immigrants. In 1992 tensions peaked, as the little sweat-shops in Chinatown were producing fake handbags which the Senegalese *vucumprà* sold in the streets, sometimes outside the very shops distributing the originals. However, the Florentines and the Chinese have struck a deal. The Chinese factories still produce handbags and leather jackets, but they buy the raw materials from Italian subsidiaries and then sell them on to Italian middle-men who, in turn, sell most of the goods to the growing eastern European market.

The story of the Albanians is not such a happy one. Universally looked down on as poor spongers, foreign without being exotic, the *cronaca nera* are filled with endless stories about their misdeeds,

such as adolescent girls kidnapped in Albania, raped for months on end and then turned out onto the streets of Italian towns. As a result, Albanians find it harder to rent a room than the Malians or Senegalese. On the other hand they speak good Italian, they look Italian, they know how to apply to the Commune or the charitable organisations for help, and they come from a country whose recent disastrous history is at least partially the result of interference by Italian criminals.

Florence responds as best it can to the arrival of hitherto unfamiliar peoples, but where ten years ago the key word describing the city of the future was the 'melting pot', in which all minorities contribute to a shared identity, the present image is that of an 'archipelago', a scattered group of independent minorities that may never coalesce. Like all Italians the Tuscans still remember the last war, when the young people of both sexes, as so many great movies tell us, were forced to take their pathetic chances as bicycle thieves or prostitutes. Tuscans face crime with a mixture of compassion and incredulity. That he (or she) should have to do such a thing!

Tuscans, notorious for their lack of curiosity about anything that takes place beyond the range of their own church bell, spare a thought for the unknown chaos of the countries whence these new faces arrive. If they'd had any choice, so the argument runs, they would have stayed at home. As we do. Because we like it. Because it is the best place in the world. Out of a particular insularity, compassion can grow. *Matthew Spender*

Tuscany by Season

The Tuscan year is packed with culinary binges, religious bashes and colourful medieval contests.

*Waiting for the dove to explode at the **Scoppio del Carro**.*

Spring

Holy Week

Date Mar.

Holy week is celebrated in many small towns all over Tuscany with religious processions, many of them in Renaissance or Medieval costumes. Some of the more important ones are Buonconvento (near Siena), Castiglion Fiorentino (near Arezzo) and Bagno a Ripoli (just outside Florence). In Grassina, near Florence, and San Gimignano, re-enactments of episodes from the life of Christ are staged on Good Friday.

Easter

Easter Sunday sees one of the most important events of the Florentine year, the **Scoppio del Carro**, an ancient ritual that dates back to the 12th century. It's a wonderfully eccentric and colourful event. A long parade of trumpeters, drummers, costumed dignitaries and flag throwers escort the *carro* (a tall, heavy wooden cart), pulled by four white oxen with garlands of flowers around their horns, through the streets from Via il Prato to Piazza del Duomo where it comes to a halt in front of the Baptistery. It is a highly tourist-friendly event, and nearby streets are always blocked by thousands of spectators. The *scoppio* (explosion) happens at 11am when a mechanical dove is 'lit' by the priest during mass. This dove flies along a wire which is stretched from the altar to the cart outside, sets off an explosion of fireworks, and returns to the altar. If all this goes smoothly, tradition has it that the harvests will be good for the year.

Car and motorbike racing

Autodromo del Mugello, near Scarperia (055 84 99 111).
Date Mar-Nov.
Top notch racing includes Formula 3 and motorcycle world championship competitions.

Mostra Mercato di Piante e Fiori

Parterra (Florence Tourist Info 055 29 08 32). **Date** 25 Apr-1 May.
Near Piazza Libertà, this huge plant and flower show attracts growers from all over the surrounding region.

Mostra Mercato Internazionale dell'Artigianato

Fortezza da Basso, Florence (055 49 721). **Date** late Apr/May.

A vast craft fair, taking in ceramics, glassware, fabrics, wood products etc-of varying quality.

Mostra Mercato Primaverile di Piante e Fiori

Greve (Florence Tourist Info 055 29 08 32). **Date** 1st Sun in May.

A large horticultural show in the pretty town of Greve near Florence. Food and drink stalls too.

Palio dei Micci

Querceta, near Seravezza (0584 20 331). **Date** 1st Sun in May.

This lower-key version of the Siena palio – held in a sports stadium and with donkeys rather than horses – is still a fine spectacle, with a parade in Renaissance costume, trumpets, drums, flag throwers and scenes of local life being re-enacted. The climax of the event is the donkey race between the various *contradas* (teams).

Cantine Aperte, Toscana

Date one Sun in late May.

A must for wine lovers. Wine-producing estates throw open their doors to the public for tastings and nibbles on one Sunday in late May from 9am-6pm. A useful guide to the various wineries is available at tourist offices.

Maggio Musicale Fiorentino

Florence (055 21 11 58). **Date** May/June.

An important international music festival with opera, concerts, ballet, chamber music and lectures given by international artists. *See chapter* **Music: Classical & Opera.**

Itinerari Sconosciuti

(055 28 08 81). **Date** May-July.

The opening of Florentine churches, palaces and monuments not normally available for public view.

Viareggio-Bastia-Viareggio International Yacht Race

(Viareggio Tourist Info 0584 48 881). **Date** May.

A major international race. There's also a powerboat race later in the year (phone above number for details).

International Iris Show

Piazzale Michelangelo, Florence (055 48 31 12). **Bus** 12, 13. **Open** 10am-12.30pm, 3-7pm, daily. **Date** May.

Spectacular floral display, with 100s of varieties of iris on display.

Summer

Una Sera al Museo

(055 28 08 81). **Date** June-Sept.

Many Florentine museums stay open in the evenings during the summer, and are used as concerts venues.

Giostra del Saracino

Arezzo (information 0575 37 76 678/tickets 0575 37 78 62). **Date** June. **Tickets** L15,000 (standing); L60-70,000 (sitting – only available for June event).

On one Sunday in mid-June, and on the first Sunday of September, this reconstruction of an ancient jousting tournament between the four *quartieri* of Arezzo is held in historic Piazza Grande. The event originated in the 13th century, and is accompanied by a parade of musicians and acrobatic flag throwers dressed in the period garb of their team's colour. The action starts in the morning at about 10am with the first of a series of parades. Another begins at 2.30pm, and, at 5pm, the procession of horses, knights and their escort arrives in the Piazza, and the tournament begins.

Calcio in Costume

Piazza Santa Croce, Florence (055 29 54 09). **Date** June.

Calcio in Costume*: football without rules, breeches without shame.*

The only fixed date for this extremely violent variation on football, in medieval costume, is 24 June. The dates of the other three matches are pulled out of a hat on Easter Sunday, but are all in June or very early July. *See also box in chapter* **Sport**.

Festa del Grillo

Parco delle Cascine, Florence. **Date** June.
Held on the day of Candlemas, this ancient symbolic event has become, like so many other events of the kind, an excuse for a big general market. However, live crickets – traditionally given to a sweetheart (to cheer them up in your absence) – are still sold in tiny hand-painted cages.

Palio, Magliano in Toscana

Magliano in Toscana (Grosseto Tourist Board 0564 45 45 10). **Date** 1st Sun in June.
One of the many smaller traditional events of the Tuscan year, this jousting match and palio (horse race) takes place in a particularly attractive town in the Maremma. The evening before the race, a torch-lit procession parades through the town, and the horses are blessed. The next day, the actual palio, raced in a field on the outskirts of the town, is at 4pm, but from 9am, the various *contradas* (teams) begin to gather and parade.

Luminaria di San Ranieri

Pisa (050 56 04 64). **Date** 16/17 June.
The visually stunning Luminaria sees tens of thousands of candles lit and displayed along the Arno and on the buildings on the Lungarni. Obviously, it should be seen after dark. The next day at 6.30/7pm is a boat race on the Arno between the four *quartieri* of the town.

Festa di San Giovanni

Florence. **Date** 24 June.
The day of Florence's patron saint is a public holiday in the municipality of Florence, and a huge fireworks display is held in the evening near Piazzale Michelangelo.

Il Gioco del Ponte

Pisa (information 050 91 03 39/tickets 050 91 05 092). **Date** last Sun in June. **Tickets** L20,000.
Another of those bizarre-to-the-uninitiated historic events. This is a kind of tug-of-war in reverse, dating from the 13th century, in which teams from Pisa and the surrounding area fight for supremacy on the Ponte di Mezzo by trying to push a metal construction on rails against an opposing team. Processions start from 4.30pm on the Lungarni near the Ponte di Mezzo, with the competition itself starting at 6pm. Tickets are available from the beginning of June.

Festa Internazionale della Ceramica

Montelupo (0571 91 75 47). **Date** 8 days from Sat to Sun in last week of June.
Tuscan ceramics are world famous, and Montelupo is one of the centres of production. This event celebrates a craft which is still very much rooted in the past, with Renaissance music and costume, and craftsmen demonstrating techniques, both past and present. Open 6pm-midnight Mon-Sat, 10am-midnight Sun.

Rassegna Internazionale di Canto Corale

Impruneta. **Date** Sats in June.
This international competition held annually near Florence attracts choirs from all over the world.

Torrita Blues

Torrita di Siena. **Date** Last week in June.
Blues festival featuring international artists.

International Polo Tournament

Ippodromo delle Cascine, Florence(055 20 47 847). **Date** late June/July.
Top flight sport action for horsey types.

Florence Dance Festival

Anfiteatro delle Cascine (055 28 92 76). **Date** July.
Three-week-long international contemporary dance festival. *See chapter* **Dance & Theatre**.

Open air cinema

Arena di Marte (Palasport) and Il Raggio Verde (Palazzo dei Congressi), Florence (055 29 31 69). **Date** July-Aug.
Two films per night are shown at these *cinema all'aperto*.

Opera Festival

Batignano (0564 28 115). **Date** July-Aug.
Near Grosseto, the tiny hilltop town of Batignano provides an idyllic setting for international opera productions.

Puccini Opera Festival

Torre del Lago (0584 35 93 22/fax 35 02 77).
Dates late July-mid Aug. **No credit cards**.
Puccini's villa on the shore of Lago di Massaciuccoli provides a magnficent setting for the staging of two or three of the Maestro's operas every year. *See also chapter* **Music: Classical & Opera**.

Effetto Venezia

Livorno. **Date** late July/Aug.
Shows, concerts and theatre productions are held in the evenings over a ten-day festival in the Venetian quarter of Livorno, so-called because of the numerous little canals in the area. Restaurants stay open late and serve local delicacies. Try the hearty Livornese speciality *cacciucco*, a thick fish soup.

Palio, Siena

Piazza del Campo, Siena. **Tickets** L250-400,000 (balconies). **Date** 2 July & 16 Aug.
The famous, and often criticised, horse race around Siena's splendid Piazza del Campo. This is Tuscan pageantry at its very best with the whole town becoming passionately involved with the race for weeks before and after. The last of the trial races is run at 9am on the morning of the big days. In the early afternoon, each horse and jockey is blessed in his team's church. At around 4.30/5pm, the historic procession (trumpets, drums, flag-throwers in costume) enters the Piazza del Campo and, after an incredible display of acrobatic flagthrowing, the often violent race is run at 7/7.30pm. Check final timings. There's no charge to stand, but you'll need to be in place very early to see the show. Tickets in the balconies overlooking the piazza are incredibly hard to come by. *See also box in chapter* **Siena**.

'On The Road Festival'

Pelago (83 26 236). **Tickets** L10,000. **Date** one weekend in late July.
This lively festival of street performers, artists, musicians, actors, mime artists, fire eaters, etc, takes place over the course of a weekend (Thur-Sun) in the second part of July. Events start at around 9pm. Pelago is 25 km east of Florence.

Sagra della Bistecca

Cortona. **Date** mid-Aug.
If meat's your thing, don't miss this orgy of steak-eating from the Valdichiana, reputedly home to the best cuts of beef in Italy.

Mostra Mercato dei Ferri taglienti e del ferro battuto

Scarperia. **Date** end Aug.
Fascinating display of knives, ancient and modern, and wrought iron from the home of this art.

Autumn

Autumn is the time when every little Tuscan village has its *sagra*. '*Sagra*' means 'rite' but these events are basically huge binges, with each having its own particular speciality (sausages, truffles, chestnuts, truffles, etc). The bigger events have stalls selling products associated with the food, and there is usually live music (often an old-fashioned band playing ballroom dancing numbers), and general merry-making. These events are invariably fun, and offer a fascinating glimpse of rural life. Many *sagre* are advertised by posters, or ask at the tourist office.

Festa della Rificolona
Florence. **Date** Sept.
Children make their own paper lanterns with a candle in the centre or else buy them in the local stationery shops. They then meet in the evening, either in Piazza SS Annunziata or along the river (posters usually inform you of the dates and whereabouts of the gatherings). For further details, *see chapter* **Children**.

Teatro Comunale
Florence (055 21 11 58). **Date** Sept-Dec.
Opera season.

Festa del Uva
Impruneta. **Date** End of Sept.
A celebration of the grape – food, wine and a parade of allegorical floats.

Rassegna Internazionale Musica dei Popoli
Auditorium Flog, Florence (055 42 20 300).
Date Oct-Nov.
Ethnic music festival.

Festa del Vino Novello
Montecarlo (Lucca). **Date** early Nov.
A celebration of the new season's wine.

Mostra Mercato del Tartufo Bianco
San Miniato. **Date** weekends in late Nov.
One of the year's top foodie events, celebrating the white truffle. Stalls sell not only bargain-priced *tartufi* but cheses, salami, olive oil, grappa and other choice comestibles. Local restaurants put on special truffle menus.

Festival dei Popoli
Florence (055 24 07 20). **Date** late Nov/early Dec.
A season of social documentary films.

Winter

The Italians go in for Nativity scenes in a big way, and many of the churches set up cribs, some of them '*viventi*' (ie with live animals). On the island of Giglio, there is even an underwater crib at Campese. In Florence, the principal ones are at San Lorenzo, Santa Croce, Chiesa di Dante and Santa Maria de' Ricci.

Settimana dei Beni Culturali
Florence (055 23 885). **Date** Early Dec.
This is free museum week, with open doors at all the city-owned museums. Phone to check details; sometimes the event happens in April.

Florence Marathon
(055 58 27 54). **Date** late Nov/early Dec.
Anyone over 18 can enter the 26+ miles. First prize is in excess of L3,000,000.

Sfilata dei Canottieri
Date 1 Jan.
Traditional parade of boats on the Arno in Florence.

Christmas Concerts
(055 28 08 81). **Date** Dec/Jan.
The antique organs of Florence are put through their paces.

Organ concerts
Sana Maria de' Ricci, Florence (055 21 50 44). **Date** Sats in Dec/Jan.

New Year's concert by the Scuola di Musica di Fiesole
Teatro Comunale , Florence (055 59 97 25). **Date** 1 Jan.

Concert and Ballet Season
Teatro Comunale, Florence (055 21 11 58).
Date Jan-Apr.
See chapters **Dance & Theatre**, **Music: Classical & Opera**.

Epiphany ('La Befana')
Date 6 Jan.
In the past, it was on the Befana (Epiphany), not at Christmas, that children in Italy got their presents (that's when the three magi brought theirs). On the eve of 6 January, a poor, old, tattered woman (the Befana), riding a broom or a donkey and carrying a sack of toys, fills children's stockings with toys, fruit and sweets (or, if they had misbehaved, a piece of coal). La Befana is a holiday throughout Italy, but nothing special happens in Florence. Some smaller towns, such as Barga and Manciano, put on more of a show. In Pisa, parachutists dressed as the Befana, drop from the sky and bring presents to children.

Viareggio Carnevale
(0584 96 25 68). *Public transport; LAZZI bus from Florence (Piazza Adua 055 35 10 61) to Viareggio or train from Florence SMN (info 1478 88 088) to Viareggio via Pisa*. **Date** Feb. **Tickets** L17,000 (for all days); L32,000 (in stands).
The precise dates of the most important Carnival celebrations in Italy outside Venice vary according to when Easter falls. Generally, however, the parades take place on four consecutive Sundays in February, the last (and most important) sometimes spilling over into March. The first three parades begin at 2.30/3 pm, and the last at 5pm, finishing around 9.30pm. The latter, an OTT procession of gigantic and elaborate floats, often lampooning political and public figures, is rounded off by a firework display and prize-giving ceremony for the best float. Tickets are available at booths in the town from 8am on the day. Tickets are bookable by phone from the above number.

February Carnivals
Many Tuscan towns hold Carnivals during February. Most consist of parades with elaborate floats, fancy dress parties, and excesses of eating and drinking. In Florence, children get dressed up and parade with their parents in the piazzas, and especially along the Lungarno Amerigo Vespucci. The younger kids scatter confetti, but beware older children with aerosol foam who squirt at anything moving. Elsewhere in Tuscany, Carnival celebrations include those in Borgo San Lorenzo (a children's event with allegorical floats, street performances, costumes, mimes, etc), Calenzano (in medieval costumes) and San Gimignano (floats and masks and costumes). The last day of Carnevale is Shrove Tuesday.

Stepping down into the past: an Etruscan tomb near Sovana that probably dates back to c700 BC. Tombs – and the odd stretch of wall – are almost all that remains of Etruscan architecture in Tuscany.

Architecture

Highlights from the last three thousand years.

This page: *The* **Roman Amphitheatre** *at Fiesole – in the 1st century AD a far more important and sophisticated town than Florence.*

Opposite page: *The astonishingly ornate 12th-14th-century façade of* **San Michele in Foro**, *Lucca – a local interpretation of Pisan Romanesque.*

This page: *The turretted Gothic might of Siena's 14th-century* **Palazzo Pubblico**, *a fine example of civic-cum-military architecture.*

Opposite page: *The light, delicate and serene arcades of Florence's 15th-century* **Convento di San Marco***: a masterpiece of the Renaissance by Michelozzo.*

Audaciously exaggerated architecture in the 16th-century courtyard of **Palazzo Pitti**, *Florence: Ammannati's mad Mannerist take on Classical architecture.*

The Tuscans

Il Toscanaccio: The Tuscan character.

Foreigners are famously in love with the beauty of Tuscany, its harmonious landscapes, Renaissance *centri storici*, Romanesque churches and all that art (all so beautiful, in fact, that the regional council are attempting to copyright its landscape, arguing that it is the work of human labour). So it's curious that one of the most distinctive features of Tuscany, to fellow Italians at least, is the one thing that imported aesthetes never take on board at all – the character of the Tuscans themselves.

Within Italy, Tuscans have long suffered from being regarded as, well, real bastards. Arrogant, sarcastic, perfidious, or just plain *cattivi* – nasty.

Much of this is envy, and an abiding sense of inferiority – after all, it was Tuscany that has contributed the lion's share to Italy's cultural and linguistic formation. Not just through the Middle Ages and Renaissance: when the Lombard Alessandro Manzoni sat down to write his classic novel, *I promessi sposi* (The Betrothed) in the 19th century, the first serious attempt to invent a modern, national language (as opposed to the plethora of regional dialects), he chose the Sienese dialect. Like Oxford English for the pre-war generation, or

Long Island Lockjaw today, the cultivated Tuscan accent speaks authority and superiority like no other in Italy – although it has long ceased to be a crucial centre of political or economic power or influence. Non-Tuscans are quick to be irritated by that presumption of "We are the real thing".

There are important historical roots to this reputation. Dante's *Divina Commedia* is not just Italy's principal literary oeuvre, it is also one of the most detailed and vituperative hit lists ever committed to paper. Apart from poetic genius, it also contains a catalogue of insults about people (rival poets and writers, but neighbours as well) with whom the sublime Dante wished to settle a score or two.

Another very important variant on Tuscan bloodymindedness, is *campanilismo* – regional chauvinism, deriving from *campanile*, as in, "Our bell tower is taller and more impressive than yours," or bitter rivalry between neighbouring towns and villages. Much of the vigour and growth of Tuscany during the Medieval/Renaissance period was fuelled by the sheer hatred engendered by rival Tuscan towns, particularly between Siena and Florence (other complex sub plots include Florence v the rest, Livorno v Pisa).

Is that a Pisan in the corner?

Campanilismo informed daily life, at all levels, from culinary skills to the size and prowess of the rival cities' standing armies.

True to their *campanilista* spirit, Tuscans can list, with amazing detail, the defects of their fellow Tuscans, and will warm to the theme over a drink or dinner. Nothing breaks the ice more effectively than a leading question (say) to a Sienese "What do you think about the Pisans?".

A spectacular modern form of this ritual hatred can be observed in football rivalry. Florence's football supporters, *i tifosi dei viola* (the team wears purple, *viola*) have long been the most aggressive supporters, and until recently, their fans have been responsible for most of the worst hooliganism at away games. Matches between serie B and serie C, or even local league teams, are worth following, but more for the action on the terraces, than that on the pitch. Franco Zeffirelli is best known abroad for his winsomely commercial, cloying epics, but in Italy he is best known for being *i viola*'s most vitriolic fan. His (and most other *viola tifosi*'s) hatred of Juventus leads him to openly advocate violence against Turin's premier team's fans, on television and in print. But there is a ritual quality to his diatribes, which makes him lovable for what might appear at first as hateful.

Likewise, Italy's other best known professional Tuscan is veteran right-wing newspaper editor, Indro Montanelli, whose caustic, unreconstructed, fogeyish views actually make him a cult figure among most of Italy's predominant left-wing cultural hegemony. He prefaces some of his outpourings with the qualifier, "*ma io sono un toscanaccio*" (but then I'm just a mean Tuscan). Well, that's all right, then.

The Tuscan sense of humour is very important, although it varies in nuance from city to city, province to province. Florentines are famous for their sarcasm, and sick humour. During the two long decades in which young couples were being murdered by the 'Mostro di Firenze' (the Monster of Florence), with police patrols and neighbourhood watch units operating particularly around the village of Scandicci, many Florentines talked about the jocularly-named 'Cicci di Scandicci', as though he were an amusing cartoon character.

Things lighten up a bit in the coastal towns of Grosseto and Livorno, where there is a long tradition of *burle* – practical jokes, sometimes cruel, at the expense of the ingenuous. A huge national drama was created in the mid 1980s by the escapades of three Livornese students, who with the aid of a judiciously wielded Black and Decker, set up Italy's most spectacular art hoax in living memory. Mindful of the legend that local sculptor Modigliani had tossed several of his tribal-looking stone heads into the local canals, they 'dredged' them up, and fooled most of Italy's art critical nomenclature for several weeks, before the sensa-

tional televised denouement, in which they created another, fourth head, with their trusty drill, in front of the cameras. Needless to say, Black & Decker wasted no time in taking out full page adverts in all the Italian papers advertising their masterpiece-creating hardware.

Livorno is also home to Italy's most scurrilous weekly newspaper, *Il Vernacoliere* (the homespun dialect). Although obtainable thoughout Italy, its deeply offensive, non-PC humour is really too much for most non-Tuscans to stomach. Tabloid in form, and etched in solid vitriol, it's largely filled with smutty news stories (often featuring female members of the Windsor family and Hollywood clans, and focusing on ill-concealed similes of their reproductive organs and the imaginative, vegetable-based use thereof). You either laugh until you cry, or you want to assault the newsvendor.

It's also widely accepted that Italy's top comic actors and TV comedians are Tuscan, although sadly most of them peddle a style and an act that doesn't travel well (though resentfully appreciated elsewhere in Italy). Actor-directors like Francesco Nuti and Alessandro Benvenuti, veteran actress-TV presenter Athina Cenci, massively popular TV personality Marco Columbro, Hollywood's darling, and latterday Pink Panther's son, comic genius Roberto Benigni, and not least Italy's current box-office smash hit comic heart throb, Leonardo Pieraccioni.

Living in Florence is not always easy for non-Tuscans, although foreigners, especially native English-speakers, may get an added degree of respect denied other Italians. During police investigations of the recent society murder of glamorous Conte Di Robilant, the Carabinieri were immensely frustrated by the way that the upper echelons of the Florentine smart set just clammed up, in a sort of snobbish *omertà* worthy of any mid-ranking Palermo hood. The prevailing attitude seemed to be, according to one inspector interviewed by the press, that it was more important to close ranks, and put on a massive display of 'class', than actually help the course of justice.

However, whatever social horrors await other Italians, kinder treatment may be in store for the British. "One of the reasons that we Tuscans so like the British, is that we perceive them to be like us in so many ways," suggests Tiziana Frescobaldi, scion of one of Florence's most distinguished families. Americans, in contrast, straightforwardly pleasant as they often seem, are viewed more as innocents abroad.

"There is a lot of closed, provincial, and presumptuous attitudes around the city, and in all social classes, largely as a result of seeing ourselves as living in the cradle of European civilization, but there is also a pervading sense of the ridiculous – we are good at poking fun at ourselves – not a quality that all other Italians share.

New Tuscan, new mobile, old Barbour.

Catching up on the gossip Tuscan-style.

Buddhism in Tuscany

The link between Roman Catholicism and Italy is so strong in most people's mind, that the idea of linking any part of the country with an oriental religion seems distinctly improbable. However, Tuscany has been, over the last couple of decades, one of the vital centres of practising Buddhism in the western world.

"When we started practising in 1976, there were about ten of us, and all in Florence. Now I'd say there's about 5,000, between adepts and sympathisers, spread throughout Tuscany". Marco Magrini, 39, is a senior journalist with *Il Sole 24 Ore*, Italy's equivalent to the *Financial Times*. "Why there are so many Buddhists in Tuscany, is a question I've often asked myself, but never found a satisfactory answer."

There are various different Buddhist sects active in Italy, and relations between them aren't always harmonious. Magrini is one of the founder members of the Tuscan branch of Soka Gakkai, the Japanese Buddhist sect whose charismatic leader is 70-year-old Daisaku Ikeda. Theirs is an essentially secular, outward looking and even ecumenical movement, and by far the largest of the various Buddhist sects active in Italy. A recent book, *Il Buddha in Noi* (Buddha Within Us) by Maria Macioti, calculated the total population of Ikeda's followers in Italy a couple of years ago as about 15,000, though Magrini reckons that it is now closer to 17,000.

Five years ago, there was a painful divorce from the more fundamentalist group Nichiren Shoshu, who preach a separatist line, and oppose dialogue of any sort with other sects or religions.

The ascetic Tibetan Buddhists are also very active in Tuscany, with an important centre at Pomaia, high in the hills, in the province of Pisa. There are also lots of Zen Buddhists in the region. "For years all the various groups had very little contact with each other, but recently a round table was organized in Milan by Johann Galtung, the American academic who specialises in organising peace conferences. It was a great success," explains Domitilla Caratti, a feisty young Florentine aristocrat, who handles international public relations for Ferragamo, the luxury leather goods label.

Although Tuscan Soka Gokkai now embraces people of all ages and backgrounds, when it started in 1976, it was curiously circumscribed. "In the first few years, about 90 per cent of us were jazz musicians in our early twenties," recalls Magrini, who is also an ace keyboard player and no mean jazz composer. "I don't think there was anyone older than 25. Being so young, our energy made us enthusiastic to spread the word." Nowadays, Tuscan Buddhists are as likely to be teachers, lawyers or manual workers. "Actually, the biggest social group we have now are women over 50 – there are lots of elderly female pensioners who chant in Tuscany."

When Ikeda made his first visit to Florence in 1981, he was so impressed by the energy and fervour of his new Italian followers, that he decided to set up the main Italian centre there. Their *centro culturale*, or headquarters, is in the impressive 13th-century Villa di Bellaggio, on the outskirts of Florence, and is surrounded by gardens and green fields. "Apart from being a wonderfully spiritual place, ideal for chanting and meetings, we also have some great parties in the grounds," enthuses Caratti, whose straightforward and energetic enthusiasm for life is quite an advertisement for the sect.

Although Japanese Buddhism has a rather patchy reputation in Britain, and is linked in some people's minds to that fateful phrase "chanting for a Porsche", and rather hyper late '80s PR Queens as spoofed in *Absolutely Fabulous*, in Italy there are no such negative or spurious connotations. As role model, there is football idol Roberto Baggio (known as *il divino codino* – the sublime pony tail), who was famously converted to chanting when he played for *i viola*, the Florentine side. "Although there are as yet no Buddhist MPs, we do have at least one city councillor in Florence, and quite a few mayors of small towns and villages in Tuscany," adds Magrini.

Inevitably, the immense growth rate of chanting among the populace has provoked curiosity and even envy among the Catholic hierarchy, some of whom are particularly miffed by the way that old ladies in Tuscany, traditionally one of the church's strongest niche groups, are 'going over' to the other side. Cardinal Ratzinger, the Vatican's ultra conservative chief ideologue, has specifically singled out contemporary Buddhism for baleful criticism, although there are known to be one or two thoughtful Jesuits within the Vatican walls who are well disposed. "Although the Catholic hierarchy officially shuns any public contact, we are actually involved in an ongoing dialogue with one or two quite interesting Vatican figures," adds Magrini discreetly.

Expats & Eccentrics

The good, the mad and the ugly.

The British presence in Tuscany goes back a long way. **John Hawkwood** (*see chapter* **History**) made his fortune as a mercenary in the 14th century, capitalising on the numerous inter-city feuds; Robert Dudley, illegtitimate son of Queen Elizabeth I's favourite, the Earl of Leicester, came here, divorced his wife and built warships for the Medici; while in the 17th century architect Inigo Jones designed a cathedral for Livorno, and used the city's main square, the Piazza Grande, as the model for Covent Garden.

Later, the Grand Tour brought Anglo-Saxons in droves, and 'safe' lodgings in the main centres sprang up to accommodate them. Such was the house of the widow Vanini, where **Tobias Smollett** stayed in the autumn of 1764 (as described in his gleefully xenophobic journal *Travels through France and Italy*). The dangers of taking pot luck were illustrated by Smollett's brief visit to Siena, of which "I can say nothing from my own observation, but that we were indifferently lodged in a house that stunk like a privy, and fared wretchedly at supper."

It was not until the beginning of the 19th century, though, that a significant English community was established. The **Shelley** circle, **Walter Savage Landor**, and the **Brownings** were all sometime residents. Florence was the main centre, followed by Pisa, Livorno, where there was a small mercantile community, and the spa town of Bagni di Lucca, where a certain Mrs Sisted successfully lobbied the Pope for permission to open Italy's first Anglican chapel. The location was not hugely convenient, as she discovered when her husband died in Rome. The only way she could get his body to Bagni for burial was to have it transported by a coachman with a permit for "used goods" (*see chapter* **Massa-Carrara and Lucca Provinces**).

Above all, Florence came to attract exiles and eccentrics who saw Italy as a land of warm Mediterranean freedom. **Byron** was fleeing a disastrous marriage, Shelley came as part of a free-loving ménage a trois, Landor ended up here after having fought with Oxford University, his father, and just about everyone else. For all their rebel credentials, though, few of these Englishmen abroad made much attempt to commune with the locals: in Bagni di Lucca, Shelley preferred to "sit on the rocks reading Herodotus" by the side of a forest pool. If they were strange when they arrived, this detached lifestyle made such exiles stranger by the year – a process explored by **Henry James** in the character of Gilbert Osmond, the brittle, cruel aesthete of *The Portrait of a Lady*.

But of all the Anglo-Saxon oddities to be found in Florence and the surrounding area, two of the oddest must certainly have been Ouida and Sir George Sitwell.

Ouida

Louisa Ramé was a sort of mid-19th-century Barbara Cartland; her pseudonym 'Ouida' came from the childhood mispronunciation of her first name. By 1867, at the age of 28, she had written no fewer than 47 romantic novels, which were so successful that she was able to set up her widowed mother and her siblings in a grand London townhouse and leave for the warm south, where she hoped to find relief from bronchitis and material for further romantic yarns.

In Florence she rented the Villa Farniola at Scandicci, and set to work living out her arcadian fantasies. She tended to identify herself with her flouncy heroines, and even dressed the part: "Ouida dressed according to the heroine she was in the process of creating, sometimes in trailing damasks of brilliant colours or else in simple dimity like the Tuscan peasants whose lives she lived in imagination" (Lina Waterfield, *Castle in Italy*). Her love life was fraught with obstacles, some of which were of her own making; after an infatuation with an Italian singer called Mario, she fell in love with a neighbouring nobleman, the Marchese della Stufa; but unbeknown to her, Stufa was already acting as *cicisbeo* (official gallant) to married Englishwoman and light history writer, Janet Ross. When she discovered the affair, Ouida was deeply wounded, but she swallowed her pride and turned the whole thing into yet another novel, *Friendship*, the publication of which split the Florentine expatriate community down the middle, with some defending her right to literary revenge and others refusing ever to speak to her again.

By this time Ouida had become an eccentric and rather lonely figure whose main companions were her beloved dogs; she even created a canine cemetery in the grounds of her villa. She lived well beyond her means, eating at Doneys (the Anglo-Florentine meeting-place) and ordering all her dresses from Worth, the Parisian designer. She was eventually evicted from the Villa Farniola and began to wander from boarding house to hotel with her aged mother, never staying very long in any one place on account of the pack of dogs she refused to part with. In 1895, she moved into a villa outside Lucca, where she continued to write (though few read her novels by this time) and take an interest in Italian politics: maverick gentleman-rebels like Garibaldi and later D'Annunzio were her heroes.

The poet Wilfred Scawen Blunt visited her here in 1900: he found her "altogether... a pathetic figure, condemned to solitude not by choice but by necessity, and regretting the cheerful society of Florence... 'The world', she said, 'takes its revenge on us, for having despised it'. Ouida died in Viareggio in 1909 after another six years of enforced wanderings. She was buried in the English cemetery in Bagni di Lucca (a place she hated), in a tomb which shows her lying down with her feet resting on a faithful dog, in imitation of a Jacopo della Quercia effigy in Lucca cathedral. As she left only debts, the tomb was paid for by the British consul in Lucca.

The Sitwells

An equally pathetic but altogether more comic variety of eccentric, Sir George Sitwell was member of parliament for Scarborough and the father of that celebrated trio of aesthetes, Edith, Osbert and Sacheverell. He must have been at least partly responsible for the brilliance of his offspring, but he was also a tyrant: on visiting DH Lawrence in his villa near Florence, Edith was quite put out by the way the Nottinghamshire miner's son harped on the difficulties of his own childhood, "as if the rich cannot have quite as miserable a time of it".

Osbert paints a grotesque but undoubtedly accurate portrait in his four-part autobiography. In *Great Morning*, the third volume, he relates how Sir George stumbled on the castle of Montegufoni, just outside the village of Montespertoli, southwest of Florence. "He apparently found it by accident in 1906 while motoring from Florence to Siena, when the driver took the wrong turning and the motor then broke down beneath the walls of an immense old castle... On the terrace above, the cellar doors were open, and the peasants could be seen treading the grapes, for it was the season of the vintage".

The castle was built by the Acciaiuoli, a noble Tuscan family who became Dukes of Athens in the 12th century. It provided the irrascible, misanthropic Sir George with an endless source of Gothick thrills. Bricked-up rooms were discovered during maintenance work, stone cannonballs were unearthed in the garden, and in what Osbert describes as "perhaps my father's happiest moment", a woman's skeleton was discovered at the bottom of the castle well.

He kept himself busy here in his Italian home. He was always writing himself brief, illegible notes about subjects which he later intended to dedicate essays to: "acorns as an article of Medieval diet", for example. One work he did finish was *The Making of Gardens* (1909), a surprisingly straight and erudite account of the laying out of formal gardens. His wife, Lady Ida – who was quite as out of touch as Sir George, in her own scatter-brained way – had her own rooms in the castle, and the two lived in blissfully separate galaxies, brought together only by the occasional disaster, as Osbert relates: "My mother... would ask 20 people to luncheon and forget to tell either my father or the butler or the chef; indeed, it would pass from her mind altogether. Suddenly, just as my father was having a quiet early luncheon, the guests would arrive, tired and hungry – that was the sort of incident which could occur regularly".

As he grew older, Sir George became increasingly distant from other people, and unable to deal with them – though his enthusiasm for gardens and history never left him. "If he did not like what was going on around him", Osbert informs us, "he just refused to perceive it, and then it could no longer exist". Thus he entirely failed to notice that Lady Ida was being blackmailed by an unscrupulous moneylender – an episode which led to a long and painful lawsuit. He was equally oblivious to the nuances of modern speech: when a friend promised to "give him a ring tomorrow", Sir George was quite put out when the promised present failed to materialise.

Though he found at Montegufoni a "comparative contentment", his end, when it came, was quite as sad as Ouida's. Sir George never listened to the radio and refused to budge when the English residents began to stream out of Tuscany in 1939. On the day he heard the news that Italy had declared war on England, writes Osbert, "he climbed the Tower of the Castle – with some difficulty for he was over 80 and had been ill for a long time – and remained up there for an hour or more". Finally he was persuaded to leave for Switzerland, where he died three years later, out of reach of friends and family.

Edith Sitwell: barmy daughter of a barking father.

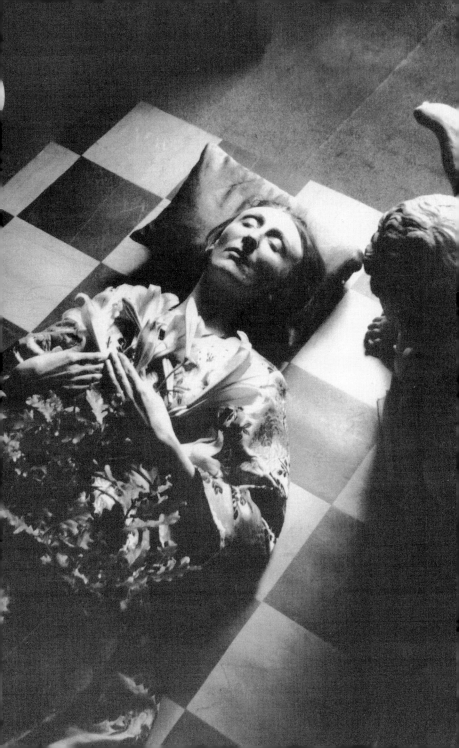

Tuscan Wines

Everything you wanted to know but were afraid to ask.

Tuscany is a major wine-producing region, making both red and white wine although traditionally the emphasis has been on red. To taste these wines you can tour the region and visit individual wineries where wine is sold direct to the public; look for the sign *'vendita diretta'*. Alternatively, almost all villages have a wine bar or *enoteca* where you can taste wine by the glass.

Classification of Italian Wine

The original classification dates back to the 1960s: **Vdt** (Vino da Tavola or table wine), **DOC** (Denominazione di Origine, indicating wines made to a specific formula in a specified geographical region). **DOCG** (Denominazione di Origine Garantita, the same as DOC but for better quality wines) was added in the 1980s. As the wine industry developed and became more experimental, winemakers became increasingly frustrated by the limitations imposed by the restrictive DOC laws. As a result they frequently ignored them, making innovative, new-style wines – the so-called **'Super Tuscans'**. Without classification these wines, under the old laws, were designated Vino da Tavola in spite of the fact that they were high-prestige products. The profusion of these new wines brought about a complete revision of the discredited wine laws in 1992. These changes are now starting to make an impact. Under the new system the most basic wines will be classified as VdT, in which no varietal or geographic claims can be made, and only a brand name can be used. The new level of classification is **IGT** (Indicazione Geografica Tipica) which will cover regional wines. They will be able to use a geographic name and a locally authorised grape. New, more specific DOC and DOCGs will be created to cover subzones, even to the extent of creating a DOC

classification for a single vineyard. The rank of DOCG has been limited to a dozen famous areas, but will now become the right of any DOC wine that performs consistently well for five years. Conversely, any wines not performing up to standard will be demoted by one rank or more. These new laws can only be good news for both the wine industry and the wine drinker.

Red Wine

The most famous of the Tuscan reds are **Brunello di Montalcino**, **Vino Nobile di Montepulciano**, **Chianti Classico** and more recently the so-called **Super Tuscans**.

Super Tuscans

This is the name that has been coined for new style wines coming out of Tuscany over the last 15 years. While the range of these wines is enormous, one can generally characterise them as being high priced, made with a large percentage of Cabernet and aged in *barrique*. As they have no DOC classification, makers have felt entirely free to label them according to their own whims and fantasies. The initial approach was an attempt to imitate French style wines and produce high priced novelty wines. However, as the wine industry has matured and developed, there has been an increasing tendency to produce experimental, innovative wines from non traditional grape varieties. Some less well known Super Tuscans worth keeping an eye out for are: Lamaione (Castelgiocondo), Olmaia (Col d'Orcia), Grifi (Avignonese), Fontalloro (Felsina), and Fontodi (Flaccianello) and Ghiaie della Furba (Capezzana); and Sassicaia, Ornellaia and Tignanello from the Antinori.

Montalcino

This hilltop town lies 40km south of Siena along the old via Cassia occupying a panoramic position overlooking the Val d'Asso and the Val d'Orcia. Wine has been produced in the area since Etruscan times but it is only recently that the business has been taken seriously. During the middle of last century enthusiastic growers started to experiment with the Sangiovese grape. The result was the development of the Brunello grape, a Sangiovese

clone, Sangiovese Grosso. It has been used, unblended, to create the wine on which Montalcino's reputation rests, **Brunello di Montalcino** (DOCG). It is extraordinary to realise that Brunello was virtually unknown outside the region up until the mid '60s, while today it has an international reputation and is considered one of Italy's top wines. The production of Brunello is strictly controlled by the local consortium, a regulatory body to which most growers belong, which determines factors such as grape variety, length of ageing and maximum yields per acre. All wine is tasted and examined before being labelled Brunello and as a result quality is very high. Brunello is made from 100 per cent Sangiovese grapes and is aged for a minimum of four years, three of which are in wood. Two types of barrel are commonly used: large Slovenian oak barrels or *botti* and smaller French oak barrels or *barrique*. After five years of ageing the wine becomes *riserva*. The wine is full-bodied, slightly tannic and well balanced with great ageing potential. The nose is fruity; blackberry, raspberry and violets predominate but there are subtle overtones of oak and vanilla. Brunello ages well and can be kept for between 10 and 30 years depending on the producer and the vintage. It goes well with red meat – especially game – mushrooms, truffles and strong cheeses.

Rosso di Montalcino (DOC) is made from the same grape as Brunello but is aged for only a year, resulting in a lively, fresh fruity wine. It is considerably less expensive than its classy relation

and is a wine for drinking young rather than laying down. It is a good accompaniment to pasta, poultry and veal dishes.

The third wine produced in the area is **Moscadello di Montalcino** (DOC) which was drunk at the English court in the 17th century. This sweet dessert wine is made from the Moscato Bianco grape, producing a fruity, fragrant, fresh dessert wine. It is made in three styles: still, sparkling (*frizzante*) and late harvest (*passito*). The wine is overwhelmingly grapey, both to the nose and to taste. The late harvest variety is made by leaving the grapes on the vine to increase sweetness. After picking they are left to dry further, before fermentation, which concentrates the raisin flavour. Producers worth looking out for are:

Altesino

Palazzo Altesino, Loc. Altesino (0577 80 62 08).
Open 8.30am-12.30pm, 2-6pm, Mon-Fri; Sat, Sun by appointment. **Credit** AmEx, EC, MC, V.
A small modern winery, with vineyards scattered throughout the region. It was founded in 1970 by Giulio Consono, one of the first northern Italians to establish themselves in the region. The winery is situated in the most northern part of the production zone, and produces an elegant well-balanced Brunello, a Brunello Riserva from their Montesoli vineyard (produced only in the best years) and two VdTs: Palazzo Altesi which is 100 per cent Sangiovese and Alte D'Altesi which is a mix of Sangiovese and Cabernet.

Villa Banfi

Sant'Angelo Scalo (0577 84 01 11/86 60 01).
Open 10am-7.30pm daily. **Credit** AmEx, EC, MC, V.
This American-owned concern is one of the largest producers in the area, with over 800 hectares of vines and producing over 5,000,000 bottles a year. It boasts one of Italy's largest, most modern wineries and it is extraordinary to realise that it has all been constructed in the last 20 years, under the dynamic direction of Ezio Rivella. Banfi produces a classic Brunello, an exceptional Riserva, Poggio all'Oro and a highly drinkable Rosso di Montalcino, Centine. Winemakers are also experimenting with Chardonnay, Pinot Noir, Syrah and Cabernet. The tasting rooms are located in the restored castle, Poggio alle Mura. The castle is also home to the fascinating Museo dei Vetri, which has a large collection of Roman glassware.

Col D'Orcia

Sant'Angelo in Colle (0577 80 80 01). **Open** 8.30am-12.30pm, 2.30-7.30pm, daily. **Credit** EC, MC, V.
The estate is located in the extreme south of the production zone, close to the village of Sant'Angelo in Colle. This tranquil estate, which looks out over Monte Amiata, dates back to the 18th century and has been owned by Conte Francesco Cinzano since 1973. Winemaking is in the capable hands of Mario Olivero who employs a high level of technology in a state-of-the-art winery to produce some superb wines. On-going research projects in co-operation with the University of Florence augur well for the future. They produce an elegant Brunello and two Riserva, produced in great vintages only – the Poggio al Vento, the 'Cru' of the estate. The VdT, Olmaia, produced from 100 per cent Cabernet Sauvignon, is also good, as is the exemplary Moscadello.

Tenuta Caparzo

Loc. Torrenieri (0577 84 83 90). **Open** 8am-1pm, 2.30-6pm, Mon-Fri. **Credit** AmEx, DC, EC, MC, V.
This innovative winery is characteristic of the cosmopolitan flavour of Montalcino, being owned by nine partners, com-

SIMPLY

Tuscany
& Umbria

The regions of Tuscany and Umbria epitomise the attractions of Italy: beautiful countryside reminiscent of the landscapes of Renaissance masterpieces, exquisite art and architecture, and wonderful food and wine.

At Simply Tuscany & Umbria, we have the specialist expertise and the necessary connections to bring you only the very best of these outstanding regions. We offer a unique range of accommodation including private villas with pools, self-catering apartments in traditional country farmhouses, and charming little hotels full of Italian character.

Whether you are searching the cultural sophistication of Florence, Siena and Lucca, or the rural simplicity of life in the country, our friendly staff can advise you with personal, in-depth knowledge of all our locations.

For those who wish to design their own itinerary we can offer our flexible "Wandering" programme, and our special interest holidays will suit those with a passion for cookery, art & architecture or watercolour painting.

For a copy of our informative brochure, please call
0181 995 9323

Simply Tuscany & Umbria, Chiswick Gate, 598-608 Chiswick High Road, London W4 5RT
ABTA V1337   ATOL 1922   AITO

ing from disparate regions of Italy. This is one of the better known wineries; their wines having been served at Italian state banquets as well as to first class passengers on Alitalia. They make a good Brunello Riserva which is aged in small casks, also an excellent white, *La Grance*, made from Chardonnay, Sauvignon and Gewurztraminer grapes. The equally good VdT, Ca'del Pazzo, is a mixture of Sangiovese and Cabernet.

Il Poggione

Sant'Angelo in Colle (0577 86 40 29). **Open** 8am-1pm, 3-6pm, Mon-Fri; 8am-noon Sat. **No credit cards**.
Located in the village of Sant'Angelo in Colle, this estate has a long tradition of making top class Brunello. Their wines already had a considerable reputation in the '20s and '30s; by the '60s their Brunello was thought to be one of the best in the region. The vineyards enjoy one of the warmest microclimates in the region and over the past few decades winemaking was in the hands of Pierluigi Talenti, a man utterly passionate about his work. Talenti has now gone on, in his retirement, to run his own winery across the road, Pian di Conte, but continues to collaborate with Il Poggione. The wines are powerful and long-lived, in the classic style; the Rosso di Montalcino and Moscadello are also good. If you are here around lunchtime, Il Pozzo in the villaage centre serves great Tuscan food and has an excellent selection of local wines.

Verbena

Loc. Verbena (0577 84 84 32). **Open** 8am-8pm daily. **Credit** AmEx, EC, MC, V.
A small working farm, located on the road between Torrenieri and Montalcino, and entirely family run. The cellars are in an 18th century famhouse that also offers *agriturismo*-style accommodation. Good Brunello and Rosso di Montalcino as well as Grappa and olive oil on sale.

Montepulciano

This graceful, dignified town, standing at 600m, is surrounded by vineyards and olive groves. Wine has been made here since at least the 6th century. The town is best known for **Vino Nobile di Montepulciano** (DOCG), the first Italian wine to gain this status. It is made from a mixture of grapes in various proportions: Prugnolo, so called because of its plummy taste, Canaiolo and Mammolo. It is aged for a minimum of two years in oak barrels, three for *riserva*. Vino Nobile goes well with roast meat and other strongly flavoured dishes. It has quite a pronounced smell of violets and a strangely attractive bitter aftertaste. In the past, high quality wines were the prerogative of aristocratic families, hence the name Nobile. Large differences in style can be noted among different producers, ranging from robust to elegant style wines.

The second string wine is **Rosso di Montepulciano**, which occupies a similar niche to Rosso di Montepulciano, a young, fruity wine which does not require cellaring. It is made from Prugnolo and Canaiolo grapes and is considerably less expensive – and less alcoholic – than Vino Nobile.The production of both Vino Nobile and Rosso di Montepulciano is overseen by the local consortium to which most producers belong.Their role is to apply standards to the processes of mak-

ing and ageing wines, supply expert assistance and promote and develop the wine industry. Some producers to look out for are:

Avignonesi

Via di Gracciano nel Corso 91, Montepulciano (0578 75 78 72). **Open** 9am-1.30pm, 2.30-7.30pm, daily. **Credit** AmEx, DC, EC, MC, V.
This 175 hectare estate was established by the Falvo family in 1974. Ettore Falvo is one of the main players on the Montepulciano wine scene and is largely responsible for improving the image and quality of the product. They have three vineyard sites; Le Cappezzine, I Poggetti and La Selva. The latter is outside the Vino Nobile production zone and grows most of the grapes for their wide range of VdTs. The Vino Nobile and the Riserva are full bodied wines which take years to reach their potential. They are also producing a range of VdTs: *Grifi* which is made from a blend of Sangiovese and Cabernet; *Marzocco* a barrique-aged Chardonnay, and a highly acclaimed Vin Santo called *Occhio di Pernice* which is aged for ten years in 13 gallon barrels. The Poliziani call this a meditative wine; it should be drunk on its own, in small quantities, out of large, wide glasses. You can taste some of these wines and visit the cellars, which date back to the 16th century, on the Corso in the centre of Montepulciano.

Gattavecchi

Via di Collazzi 72, Montepulciano (0578 75 71 10). **Open** 9am-1pm, 3-7pm, daily. **Credit** AmEx, EC, MC, V.
For a truly Italian experience, a visit to the Gattavecchi cantina is highly recommended.This small company is enthusiastically run by the Gattavecchi family. They have 15 hectares of vineyards and have been producing wine for 15 years. The cantina, next to the church of Santa Maria dei Servi, is especially worth a visit as it is situated directly over an Etruscan tomb. You can descend into the bowels of the earth to visit it, before tasting some of the excellent wines on

offer in the cantina. They make two quite different Vino Nobiles; one a traditional-style wine, the other, *Piazza Grande*, which contains 90 per cent Sangiovese. Their Rosso di Montepulciano is both highly drinkable and incredibly good value. They also make Aleatico, a traditional red wine dating back to the Renaissance that has recently been revived. Made from the Aleatico grape, it is smooth, rich and slightly sweet.

Poliziano

Via Fontago 11, Montepulciano (0578 73 81 71). **Open** 8.30am-noon, 2.30-6pm, Mon-Fri. **No credit cards**.

One of the longest established estates in Montepulciano, with 80 hectares of vineyards on three sites. The company was established in 1962 and has been run by Federico Carletti since 1984. They produce three different Vino Nobiles, two of which are single-vineyard wines. The two VdTs are Le Stanze, mainly Cabernet Sauvignon with a small addition of Cabernet Franc, and Elegia which is 100 per cent Sangiovese. The Rosso di Montepulciano is fresh and fruity and very reasonably priced.

Fattoria del Cerro

Via Grazianella 5, Montepulicano (0578 76 77 22). **Open** 8.30am-12.30pm, 2.30-6.30pm, Mon-Fri. **Credit** AmEx, EC, MC, V.

This is one of the largest estates in the region with over 140 hectares of vines, with many more under plantation. The vineyards are spread out over the hills of Argiano, recognised as one of the best areas for the production of Vino Nobile. They are at the forefront of innovative viticulture, setting up experimental projects to select the most valid biotypes in terms of ageing qualities. You can visit the vineyard and take a tour of the high-tech wine-making cellar or visit the tasting rooms in Montepulciano's Piazza Grande. They make full bodied wines, especially Vino Nobile and Vino Nobile Riserva as well as two very good VdTs; *Cerro Rosso* which is 100 per cent Cabernet and a Chardonnay, *Cerro Bianco*. Both are aged in barrique.

Vin Santo

Vin Santo is sweet dessert wine which is made all over Tuscany. It is made from Malvasia (and also white) grapes which are left to dry after picking. They are then crushed, and fermented in *caratelli*, brandy casks which contain the remains of the previous year's wine, known as *madre*. The barrels are then sealed and the wine is left to age for a minimum of three years, but often much longer. The wine is a deep golden colour and usually served with *cantucci* or almond biscuits. The good quality Vin Santo is usually expensive and always hard to come by.

Notable producers include Avignonesi, Capezzana, Contucci, Poliziano, Selvapiana and Isole Olena.

Chianti Classico

Chianti is the region that lies between Florence and Siena. It is a hilly region of vineyards and olive groves, dotted with castles and medieval villages. The region has also given its name to the famous red wine, Chianti. Of the many different wines calling themselves Chianti, only the wine produced in the Chianti heartland can call itself Chianti Classico (DOCG). It is produced in seven districts

or *commune*: Greve and Panzano, Castellina, Radda, Gaiole, Barberino, San Casciano and Castelnuovo Berardenga. As a result of the mutable nature of the Sangiovese grape each of these regions produce distinctly different wines. Chianti is made predominantly from the Sangiovese grape, with the addition of small quantities of Canaiolo, Trebbiano and Malvasia grapes. The original recipe or formula was devised in the mid-19th century by Barone Bettino Ricasoli, whose ancestors still make Chianti at Castello di Brolio.

There has been a huge improvement in quality since the 1970s when most Chianti was sold as quaffing wine, in straw covered bottles. In the last twenty years the DOC laws have been overhauled, production has been halved and a greater emphasis has been placed on making quality wines. There has also been a change in style, with a tendency to produce either lighter, fruitier wines or darker, tannic wines rather than traditional lean, astringent wines. The production of Chianti Classico is governed by two regulatory bodies: Consorzio del Chianti Classico and Consorzio del Marchio-Storico. The first is responsible for the quality of Chianti, bestowing the pink DOCG labels to those wines judged to be up to scratch. The second body is responsible for the marketing and promotion of Chianti and has the black rooster as its symbol. Some outstanding Chianti Classico producers are listed below.

Felsina

SS 484 Chiantigiana (nr Castelnuovo Berardenga) (0577 35 51 17). **Open** 8.30am-7pm Mon-Sat. **Credit** EC, MC, V.

This winery on Chianti Classico's southernmost border produces some of the region's best wines. The site has probably been continuously inhabited since Etruscan times and was bought by the Poggiali family in 1966, with the aim of making great wines with the Sangiovese grape. The winery is run by Giuseppe Mazzocolin with the assistance of wine consultant Franco Barnebei. Since 1983 the story has been one of uninterrupted sucess and the estate is widely regarded as a trendsetter in the wine world. As well as making great Chianti Classico, including single vineyard wines, Vigneto Rancia they are also producing a range of highly acclaimed VdTs: *Fontalloro* which is 100 per cent Sangiovese, *I Sistri* made from Chardonnay and *Maestro Raro* made from Cabernet. The winery and tasting rooms are located 3km outside the small town of Castelnuovo Berardenga.

Casa Emma

S. P. Castellina in Chianti 3, San Donato in Poggio (0577 807 22 39). **Open** 9am-7pm Mon-Sat; 9am-noon Sun. **Credit** EC, MC, V.

This 13 hectare estate is located midway between Castellina in Chianti and San Donato, a particularly good region for Sangiovese. The estate has been owned by the Bucalossi family since 1971 but it is only recently that the wines have begun to receive public attention. Up until ten years ago much of the harvest was sold to other producers who recognised the superior quality of the grapes, due in part to immaculate viticulture practices. Winemaker, Nicola D'Afflitto has recently started to experiment with a series of interesting wines: Selezione, a selection of Sangiovese grapes and Soloio, made from 100 per cent Merlot. They also make good Chianti Classico and Chianti Classico Riserva. Tasting and direct sales at the winery.

The wine is made from a minimum of 85 per cent Sangiovese, which is known locally as Morellino, but can be made exclusively from Sangiovese. Grape varieties added to the Sangiovese include Canaiolo, Alicante and Malvasia in varying proportions determined by the winemaker. It produces a lively, cherry red wine that is softer than Chianti, reflecting in part the warmer climate in this part of Tuscany. The *riserva* is aged for at least two years in oak. Good producers are:

Le Pupille
Loc. Pereta, Magliano in Toscana (0564 50 51 29). **Open** 8am-noon, 1-5pm, Mon-Fri. **No credit cards**.
Possibly the best producer in the area with very good *riserva* and experimental VdTs, especially Saffredi.

Mantellassi
Loc. Banditaccia 26, Magliano in Toscana (0564 59 20 37). **Open** 8.30am-1pm, 2.30-7.30pm, Mon-Fri; 8.30am-1pm Sat. **No credit cards**.
The oldest estate in the region making traditional Morellino di Scansano.

White Wine

Tuscany is a predominantly red wine region although some good white wines are produced and with the change in the DOC laws this situation will probably improve. The traditional Tuscan white grape is Trebbiano which is used in Galestro and Bianco della Toscana. It requires expert handling to make good wine. Winemakers are starting to experiment with non traditional grape varieties such as Chardonnay and Sauvignon. It is probable that there will be rapid developments in the next few years.

Vernaccia

Vernaccia di San Gimignano (DOCG) has been made since at least the 13th century and was thought to be Michelangelo's favourite wine. A lot of ordinary wine has been sold under this label but the quality has improved recently with the revival of interest in white wine production. The wine is made from the Vernaccia grape in two distinct styles: a heavier style which is gold in colour and rich in flavour and a lighter which is pale, fresh and dry. Good producers are: Teruzzi e Puthod who make good Vernaccia but are also experimenting with other grape varietals. Panizzi One of the up and coming wineries in the area making Vernaccia Riserva and Chianti Colli Senesi. Falchini Makes good traditional wines and Vin Santo, also leading the way with innovative VdTs

To taste in San Gimignano try **Bar Enoteca Chianti Classico** in Via San Matteo which has a range of Vernaccia as well as other Tuscan wines available by the glass.

Badia a Coltibuono
Gaiole in Chianti (0577 74 94 98). **Open** *cellars* 2.30-4.30pm daily; *shop* 9.30am-1pm, 2-7pm, daily.
Credit MC, V.
The winery is on the site of the 700-year-old abbey and wine has been made here for hundreds of years. The abbey is now owned by the Stucchi Prinetti family, which runs the winery, a restaurant and a well known cooking school. They also produce a good VdT, *Sangioveto*, which is 100 per cent Sangiovese and aged in *barrique*. You can taste wine and other products from the estate, such as honey and olive oil, at the abbey's restaurant, Osteria di Badia a Coltibuono. Closed on Mondays.

Riecine
Gaiole in Chianti (0577 74 95 27). **Open** 9am-6pm daily.
Credit AmEx, EC, MC, V.
This small estate is owned by Englishman, John Dunkley. After a discouraging start in 1972 – one of the worst harvests since the war – he has gone on to be counted as one of the best small producers in Chianti. The '80s and '90s have seen further improvements with the arrival of *barrique* and a young winemaker, Sean O'Callaghan. The Chianti Classico is elegant and intense and the SuperTuscan, *La Gioia* is 100 per cent Sangiovese. Tastings by appointment.

Morellino di Scansano (DOC)

This wine is made on the southern Tuscan coast, in the hills above the plains of Maremma – an area hitherto more famous for its cattle and sheepdogs than its wine. Morellino has recently started to receive considerable attention in the wine world.

Food in Tuscany

Raw ingredients, simple pleasures.

It makes more sense to talk about food in Tuscany than about Tuscan cuisine, because cuisine implies cooking, whereas much of what is tastiest in this region involves little or no cooking at all. The three staples of the Tuscan diet are bread, olive oil and wine; add to these locally cured meats and salamis, subtle sheep's milk cheeses, and local vegetables preserved in oil and you have the ingredients for a delicious picnic or a feast of *antipasti*.

Summer, autumn, winter and spring are clearly differentiated in this region, and each brings with it particular foods that the Tuscans will have looked forward to for several weeks and will finally consume with an eagerness bordering on ritual celebration. The very first pressing of olive oil will be mopped up on cubes of bread; the first broad beans of the season will be eaten with olive oil and pieces of week-old *pecorino* cheese; the first porcini mushrooms will be grilled over wood and served with nothing but bread and olive oil; and even chestnuts – so common in Tuscany – will be eaten as a delicacy the first time they appear. So if you're in a restaurant, look around to see what the locals are eating before ordering.

L'ANTIPASTO

Meals generally start with the *antipasto*, literally, 'before the meal'. In Tuscany, the most common *antipasto* is *crostini*, chicken liver pâté on bread or toast. Cured meats are a regional speciality – usually pork and wild boar, which are butchered or hunted during the cold winter months. *Prosciutto crudo* comes from a pig haunch that has been buried under salt for three weeks, then swabbed with spicy vinegar, covered with black pepper and hung to dry for a further five months. *Capocollo* is a neck cut cured the same way for three days, then covered with pepper and fennel seed and rolled round in yellow butcher's paper and tied up with string so that it looks sausage-shaped. It's ready for eating by April. The most typical Tuscan salami is *finocchiona*, made of pork and flavoured with fennel seed and whole pepper corns. *Salamini di cinghiale*, or small wild boar salamis, include plenty of chilli pepper and a little fatty pork to keep them from going too hard (wild boar is a very lean meat). Look out as well for *milza*, a delicious pungent pâté, made from spleen, herbs, spices and wine.

Fresh and flavoursome: a panoply of just-picked Tuscan produce.

Wild Foods

Foraging for wild food is a popular countryside pursuit. In September and October, when the first autumn rains have dampened the hot earth, *funghi* (mushrooms) and *tartufi* (truffles) are the main attractions. Of the former, *porcini* (*Boletus edulis* or ceps) are the most highly prized. They can be eaten raw dressed with oil and lemon, cooked in a pasta or meat sauce, or turn up with other *funghi* in a warming soup. The *Cantharellus cibarius* (chanterelle) is also delicious – local names vary, but *giallarello* is a fairly common one. As for truffles, apart from the precious autumnal *bianco pregiato* (*Tuber magnatum pica*), there is also the *marzolo* truffle found from February to March, and a summer truffle, the *scorzone*, which is less tasty but still quite acceptable. Alas, many restaurants use a doctored olive oil (*olio tartufato*) to invest their dishes with more truffle flavour. *Castagne* (chestnuts) are another much-prized product of autumn They are not only served roasted, but are also ground into a flour which is used to make pasta and a

sweet-savoury cake, *castagnaccio*, that contains raisins, pine nuts and rosemary as well.

Spring is the season of the *sparagini* or wild asparagus, a thinner, tastier version of its cultivated nephew that is used in pasta sauces, soups and *frittata* (an unfolded omelette cooked on both sides). *Fiori di sambuco* (elder flowers) are exquisite fried in a light batter. *Vitalbini*, or the young shoots of *Clematis vitalba* (Old Man's Beard in its Spring array), make utterly delicious *frittata*. A little later, tightly closed thistle flowers (*cardaccio* or *carciofo selvatico* which were once used to curdle milk in cheese-making) can be picked (with gloves) and eaten as you would artichokes, by removing the hard outside and dipping the crunchy centre in oil and salt. Of the many species of wild salad, the sweetest and most delicate is the *gallinella* (*Valerianella carinata*); mixed wild salads (*insalata di campo*) are quite often available at family-run country trattorias because a quiet walk through the fields armed with a penknife and plastic bag is the sort of thing *i nonni* (the grandparents) like to do of an afternoon.

IL PRIMO

The *primo*, or first course, is carbohydrate-based. In most parts of Italy the carbohydrate will be pasta or rice. Here in Tuscany it's as likely to be a bread-based salad or soup. Old bread is never thrown away, but is mixed with what could be called the second tier of Tuscan staples – tomatoes, garlic, cabbage and *fagioli* (Tuscan white beans). These form such dishes as *panzanella* (stale bread that is soaked in water, squeezed out, mixed with raw onion, fresh tomato, basil, the odd salad leaf, and dressed with oil, salt and pepper), *ribollita* (rich bean and cabbage soup with bread), *acqua cotta* (toasted bread rubbed with garlic and covered with crinkly dark green cabbage and the water it was cooked in topped with premium olive oil, sometimes with an egg broken into it), *pappa al pomodoro* (an exquisite porridge-like mush of a soup made with onion, garlic, plenty of tomatoes, basil, a touch of chilli pepper and dressed with a swirl of olive oil). To say nothing of the ultimate winter ritual: *bruschetta* (not pronounced

'brooshetta' but 'brooosketta'), which is nothing more than toasted bread rubbed with garlic and soaked in freshly-pressed olive oil with a sprinkle of salt on top.

Fresh pasta in Tuscany usually takes the form of *tagliatelle* (flat ribbons made with flour, water and egg), *ravioli* (envelopes of the same mixture containing ricotta and spinach); *tordelli* (from around Lucca, stuffed with chard, meat and ricotta); in the south you'll find *pici* (just flour and water extruded into fattish strings) and in the Mugello *tortelli* (a double carbohydrate whammy stuffed with potato and bacon). *Ravioli* are best eaten with a topping of *burro e salvia* (butter and sage) or with a sprinkling of parmesan or *pecorino*, while flat ribbony pastas (like *papardelle*) go well with gamey sauces such as *lepre* (hare) and *cinghiale* (wild boar), and also *anatra* (duck), as well as the ubiquitous *ragù* (made with minced beef and tomato or, occasionally, lamb) and *salsa di pomodoro* (tomato sauce, usually spiced up with chilli pepper).

IL SECONDO

Cacciagione (game), *salsicce* (sausages) and *bistec-ca* (beef steak) are the main meats eaten in the region, though there is good lamb in some areas (look out for *agnellino nostrali*, with means young, locally raised lamb). Also common are *coniglio* (rabbit, usually roasted, sometimes with pine nuts, sometimes rolled around a filling such as egg and bacon) and *pollo* (chicken, look out for *ruspante*, free-range). During the winter you'll find plenty of slowly stewed and highly spiced *cinghiale* (wild boar). This is a species that was cross-bred with the domestic pig about 20 years ago, producing a largely herbivorous creature so prolific that it has become a threat to crops and has to be culled. Other common game includes *lepre* (hare) and *fagiano* (pheasant). The famous *bistecca fiorentina* is a vast T-bone steak that tends to be served very rare and is quite enough for two or even three people. Though a *fiorentina*, grilled over a herby wood fire, might now seem synonymous with Tuscany, the habit of eating huge beef steaks is in fact, introduced last century by English aristocrats homesick for roast beef. Have no qualms: the *Chianina* breed of cattle found locally are a salubrious lot.

IL CONTORNO

To accompany your meat course you're normally offered a side plate of vegetables or a salad. *Bietole* (Swiss chard) is available almost throughout the year. It is scalded in salted water and then tossed in the pan with olive oil, garlic and chilli pepper. *Fagiolini* (string beans) are more likely to be boiled and then dressed with oil and lemon or vinegar. The ubiquitous and sublime white Tuscan *fagioli* (white beans about the size of British baked beans) are served luke warm with a swirl of good olive oil and a sprinkle of black pepper on top. *Patatine fritte* (French fries) are available almost everywhere, though boiled potatoes dressed with oil, pepper and a few capers are often much tastier. *Pomodori* (tomatoes) and *cipolle* (onions) that are sliced, spiced and baked *al forno* (in the oven) are highly recommended. To those accustomed to watery lettuce, radicchio salads may at first seem bitter: an acquired taste that will soon lead you to an appreciation of the many wild salad varieties (*see box above*). In early summer artichokes are often eaten raw, stripped of their tough outer leaves and dipped into olive oil and salt.

IL FORMAGGIO

The one true Tuscan cheese is *pecorino*, made with ewe's milk. In fact the sheep you see grazing on the hillsides are not often there for mutton, lamb or wool, but for their milk. Thirty years ago each small farm would have raised enough sheep to provide the household with sufficient rounds of *pecorino*, which can be eaten *fresco* (up to a month old) *semi-stagionato* after about a month of ripening, or up to six months later when the cheese is fully *stagionato*, and thus drier, sharper and tastier. Nowadays sheep farming, milk collecting and cheese-making are mostly the province of Sardinians, who came over to work the land abandoned by the Tuscans drawn to towns and factory employment.

Fresh *ricotta*, which is made from whey and is thus not strictly speaking a cheese, is soft, mild and wet and should be eaten with a sprinkling of black pepper and a few drops of olive oil on top.

LA FRUTTA

Cherries, then apricots and peaches, are readily available in the summer, grapes in the late summer, and apples and pears in the early autumn. Although citrus fruits imported from the south now take pride of place in the winter months, the indigenous fruits are quinces (*mele cotogne*, excellent baked, stewed or turned into a sort of jelly) and persimmons (*cachi*) – each sloppy sweet spoonful of which helps keep out the winter cold. However, for visitors to Tuscany fruit is perhaps at its most interesting in sweet/savoury combinations: *il cacio con le pere* (cheese with pears), *i fichi con il salame* (figs with salami), *melone* (or *popone*) *con prosciutto* (melon and cured ham).

IL DOLCE

Although the Tuscans are not great purveyors of desserts, they do like to conclude festive meals with a glass of a dry raisin wine called *vin santo* into which they dunk *cantucci*, little dry biscuits packed with almonds. *Vin santo* is made with a special white grape variety which is dried out in bunches for a month, then crushed to obtain a sweet juice which is aged for at least five years in casks containing enough of the previous year's sediment to encourage fermentation. All this is highly uneconomical (you could get five bottles of wine out of the grapes you need for one bottle of *vin santo*), so that to offer a glass of *vin santo* is to honour a guest with the essence of hospitality. Country folk in Tuscany still make their own *vin santo*, though what you find in restaurants is more likely to be a slightly sweeter semi-industrial product.

IL CAFFÈ

A short, sharp *espresso* may help you digest so much gastronomic indulgence, whereas asking for a *cappuccino* at the end of a meal is like gulping down a bowl of porridge after a banquet: it is considered substantial breakfast fare, and no Italian would ever wish to see brought to the lunch or dinner table. If the caffè seems too dauntingly dark and strong, ask for *un po' di latte da parte*, a little milk with which to temper the bitter brew, or a *macchiato*, an *espresso* literally stained with a little frothy milk.

Olive Oil - Virgin Territory

To many Italians, Lucca is synonymous with olive oil. Nearly all the big Italian manufacturers and bottlers are located around the city, and the surrounding hills are patchworked with countless tiny groves, often producing just enough oil for family and friends. What makes Lucchese oil so fine is that elusive combination of soil, climate, topography and olive variety – typically a blend in which Frantoio and Leccino olives are prominent, although some innovative makers are now producing single varietals. Typical central Tuscan olive oil is powerful stuff – green, pungent, fruity and a little bitter; the oil of Liguria, in contrast, is far lighter, sweeter and less fruity; Lucchese oil falls somewhere between the two – yellowish, well flavoured but not overpowering, fruity but with no trace of bitterness.

However, all is not as it seems in the world of olive oil. The primary business of many of the big Tuscan oil companies (such as Cirio, Bertolli and Salov) is not producing, but bottling much cheaper oil they buy from countries like Spain, Greece and Tunisia, and then slapping their own label on the bottle. It's not illegal – they take care not to put 'Produce of Tuscany' on the label – but shoppers who see an Italian label on a bottle of oil will naturally assume that it contains Italian oil. Worse, according to Giuseppe Grappolini, President of MICO, an organisation dedicated to promoting quality olive oil, is that sometimes retailers buying the olive oil are taken in. The finely tuned noses and palates of Grappolini and his team of experts can detect the origin of any oil with remarkable accuracy. Often they discover that an oil labelled as Tuscan is, in fact, not from Tuscany at all. The problem, says Grappolini, is that there is a total absence of tests during the harvest and pressing, and that most consumers have no idea what genuine extra virgin olive oil tastes like.

So what is extra virgin olive oil? Under a 1992 law, olive oil is assessed according to 24 chemical parameters, the most important of which is the oil's acidity level (measured in terms of oleic acid content). Oils with a high acidity level deteriorate quickly, so low acidity is more an indication of how well an oil will hold its qualities, than of the qualities themselves. An 'extra virgin' oil must have an acidity level no higher then one per cent, 'virgin' oil is up to 1.5 per cent, while 'olive oil' can have an acidity level between 1.5 and 3.3 per cent. Sadly, the law is pretty useless as far as qual-ity control goes: Grappolini points out that if a producer creates an extra virgin olive oil with an acidity level of, say, 0.5 per cent, then he can blend it with lower quality virgin oil with an acidity level of perhaps 1.2 per cent, and still legally sell it as extra virgin.

Doubtless bearing this in mind, the 1992 regulations recommended that there should also be a qualitative test by a panel of oil experts. Unsurprisingly, this requirement is being opposed by many producers – who claim that tasting is too subjective. Grappolini disagrees. "If you have a range of people tasting oils, they will always come to the same conclusion. It just never happens that one person thinks an oil is terrible and another loves it." At a tasting in Lucca a few years ago of 20 'extra virgin' oils (all with less than one per cent acidity), oil experts rated only two as being of a high enough standard to deserve the appellation.

Some of the big bottlers can sense which way the wind's blowing and are starting to plant and grow their own olives. It will be tough for the small commercial producers to survive. A grower like Tenuta di Valgiano, northeast of Lucca, makes only 1,500 litres of olive oil a year, with each olive tree yielding just one litre of oil. The quality of the oil is superlative, but costs are inevitably huge (picking costs alone are about L12,000 per tree – Valgiano did once hire a helicopter to hover over the trees to hopefully shake the olives off the branches but, alas, it was "bloody useless, and expensive"). But such producers will survive as long as people are prepared to pay for quality.

Many operate plants as modern as those of the big boys. Banish from your mind the image of worthy peasants laboriously grinding olives with massive stones then pressing the resultant paste to extract the oil. Too often traditionally ground and pressed oil is dirty (the grinding stones can never be thoroughly cleaned) and partially oxidized (as the process takes so long). It may not be very romantic, but speedy mechanised olive crushing, and oil separation using cool water and centrifugal force, will always produce a better quality oil.

Lucchese oils to look out for: Tenuta di Valgiano, Colle Verde, Fubbiano, Maionchi (traditional method).

With thanks to Saverio Petrilli, Giuseppe Grappolini of MICO (*olivarte@val.it*) and Charles Carey of The Oil Merchant, London (*mail order 0181 740 1335*).

Florence Essentials

Essential Information

All you need to know about bureaucracy and dentistry, praying and paying, driving and surviving in the city by the Arno.

Visas

EC nationals and citizens of the USA, Canada, Australia and New Zealand do not need visas for stays of up to three months, but all non-EC citizens must have full passports. All non-EC visitors, and EC nationals working in Italy have to declare their presence to the police within eight days of arrival. If you're staying in a hotel, this will be done for you. If not, contact the *Questura Centrale*, the main police station, for advice.

Any foreigners staying for longer than three months (or eight days if non-EC) or intending to work or study in Italy, need to register and procure additional documents. For details of the *Questura* and information on negotiating Italian bureaucracy, *see below* **Bureaucracy**.

Customs

Since the introduction of the Single European Market EC nationals no longer have to declare goods imported into Italy for their personal use, but random checks are still made for drugs.

For non-EC citizens the following limits apply:
- 400 cigarettes **or** 200 small cigars **or** 100 cigars **or** 500 grams (17.64 ounces) of tobacco
- 1 litre of spirits (over 22 per cent alcohol) **or** 2 litres of fortified wine (under 22 per cent alcohol)
- 50 grams (1.76 ounces) of perfume

There are no restrictions on the import of cameras, watches or electrical goods. Visitors are also allowed to carry up to 20 million lire in cash.

Insurance

EC nationals are entitled to reciprocal medical care in Italy, provided they have an E111 form, available in Britain from post offices, Health Centres and Department of Social Security (DSS) offices. This will cover you for emergencies, but using an E111 naturally involves having to deal with the intricacies of the Italian state health system, and for short-term visitors it's better to take out health cover under private travel insurance. .

Non-EC citizens should take out private medical insurance for all eventualities before their visit. For more information on all health matters *see below* **Health**.

As always when journeying abroad, visitors should ensure they have adequate travel insurance before leaving for Italy. If you rent a motorcycle or moped, pay the extra charge for full insurance cover, and sign the collision damage waiver when renting a car.

Money

The Italian currency is the lira (plural lire), often abbreviated to £ or L. As well as the new, tiny coins for L50 and L100, and the traditional L200 and L500 coins, you may also come across the bronze *gettone*, worth L200, originally a token only for use in the old-fashioned slot telephones that are still found in some bars. Notes start with the multicoloured L1,000 and go through L2,000, L5,000, L10,000 and L50,000 up to the brown and green L100,000, which sports a portrait of Caravaggio.

Prices are rounded up to the nearest 50 lire, and by law after any transaction you must be given a full receipt (*scontrino fiscale*). Some places will insist you take it, but others (especially old-fashioned trattorias, where your bill is added up on the paper tablecloths) may try to avoid giving you a receipt for tax reasons, in which case it is your right to ask for one.

Banks and foreign exchange

Banks usually have better exchange rates than the private bureaux de change (*cambio*). The main Florence offices of most of the banks are around Piazza della Repubblica. To change travellers' cheques you will need a passport or other identity document. Commission rates vary considerably between banks and between bureaux de change, and you can pay from nothing to L10,000 for each transaction. Beware of any apparently generous 'no commission' sign as the rate of exchange will generally be terrible.

Bank cash machines can also be used with major credit cards. There are several automatic cash exchange machines around the city which accept notes in most currencies. Notes need to be in good condition for the machine to take them. If you need to have money sent over to you, the best method is through American Express, Thomas Cook or Western Union.

Opening Times

Most banks are open from 8.20am to 1.20pm and 2.35pm to 3.35pm Monday to Friday, although these times may vary slightly from bank to bank. All banks are closed on public holidays and staff work reduced hours the day before a holiday, usually closing at around 11am.

Credit Cards

Italy is still mainly a cash economy and it is estimated that only ten per cent of the population carry credit cards. However, this is changing somewhat and most hotels of two stars and up, and increasing numbers of shops and restaurants, will now take plastic. If you find yourself in an establishment that does not, Eurocheques are widely accepted when accompanied by the appropriate guarantee card. While we have tried to indicate the credit cards accepted by each of the hotels, restaurants and so on listed in this guide, this is something that in Italy can change without warning, and the stickers festooning a restaurant window are not necessarily an accurate indication of what is acceptable inside. If in doubt, check it out beforehand or take cash.

Most automatic cash machines (*Bancomat*) accept Eurocheque cards (for amounts up to L300,000 per day) and Access/MasterCard and Visa credit and debit cards. However, they are quite often out of order, with the added twist that, as the machines are all centrally linked, when one goes out of action this tends to affect every one of them. Most banks will also give cash advances against a credit card, but this varies according to the bank, and only some will do so without a PIN number.

If you lose a credit or charge card, phone one of the emergency numbers listed below. All lines are freephone (1678) numbers, have English-speaking staff and are open 24 hours daily.

American Express *(card emergencies 1678 64 046/travellers' cheques 1678 72 000).*
Diners Club *(1678 64 064).*
Mastercard/Access/Carta Sí/Eurocard *(1678 68 086).*
Mastercard *(1678 70 866).*
Visa *(1678 77 232).*

American Express

Via Dante Alighieri 22r (50 981). Bus 23. **Open** 9am-5.30pm Mon-Fri; 9am-12.30pm Sat.
All the standard AmEx services are available, such as a travellers' cheque refund service, card replacement, poste restante and a cash machine usable with AmEx cards. Money can be transferred from any American Express office in the world within 24 hours. Charges are paid by the sender who must be in possession of an AmEx card. This office also offers a travel agency service.

Deutsche Bank

Via Strozzi 16r (27 061). Bus 6. **Open** 8.20am-1.20pm, 2.40-4pm, Mon-Fri.
Visa and Mastercard holders can withdraw money without a PIN number, and cash and travellers' cheques can be changed for a standard charge of L10,000.
Branch: *Via Porta Santa Maria 50 (28 38 32).*

Thomas Cook

6/12 Lungarno Acciaiuoli (28 97 81). Bus B, C or to Ponte Vecchio. **Open** 9am-6pm Mon-Sat; 9am-2pm Sun.

One of the few exchange offices open on a Sunday, a 4.5 per cent commission is charged on each cash transaction with a minimum of L4,500. No commission is charged for cash withdrawal via Mastercard, Eurocard or Visa. Money can be transferred to the Florence office from any Thomas Cook branch in the world. This will take 24 hours within Europe and 48 hours outside. Charges are paid by the sender.

Western Union

(Toll-free number 1670 16 840).
Agenzia STS *Via Zanetti 18 (28 41 83). Bus 1, 17.* **Open** 10.30am-1pm, 3.30pm-6.30 pm, Mon-Fri.
Agency Prime Link *Via Panicale 18 (29 12 75). Bus to Santa Maria Novella station.* **Open** 9.30am-1pm, 3-8.30pm, daily.
The quickest, but certainly not the cheapest way to send money anywhere in the world. A money transfer will take just 20 minutes and charges are on a sliding scale, payable by the sender; the more you send, the more commission you pay. There is no charge for receiving money.

Other offices offering exchange facilities:

Change Underground

Piazza Stazione 14, interno 37 (29 13 12). **Open** 9am-7.30pm Mon-Sat; 9am-12.30pm Sun.
In the new underground shopping mall under Santa Maria Novella train station.

Frama

Via Calzaiuoli 79r (21 40 03). Bus to the Duomo. **Open** 9am-7pm Mon-Sat; 10am-6.15pm Sun.
A hefty 9.6 per cent is charged on larger transactions, or a minimum of L4,000.
Branch: *Via Martelli 9r (28 82 46). Bus 11, 17.* **Open** 8.30am-7.30pm daily.

Universal Turismo

Via Speziali 7r (21 72 41). Bus 11, 17. **Open** 9am-1pm, 2.30pm-6.30pm, Mon-Fri; 9am-noon Sun.
Here there is a five per cent standard commission, and they don't accept credit cards against cash withdrawals.

Main Post Offices

Via Pellicceria 3 (1st floor). Bus to Piazza della Repubblica. **Open** 8.15am-6pm Mon-Sat.
Via Pietrapiana 53. Bus B. **Open** 8.15am-6pm Mon-Fri; 8.15am-12.30pm Sat.
Via Cavour 71r. Bus to Piazza San Marco. **Open** 8.15am-1.30pm Mon-Fri; 8.15am-12.30pm Sat.
The main post offices (and even some smaller ones) have exchange bureaux and these offer good rates. The commission on cash transactions is L1,000. For travellers' cheques, commission is L2,000 up to the value of L100,000, and L5,000 above that. These offices will only accept American Express travellers' cheques.

Tourist information

The offices of Florence's provincial tourist board, the APT, and the municipally run *Ufficio Informazione Turistiche* have English-speaking staff but, while trying to be helpful, the information they supply is not always reliable and up to date. Unfortunately, there is no central information service for other cities and sights in Tuscany. You have to contact the tourist offices (*Azienda Turistica*) in each area concerned. The local English-language press is a useful source of information (eg *Vista, Events, Florence Concierge Information*). The international *English Yellow*

Pages, although published in Rome, has a Florence section and lists English-speaking services and useful numbers. It is obtainable from all the main bookshops, and many hotels have copies which you can borrow. For a list of English-language bookshops, *see chapter* **Shopping: Bookshops**.

Azienda Promozionale Turistica Firenze (APT)

Head office:*Via Manzoni 16 (23 320). Bus 6.*
Open 8.30am-1.30pm Mon-Sat.
This is the headquarters of the APT and has an information office open to the public. However, it is rather out of the way, and it is usually easier for visitors to go to the more central office in Via Cavour. There are also offices in Florence and Pisa airports. The APT provides information and free brochures on events – cultural and otherwise – in Florence and the surrounding province (NB this does not mean the whole of Tuscany; the *Provincia di Firenze* incorporates Florence and the immediate surrounding area). It distributes several free maps, the more comprehensive of which has a good street guide as well as lists of useful phone numbers, emergency services, hospitals, chemists, markets and so on. Also listed are the main galleries and museums with their opening hours. The office will provide hotel lists but not a booking service.
Branches:*Via Cavour 1r (29 08 32). Bus 17.*
Open *Nov-Feb* 8.15am-1.45pm Mon- Fri; *Mar-Oct* 8.15am-7.15pm Mon-Sat; 8.15am-1.45pm Sun.
Piazza Mino 37, Fiesole (59 87 20). Bus 7.
Open 8.30am-1.30pm daily.

Consorzio Informazioni Turistiche Alberghiere (ITA)

Stazione di Santa Maria Novella (28 28 93).
Open *summer* 9am-9pm daily; *winter* 9am-8pm Mon-Sat; 9am-7pm Sun.
This organisation offers a hotel booking service and only accepts personal callers. It provides a full list of hotels in all categories, and a charge of between L3,000 and L10,000 is made according to the category of hotel being booked. It is obligatory to pay the first night in advance at the time of booking. Payment can be made by credit card, travellers' cheque or foreign cash. The Florence airport branch does not provide a booking service.
Branches: *AGIP service station at Peretola (42 11 800) on the A11 'Firenze-Mare' motorway.*
Open 10am-1.30pm, 2-4pm daily. In the summer, the hours are extended.
Chianti Est service station (62 13 49) on the A1 'Autostrada del Sole' motorway. **Open** *Easter-31 Oct* 10.30am-6.30pm daily.
Florence airport (31 58 74). **Open** 8.30am-10.30pm daily.

SOS Turistica

Via Cavour 1r (27 60 382). Bus 17. **Open** *summer* 10am-1pm, 3-6pm, Mon-Sat; *winter* 10am-1pm Mon-Sat, but times may vary from year to year.
The APT also runs this consumer complaints office specifically for tourists who feel that they have been unfairly treated (usually involving over-charging) at a hotel, restaurant, shop or other tourist facility.

Ufficio Informazione Turistiche

Borgo Santa Croce 19 (no phone yet). **Open** *winter* 8.15am-2pm Mon-Sat; *summer* 8.15am-7.15 Mon-Sat; 8.15am-1.45pm Sun.
Piazza Stazione (21 22 45). Bus to Santa Maria Novella station. **Open** 8.15am-7.15pm daily.
Run by the City of Florence, these offices provide general tourist information, free maps, restaurant and hotel lists. The Borgo San Croce office opened in late 1997 and its phone number was unknown at the time of going to press.

Florence: closed for lunch.

Maps

A reasonably comprehensive street map is available free from APT offices, but better ones can be bought at newspaper stands and bookshops. The ATAF city bus company distributes a free bus map which, while looking like a plate of multi-coloured spaghetti, covers all routes and gives basic information in English on tickets and fares. This is available at the ATAF information office at Santa Maria Novella train station and some bars, post offices and hotels. The telephone company, Telecom Italia, supplies subscribers with a free street atlas, *Tutto Città* which is very detailed; most bars and hotels will have one for perusal.

Opening times

Shops

For shops, standard opening times are from 4pm or 5pm to 7.30pm on Monday, and from 8.30am to 1pm, and 4pm or 5pm to 7.30pm, Tuesday to Saturday. Nothing is simple in Italy, and different types of shops observe different opening hours and have a different day off during the week. Clothes shops tend to open later in the mornings, and food shops are open on Monday morning but closed on Wednesday afternoon. Hours also change slightly from mid-June to mid-September with most shops staying open a bit later on weekday evenings and closing on Saturday afternoons. Larger chain stores and many supermarkets stay open all day (*orario continuato*). Food and other small shops will shut completely at some point during July or August for anything from a week to a month.

Restaurants & bars

Most restaurants are open from about 12.30pm to 2.30pm for lunch, and from 8.30pm to 10.30pm in the evening. They also each have an official day off during the week (*riposo settimanale*; most commonly Monday), which is posted outside. Bars are much less predictable. During August a great many bars and restaurants are shut completely, and throughout the summer opening times are more than usually erratic.

Offices

Offices are usually open from 8am to 1pm and 2pm to 5pm or 6pm. Many now operate the so-called *orario continuato* and work through the middle of the day, but you may still not find anyone answering the phone at lunch-time. On the other hand, it is also quite common to find people still at work outside their regular hours.

Public holidays

On public holidays (*giorni festivi*) virtually all shops, banks, and businesses are closed, though most bars and restaurants stay open. The many public holidays are:

New Year's Day (Capo d'anno) 1 January; **Epiphany (La Befana)** 6 January; **Easter Monday (Lunedì Pasqua)**; **Liberation Day (Venticinque Aprile)** 25 April; **May Day (Primo Maggio)** 1 May; **Saints' Day (San Giovanni)** 24 June; **Feast of the Assumption (Ferragosto)** 15 August; **All Saints' (Tutti Santi)** 1 November; **Immaculate Conception (Festa dell'Immacolata)** 8 December; **Christmas Day (Natale)** 25 December; **Boxing Day (Santo Stefano)** 26 December.

There is very limited public transport on 1 May and Christmas afternoon. Holidays falling on a Saturday or Sunday are not celebrated the following Monday, but if a holiday falls on a Thursday or Tuesday many people make a long weekend of it, and take the intervening day off as well. A weekend like this is called a *ponte* (bridge). Most people also disappear for the whole month of August, when *chiuso per ferie* (closed for holidays) signs appear on shops and restaurants, with the dates of closure. For a calendar of Tuscany's traditional and modern festivals, *see chapter* **Tuscany by Season**.

Street crime

Serious street crime is not a problem in Florence, and it remains a relatively safe city to walk in, even late at night. Streets in the centre are well-lit and, particularly in the summer, there are usually plenty of people around. However, in common with most cities, the area round the station should be avoided at night as there are usually shady characters hanging around. It is said that crime is on the increase, but as a tourist, you are unlikely to come up against any serious problems. Your biggest hassle will probably be the gangs of pickpockets, often in the form of gypsies (*zingari*) with their kids who hang around the main tourists spots waiting to prey on unwary visitors. One particularly popular technique is to distract their victims – often by waving a piece of card – and then slip deft hands into bags or pockets. These gangs can be very insistent. If you are approached, just keep walking, keep calm, and hang on to your valuables.

For details of what to do if you are a victim of crime, *see below* **Police & Security**. You will find that a few basic precautions will greatly reduce a street thief's chances:

• Do not carry wallets in back pockets, particularly on buses, and if you have a bag with a carrying strap wear it across the chest, not on the shoulder.
• Keep bags closed and keep a hand on your bag, and, if you stop at a pavement café, do not leave bags or coats on the ground or the back of a chair where you can't see them.
• Avoid attracting unwanted attention by pulling out large notes to pay for things at street stalls.
• When walking down a street, hold cameras or bags on the side of you toward the wall, in order to avoid becoming the prey of a motorcycle thief or *scippatore*.

Reference points

Electricity

The world of plugs and sockets in Italy is varied and complex, but there is only one electrical current, 220V, which works with British and US-bought products. Buy two-pin travel plugs before leaving, as they will be hard to find in Italy. Adaptors for different Italian plugs can be bought at any electrical shop (look for *Casalinghi* or *Elettricità*).

Queuing

Lining up in an orderly fashion and patiently waiting your turn is not something that comes easily to most Italians. You have to have your wits about you and your elbows sharpened in shops, bars and banks in order not to be left standing while others pass in front of you. Some shops and information services now use a ticket dispenser; go in and take a number (*numerino*) and wait for that number to be displayed. If there is no such machine, be aware of who is in front of and behind you, and when it is your turn, be assertive. Queues at ticket offices are usually more orderly.

Time & weather

Florence is one hour ahead of Greenwich Mean Time, and clocks change at the beginning and end of summer on the same date as the UK. The city does not enjoy an easy climate; the surrounding hills mean that it can be cold and humid in the winter and blisteringly hot and humid in the summer with temperatures soaring to 40 degrees plus in late July and August. For this reason, the city will be relatively empty of Florentines in these months, and for good reason. Spring and autumn are often warm and pleasant but not without the risk of rain, particularly in March and April. Between November and February the weather cannot be relied upon, but the scarcity of fellow tourists is some compensation and, with luck, days will be crisp with clear blue skies.

Tipping

Foreigners are expected to tip more than Italians, but the ten per cent customary in many countries would be considered generous even for the richest-looking tourist. Most locals will leave L100 or L200 on the bar counter for a *cappuccino* and, depending on the standard of the restaurant, L2,000 to L10,000 for the waiter after a meal. Many of the larger restaurants now include a service charge. Tips are not expected in family-run restaurants, nor is it usual to tip taxi drivers.

Bureaucracy

The Italian state loves documents, and the more documents the better. Luckily, EC nationals and (in practice) citizens of other first-world countries staying for less than three months no longer need bother with permits. However, anyone intending to be in Italy for any length of time will have to bite the bullet and try to acquire the bewildering array of papers needed to get a *permesso*.

The most important documents listed below are obtained from the main police station, the **Questura Centrale** (*see below* **Police & Security**). Officially, all non-EC citizens and EC nationals who are working in Italy should register with the police within eight days of arrival and apply for a 'permit to stay'. At the *questura* there is a useful computer that prints out lists (in various languages) of the documents you need for every type of *permesso*. Theoretically information can also be obtained by phone, but as the line is near-permanently engaged it's usually easier to go along in person. EC citizens now usually receive their permits the same day, but anyone else might face a longer wait. For information on working in Italy, *see below* **Working in Florence**.

Questura Centrale
Via Zara 2 (49 771). **Open** 24 hours daily.
Foreigners' Section: *Via San Gallo 81 (49 771, ask for 'Ufficio Stranieri').* **Open** 8.30am-noon Mon-Fri.
To report a crime, go to the Ufficio Denuncie in the main entrance in Via Zara where you will be given a form to fill in (hopefully in your native language). This office is open from 8.30am-8pm daily. To apply for your documents, go to the Foreigners' Section early in the day (there are often long queues) where English-speaking staff are usually available. Applications are dealt with at one of eight desks; be prepared to wait.

Codice Fiscale (Employment Number)
Essential if you are working legally, this can be obtained with relatively little hassle from the tax office, the **Ufficio Imposte Dirette** in Via S Caterina d'Alessandra 23 (47 28 51). The office is on the 3rd floor and is open from 9am to 1pm Monday to Saturday.

Partita IVA (VAT Number)
Anyone doing business in Italy may also need a VAT number. To obtain one costs L100,000 or 250,000, depending on whether the application is from an individual or a company. Most people pay an accountant to do this for them.

Permesso di Soggiorno (Permit to Stay)
Anyone, including EC citizens, wishing to work legally, enrol on a course, open a bank account, rent a flat or do anything much in Italy other than be a tourist will need at least this document. To obtain one you will need a photocopy of your passport, three passport-style photographs and (for non-EC nationals) a *marca da bollo* (an official stamp) which costs L20,000 and is available from *tabacchi*.

Permesso di Soggiorno per Lavoro (Work Permit)
Despite the Single European Market this is still required by EC nationals working in Italy. The requirements are the same as for the Permit to Stay, plus a letter from your employer.

Permesso di Soggiorno per Studio (Students' Permit)
The same requirements as the Permit to Stay, plus a guarantee that your medical bills will be paid (an E111 form will do), evidence that you can support yourself (such as a photocopy of your credit card or a letter from your bank or parents) and a letter from the educational institution at which you will be studying in Italy.

Residenza (Residency)
Necessary if you want to buy a car or get customs clearance on goods brought into Italy, and obtained but from the municipal office for the district (*circoscrizione*) where you are living. They are listed in the *TuttoCittà* street atlas. To apply you will need photocopies of your *permesso di soggiorno* (which must be valid for at least a year) and passport. The municipal police will then come round, without an appointment, to check that you live where you say you do.

Communications

Post

The Italian postal system is notoriously unreliable. It is, of course, unfair to make blanket statements, and letters often do arrive in reasonable time, but unpredictability is a key word, so be prepared for delays. If it is essential that a letter or parcel should arrive at its destination on time, use one of the supplementary or courier services listed below.

Stamps & charges
Stamps can be bought at *tabacchi* or from post offices. A letter or postcard to any destination in the EC costs L80 0, and to the USA both cost L1,300 airmail. Post boxes are red and have two slots, *Per la Città* (for Florence) and *Tutte le altre Destinazioni* (for everywhere else). With luck, a letter should take about five days to reach the UK, and eight to the USA, but be prepared for delays. To speed things up, mail can also be sent *espresso* (express, the quickest, L3,600 extra), *raccomandata* (registered, L4,000 extra) or *assicurata* (insured, L7,400 extra). The latter two services are only available from post offices.
Charges are calculated by weight. Within Europe, a letter or parcel under 500g will cost L30,000, between 500g and 1 kilo, L34,000, between 1 and 2 kilos, L40,900 and so on. Within Italy, charges are about half of this. To the USA, add about 50 per cent more.

Postal information
(160).
Based at the main post office, this phone line (with some English spoken) will answer all queries on the postal system. A call will cost 3 *scatti* (L600).

CAI Post courier service
Via Alamanni 20r (21 63 49/23 81 065). Bus to Santa Maria Novella station. **Open** 8.15am-1pm, 1.35-7pm, Mon-Fri; 8.15am-12.30pm Sat.
This express letter and parcel service is run by the *Poste Italiane*. You get what you pay for; within Europe, delivery is guaranteed between one and three days, and to the USA between two and four days. The same service within Italy is called *Post Accelere Interno.*
Branch: *Via Pellicceria 3 (within the main post office) (21 61 22). Bus to Piazza della Repubblica.* **Open** 8.15am-1pm, 1.35pm-7pm, Mon-Fri; 8.15am-noon Sat.

Post offices

There are local post offices (*ufficio postale*) in each district, and these are open from 8.25am-1.50pm Monday to Friday, and from 8.15am to 12.30pm on Saturday. They close one hour earlier than normal on the last day of each month. The main office in the centre of town has longer opening hours and a range of additional services.

Posta Centrale (Main Post Office)
Via Pellicceria 3 (information 160). Bus to Piazza della Repubblica. **Open** 8.15am-7pm Mon-Sat.
This vast building on two floors is always busy and offers a full range of postal and telegraph services. There is also a CAI Post courier office here (*see above*), and Telecom Italia

run their mobile phone centre in the building. Letters sent Poste Restante (in Italian, *Fermo Posta*) should be sent here and addressed '*Fermo Posta Centrale, Firenze*'. To collect mail, you will need a passport and may have to pay a small charge. There is also a 24-hour **fax** service, available from 8.15am to 7pm, Monday to Saturday. (*Tabacchi* often also offer fax services but they are expensive to use.)
Other offices in the centre of town: *Via Pietrapiana 53. Bus B*. **Open** 8.15am-6pm Mon-Fri; 8.15am-12.30 Sat. *Via Cavour 71r. Bus 11,17*. **Open** 8.15am-1.30pm Mon-Fri; 8.15-12.30 Sat. *Via Barbadori 40r. Bus to Ponte Vecchio*. **Open** 8.15am-1.30pm Mon-Fri; 8.15am-12.30pm Sat.

Telegrams & telex

Telegrams and telexes can be sent from 11 post offices and by phone (dial 186). The telegraph office at the Posta Centrale in Via Pellicceria is open from 8.15am to 7pm Monday to Saturday, and from 8.15am to 12.30pm on Sunday. Charges vary according to destination. To Britain, up to three words (including the name and address) will cost about L12,870 and L430 for each additional word. To the USA, you will pay L7,600 for seven words and L1,090 per word over that. For telegrams sent by phone, there is an additional charge of L1,000.

Telephones

Telecom Italia, the Italian phone company, operates one of the most expensive systems in Europe, particularly for international calls. From a public call box, the minimum charge for a local call is L200, but the normal daytime rate to the UK is L1,070 for the first minute, and L582 per minute thereafter. At off-peak times this falls to L1,016 and L526 respectively. One way to keep costs down is always to phone off-peak (from 10pm to 8am Monday to Saturday, and all day Sunday). Another is to use private phones instead of public phone booths or phones in hotels, which carry extortionate surcharges. Phoning from a telephone centre costs the same as from a phone box, but is more convenient for long-distance calls as you avoid the need for large amounts of change or several phone cards. Additional services are listed in the local phone book, the *Elenco Telefonico*.

Phone numbers

All numbers beginning with 167 or 1678 are freephone lines. Local numbers have 6 or 7 digits.

Public phone boxes

Many public phones only accept phone cards (*carte telefoniche*) or Telecom Italia credit cards. They cost L5,000, L10,000 or L15,000 and are available from *tabacchi*. When you use a new card, break off one corner as marked and insert the card into the slot in the phone. The available credit is shown on a digital display. To use public phones that accept coins, you will need L100, L200 or L500 pieces. The minimum for a local call is L200. A few bars still have phones that only accept special tokens called *gettoni*, worth L200 each.

International calls

To make an international call from Florence, dial 00, and the appropriate country-code: **Australia** 61; **Canada** 1; **Eire** 353; **New Zealand** 64; **United Kingdom** 44;

United States 1, followed by the area code and individual number. To phone Florence from abroad, dial the international code (00 in the UK), then 39 for Italy and 55 for Florence, followed by the individual number. To make a reverse charge (collect) call, dial 172 followed by the country code (ie, 17 20 044 for the UK, 17 20 01 for the US) and you'll be connected directly to an operator in that country. In a phone box you will need to insert L200, which will be refunded after your call.

Phone centres

Via Cavour 28r. Bus 11, 17. **Open** 8am-9.45pm daily.
At this Telecom office, you are allocated a booth and can either use a phone card or pay cash at the desk after you have finished making all your calls. They also supply phone directories from all over Europe, information on telephone charges and sell phone cards.

Operator services

All these services are open 24 hours daily.

Operator & Local Directory Enquiries *(12)*.
International Operator (Europe) *(15)*.
International Operator (rest of world) *(170)*.
Directory Enquiries (Italy) *(175)*.
International Directory Enquiries (Europe) *(176)*.
Intercontinental Directory Enquiries (the rest of the world) *(1790)*.
Communication Problems on Local Calls *(182)*.
Communication Problems on International Calls *(17 23 535)*.
Alarm Calls *(114)*.
An automatic message will ask you to dial in the time you want your call (with four figures, on a 24-hour clock) followed by your phone number.
Tourist Information *(110)*.
Financial markets: Milan *(19 31)*; **Rome** *(19 32)*.

Disabled travellers

Facilities for the disabled are generally poor in Florence, but things are improving slowly. City buses all have special seats, slightly lower than normal, placed near the front. There are now new buses (orange, grey and green in colour) which share routes 9, 27, 28, 30 and 35 with the old, non-accessible, (orange) buses, and these are fully wheelchair accessible with an electric platform at the rear door and space for a wheelchair on board. The driver will assist if help is needed. Many of the newer trains are also equipped for wheelchairs with space in the compartments and disabled loos. Such trains have a wheelchair logo on the side. The trouble is that there is no access up the very steep steps. If you should need assistance, call the English-speaking information office (*23 52 275*). Taxis will take wheelchairs, but it is advisable to warn them when phoning to book. Disabled parking places are found throughout the city, and are free.

There are toilets for the disabled at Florence and Pisa airports and at Florence's Santa Maria Novella train station, as well in a handful of the city's main sights. However, be warned that, in general, very little effort has been made to make the city wheelchair friendly.

Driving in Florence

You do not really need a car to get around Florence as the city centre is so small, and the public transport sytem is efficient (*see chapter* **Getting Around**). However, if you arrive or leave by car, or if you hire one while there for an out of town trip, you will inevitably be obliged to do battle with the Florentine traffic which can seem daunting to the uninitiated. Driving in Italy tends to deteriorate as you move from north to south. Being at close to the mid-way point, Florentine drivers, while not conforming 100 per cent to the highway code, certainly do not display the chaotic, anarchic tendencies on the road that typify, say, Naples. A red traffic light in Florence is generally perceived as meaning 'stop'. Drivers are skillful and accidents are not commonplace, but you will need to keep your wits about you; and be decisive.

Parking is always a problem, and not all of the city is accessible by car. Driving is expensive in Italy, with petrol prices the highest in the EC. Car break-ins are fairly common.

If you do use a car in the city, some tips to be born in mind are listed below. It is essential to have an **international driving licence** or an **Italian licence** after you have been in the city for a year. An international licence is available in Britain over the counter at AA and RAC offices if you produce your normal licence and a passport-size photo. For car and scooter hire companies, *see chapter* **Services**.

• It is required by law to wear safety belts at all times (no-one does!) and carry a warning triangle in your car.
• Keep your driving licence, Green Card, vehicle registration and personal ID documents on you at all times.
• Do not leave anything of value (including a car radio) in your car, and never leave bags or jackets visible on the seats. Take all your luggage into your hotel when you park your car.
• Flashing your lights in Italy means that you will *not* slow down (contrary to British practice).
• After 10.30 at night most of the traffic lights flash amber, in which case you should STOP and give way to the right.
• Try and look at the other drivers around you to see where they are looking, and watch out for mopeds and pedestrians. By local convention, pedestrians usually assume they have the right of way in the old streets without clearly-marked pavements.

Restricted areas
See chapter **Getting Around**.

Breakdown services

It is advisable to join a national motoring organisation, like the AA or RAC in Britain or the AAA in the US, before taking a car to Italy. They have reciprocal arrangements with the **Automobile Club d'Italia** (**ACI**), who will tell you what to do in case of a breakdown, and provide useful general information on driving in Europe. Even for non-members, the ACI is the best number to call if you have any kind of breakdown.

If you require extensive repairs and do not know a mechanic, pay a bit more and go to a manufacturer's official dealer, as reliable garages are hard to find in Rome. Dealers are listed in the *Yellow Pages* under *auto*, along with specialist repairers under classifications like *gommista* (tyre repairs), *marmitte* (exhaust repairs) and *carrozzerie* (bodywork and windscreen repairs). The *English Yellow Pages* has a list of English-speaking mechanics.

Automobile Club d'Italia (ACI)
Viale Amendola 36 (24 861/24-hour emergency line 116/24-hour information line in English 06 44 77).
Bus 8, 14, 31. **Open** 8.30am-1pm, 2.30-5.15pm, Mon-Thur; 8.30am-1pm Fri.
The ACI has English-speaking staff, and while no longer providing free service for all foreign drivers, their prices are reasonable. Members of associated organisations are entitled to basic repairs free, and to other services at preferential rates. Non-members will be charged, but prices are generally reasonable. Phone 44 77 for information on ACI services, driving regulations and customs formalities in Italy and for traffic and weather information. Membership is not needed to use the phone lines.

Autofficina Inglese
Via Cittadella 4r (35 56 93). Bus to Porta al Prato. **Open** 8.30am-12.30pm, 2-9.30pm, Mon-Sat. **No credit cards**.
Domenico Giannitti lived in England for many years and trained there as a mechanic. He speaks fluent English (with more of a Cockney than a Florentine accent), he will deal with all your car problems; what he can't manage himself he will send out to a colleague.

Parking

The safest place to leave a car in Florence is in one of the underground car parks, although this can be costly. The following two are equipped with surveillance cameras, and are open 24 hours a day.

Parcheggio Parterre *Via Madonna delle Tosse 9 (50 01 994). Bus to Piazza della Libertà.* **Open** 24 hours daily. **Rates** L2,000 per hour; L25,000 24 hours; L70,000.
A guest of any Florentine hotel can park their car here for L12,000 a day if they present a receipt from the hotel. An additional bonus is the free loan of a bike while the car is parked.
Parcheggio Piazza Stazione *Via Alamanni 14/Piazza Stazione 12/13 (23 02 655).* **Open** 24 hours daily. **Rates** L3,000 per hour; L2,500 per hour 9pm-7am Mon-Thur; L140,000 for five days.
The following car parks are smaller and more centrally located. The exact cost depends on the size of the car.
Garage Lungarno *Borgo San Jacopo 10 (28 25 42). Bus to Ponte Vecchio.* **Open** 7am-midnight. **Rates** L10,000 for first two hours; L30,000 24 hours.
International Garage *Via Palazzuolo 29 (28 23 86). Bus to Ponte Vecchio.* **Open** 7am-midnight Mon-Sat; 6pm-midnight Sun. **Rates** L8,000 for first two hours; L34,000 24 hours.
Garage del Centro *Piazza Duomo 38/39r (21 66 72). Bus to Duomo.* **Open** 7am-midnight Mon-Sat; 8am-noon, 6-10pm, Sun. **Rates** L15,000 for first two hours; L3,000 per hour thereafter; L40,000 24 hours.

Street parking
If you ever manage to find a space in an unrestricted area, parking is free in most of the side streets, but most main streets are strictly no-parking zones. Watch out for signs

saying *Passo Carrabile* (access at all times) by entrances, *Sosta Vietata* (no parking), and disabled parking spaces marked by yellow stripes on the road. The sign *Zona Rimozione* (tow-away area) at the end of a street means no parking, and is valid for the length of the street. If a street or square has no cars parked in it, then it's a no-parking zone. Blue lines on the road indicate a paid parking area, and here an attendant will issue you with a ticket.

Car pounds

If you do not find your car where you left it, it has probably been towed away. Phone the municipal police (*vigili urbani*) on 32 831, or the central car pound number (30 82 49) to find out which of the three pounds it has been taken to, quoting your number plate.

Depositeria Comunale (Car Pound) *Viale Strozzi-Tourist Bus Park. Bus 8, 20, 67.* **Open** 24 hours daily. *Via Arcovata 6. Bus 23, 33 to Viale Corsica.* **Open** 7am-9pm Mon-Sat.

Parcheggio Parterre *Via Madonna delle Tosse 9. Bus to Piazza Libertà.* **Open** 7am-1am daily.

You will have to pay a towing charge when you collect your car, and this depends on whether it was towed away during the day or at night. Rates are L90,000 and L104,000 respectively for the first 24 hours, and L12,000 per day after that. Payment can be made by Eurocheque or in cash, including foreign currency. On top of these charges, you will also be liable for a parking fine, but tourists can normally get away without paying this.

Petrol

Most petrol stations sell unleaded petrol (*senza piombo*) and regular (*super*). Diesel fuel is *gasolio*. All petrol stations have full service during weekdays. Pump attendants do not expect tips. At night and on Sundays most stations have automatic self-service pumps that accept L10,000 or L50,000 notes, in good condition. Unofficial 'assistants' will do the job for you for a small tip (L500-L1,000).

There are petrol stations on most of main roads out of town, and their normal opening hours are 7.30am to 12.30pm, 3-7pm, Monday to Saturday. They are open half an hour earlier in the morning and half an hour later in the afternoon during the summer. On Saturday afternoons and Sundays there is a rota system. There are no permanently staffed 24-hour petrol stations in Florence; the nearest are on the motorways. However, the following **AGIP** stations have 24-hour self-service machines: Via Bolognese, Via Aretina, Viale Europa, Via Senese, Via Baraca.

Embassies & consulates

There are no embassies in Florence, but some countries have consular offices in the city although these may offer limited services. Below are the only three consulates of English-speaking countries, but we have also listed the embassies in Rome of countries not represented in Florence.

American Consulate

Lungarno A Vespucci 38 (23 98 276). Bus C. **Open** 9am-2pm Mon-Fri.
In case of emergency outside these hours, call the above number and a recorded message will refer you to the current emergency number.

British Consulate

Lungarno Corsini 2 (21 25 94). Bus 6, 11, C. **Open** 9.30am-12.30pm, 2.30-4.30pm, Mon-Fri. Telephone enquiries 9am-1pm, 2-5pm, Mon-Fri. In emergency, call 06 48 25 441/551 5-7pm, 06 48 25 400/06 48 28 893 9pm-9am Mon-Fri; 06 48 25 400/06 48 28 893 weekends and holidays.
A duty officer will get back to you within the hour.

South African Consulate

Piazza dei Salarelli 1 (28 18 63). Bus to Ponte Vecchio. No office; call to make an appointment.

Australian Embassy

Via Alessandria 215, Rome (6 85 27 21). Bus to Via Nomentana. **Open** 9am-noon, 2-4pm, Mon-Thur; 9am-noon Fri.

Canadian Embassy

Via GB de Rossi 27, Rome (06 84 15 341). Consulate: *Via Zara 30, Rome (06 44 59 81/emergency phone line (06 44 59 84 21/84 18). Bus to Viale Regina Margherita.* **Open** 10am-noon, 1-4pm, Mon-Fri.

Irish Embassy

Largo del Nazareno 3, Rome (06 67 82 541). Metro Barberini/bus to Largo del Tritone. **Open** 10am-12.30pm, 3-5pm, Mon-Fri.

Health

Emergency health care is available for all travellers through the Italian national health system. EC citizens are entitled to most forms of treatment for free, though many specialised medicines, analyses and tests will be charged for. To obtain treatment you will have to produce an E111 form (*see above* **Insurance**) and for hospital treatment, you have to go to one of the casualty departments listed below. If you want to see a doctor, take your E111 to the state health centre or **USL** for the district in which you are staying. The USL are listed in the local phone book and are usually open 9am to 1pm and 2pm to 7pm, Monday to Friday.

Using the state system inevitably means dealing with a whole series of bureaucratic hurdles, and short-term visitors are recommended not to rely on the E111 form but to use private travel insurance. Embassies provide lists of English-speaking doctors and clinics, and they are also listed in the *English Yellow Pages*.

Non-EC citizens with private medical insurance can make use of state facilities on a paying basis, but for anything other than emergencies, it will be more convenient to go directly to private medicine.

Enrolling in the State System

If you are staying in Rome for any length of time, you will need to enrol fully in the state system. EC nationals should take their E111 to the local USL and ask for form 503E. Non-EC citizens can also subscribe to the system. They should go to the local office of the **INPS**, the Italian national insurance department (listed in the phone book), and have with them a *permesso di soggiorno*, *residenza* and *codice fiscale*. At time of writing the cost is L750,000 per year, which is significantly less than private health insurance. If you are working legally this will be paid by your employer, who must also provide a letter confirming your employment.

Emergencies/hospitals

If you need urgent medical care, it is best to go to the *Pronto Soccorso* (casualty) department of one of the hospitals listed below. They are open 24 hours daily. If this is impossible, phone for an ambulance (*ambulanza*) on 113 or 21 22 22/21 55 55. You can also call 118 to find a doctor on call in your area (emergencies only). One of the obvious anxieties involved with falling ill abroad is the language problem. If you need a translator to help out at the hospital, see below.

Arcispedale di Santa Maria Nuova

Piazza Santa Maria Nuova 1 (27 581). Bus 11, 14, 17, 23.
This is the most centrally located hospital in Florence.

Ospedale Istituto Ortopedico Toscano (Orthopedics)

Viale Michelangelo 41 (65 881). Bus 12, 13.

Ospedale Meyer (Children)

Via Luca Giordano 13 (56 621). Bus 11, 17.

Ospedale Torregalli

Via Torregalli 3 (71 921). Bus 83, 59.

Policlinico di Careggi

Viale Morgagni 85 (42 77 11). Bus 2, 14.

IAMAT – Associated Medical Studio

Via Lorenzo il Magnifico 59 (47 54 11). Bus 8, 13.
Clinic **open** 11am-noon, 5-6pm, Mon-Fri; 11am-noon Sat. Phone service open 24 hours.
IAMAT is a private medical service which organises home visits by doctors. Catering particularly for foreigners, they will send a GP or specialist to your hotel or temporary residence within an hour and a half. English and French are spoken fluently by the medical staff. A home visit will cost about L80,000. IAMAT also runs a clinic where a consultation will cost L60,000 (or L50,000 for students).

AVO (Association of Hospital Volunteers)

(42 50 126/23 44 567). **Open** 4-6pm Mon, Wed and Fri; 10am-noon Tue and Thur.
If you are unfortunate enough to need hospitalisation while staying in Florence and do not speak Italian, there is a group of volunteer interpreters who will come to your rescue by helping out with explanations to doctors and hospital staff. They also provide support and advice on what to do in this situation. 22 languages are spoken. The above opening times are office hours. At other times call the first listed number.

Dentists

The following dentists speak English. Call for an appointment.

Dr Derek Murphy *Via Maffei 39 (57 75 45). Bus 1.* **Open** 9am-noon, 3.30-6.30pm, Mon, Wed, Thur.

Dr Maria Peltonen Portman *Via Teatina 2 (21 85 94).* **Open** 9.30am-7pm Mon-Fri.

Pharmacies

Pharmacies (*farmacia,* identified by a large red or green cross) function semi-officially as mini-clinics, with their staff giving informal medical advice and suggesting medicines as well as making up prescriptions from your doctor. Normal opening hours are from 8.30am to 1pm and from 4pm to 8pm, Monday to Saturday. At other times, a duty rota system is in operation. The shops listed here all have permanent or extended out-of-hours services.

Duty pharmacies

A list by the door of any pharmacy indicates the nearest one which is open outside normal hours. The daily rota is also published in all the local papers, and there are phone lines for information on which chemists are open in each district (call *182*; operators do not usually speak English). At duty pharmacies there is a surcharge of L5,000 per client (though not per item) when the main shop is shut and only the special duty counter is open, which in most cases is between midnight and 8.30am. The following pharmacies all provide a 24-hour service, and there is no supplement for night service:

Farmacia Comunale

n13 Interno Stazione Santa Maria Novella (28 94 35). Bus to Santa Maria Novella station. **Open** 24 hours daily. **No credit cards.**

Farmacia Molteni

Via Calzaiuoli 7r (21 54 72). Bus to Duomo. **Open** 24 hours daily. **Credit** AmEx, EC, MC, V. English spoken.

Farmacia all' insegna del Moro

Piazza San Giovanni 20r (21 13 43). Bus to Duomo. **Open** 24 hours daily. **Credit** V. Some English spoken.

AIDS/HIV

AIDS tests are available at all the main hospitals. A charge will normally be made as they are not free under EC reciprocal arrangements. There are,

---

Emergencies

The following emergency services are open 24 hours daily.

Police/Fire/Ambulance *(113).*
Ambulance/Mobile Coronary Unit/Ambulanza/ Unita Coronarica Mobile *(118/21 22 22).*
Carabinieri *(112).*
Central Police Station/Questura Centrale *(49 771).*
Fire Service/Vigili del Fuoco *(115).*
Municipal Police/Vigili Urbani *(32 831).*
Police (Road Accidents) *(57 77 77).*
Police (Motorway Accidents) *(50 551).*
ACI Auto Assistance/Automobile Club d'Italia *(116).*

EMERGENCY REPAIRS

If you need to report a malfunction in any of the main services, the following emergency lines are open 24 hours daily.

Electricity-ENEL *(167 86 12 86).*
Fiorentina Gas *(167 86 20 48).*
Telephone (Telecom Italia) *(182).*
Water (Aquedotto) *(57 92 22).*

however, a number of free counselling services available throughout the city, and one or two even have English-speaking staff.

Linea Verde Aids
(12 78 61 061/freephone 1678 61 061).
This is the national help and information line dedicated to HIV-related problems. Some English may be spoken.

Consultorio per la Salute Omosessuale
Via San Zanobi 54r (48 82 88). Bus 11, 17.
Run by the ARCI Gay organisation, this centre provides various services relating to AIDS/HIV, and English is spoken. Telephone counselling is offered from 4pm to 8pm Monday to Friday, and counsellors are also available in person. AIDS tests are carried out on Wednesdays from 4 to 5pm. Staffed by volunteers, all these services are free.

Contraception & abortion

Condoms and other forms of contraception are widely available in pharmacies and some supermarkets. If you are in need of further assistance, the *Consultorio Familiare* at your local USL state health centre (*see above*) will provide advice and information free of charge, though for an examination or prescription you will need an E111 form or private insurance. An alternative is to go to a private clinic like those run by the AIED.

AIED
Via Ricasoli 10 (21 52 37). Bus to Duomo.
Open 3-6.15pm Mon-Fri.
The clinics run by this private family-planning organisation provide help and information on contraception and related matters and low-cost medical care. Treatment is of a high standard and service is often faster than in state clinics. An examination usually costs around L55,000 plus L20,000 compulsory membership, payable on the first visit and valid for a year.

Complementary medicine

Most conventional pharmacies also sell some alternative medicines which are quite commonly used in Italy. These medicines are, however, expensive; bring supplies from home if you use them regularly.

Antica Farmacia Sodini
Via dei Banchi 18/20r (21 11 59). Bus to Piazza Santa Maria Novella. **Open** 9am-1pm, 4pm-8pm, Mon-Sat. **No credit cards.**
The English-speaking staff at this homeopathic pharmacy are very helpful. They carry a huge range of medicines and make up prescriptions as well as giving advice.

Ambulatorio Santa Maria Novella
Piazza Santa Maria Novella 24 (28 01 43). Bus to Santa Maria Novella station. **Open** 9am-1pm, 3-7.30pm, Mon-Fri. **No credit cards.**
This is a large group practice where several homeopathic doctors have consulting rooms and offer a range of alternative health services. A full check-up will cost from about L100,000, and some English is spoken. Call to make an appointment first.

Veterinary care

Ente Nazionale Protezione Animale
Via Ricasoli 73r (21 32 96). Bus to the Duomo.
Open 4-7pm Mon-Fri; 9.30-11.30am Sat, emergencies only.

This Italian equivalent of the RSPCA is centrally located, and some English is spoken. An examination of a dog will cost L30,000.

Clinica Veterinaria Campo di Marte
Viale Righi 19 (61 05 52/emergency line 167 01 30 75 for name of clinic on call). Bus 17. **Open** 9am-noon, 4-8pm, Mon-Sat.
It is essential to make an appointment at this friendly surgery (except in emergencies). Several of the vets speak English. The examination of a dog costs about L40,000.

Alcohol & drugs

Alcoholics Anonymous
(65 03 254). English-speaking group: St James' Church, Via Rucellai 9 (35 36 254). Bus to Santa Maria Novella station.
The English-speaking branch of AA in Florence is attached to the American Church. Meetings are held on Tuesdays and Thursdays at 1.30pm, and on Saturdays at 5pm. These are also open to anyone with drug-related problems.

SOS Droga
(1678 62 278). **Open** 24 hours daily.
A freephone drugs counselling service run by the state health service. Some staff may speak English.

Drogatel
(167 01 66 00). **Open** 9am-9pm daily.
Another national freephone number with English speakers who can refer you to the correct number to call in Florence if you should need help

Anything mislaid on public transport, or stolen and subsequently discarded, may turn up, if you're lucky, at one of the lost property offices (*ufficio oggetti rinvenuti*) listed below.

For the emergency numbers to call if you lose (or have pickpocketed or stolen) a credit or charge card or travellers' cheques, *see above* **Money.**

ATAF
Via Circondaria 17b (32 83 942). Bus 23 to Viale Corsica. **Open** 9am-noon Mon-Sat.
This is a municipal office, and anything found on ATAF city bus network should, with luck, end up here.

FS/Santa Maria Novella (SMN) Station
Interno Stazione Santa Maria Novella (23 52 190).
Bus to Santa Maria Novella station. **Open** 4.15am-1.30am daily.
This office is on platform 16, next to the left luggage deposit. Articles found on the state railways in the Florence area are sent here. The staff speak minimal English.

Italian police forces are divided into four colour-coded units. The municipal police (*vigili urbani*) wear navy blue. They are the only unarmed force and deal with all traffic matters within the city. The two forces with primary responsibility for dealing with crime are the state police, the *polizia*

is not always what could be desired. If you are out and about, there are public toilets in Santa Maria Novella station, the Palazzo Vecchio, the Palazzo Pitti and in the coach park to the west of the Fortezza da Basso.

Religion

There are numerous Catholic churches all over the city (*see chapter* **Churches**), and even if you are not a practising Catholic, it is worth attending mass for the atmosphere. A few churches still sing mass, and if you want to hear some Gregorian Chant, go to **San Miniato al Monte** (Bus 12 or 13). Catholic mass is held in English at **Santa Maria del Fiore** on Saturdays at 5pm and at the **Chiesa dell' Ospedale San Giovanni di Dio** at Borgo Ognissanti 20 on Sundays and holidays at 10am. Some of the non-Catholic religions represented in Florence are listed below.

American Episcopal Church
St James', Via Rucellai 9 (29 44 17). Bus 1, 17 or Santa Maria Novella station. **Services** (in English) 9am, 11am Sun.

Anglican
St. Mark's, Via Maggio 16 (29 47 64). Bus C, 11. **Services** 9am Eucharist, 10.30am Sung Eucharist, Sun; 6pm Eucharist Thur; 8pm Eucharist Fri.

Jewish
Comunita Ebraica, Via Farina 4 (24 52 52/24 52 53). Bus 6. **Services** 8.30/8.45am Sat. For Fri and Sat evening services, call for details as times vary.

Methodist
Chiesa Metodista, Via dei Benci 9 (24 31 16). Bus 23, B. **Services** 11am Sun.

Working in Florence

Gone are the days when a foreigner could arrive in Florence and stand a pretty good chance of finding a decent job. Nowadays, you have to be prepared to teach English to children, or possibly pick up casual work in a bar or a leather store, but it's not easy. Officially, all non-Italians working in Italy need a work permit (*see above* **Bureaucracy**), and to get a work permit you need a job. Most of the lower-paid jobs available are not declared to the authorities, and so do not require documentation. Jobs like this make up quite a sizeable sector of the economy, and checks on undeclared labour-pool are not particularly rigorous.

The classified ads paper *La Pulce* has job listings, and it's worth looking in the local English-language press. English-language bookshops have noticeboards where ads are sometimes placed, or can be placed. For a serious job, look in the 'Firenze' section of *La Repubblica*, or in the local *La Nazione*.

statale, also in blue, though with lighter trousers, and the normally black-clad *carabinieri*, officially part of the army. Their roles overlap, and distinctions are hard to establish. The *guardia di finanza* (financial police) are in grey and deal with financial and customs irregularities. They have little to do with tourists.

In an emergency call on any of the police forces for help, but if you are robbed, go immediately to the nearest *carabinieri* post (*commissariato*) or police station (*questura*), and say you want to report a *furto*. A *denuncia* (written statement) of the incident will be written by or for you. It is unlikely that your things will be found, but you will need the *denuncia* for making an insurance claim. A lost or stolen passport should be reported immediately to your embassy or consulate.

The best place to report a crime in Florence is at the **Questura Centrale** (*see above* **Bureaucracy**).

Commando Regione Carabinieri
Borgo Ognissanti 48 (24 811). Bus B, C. **Open** 24 hours daily. A *carabineri* station near the centre of town.

Public lavatories

Florence is not well equipped with public loos, and the easiest thing to do is go to a bar where you may or may not find loo paper. The level of cleanliness

Getting Around

Those boots were made for walking.

Florence's streets are so jammed with traffic, and the air quality has become so poor, that the municipal council has recently started taking steps to improve the situation. When pollution levels reach a certain limit, cars that do not use unleaded fuel are banned altogether from within a large radius of the city (those that are eco-friendly have special window stickers). Digital information boards suspended above the main roads into town give notice of such a ban (and all street lights go on for 15 minutes at noon, 2pm and 4pm the preceding day). On these days, if you do not have the appropriate vehicle, you cannot drive between 8am and 6pm. However, as hire cars and any vehicles with foreign number plates are excluded from the ban, tourists need not worry.

Added to this are the limits imposed by the permanent Traffic Free Zones (ZTL). These areas (lettered A-E), include the *centro storico* and are gradually expanding outwards. Only residents or permit-holders can enter from 7.30am to 12.30pm and from 3pm to 6.30 pm, Monday to Saturday. This is extended in the summer to exclude cars from the city centre in the evenings (times vary from year to year) from Friday to Sunday. Access to hotels on arrival and departure is permitted.

Parking is another major problem and is severely restricted in the centre of town. You are advised to use one of the car parks rather than risk a fine or being towed away. For further information on car parks, *see* **Essential Information: Driving in Florence**. Everything considered, the best, and quickest way to get around Florence is on foot; the historic centre (*centro storico*) is relatively compact. In pedestrian areas, beware of speeding bicycles and mopeds, and do not be surprised if you meet two-wheeled vehicles zooming the wrong way up a one-way street. Don't expect cars to stop instantly for a traffic light, and expect cars making right turns from side streets to ignore red lights. If you really want to take your life in your hands, hire a bicycle or scooter. For further details of vehicle hire, *see chapter* **Services**.

Arriving in Florence
By Air

If you are arriving in Tuscany by air, you will most likely land at either Pisa's **Galilei Airport** or at the tiny-but-busy **Vespucci Airport** just outside Florence at Peretola.

From Pisa Airport

Galilei Airport information (050 50 07 07).
Open 6.30am-8.30pm daily. *Flight information (21 60 73).* **Open** 7am-5.30pm daily. Airport **open** 5am-midnight daily.
Pisa Airport lies just south of Pisa, 80 kilometres (50 miles) west of Florence. It handles national and international (but not intercontinental) flights, both scheduled and charter. The journey into Florence by car is along the 'Firenze-Pisa-Livorno' dual carriageway (*superstrada*) which runs into the airport and into the west of the city. There is also a direct train service to Florence's Santa Maria Novella station which takes just over one hour, stopping at Pisa Centrale and Pontederra on the way. Tickets cost L7,400, and can be purchased at the information desk in the main airport concourse (open 6.30am-8.30pm daily). This service is rather erratic and departures have little to do with incoming flights; trains run roughly every hour from 10.44am to 5.44pm. There is another service – albeit less direct – into Florence from Pisa Airport via Lucca, but trains are even less frequent and the journey time is nearly two hours. If the arrival of your flight does not coincide with a direct train to Florence, it is worth looking into departures from Pisa Centrale station. The information desk has a timetable, and a taxi into Pisa will cost about L12,000. There is also a city bus link; the CPT bus 7 leaves for the city centre and train station every 15 minutes. Tickets are available at the information desk.

For the return journey, the first departure from Florence is at 6.47am, and trains run almost every hour between 11.05am and 5.05pm. There is a passenger and baggage check-in facility at Santa Maria Novella station on platform 5. Minimum check-in time is 15 minutes before your train for Pisa Airport is due to leave, or 5 minutes for hand baggage only. Tickets to the airport are on sale here but you will pay a L2,000 supplement on the normal fare. A flight information service is also provided.

From Florence Airport

Vespucci (Peretola) Airport Information (37 34 98).
Open 7.30am-10pm daily. *Flight Information (30 61 700, recorded message, also in English).* **Open** 24 hours daily. Airport **open** 24 hours daily.
Florence now has its own small, but very busy airport. Known locally as Peretola (after the nearby suburb), the decision to expand what was, until relatively recently, a small airfield, has excited much controversy. In 1996 the runway was lengthened, and the airport handles over 70 national and international scheduled flights a day. Situated about 5 kilometres (3 miles) west of central Florence, there are two bus lines that service the airport. The SITA coach stops right outside the arrivals building, and goes to the SITA bus station in Via S Caterina da Siena, adjacent to Santa Maria Novella train station. It runs every 45 minutes/hour from 9.45am to 10.35pm and tickets, costing L6,000, can be bought on board. The ATAF city bus number 62 stops just outside the main gate (which is a bit of a trek with heavy bags). This runs every 20/25 minutes from 6.30am-10.45pm and tickets cost L1,500. These are available form the automatic machine by the exit or from the bar/tabacchi on the first floor of the departures building.

A taxi from the airport into the centre of Florence will cost from about L25,000 plus extras for luggage and surcharges for nights or public holidays.

The journey time into Florence is from 20 minutes to half an hour, depending on the traffic.

Airport Information & Services

For general enquiries, ring the airport information numbers given above. If you manage to get through (not always easy), some of the staff should be able to answer queries in English. At both Florence and Pisa airports there are offices of the Tuscan Tourist Board (the APT; open 8.30am-10.30pm daily and 11am-5pm Mon-Sat, 11am-2pm Sun in Pisa), and both airports have exchange facilities.

The major airlines serving Florence and Pisa can be reached at the following numbers:

Alitalia

Lungarno Acciaiuoli 12/12r (27 889). 24-hour international flight information line (1478 65 642). Bus to Ponte Vecchio. **Open** 9am-4.30pm Mon-Fri. **Credit** AmEx, DC, EC, MC, V.

British Airways

Pisa Airport (050 40 866). **Open** 8am-8pm Mon-Fri, 9am-5pm, Sat. *International flight information and general enquiries (167 21 52 15).* **Open** 8am-8pm Mon-Fri; 9am-5pm Sat. British Airways no longer has an office in Florence.

Meridiana

Lungarno Vespucci 28r (32 961). Bus C. **Open** 9am-1pm, 2-5pm, Mon-Fri. **Credit** AmEx, DC, EC, MC, V.

By Bus

If you come to Florence by coach, you will probably arrive at either the SITA or LAZZI bus stations, both near Santa Maria Novella train station. For information, including services to Tuscany:

SITA

Via S Caterina da Siena 15 (Information 48 36 51). **Open** 8.30am-12.30pm, 2.30-5.30pm, Mon-Fri; 8.30am-1pm Sat, Sun.

LAZZI

Piazza Stazione 47r. (Information 166 84 50 10). **Open** 6am-10pm daily.

By Train

Virtually all long distance trains arrive at the main Santa Maria Novella station (Firenze SMN). Like most city stations, it is an obvious target for pickpockets and thieves, so keep a close eye on your bag and luggage. Taxis service the station on a 24 hour basis, and many of the city buses stop here. If you are travelling light, it is only a ten-minute walk into the centre of Florence. If you arrive late, head for the taxi rank (avoiding the touts), or for one of the night buses – 67, 70 or 71 – that stop here (*see below* **Night Buses**). Most long-distance trains arriving during the night stop at Campo di Marte station to the northwest of the city where the number 67 and 70 buses also stop. Some of the new high-speed trains (*pendolino*) stop at Rifredi station (as well as Santa Maria Novella).

If you are boarding a train in Florence (or, indeed, in any other Italian city), make sure you stamp your

ticket and any supplements in the not-very-obvious machines at the head of the platforms. Failure to do this may result in a fine. Left luggage facilities are available at Santa Maria Novella station. The principal stations in Florence are:

Stazione Campo di Marte

Via Mannelli (24 33 44). Bus 6, 12, 20, 91. This is the principal station in Florence when Santa Maria Novella is closed during the night, and many long distance trains stop here. The ticket office is always open.

Stazione Rifredi

Via dello Steccuto 1 (23 52 863). Bus 28. Some local trains stop here as well as the high-speed *pendolino* which runs between Milan and Rome.

Stazione Santa Maria Novella

Piazza Stazione (23 52 061). Bus to Santa Maria Novella station. **Open** 4.15am-1.30am daily. Most national and international services serve this terminus. The information office, open from 7am to 9pm daily, is for personal callers only, and staff speak English. The ticket office is open from 5.45am to 10pm daily.

Train information

(1478 88 088). **Open** 7am-9pm daily. This is the centralised information service of the state railways (the FS – Ferrovie dello Stato) and provides information on trains throughout Italy. Calls are answered and put on a queuing system, so you may have a long wait. Information is given for both national and international routes, and some English is spoken.

Public transport

Buses

Florence is a small city and relies on buses for public transport. The city bus network, run by the ATAF bus company, is comprehensive and reasonably efficient. Travelling by bus is pretty safe, even at night, but keep an eye on your bag or wallet when there is a crowd. For most of the places mentioned in this guide, we have given the bus routes that serve that destination where relevant. Bearing in mind that Florence is small, it is often easier, and quicker, to go on foot. When several bus routes serve the same area, we have given the name of the destination to look out for. The most useful, or interesting, routes are also given below.

ATAF

Information: *Piazza Stazione (56 50 222). Bus to Santa Maria Novella station.* **Open** 7am-8pm daily for telephone and personal callers.

The main ATAF information desk has English-speaking staff, although if you make your enquiry by phone, you may not be so lucky. Here you can buy a variety of bus tickets (*see below* **Tickets**), and obtain a helpful bus map with details of all routes and the different tickets. Basic information on prices is also available in English.

Daytime services

Most ATAF routes run between 5.30am and 9pm with a frequency of between 10 and 30 minutes depending on the route. After 9pm, routes are compressed into four night-time services (*see below* **Night Buses**). Surprisingly, buses usually leave their departure point on time, but heavy traffic can cause delays en route. The newer orange and white bus stops (*fermata*) list the stops along the route to be followed, and each stop has its name (relative to the street or landmark concerned) written on the top. You are expected to board the bus by the front and rear doors, and to get off through the middle doors. When the bus is really crowded (and it often is), it can be impossible to squeeze your way to the right door, so use the nearest exit. If you are not sure where to get off, fellow passengers are usually happy to help. You must have a ticket before boarding as they are not available on the bus (with the exception of the 70, *see below* **Night Buses**).

Useful routes

The following daytime routes might be useful for visitors: **7** from the Santa Maria Novella station, via the Duomo and Piazza San Marco to Fiesole; **13** from the station takes a cicular route to Piazza della Libertà, accross the river, up the tree-lined Viale Michelangelo with its fabulous villas, to Piazzale Michelangelo and San Miniato; **62** to the airport (*see p66* **Arriving in Florence**); **10** to Settignano.

The ATAF has recently introduced a number of eco-friendly electric buses which run three routes: **B**, **C** and Sunday and holiday service, **D**. Their diminutive size means that they can cope with the narrower streets (something which is impossible for their larger counterparts), and these routes make for wonderful unofficial sightseeing tours, taking in between them most of the important sights, both north and south of the river. The routes are detailed in ATAF's brochure.

Night buses

Three bus routes operate until 12.30am/1am (the **67**, **68** and **71**), but only one – the **70** – runs all night and this leaves Sant Maria Novella every hour. It passes through the centre of town, turns north, calls at Campo di Marte station (useful for night-time train departures and arrivals), and returns to Santa Maria Novella via a long, circular route. Tickets are available on board, but will set you back double what they would normally cost.

Tickets

There is a variety of ATAF bus tickets, all of which must be bought in advance. These are available from the ATAF office in Piazza Stazione (open 7am-8pm daily). Excepting the monthly season ticket (*see below*), tickets can also be purchased from automatic machines (the most central of which are in Piazza Stazione, Piazza San Marco and Piazza Unità, as well as Piazza Mino, Fiesole), *tabacchi*, newsstands and some bars, all of which display an orange ATAF sticker. When you board the bus, stamp the single ticket in one of the machines, usually placed by the front and rear doors. Many people try to avoid paying fares, but plain-clothes inspectors circulate frequently and anyone without a ticket will be fined L75,000 on the spot.

60-minute ticket (*biglietto 60 minuti*)

Costing L1,500, this is just what it says; valid for an hour of travel on all buses. You can use as many different routes as you want within this time.

Multiple ticket (*biglietto multiplo*)

This costs L5,800 and consists of four single tickets, each one of which is valid for 60 minutes, and must be stamped.

3-hour ticket (*biglietto 3 ore*)

Again, this is self explanatory, and costs L2,500.

24-hour ticket (*biglietto 24 ore*)

This ticket, which costs L6,000, is good value and must be stamped at the beginning of the first journey.

Monthly pass (*abbonamento ordinario*)

A passport-sized photo is required for this season ticket which costs L53,000. Available to anyone, it can be bought from the ATAF office at Santa Maria Novella station, or from any of the normal outlets displaying an *Abbonamenti ATAF* sign. It is valid for a month's unlimited travel on all ATAF routes.

Taxis

Licensed taxis are painted white with yellow graphics and have a meter. Each one will have its code name of a city or country plus a number on the door by way of identification; for example, *Londra 6*. If you have any problem, you should quote this number. Always avoid the shifty-looking characters muttering "Taxi?" at the stations; they will charge huge rates. Official taxis are normally found at a rank; it's difficult to flag one down in the street.

Taxi fares & surcharges

Taxis are expensive in Florence, but fares are standard for all the legitimate companies working in the city. When you get into a cab, the meter will never read less than L4,300; this is a minimum charge which begins to rise immediately at a rate of L1,350 per kilometre. There is an overall minimum fare of L7,000. Between 10pm and 6am, a L4,000 night supplement is applicable, and on Sundays and public holidays, this runs at L3,000 going up to the normal night rate after 10pm. You will also be charged extra for every piece of luggage placed in the boot, and destinations outside the official city limits (Fiesole, for example), will cost considerably more. A trip to Florence airport will cost about L25,000 plus extras where relevant. Tipping is not required, but if you feel like it, round up to the nearest L1,000 or so.

Taxi ranks

Ranks are indicated by a blue sign with 'TAXI' written in white, but this is no guarantee that it will be well-stocked with waiting cars, particularly when it is raining or during the rush hours when you may have to wait a considerable time. In the centre of town, there are ranks in Piazza della Repubblica, Piazza Stazione, Piazza Santa Maria Novella, Piazza Duomo, Piazza San Marco, Piazza Santa Croce and Piazza Santa Trinità.

Phone cabs

You can phone for a taxi from any of the numbers listed below, but again, during rush hour or in the rain, you may have to wait a while. Rates are standard, and operators probably speak sufficient English for you to make yourself understood. If you want an English-speaking driver, they can oblige. When your call is answered, name the street and number, or the bar, restaurant or club from where you want to be picked up. You will be given the code name of the taxi and a time; for example, "*Londra 6 in tre minuti*". Londra 6 will be there in three minutes. The taxi meter will start running from the moment your call is answered, so do not be surprised if there is already a hefty sum on the clock when you get in. It is not normal to book taxis in advance; ring when you are ready to leave, and allow extra time for adverse weather conditions.

Radio taxi numbers: *43 90, 47 98, 42 42, 43 86.*

Accommodation

Romantic rooms with a view aren't just confined to fiction – Florence has many wonderful hotels, but expect to pay for the pleasure.

Old world opulence at the **Grand Hotel Villa Cora** *(see page 71).*

Florence is one of the most expensive cities in Italy in which to stay, possibly surpassed only by Venice. However, many of its hotels are wonderfully atmospheric and there is a merciful lack of international chains. It pays to shop around as there is an enormous disparity in prices, even among hotels within the same star rating. Once you have decided on a hotel, don't be afraid to ask to see the room before accepting it, and ask to see another if it's not satisfactory in any way. One thing to seek out if you are visiting during the summer is a terrace or garden; it can make a huge difference after a long day's sightseeing to be able to relax al fresco with a Campari.

The hotels listed below have been chosen for the good value they offer within their category. Italian hotels are classified on a star system (from one to five) and this will give you some idea of the price and facilities to expect, but as many hotels choose to use a lower rating than they deserve (and so pay lower taxes), this is only a rough guideline.

Few Florentine hotels have even heard of non-smoking areas, and there aren't many places with access for the disabled. Although the staff are more than willing to help, most places have so many steep stairs there's not much they can do, but we've indicated the few places that do have special facilities. Many hotels reduce their prices by as much as 50 per cent in the off season. In Florence, this means roughly from January to March, or a couple of weeks before Easter, and late July and August. Even outside these times, you may find that a hotel will give you a better price if it has plenty of room; it's worth haggling a bit.

Hotels are either in the tourist-packed *centro storico*, the quieter, often cheaper, but still convenient residential outskirts, or away from the crowds in the relative cool and calm of nearby hills. As with many European cities, the area around the railway station can be unsavoury at night but is packed with cheap *pensioni* (particularly in Via Faenza). Hardly any hotels have their own parking, and garages are pricey.

florence
& Tuscany

ADVANCE BOOKINGS

Always book well in advance, whatever time of the year you are visiting, as Florence fills up very quickly. If you arrive without a place to stay, go to the **APT** office (*see chapter* **Essential Information**), the **Ufficio Informazione Turistiche** in Piazza Stazione where they provide hotel lists but not a booking service, or directly to the **ITA** office in the station where they will, for a fee, find and book you a hotel.

Unless stated, prices (which are subject to change) are for a single or double room with its own bathroom, and include breakfast. Nearly all of the hotels and *pensioni* will put at least one extra bed into a double room – you'll have to pay extra, but it's a lot cheaper than taking an extra single room.

The sky's the limit (over L450,000)

Brunelleschi

Via de Calzaioli, Piazza Santa Elisabetta (56 20 68/fax 21 96 53). Bus to the Duomo. **Rates** *single* L350,000; *double* L470,000; *suite* L580-700,000. **Credit** AmEx, DC, EC, JCB, MC, V.

The Byzantine tower which now forms part of this centrally located hotel was once a prison, and is believed to be the oldest standing structure in Florence. Inside, however, the Brunelleschi is a thoroughly modern, well-run establishment, offering all the amenities of a luxury hotel. The 95 bedrooms are comfortably, if rather uniformly, furnished. Part of the restaurant is in the tower, and two penthouse suites on the fifth floor enjoy 360° views of the city. Many objects of archaeological interest were unearthed during reconstruction work in the '80s, and are now on display in a little museum in the hotel basement.

Hotel services *Air-conditioning. Babysitting. Bar. Car park (nearby garage, extra cost). Conference facilities (for up to 140). Currency exchange. Fax. Laundry. Lifts. Multi-lingual staff. Non-smoking rooms. Restaurant.* **Room services** *Air-conditioning. Hair drier. Jacuzzi in penthouse suites. Mini-bar. Radio. Room service (24-hour). Telephone. TV (satellite).*

Excelsior

Piazza Ognissanti 3 (26 42 01/fax 21 02 78). Bus B, C. **Rates** *single* L340-400,000; *double* L570,000/640,000/720,000; *suite* L900,000/1,500,000/2,200,000; L60,000 supplement for view of Arno. **Credit** AmEx, DC, EC, JCB, MC, V.

Napoleon's sister once lived in part of the building which, since 1927, has been the Hotel Excelsior; today the occupants are no less illustrious. More 'old world' in atmosphere and style than the Grand across the piazza, the hotel offers luxury accommodation without being stuffy; the green-liveried staff are charming and helpful. Public rooms are on a grand scale with polished marble floors and neoclassical columns, stained glass and painted wooden ceilings. The 163 bedrooms are sumptuously decorated, with fine antiques and marble bathrooms. Those on the fifth floor have been renovated recently and some boast spacious terraces with views over the river to the rooftops of Oltrarno.

Hotel services *Air-conditioning. Babysitting. Bar. Car park (nearby garage, extra cost). Conference facilities (for up to 180). Currency exchange. Fax. Laundry. Lifts. Multi-lingual staff. Non-smoking rooms. Restaurant. Tours arranged.* **Room services** *Air-conditioning. Hair drier. Mini-bar. Radio. Room service (24-hour). Safe. Telephone. TV (satellite).*

Grand Hotel

Piazza Ognissanti 1 (28 87 81/fax 21 74 00). Bus 9, B, C. **Rates** (breakfast L29,000) *single* L410-450,000; *double* L620-690,000; *suite* 1,000,000-1,900,000. **Credit** AmEx, DC, EC, JCB, MC, V.

Favoured hangouts of the rich and famous, the two sister hotels facing each other across Piazza Ognissanti are equally 'grand' but different in character. The slightly smaller (and arguably more personal) Grand has recently been restored and glories in its unashamed luxury. The vast hall, with its original 15th-century stained glass ceiling, elaborate marble floor, *pietra serena* columns, rich brocades, statues and potted palms, combines restaurant, bar, salon and piano bar. Many of the 107 bedrooms look over the Arno (the river view costs an extra L60,000 per night), and are decorated in early Florentine style with frescoes and traditional paintwork (all hand done by local master craftsmen), repro wooden furniture, marble inlay, and rich fabrics. Bathrooms, as one might expect, are symphonies in marble. Other rooms are decorated in plainer Empire style but are equally comfortable.

Hotel services *Air-conditioning. Babysitting. Bar. Car park (nearby garage, extra cost). Conference facilities (for up to 200). Currency exchange. Fax. Laundry. Lifts. Multi-lingual staff. Non-smoking rooms. Restaurant. Safe. Tours arranged.* **Room services** *Air-conditioning. Hair dryer. Mini-bar. Radio. Room service (24-hour). Telephone. TV (satellite).*

Grand Hotel Villa Cora

Viale Machiavelli 18 (22 98 451/fax 22 90 86). Bus 13. **Rates** *single* L420,000; *double* L680-780,000; *suites* L1,000,000-1,800,000. **Credit** AmEx, DC, EC, JCB, MC, V.

This impressive villa, set in spacious gardens with statues, green lawns and huge terracotta flower pots, dates from the mid-19th century. It is now a luxury hotel, but its relatively small size – 49 rooms – means that it is able to maintain the feel of a grand country house. Public rooms are lavish; ornate plasterwork, lashings of gold, frescoes, outrageous Venetian chandeliers (the only survivors of the original decor), huge mirrors, intricately carved woodwork, and rich fabrics. Downstairs, everything is on a grand scale. The bedrooms vary enormously, from the cleaner, classical (and some may feel less oppressive) lines of the second and third floors, to the formal grandeur of the first, where the walls are hung with pale silks, furniture is elaborate reproduction, and dimensions are more in keeping with the public rooms. Porta Romana is only a ten minute walk down the hill, but a courtesy limo service to and from the Ponte Vecchio is provided for guests.

Hotel services *Air-conditioning. Bar. Car park. Conference facilities (for 120). Currency exchange. Fax. Garden. Laundry. Lifts. Multi-lingual staff. Non-smoking rooms. Pool. Restaurant.* **Room services** *Air-conditioning. Hair drier. Mini-bar. Radio. Room service (24-hour). Telephone. TV (satellite). Video (on request).*

Helvetia & Bristol

Via dei Pescioni 2 (28 78 14/fax 28 83 53). Bus to Duomo. **Rates** (breakfast L32,000) *single* L335,000; *double* L451-572,000; *suite* L726-1,540,000. **Credit** AmEx, DC, EC, MC, V.

Built as a hotel in the 19th century, and completely renovated between 1987-89, the Helvetia & Bristol is arguably central Florence's finest hotel. Illustrious past guests include Gabriele D'Annunzio, Luigi Pirandello, Stravinsky and Bertrand Russell, and the building preserves a strong sense of a long and distinguished history. No expense has been spared to create a supremely comfortable hotel in exquisite taste. The salon, with its welcoming fireplace and deep green velvet sofas and armchairs, is brimming with antique furniture. Breakfast and lunch are served in the delightful and informal 'Winter Garden', a meeting place for the intelligentsia of the 1920s and now an airy room with a pale green stained glass roof, wicker furniture, stone fountain and lush

*Room with a view at the **Lungarno**.*

green plants. The Bristol's restaurant is an intimate, sober room decorated in rich dark colours, with vast gilt mirrors, and dominated by two extraordinary lamps which came from Mona Bismarck's villa on Capri. Bedrooms are sumptuous with heavy, ornate fabrics adorning walls, beds and windows. Every one is different but they are all furnished with antiques, Venetian lamps and mirrors. The luxury bathrooms are, inevitably, kitted out in Carrara marble. Prints and original paintings hang throughout the hotel, including some important works of 15th-century Tuscan School. One of the most attractive things about the Helvetia & Bristol is that, in spite of its undeniable exclusivity, it manages to avoid any hint of stuffiness.
Hotel services *Air-conditioning. Bar. Car park (nearby garage, extra cost). Currency exchange. Fax. Laundry. Lift. Multi-lingual staff. Non-smoking rooms. Restaurant.* **Room services** *Air-conditioning. Hair drier. Jacuzzi (in half of rooms). Mini-bar. Radio. Room service (24-hour). Safe. Telephone. TV (satellite). Video.*

Expensive (L300-450,000)

Berchielli
Lungarno Acciaioli 14/Piazza del Limbo 6 (26 40 61/fax 21 86 36). Bus to Ponte Vecchio. **Rates** *single* L250-300,000; *double* L330-420,000. **Credit** AmEx, DC, EC, JCB, MC, V.
This hotel, occupying what were three 14th-century palazzi, enjoys a fabulous position on the river, and many of its 76 rooms have a waterfront view. The great slabs of black and white polished marble in the lobby are jarring; but upstairs the rooms are spacious, comfortable and furnished in traditional style and restful colours. Prices are reasonable for a four-star hotel.
Hotel services *Air-conditioning. Bar. Car park (nearby garage, extra cost). Conference facilities (up to 80). Fax. Laundry. Lifts. Multi-lingual staff. Roof garden.* **Room services** *Air-conditioning. Hair dryer. Mini-bar. Radio. Room service. Safe. Telephone. TV (satellite).*

Hermitage
Vicolo Marzio 1 (Piazza del Pesce) (28 72 16/fax 21 22 08). Bus to Ponte Vecchio. **Rates** *single* L190,000; *double* L290,000. **Credit** EC, MC, V.
Book well in advance to be sure of one of the 28 rooms in this delightful hotel. Its superb location (by the Ponte Vecchio),

warm welcome and superior facilities make it a winner. Public areas – plant-filled roof garden, sunny breakfast room and cosy sitting room – are on the top floors, while the comfortable and intimate bedrooms with their tasteful fabrics and antique furniture occupy the lower three floors. Some bedrooms enjoy the view of the river but, in spite of double glazing, these are not the most peaceful. Prices are a little above average for this category, but well worth the outlay.
Hotel services *Babysitting. Bar. Currency exchange. Fax. Laundry. Lift. Multi-lingual staff. Non-smoking rooms. Roof garden.* **Room services** *Air-conditioning. Hair drier. Jacuzzi (in 8 rooms). Room service. Telephone. TV.*

J and J
Via di Mezzo 20 (23 45 005/fax 24 02 82). Bus C to Piazza dei Ciompi. **Rates** *doubles* L300-500,000. **Credit** AmEx, DC, EC, MC, V.
The simple façade of this former convent, and its location in a quiet residential street in the old city near Sant'Ambrogio, belies the luxury accommodation that lies within. Its owner is an architect, and this is apparent throughout the chic interior. Old and new are effectively combined, with many original architectural features visible in the public rooms (comfortably furnished in pale modern fabrics) and in the arched cloister where breakfast is served in the summer. No two bedrooms are alike; some are enormous, with split levels and sitting areas. All are furnished with antiques and hand-woven fabrics, and mellow lighting gives a romantic touch. A supremely comfortable and discreet small hotel for those who appreciate individual attention.
Hotel services *Air-conditioning. Babysitting. Bar. Car park (nearby extra cost). Fax. Laundry. Multi-lingual staff. Safe.* **Room services** *Air-conditioning. Hair dryer. Mini-bar. Room service. Telephone. TV (satellite).*

Kraft
Via Solferino 2 (28 42 73/fax 23 98 267). Bus C. **Rates** *single* L180-290,000; *double* L290-410,000; *triple* L360-480,000. **Credit** AmEx, DC, EC, JCB, MC, V.
Extensive renovation work has given this 80-room hotel a contemporary look. Situated west of the city centre, near the Arno and convenient for Santa Maria Novella rail station, you are likely to be rubbing shoulders with conductors and opera singers from the Teatro Comunale just over the road. The colour scheme in the smart public rooms is deep terracotta and green; the comfortable bedrooms are traditionally

furnished with bright fabrics on the beds and windows, and warm-coloured papers on the walls. One of Kraft's major pluses is its big roof garden and pool where, under white umbrellas, you can escape from the city heat. Adjacent is an attractive breakfast room. The five junior suites enjoy panoramic views from the top floor.

Hotel services *Air-conditioning. Babysitting. Bar. Conference facilities. Currency exchange. Fax. Laundry. Lift. Multi-lingual staff. Non-smoking rooms. Pool. Restaurant. Roof garden. Safe.* **Room services** *Air-conditioning. Hair drier. Mini-bar. Room service. Telephone. TV (satellite). Safe (in some rooms).*

Lungarno

Borgo San Jacopo 14 (26 42 11/fax 26 84 37). Bus to Ponte Vecchio. **Rates** (breakfast L25,000) *single* L280,000; *double* L380,000, *suite* L540-570,000. **Credit** AmEx, DC, EC, JCB, MC, V.

The location of this hotel – in a '60s building with a medieval tower in the middle – couldn't be more central. Two minutes walk from the Ponte Vecchio in the Oltrarno, it is right on the river, and the most coveted rooms have flower-clad terraces directly over the water. The comfortable sitting room area, where you can also have breakfast, has huge picture windows which take full advantage of the waterside setting. The hotel has been in business for 30 years and many of the staff have been there since day one. Pride is taken in the fact that many guests are regulars; some have the furniture in their favourite rooms re-arranged according to whim, and others even store their summer or winter wardrobes at the hotel. The sitting and bar area is on two levels and overlooks the river. Furniture is traditional with comfortable chairs and sofas in elegant fabrics which mix well with some antique pieces, prints on the walls and lots of fresh flowers. Bedrooms – on 8 floors – are not particularly spacious, but extremely comfortable; those in the medieval tower have original stone walls. At the time of going to press the Lungarno was being refurbished, but the management guarantees to maintain standards.

Hotel services *Bar. Babysitting. Currency exchange.* *Car park (nearby garage, extra charge). Fax. Laundry. Lifts. Multi-lingual staff.* **Room services** *Air-conditioning. Hair dryer. Mini-bar. Radio. Room service. Safe. Telephone. TV (satellite).*

Monna Lisa

Borgo Pinti 27 (24 79 751/fax 24 79 755). Bus B. **Rates** *single* L200-280,000; *double* L300-450,000. **Credit** AmEx, DC, EC, JCB, MC, V.

There is little evidence, from the plain façade, of the existence of this up-market hotel located on a narrow street near Santa Croce. The present owners are descendants of the sculptor Giovanni Dupre, and the Renaissance palazzo is crammed with their superb collection of precious paintings, sculptures and furniture. There is a maze of public rooms on the ground floor, many of them with original waxed terracotta floors and ornate wooden ceilings. One of the great assets of this hotel is the delightful courtyard garden (with ample parking at one side) where breakfast is served in summer. The 30 bedrooms vary considerably in size and style, from the huge and ornate to the more cramped and ordinary. The best of them look onto the garden, and some have little terraces. On the down side, the reception from the staff is inclined to be a little cold.

Hotel services *Air-conditioning. Babysitting. Bar. Car park (extra charge). Laundry. Lift (in annexe). Multi-lingual staff. Non-smoking rooms. Safe.* **Room services** *Air-conditioning. Hair dryer. Jacuzzi (in 6 rooms). Mini-bar. Room service. Telephone. TV (satellite).*

Torre di Bellosguardo

Via Roti Michelozzi 2 (22 98 145/fax 22 90 08). Bus to Porto Romana then 15 min walk. **Rates** (breakfast L25,000) *single* L250-290,000; *double* L390,000; *suite* L490-590,000. **Credit** AmEx, DC, EC, MC, V.

Of all the havens of escape from the torrid summer heat, this exceptional hotel at Bellosguardo (beautiful view) about five minutes drive up the hill near Porta Romana, is possibly the most appealing. The honey-coloured Renaissance villa, with its solid central tower, has been the family home of Amerigo

The exceptionally atmospheric **Torre di Bellosguardo**.

BRIDGEWATER'S
Idyllic Italy

COUNTRYSIDE TO COAST

The complete selection of private rental accommodation
throughout Tuscany, Umbria and beyond, including:

PRIVATE VILLAS BY THE SEA
in Marina di Pietrasanta on Tuscany's golden coast

COUNTRY VILLAS & FARMHOUSES WITH POOLS
in the heart of Tuscany and Umbria

CASTLES & COUNTRY HOUSE HOTELS
in the Chianti Hills, Florence, Siena, Arezzo and Cortona

MOUNTAIN VILLAGE COTTAGES & APARTMENTS
with spectacular views of the coast in Capezzano and Argentario

LAKE GARDA HOTELS
superb 3 & 4 star lakeside hotels

CITY APARTMENTS
in the Roman amphitheatre of Lucca and the heart of Rome itself

For reservations, information or a copy of our 100 page brochure,
call the Italian accommodation experts:

BRIDGEWATER'S IDYLLIC ITALY
217 MONTON ROAD, MONTON, MANCHESTER M30 9PN. ENGLAND
TEL: 0161 787 8587 FAX: 0161 787 8896

E-Mail: italy@bridgewater-travel.co.uk

ABTA
V7278

Franchetti for generations. Now carefully restored, it maintains its historic atmosphere while offering supreme comfort. The spacious public rooms, vaulted and frescoed, contain fine antique furniture and massive carved *pietra serena* fireplaces. Each bedroom is different, and each has its own charm. The suite in the top of the tower enjoys a 360° view of the Florentine hills, while another displays remarkable wood craftsmanship, the sitting room being entirely panelled in intricately worked pieces of wood. The real appeal, however, lies in the setting. Wander through the ornamental gardens, or laze by the side of the pool, possibly nibbling at one of the light lunches which are served during the summer months, and thank your lucky stars that you are not down in the sweaty, crowded city laid out below.

Hotel services *Babysitting. Bar. Car park. Fax. Garden. Laundry. Lift. Multi-lingual staff. Pool. Safe.* **Room services** *Air-conditioning (in 3 suites). Room service. Telephone.*

Moderate (L180-300,000)

Annalena

Via Romana 34 (22 24 02/fax 22 24 03). Bus 11, 36, 37 to Boboli Gardens. **Rates** *single* L175,000; *double* L250,000. **Credit** AmEx, DC, EC, MC, V.

Annalena, a young Florentine noblewoman, inherited this 15th-century palazzo from the Medici family, although she subsequently donated it to an order of nuns for use as a refuge for young widows. During the Mussolini years, refugees from the fascist police were lodged here. Today it is an old-fashioned and comfortable *pensione*. The bedrooms are of various sizes, but all have some antique furniture; the best have terraces and views over the adjacent horticultural centre. The Palazzo Pitti and Boboli Gardens are nearby.

Hotel services *Bar. Car park. Currency exchange. Fax. Laundry. Multi-lingual staff. Safe.* **Room services** *Room service. Telephone. TV.*

Aprile

Via della Scala 6 (21 62 37 or 28 91 47/fax 28 09 47). Bus to Santa Maria Novella station. **Rates** *single* L100,000; *double* L220,000. **Credit** AmEx, EC, JCB, MC, V.

This 29-room hotel occupies a Medici palace dating from 1470; there is a bust of Cosimo I above the entrance. Convenient for the station, the hotel has an old-fashioned feel to it, and some of its varied bedrooms feature frescoes, vaulted ceilings and scraps of 15th-century graffiti. Some rooms are a little gloomy, but there is an attractive bar and dining room for breakfasts, and a shady courtyard where you can retreat in warmer weather.

Hotel services *Bar. Babysitting. Car park (nearby garage, extra cost). Currency exchange. Fax. Lift. Multi-lingual staff. Safe.* **Room services** *Air-conditioning (15 double rooms). Hair dryer (15 rooms). Mini-bar. Room service. Telephone. TV.*

Bencista

Via Benedetto di Maiano 4, Fiesole (tel/fax 59 163). Bus 7. **Rates** *per person per night, half board* L130,000; *without bath* L110,000; half board (lunch or dinner) obligatory; full-board L15,000 extra. **No credit cards.**

The oldest part of this former convent dates from the early 14th century, and it has been run as a hotel by the Simoni family since 1925. Situated among the cypresses, olive groves and magnificent villas on the hillside just below Fiesole, the flower-clad terraces offer fabulous views of Florence and a true haven of peace and quiet for the weary traveller. Inside, a comforting, old-fashioned atmosphere pervades. The three salons are furnished with antiques, and one has a cosy fireplace and bookshelves stuffed with early editions of English books. The 47 bedrooms are reached along a rabbit warren of passages and stone stairways. No two are alike, but each has its share of solid antique furniture. Those

at the front of the building enjoy the views of the city; others look onto the hillside; two have little terraces. This is a *'pensione'* in the true sense of the word; prices are based on half board, and you are expected to eat either lunch or dinner in the sunny restaurant overlooking Florence.

Hotel services *Bar service. Car park. Exchange. Fax. Garden. Laundry. Multi-lingual staff. Restaurant. Safe. TV.* **Room services** *Telephone.*

Guelfo Bianco

Via Cavour 29 (28 83 30/fax 29 52 03). Bus 1, 11, 17. **Rates** *single* L185,000; *double* L260,000; *triple* L320,000; *family* L300-370,000; *suite* L400-500,000. **Credit** AmEx, EC, MC, V.

This attractive hotel is situated just north of the Duomo, and is popular with young business travellers. The recent renovation of the two adjacent 15th-century houses has preserved many of the original features, particularly in the annexe. The 39 bedrooms are tastefully and comfortably furnished in traditional style, and some are very spacious, allowing for a sitting area or two extra beds. Those facing onto busy Via Cavour have soundproofing; those at the back are quieter. One single room has a terrace – be prepared to fight for it! Two courtyards offer a peaceful respite from city noise, and a smart little breakfast room provides a contemporary setting in which to start the day.

Hotel services *Air-conditioning. Babysitting. Bar. Car park (nearby garage, extra cost). Currency exchange. Fax. Laundry. Lift. Multi-lingual staff. Non-smoking rooms.* **Room services** *Air-conditioning. Hair dryer. Mini-bar. Radio. Room service. Safe. Telephone. TV (satellite).*

Loggiato dei Serviti

Piazza SS Annunziata 3 (28 95 92/fax 28 95 95). Bus 6, 31, 32. **Rates** *single* L195,000; *double* L270-295,000; *suite* L345-475,000. **Credit** AmEx, DC, EC, JCB, MC, V.

This 29-room hotel occupies a wonderful position in one of Florence's most beautiful piazzas, now enjoying traffic-free status, and is one of the city's most charming small hotels. The tasteful interior decoration combines original architectural features (it was a convent in the 16th century) with superb antique furniture and all the comforts of an up-market hotel. Bedrooms are all different, varying enormously in size, but are furnished with antiques, rich fabrics in co-ordinated colours, prints and mirrors. The four suites have two bedrooms and two bathrooms so are ideal for families. The generous breakfast is served in a bright and elegant room with vaulted ceilings, and there is a cosy bar/sitting room for drinks away from the fray.

Hotel services *Air-conditioning. Babysitting. Bar. Car park (nearby garage, extra cost). Fax. Laundry. Lift. Multi-lingual staff.* **Room services** *Air-conditioning. Hair drier. Mini-bar. Radio. Room service (24-hour). Safe. Telephone. TV (satellite).*

Mario's

Via Faenza 89 (21 68 01/fax 21 20 39). Bus to Santa Maria Novella station, then 10 min walk. **Rates** *single* L180,000; *double* L220,000; *triple* L280,000. **Credit** AmEx, DC, EC, MC, V.

Of the many hotels in this street – convenient for the station and central sights – Mario's is one of the most attractive. On the second floor of an unremarkable building, the atmosphere is old-fashioned and friendly. The cosy reception and bar set the scene for the traditional Florentine-style rustic decor, and there are lots of fresh flowers. The 16 bedrooms are along the same lines with rustic wooden furniture, wrought iron bedheads, pretty fabrics and spotless new bathrooms. Those looking onto the street are double glazed while others at the back are quieter.

Hotel services *Bar. Car park (nearby garage, extra charge). Currency exchange. Fax. Laundry. Safe.* **Room services** *Air-conditioning. Hair dryer. Room service. Radio. Telephone. TV (satellite).*

Morandi alla Crocetta

Via Laura 50 (23 44 747/fax 24 80 954). Bus 6, 31, 32 to Piazza SS Annunziata. **Rates** (breakfast L18,000) *single* L110,000; *double* L190,000; *triple* L250,000.
Credit AmEx, DC, EC, MC, V.

This quiet ten-room hotel is housed in a former 16th-century convent in the university area. Kathleen Doyle Antuono and her family offer friendly, informal but comfortable accommodation at very reasonable prices. Rooms are furnished with antiques and prints, manuscripts and icons, with colourful rugs on warm parquet floors. Two rooms have private terraces, and one has an original 16th-century fresco (discovered quite by chance during renovation work) filling one wall. Particularly popular with gay couples.
Hotel services *Air-conditioning. Babysitting. Bar. Car park (nearby garage, extra cost). Fax. Laundry. Multi-lingual staff.* **Room services** *Air-conditioning. Hair dryer. Mini-bar. Radio. Room service. Safe. Telephone. TV (satellite).*

La Residenza

Via Tornabuoni 8 (28 41 97 or 21 86 84/fax 28 41 97). Bus B, C. **Rates** *single* L150,000; *double* L250,000; *triple* L330,000; dinner L35,000.
Credit AmEx, DC, MC, V.

Arrival at the Residenza which inhabits the top three floors of a 15th century palazzo, is via an old-fashioned wood and glass lift with brass rails. In a highly prized location, one of the main advantages of the hotel is its roof garden and adjacent sitting room. Recent renovation work has resulted in huge disparity in the 25 bedrooms. The newer ones have pretty co-ordinating fabrics, fresh paintwork in warm colours, and modern lighting, whereas those still waiting for redecoration are simpler, unimaginatively furnished and occasionally a bit drab. But it is the latter that have private terraces. Essentially a family-run establishment, it is one of the very few Florentine pensioni to offer half board. Double glazing keeps out the worst of the noise from Via Tornabuoni.
Hotel services *Air-conditioning. Bar. Babysitting. Car park (nearby garage, extra cost). Currency exchange. Fax. Laundry. Lift. Multi-lingual staff. Restaurant. Roof terrace. Safe.* **Room services** *Air-conditioning. Hair dryer. Room service (24-hour). Telephone. TV.*

Silla

Via de' Renai 5 (23 42 888 or 23 42 889/fax 23 41 437). Bus B, C. **Rates** *single* L160,000; *double* L220,000; *triple* L270,000.
Credit AmEx, DC, EC, MC, V.

This old-fashioned *pensione* is housed in an elegant 16th-century palazzo south of the river, and just east of the Ponte Vecchio. From its ample terrace (where breakfast or afternoon tea is served in the summer) guests look over the Arno and to Florence's skyline beyond. Public areas have an almost Venetian feel to them with polished marble floors, chandeliers and painted furniture. Bedrooms are furnished in traditional style and are spotlessly clean; those facing the Lungarno can be noisy. A good location for those needing a little greenery in their surroundings, and only a short walk from the sights.
Hotel services *Air-conditioning. Bar. Car park (extra cost). Fax. Lift (within the hotel, but not up the two flights to get to it). Multi-lingual staff. Terrace.* **Room services** *Air-conditioning. Hair drier. Mini-bar. Room service. Telephone. TV.*

Splendor

Via San Gallo 30 (48 34 27/fax 46 12 76). Bus to Piazza San Marco. **Rates** *single* L135,000; *double* L200,000 (L150,000 without bath); *triple* L270,000 (L235,000 without bath). **Credit** AmEx, MC, V.

There are flowers adorning every window sill on the façade of this modest but elegant little late 19th-century palazzo in the university area of the city, near Piazza San Marco. Public room are surprisingly lavish with intricate original parquet floors, frescoed ceilings, chandeliers and plants and flowers everywhere. The comfortable sitting room is painted in rich, deep reds from floor to ceiling, while the breakfast room, with its elegant painted panels, is full of light, and looks onto a pretty terrace where you can enjoy a drink after a weary day in the city. Breakfast is a generous buffet. The 31 bedrooms are plainer with some antique furniture – all but a few have private bathrooms. The triples are huge and light with views over San Marco.
Hotel services *Car park (nearby garage, extra cost). Fax. Multi-lingual staff. Terrace.* **Room services** *Air-conditioning (in most rooms). Hair drier. Room service. Safe. TV (satellite).*

Torre Guelfa

Borgo SS Apostoli 8 (23 96 338/fax 23 98 577). Bus to Ponte Vecchio. **Rates** *single* L170,000; *double* L230,000.
Credit AmEx, MC, V.

Enthusiastic new management has put fresh life into this hotel which boasts the tallest privately-owned tower in Florence. From the top you can enjoy an aperitif (there is bar service in the summer) while marvelling at the 360° view of the city rooftops and surrounding hills. Bedrooms are decorated in different pastel shades and furnished with wrought iron beds (several four-posters), pretty white cotton embroidered curtains and bedspreads, and traditional hand-painted Florentine furniture. One room, with access up a little private stairway, has its own roof garden. Some of the bathrooms have been refurbished in grey marble and are quite grand. A sunny glassed-in breakfast room provides a good spot from where to start the day, and the impressive double salon, with its intricate wooden ceiling, adds elegance. This is a classy place, popular with the designer crowd who come over for the fashion shows.
Hotel services *Bar. Car Parking (nearby garage, extra cost). Fax. Lift. Multi-lingual staff. Terrace.* **Room services** *Air-conditioning (eight rooms). Mini-bar. Room service. Telephone. TV (in five rooms).*

Villa Belvedere

Via Benedetto Castelli 3 (22 25 01 or 22 25 02/fax 22 31 63). Bus 11. **Rates** *single* L230,000; *double* L280-320,000; *suite* L400,000. **Closed** end Nov-1 Mar. **Credit** AmEx, DC, EC, MC, V.

Not everybody who visits Florence wants to stay in the centre of town, especially in the summer when temperatures soar. The Villa Belvedere offers a pleasant alternative and, while not providing the thrill of staying in a genuine 15th-century castle (*see* **Torre di Bellosguardo**), it is a comfortable hotel with the added advantage of a pool and tennis court, set in a well-kept garden on the Poggio Imperiale, above Porta Romana. The rather plain building dates from 1932, and the 25 rooms are spacious and modern with parquet floors and lots of wood. The best have large terraces and enjoy spectacular views of the city.
Hotel services *Air-conditioning. Bar. Car park. Currency exchange. Fax. Garden. Laundry. Multi-lingual staff. Pool. Restaurant (light meals). Tennis court.* **Room services** *Air-conditioning. Hair drier. Radio. Room service. Safe. TV (satellite).*

Villa Betania

Viale del Poggio Imperiale 23 (22 05 32 or 22 22 43/fax 22 05 32). Bus to Porta Romana. **Rates** *single* L140,000; *double* L190,000; *triple* L220,000. **Credit** AmEx, DC, EC, MC, V.

Hidden away in a secret garden, ten minutes walk from Porta Romana, the Betania's setting is its main advantage. The building dates from the late 15th century and now houses this rather run-down but welcoming and laidback hotel. The 15 rooms (nearly all with private baths) are simply furnished and a little shabby, but wonderfully peaceful. The most

pleasant are those in the tower which enjoy a view over gardens and fields. Downstairs, the sitting rooms and bar are a mish-mash of cheerful '70s furniture, lush pot plants, huge lamps and the odd antique. A generous breakfast buffet can be taken on one of the two shady terraces, and loungers are available for relaxation in the garden.
Hotel services *Bar. Car Park. Currency exchange. Fax. Garden. Multi-lingual staff. TV (satellite).* **Room services** *Radio. Room service. Safe. TV.*

Villa Villoresi

Via Campi 2, Colonnata di Sesto Fiorentino (44 36 92/fax 44 20 63). Bus 2, 28. **Rates** *single* L160,000; *double* L250-350,000; *de-luxe double* L450,000; half board L180-230,000 (L280,000 *de-luxe*) per person.
Credit AmEx, DC, MC, V.
Contessa Cristina Villoresi's aristocratic family home was once a country retreat. It has now been engulfed by the sprawl of Florentine suburbia, but remains an oasis of calm elegance and a delightful alternative to a lodging in the city. The villa has maintained the feel of a grand, if rather faded, private home with impressive interiors; the frescoed and chandeliered entrance hall, the ground floor bedroom with its frescoes and glittering crystal and the five splendid bedrooms leading onto the longest loggia in Tuscany. Other (cheaper) rooms are smaller and relatively plain. If you choose to make the journey to Sesto Fiorentino, you will be sure of a warm welcome. You could also join one of the courses on Italian renaissance culture organised at the villa.
Hotel services *Babysitting. Bar. Car park. Fax. Laundry. Pool. Restaurant.* **Room services** *Room service. Telephone. TV.*

Budget (L75-180,000)

Alessandra

Borgo SS Apostoli 17 (28 34 38/fax 21 06 19). Bus C or to Ponte Vecchio. **Rates** *single* L110,000 (L80,000 without bath); *double* L165,000 (L120,000 without bath); *triple*

L225,000 (L160,000 without bath); *quad* L260,000 (L190,000 without bath). **Credit** AmEx, EC, MC, V.
A good location on a quiet back street between Santa Trinità and the Ponte Vecchio makes this modest hotel worth considering. The 25 rooms are spacious, many have polished parquet floors and antique furniture, and prices are good.
Hotel services *Currency exchange. Fax. Non-smoking rooms. Safe.* **Room services** *Air-conditioning (7 rooms). Room service. Telephone. TV.*

Belletini

Via de' Conti 7 (21 35 61/28 29 80/ fax 28 35 51). Bus 11, 17. **Rates** *single* L105,000; *double* L170,000; *triple* L229,000; *quad* L289,000.
Credit AmEx, DC, EC, MC, V.
Near to the Medici chapels and San Lorenzo, this bustling hotel is run by the delightful Signora Gina. She will do all within her power to make your stay pleasant, and offers all sorts of extras; toys, games and videos for bored children, day membership of a nearby swimming pool or gym at discounted prices, a theatre booking service and travel arrangements. The 27 rooms are simply furnished in Florentine style, and the two at the top of the building have a close up view of the domes of the Duomo and the Medici chapel. One single has a spacious terrace. Breakfasts, with homemade cakes, are varied and generous. The hotel has an interesting history – dating from the 15th century, it holds one of the oldest hotel licences in the city. It originally hosted labourers in the employ of the Medici family, as testified to by the symbol of the crossed keys carved into the original stone plaque in the breakfast room.
Hotel services *Babysitting. Bar. Car parking (nearby garage, extra cost). Currency exchange. Fax. Laundry. Lift (to first floor). Multi-lingual staff. Non-smoking rooms. Video.* **Room services** *Air-conditioning. Room service. Telephone. TV (in most rooms).*

Casci

Via Cavour 13 (21 16 86/fax 23 96 461). Bus 1, 11, 17. **Rates** *single* L110,000; *double* L160,000; *triple* L215,000;

The gorgeous garden of the **Classic Hotel**.

quad L270,000. **Closed** 3 weeks in Jan. **Credit** AmEx, DC, JCB, MC, V.

This 15th-century palazzo once belonged to Giacomo Rossini, and you may find yourself sleeping in his bedroom. The Lombardi family now runs a cheerful *pensione*; the 25 bedrooms have recently been redecorated with modern wooden furniture and colourful bedcovers, and many bathrooms are new. The quietest rooms are at the back of the building although effective double glazing deals with traffic noise on the busy Via Cavour. The breakfast room and bar have frescoed ceilings, and bookshelves are well stocked with guide books and maps. A real bargain with a welcoming family atmosphere.

Hotel services *Babysitting. Bar. Car park (nearby garage, extra cost). Currency exchange. Fax. Laundry. Lift. Multi-lingual staff. Safes.* **Room services** *Hair drier. Telephone. TV (satellite).*

Cimabue

Via Bonifacio Lupi 7 (tel/fax 47 19 89 or 47 56 01). Bus to Piazza San Marco. **Rates** *single* L130,000; *double* L176,000; *triple* 210,000. **Closed** 2 weeks in Dec. **Credit** AmEx, DC, EC, MC, V.

The Rossis rescued this little hotel from oblivion in the mid-1990s and have taken great care to create a welcoming and friendly atmosphere for their guests. Only ten minutes walk north of the Duomo, the hotel offers more than you might expect for two stars. The 16 rooms are all different, but each has antique furniture and bright bedspreads; the best are the doubles and triples with impressive frescoed ceilings. Bathrooms are mostly on the small side, but each room has its own. The generous breakfast buffet is served on a bright little ground floor room where there is lots of tourist information thoughtfully supplied by the owners.

Hotel services *Babysitting. Bar. Currency exchange. Fax. Multi-lingual staff. Safe. Car park (nearby garage, extra cost).* **Room services** *Hair drier. Room service. Telephone. TV.*

Classic Hotel

Viale Machiavelli 25 (22 93 51/fax 22 93 53). Bus 11, 36, 37 to Porta Romana. **Rates** *(breakfast L10,000) single* L120,000; *double* L160,000; *suite* L250,000. **Closed** one week mid-Aug. **Credit** AmEx, EC, MC, V.

Standing in a lush, mature garden, this attractive pink-washed villa is situated on a leafy avenue just outside the old city walls at Porta Romana. With 21 rooms, the hotel has been carefully refurbished and the result is elegant and tasteful; white walls, parquet floors, original plaster work, frescoes, a mix of old and new paintings, antique furniture, cheerful fabrics – everything is pristine. A delightful conservatory, where breakfast is served in the summer, leads into the garden where tall trees provide shade for the terrace. For romantics, a little annexe suite (for the same price as a double) is tucked away in a corner of the garden with its own terrace. The friendly and helpful staff, and high standard of accommodation for the price make the Classic a real bargain.

Hotel services *Bar. Babysitting. Car park. Currency exchange. Fax. Laundry. Garden. Lift. Multi-lingual staff.* **Room services** *Room service. Safe. Telephone. TV.*

Dei Mori

Via Dante Alighieri 12 (tel/fax 21 14 38). Bus 14, 23. **Rates** *single* L110,000; *double* L140,000; reduced rates for longer stays. **Credit** AmEx, MC, V.

This 15th-century town house in a central pedestrian area offers peace and quiet with self-catering facilities. The charming hosts, Daniele and Franco, welcome guests as friends into their own home. Rooms are on the small side, but have been attractively decorated in pastel shades with brightly-coloured bedspreads, pictures on the walls and lots of attention to detail. Nice touches include feather duvets, dressing gowns and coloured towels. Only two rooms have private baths. The welcoming sitting room has a TV, books,

magazines and a stereo. There is a small flower-decked terrace from which you can see the top of the cupola of the Duomo while enjoying a coffee or aperitif. Good value.

Hotel services *Fax. Kitchen. Laundry. Multi-lingual staff.* **Room services** *Telephone.*

Firenze

Via del Corso/Piazza Donati 4 (26 83 01/fax 21 23 70). Bus 14, 23 to Via del Corso. **Rates** *single* L70,000; *double* L100,000; *triple* L135,000; *quad* L170,000; *quin* L190,000. **No credit cards.**

This simple and centrally located hotel offers clean, if not very imaginative, accommodation at budget prices. Its 60 rooms have been recently renovated, and all have private bathrooms. Rooms on the top two floors have more light.

Hotel services *Car park (nearby garage, extra cost). Currency exchange. Fax. Lift. Multi-lingual staff. Safe.* **Room services** *Hair dryer. Telephone. TV.*

Liana

Via Alfieri 18 (24 53 03/fax 23 44 596). Bus 8, 80 to Piazza Donatello. **Rates** *single* L130,000; *double* L170,000; *triple* L230,000; 20 per cent discount in low season and four nights for the price of three; anyone arriving with a copy of the guide will get a five per cent discount. **Credit** AmEx, DC, EC, MC, V.

This 19th-century Liberty style (Art Nouveau) house was once owned by the Albizzi family. Standing in its own garden on one side, and on a rather noisy road on the other, it is worth considering if you want to be within reach of the sights but don't want to be in the centre of town. Bedrooms vary enormously from the plain to the more interesting and quite elegant 'Count's Room' with its fireplace, parquet floor, balcony and comfortable furniture. There is an attractive first floor breakfast room where classical music plays, and the hotel is full of fresh flowers. New management took over in January 1997 to rescue a hotel somewhat gone to seed. A bit shabby but not without its attractions.

Hotel services *Bar. Car parking (extra cost). Currency exchange. Fax. Laundry. Multi-lingual staff. Garden. Safe.* **Room services** *Room service. Telephone. TV.*

Residence Johanna

Via Bonifacio Lupi 14 (48 18 96/fax 48 27 21). Bus 8 to Piazza Libertà. **Rates** *single without bath* L60,000; *double* L110,000 (L100,000 without bath). **No credit cards.**

A welcome addition to the all-too-expensive hotel scene in Florence, this discreet home-from-home offers comfortable and stylish accommodation at rock bottom prices. A little removed from the centre of town, the 'no frills' formula (no telephone or TV in room) keeps rates down, and yet bedrooms are beautifully decorated with floral fabrics, country furnishings and prints. Each room has coffee/tea making facilities and the wherewithal for a simple breakfast. Guests are given their own keys, mobile phones are available for rental and there is a good supply of books and magazines.

Hotel services *Car park (nearby, extra cost). Fax. Lift. Multi-lingual staff. Safe.* **Room services** *Coffee and tea making facilities/breakfast.*

La Scaletta

Via Guicciardini 13 (28 30 28 or 21 42 55/fax 28 95 62). Bus C. **Rates** *single* L90,000 (L60,000 without bath); *double* L150,000 (L115,000 without bath); *triple* L185,000; *quad* L220,000; dinner L20,000. **Credit** MC, V.

This budget hotel has two main advantages; its vicinity to the greenery of the Boboli Gardens and its delightful roof garden. Otherwise it is a family-run, friendly but simple hotel which has a real lived-in feel. The building dates from the 15th century, and is a stone's throw from the Pitti Palace and the Ponte Vecchio. The public rooms retain the atmosphere of the origins of the building, and meals are served in a high-ceilinged dining room. The 12 bedrooms are all different and a mish-mash of styles. Some are very '70s with a predominance of browns and clashing patterns, while others are airier with some period furniture. Those on the busy Via Guicciardini have double glazing and some have lovely views onto the adjacent Boboli Gardens.

Hotel services *Bar. Car park (garage nearby, extra cost). Currency exchange. Fax. Lift. Multi-lingual staff. Restaurant. Roof garden. Safe.* **Room services** *Hair dryer. Telephone.*

Sorelle Bandini

Piazza Santo Spirito 9 (21 53 08/fax 28 27 61). Bus 11, 35, 36. **Rates** *(breakfast L15,000) double* L136,000 (L104,000 without bath). **No credit cards.**

This simple but rather overpriced *pensione* enjoys a superb situation on Piazza Santo Spirito with its morning market and night-time revelry. It occupies the top floors of a 15th-century palazzo, and started life as a hotel 60 years ago when it was run by the Bandini sisters. Since 1978 it has been in the care of the present, slightly bizarre, incompetent management. The hotel offers shabby charm in a wonderful setting, and a great loggia which runs along the two sides of the building (ask for room no. 4 if you want direct access) with its creaky cane furniture makes up for the rather dilapidated interior. Wonderful mirrors and chandeliers provide a touch of class. The 12 rooms come in all shapes and sizes; several are huge, some are more cosy, and many enjoy superb views over the Florentine skyline. Don't rely on being provided with blankets or having the central heating switched on in winter.

Hotel services *Currency exchange. Fax. Lift. Loggia. Pay phone. Safe.* **Room services** *Room service (breakfast).*

Villa Natalia

Via Bolognese 106/110 (49 07 73/fax 47 07 73). Bus 25. **Rates** *single* L90,000; *double* L140,000; *triple* L190,000. **Credit** AmEx, EC, MC, V.

Some way north of the city centre, but near a bus stop, Villa Natalia (once home to Natalia, Queen of Serbia) is an impressive, if slightly crumbling, ochre-coloured building standing in a *'Giardino al'Italiano'*. The public rooms are a bit institutional (the canteen is shared by employees of the nearby Olivetti headquarters), but bedrooms are more comfortable and are filled with wonderful antiques, painted wood panels, mirrors and pictures. Given the low prices, this is a real bargain but, as the hotel has an arrangement with one of the American universities, rooms can be very hard to come by.

Very cheap (under L75,000)

Hostel Archi Rossi

Via Faenza 94r (29 08 04/fax 23 02 601). Bus to Santa Maria Novella station. **Rates** *(breakfast L2,500, dinner from L12,000)* L23,000 *per person* (L23,000 without bath). **Closed** one week at Christmas. **No credit cards.**

A new hostel and only a five minute walk from the station, the Archi Rossi is purpose-converted, and unusually well-equipped for the disabled. Rooms, some with private bathroom, are mostly spacious and light, and are not over-crowded. The walls of the reception area and corridors are covered in colourful graffiti – add your own before you leave. There's a big terrace at the back of the building, a restaurant, and vending machine with microwave for snacks. The hostel opens at 6.30am and curfew is at 12.30am. A popular place, so book early.

Istituto Gould

Via dei Serragli 49 (21 25 76/fax 28 02 74). Bus 11, 36, 37 to Serragli. **Rates** *single* L50,000 (L45,000 without bath); *double* L74,000 (L66,000 without bath); *triple* L96,000; *quad* L120,000; *quin* L125,000. **No credit cards.**

Very pleasant and superior budget accommodation in a convenient part of town. This 17th-century palazzo, with its arched courtyard, cool stone staircases, white walls and terracotta floors has plenty of atmosphere. Rooms are bright and comfortable, and many are newly decorated. If you want to avoid noisy Via dei Serragli, ask for a room at the back; some of these have access onto a terrace. The only drawback

Simplicity at **Residence Johanna**. *See page 79.*

*Lodger in the loggia at **Sorelle Bandini**.*

is that you must check in during office hours (9am-1pm, 3pm-7pm Mon-Fri; 9am-1pm Sat; closed Sun), but there is no curfew and you will be given a key. Very popular.
Hotel services *Multi-lingual staff. Safe. Wheelchair access.* **Room services** *Telephone.*

Locanda Orchidea
Borgo degli Albizi 11 (tel/fax 24 80 346). Bus 14, B.
Rates *single without bath* L50,000; *double without bath* L75,000; *triple* L110,000. **Closed** 6-22 Aug, 3 days over Christmas. **No credit cards.**
Dante's wife was born in the 12th-century palazzo which now houses the simple but cosy Locanda Orchidea. In a lively area near Santa Croce, the hotel has seven bright rooms, the best of which overlook a wonderful overgrown garden (one even has a tiny terrace). Book way ahead for one of these or be prepared to risk the street noise on the other side. Only one room – a triple – has a private shower; the rest share the two communal bathrooms. Friendly Anglo-Italian owners.
Hotel services *Multi-lingual staff. Telephone in reception.*

Ostello per la Gioventù
Viale Augusto Righi 2/4 (60 14 51/fax 61 03 00). Bus 17, A or B. **Rates** *bed and breakfast* L23,000; *family rooms (double)* from L64,000; *extra meals* L14,000.
No credit cards.
An impressive setting for a youth hostel – a grand façade, loggia and ranks of massive lemon trees in terracotta pots. The grounds are extensive (it's a bit of a trek up the hill from the bus) and the views are of olive groves and cypresses. Well-kept with multi-bedded rooms, the facilities are good. There are some smaller rooms, strictly for use by families. Worth the 20 minute bus ride from the centre of town if you want peace and quiet. There's a bar, restaurant and TV room, and it's wheelchair accessible. Curfew is at 11.30pm.

Pensionato Pio X
Via de' Serragli 106 (22 50 44). Bus 11, 36, 37 to Serragli. **Rates** *single* L25,000; *doubles, triples, quads & quins* L22,000 per person. **No credit cards.**

This state-owned *pensione* (housed in a 13th-century former-convent) provides a quiet, pleasant alternative to a youth hostel as a budget option. Singles are remarkable value. Rooms, while simply furnished, are less barrack-like than at the nearby Santa Monaca hostel, and are mostly three- and four-bedded – there are no bunks. All rooms have a basin and several have a little terrace overlooking the garden at the back of the building. There is a cheerful sitting room and a dining room where guests can picnic. There's a midnight curfew and minimum two-day stay, but the place has one huge advantage over the hostels – it is open all day.
Hotel services *Hair driers (in bathroom). Safe. Telephone. Vending machine (hot and cold drinks).*

Santa Monaca
Via Santa Monaca 6 (26 83 38/fax 28 01 85). Bus 11, 36, 37 to Carmine or Santa Spirito. **Rates** L21,000 per person. **No credit cards.**
This 15th-century convent was converted to a hostel in 1968. It is convenient for anybody who wants to stay in trendy Oltrarno, south of the river, but is a bit gloomy. There are cooking facilities, washing machine and a TV room. Curfew at 12.30am.

Scoti
Via Tornabuoni 7 (tel/fax 29 21 28). Bus 6, 11, C.
Rates (no breakfast) *single* L48,000; *double* L75,000; *triple* L100,000; *quad* L125,000. **No credit cards.**
This simple *pensione* is housed on the second floor of a 15th-century palazzo on chic Via Tornabuoni. In spite of its vicinity to Gucci, Ferragamo, YSL, it is one of the best bargains in town if you are interested in atmosphere rather than creature comforts and are travelling on a tight budget. New, young owners have given a much-needed lick of paint throughout and bedrooms are light and airy, if basically furnished. None have private baths. The sitting room, with its 19th-century floor-to-ceiling frescoes is from another world. Book well ahead if you want to be sure of securing one of the more intimate single rooms.
Hotel services *Lift. Multi-lingual staff.*

Sightseeing in Florence

By Area

The good, the bad and the ugly: your guide to the city and its sights.

Sights are arranged in a suitable order for a walking tour.

Central Florence

Home to the Duomo, Piazza della Signoria and the Uffizi, there are probably more tourists per square centimetre in central Florence than in any other city in Italy. Even in November, it's virtually impossible to walk down a street without hearing an English, American or Aussie gushing over gelato, Gucci, Giotto or gigolos. Piazzas are full of backpackers snacking on take-away pizza; café terraces are packed with the middle classes of northern Europe and America lingering over L10,000 cappuccinos; and all over, vying with one another to lighten the purses of visitors, are gaudy fast food and ice cream joints, fake Louis Vuitton, fake Gucci and fake Chanel vendors, and shops selling posters, postcards and T-shirts printed with images from Botticelli, Leonardo and Michelangelo.

Orsanmichele & the Museo di Orsanmichele

Via Arte della Lana (28 49 44). **Open** 9am-noon, 4-6pm, daily. **Closed** 1st & last Mon of the month. **Admission** free.

The relationship between art, religion and commerce hardly gets closer than in the church of Orsanmichele. The site was first occupied by a church – San Michele in Orto – then by a grain market where grain traders mingled with money lenders, beggars and locals who'd come to seek solutions to life's problems from a miracle-working painting of the Madonna, or free singing lessons from the religious brotherhood associated with the building. In 1336, the city council decided to replace the ancient market hall with a building that contained an oratory on its ground floor and a store for the city's emergency grain supplies on its two upper storeys. In 1380 the arcades of the lower storey were walled in.

From the outset, the council intended Orsanmichele to be a magnificent advertisement for the wealth of the city's guilds and, in 1339, each guild was instructed to fill one of the loggia's niches with a statue of its patron saint. Only the wool guild obliged (with a stone statue of St Stephen) so, in 1406, the council presented the guilds with a ten-year deadline. In 1412, the Calimala, the wealthiest guild (of cloth importers) commissioned Ghiberti to create a life-sized bronze of John the Baptist, the largest statue ever to have been cast in Florence. From then on, the other major guilds fell over themselves to produce the finest statue. The guild of armourers were represented by a tense, nervous *St George* by Donatello (now in the **Bargello**, *see chapter* **Museums**) one of the first psychologically realistic sculptures of the Renaissance; while the Parte Guelfa had Donatello gild their bronze, a *St Louis of Toulouse*, later removed by the Medici to Santa Croce (*see below*) in their drive to expunge all memory of the Guelphs from the public face of the city (*see chapter* **History: Guelph v Ghibelline**). Most of the statues are now replicas – the originals are on display either in the

Orsanmichele, *a monument to mercantile wealth.*

Raping the Sabine Women on **Piazza della Signoria**.

Duomo, Campanile & Baptistery

Nowhere in Italy is there a city centre quite as magnificent as Florence's Piazza del Duomo. The cathedral itself, lacily inlaid with pink, white and bottle green marble, soars above the surrounding buildings, so huge that there is no point nearby from which you can see the whole building. To do so, you either have to climb the campanile, or head out to Piazzale Michelangelo on the hilly brink of town.

Duomo

In the 13th century it was decided that the old cathedral of Santa Reparata was no longer fit to represent the city's power, wealth and excellence. A competition was held to find an architect, and the prize went to Arnolfo di Cambio, a sculptor and architect who had trained in Pisa with Nicola da Pisano (*see chapter* **Pisa**). The building was financed from various sources – including fines levied on roisterers and gifts from userers who repented of their greed – and work began in 1296. The cathedral was consecrated just over a century later, in 1436, but did not get a façade until the 19th century.

The dome, by **Brunelleschi**, was a triumph of faith-in-engineering over gravity, built without the use of outer scaffolding. The design consisted of an outer dome (30 inches thick) and an inner dome (13 feet thick) with eight major and 16 minor ribs springing up towards the lantern. The real stroke of genius was making the dome support itself as it was built: bricks were laid out in herringbone-pattern rings, each ring jutting out sufficiently to carry the ring above. In order not to waste time over lunch, a kitchen was installed in the space between the two shells. Consequently, the job, started in 1420, took only 16 years – fast for medieval Italy.

After the splendour of the dome and the sugar candy intricacy of the walls, the interior looks gloomy and Gothic. There are, however, a couple of features worth examining – notably two trompe l'oeil frescoes of tombs mounted by equestrian statues on the left hand wall. The first is of Niccolò da Tolentino by Andrea del Castagno, the second of English soldier of fortune **John Hawkwood** (*see* *chapter* **History: Medieval Mercenary**) by **Paolo Uccello**. The Uccello, created in 1436 is slightly muddled: the horse and rider are painted as if seen from the side; the tomb as if seen head on. Beyond, is Domenico do Michelino's well-known *Dante Explaining the Divine Comedy*, featuring the poet dressed in pink, and the recently completed Duomo vying for prominence with the mountain of purgatory.

Further down the aisle is the entrance to the dome itself, a stiff climb up staircases squeezed in between its two shells, but worth the effort for the fantastic views of the city from the top.

Campanile

The Campanile was designed by Giotto in 1334, and was continued after his death three years later by Andrea Pisano, who took the precaution of doubling the thickness of the walls. Inlaid, like the Duomo, with pretty pink, white and green marble, it is decorated with bas reliefs designed by Giotto and executed by Pisano recounting the Creation and Fall of Man and his Redemption through Industry. Look carefully and you should be able to make out Eve emerging from Adam's side, a drunken Noah and various professions, including building, shopkeeping and weaving. There are great – if troublingly vertiginous – views of the Duomo and city from the top.

Baptistery

For centuries, Florentines (including such well educated characters as Brunelleschi and Alberti) believed that the Baptistery was converted from an ancient Roman

Shooting up.

The sugar candy **Duomo**.

temple dedicated to Mars. In fact, although there are the relics of an ancient pavement below the building, these probably belonged to a bakery. The Baptistery was actually built between 1059 and 1128 as a remodelling of a 6th- or 7th-century version. Today, the gaily striped octagon is best known for its bronze doors, though you might want to go inside to see the vibrant *Last Judgement* mosaic lining the vault.

In the 1330s Andrea Pisano completed the south doors, with 28 Gothic quatrefoil-framed panels depicting incidents from the life of St John the Baptist and the eight Theological and Cardinal Virtues. In 1400, the Calimala guild held a competition to find an artist to create a pair of bronze doors for the north entrance, and eventually, having seen trial pieces by Brunelleschi, Ghiberti and five others (the Brunelleschi and Ghiberti pieces are in the Bargello, *see chapter* **Museums**), gave the commission to Ghiberti, then only 20. Relief panels displaying a masterful use of perspective, retell the story of Christ, from the Annunciation to the Crucifixion. The eight lower panels show the four evangelists and four doctors. Even more remarkable are the east doors, known as the Gates of Paradise. No sooner had the north doors been installed than the Calimala commissioned Ghiberti to make another pair. The doors you see here are copies (the originals are in the Museo dell'Opera del Duomo, *see chapter* **Museums**) but the casts are fine enough to appreciate Ghiberti's achievement. Perspective, supple modelling, composition and deftly evocative gesture all unite to create a fascinating narrative of Old Testament events. From left to right, top to bottom the panels are: The

Duomo Restoration

About halfway down Via dello Studio – one of the lanes that meanders from the side of the Duomo down towards Piazza della Signoria – there is a low building with grimy windows. Anyone who bothers to stop and peer in is met by an intriguing sight. Going by the haircuts, the overalls and the radio, this could be a local panel-beaters'. But look more closely, and you realise that these young lads are stooped over fluted columns and flowery baldacchinos, not car doors. For this nondescript workshop belongs to the stonemasons of the Opera di Santa Maria del Fiore – the cathedral's own conservation and maintenance wing.

The ten stonemasons who work here – all in their twenties and thirties – carry out running repairs to the fabric of Florence's most prominent landmark. Paolo Bianchini, head of the technical staff of the cathedral works office, estimates that over the last seven centuries around 70 per cent of the exterior stonework has been replaced. "A cathedral is a living organism – but a very delicate one," he says. "It needs constant check-ups, the right medicine in the right places, and the occasional more serious operation if it is going to stay in good health".

Fifteen years ago there were only two permanent stonemasons on the cathedral books, with much of the restoration work being farmed out to outside contractors. The revival of this ancient craft has been made possible by the revenues generated by the Duomo's star attractions: the cathedral museum, where precious works such as Lorenzo Ghiberti's original bronze reliefs for the doors of the Baptistery are displayed; Giotto's campanile or bell-tower; and the ascent to the top of Brunelleschi's dome, with its breathtaking view.

Candidates for the job of cathedral stonemason should be prepared to take the long view. "There are no schools that teach what we're doing here, so we have to do it ourselves," Bianchini explains. "These days, young people expect to pick up the necessary skills in a few months at most. In this job, it can take 20 years. But when you remember that eight generations of stonemasons were involved in building the Duomo, it puts the whole thing in perspective. If I stayed here for my whole working life, I would just manage to supervise one complete 'restoration tour' of the cathedral, which will take around fifty years at our present speed. But that's still something to be proud of."

If the pace is slow, the job satisfaction is correspondingly high. Each stonemason follows a piece of work through from the moment the old section is removed to the nerve-racking day when his lovingly carved marble replacement is hoisted into place. And if it doesn't fit? "Then we start again," says Bianchini. After all, when you've waited seven hundred years for a new baldacchino, what's another few months?

Creation of Adam and Eve, Cain and Abel, Noah's Ark, the Story of Abraham, Jacob and Esau, the Story of Joseph, Episodes from the Life of Moses, the Story of Joshua, the Story of Saul and David, and the Temple of Solomon.

museum above or in the Bargello. Inside the church an elaborate glass and marble tabernacle by Orcagna, frames a *Madonna* by Bernardo Daddi, painted in 1347 to replace the miraculous Madonna which had been burnt in a fire in 1304.

SS Apostoli and Piazza del Limbo

Piazza del Limbo (29 06 42). **Open** 3-7pm Mon-Sat; 9am-noon, 3-7pm Sun.

SS Apostoli, tucked below the long, dark Borgo of the same name, is one of the oldest churches in the city, still retaining much of its original 11th-century façade. The church's design, like that of the early Christian churches of Rome, is based on that of a Roman basilica: rectangular, with columns and a flat ceiling. Piazza del Limbo outside is so-called because it occupies the site of a graveyard for unbaptised babies.

Badia Fiorentina

Via del Proconsolo. **Open** 4.30-6.30pm Mon-Sat; 10.30am-11.30am Sun. **Admission** free.

The Badia, an ancient Benedictine abbey founded by Willa, mother of Ugo, Margrave of Tuscany, was the richest religious institution of medieval Florence. Willa had been deeply influenced by a certain Romuald, a monk who travelled around Tuscany denouncing the wickedness of the clergy, flagellating himself, and urging the rich to build monasteries and hermitages. Eventually Romuald persuaded Willa to found an abbey within Florence, which she did in 978. Ugo also lavished money and property on the abbey, and was eventually buried there in a Roman sarcophagus, later replaced by a tomb by Renaissance sculptor Mino da Fiesole. Just across the street from Dante's probable birthplace (*see chapter* **Museums**), it was in the Badia that the poet first set eyes on Beatrice attending a May feast in 1274. He was nine,

she eight, and he fell instantly in love with "the glorious Lady of my mind". His life was for ever blighted when her family arranged her marriage at the age of 17 to one Simone de Bardi. She died seven years later at the age of 24 and Dante attempted to forget his pain by throwing himself into war, fighting in battles against Arezzo and Pisa. As for the Badia, it has been rebuilt many times since Dante's day, but still retains a graceful Romanesque campanile. The Chiostro degli Aranci, where the Benedictine monks grew oranges (*aranci*) dates from 1430 and is frescoed with scenes from the life of St Bernard. Inside the church Bernard is again celebrated, this time in a painting by Filippino Lippi. Ugo lies in a 15th-century tomb by Mino da Fiesole.

Piazza della Signoria

Florence's civic showpiece, Piazza della Signoria is dominated by the crenellated and corbelled Palazzo della Signoria or Palazzo Vecchio (*see chapter* **Museums**), built at the end of the 13th century (probably to a design by Arnolfo di Cambio) as the seat of the Signoria, the top tier of the city's government. The piazza itself was the focus of civic activity. Life in medieval Florence was beset with political and personal vendettas, and it didn't take much to ignite a crowd. On one occasion in the 14th century, a man who aroused the hatred of the crowd was actually eaten to death. More constructively, whenever Florence was threatened by an external enemy, the bell of the Palazzo della Signoria (known as the '*Vacca*', after its moo-ing tone) was tolled to summon the citizen's militia. Part of the militia's training included playing a a rough tough ball game similar to rugby (*see chapter* **Sport**) which until recently was staged every June on the Piazza. It was here that Savonarola (*see chapter* **History: Savonarola**) lit his famous Bonfire of Vanities in 1497, and

The Flood of 1966

During the night of 3-4 November, 1966, it started to rain. Within the next 48 hours, 19 inches (200mm) of rain fell on Florence and the surrounding hills. At 7.26am on 4 November the embankments along the Arno broke and water poured into the city at a rate of 35 miles (56km) an hour. By the time the rain eventually abated 39 people had died and the city centre was under water as far as San Marco with levels as high as 20 feet (6.2m) in Piazza Santa Croce.

The waters were so ferocious that they ripped off five panels from Ghiberti's Baptistry doors, and severely damaged Cimabue's crucifix in Santa Croce and Uccello's frescoes in Santa Maria Novella's Chiostro Verde. In all the flood damaged 221 oil paintings, 413 textiles, 11 fresco cycles, 39 single frescoes, 14 sculpture series, 122 single sculptures and 23 illuminated manuscripts. At the Biblioteca Nazionale Centrale (National Library) 1,300,000 volumes, journals and periodicals were damaged and 60km of books on Florentine history were lost at the Archivio di Stato (State Archive).

All the major piazzas were transformed into lakes; their surfaces covered in oil slicks from ruptured heating fuel tanks. When the waters

finally fell, the streets were all but unrecognisable, piled with rubble and mud, and littered with twisted cars, dead animals and other detritus. The Florentines set to the immense task of cleaning up the city with impressive solidarity and graft. Nearly everyone donned rubber boots and shovelled, scrubbed and carted tirelessly. Youths from all over Europe descended on Florence to "save culture", as one of them commented, earning for themselves the title of *angeli di fango* (the mud angels).

Much has been done since 1966 to prevent such a catastrophe recurring, but Florentines remain fearful of the petulant Arno. The river has been significantly widened and embankments have been heightened and strengthened. However, increased urbanisation of the area around the Arno has exacerbated various hydrogeologic problems such as sedimentation. The possibility of another devastating flood continues to loom over Florence.

For more information about the flood and the current condition of the Arno, contact the Legambiente (*24 78 599*) or look up their web site at http://www.mega.it

The polished porcellino *of* **Mercato Nuovo**.

here too that he was himself immolated the following year. In 1924, a Fascist march through the city, intended to intimidate people mourning the murder of anti-fascist Giacomo Matteotti, ended up in the piazza. In the 1970s it was decided to take up and restore the piazza's ancient paving stones and, in the course of the work, the mazy ruins of 12th-century Florence were discovered beneath the piazza, built over bits and pieces of Roman and Etruscan Florentia. The state-run Soprintendenza di Bene Archeologica ordered the excavation of the ruins; local government, faced with the prospect of their showpiece piazza becoming a building site, and losing them valuable tourist denaro, objected. The result was a shambles. The company charged with restoring the ancient slabs turned out to have won the contract by bribing the city's chief engineer. They not only had no idea how to restore stone properly, but managed to 'lose' some of the slabs, now apparently to be spotted gracing the courtyard of the occasional Tuscan villa.

The Piazza's Statues

Dominating the piazza are a copy of Michelangelo's *David* (*see chapter* **Museums**), and an equestrian bronze of Cosimo I by Giambologna. Giambologna also created some sexy nymphs and satyrs for Ammannati's Neptune fountain, a Mannerist monstrosity of which Michelangelo is said to have said "Ammannato, Ammannato, che bel marmo ha rovinato" (Ammanato, Ammanato, what beautiful marble you have ruined). Even Ammannati eventually admitted the piece was a failure. This was in part because the block of marble used for Neptune lacked width, forcing Ammannati to give the god narrow shoulders and to keep his right arm close to his body. Beyond is a copy of Donatello's *Marzocco* (the city's heraldic lion, original in the Bargello (*see chapter* **Museums**) and his *Judith and Holofernes* (original in the Palazzo Vecchio, *see chapter* **Museums**). Judith, like David, was a symbol of the power of the people over tyrannous rulers, a Jewish widow who inveigled her way into the camp of Israel's enemy, Holofernes, got the man drunk, then sliced off his head. Beyond David is a *Hercules and Cacus* by Bandinelli, described by the ever outspoken Benvenuto Cellini as a "sack of melons". Donatello cast the bronze in sections – the gown was cast from a wax model of real cloth. Cellini himself is represented by another monster-killer, a fabulous *Perseus* holding the snaky head of Medusa. The statue stands in the adjacent **Loggia dei Lanzi**, built in the late 14th century to shelter civic bigwigs during ceremonies. By the mid 15th-century it had become a favourite spot for old men to gossip and shelter from the sun, which the architect Alberti noted with approval, had a restraining influence on the young men engaging in the "Mischievousness and Folly natural to their Age". It was named for Cosimo I's brigade of Swiss lancers who had their barracks nearby in Via Lambertesca. Also in the Loggia is Giambologna's acrobatically spiralling *Rape of the Sabine Women*, carved in 1582, a virtuoso attempt by the artist to outdo Cellini.

Mercato Nuovo

The Mercato Nuovo is a fine stone loggia erected between 1547 and 1551 on a site where there had been a market since the 11th century (the Mercato Vecchio, or old market, occupied the area now covered by Piazza della Repubblica). It now houses stalls selling expensive tourist tat – bags, T-shirts, fancy stationary and the like – but in the 16th century it would have been full of silk and gold merchants and money-changers. The market is popularly known as the *Porcellino*, or piglet, after a bronze statue of a boar, a copy of an ancient statue now in the Uffizi (*see chapter* **Museums**). It is considered good luck to put a coin in the animal's mouth and get it to drop through the grille below – all proceeds go to support abandoned children.

Palazzo Antinori

Not open to the public (apart from the wine bar).
This austere mid-15th-century palace of neat stone blocks was bought by the Antinori family in 1506, and today houses an upmarket wine-bar/restaurant selling wines from the extensive Antinori estates (*see chapter* **Cafés & Bars**). There is a pretty courtyard inside.

Piazza della Repubblica

In 1890, the ancient heart of Florence was demolished and replaced with Piazza della Repubblica, an urban space that would be more at home in Milan or Turin, surrounded by pavement cafés (*see chapter* **Cafés & Bars**) and dominated at night by a neon Martini ad clamped to an ersatz triumphal arch. The ancient Roman Forum once occupied about a quarter of the piazza, while nearby there were two bath complexes. In the medieval period the area covered by the piazza was given over to a huge market frequented by merchants, housewives, farmers, and, naturally, pickpockets and beggars from all over the region. You could change money, buy a hawk or falcon, pay over the odds for a quack remedy, or pick up a prostitute (distinguished by wearing bells on their hats and gloves on their hands). Criers were hired to advertise domestic vacancies, and heralds announced death sentences, news of wars and bankruptcies. A 14th-century town-crier, Antonio Pucci, wrote a poem about the market, that included the lines:
"The women who sell fruit here might give some fright
Tough as they are they surely know their parts
And, just for two dried chestnuts, morning to night
They'll bawl and brawl and call each other tarts..."

Ponte Vecchio

There has been a bridge spanning this point of the Arno – its narrowest in the city – since Roman times. The current structure, however, was built in 1345 to replace a 12th-century bridge swept away by flood in 1333. By the 13th century there were wooden shops on the bridge. These frequently caught fire and, consequently, when the bridge was reconstructed, the shops were built of stone. Now occupied by gold and gem merchants, the Ponte Vecchio was originally favoured by butchers and tanners. As the latter trade involved soaking the hides in the Arno for eight months, then curing them in horse urine, the bridge was a pretty smelly place. Eventually, in 1593, Grand Duke Ferdinando I, fed up of retching every time he walked along the Vasari Corridor (*see below*) on his way to or back from the Pitti Palace, decided to ban all vile trades, as he called them, and permit only jewellers and goldsmiths on the bridge.

Palazzo Strozzi

Piazza Strozzi (28 83 42). **Open** varies according to exhibitions; *library* 9am-12.30pm, 3-6.30pm, Mon-Fri; 9am-12.30pm Sat.
Mercantile Florence was at its zenith in the 1400s, and in the course of the century over 100 palaces were built. The largest and most magnificent was Palazzo Strozzi, whose three tiers of golden rusticated stone still dominate Via Tornabuoni. Work began on the palace in 1489 on the orders of Filippo Strozzi. The Strozzi family had been exiled from Florence in 1434 for opposing the Medici, but made

Dwarfed by **Palazzo Strozzi**.

*Worshipping the sun on **Ponte Santa Trinita**. See page 97.*

good use of the time, moving south and becoming bankers to the King of Naples. By the time they were permitted to return to Florence in 1466, they had amassed a huge fortune. In 1474 Filippo began buying up property in the centre of Florence, until he had acquired enough to build the biggest palace in the city. Fifteen buildings were demolished to make room for it, playing havoc with local traffic and covering the city in dust, according to local shopkeeper and diarist Landucci. Finally an astrologer was asked to choose an auspicious day on which to lay the foundation stone: August 6, 1489. Conveniently enough, a few months earlier, Lorenzo de' Medici had passed a law exempting anyone who built a house on empty sites from 40 years of communal taxes. Three architects were involved in the design of the palazzo, Giuliano da Sangallo, Benedetto da Maiano and Simone del Pollaiuolo. Lorenzo de' Medici is thought to have suggested the rustication. Unfortunately, in 1491 Filippo died, leaving his heirs with the responsibility of completing the project, which eventually bankrupted them. The palace now houses a number of learned institutions and stages prestigious exhibitions. Incidentally, the huge iron rings embedded in the facade were for tethering horses, while the spiky iron clusters on the corners are torch holders.

Oltrarno

Oltrarno literally means 'on the other side of the Arno', and this area, like Paris's Left Bank, was first the working class, and then the alternative centre of the city, despite the fact that the Medici's gargantuan Palazzo Pitti was bang in the middle. Nowadays, however, although there are still plenty of artisans' workshops, a couple of trattorias serving astonishingly cheap food, and a monthly flea market, gentrification is well underway. The bars and restaurants of Piazza Santo Spirito are among the hippest in town, the flea market alternates with an organic produce market, and opening among the neighbourhood household and food shops are boutiques selling trendy crafts, clothes and jewellery. An air of rusticity is retained by the daily food market when farmers from the surrounding area come into town to sell their produce. The area immediately around Palazzo Pitti is devoted to shops selling expensive paper, crafts and jewellery, while Borgo San Jacopo is lined with a mix of high and low class clothes and food shops.

Over towards the church of Santa Maria del Carmine (stupendously frescoed by Massaccio and Masolino) and stretching down to the Porta Romana at the start of the road to Rome, and west to Porta San Frediano, is the still working class area of Borgo San Frediano. Here, locals live in small terraced cottages, and you can still eat in osterias and trattorias where you will be the only foreigner.

Santa Felicita

Piazza Santa Felicita (21 30 18). Bus C.
Open *summer* 8am-noon, 3.30-6.30pm, daily;
winter 7am-noon, 4-7pm, daily.
This little church occupies the site of the first church in Florence, founded in the 2nd century AD by Syrian Greek tradesmen who settled in the area. There are, however, no traces of its ancient beginnings – the interior is largely 18th-century, and the portico was built by **Vasari** in 1564 to support the Corridoio Vasariano, an overhead walkway that connected the Palazzo Pitti with the Palazzo Vecchio and the Uffizi (*see chapter* **Museums**). The reason to step inside is to see **Pontormo's** *Deposition*, the descent from the cross looking as it might if choreographed by Frederick Ashton with a colour scheme courtesy of Opal Fruits.

Medici Munchies

Flashness has never really been a Florentine characteristic, but a family as self-regardingly important as the Medici felt that they had to put on a bit of a show every now and again to impress the plebs and their peers. In June 1469, when Lorenzo il Magnifico married Clarice Orsini, there were no fewer than five celebratory banquets spread over three days. More than 4,000 chickens and geese and 150 calves were consumed (some being kept in the courtyard of the Palazzo Medici prior to being slaughtered) as well as huge quantities of fish and game birds and gallons of wine. Typical menus of the time often started with some sort of gelatine-based salad, followed by a hot pasta or grain dish, then roasted meat, *cialdoni* (pastries), *frittellette* (fried pastries), squash, marzipan, roasted almonds and pine nuts, and plenty of wine and *vin santo*. For a *calendimaggio* feast (a May festival), wealthy Florentines might eat spit roasted goat, calf's stomach, pigeons, cockerels and the innards of *castrati* (various castrated beasts). A favourite 15th-century dish was the sorbet (*sorbetto*); easy and economical to make thanks to the preponderance of local lemon and orange trees (there was a 3,500-tree orchard on Borgo Pinti).

Palazzo Pitti

*Piazza Pitti, Via Romana. Bus C. (See chapter **Museums** for opening times of individual museums.)*
Palazzo Pitti's chunkily rusticated facade bears down on its sloping forecourt, dwarfing the tourists who've come to visit its many museums, or wander around the Boboli Gardens behind. It was built in 1457 for Luca Pitti, a rival of the Medici, probably to a design by Brunelleschi that had been rejected by Cosimo il Vecchio as too grandiose. It was also too grandiose for the Pitti, and less than a century later they were forced to sell out to the doubtless gleeful Medici. The palace was far more luxurious than the draughty old Palazzo Vecchio and, in 1549, Cosimo I and his wife Eleonora di Toledo moved in. Huge as it was, it wasn't huge enough for the Medici, and Ammannati (he of the hideous Neptune fountain, *see above* **Piazza della Signoria**) was charged with remodelling the façade and creating the courtyard, a manic Mannerist space, with columns threaded through huge stone doughnuts. The façade was extended in the 17th century (it was originally seven windows wide) and two further wings were added in the 18th century. The palazzo now holds the vast, opulent and not-very-tasteful collection of Medici paintings, silver and other *objets d'art* (*see chapter* **Museums**).

Boboli Gardens

Piazza Pitti, Via Romana (21 87 41). Bus C. **Open** *Nov-Feb* 9am-4.30pm daily; *Mar* 9am-5.30pm daily; *Apr, May, Sept, Oct* 9am-6.30pm daily; *June-Aug* 9am-7.30pm daily; closed first and last Mon of the month. **Admission** L4000.
The Boboli, the only park in central Florence, was laid out by a number of artists for Eleonora di Toledo and Cosimo I. Bandinelli created a grotto for Eleonora, complete with casts of Michelangelo's *prigionieri* (*see chapter* **Museums**) and Ammannati and Giambologna designed fountains. The gardens run right up to the Forte del Belvedere (there is no longer access to the fortress from the gardens) and down to the Porta Romana. Beautifully kept, it makes the most of its hilly site. Be sure to wander along the **Viottolone**, a long avenue lined with cypresses, and in summer to have a snack and a coffee at the rococo **Kaffeehaus**, built in 1776, while gazing out over the city. Other highlights include the **L'Isolotto**, a miniature island in a circular lake with a copy of Giambologna's *Oceanus* charging through the waters on a horse; the **Amphitheatre**, created in the gap left after stone had been quarried for the Palazzo, where Jacopo Peri's opera, *Euridice*, was staged for the Medici in 1600 (his earlier work, *Dafne*, is considered to be the first ever opera); and the repulsively obese Bacchus fountain, a copy of a 16th-century statue showing Cosimo I's dwarf as a nude Bacchus (by the grotto). The entrance to the Boboli is via the main palace entrance.

Santo Spirito

Piazza Santo Spirito. Bus B, 36, 37. **Open** 8am-noon, 4-6pm, Mon, Tue, Thur-Sun; 8am-noon Wed.
Santo Spirito is one of **Brunelleschi**'s most remarkable buildings, although you wouldn't know so from its yellow 18th-century façade, blank and featureless as a slab of

The **Boboli Gardens**.

Checking out perspectives at **Santo Spirito**.

Piazza Santo Spirito's Sunday flea market.

marzipan. Step inside, however, and you enter a world of perfect proportions, a Latin-cross church surrounded by a continuous colonnade of dove grey *pietra serena* columns. Almost inevitably, there will be a couple of architecture students, squinting at vanishing points, calculating ratios or simply pacing glassy-eyed down the aisles and around the choir, mesmerised by the ever-moving pattern of column on column. There had been an Augustinian church on the site since 1250, but in 1397 the monks decided they wanted to replace it with a new one. To finance the project, they cut out one meal a day. Eventually they commissioned Brunelleschi to design it. Work started in 1444, two years before Brunelleschi died. The façade and exterior walls were never finished – the art critic Vasari reckoned that if the church had been completed to Brunelleschi's plans it would have been "the most perfect temple of Christianity". It is hard to disagree.

Piazza Santo Spirito
Bus B, 36, 37.
Piazza Santo Spirito is a low-key, laid-back space that – by day at least – still very much belongs to the locals. Furniture restorers have workshops just off the square, nearby trattorias serve good, cheap, working-class food, there is a daily morning market, an organic food market on the third Sunday of the month, and a huge flea market that spills over the piazza on the second Sunday of the month. Until quite recently the square was full of dope pushers; nowadays things have been cleaned up considerably, and it has become one of the crucial rendezvous points for the city's pre-clubbers (*see chapter* **Nightlife**).

Santa Maria del Carmine & the Brancacci Chapel
Piazza del Carmine. Bus B. **Open** *Brancacci Chapel* 9am-5pm Mon, Wed-Sat; 1-5pm Sun. **Admission** L5,000.
Santa Maria del Carmine is a blowsy Baroque edifice, an 18th-century replacement for a medieval church belonging to the Carmelite order, most of which burnt down in 1771. Miraculously, the Brancacci Chapel, matchlessly frescoed in the 15th century by **Masaccio** and **Masolino**, escaped. Masolino and Masaccio were an odd pair with little in common other than the fact that they were both born down in the Val d'Arno. Masolino, 18 years older than Masaccio, was a court painter, his style graceful, and still in tune with the highly decorative International Gothic traditions of artists like Gentile da Fabriano (*see chapter* **Museums: Uffizi**). Masaccio was a more modern, innovative painter, who had worked mostly for monks and local priests – his work is far more realistic, driven and emotive. Compare Masolino's elegant Adam and Eve in the *Temptation*, with Masaccio's ghastly horror-stricken couple in *Expulsion from Paradise*, or Masolino's dandified Florentines in their silks and brocades with Masaccio's simply clad saints. There are two themes to the paintings: the redemption of sinners and scenes

from the life of St Peter. Masaccio died aged 25, and work on the frescoes stopped for 60 years, when it was taken up again by **Filippino Lippi**, whose most striking contribution was *The Release of St Peter*. The frescoes were restored during the 1980s, financed by Olivetti, and there are now strict rules about how many people can visit at a single time, and how long they can stay (15 minutes).

Piazzale Michelangelo
Bus 12, 13.
Popular with lovers in cars, Piazzale Michelangelo is the city's balcony, a large, open square with views over the entire city. Laid out in 1869 by Giuseppe Poggi, it is dominated by a bronze replica of Michelangelo's *David*, and crammed all day with coaches. The pleasantest way of approaching from the lower city is to walk along Via San Niccolo until you reach Porta San Miniato, and climb up Via del Monte alle Croce, winding between the gardens of villas. Alternatively, walk up the rococo staircase Poggi designed to link Piazzale Michelangelo with his namesake, Piazza G Poggi below.

Forte del Belvedere
Via San Leonardo (23 42 425). Bus B, C, then 10-minute uphill walk. **Open** *summer* 9am-7pm daily; *winter* 9am-4.30pm daily. **Admission** free.
Now used as an exhibition space, the star-shaped fortress was built by Bernardo Buontalenti in 1590. Originally intended to protect the city from foreign enemies or insurgent natives, it soon became a place of refuge for the Medici Grand Dukes. The views over the city from the ramparts are stupendous.

San Miniato al Monte
Via Monte alla Croci (23 42 731). **Open** *summer* 8am-noon, 2-7pm, daily; *winter* 8am-noon, 2.30-6pm, daily.
The exquisite façade of San Miniato, delicately inlaid with white Carrara and green Verde di Prato marble, looks down on the city from high; a delicate, almost frail landmark, visible throughout the west of Florence. There has been a chapel on the site since at least the 4th century, erected on the spot where, according to legend, the recently beheaded San Miniato took up his head and walked from the banks of the Arno (where he had been killed) up the hill, where he finally expired. The chapel was replaced with a Benedictine monastery in the early 11th century, built on the orders of the reformer, Bishop Hildebrand. The interior of the church is one of the most beautiful in Tuscany, its walls patchworked with faded frescoes, its choir (dominated by an austere, almost Byzantine, mosaic of Christ) raised above a serene 11th-century crypt. Occasionally a door from the crypt is open, leading down to an even earlier chapel, used for special services. One of the church's most remarkable features is the marble pavement of the nave, inlaid with signs of the zodiac, and stylised lions and lambs. Other highlights include the pretty tabernacle between the choir stairs designed by **Michelozzi**, and the Cappella del Cardinale del Portogallo to the left of the choir, designed by a pupil of Brunelleschi, with an altar by the Pollaiuolo brothers, a tomb by Antonio Rossellino and a glazed terracotta ceiling by Luca della Robbia. To the right of the choir is the sacristry, frescoed with eerie, almost monochrome scenes from the *Life of St Benedict* by Spinello Aretino.

Santa Maria Novella to Ognissanti

Stretching from the striking modernist main railway station (designed by Michelucci in 1935), through a maze of dark, twisting backstreets to the river, this is a richly varied area of Florence. Round the railway station (as seems the case in virtually every European city) sleaze is conspicuous, with a chaos of beggars, tramps, men-on-the-pull, chest-

*See Florence and die: the graveyard at **San Miniato al Monte**.*

nut vendors, bewildered backpackers, swingeing buses and dodgeming taxi drivers. Across from the station, Alberti's façade for the church of Santa Maria Novella looks out on a piazza where tour groups thread their way through Africans, Asians and Filipinos hanging out. Down below the church, narrow streets twist down to the designer clothes shops of Via della Vigna Nuova.

Santa Maria Novella

Piazza Santa Maria Novella (21 01 13). **Open** 7am-12.15pm, 3-6pm, Sun-Fri; 7am-12.15pm, 3-5pm Sat.

Santa Maria Novella was the Florentine seat of the Dominicans, a fanatically inquisitorial Order, fond of leading street brawls against suspected heretics, and encouraging the faithful to strip and whip themselves before the church's altar. The piazza outside – one of Florence's biggest – was enlarged in 1244-5 in order to accommodate the crowds who came to hear St Peter Martyr, one of the viler members of the saintly canon, who made his name persecuting so-called heretics in the north of Italy (and ended up with one of their axes in his head).

The interior of the church – designed by the Order's own monks – is appropriately cheerless, but the façade is a light, elegant green and white marble affair. This is thanks to **Alberti** (*see chapter* **History: A Renaissance Man**) who in 1465, at the request of the Rucellai family, incorporated the Romanesque lower storey into a refined Renaissance scheme. To the right of the church is a cemetery surrounded by *avelli*, the grave niches of Florence's wealthy families. Until Vasari insisted they were whitewashed in the mid-16th century, the walls of the church were covered with frescoes. Fortunately he left alone Masaccio's *Trinity*. Painted in 1427, this was the first time that Brunelleschi's mathematical rules of perspective were applied to a painting, and the result is a solemn triumph of *trompe l'oeil*, with God, crucified Christ and two saints appearing to stand in a niche, watched by the two donors, Lorenzo Lenzi (a *gonfaloniere*) and his wife.

Over the next few decades the Dominicans appear to have loosened up a bit and, in 1485, allowed Ghirlandaio to cover the walls of the **Cappello di Tornabuoni** with scenes from the life of John the Baptist, featuring lavish contemporary Florentine interiors and supporting actors cast from members of the Tornabuoni family. At about the same time, Filippino Lippi was at work next door in the **Cappello di Filippo Strozzi**, painting scenes from the life of St Philip set among a fantasia of weird, vaguely Roman buildings that could have been dreamed up by Mervyn Peake.

To compare Masaccio's easeful use of perspective with the contorted struggles of Paolo Uccello, pop outside to the **Chiostro Verde**, to the left of the church. The cloister is so-called because of the green base pigment Uccello used, giving the flood-damaged frescoes a chill, deathly hue. The best preserved example of how not to do perspective is *The Flood*, looking as it might from deep down inside a plug hole. Beyond the Chiostro is the **Cappella degli Spagnuoli**, named because Cosimo I's wife Eleonora di Toledo reserved it for the use of her Spanish cronies, and decorated it with vibrant scenes celebrating the triumph of Dominicans and the Catholic Church.

Palazzo Rucellai

Via della Vigna Nuova. Bus C.

When **Alberti** created the façade of Santa Maria Novella for the Rucellai family, he had already designed their palazzo, the most refined in the city. Its subtle façade was inspired by the Colosseum: the pilasters that section the bottom storey have Doric capitals, those on the middle storey Ionic, and those on the top storey capitals based on the Corinthian. There is no rustication: Alberti loathed rustication, considering it pompous, arrogant and fit only for tyrants. The Rucellai were a family of wool merchants who had grown rich from importing from Majorca a red dye derived from lichen, known as *oricello*, from which their surname was derived. The palazzo now houses the **Museo Alinari** (*see chapter* **Museums**).

Striped vaults at **Santa Maria Novella**.

Santa Trinita

Piazza Santa Trinita (21 69 12). **Open** 8am-noon, 4-6pm, Mon-Sat; 4-6pm Sun.

Santa Trinita is a rather plain church, built in the 13th century over the ruins of two earlier churches belonging to the Vallombrosans. The Order was founded by San Giovanni Gualberto Visdomini in 1038, in an attempt to persuade pious aristocrats to surrender their wealth and live a life of austerity. In fact, the Order became extremely wealthy and powerful, reaching a peak in the 16th and 17th centuries when their huge fortress abbey at Vallombrosa was built (*see chapter* **Around Florence & Pisa**). The church is worth a visit for the **Sassetti Chapel**, frescoed by **Ghirlandaio**, with scenes from the life of St Francis, including one (above the altar) set in the Piazza della Signoria (you can clearly see the Palazzo della Signoria and the Loggia dei Lanzi) and featuring Lorenzo il Magnifico and his children.

Piazza & Ponte Santa Trinita

Piazza Santa Trinita is little more than a bulge in Via Tornabuoni, used as a taxi rank and dominated by an ancient column taken from the Baths of Caracalla in Rome, a gift to Cosimo I by Pope Pius I in 1560. The porphyry statue of Justice on top was designed by Ammannati. Ponte Santa Trinita is an elegant bridge with an elliptical arch, linking Piazza Santa Trinita with the Oltrarno. It was built by Ammannati in 1567, possibly to a design by Michelangelo. The statues at either end represent the Four Seasons and were placed there in 1608 to celebrate Cosimo II's marriage to Maria of Austria.

Ognissanti

Via Borgognissanti 42. Bus C. **Open** 8am-noon, 4-7pm, daily; *Cenacolo* 9am-noon Mon, Tue, Sat.
Admission free.

Ognissanti, or All Saints, was founded in the 13th century by a group of monks from Lombardy known as the Umiliati. They were responsible for introducing the wool trade to Florence and, as the city's wealth was built on wool, it could be argued that without the Umiliati there would have been no Florentine Renaissance. As well as building their church and monastery, the Umiliati had 30 houses that they rented out to wool workers. They also built a sturdy bridge across the Arno to the Borgo di San Frediano, where most of the wool workers lived. It is still known as the Ponte alla Carraia after the *carri* or carts that carried fleeces and wool back and forth across the Arno. By the 14th century, the Umiliati were so rich that they commissioned Giotto to paint the *Maestà* (now in the Uffizi, *see chapter* **Museums**) for their high altar. Within 50 years they had decided they needed a far flashier altar, and commissioned Giovanni da Milano to create an altarpiece with a lot more gold (now also in the Uffizi).

Ognissanti was also the parish church of the Vespucci, a family of merchants who came from Peretola (now near the airport) and dealt in silk, wine, wool, banking and goods from the Far East. One of their number was the 15th-century navigator, Amerigo, who sailed to the Venezuelan coast in 1499 and ended up having two continents named after him. Founded in the 13th century, it has been rebuilt on numerous occasions, and is now worth visiting mainly for the paintings by **Ghirlandaio**. As ever, biblical incidents are restaged in late 15th-century Florence with a cast of wealthy merchants. Amerigo himself appears as a young boy dressed in pink in the *Madonna della Misericordia*. Other paintings worth seeing include a *St Augustine* by Botticelli, a *St Jerome* by Ghirlandaio, and on a wall of the refectory, a *Last Supper*, also by Ghirlandaio.

San Lorenzo and San Marco

This is a vibrant, colourful area, stretching from the huge market around the church of San Lorenzo, with hundreds of stalls selling identical leather

*Some saints in All Saints – **Ognissanti**.*

gloves, leather bags, T-shirts and jewellery to the lively student area of San Marco, where cars are for once outnumbered by cycles and vespas.

San Lorenzo

Piazza San Lorenzo (21 66 34). **Open** 7am-noon, 3.30-6.30pm, daily.

San Lorenzo was the parish church of the Medici, who largely financed its construction, and for centuries continued to lavishly endow the place. It was built between 1419 and 1469 to a design by **Brunelleschi**. Its huge dome is almost as prominent as that of the Duomo, and the building itself sprawls, heavy and imposing, between Piazza di San Lorenzo and Piazza di Madonna degli Aldobrandini, surrounded by the hubbub of Florence's biggest street market.

Despite the fortune spent on the place, the façade was never finished, hence the digestive-biscuit-bricks. In 1518, the Medici Pope Leo X commissioned Michelangelo to design a façade (the models can be seen in the **Casa Buonarroti**, *see chapter* **Museums**). The Pope decided that the marble should be mined at Pietrasanta, which was part of Florence's domain. Michelangelo, however, wanted to use high quality Carrara marble. In the end it didn't matter as the whole scheme was cancelled in 1520.

San Lorenzo was the first church in which Brunelleschi applied his theory of rational proportion. The design for the entire building is based on the square of the transept crossing. The nave, for example, is four times the length of the crossing; the bays in the side aisles are half the length. The rhythm is emphasised by the use of grey *pietra serena*, with cream rough-cast plaster in between. Like Santo Spirito, this is a church to stroll slowly around and savour, though there are a couple of artworks you might want to look at more closely. First of these is **Donatello's bronze pulpits**, from which Savonarola (*see chapter* **History: Savonarola**)

More balls than most

The Medici have long been associated with a load of balls. Their family emblem – a number of red balls, the *palle*, on a gold shield – is prominently displayed on buildings all over Florence and Tuscany which have Medicean connections or which were financed with Medici money. One outraged contemporary of Cosimo il Vecchio declared that "He has emblazoned even the monks' privies with his balls." In times of danger, Medicean supporters were rallied with cries of *Palle! Palle!* The most romantic (and far-

fetched) explanation of the origin of the *palle* is that the balls are actually dents in a shield, inflicted by a fearsome giant in the Mugello on one of Charlemagne's knights, Averardo. The knight eventually vanquished the giant and, to mark his victory, Charlemagne permitted Averardo to use the image of the battered shield as his coat of arms. Rather more probable is that, as the name Medici suggests, the balls have a medical connection, perhaps representing pills or cupping-glasses.

---

snarled his tales of sin and doom. The reliefs are pretty powerful stuff too: you can almost hear the crowds scream in the *Deposition*. On the north wall is a *Martyrdom of St Lawrence* by Mannerist *par excellence* **Bronzino**, a decadent affair in which the barbequeing of the saint is attended by lots of muscle-bound men and hefty women with masculine shoulders and red-gold hair dressed in pink, lime green, yellow and lilac. In the second chapel on the right is another Mannerist work, a *Marriage of the Virgin* by Rosso Fiorentino, elegantly choreographed, with the cast dressed in bright pastels. In the north transept is a lucid *Annunciation* by Filippo Lippi, with a clarity of line and depth of persective that make it a perfect painting for this interior.

Opening off the north transept is the **Sagrestia Vecchia**, or old sacristy, another Brunelleschi design, with a dome segmented like a tangerine, and proportions based on cubes and spheres. The doors by Donatello, feature martyrs, apostles and Church fathers, while to the left of the entrance is an elaborate tomb of serpentine, porphyry, marble and bronze filled with the remains of Lorenzo il Magnifico's father and uncle, and designed by Verrochio. The **Biblioteca Laurenziana** was built to house the Medici's considerable library and is reached via the door to the left of the façade and up one of Europe's most elegant stairways, a slick Michelangelo design in *pietra serena*.

There are more Medici tombs in the **Cappella dei Principi**, entered from the side of the church on Piazza Madonna di Aldobrandini. Designed by **Michelangelo** as the Medici mausoleum, the floor-plan was based on that of Florence's Baptistry, and possibly of the Holy Sepulchre in Jerusalem. It is inlaid with brilliantly-hued *pietra dura*, which kept the workers of the the **Opificio** (*see chapter* **Museums**) busy for several centuries, and made of huge hunks of porphyry and ancient Roman marbles hauled into the city and sawn into pieces by Turkish slaves. At one time it was hoped that the tombs of the Medici would be joined by that of Christ – but, unfortunately for the Medici, the authorities in Jerusalem refused to sell it. The adjoining **Sagrestia Nuova** is dominated by the tombs of Lorenzo il Magnifico's far from magnificent cousins, Giuliano, Duke of Nemours, and Lorenzo, Duke of Urbino (*see chapter* **History: Medici Who's Who**), designed by Michelangelo with ghastly figures of Night and Day, and Dawn and Dusk reclining atop the two sarcophagi.

Giardino dei Semplici

Via Micheli 3 (27 57 402). Bus 11, 17. **Open** 9am-noon, 2.30-5pm, Mon, Fri; 9am-noon Wed, some Sundays. **Admission** free.
The Giardino dei Semplici, or garden of samples, was planted in 1545 on the orders of Cosimo I, on lands seized from an

order of Dominican nuns, for the cultivation of exotic plants and research into their uses. Essential oils were extracted, perfumes distilled and cures sought for various ailments and as antidotes to poisons. Nowadays it makes a pleasant place to wander in spring or summer, an escape from both crowds and high culture.

Palazzo Medici Riccardi

Via Cavour 1. **Open** 9am-1pm, 3-5pm, Mon-Sat; 9am-noon Sun. **Admission** free. *Capella dei Magi* **open** 9am-1pm, 3-6pm, Mon-Tue, Thur-Sat; 9am-1pm Sun. **Admission** L6,000.
A demonstration of both Medici muscle and Medici subtlety, Palazzo Medici Riccardi was home to La Famiglia until they moved into the Palazzo Vecchio in 1540. Not wishing to appear too ostentatious, Cosimo il Vecchio rejected a design by Brunelleschi as too extravagant. He plumped instead for one by **Michelozzo**, with a heavily rusticated first storey – in the style of many military buildings – but a smoother, more refined first storey and an even more restrained second storey, crowned by an overhanging cornice. The palazzo doubled as fortress and home, and was widely copied throughout Italy. It was massively expanded and revamped in the 17th century by its new owners the Riccardi, but retains a chapel frescoed by Benozzo Gozzoli, featuring a vivid *Journey of the Magi*. The palace now hosts various cultural exhibitions.

San Marco

Piazza San Marco. Bus to Piazza San Marco. **Open** 7am-12.30pm, 4-6.30pm, daily.
The Medici lavished even more money on the church and convent of San Marco, than they did on San Lorenzo. In 1434, Cosimo il Vecchio returned from exile and organised the handing over of the monastery of San Marco to the Dominicans. He then funded the renovation by **Michelozzo** of the decaying church and convent. Whether to ease his conscience (banking was still officially forbidden by the church), or to cash in on the increasing popularity of the Dominicans, is uncertain, but Cosimo agreed to foot the bill no matter how high it was. He also founded a public library, full of classic Greek and Latin works, the source of much influence on Florentine humanists. Ironically, later in the 15th century, San Marco became the base of religious fundamentalist Savonarola (*see chapter* **History: Savonarola**).

The reason for visiting San Marco is to see the so-called **Museo di San Marco**, housed in the various buildings

Icons for sale at **SS Annunziata**.
Devil spewing on **Piazza della Annunziata**.

of the convent alongside the church, and largely dedicated to the ethereal paintings of **Fra Angelico**, arguably the most spiritual artist of the 15th century. Walk up the steps to the first floor of the convent, and you are greeted by one of the most famous images in Christendom, an *Annunciation* that is, for once, entirely of another world, rather than looking as if a Renaissance fop with wings had dropped by a Florentine palazzo. The same is true of the other images Fra Angelico and his assistants frescoed on the walls of the monks' white, vaulted cells. Most of the cells on the outer wall of the left corridor are by Fra Angelico himself. Particularly outstanding are a lyrical *Noli Me Tangere* showing Christ appearing to Mary Magdalene in a field of flowers – she moves to touch him, he gently gestures that she should not; and the surreal *Mocking of Christ*, in which Christ's torturers are represented simply by relevant fragments of their anatomy: hands holding a whip, and a sponge; a face spitting. Carry on walking around the cells, and you'll come to the cell occupied by Savonarola, with portraits of the rabid reformer by Fra Bartolommeo.

Back down on ground level, there are more works by Fra Angelico in the **Ospizio dei Pellegrini**, or pilgrims' hospice, many of them collected from churches around the city: his first commission, the *Madonna dei Linaiuoli*, painted in 1433 for the Guild of Linen Makers, is here, along with a superb *Deposition* and a *Last Judgement* in which the Blessed dance among the flowers and trees of Paradise, while the Damned are boiled in cauldrons and pursued by monsters. By way of contrast, pop into the refectory, dominated by a Ghirlandaio *Last Supper* in which the disciples – by turn bored, praying, crying or haughty – pick at a frugal repast of bread, wine and cherries, against a background of orange trees, a peacock, a Burmese cat and flying ducks.

Piazza Santa Croce.

SS Annunziata

Piazza SS Annunziata (23 98 034). Bus 6, 31, 32.
Open 7.30am-12.30pm, 4-6.30pm, daily.
SS Annunziata, the church of the Servite Order, is a place of popular worship rather than perfect proportion, cosy and candlelit, with a frescoed Baroque ceiling and an opulent shrine built around a miraculous icon of the Madonna, said to have been painted by a 13th-century monk and finished by angels. Surrounding it are bouquets of flowers, silver lamps and pewter body parts – mostly limbs and hearts – ex-votives left in the hope that the Madonna will cure the dicky heart or gammy leg of a loved one. Despite its Baroque appearance the church was actually built by Michelozzo in the 15th century, as can be seen in the light, arcaded atrium. Early the following century it was frescoed by Pontormo, Rosso Fiorentino and, most strikingly, **Andrea del Sarto**, whose *Birth of the Virgin* is set between the refined walls of a Renaissance palazzo, with cherubs perched on a finely carved mantelpiece and on the festooned canopy of the bed. There is another fresco by del Sarto in the **Chiostro dei Morti**, or Cloister of the Dead, so-called because it was originally a burial ground, but you will need to get permission from the sacristan to see it.

Piazza SS Annunziata

Bus 6, 31, 32.
Piazza SS Annunziata is one of the most pleasing in the city, surrounded on three sides by delicate arcades, and with a powerful equestrian statue of Grand Duke Ferdinando I by Giambologna in the the centre. Opened in 1445, the **Spedale degli Innocenti** on the eastern side was the first foundling hospital in Europe, commissioned by the Guild of Silk Weavers and designed by **Brunelleschi**. The powder blue medallions in the spandrels, each of them showing a swaddled baby, are by **Andrea della Robbia**. Babies, many of them the offspring of the city's numerous domestic slaves, were left in a small revolving door, set into the wall at the left. Brunelleschi envisioned creating a perfectly symmetrical piazza, which would have been modern Europe's first, but died before he could realise the dream. However, in the 17th century, the porticos were later continued around two further sides of the square, giving the piazza a human scale and unity otherwise lacking in the city – making it an understandably popular hangout for students from the nearby university and mums waiting to collect children from the school.

Santa Croce and Sant'Ambrogio

The streets leading from central Florence to the church and piazza of Santa Croce are devoted to tourism – at least every other shop is a leather-goods emporium. Behind Santa Croce, however, there's a totally different scene – a working class district with a funky alternative element manifesting itself in ads for tattooists, graffitied self-advertisements from conceptual artists and flyers for gigs and benefits at the *centri sociali*. At the heart of the district is the fruit and vegetable market of Sant'Ambrogio, best seen on a Saturday, followed by an aperitif at *Caffè Cibreo* with the area's myriad foodies.

Santa Croce

Piazza Santa Croce (24 46 19). Bus 14. **Open** *summer* 8am-6.30pm Mon-Sat; 3-6pm Sun; *winter* 8am-12.30pm, 3-6.30pm, Mon-Sat; 3-6pm Sun.
Santa Croce is filled with the tombs of the city's illustrious; oddly so, given that it belonged to the Franciscans, the most unworldly of the religious orders. They founded the church in 1228, ten years after they arrived in the city. A recently established order, the Franciscans were supposed to make

The Arno from **Ponte delle Grazie.**

their living by manual work, preaching and begging. At the time, Santa Croce was a slum, full of the city's grossly underpaid dyers and wool-workers. Franciscan preaching, with its message that all men were equal, had a huge impact on the poor people of the quarter. Indeed it was doubtless in part because of the confidence given them by the Franciscans that in 1378 the dyers and wool-makers revolted against the all-powerful guilds and were finally allowed to organise their own guilds. As for the Franciscans, their vow of poverty slowly eroded over the years: in fact, by the late 13th century, the old church was felt to be inadequate, and a new one was planned – intended to be one of the largest in Christendom, and probably designed by Arnolfo di Cambio, architect of the Duomo and the Palazzo Vecchio. It was financed partly by property confiscated from Ghibellines (*see chapter* **History: Guelph v Ghibelline**) who had been convicted of heresy.

It remains the richest medieval church in the city, with frescoes by Giotto, a chapel by Brunelleschi, and one of the finest of all early Renaissance tombs. At first sight, however, the interior of the church is a bit of a disappointment, too big, too gloomy and with too many overbearing marble tombs clogging the walls. Not all the tombs contain bodies: **Dante's** (right aisle) is simply a memorial to the writer, who is buried in Ravenna. In the niche alongside is the **tomb of Michelangelo** – he died in Rome, but his body was brought back to Florence – and further down, the **tomb of Leonardo Bruni** by Bernardo Rossellino, the sculpture so realistic, that he could almost be snoozing. Back at the top of the left aisle is **Galileo's tomb** – a polychrome marble confection created over a century after his death in 1737, when the Church finally permitted him a Christian burial.

Things get considerably more interesting once you hit the **Cappellas Bardi** and **Peruzzi**, completely frescoed by **Giotto**. Unfortunately, they are not in great condition – a result of Giotto painting on dry instead of wet plaster, and of them being daubed with whitewash in the 18th-century. The most striking of the two chapels is the Bardi, with scenes from the life of St Francis, in haunting, virtual monotone, the figures just stylised enough to make them other-worldly, yet

individual enough to make them human. On the far side of the high altar is the **Cappella Bardi di Vernio**, frescoed by one of Giotto's most interesting followers, **Maso di Banco**, but under restoration at the time of writing.

To get to the **Cappella dei Pazzi**, Brunelleschi's geometric *coup de grace*, you have to leave the church, and pass through the cloister. Planned in the 1430s, and completed some 40 years later, it is based on a central square topped by a cupola, flanked by two barrel-vaulted bays, and with the decorative arches on the white walls perfectly echoing the structural arches. Across the courtyard is a small museum of church treasures, including a 13th-century crucifix by **Cimabue** badly damaged in the 1966 flood (*see* **Box** *above*) and Donatello's *St Louis of Toulouse* from Orsanmichele.

Ponte alle Grazie

Until they were demolished last century, the Ponte delle Grazie had several oratories and chapels built upon its piers. One of them, devoted to Santa Maria delle Grazie, was much visited by distraught lovers seeking solace, and gave the bridge its name. Also on the bridge was a tiny convent where several nuns cloistered themselves for life, never leaving, and never seeing anyone. The architect Alberti (*see chapter* **History: A Renaissance Man**) died in another of the bridge's chapels. The original stone bridge, built in 1227, the only one to survive a disastrous flood in 1333. It was destroyed by mines in 1944, and replaced by the present structure in 1957.

Piazza dei Ciompi

Bus B.

Named after the dyers and wool-workers revolt of 1378, Piazza dei Ciompi is now given over to a junk/antiques market during the week, and is flooded by a huge day-long flea market on the last Sunday of every month. It is dominated by a loggia, built by Vasari in 1568 for the Mercato Vecchio, which occupied the site of Piazza della Repubblica (*see above*). It was dismantled in the 19th century and re-erected here. It now shelters a book cart which often has some good value art and history books (*see chapter* **Students**).

Museums

Florence's art behemoths are deservedly world-renowned but the city's clutch of lesser known quirky collections can be equally rewarding – and blessedly crowd-free.

Good enough to kiss: the arse of Donatello's David in the **Bargello**. *See page 107.*

Florence's museum collections are unrivalled, and it would take several intensive weeks and much shoe leather to see them all properly. Many have private collections at their core: whether that of a mega-family like the Medici (**Uffizi** and **Palazzo Pitti**) or of a lone connoisseur (Museos **Horne**, **Bardini** and **Stibbert**). Add to these the museums founded to preserve treasures too precious to expose to the elements (**Bargello**, **Museo dell'Opera del Duomo**, the **Accademia** and **Museo Archeologico**) to say nothing of the scholarly collections you would expect to find in any university town (mounds of gems, bones, stuffed animals and anatomical models) and you have a selection as eclectic as the Renaissance itself. Few people visit Florence without seeing the Uffizi, the Accademia and the Bargello, but most people miss out on some of the city's most inspiring collections: the **Museo Archeologico**, for example, with its mind-blowing collection of Etruscan ceramics; the **Museo di Storia della Scienza**, which focuses on the huge scientific and technical innovations of Renaissance Florence; or the **Palazzo Davanzati**, where you can glimpse the lifestyle of a 15th-century wool merchant.

There is a collective ticket available (L15,000) for the six city museums, including the Museo Bardini, the Museo di Santa Maria Novella (*see chapter* **Florence By Area**), the Museo Firenze com'era and the Palazzo Vecchio. The ticket is valid for one visit to each museum within a six-month period.

Ticket offices stop issuing tickets about half an hour before the museum closes. Entrance to all state museums is free to EC citizens under 18 and over 60. On 2 June and for one week (usually in November), state museums are free for all.

Writhing limbs and fluffy clouds in the excessive **Palazzo Pitti**. *See page 108.*

The Uffizi

Piazzale degli Uffizi 6 (23 885). **Open** 8.30am-6.50pm
Tue-Sat; 8.30am-1.50pm Sun. **Admission** L12,000.
If you're at all fond of Renaissance art, prepare to step into
heaven. A crowded heaven, maybe, but one in which there
are more gorgeous daubings to drool over than any other
gallery in Europe. Picking a time when the gallery is not
busy is hard, but try lunchtime and an hour before closing.
The name, incidentally, means offices, which is precisely
what Vasari designed the building to be used for in 1550.

The collection begins, gloriously, with three *Maestàs* by
Giotto, **Cimabue** and **Duccio** in **room 2**, painted in the
late 13th and early 14th centuries. All three are still part of
the Byzantine tradition: even Giotto's Virgin – painted for
Ognissanti – with the mounds of her breasts discernible
beneath her gauzy dress, is still very much of another, icon-
ic world. Stepping into **room 3** is to enter the magical
world of 12th-century Siena, most exquisitely evoked by
Simone Martini's fairy-tale *Annunciation (see picture
right)*, with breathtakingly beautiful angel, coy Virgin, and
a room with a marble floor, marquesite throne and lilies
standing in a gold vase. Such delight in detail reached its
zenith in the International Gothic movement (**rooms 5** and
6), most particularly in the work of **Gentile da Fabriano**
(1370-1427), whose *Adoration of the Magi*, painted for one
of the Strozzi family, is little more than an excuse to paint
sumptuous brocades and intricate gold jewellery.

It is something of a surprise, then, to turn to an almost
contemporary *Madonna and Child with St Anne*, by
Masolino (1383-1440) and **Masaccio** (1401-28) in **room
7**. Although Masolino was not averse to a bit of
International Gothic frivolity (witness some of the costumes he dreamed up for the Brancacci Chapel; *see chapter* **Florence by Area**) here he is totally restrained. The
younger Masaccio made the Virgin, whose severe
expression and statuesque form make her an indubitable
descendent of Giotto's *Maestà*. In the same room is
*Madonna and Child with Saints Francis, John the Baptist,
Zenobius and Lucy* by **Domenico Veneziano** (1405-61),
a Venetian artist who died a pauper in Florence, and had
a remarkable skill for rendering the way in which light
affects colour. If you are familiar with his pupil **Piero
della Francesca**'s work, his influence on the younger
artist will be clear. Piero has just one painting in the Uffizi,
a pair of portraits in profile of The Duke and Duchess of
Urbino. Still in room 7, **Paolo Uccello** (1397-1475) is represented by one of three original panels of *The Battle of
San Romano* (the others are in the National Gallery,
London and the Louvre, Paris). A work of tremendous
energy and action, the chaos of battle is only reinforced
by Uccello's intense, contorted use of perspective.

The next two rooms are dominated by **Filippo Lippi** and
the **Pollaiuolo** brothers. The exquisite Madonna in Lippi's

Madonna and Child with Two Angels is a portrait of the
astonishingly beautiful Lucrezia Buti, a nun he abducted,
impregnated with Filippino and eventually married. The
more talented of the Pollaiuolo brothers, Antonio, was one of
the first artists to dissect bodies in order to study anatomy.
There is the subtle sense of a skull beneath the skin of the
beauty in *Portrait of a Lady*, though you really need to look
at something like his small panel showing *Hercules Slaying
the Hydra*, for evidence of his familiarity with musculature.

The two most famous paintings in the Uffizi are in **room
10**. **Botticelli**'s *Birth of Venus* (c1485) *(see picture below)*,
the epitome of Renaissance romance, in fact depicts the birth
of the goddess from a sea impregnated by the castration of
Uranus, an allegory of the birth of beauty from the mingling
of physical world (the sea) and spirit (Uranus). If you want
to scatter the old dears cooing sentimentally over her porcelain skin and ropes of red hair, just try retelling the myth in
a loud voice with lots of gory detail. Scholars have been
squabbling over the meaning of *Primavera (see picture opposite)* almost since the thing was painted in 1478, but most
agree now that it is meant to celebrate the triumph of Venus
(in the centre) with the Three Graces representing her beauty, and Flora her fecundity.

Beyond, in **Room 15**, are several paintings by
Leonardo, including an *Annunciation* with an angel who
could be Mona Lisa's brother. The octagonal tribune
beyond is dominated by portraits by **Bronzino**, most
strikingly that of Eleonora di Toledo, assured, beautiful
and very Spanish in an opulent gold and black brocade
gown. Walk on, and you'll eventually come to **room 25**,
and **Michelangelo**'s *Doni Tondo (see cover)*, a huge leap
into Mannerism, with its virtuoso composition, sculptural bodies and luscious palate. To realise how radical this
painting was, just compare it to his peer **Raphael**'s con-
ventionally sentimental *Madonna of the Goldfinch*.

Room 28 has works by **Titian**'s steamy *Venus of
Urbino*. For more Venetian works skip on to **rooms 31**
to **35**, but don't miss Parmigianino's *Madonna with the
Long Neck* en route, one of the weirdest of all the weird
emanations of the febrile Mannerist imagination, with the
Madonna and Child looking as they might distorted in a
hall of mirrors.

Shooting David *at the* **Accademia**.

Art & sculpture

Accademia
Via Ricasoli 60 (23 88 609). **Open** 8.30am-6.50pm Tue-Sun. **Admission** L12,000.

They queue and they queue. In fact they queue so much that the road outside has been pedestrianised. And what they queue to see is Michelangelo's *David*. The real thing. The only problem is that looking at the real thing, it's difficult not to think of fridge magnet Davids with boxer shorts, or the Davids stretched across the ample bosoms of ladies from Cleveland. You almost expect it to wink.

The poor misunderstood thing started life as a serious political icon, a symbol of brave little Florence pitted against big bad Goliaths like France (Charles VIII had invaded Italy in 1494, a decade before *David* was sculpted). Michelangelo, however, seems more likely to have considered it a monument to his genius, a triumph of skill over the restriction of carving a figure from a slab of marble five metres high, but exceptionally narrow. Not without cause has it been suggested that its chill arrogance and self-satisfied smugness may have been inspired by what Michelangelo saw when he looked in the mirror.

Intended to stand on the Piazza della Signoria, its proportions seem distorted in an enclosed space: the head looks too big, the arms too long. Far more exciting are Michelangelo's so-called slaves, unfinished sculptures struggling to emerge from their slabs of marble. They were intended for Pope Julius II's tomb, a project that Michelangelo was eventually, much to his irritation, forced to abandon in order to paint the Sistine Chapel ceiling.

Bargello
Via del Proconsolo 4 (23 88 606). **Open** 8.30am-2pm Tue-Sun; 1st, 3rd & 5th Mon of the month. **Admission** L8,000.

This dour fortified building started life as the Palazzo del Popolo in 1250, and soon became the seat of the *Podestà*, the chief magistrate. *Podestàs* were noblemen from other cities – the theory being that they would remain neutral in conflicts between rival factions. In the 14th century the bodies of executed criminals were displayed here and, in the 15th century, law courts, prisons and torture chambers were set up inside. It didn't get its present name until the 16th century, when the Medici made it the seat of their chief of police, known as the Bargello. In 1865, the Bargello was opened as a museum.

The collection is one of the most eclectic and prestigious in the city, ranging from prime sculptures by Michelangelo, Donatello, Cellini and Giambologna, to Turkish suits of armour, Scandinavian chess sets and Egyptian ivories. The most famous works are Giambologna's fleet-of-foot *Mercury* and a tipsy, lolling *Bacchus* by Michelangelo (on the ground floor); and Donatello's campish *David* and tense, nervous *St George* (on the first floor). Also worth seeing are Giambologna's virtuoso aviary of bronze birds, including a madly exaggerated turkey, Medici majolica and glazed terracotta Madonnas by Luca Della Robbia. If you like oddities, don't miss the collection of late 16th-century anatomical figures, nor the lifesized gaudy wooden statue of a baggy trousered Saracen.

Museo dell' Opera del Duomo
Piazza Duomo 9 (23 02 885). **Open** *summer* 9am-6.50pm Mon-Sat; *winter* 9am-6.20pm Mon-Sat. **Admission** L8,000.

This museum, just behind the duomo, contains instruments used to build the Duomo, and sculpture deemed too precious and vulnerable to be left to the mercy of the elements. On the ground floor are brick stamps and forms, and the pulleys and ropes by which building materials (and workers) were winched up to the dome of the Duomo. There are also bits and pieces from Santa Reparata, an earlier church on the site, including a Classical-style Madonna with spooky glass eyes by Arnolfo di Cambio, and a series of 1587 models of proposals for the façade by, among others, Giovanni de' Medici and Giambologna.

Half way up the stairs is a *Pietà*, a late work by Michelangelo showing Christ, dead and disjointed, slithering from the grasp of Nicodemus. The sculpture was never

*Keeping an eye on things in the **Palazzo Pitti**'s Galleria Palatina. See page 108.*

finished, supposedly because Michelangelo got so frustrated by his servant nagging him about it, and with the poor quality of the marble, that he eventually smashed off the arm of Christ in frustration. According to Vasari, Nicodemus is a self-portrait.

Upstairs is an extraordinary wood sculpture of *Mary Magdalene* by Donatello, dishevelled and ugly, with coarse, dirty hair so realistic you can almost smell it. His *Habbakuk*, bald, emaciated and caught in a vision, is another uncomfortable work: indeed Donatello himself is said to have gripped the statue and screamed at it, 'Speak, speak, speak!' It's a relief then to turn to the *cantorias* (choir lofts). One by Donatello carved with cavorting putti, the other full of angel musicians by Luca della Robbia. Beyond, are the reliefs Giotto carved for the campanile and, most strikingly, some of the original panels created by Ghiberti for the Baptistry doors (*see chapter* **Florence by Area**).

Museums of the Palazzo Pitti

Galleria del Palatina/Appartamente Reale (23 88 614). **Open** 8.30am-6.50pm Tue-Sat; 8.30am-1.50pm Sun. **Admission** L12,000.
Galleria del Costume/Galleria d'Arte Moderne (23 88 713/23 88 616). **Open** 8.30am-1.50pm Tue-Sat; 1st, 3rd & 5th Sun of the month; 2nd & 4th Mon of the month. **Admission** L8,000.
Museo degli Argenti (23 88 710). **Open** 8.30am-1.50pm Tue-Sat; 1st, 3rd & 5th Sun of the month. **Admission** L4,000.

There's no two ways about it: the Pitti museums are heavyweight stuff, and you'd be mad to try to see them all on one visit. The most famous is the **Galleria del Palatina**, with paintings hung four or five high in huge gilt frames on its damask walls, in rooms busy with *pietra dura* and malachite tables. This may be the way the Medici liked it, but it doesn't make seeing the things particularly easy. Highlights – if you've the patience to find them – include Tintoretto's *Entrance of Christ into Jerusalem*, an exquisite *Madonna and Child* by Filippino Lippi, portraits by Botticelli, a lustrous-haired *Magdalene* and the famous *Concerto* by Titian. Most people, however, seem to come for the Raphaels: *Portrait of a Pregnant Woman*, a serene *Madonna del Granduca* with Leonardesque eyes, the famous coyly sweet *Madonna della Seggiola*, and portraits of Angelo and Maddalena Doni.

The Galleria runs into the **Appartamente Reale**, or royal apartments, decorated in the worst possible taste in the 19th century, first by the Lorraine Dukes, then by Italy's first royals, King Umberto I and Queen Margherita (of pizza fame) who lived here during Florence's brief stint as capital (1865-70). Rooms are walled with garish silk brocade, anything that can be gilded is gilded, and anything that is not, is smothered in precious gems and marbles. The *pièces de résistance* are the royal couple's ebony *prie dieus*, Maggie's encrusted with gilded bronze and *pietra dura*, and Bert's with ghoulish porcelain dolls' heads.

Far more fun is the **Galleria del Costume**, ranging from fin de siècle clothes by Rosa Genoni, inspired by Botticelli and Pisanello, to a Pucci dress of 1982. In the same block as the costume gallery is the unspeakable **Galleria d'Arte Moderne**, full of sugary *macchiaiuoli* ladies and blossomy trees, Italy's unnecessary contribution to French Impressionism.

The **Museo degli Argenti** is glutted with the treasures the Medici amassed over the centuries: case upon case of *pietra dura* knick knacks, Roman glassware, ivory and, refreshingly, speaking of another time, place and taste entirely, Chinese porcelain and ceramics.

Palazzo Vecchio

Piazza Signoria (27 68 465). **Open** 9am-7pm Mon-Wed, Fri, Sat; 8am-1pm Sun. **Admission** L10,000.
Still Florence's town hall, the 13th-century Palazzo Vecchio (*see chapter* **Florence by Area**) was seat first of the

Signoria, the city's ruling body *(see box* **Florence by Area**) then, for nine years, of the Medici (1540-9). The Medici's stay may have been brief, but they nevertheless instigated a huge Mannerist makeover of the palace's interior, under the direction of Giorgio Vasari, court architect from 1555 until 1574. To be frank, unless you are a die-hard fan of Mannerism, you may find the visit a bit of a slog.

The **Salone dei Cinquecento**, or hall of the 500, where the (actually six or seven hundred) members of the Great Council held meetings, should have been decorated with battle scenes by Leonardo and Michelangelo, not the dull, dutiful scenes of victory by Vasari that actually cover the walls. Unfortunately Leonardo (typically) abandoned the *Battle of Anghiari*, and Michelangelo had only completed the cartoon for the *Battle of Cascine*, when he was summoned to Rome by Pope Julius II. One of Michelangelo's commissions for Pope Julius did, however, end up here: *Victory*, a statue carved for the pope's never-finished tomb. Victory, a muscle-bound young man, apparently started out as a woman, proof if any were needed, that Michelangelo's women are simply men with breasts.

Off the Salone is the **Studiolo di Francesco I**, where weedy Francesco I hid away and conducted alchemical experiments. The room, decorated by Vasari, includes a scene from an Alchemist's laboratory, and illustrations of the four elements while, on the vaults, portraits of Francesco's parents, Cosimo I and Eleonora di Toledo by Bronzino, look down.

Upstairs is the palazzo's most beautiful room, the **Sala dei Gigli**, so-called for the gilded lilies (*gigli*) that cover the walls. Decorated in the late 15th century, it has a ceiling by Giuliano and Benedetto da Maiano, and frescoes of great Roman statesmen by Ghirlandaio: a refreshing change from too much Mannerist bombast.

Beyond is the **Sala d'Udienza**, with another lovely da Maiano ceiling, and Donatello's original *Judith and Holofernes*.

Individual collections

Museo Bardini

Piazza de' Mozzi 1 (23 42 427). **Open** 9am-2pm Mon, Tue, Thur-Sat; 8am-1pm Sun. **Admission** L6,000.
The art dealer Stefano Bardini bequeathed his huge collection to the city on his death in 1923. Bardini built the palazzo in 1881, on the site of a ruined 13th-century church: the first-floor windows incorporate altar stones from a church at Pistoia, and the ceilings, doors, fireplaces and other architectural details, were salvaged from other palaces. The collection itself is still partly uncatalogued, so staff may be as much in the dark about certain pieces as you are. The pleasingly eclectic pieces on display include fine Persian and Anatolian carpets, Turkish ceramics, a headless *Virgin* by Giovanni Pisano and musical instruments including a Neapolitan *tabarda* and three serpents.

Museo Horne

Via dei Benci 6 (24 46 61). **Open** 9am-1pm Mon-Sat. **Admission** L8,000.
The 15th-century Palazzo Corsi-Alberti was bought by English architect and art historian Herbert Percy Horne in the late 19th century. When he died he bequeathed the palazzo and his vast, magpie-ish collection to the state, and in 1922 it opened as a museum. Objects on the ground floor range from ceramics and coins to a coffee grinder and spectacles. Upstairs is a damaged wooden panel by Masaccio, relating the story of San Giuliano, a medieval Oedipus who came home early one day to find his mother in bed with a man, and killed the two of them without troubling to find out that the man was his dad. In repentance, Giuliano cut off his own right arm, and became a devout Christian. Also here is an exorcism by the Maestro di San Severino and, pride of the

collection, a gold-backed *Santo Stefano* by Giotto. There is also a limbless statue of an athlete by Giambologna, a pom-pom hat and a painted wedding chest.

Museo Stibbert

Via Stibbert 26 (48 60 49). **Open** 9am-1pm Mon-Wed, Fri, Sat; 9am-12.30pm Sun. **Admission** L5,000.
Like Museos Horne and Bardini, the Stibbert is devoted to the collection of one man, a certain Frederick Stibbert (1838-1906) who fought for Italian unification with Garibaldi. He had an English father and an Italian mother, who conveniently left him her 14th-century house. Considering it too small, he bought a neighbouring mansion and had the two joined together. The 64 rooms are crammed with 50,000 or so items, ranging from snuff boxes and silver basins to a painting attributed to Botticelli. Stibbert's real passion, however, was for armour, as you can see if you walk into the Sala della Cavalcata, with its serried ranks of fully kitted up knights and footmen.

Florence life

Museo di Bigallo

Piazza San Giovanni 6 (21 54 40). **Open** Tue-Sun, by appointment only. **Admission** free.
This is a tiny museum, housed in a Gothic loggia, built for the Misericordia, a charitable organisation which cared for unwanted children and looked after victims of the plague. The Misericordia still exists – its ambulances are usually to be seen outside its headquarters next door. There's not much to see inside: most curious is the *Madonna della Misericordia*, an anonymous work of 1342, showing the Virgin suspended above the earliest known painting of the city. There are plans to open the museum fully to the public, but no details were available at the time of going to press.

Museo di Firenze com'era

Via dell'Oriuolo 24 (23 98 483). **Open** 9am-2pm Mon-Wed, Fri, Sat; 8am-1pm Sun. **Admission** L5,000.
The charmingly named museum of 'Florence how it was', is in fact a collection of maps and paintings tracing the development of the city. As labelling is perfunctory, even in Italian, it is not hugely accessible, and parts of it are closed when temporary exhibitions are hosted. If you are lucky you will be able to see the famous lunettes of Medici villas created in 1599 by the Flemish artist Giusto Utens; and the room devoted to the vainglorious plans of Giuseppe Poggi in the late 1860s to destroy the centre of Florence and replace it with buildings fit for a modern capital.

Palazzo Davanzati: Museo della Casa Fiorentina Antica

Via Porta Rossa 13 (23 88 610). **Open** 8.30am-1.50pm Tue-Sat; 1st, 3rd & 5th Sun of the month; 2nd & 4th Mon of the month. **Admission** L6,000. **Closed until 1998 for restoration. All details are subject to change.**
Palazzo Davanzati, decorated and furnished as it would have been as a medieval family house, is many people's favourite Florentine museum. Built in the 14th century for a family of wool merchants, it was bought by the Davanzati family in 1578. In 1838, after the last surviving Davanzati leapt to his death from a window, it was split up into apartments. In 1904 it was bought by an art collector, artist and restorer, Elia Volpi, who restored it and installed her collection inside. It opened as a museum in 1956.
The palazzo was well prepared for the volatile nature of life in medieval Florence, with impenetrable doors, a private well, and hatches in the otherwise elegant Sala Grande, through which all manner of nasty objects could be thrown on the heads of an enemy. More luxuriously, lavatories were installed on each storey in the 15th century, and water winched in buckets from floor to floor by a pulley system.
The main rooms have beautifully painted walls: the din-

ing room was known as the *Sala dei Pappagalli* (Room of the Parrots) for its parrot-patterned trompe l'oeil wall hangings, and the *camera da letto* (bedroom) is frescoed with scenes from a French Romance, *La Châtelaine de Vergi*. Look out as well for the fabulously decorated *cassoni* in which a wife's dowry would be stored. On the top floor – to limit the damage that would be caused by a fire – is the covetable kitchen, packed with utensils, and with a medieval dumb-waiter connecting it with the floors below.

Science & natural history

Museo di Geologie e Paleontologie

Via La Pira 4 (23 82 711). **Open** 2-6pm Mon; 9am-1pm Tue-Thur, Sat; 9.30am-12.30pm 1st Sun of the month. **Admission** L5,000.
One of the best fossil collections in Italy, this is the sort of old-fashioned museum that looks like the hoard of some mad Enid Blytonesque uncle. One highlight is the remains of elephant-like creatures found in the Valdarno.

Museo di Mineralogie e Lithologie

Via La Pira 4 (27 57 537). **Open** 9am-1pm Mon-Fri; Sat by appointment only; 1st Sun of the month. **Admission** free (L5,000 on Sun).
Let's rock. A delightfully old fashioned university museum stuffed with immense chunks of strange and lovely gems, including a 360lb topaz from Brazil. Fantastic agates, chalcedony, tormaline and quartzes, acid yellow *zolfo celestina*, irridescent limonite from Elba, glass models of famous stones like the Koh-i-noor, and a jade cup and Ming lotus flower bowls made of nephrite from the Granducal collection.

La Specola

Via Romana 17 (22 88 251). **Open** 9am-noon Mon, Tue, Thur-Sat; 9am-1pm Sun. **Admission** L6,000.
Known as La Specola because of the telescope on its roof, this is actually Florence's museum of zoology. At first glance it looks like any other old-fashioned natural history museum, crammed with stuffed and pickled animals, including a hippopotamus, a gift to Grand Duke Pietro Leopoldo, that used to be kept in the nearby Boboli Gardens. But then you pass through the door marked 'Cere Anatomiche', and everything changes. In a laboratory fit for Frankenstein, wax corpses lie on beds covered with satin, each one a little more dissected than the former, and walls are covered with dismembered body parts: limbs, organs and body slices, all of them perfectly realistic. They were made between 1775 and 1814 by Clemente Susini, an artist, and Felice Fontana, a physiologist, to be used as teaching aids. Also here are four unflinchingly gory tableaux devoted to Florence during the plague: definitely not for sensitive souls.

Museo di Storia della Scienza

Piazza dei Giudici 1 (23 98 876). **Open** 9.30am-1pm Mon-Sat; 9am-1pm, 2-5pm, Mon, Wed, Fri. **Admission** L10,000.
The museum of the history of science is without doubt one of the best in Florence – a chance to look at the Renaissance and beyond from a viewpoint that, for once, is not limited stone, paint and canvas. One of the most fascinating rooms is that devoted to Galileo, including a reliquary containing his right-hand middle finger, cut from his corpse as it was moved to Santa Croce. In 1608 Galileo developed a telescope with 30x magnification, and in 1609 discovered that there were mountains on the moon. The following year he saw what he believed to be three small stars aligned with Jupiter, but observing them over the next few days realised that they, plus a fourth, were actually moons orbiting the planet. Eventually he came up with evidence to back his – until then private – belief that the earth orbited the sun. Copernicanism,

as it was called, after the Pole who first posited the theory, was then anathema to the Church, and eventually Galileo was tried and convicted of heresy, and placed under house arrest.

In the following rooms are a collection of lenses, prisms and optical games, followed by a hall devoted to armillary spheres, most of them with the earth orthodoxly at the centre of the universe, surrounded by seven spheres of the planets, and the sphere of the Prime Mover. Beyond are instruments used by the Accademia del Cimento, founded in 1657 by Ferdinando II for the study of science. Among the exhibits are glass instruments made at a kiln in the Boboli Gardens. On the second floor are magnetic instruments, pneumatic pumps, and anatomical models in wax or painted wood, showing the development of the foetus (including Siamese twins) and different delivery techniques.

Anthropology & archaeology

Museo Antropologia e Etnologia

Proconsolo 12 (23 96 449). **Open** 9am-1pm Thur-Sat; one Sun per month (variable). **Admission** free.
A fascinating muddle of goodies from all over the world. Everything from intricate Abyssinian basketwork and fantastic Polynesian wood carvings to Peruvian mummies in foetal position, shadow puppets from the Nicobar Islands, and anoraks from the Arctic circle made by sewing together strips of intestines from whales, dolphins and porpoises.

Museo Archeologico

Via della Colonna 38 (23 575). **Open** 9am-2pm Tue-Sat; 9am-1pm Sun; 1st, 3rd & 5th Mon of the month. **Closed** 1st, 3rd & 5th Sun of the month. **Admission** L8,000.
One of the best museums in Florence, and just the place to come when you begin to tire of studied Renaissance smug-

The garden of the **Museo Archeologico**.

Casa di Dante – *don't bother.*

ness. Heralding the collection is a dynamic Etruscan bronze chimera, its flesh tensed against its rib cage, its mane violently diamond-pointed. Continuing, there is a selection of Etruscan jewellery, including a case of fakes bought by the museum in 1911. On the first floor are shelves of Etruscan kitchen utensils – including a cheese grater – and miniature Etruscan bronzes, most notably an attenuated Giacometti-like figurine. Some of the most intriguing tomb finds are on display in the new wing, the best of them dramatically fusing the abstract and figurative: schematic horned animals with babies on their backs, a jug with its neck bent back to form a swan's neck handle, an urn with human features scored on its lid and hands growing from its handles.

Artists & writers

Casa Buonarroti

Via Ghibellina 70 (24 17 52). **Open** 9.30am-1.30pm Wed-Mon. **Admission** L10,000.
Michelangelo never actually lived in this house, although he did own it, and the collection of Michelangelo memorabilia, put together by his great-nephew, is a little contrived. However, among the reproductions, attributions and scenes from the life of the master, are two early works, a bas-relief, *Madonna della Scala*, modestly breastfeeding at the foot of a flight of stairs, and an unfinished *Battle of the Centaurs*, an energetic tangle of writhing limbs.

Museo Casa di Dante

Via Santa Margherita 1 (21 94 16). **Open** *summer* 9am-6pm Wed-Mon; *winter* 10am-4pm Wed-Mon. **Admission** L5,000.
An utter rip off. The house where Dante is thought to have been born in 1265 is now full of facsimiles of archive material. Treasures include a photocopy of a document in which Dante's great-great-grandfather promised to cut down a fig tree; a photograph of a field where Dante may have fought at the Battle of Campaldino in 1289; and copies of the *Divine Comedy* in Greek and German.

Modern arts & ancient crafts

Museo Alinari

Via della Vigna Nuova 16 (21 89 75). **Open** 10am-7.30pm Sun-Thur; 10am-11pm Fri, Sat. **Admission** L10,000.
The Alinari brothers began taking photographs in the 1840s, and in 1852 founded the world's first photography firm. Most of their business came from supplying postcards, prints and art books to foreigners on the Grand Tour. The museum, on the ground floor of the Palazzo Rucellai (*see chapter* **Florence by Area**) mounts exhibitions throughout the

year from the Alinari archives, and occasionally hosts exhibitions of other major photographers' work.

Museo Ferragamo

Via Tornabuoni 2 (33 60 456). **Open** 9am-1pm, 2-6pm, Mon, Wed, Fri, by appointment only. **Admission** free.
The small museum above Ferragamo's shop in the Palazzo Spini Ferroni is excellent. Not only for the opportunity to drool over the most beautiful shoes in the world, but also for the insight it gives into the links between fashion and society during the first half of the century. Ferragamo was born in a small village outside Naples in 1898. After serving his apprenticeship, he opened his first shop at the age of 14, emigrated to the USA at 16, and was soon designing shoes for the movies. Commissions for anything from Roman sandals to shoes for Cecil B deMille's *Cleopatra*, gave him a unique opportunity to experiment (look out for shoes with pyramid heels and prow-shaped toes). In 1927, Ferragamo moved to Florence, the only place he knew where there were enough craftsmen available for him to put together a factory that could produce hand-made shoes *en masse*. Momentarily set back by bankruptcy in 1933, he had sufficiently recovered by 1938 to buy the Palazzo Spini Ferroni. Sanctions against Italy during the war forced Ferragamo to improvise and resulted in some of his most innovative creations: on display in the museum are shoes made of gold and silver thread covered with cellophane sweet wrappings, and shoes made of fish skin, raffia, and synthetic leather. Most significant, perhaps, was the invention of a wedge heel made of Sardinian cork because there was no steel to make stilettos. After the war, Ferragamo invented the invisible sandal (kept on the feet with transparent threads) in the same year that Dior launched the New Look, and continued to make fantastic footwear for the rich and famous (like Audrey Hepburn, the Duchess of Windsor and Lauren Bacall) until his death in 1960.

Museo Marino Marini

Piazza San Pancrazio (21 94 32). **Open** *summer* 10am-5pm Wed, Fri, Sat; 10am-11pm Mon, Thur; *winter* 10am-5pm Mon, Wed-Sat; 10am-1pm Sun. **Admission** L8,000.
Housed in the stylishly converted former church of San Pancrazio, this museum is devoted to the work of Marino Marini (1901-80). A household name in Italy, Marini's sculptures deserve to be far more widely known. Many of them are variations on the theme of horse and rider, powerfully emotional works inhabiting a world where abstract becomes figurative, or figurative verges on the abstract. There is also a good book shop.

Opificio delle Pietre Dure

Via degli Alfani 78 (21 01 02). **Open** 9am-2pm Mon-Sat. **Admission** L4,000.
Founded in 1588 by Grand Duke Ferdinando I, the name literally means the workshop of hard stones. *Pietra dura* is the craft of inlaying gems or semi-precious stones in intricate mosaics to be used as table tops, wall panels, etc. Nowadays most of the work undertaken is restoration, but some of the finest pieces are exhibited in a small museum. There are landscapes where the natural gradations of colour in the stones are used to convey light and shadow, and bowls of fruit with uncannily realistic semi-translucent muscat grapes and blush-peaches. On a mezzanine are samples of stones, tools and designs.

The brothers Alinari.

Eating & Drinking in Florence

Restaurants

How not to get ripped off for your nosh.

Centuries as a tourist destination have done nothing for the standard of Florence's restaurants. And why should it be otherwise? The restaurateurs know they have an eternally self-renewing captive market. One suspects they know as well that most tourists are so dewy-eyed about being in 'Idderly', and so convinced that it is impossible to eat badly in the country, that all a restaurateur need do for success is find a central location, hang some hams, salamis and strings of garlic from the beams, stuff some dusty old Chianti bottles on the shelves, and find a few exuberant good-looking waiters. In these surroundings, most tourists won't even notice that the wine is crap, the *crostini* soggy and the pasta sauce made from nothing more than tinned tomatoes.

So, are you likely to have more luck if you avoid the rustic tourist traps and head instead to a local tratt, neon-strip-lit, with a Pirelli calendar on the wall, plaster Madonna on the bar, and lots of old men in flat caps stubbing fags out in their tripe? Maybe. Sometimes. But, well, more often than not, the wine is just as crap, and the *crostini* just as soggy.

There are, of course, some superb places. The refreshingly unpretentious **Cibreo** for example, is one of the best Italian restaurants in Europe, and there are little gems, like **Casalinga** and **Alla Vecchia Bettola** in the Oltrarno, and **Da Stefano** out in the suburb of Galluzzo. But Florence is sadly not a city where you can pop into a place on spec, and be 90 per cent sure of having a good feed.

L40,000 and under

Alla Vecchia Bettola

Viale Ariosto 32-34r (22 41 58). **Open** 7.30am-3.30pm, 7.30-10.30pm. Tue-Sat. **No credit cards.**
A few blocks south of Santa Maria del Carmine, Alla Vecchia Bettola is popular with locals and foodies. You sit on stools and benches at marble tables, and are given a flask of house red or white – you simply pay for what you drink. The menu changes daily, but regular fixtures include *tagliolini con funghi porcini*, and what is possibly the best *carpaccio* in Tuscany, with thin slices of tender, juicy top-quality raw beef topped with shredded rocket and parmesan. For dessert, plump for *vin santo* and home-made *cantuccini*, or ice cream, which comes from Vivoli (*see chapter* **Cafés and Bars**).

Borgo Antico

Piazza Santo Spirito 6r (21 04 37). **Open** 12.45-2.30pm, 7.45pm-midnight, daily. **Average** L40,000. **Credit** AmEx, DC, EC, MC, V.
This pizzeria-trattoria has become a lively hang out for the young Florentine *beau monde*. Under the same ownership as Osteria Santo Spirito, it has hit on a winning formula; a

Go for the carpaccio: **Alla Vecchia Bettola**.

fixed menu of pizzas, salads and a selection of interesting and well-cooked pasta, meat and fish dishes (most of them substantial enough to constitute a meal in itself), nicely served on oversized ceramic plates. The daily menu presents a pizza of the day as well as a selection of *antipasti, primi* and *secondi* which go with seasonal availability. Fish is often on offer (try the *spaghetti alla vongole,* a steaming pile of pasta tossed with clams, garlic and parsley), or the *antipasto caldo di mare* (a mountainous pile of steamed shellfish and crustaceans). For vegetarians, the mixed grilled vegetables baked in the oven with a melting baby camembert is a good choice, and pizzas are good, with crisp, light bases, and interesting toppings. Don't go here if you object to noise; the music is almost always too loud for decent conversation, and the human noise level rises accordingly. In the summer, however, tables are laid outside where relative peace reigns. Be prepared for a wait - Borgo Antico is very crowded.

La Casalinga

Via del Michelozzo 9r (21 86 24). **Open** noon-2.30pm, 7-9.45pm, Mon-Sat. **Average** L25,000. **Credit** AmEx, DC, EC, MC, V.
One of the best traditional neighbourhood restaurants in the city, run for decades by a family that are now an essential part of the Oltrano neighbourhood: they even feed locals who have hit hard times for free. Inevitably full of regulars, along with a smattering of tourists and ex-pats, it's a vibrant, bustling place, brightly lit with varnished pine walls, tables covered with paper cloths (on which your bill with eventually be calculated), and carafes of wine, ready poured, to ensure swift service. On some nights there is home-made pasta. Not every dish is good – for example the rather bland *penne all'arrabbiata* – but the *ribollita* and *pappa al pomodoro* are excellent, the roast meat good, and the *bollito misto* comes with a deliciously fresh and pungent *salsa verde*. Other good dishes are the *bruschetta al pomodoro* and *fagioli*, Tuscan white beans (especially if you drizzle the sweet, fruity house olive oil over them), and the guinea fowl. *Tiramisù* is home-made and delectable.

Gauguin

Via degli Alfani 24r (23 40 616). **Open** 7pm-11.30pm daily. **Average** L32,000. **Credit** AmEx, EC, MC, V.
Recommended here solely because it is one of Florence's very few vegetarian restaurants. The best of the dishes are the

North African-influenced couscous and mezes, and traditional Italian vegetable dishes, such as a purée of Pugliese *fava* beans. The Gauguin chef on duty when we visited seemed to lack the knack of making genuinely tasty vegetarian versions of dishes tradtionally made with meat, so avoid such dishes as onion soup. Raw ingredients are not always of the best quality, and some of the dishes suffer from lack of attention to detail. The restaurant may have started opening for lunch by the time this guide is published; phone for details

India

Via Gramsci 43A, Fiesole (59 99 00). Bus 7. **Open** 7.30pm-midnight daily. **Average** L40,000. **All major credit cards.**
It may never happen, but if you should tire of pasta and feel the need of a hit of something more spicy, Fiesole could be the place to go. The interior of the restaurant is totally incompatible with its surroundings: rich fabrics draped across the ceiling and walls, a rickshaw straight off the streets of Delhi, brightly coloured tables, wide seats with rush seating and waiters dressed in Indian gear. The tandoori oven is on show behind a glass screen.

Tramvai

Piazza T Tasso 14r (22 51 97). **Open** noon-3pm, 7-10.30pm, Mon-Fri. **Average** L23,000. **Credit** V.
A good place to go if there's a group of you on a tight budget wanting to eat in a tourist-free zone. Tramvai (so-called because the old tram terminus was nearby) is a hectic, animated hostelry popular with students and alternative types. Long and narrow, tables are tightly packed along each wall. Food is so-so: *penne al pomodoro piccante* was rough and ready and needed cooking longer, a chicken casserole was quite pleasant but nothing special. House red is light and fruity.

Osteria dei Benci

Via de' Benci 13r (23 44 923). **Open** 12.45-2.25pm, 7.45-10.45pm, Mon-Sat. **Average** L25,000 (lunch), L40,000 (dinner). **Credit** AmEx, DC, EC, JCB, MC, V.
A small, fairly new restaurant where you dine in pleasant-brick vaulted rooms. The food is delicious, the menu, which changes every month, is inventive, and there is a daily menu

which depends on availability at the market. Winter and summer vary considerably. During warmer months, the emphasis is on light, fresh ingredients; *carpaccio di zucchine con scaglie di parmigiano* is a plate of thinly sliced, raw courgette topped with grainy parmesan and dressed with fruity olive oil. Milky slices of buffalo mozzarella come dressed with olive oil and garnished with finely grated courgettes. *Tagliolini al pesto* (home made, of course), is a deliciously aromatic concoction, as is pasta with fresh tomato, ricotta cheese and *pecorino romano* grated over the top. Autumn and winter dishes are absolutely right for cold days. Don't miss the *crostone di piccione* – hot toast piled with a warm flavoursome pigeon pâté (something like a much reduced pigeon stew). Just as good is the *fettunta con fagioli* – a slice of thick rustic toast piled with hot, perfectly cooked white Tuscan beans and dressed with freshly crushed garlic and fruit olive oil. There are also good soups, stews and grilled meats. Desserts include a fantastically light, towering baked cheesecake.

Osteria Santo Spirito

Piazza Santo Spirito 16r (23 82 383). Bus 11, C. **Open** 12.30-2.30pm, 7.30-11.30pm, daily. **Average** L35,000. **Credit** MC, V.
This recent addition to the Oltrarno eating scene is a refreshing change from the white table cloth trattoria style. Flame red walls contrast with deep blue paint work, lighting is contemporary and original. Downstairs, you have a choice of small tables for two or four, or larger tables such as the big round one in the window; upstairs is a little cramped. Being an osteria, you don't have to eat a full meal here, and there is plenty of choice between snacks and more substantial dishes. The fixed menu features a series of salads and cold dishes (such as *caprino con pomodori secchi* – soft goats' cheese with sun-dried tomatoes). Moving onto the *primi piatti*, a favourite is the *gnocchi di patate gratinati con formaggio morbido e profumo di tartufo*, a bubbling concoction of *gnocchi* doused in truffle-scented melted cheese and browned under the grill, and to follow, you might try the *tagliata con rucola*, tender slices of grilled steak, topped with peppery green rocket. The daily menu reflects the season, and there is often fish on offer. The choice of wines is reasonable with some excellent reds; three or four of each colour are avail-

Cibreo

Via de' Macci 118r (23 41 100). Open 12.50-2.30pm, 7.30-11.15pm Tue-Sat. **Average** L65,000 (restaurant), L40,000 (trattoria). **All major credit cards.**
Cibreo is a legend among the world's foodies, for once justifiably so. The food is a winning combination of traditional Tuscan and creative cuisines, based on the use of prime ingredients; and the owner, Fabio Picchi, understands that when people who really love food come to a restaurant, they want to relax and enjoy it, not feel under pressure to pose. In keeping with this philosophy, Cibreo has two dining rooms: one, a trattoria with marble tables, where no bookings are taken – you just arrive and join the queue; the other, an elegant panelled restaurant in which service is relaxed, friendly and alert, and prices are double.
The restaurant is so popular that you may have to wait for your table, even if you have booked. However, you will be given a complImentary glass of white wine, and every so often, a plate of nibbles. If you are going to have a lengthy wait, you can drink in the Cibreo Caffè opposite, and a member of staff will come and get you when your table is ready.

There are no antipasti at Cibreo, but a generous selection of *amuse-gueules*. These will probably include a triumphant soft, tomato jelly gently spiced with basil and chilli; a ricotta and parmesan soufflé; and a gelatinous, spicy tripe salad. Unusually, there is no pasta on the menu in Cibreo, instead there is a fantastic selection of soups, soufflés and polentas. There is a yellow pepper soup (*passato di peperoni gialli*) with all the sweet, luscious flavours of sun-ripened peppers; *polenta all'erbe*, a wickedly buttery bowl of polenta, deep green and zinging with fresh aromatic herbs; and *pasatelli in brodo*, an intensely flavoured broth, with fat, textured noodles of parmesan and breadcrumbs.
For *secondi*, look out for *inzimino*, a Tuscan dish that sounds horrid, but is utterly delicious, a spicy stew of squid, spinach and chard, served with triangles of toast; or spicy sausages with Tuscan white beans; or fish cooked with a spicy tomato sauce. Desserts are a must, and if you like, you can have half-portions of two. The cheese cake with tangerine marmalade, the flour-less chocolate cake, and the *torta di pere* are such that you will probably remember them on your death bed.

Doing lunch

It's more than likely that you won't want to eat two full restaurant meals a day. Unfortunately, the alternatives most immediately on offer in the centre of Florence mean facing a crowded touristy bar or fast food joint serving cardboard triangles of pizza, tasteless sandwiches, overcooked pasta and wilting salads. Don't despair, there *are* better places in or near the centre where you can get a good, light meal without making big dents in the budget. Many bars now serve more than just sandwiches, sometimes preparing a few dishes in a back kitchen to serve to regular customers. Often, these places do not over-advertise the fact, but keep your eyes open as they can be great value.

Cantinetta da Verrazzano

Via Dei Tavolini 18/20r (26 85 90). **Open** 8am-9pm Mon-Sat. **Average** L15,000. **No credit cards**.
A wine bar belonging to the Castello da Verrazzano, one of Chianti's major vineyards. Wood-panelled, with two rooms – one smoking, the other non – it gets uncomfortably packed at lunchtime; hardly surprising, as both wine and food – primarily pizza and focaccia fresh from the oven – are absolutely top notch. There's no table service: instead, you choose what you want, pay at the bar, and take the receipt to the section selling wine and food. Wine is excellent value for money: L3,000 for a glass of Chianti, L20,000 for a bottle.

Le Volpi e L'Uva

Piazza de' Rossi (23 98 132). **Open** 10am-8pm Mon-Sat. **Average** L20,000. **Credit** AmEx, EC, MC, V.
A fine, five-year old enoteca specialising in the wines of small producers, with ten wines to drink by the glass at any one time. This is a fine place for lunch – sit at the bar and feast on *pate al perigord*, carefully selected cheeses, smoked duck and other goodies accompanied by breads that include wholegrain focaccia and schiacciata.

Il Cantinone del Gallo Nero

Via Santo Spirito 6r (21 88 98). **Open** 12.30-2pm, 7.30-10.30pm, Tue-Sun. **Average** L35,000. **Credit** EC, MC, V.
A huge vaulted cellar in the bowels of the Oltrarno, with long narrow wooden tables and benches and a terracotta-tiled floor. Although hugely popular, it has to be said that portions are small, and prices quite high for food of such

simplicity. As you might expect, the wine list is extensive, with a huge choice of Chiantis. Food is traditional wine bar fare: there is a good selection of *crostoni* and *fettunta* – with various cheeses, *funghi porcini*, *prosciutto* or canellini beans. There is also a limited number of *primi*: *ribollita*, a delicious *zuppa di farro e funghi* (a soup made with spelt and mushrooms), *pappa al pomodoro* and a couple of pasta dishes. Portions are small, and service can be brusque.

Tavola Calda da Rocco

Mercato di Sant'Ambrogio (no phone). **Open** noon-2.30pm Mon-Sat. **Average** L15,000 for a full meal incl wine. **No credit cards**.
A tiny kitchen and a few formica-covered tables and benches right in the middle of Sant' Ambrogio market, Rocco's is a great place for a cheap, no-frills lunch. You will be seated wherever there is space, usually sharing a table, and your fellow-lunchers will be workers from the market. Rocco and his children dole out the grub; the menu is written on a board on the wall, and prices are rock-bottom. Pastas or soup are L6,000 (the hearty *pappa al pomodoro* is particularly good), while for *secondi* try the *polpette* – meat balls, fried or in tomato sauce *alla pizzaiola* – or *spezzatino con le patate*, a rich meat stew with potatoes. House wine, in plastic cups, is rough but ready.

Caffé Ricchi

Piazza Santo Spirito 9r (21 58 64). **Open** *summer* 7am-1am Mon-Thur, 7am-2am, Fri, Sat; *winter* 7am-8pm Mon-Sat. **Average** L20,000. **No credit cards**.
Well known as a gelateria, bar and general hang out, Bar Ricchi is a great place for a light and inexpensive lunch. In the summer, tables are set out in the Piazza under white umbrellas, and in the winter, there is a good-sized room in the back for eating. The menu changes daily, and there is always a selection of pasta and other *primi* (both hot and cold) from L6,000; try the *strozzapreti* (literally 'priest stranglers' – delicate spinach and ricotta balls served with melted butter and parmesan) if they are on offer. *Secondi*, at L8,000 or L12,000 could be *spezzatino con patate* (a hearty stew), roast beef, or stuffed rabbit. Vegetables are excellent; there is a daily *sformato* (a kind of flan without the pastry), from L4,000 and a selection of salads at L8,000. For afters, there is good ice cream.

Fuori Porta

Via Monte alle Croci 10r (23 42 483). **Open** noon-12.30am, Mon-Sat. **Average** L20,000. **Credit** EC, MC, V.
So- called because of its location just outside the old city gate of San Niccolò, the Enoteca Fuori Porta is a popular

able by the glass. In the summer, tables are set outside in the glorious Piazza Santo Spirito.

La Libra

Via Carducci 5 (24 47 94). **Open** 12.30-2.30pm, 8pm-midnight, Mon-Fri; 8pm-midnight Sat; call ahead if you want to dine after 10.30pm. **Average** L30,000. **Credit** EC, MC, V.
Run by a gastronomic association devoted to the produce of the Mediterranean, La Libra is housed in a huge industrial hall up near the Sant'Ambrogio market, made homelier by the addition of a few plants, a grand piano and a TV set. What the place lacks in finesse, it makes up for in the quality and value of the food and wine. Menus change frequently, explor-

ing different regional Italian and Mediterranean cuisines. Antipasti can be a little mundane (an *antipasto misto* was let down by tasteless commercial pitted Spanish olives) so you may prefer to stick with bread (crusty and springy) and ask to sample some of the various olive oils they have in stock. *Primi* are usually delicious: Pugliese *orecchiette* with a thick spicy tomato sauce and crumbled ricotta; *fusilli* with vegetables; or a fennel soup. *Secondi* might include sardines baked with potato and tomato, mixed grilled meats or roast duck.

Sabatino

Borgo San Frediano 39r (28 46 25). **Open** noon-2.30pm, 7.30-10pm, Mon-Fri; closed Aug. **Average** L20,000 incl house wine. **No credit cards**.

Cantina del Verrazzano: *nowhere better for a vinous lunch.*

place in the evenings, especially in the summer when it has tables outside. Foodwise, the speciality of the house are tasty *crostoni*: hunks of Tuscan bread, topped with a vast choice of cheeses, hams and salamis, or vegetables and toasted to melting point under the grill. At lunchtime, there is also a choice of pastas. Particularly good are the *taglierini* with porcini mushrooms. The choice of wines here is superb; there are at least 600 different labels available, and every five days, the choice of those on offer by the glass – eight reds and eight whites – changes.

Trattoria Bordino

Via Stracciatella 9r (21 30 48). **Open** noon-2.30pm Mon-Sat. **Average** L10,000. **Credit** AmEx, DC, EC, MC, V.

This cosy little trattoria is tucked away off a piazza just south of the Ponte Vecchio. In the 16th century, it was an animal stall, but the vaulted ceiling and rough stone walls are now covered in old wood and iron kitchen utensils, baskets, banners and other memorabilia, and there are a few tables outside. Lunch is a real bargain here, and for L10,000 you can eat *primo, secondo* and *contorno*. Dessert and drinks are extra. Every day, there is a choice of four first courses (soup, rice, or pastas of the day), four main courses (maybe roast beef, fried lamb cutlets or a simple

insalata caprese) and a couple of vegetable dishes. This is a high quality restaurant, and although the lunch menu is simpler than that in the evenings, the food is still of a high standard. Not surprisingly, it is very crowded with workers from the surrounding shops and offices, so try to avoid from 1-2pm. Bookings are not accepted for lunch.

Caffè Italiano

Via Condotta 56r (29 10 82). **Open** 12.30-2.45pm, 9.30pm-1am, Mon-Sat. **Average** L20,000. **No credit cards.**

Under the same ownership as the **Alle Murate** (*see above*), this elegant bar, near Piazza Signoria, is a good lunch stop. Downstairs is a dark wood-panelled bar with a few tables for a cafe or *aperitivo*, and upstairs is a pleasant space, where light lunches are served. The menu changes daily and with the season. In the summer, there is a choice of over twenty different salads along with some interesting *primi* and *secondi*. *Carpaccio di pesce spada affumicato* is a plate of delicately smoked swordfish; *sformati di verdura misti* offers a choice of light vegetable flans, and *boccini di pollo alla contadina* are bite-sized pieces of tender chicken in a fresh tomato sauce. With its central location, the Caffè Italiano is very crowded between 1 and 2pm, so try and avoid these times.

Walking into the old-fashioned yellow tiled front room of this modest trattoria in the Oltrarno is like taking a step back in time. It has been in the present owner's hands for more than 40 years, and little has changed. Some of your eating companions will also look as if they have been coming here for forty years. The decor – green and brown paintwork, worn terracotta floors, old-fashioned wooden tables and chairs – has been carefully maintained, the menu and cooking methods – pure *casalinga* – are much as they were, and prices are still extremely modest. Although they serve standard Italian dishes such as pasta with tomato sauce, roast meats and so on, it is worth going for the Florentine specialities here. *Ribollita* and *pappa al pomodoro* (bread-based soups), *pasta e fagioli* (another hearty soup of puréed Tuscan beans and

pasta) or cabbage and rice soup (made with rich meat stock) are all deliciously warming and rustic. For offal-lovers, *trippa alla fiorentina* (tripe in a tomato sauce), *lampredotto* (lamprey), or stewed kidneys are all typically Florentine.

Trattoria del Carmine

Piazza del Carmine 18r (21 86 01). **Open** noon-2.30pm, 7-10.30pm, Mon-Sat. **Average** L30,000 incl house wine. **Credit** AmEx, DC, EC, MC, V.

Piazza del Carmine would be a more peaceful place if it weren't for the car park that now occupies it. However, the few outside tables on offer at this traditional trattoria are still a pleasant place to sit and enjoy a meal. The long menu is very reasonably priced (*antipasti* from L5,000, *primi* from

Il Latini

Via dei Palchetti 6r (21 09 16). **Open** 12.30-
2.30pm, 7.30-10.30pm, Tue-Sun. **Average** L50,000.
Credit AmEx, DC, EC, MC, V.

Latini, a legend in Florence, is one of the few places
where you are equally likely to find a Florentine at
your table as a fellow tourist. Tucked away in a back
street behind Via della Vigna Nuova, there will probably be a huge crowd outside the door clamouring to
get in. They come from far and wide to eat here and
it's difficult to book (you have to do it before 8pm or
after 9.30pm) so the tendency is to show up and hope
to be lucky.

Once inside, Narciso Latini (the head of the family
and well into his eighties), or one of his sons is likely
to be slicing a huge ham or salami for *antipasto*, and
may slosh you out a glass of house wine if you are in
for a wait. The decor is rustic – *prosciuttos* hang from
the ceiling (they apparently get through 3-4 whole ones
on any given day), garish paintings and certificates
cram the walls, tables are long and white-clothed; the
noise level is high. Once seated in one of the four
rooms, things happen fast, and often without a menu.
The *antipasto misto* is standard Tuscan *prosciutto*,
salami, *salsicce di cinghiale* (wild boar salami) and *crostini* with liver pâté. Moving on, the *primi* are possibly
the weakest point on the menu, although the *ribollita*,
pappa al pomodoro, and *zuppa di farro* (three of the
great, traditional rustic Tuscan soups) are all excellent. Meat is the great thing here, and is of high quality. The '*Gran Pezzo*' is a massive and succulent piece
of rib of beef, roasted on the bone in the oven – almost
enough for two. Alternatives are good roast lamb and
rabbit, *salsicce con fagioli*, a hearty Tuscan dish of
country sausage and beans stewed in garlic and tomato, *bistecca alla fiorentina*, and *lombatina di vitella* (veal
steak done over the grill). Vegetables vary according
to season, and are usually reliable. Particularly good
are the *fiori* or *carciofi fritti*; crisp, golden deep-fried
courgette flowers or artichokes. The Latini family are
prolific producers of a fine, sludgy green olive oil, and
of some very good wines. The house red is full-bodied
and very drinkable, but if you want something a bit
special, go for one of the *riservas*. Wash it all down
with their own delicious, dry-ish *vin santo* (to accompany the excellent *biscotti di Prato*) and, if you have
the stamina, ask for the house grappa. A meal here is
definitely an experience, but not a peaceful one, so
don't choose Latini for a romantic '*cena à due*'.

L6,000, *secondi* from L10,000-L18,000, house wine – a
respectable, fruity Montespertoli – at L8,000 a litre), and the
cooking is reliable. *Penne della Casa* are a delicious combination of tomato, baby green peas, mushrooms, with a little
pancetta, and a drop of cream. Depending on the season, you
may find home-made ravioli stuffed with either *porcini*
mushrooms, asparagus or truffles. Pesto, although not a
regional speciality, is home-made and suitably pungent.
Other dishes to go for include rabbit, stewed in a rich tomato sauce (*coniglio alla Maremmana*), tasty roast pork, stuffed
courgettes, *carpaccio* (thinly-sliced raw beef with either artichokes or rocket topped with shavings of fresh parmesan),
or *vitella tonnata* (a classic summer dish consisting of thinly sliced roast veal topped with a delicate tuna mayonnaise),
or a simple mozzarella and tomato salad. *Dolci* are all home
made and, apart from the house wine, there is a good list of
Tuscan labels.

Za Za

Piazza del Mercato Centrale 26r (21 54 11). **Open** noon-
3pm, 7-11pm, Mon-Sat. **Average** L25,000. **Credit** AmEx,
DC, EC, MC, V.

Everyone's idea of what an Italian trattoria should be, with
wine poured from straw-covered flasks, huge jars of preserved vegetables on a marble counter, and an ebullient,
earthy Tuscan mama in the shape of Za Za, overseeing all.
Long popular with both locals and tourists, there are often
queues in the evenings or on Saturday lunchtime. Food is
traditional Tuscan: *crostone* with *funghi porcini* (a thick slice
of toast with ceps), *fettunta con fagioli* (toast with white
Tuscan beans), *ribollita*, *pappa al pomodoro* and, from the
chargrill, chicken, *bistecca* or *salsicce e fagioli* (sausage and
beans). Desserts are home-made: try the delicious *torta di
miele*, *tiramisù* or *vin santo* and *cantucci*.

L40,000-L70,000

Albergaccio Machiavelli

Sant'Andrea in Percussina (82 84 71/82 00 27). **Open**
12.30-1.30pm, 8-11pm, Wed-Sun. **Average** L55,000.
Credit V.

Less than 30 minutes' drive from Florence, this is an old stone
inn in which Machiavelli spent his exile, by day killing time
playing tric-trac and complaining about the local peasants,
and by night writing *The Prince*. You dine in a heftily beamed
room with whitewashed walls and pink tablecloths. Food is
high quality Tuscan; the speciality is meat (especially *bistecca alla fiorentina*, guinea fowl, duck and Tuscan sausages)
grilled or roast over a wood fire. Other courses are great as
well, an *antipasto misto* consists of local *prosciutto*, *finocchiona*, *salame*, and in summer there's a lovely, refreshing *panzanella*; pasta dishes include an unbeatable *tortelloni
all'ortolano* – ricotta filled *tortelloni* with ceps, spring green
vegetables and tomato; and *tortelli di patate mugellese*, a dish
from north of Florence, of potato-filled pasta with a tasty lamb
ragù.

Bibe

Via delle Bagnese 1r (20 49 085). **Open** 12.30-1.45pm, 7.30-
9.45pm, Mon-Sat. **Average** L50,000. **Credit** AmEx, V.

If you have a car, or are prepared to foot a taxi, this restaurant, some 3km from Porta Romana, is well worth the trip.
An old Casa Colonica (farmhouse) in a lovely garden (tables
are set on the flower-filled terrace in summer), it serves creative as well as traditional food, and there is always something interesting on offer. If you can't stand the sight of
another slice of prosciutto, try the *torta di caprino e olive nere*
(dark olive paste sandwiched between creamy goat's cheese)
or oven-baked, garlicky tomatoes. One of the best *primi* is
the cep soup with chick peas, but home-made ravioli with
spinach and ricotta are excellent, as are the *crespelle alla
fiorentina* (delicate crepes filled with the same mixture,
topped with a dollop of bechamel, a little tomato sauce, and

*Things get steamy at **Da Stefano**.*

bean purée. For dessert there is an excellent pear and almond tart. There is a limited lunchtime menu, but you should always find a pasta dish and salad.

Taverna del Bronzino
Via delle Ruote 25r (49 52 20). **Open** 12.15-2.30pm, 7.30-10.30pm, Mon-Sat. **Average** L60,000 incl wine. **Credit** AmEx, DC, EC, MC, V.
The 16th-century palazzo which houses the Bronzino is set in an unremarkable street some ten minutes walk north of San Lorenzo. The interior is classic Tuscan – vaulted ceilings in the three airy rooms and terracotta on the floors. Its reputation is well-earned, and it was a favourite haunt of Sandro Pertini, late ex-president of Italy. The regular menu offers such classics as *bistecca alla fiorentina, risotto* with asparagus, *tortellini* subtly flavoured with truffles, and *ossobuco alla fiorentina.* The daily menu is more adventurous. *Insalata di pesce spada e gamberetti* is a delicate dish of smoked swordfish on a bed of fresh shrimp and raw julienned spring vegetables, simply dressed with fruity olive oil and lemon juice. Of the *primi, risotto* with shrimp, saffron and courgette is creamy and subtle; *pici alla portofino* is a hearty, pungent dish of home made spaghetti tossed in tomato pesto; and *cappelacci* (a kind of ravioli) come in a delicate citron-flavoured sauce.

Over L70,000

Alle Murate
Via Ghibillina 52r (24 06 18). **Open** 7.30pm-midnight Tue-Sun. **Average** L110,000; minimum 55,000 per person. **Credit** AmEx, DC, EC, MC, V.
Highly regarded in Florence, Alle Murate may seem rather too pretentious for London or New York tastes. Like – indeed probably inspired by – Cibreo, there are two dining rooms at Alle Murate, a posh one, with pastel walls and crisp linen napery, and a so-called wine bar, with wooden tables (open in the winter months), where prices are halved. Unfortunately management seem rather reluctant to allow foreigners into the wine bar – so try getting an Italian to book for you. Reception can be a little brusque, and you may have to wait at the bar for some time even if you have booked: though if the waitresses are in a generous mood they may decide you deserve a glass of *prosecco* to pass the time. The menu is divided into three sections: *antipasti,* fish, and meat, but there is also a *menu degustazione* (which is only served if taken by everyone on the table). Food is what is known as creative-traditional, including dishes like lasagne with tomato and buffalo mozzarella, spaghetti with seabass and a velvety *crema di verdura,* served with a swizzle of basil-suffused *caponata.* The fish course might have steamed octopus or squid with mangetout, and the meat course tender, succulent Chianina steak braised in Brunello di Montalcino or duck breast with herbs and orange. Desserts might include a soft, intensely flavoured *torrone di pistacchio* served with an acacia honey sauce or an American-influenced ricotta cheesecake (*torta di formaggio*) drizzled with raspberry coulis. Wines range in price from L30,000 for a 1994 Chianti Classico (by La Massa) to L250,000 for a 1988 Brunello di Montalcino from La Chiesa di Santa Restituta.

Da Stefano
Via Senese 271, Galluzzo (20 49 105). **Open** 7.30-10pm Mon-Sat. **Average** L70,000. **All major credit cards**.
It's well, well worth making the 5-minute drive outside town to Galluzzo, to eat in this excellent fish restaurant. Just starve yourself first. Most people plump for a *degustazione,* at either L70,000 or L90,000, both based on having an *antipasto, primo* and *secondo,* the first with house wine, the second with more elaborate dishes and a more sophisticated wine. It is advisable to put yourself in Stefano's hands, as dishes depend on the catch of the day. Triumphs include *spaghetti alla Stefano,* a steaming platter of perfectly cooked spaghetti, with buttery, chilli-spiked lobster, langoustines and prawns; and the aptly named *gran piatto,* a mountain of perfectly steamed seafood.

browned under the grill). *Secondi* are classic Tuscan: excellent steak or veal steak done over an olive wood grill, roast pigeon or deep-fried chicken (eat your heart out Colonel Sanders) or brains. Deep fried mixed veg – courgettes and their flowers, artichokes, cauliflower – are a melt-in-the-mouth must. Puddings here are a dream. A favourite is the home made ice cream with a honeycomb case. The selection of wines, both Tuscan and otherwise, is good and the house red is well worth trying.

Osteria del Bricco
Via San Niccolò 8r (23 45 037). **Open** 11.30am-3pm, 7pm-10.30pm, Tue-Sun; can eat until 1am if you book first. **Average** L50,000. **Credit** EC, MC, V.
A recently-opened family-run place, with excellent, straightforward food cooked by the owner's mum. Refreshingly unpretentious, it attracts an arty crowd. Twists on traditional food are inspired: crostini are served as a basket of toasted bread, with a variety of toppings in little bowls; and a *sformatina* comes with the slightest pinch of chilli. *Zuppa di porcini* (cep soup) is rich, earthy and pungent, and *penne al fattore* is a delicious combination of mild creamy ricotta and artichoke. *Secondi* are all meat-based.

Pane e Vino
Via San Niccolò 70r (24 76 956). **Open** 12.30-2pm, 7.30pm-midnight, Mon-Sat. **Average** L50,000. **All major credit cards**.
A calm, informal restaurant that started out as a wine bar and enoteca, with amenable staff, good wines and an enticing menu. The day's *degustazione* menu is highly recommended, as the waiters will bring wines to match each course. Highlights include an extraordinary *porcini* mousse, and a smoked duck salad; exceptionally good miniature dumplings of shredded pumpkin, with butter, sage and parmesan; spaghetti with anchovies, breadcrumbs and fennel; and tender young lamb with rosemary-spiked broad

The Menu

GENERAL

Posso vedere il menù? – Can I see the menu?
Mi fa il conto, per favore? – Can I have the bill, please?
Dov'e il bagno? – Where's the loo?
Aceto – vinegar
Al forno – cooked in an oven
Affumicato – smoked
Arrosto – roast
Burro – butter
Fatto in casa – home-made
Focaccia – flat bread made with olive oil
Fritto – fried
Ghiaccio – ice
Griglia – grill
Miele – honey
Nostrali – locally grown/raised
Olio – oil
Pane – bread, usually thick crusted, unsalted Tuscan
Panini – sandwiches
Panna – cream
Pepe – pepper
Ripieno – stuffed
Sale – salt
Salsa – sauce
Senape – mustard
Uovo – egg

ANTIPASTI

Antipasti misto – mixed *antipasti*
Bruschetta – bread toasted and rubbed with garlic, sometimes drizzled with olive oil. Often comes with tomatoes or white tuscan beans.
Crostini – small slices of toasted bread, crostini toscana are inevitably smeared with chicken liver pate.
Crostone – a big crostino
Fettunta – basically another name for bruschetta
Olive – olives
Prosciutto crudo – cured ham – similar to what the British call Parma ham, but saltier

PRIMI

Acquacotta – cabbage soup usually served with a *bruschetta*, sometimes with an egg broken into it
Agnolotti – stuffed pasta, roughly triangular shaped
Brodo – broth
Cacciucco – chilli-spiked fish stew: Livorno's main contribution to Tuscan cuisine
Cecina – flat crispy bread made of chickpea flour
Fettuccine – long, quite narrow ribbons of egg pasta
Frittata – type of substantial omelette
Gnocchi – tiny potato and flour dumplings, served with a sauce
Infarinata – Garfagnana dish of polenta mixed with beans and vegetables
Minestra – soup, usually vegetable
Pappa al Pomodoro – bread and tomato soup
Pappardelle – broad ribbons of egg pasta, usually served with *lepre* (hare)
Panzanella – typical Tuscan bread and tomato salad
Passato – puréed soup
Pasta e fagioli – pasta and beans, a quintessential peasant dish
Ribollita – literally a twice-cooked bean, bread, cabbage and vegetable soup
Taglierini – thin ribbons of pasta

Tordelli/Tortelli – stuffed pasta
Zuppa – soup
Zuppa frantoiana – literally, olive press soup, another bean, bread and cabbage soup, distinguished by being served with the very best young olive oil

FISH & SEAFOOD

Acciughe/Alici – anchovies
Anguilla – eel
Aragosta – lobster
Aringa – herring
Baccalà – salt cod
Bianchetti – little fish, like whitebait
Bonito – small tuna
Branzino – sea bass
Calamari – squid
Cappe sante – scallops
Cefalo – grey mullet
Coda di rospo – monkfish tails
Cozze – mussels
Dorato – gilt head
Fritto misto – mixed fried fish
Gamberetti – shrimps
Gamberi – prawns
Granchio – crab
Insalata di mare – seafood salad
Merluzzo – cod
Nasello – hake
Ostriche – oyster
Pesce – fish
Pesce spada – swordfish
Polpo – octopus
Ricci – sea urchins
Rombo – turbot
San Pietro – John Dory
Sarde – sardines
Scampi – langoustines
Scoglio – shell- and rock-fish
Scombro – mackerel
Seppie – squid or cuttlefish
Sogliola – sole
Stoccafisso – stockfish
Tonno – tuna
Triglia – red mullet
Trota – trout
Trota salmonata – salmon trout
Vongole – clams

MEAT, POULTRY, GAME

Agnellino – young lamb
Agnello – lamb
Anatra – duck
Animelle – sweetbreads
Arrosto misto – mixed roast meats
Beccacce – woodcock
Bistecca – beef steak
Bresaola – raw, dried pork, served in thin slices
Caccia – general term for game
Carpaccio – raw beef, served in thin slices
Capretto – kid
Cervo – venison
Cinghiale – wild boar
Coniglio – rabbit
Cotoletta/Costoletta – chop
Fagiano – pheasant
Fegato – liver

Filetto – fillet
Lepre – hare
Maiale – pork
Manzo – beef
Ocio – goose
Ossobuco – veal shank stew
Pancetta – like bacon
Piccione – pigeon
Pollo – chicken
Porchetta – roast pork
Rognone – kidney
Ruspante – free range
Salsicce – sausage
Tacchino – turkey
Trippa – tripe
Trippa alla fiorentina – tripe stewed with mint and tomato
Vitello – veal

HERBS, PULSES & VEGETABLES

Aglio – garlic
Asparagi – asparagus
Basilico – basil
Bietola – Swiss chard
Capperi – capers
Carciofi – artichokes
Cardi – cardoon
Carote – carrots
Castagne – chestnuts
Cavolfiore – cauliflower
Cavolo nero – a dark variety of cabbage
Ceci – chick peas
Cetriolo – cucumber
Cipolla – onion
Dragoncello – tarragon
Erbe – herbs
Fagioli – Tuscan white beans
Fagiolini – green string or French beans
Farro – spelt (a hard wheat), a popular soup ingredient around Lucca and the Garfagnana
Fave or **Baccelli** – broad beans
Finocchio – fennel
Fiori di zucca – courgette flowers
Funghi – mushrooms
Funghi porcini – ceps
Funghi selvatici – wild mushrooms
Lattuga – lettuce
Lenticchie – lentils
Mandorle – almonds
Melanzane – aubergine
Menta – mint
Patate – potatoes
Peperoncino – chilli pepper
Peperoni – peppers
Pinoli – pine nuts
Pinzimonio – selection of raw vegetables to be dipped in olive oil
Piselli – peas
Pomodoro – tomato
Porri – leeks
Prezzemolo – parsley
Radice – radish
Ramerino/Rosmarino – rosemary
Rapa – turnip
Rucola or **Rughetta** – rocket
Salvia – sage
Sedano – celery
Spinaci – spinach
Tartufo – truffles
Tartufato – cut thin like a truffle
Zucchini – courgette

FRUIT

Albicocche – apricots
Ananas – pineapple
Arance – oranges
Banane – bananas
Ciliege – cherries
Cocomero – watermelon
Datteri – dates
Fichi – figs
Fragole – strawberries
Lamponi – raspberries
Limone – lemon
Macedonia di frutta – fruit salad
Mele – apples
Melone – melon
More – blackberries
Pera – pear
Pesca – peach
Pompelmo – grapefruit
Uva – grapes

DESSERTS & CHEESE

Amaretti – macaroons
Brutti e buoni – literally, 'ugly and beautiful'; knobbly biscuits made of hazelnuts and egg white
Cantuccini – hard almond biscuits, to be dunked in Vin Santo
Castagnaccio – chestnut flour cake, made around Lucca
Cavallucci – spiced biscuits from Siena
Gelato – ice-cream
Granita – flavoured ice
Mandorlata – almond brittle
Necci – chestnut flour pancakes, served with ricotta and preserves
Ossi di Morto – literally, 'bones of the dead'; brittle biscuits with almond and egg white from Elba
Panforte – heavy cake of dried fruit
Pecorino – sheep's milk cheese
Ricciarelli – almond biscuits from Siena
Tiramisù – sponge, mascarpone, coffee and chocolate
Torrone – nougat
Torta – tart, cake
Vin Santo – raisiny dessert wine
Zabaglione – hot whipped egg and Marsala
Zuppa Inglese – trifle

DRINKS

Acqua – water, either *gassata* (fizzy) or *senza gas* (still)
Birra – beer
Bottiglia – bottle
Caffè – coffee
Cioccolata – hot chocolate
Latte – milk
Succo di frutta – fruit juice
Tè – tea
Vino rosso/bianco/rosato – red/white/rosé wine

Cafés & Bars

From early morning cappuccino to early hours nightcap, Florence has a café or bar to fit the bill.

Ever wondered why Italians are so manic and volatile? The national addiction to caffeine could be the answer – and Florence provides a huge variety of venues where its citizens can get their fix. There are any number of fairly generic coffee bars, usually reasonably cheap, which also sell alcohol and decent food. It is here you'll find Florentines downing espressos while standing at the bar – far too busy to sit down but not so busy that they can't shoot the breeze with each other. Alternatives include *pasticcerias*, which sell freshly made biscuits, cakes and other delicacies to nibble on. *Fiaschiatterias* specialise in wines and food, but will always serve the obligatory espresso. Depending on their licences, some cafés sell fresh milk products (*latterie*), cigarettes (*tabacchi*) and groceries (*drogherie*). Many will also provide a full, 3-course lunch menu.

Antico Noe

Volta di San Piero 6r (23 40 838). **Open** 11am-8pm Mon-Sat.
A squeeze of a wine bar, lurking within a seedy old arcade full of falafel shops, winos and junkies, which nevertheless pulls in Florentines from all walks of life thanks to the high quality and low prices of its food and wine. Inside, it's standing room only at the bar – though there is a restaurant behind – which serves a selection of local wines (from L2,000 a glass) and huge sandwiches (from L3,000), made to order. The salamis are great – especially the fennel-seed spiked Tuscan *finocchiona* – but there are lots of veggie options as well, including sun-dried tomatoes, spinach and cheeses.

La Badia

Via Del Proconsolo, corner of Piazza San Firenze (29 43 96). **Open** *summer* 7.30am-midnight daily; *winter* 7.30am-8pm daily.
A small, rather touristy café with a well stocked bar plus pizzas, sandwiches and a limited ice-cream selection. There's no seating inside the café although, as usual, you can take your drinks standing and pay at least half of the table price. The modern, clean interior doesn't provide much space to relax, so most people sit outside facing the Bargello. Prices are high – L8,000 for a small ice-cream, L5,000 for a cappuccino – particularly when you have to put up with constant traffic hurtling by.

Bar La Ribotta

Borgo degli Albizi 80/82r (23 45 668). **Open** 9am-1am Mon-Sat.
This is a very friendly, busy café, with plenty of tables. The sandwiches are delicious – try goat's cheese with aubergine. There's also hot food and salads at lunch-time. Seats are tucked away in alcoves so, despite the bustle, you can have a fairly peaceful lunch. The staff are lively and efficient and there is always info here about local clubs, music and theatre events. Discounts for students with student cards.

Bar S. Firenze

Piazza San Firenze 1r (21 14 26). **Open** 7am-8pm Mon-Sat.
This bar is located within a 15th-century Renaissance palace built by Giuliano da Sangallo and stands opposite the elaborate Civil Court building. Inside, there's ample seating and the very high ceilings create a cool tranquil space. The vast range of culinary delights on offer includes chocolates, ice-creams, pizzas and 3-course meals. You can also buy *cantuccini* (almond biscuits for dipping in vin santo) and the Sicilian speciality of marzipan fruits. Prices are reasonable, although you'll pay double to sit outside in the sun. Cocktails start at around L6,000.

Bar Tiratoio

Piazza dei Nerli 1 (21 35 78). **Open** 6.30am-8pm Mon; 6.30am-midnight Tue-Sun.
Tiratoio is a stylish bar on the Santo Spirito side of the river. Staff are congenial and efficient and, as Tiratoio is not particularly central, the prices are cheap. They serve a selection of scrumptious *dolce* including an amazing lemon mousse cake, and savouries such as courgette pizza drizzled with olive oil. The bar has a large selection of liqueurs, aperitifs, coffees and cold drinks. The hot chocolate with cream is so rich and thick you have to eat it with a spoon.

Buffet Boomba

Via de' Neri 2r (21 68 87). **Open** 9am-9pm Mon-Sat.
This *fiaschetteria* serves a good choice of Italian wines and excellent home-made hot and cold grub. *Melanzane sott'olio* and *carciofi polpette* (aubergine in olive oil and artichoke heart rissoles) are specialities. Chianti, served in enormous glasses, is the drink to go for here, at just L2,000 a glass. The decor is rustic and welcoming. This is a favourite lunch-time stop for trendy Florentines and businessmen. It is not a huge café but there is adequate seating.

Caffè Amerini

Via Della Vigna Nuova 63r (28 49 41). **Open** 8.30am-8.30pm Mon-Sat.
An elegant but cosy place in which to breakfast, lunch or take an aperitif. With agreeable modernist art covering pastel blue walls, mosaics, comfy seats and an abundance of mirrors you could find yourself forgetting the sights and holing up here all day, watching brusque locals mingle with ladies who shop. Sandwiches and cakes are all around L6,000, alcoholic and non-alcoholic beverages cost from L2-10,000.

Caffè Cibreo

Via A del Verrocchio 5r (23 45 853). **Open** 8am-1am Tue-Sat; lunch served 1-2.30pm.
This pleasant café was founded in 1989 as the third outpost of Cibreo, to complement the restaurant and trattoria on the street (*see chapter* **Restaurants**). Also round the corner from the Sant'Ambrogio produce market, it's a peaceful, non-touristy place much frequented by chefs, restaurant reviewers and others in the food trade. The decor is simple yet striking: dark, coffered wood ceilings, Liberty-style light fixtures, and tables tucked intimately into the corners. The café also benefits from the Cibreo kitchen, which turns out some phenomenal desserts; notably a cheesecake served with mandarin sauce and a dense, too-good-to-be-true chocolate torte. There is also a full bar. Outside seating in the summer.

Early hours

Florence goes to bed early. Few bars or restaurants are open long after midnight, and night owls have to search hard for signs of life in the early hours. Some bars open again around 3-3.30am.

Nicotine fix

Fortunately for nicotine addicts a few bars have recently set up cigarette machines outside their premises (and they actually work – never something to be taken for granted in Italy). Three within the centre are in:

Piazza degli Ottaviani 23r.
Piazza G Salvemini.
Corner of Via Verdi & Borgo dei Greci.

Midnight munchies

Unfortunately there aren't any food automats yet, so if you're hungry after the curfew, it's going to be pretty hard to find something to eat.

Almost no restaurants serve food after midnight, but there are some exceptions (although they tend to be pricey):

Capocaccia *Lungarno Corsini 12/14r.*
Serves dinner and elaborate sandwiches until 1.15am (1.30am Sat). Pleasant ambience, but expensive.

La Torre *Piazza G Poggi 20..*
It's possible to get dinner and salads here long after 1am. Not as funky **Capocaccia** but with the same scary prices. Better known as a bar than a restaurant.

There are a few other places, but they're far from the centre, and you will need a car to reach them. The most well known is a pizzeria:

Il Bivio *Corner of Via Pistoiese and Via Baracca.*
This place looks like a trashy soft-core movie set, and the owners are conspicuously unfriendly, but it's always open, produces a decent pizza for a decent price, and also sells cigarettes.

Early breakfast & after-hours

A popular ritual for clubbers is the early morning *colazioni* (breakfast). Crowds of Italians, ears still buzzing from the latest techno anthem, meet in front of some *panificio* or *pasticceria* for *cornetti* before moving on to the newest and hottest after- hours venue.

Florentines like their sleep, so by necessity these after-hours joints have to be low key, and their locations are not widely known.

Via Campo d'Arrigo 14r.
Located behind Campo di Marte rail station, this is Florence's most famous after-hours venue. It has no official signs, but you can't miss the crowd outside. Opening hours are not fixed, but start early, around 2am. While waiting in line you might get some free tips about parties and night clubs.

Canto del Rivolto.
A lesser known place. They must have had some problems with protesting neighbours – your pasta and *cornetto* comes in a bag with *'Fate Silenzio'* (keep silent) written on it (not bad as an unusual souvenir). It opens after 3am.

Late-night drinking

Finally, there are the late-night bars – but not many of them.

Bar Mercato Ortofrutticolo *Viale Gudoni 46, Novoli.*
Florence's most famous late-night drinking den, in the western suburb of Novoli, is open every day (except Saturday) until 2.30-3am. On Saturdays, you can drink at the **Gran Bar** on the opposite side of the street.

Booth bars are also *tabacchi* and have a small news stand. Expect a motley, and occasionally unsavoury, clientele.

Bar Latteria *Viale Petrarca 39r.*
Roughly the same opening hours as **Bar Mercato Ortofrutticolo**, but nearer to the centre, right behind Porta Romana. It doesn't sell cigarettes.

TRATTORIA-PIZZERIA
BALDOVINO

REAL NEAPOLITAN PIZZA
FROM THE WOOD OVEN

FRESH SEAFOOD
& GOURMET SALADS

CHAR-GRILLED TUSCAN
"CHIANINA" BEEF

MODERN ITALIAN COOKING

A FINE SELECTION OF ITALIAN WINES

**VIA S. GIUSEPPE 22R (PIAZZA S. CROCE)
FIRENZE - TEL. (055) 241773**

Caffè Concerto Paszkowski

Piazza della Repubblica 31-35r (21 02 36). **Open** 8am-1am Tue-Sun.

Caffè Concerto Paszkowski was founded in 1846 as a beer hall, and during the second half of the 19th century it was a meeting point for artists, performers and writers. Its name commemorates the live nightly concerts given here during the summer months; alas, now it is simply another over-priced café on the Piazza della Repubblica. Less popular than both **Caffè Gilli** and **Le Giubbe Rosse** (*see above* and *below*), you will at least always find an empty seat, and there are still regular concerts here. The café was declared a national monument in 1991. Outside seating during the summer.

Caffè Curtatone

Via Borgognissanti 167r (21 07 72). **Open** 7am-1am Wed-Mon.

A vast, stylish café serving a decadent selection of pastries, cakes and savouries. You can take a full 3-course meal here from 12.30-2.30pm or sip on a selection of liqueurs and aperitifs. The faux-Gothic frescoes may not be to your taste, but the local business people and stylish Florentines don't seem to mind. Always busy, but service is efficient.

Caffè Gilli

Piazza della Repubblica 36-39r (21 38 96). **Open** 8am-midnight Wed-Mon.

Caffè Gilli's history dates back to 1733, when a *pasticceria* of the same name was founded on Via degli Speziale, near Via dei Calzaiuoli. It moved to its present site in 1910. The Belle Epoque interior and furnishings are original, and the café continues to attract Florentines as well as tourists. Not to be missed are Caffè Gilli's five flavours of hot chocolate – cacao, gianduia, almond, orange and coffee – served in ceramic pitchers; they are so thick and rich that they are best slurped down with a spoon. The spread of free aperitifs at lunchtime and early evening are among the best in town. In addition, the waiters at Caffè Gilli are among the most cordial in Florence. Outside seating in warm weather.

Futurism & Florentine Café Society

Café society didn't take off in Florence until the beginning of the 20th century, relatively late in comparison with other European cities. Prior to this time, the only café of note was Caffè Michelangelo in Via Cavour, which was an artists' and intellectuals' haven between 1848 and 1866 (*see chapter* **History: Florence During the Risorgimento**).

Although most cafés of the time, especially those on Piazza della Repubblica, had artistic, literary and social connections (for example, Caffè Giocosa was a favourite with aristocrats and **Caffè Concerto Paszkowski**, *see above*, was a haunt of musicicans), **Le Giubbe Rosse** (*see above*) was by far the best known. Founded as a German beer hall in 1897, it got its name from the red jackets the waiters wore. Futurist leaders such as Marinetti, Papini and Montale treated Le Giubbe Rosse as their own intellectual enclave, actually launching the movement from there in 1909, with the publication of the Futurist Manifesto. From their cosy café the Futurists planned a brave, violent and agressive new world: "We intend to sing the love of danger... We intend to exalt the agressive movement, feverish insomnia, the mortal leap... We affirm that the world's magnificence is enriched by a new beauty: the beauty of speed... The only thing more beautiful than speed is struggle. We intend to glorify war – the only 'hygiene' in the world – militarism, patriotism, the destructive actions of the libertarians, the great ideas for which one dies." It is no surprise that the Futurists and Mussolini were deeply impressed by each other – with many members of the movement fighting for Mussolini.

Caffè Italiano

Via della Condotta 56r (29 10 82). **Open** 8am-8pm, 9.30pm-1am, Mon-Sat; lunch served 1-3pm.

Caffè Italiano is one of Florence's hidden secrets – centrally located, but tranquil and still to be overrun by tourists. The café is spread over two levels, with the lower reserved for bar and stand-up service and the upper for those wishing to dally awhile. Dark wood tables, red velvet seats and a soundtrack of classical or jazz music create a classy atmosphere. Regularly changing photography and art exhibitions hang from the walls, and there's a wide selection of international newspapers to browse. Downstairs is frequently a venue for cultural presentations and gatherings. Coffee and desserts are some of the best in town – though the service can be quite poor at times. The caffè-choc is a must – espresso laced with pure bitter chocolate powder – or go for their *acqua antica*. Both drinks come with a complimentary plate of delicious homemade *biscotti*; depending on the day they may be butter, walnut, cinnamon, chocolate or orange-flavoured. In addition there are more trad desserts; the *torta di mela* is particularly good, and the *torta di cioccolato amaro* is as good as any in Florence. No outside seating.

Caffèllatte

Via degli Alfani 39r (24 78 878). **Open** 8am-1am Mon-Sat.

Caffèllatte was originally licensed in 1920 as a shop to sell "coffee and milk beverages"; prior to that it was home to a butcher's shop (look for the bas-relief cow visible on the large marble counter). The café's primary function was as a neighbourhood milk supplier, a task which it continues to perform today. In 1984, an organic bakery was added, and the current Caffèllatte was born. The café consists of one tiny room kitted out with a few rustic wooden tables and chairs. Jazz music is usually playing, and there are rotating photography exhibits and plenty of magazines and papers to peruse. In line with its name, Caffèllatte's *caffè lattes* (L3,500) are the city's best; served piping hot in giant coffee bowls. The bakery offers a wide variety of tarts, breads and cookies, and there is always a macrobiotic selection. Highly recommended are the chocolate-banana bread and the apple tart served with honey and cream. No outside seating.

Caffè Megara

Via della Spada 15-17r (21 18 37). **Open** 7am-1am Mon-Sat; lunch served 1-2.30pm.

Caffè Megara is situated on one of Florence's trendiest shopping streets, yet feels strangely dislocated from its setting. You can lose yourself among the mounds of international newspapers and magazines that are there to dip in to, and enjoy the impeccably friendly service. The café attracts a large (primarily Italian) lunch crowd, who flock for such specialities as *farfalle con pomodori, melanzane e noci* (butterfly pasta with a sauce of tomatoes, aubergines and walnuts) for L5,500. They also serve substantial breakfasts and a mean

Philadelphia cheesecake. Definitely a worthwhile stop for a taste of New York in Italy. No outside seating.

Caffè Nuovo Poste

Via Verdi 73r (24 80 424). **Open** *Sept-June* 7am-1am Mon-Sat; *July, Aug* 7am-1am daily.

A newly refurbished café, with spooky blue strip lighting, popular with local students and arty types. Huge patio windows open out onto the street, and there is a seating area outside – unfortunately on a busy road. Prices are average: L2,500 for a cappuccino and L3,000 for a hot pizza slice or sandwich.

Caffè Piansa

Borgo Pinti 18r, near Piazza Salvemini (23 42 362). **Open** 7am-1am Mon-Sat; lunch served noon-2.30pm.

Unobtrusively located on a quiet street, this café is a favourite with students, local business types and only the occasional wandering tourist. Wooden tables line the walls, and seating is rarely a problem outside of the lunch period. The café operates on a self-service basis, which means that the service is quicker and the prices more reasonable (espresso L1,400, cappuccino L1,800, pastries L2-4,000, sandwiches L3-5,000, pasta L5,500) than in waiter-service cafés. In addition, there's a full bar, and you can take away packets of Piansa's own famous coffee beans. No outside seating.

Caffè Rivoire

Piazza della Signoria 5r (21 44 12). **Open** 8am-midnight Tue-Sun.

Caffè Rivoire was founded in 1872 as a Fabbrica di Cioccolata a Vapore (literally, 'steamed chocolate factory') and is still famous for its chocolate concoctions. It also has the most picturesque location in town – directly across from the Palazzo Vecchio, with a commanding view of Piazza della Signoria. Aside from chocolate, the Rivoire's food and drink are much like those found anywhere else – though the *gelato* is better than most. Outside seating year-round.

I Fratellini

Via dei Cimatori 38r (23 96 096). **Open** 8am-8.30pm Mon-Sat.

A real hole in the wall, serving tasty sandwiches and wines from the best vineyards in Italy. On the outside wall are shelves for you to rest your wine glass on as you stand in the street and enjoy your grub. Look out for wild boar salami, artichokes in olive oil and a delicious selection of cheeses – feta, pecorino, gorgonzola – and truffle and asparagus sauces. If your legs are up to it, this is definitely an experience worth seeking out.

Le Giubbe Rosse

Piazza della Repubblica 13-14r (21 22 80). **Open** 7.30am-3am daily. **No credit cards.**

This famous café dates from the end of the 19th century and was in its heyday between 1910 and 1920. Always popular with the *literati* and the international set, it nevertheless declined after World War II, and the trend was only arrested when new management took over in 1991 and breathed life back into the place. The café's food and drink are fairly standard (and expensive); the reasons to come here are more historic and social than gastronomic. Outside seating in the summer.

Gran Caffè San Marco
Piazza San Marco 11r (21 58 33). **Open** 6am-midnight daily.
This mammoth establishment is equipped with a gelateria, a self-service restaurant, a pizza slice and sandwich bar and a sophisticated café. Decor is tacky pink with plastic chandeliers dripping from high ceilings. There are tables outside which sprawl out onto the busy, noisy piazza, although strategically placed bushes offer a little cocooning from the chaos. However, the central garden hidden within the café offers a prettier and much quieter space to relax in. The daytime clientele are mainly business people and well-dressed locals who sip on spumanti and nibble on the delicious tapas which are always on the bar. Table service at least doubles the prices. The cocktail list includes the delicious Papaya Sunrise from Barbados, and the fruit ice-cream and liqueur concoctions (called *I mangiabevi*) are a real treat – but, at L16,000, expensive. The self-service restaurant and *pizza a taglia* are considerably better value, if less glamorous. A warning: behind the supposedly classy appearance of Gran Caffè lurks one of the filthiest toilets in Florence.

Hemingway
Piazza Piattellina 9r (28 47 81). **Open** 4pm-1am Tue-Thur; 4pm-2am Fri, Sat.
The owners of this stunningly beautiful café seem to be under the misapprehension that Ernest Hemingway was English, to judge by the anglo-centric decor. Walls are painted in duck-egg blue with cabinets full of Twinings tea, wicker chairs and giant black and white prints of Ernie. The menu is extensive with an amazing selection of teas (including Fortnum & Mason's, of course, daaaahling), at least 20 different types of coffee and stunning tea cocktails – the Victorian Tea (vanilla tea, Southern Comfort and milk) must not be missed. The bar's main attraction (for chocoholics, at least) is that the owner is a member of the Chocolate Appreciation Society, so the choccies here are to die for. There's also a special section of the menu which explains which wines go best with which chocolates. Prices are fair considering the quality, ranging from L1,400 for a coffee to L10,000 for a cocktail and L6,000 for a tea. The hand-made chocolates go for around L14,000 for 100g. They also serve a cream tea which includes ten different nibbles.

Massimo Bar
Via Dei Benci 49r (24 19 04). **Open** 8am-9pm Mon-Wed, Sun; 8am-1.30am Fri, Sat.
This café near Santa Croce is part of the huge 'Jolly Café' chain. Most are anything but jolly, but this is an exception. Cheap cappuccino, sandwiches and pizza slices are all served up by a rosy-faced waitress and the atmosphere is relaxed and friendly. There isn't much seating space, so don't go with a wedding party, but if there are no more than five of you, this café is an ideal place to nibble on a *pannini* and study your guide book.

Pitti Caffè
Piazza Pitti 35r (23 96 241). **Open** 9.30am-late daily.
Opposite the Pitti Palace and a stone's throw from the Boboli Gardens, this is a good place to pause for a coffee while in the Oltrarno. There are lots of tables, and a high, vaulted ceiling that keeps the place cool in summer. Prices are as high as you would expect in a café opposite a major tourist site, and food is not as good as it should be. Expect to pay around L10,000 for a sandwich and L5-10,000 for drinks.

Ruggini Pasticceria
Via de' Neri 76r (21 45 21). **Open** 7.30am-8pm Tue-Sat; 7.30am-1.30pm Sun.
This much-loved *pasticceria* is packed with glass display boxes, fridges and shelves crammed with exquisite selections of gastronomic delights – delicious hand-made chocolates, pastries, ice-creams, gateaux and cakes. The kiwi bavarese, a delicate mousse cake (L1,500), is well worth adding to your love handles for. At the far end of the shop there's a curved coffee bar (no seating).

Vecchio Casentino
Via Dei Neri 17r (21 74 11). **Open** 11.30am-3pm, 6pm-midnight Tue-Sun.
A tranquil wine shop with plenty of seats where you can feast on toasted sanwiches and pasta dishes. Dark and quiet, the café is kitted out with large wooden benches and decorated with copper pots and pans, 1930s' pictures and bottles and bottles of wine. You have to order your food at the bar, but it is brought to your table when it is ready. If you don't specify which wine you want you'll end up with cheap plonk. *Pannini* cost L3-6,000 and pasta is L6-L10,000.

Vivoli
Via Isole delle Stinche 7r (29 23 34). **Open** 8am-1am Tue-Sun.
The best ice-cream in town, in fact, virtually the only gelateria worth bothering with. Flavours change with the season – they do magnficent *noce* (walnut) and *marrone* (chestnut) in late autumn. Either take away, or eat for no extra charge at the high tables at the back.

Consumer's Florence

Where do you find out what's happening in London?

RED ROUTE
No stopping
Mon-Sat
8am-7pm

http://www.timeout.co.uk

Time Out

Your weekly guide to the most exciting city in the world

Shopping

Forget the Renaissance for a while and start indulging in some serious retail therapy.

Forget Michelangelo and Botticelli. One of the reasons Florence is such a popular holiday destination is that wealthy Japanese and American tourists just *lurve* shopping in the city. So some mornings the queue outside Gucci is as long as the Uffizi's. Unfortunately, the presence of vast droves of moneyed, middle-aged M-O-R foreigners combined with the natural conservatism and snobbishness of the Florentines means that most of the stuff on sale is deeply conventional. Consequently, Florence is not really a place to shop for clothes: there's no street or club fashion to speak of, and even the big name designers tend to be represented by their most conservative creations. If you do want to clothes-shop, the main areas are Via Tornabuoni (*see box*), Via della Vigna Vecchia, the Corso, Via Roma and Via de' Calzaiuoli.

On the plus side, Florence has a strong tradition of artisans. Leather goods and hand-made hand-marbled paper are its great specialities, and although some of what you see is mass-produced, there are still genuine craftsmen and women at work in the city, many of them in the Oltrarno.

Unless the lire is particularly weak, prices are quite high, although the two major sales periods in January/March and July/August make a drastic difference. Keep your official receipt (*scontrino*) as non-EC visitors are entitled to a VAT rebate on purchases of personal goods over L300,000 if exported unused and bought from a shop displaying the 'Europe Tax Free' sticker. The shop will give you a form to show to customs when leaving Italy.

Though many large upmarket stores now stay open throughout the day, most shops still operate similar hours (*see chapter* **Essential Information**), closing at lunchtime and (food shops excepted) Monday mornings. Food stores usually close on Wednesday afternoons, except in the summer (usually interpreted in Florence as being from the middle of June to the end of August) when they close on Saturday afternoons. Indeed virtually all shops in the city close on Saturday afternoons in the summer, though they stay open later during the rest of the week to compensate. The times listed below are those stated to us at time of writing

Patti, *an eclectic Florentine treasure trove. See page 133.*

as being each shop's opening hours for the greater part of the year. However, note that times here are often unreliable, and shops – particularly the small ones that are individually owned and run – may well open or close at other times.

Department stores

COIN
Via de' Calzaiuoli 56r (28 05 31). **Open** 9.30am-8pm Mon-Sat; 11am-8pm Sun. **Credit** AmEx, DC, EC, MC, V.
Fairly middle-of-the-road department store: the sort of place Florentines come for sets of bed linen, sensible clothes, pairs of socks or bargain make-up. This may not be high fashion, but it is not frumpy either.

Rinascente
Piazza della Repubblica 1 (23 98 544).
Open 9am-9pm Mon-Sat; 10.30am-8pm Sun.
Credit AmEx, DC, EC, MC, V.
Opened in 1996, Rinascente is more upmarket than Coin with a perfume and cosmetics department on the first floor and clothes, both men's and women's, on the upper floor, plus kitchenware and bedding.

Standa
Via Pietrapiana 42/440 (24 08 09). Bus B. **Open** 7.30am-8pm Tue-Sat; 2-8pm Mon. **Credit** AmEx, DC, EC, MC, V.
Scruffy supermarket worth visiting only if you want cheap toiletries or basic foods.
Branch: *Via Panzani 31r (23 98 963)*. **Open** 2-8pm Mon; 9am-8pm Tue-Sat. There is no food at his branch but plenty of clothes, toiletries and hardware.

Art, style, antiques

Arredamenti Castorina
Via di Santo Spirito 13/15r (21 28 85). Bus 6, 31, 32.
Open 9am-1pm, 3.30-6.30pm, Mon-Fri; 9am-1pm Sat.
No credit cards.
Founded in 1895, and still partially housed in an art nouveau shop, Castorina stocks all you need to transform your council flat into a mock Baroque boudoir: carved and

Via Tornabuoni

Most of the city's international designer shops are strung along Via Tornabuoni and Via Vigna Nuova. Addresses are as follows:

Ferragamo *Via Tornabuoni 16r (29 21 23)*. **Open** 3.30-7.30pm Mon; 9.30am-7.30pm, Tue-Sat. **Credit** AmEx, DC, EC, JCB, MC, V.
Fantastic shoes from the company founded by Salvatore Ferragamo in the 1920s. Nowadays they also design clothes and accessories, but it's the shoes that are worth splashing out on.

Louis Vuitton *Via Tornabuoni 24-26r (21 43 44)*.
Open 3-7.30pm Mon; 9.30am-7.30pm, Tue-Sat.
Credit AmEx, DC, EC, JCB, MC, V.
Purveyors of the genuine brown orange-peel bags, luggage and accessories, most of it indistinguishable from the fakes sold on nearby Via Calzaiuoli.

Trussardi *Via Tornabuoni 36r (21 99 02)*.
Open 3-7pm Mon; 10am-7pm, Tue-Sat. **Credit** AmEx, DC, EC, JCB, MC, V.
Classic leather jackets, tweed trousers, men's and women's overcoats, and leather bags. Italians would think the style very English, while to English eyes the look is *molto italiano*.

Bulgari *Via Tornabuoni 61-63r (23 96 786)*.
Open 3-7.30pm Mon; 10am-1pm, 3-7.30pm, Tue-Sat.
Credit AmEx, DC, EC, JCB, MC, V.
Astronomically priced, often rather vulgar jewellery.
Scarves and perfume as well.

Gucci *Via Tornabuoni 73r (26 40 11)*. **Open** 3-7pm Mon; 9.30am-7pm Tue-Sat. **Credit** AmEx, DC, EC, JCB, MC, V.
Queues of middle-aged Japanese form every morning at the doors of the huge Gucci – most of the clothes seem aimed at them; few of the catwalk triumphs are to be seen here. Shoes of course, too.

Enrico Coveri *Via Tornabuoni 81r (21 12 63)*.
Open 3.30am-7.30pm Mon; 10am-1pm, 3.30-7.30pm Tue-Sat. **Credit** AmEx, DC, EC, JCB, MC, V.

Tuscan designer from nearby Prato, who creates loud, brash clothes: last season sequinned tweed dominated.

Armani *Via Vigna Nuova 51r (21 90 41)*.
Open 3.30-7.30pm Mon; 10am-7.30pm Tue-Sat.
Credit AmEx, DC, EC, JCB, MC, V.
All the usual Armani favourites.

Pucci *Via Vigna Nuova 97r (29 40 28)*. **Open** 3.30-7.30pm Mon; 9am-1pm, 3.30-7.30pm, Tue-Sat. **Credit** AmEx, DC, EC, JCB, MC, V.
Psychedelic printed shirts and leggings – first designed in the 1950s by aristocrat Emilio Pucci.

Emporio Armani *Piazza Strozzi 14-16r (28 43 15)*.
Open 3.30-7.30pm Mon; 10am-2pm, 3.30-7.30pm, Tue-Sat. **Credit** AmEx, DC, EC, JCB, MC, V.
Armani's diffusion line. Some of the clothes are very poorly made, so check the seams before you splash out.

gilded balustrades, columns, capitals, mouldings, frames, cherubs and candelabra, along with intarsio veneers, trompe l'oeil tables and fake malachite and tortoiseshell obelisks.

Arte della Scagliola
Via di Santo Spirito 11 (23 96 150/fax 0574 60 93 76). **Open** 12.30-6.30pm Mon-Sat. **No credit cards.**
Mohammed Al-Fayed and the queen of Saudi Arabia have both bought from this tiny shop tucked into the gateway of a palazzo. The craftsmen here make table tops, either inlaid with *pietra dura* or made to look as if they are inlaid with *pietra dura*. The latter technique is known as *scagliola*, and involves using pulverised marble, gesso and tints, rather than pieces of gems and marble. A s a guide, a *scagliola* table top takes 40 days to make, a *pietra dura* table several months. Consequently, expect to pay L10,000,000 for a *scagliola* table and ten times that for a *pietra dura* piece.

Kashi
Via Cesare Battisti 7r (28 43 99). Bus 6, 31, 32. **Open** 10am-1pm, 4-8pm, Tue-Sat; 4-8pm Mon. **No credit cards.**
Nepalese masks; bronzes and terracottas from Bhutan, Nepal and Tibet; shamanistic objects; and Tibetan tantric temple hangings (*thangkas*).

Patti
Borgo degli Albizi 64r (234610). **Open** 4-7.30pm Mon; 10am-1pm, 4-7.30pm, Tue-Sat. **Credit** AmEx, DC, EC, MC, V.
Restrained contemporary African textiles, antique Russian textiles, Japanese lacquer bowls, Japanese rice bowls (which Italians like to use for cappuccino), Japanese teapots, along with other stylish items such as ricepaper books, glassware, jewellery, mosaics and ceramics.

Sakura
Via del Melarancio 4r (26 40 45). **Open** 4-7.30pm Mon; 9am-7.30pm Tue-Sun; closed Sun in winter. **Credit** AmEx, DC, EC, MC, V.
Shop specialising in tasteful Japanese goods – rice bowls, tea sets, lacquer bowls, brushes, calligraphy pens, cotton kimonos and hand-made paper. However, there's also some very run-of-the-mill tourist fodder too.

Siddhartha
Via Cesare Battisti 5r (no phone). **Open** 4-8pm Mon; 10am-1pm, 4-8pm, Tue-Sat. **No credit cards.**
Hippy trail textiles, bags, tarot cards and jewellery.

Le Stanze
Borgo Ognissanti 54r (28 89 21). Bus 12, C. **Open** 10am-7.30pm Tue-Sat. **Credit** AmEx, DC, EC, MC, V.
Stylish design emporium. Covetable objects include cerulean-glazed clay pots squeezed into weird and wonderful shapes, elegantly lipped carafes, cubic candles and canvas magazine racks.

Studio X
Piazza N Sauro 16r (21 99 48). **Open** 4-8pm Mon; 10.30am-1pm, 4-8pm, Tue-Sat. **Credit** AmEx, DC, EC, MC, V.
Contemporary Italian ceramics, jewellery and textiles (mostly scarves and sarongs) along with a selection of furniture that can range from a 1950s barber's chair or 1940s wooden kitchen cabinet (complete with built-in coffee grinder) to 17th-century rustic tables.

Zona
Via di Santo Spirito 11 (23 02 272). Bus 11. **Open** 3.30-7.30pm Mon; 9.30am-1.30pm, 3.30-7.30pm, Tue-Sat. **Credit** AmEx, DC, EC, JCB, MC, V.
A hideously expensive shop packed with covetable goodies. Imports from the US and Mexico with an emphasis on nat-

ural materials. Carefully chosen crafts from closer to home include textiles, glassware, furniture, wrought iron and pewterware, hand-made books, children's toys and clothes.

Books

After Dark
Via de' Ginori 47r (29 42 03). **Open** 10am-2pm, 3-7pm, Mon-Sat. **Credit** AmEx, DC, EC, MC, V.
English language bookstore with Florence's best selection of magazines (including *Time Out*, *Dazed & Confused*, *i-D* and *Vogue*). Good selection of novels set in Italy, along with reasonable psychology, philosophy, new age and gender sections.

Alinari
Via della Vigna Nuova 148r (21 89 75). **Open** 10am-7.30pm daily. **Credit** AmEx, DC, V.
The Alinari brothers' photographic firm, established in 1852, was the world's first. The bookshop in the Palazzo Rucellai, which now houses the Alinari museum (*see chapter* **Museums & Galleries**) is well worth a visit for its photography books, exhibition catalogues and the opportunity to order prints of virtually anything in the Alinari archives.

BM
Borgo Ognissanti 4r (tel/fax 29 45 75). **Open** 9am-1pm, 3.30-7.30pm, Mon-Sat. **Credit** AmEx, DC, EC, MC, V.
A cosy English-language bookshop with a good selection of guidebooks, novels set in Italy, Italian literature in translation, art books and cookery books.

CIMA Libreria Caffeteria
Borgo degli Albizi 37r (24 77 245). Bus 14, 23. **Open** 9.30am-7.30pm Mon-Sat, last Sun of the month; 9.30am-7.30pm, 9.30pm-1am, Tue, Thu, Sat. **Credit** A, AmEx, V.

The **Paperback Exchange**. *See p135.*

Florence's first internet café-cum-bookshop. The book selection is strong on art, music, alternative medicine and alternative philosophy. The café serves light snacks and cakes. Rates on the internet are L10,000 for one hour, L28,500 for three hours and L45,000 for five hours.

Feltrinelli
Via Cerretani 30r (23 82 652). **Open** 9am-7.30pm Mon-Sat. **Credit** AmEx, DC, EC, MC, V.
Branch of Italy's foremost chain of bookshops, owned by radical publishing company Feltrinelli. Modern, well organised, and with a good selection of art, photography and Italian comic books, along with a range of cool T-shirts, postcards and posters.

Feltrinelli Internazionale
Via Cavour 12-20r (21 95 24). **Open** 9am-7.30pm Mon-Sat. **Credit** AmEx, DC, EC, MC, V.
A fashionable, cosmopolitan bookstore with a good range of books, magazines and vids in English and other languages. *http://www.vol.it/icone*

Geographica
Via dei Cimatori 16r (23 96 637). **Open** 10am-1pm, 4-7.30pm, Mon-Sat. **No credit cards**.
The city's best source of maps, including large-scale walking maps and military maps. There are also a few guidebooks in English.

Libreria del Cinema "Crawford"
Via Guelfa 14r (21 64 16). Bus 6, 11. **Open** 9.30-1.30pm, 3.30-7.30pm, Mon-Sat. **Credit** V.
The first cinema bookshop in Florence – it opened mid 1996 – stocks videos, soundtracks, postcards, posters and English and Italian books about cinema.

Libreria delle Donne
Via Fiesolana 2b (24 03 84). Bus B. **Open** 3.30-7.30pm Mon; 9am-1pm, 3.30-7.30pm, Tue-Sat. **Credit** EC, MC, V.
Florence's women's bookshop, with a supply of feminist literature mostly in Italian. There is also a useful notice board, for those wishing to key in to the lesbian and feminist scenes in the city.

Thread Zone: affordable clothes-shopping in Florence

Most people in Italy would be horrified by the prospect of wearing another person's cast-offs, but not everyone wants or, more to the point, can afford to be clothed from head to foot by Valentino or Armani. Market stalls are usually the best source of cheap and second-hand clothes – woollen sweaters, leather jackets, silk scarves, T-shirts, skirts and shoes are the items you will come across most often. Quality is highly variable. The main market is at **San Lorenzo** (*Open 9am-7.30pm daily; closed Sun, Mon in winter*), but the smaller **Mercato del Porcellino** (Mercato Nuovo) and the stalls along Via dei Neri are also good bets (*same hours as above*).

The best places for affordable clothes are around Borgo San Lorenzo, Via della Vigna Nuova and Corso Italia, with the former offering probably the most funky styles. Particularly recommended for women are **Ritratto Donna**, Borgo San Lorenzo 26r (*No phone. Open 3.30-7.30pm Mon; 9am-1.30pm; 3.30-7.30pm Tue-Sat*), and **Diva**, Borgo San Lorenzo 5r (*21 50 61. Same hours as above*), while for men there's **Desii**, Borgo San Lorenzo 4-6r (*21 12 22/29 23 21. Open 3.30-7.30pm Mon; 9.30am-7.30pm Tue-Sat*). Casual unisex clothing is available at **14 Onze**, Borgo San Lorenzo 9r (*No phone. Open 3.30-7.30pm Mon; 9.30am-7.30pm Tue-Sat*).

Most Via della Vigna Nuova shops are high fashion-dedicated but a couple offer a little more originality and affordability – **Il Triangolo**, Via dell Vigna Nuova 58r (*No phone. Open 10am-7.30pm Mon-Sat*) and **Alex**, Via della Vigna Nuova 17r (*21 49 52. Open 3.30-7pm Mon; 10am-7pm Tue-Sat*), which sells a good selection of clothes by lesser known designers.

Taking a stroll down the Corso or Via dei Neri is also likely to turn up some clothing bargains. **The End** chain of stores, Corso 39r (*21 59 48. Open 3.30-7.30pm Mon; 10am-7.30pm Tue-Sat*), and **Solomoda**, Via dei Neri 51r (*No phone. Same hours as above*) are good places to start.

There are only a couple of shops that sell second-hand clothes: **C Mazzanti** at Borgo degli Albizi 48r (*23 40 537. Open 3.30-7.30pm Mon; 10.30am-1.30pm, 3.30-7.30pm, Tue-Sat*) offers a little bit of everything, including Levis and some rather fetching antiquey items; and an unnamed shop at Borgo Pinti 37r (*No phone. Open 4-6.30pm Mon; 10am-1pm, 4-6.30pm, Tue-Sat*) stocks a good range of '70s and other funky retrowear.

One final recommendation for women is **Echo**, behind the Duomo at Via Dell'Oriuolo 31r (*No phone. Open 3.30am-1pm, 3.30-7.30pm, Mon-Sat*), with its excellent range of striking sweaters, skirts and evening wear, made-to-order or off-the-rack at startlingly low prices – one of Florence's hidden clothing gems. And, as a last resort perhaps, there's always the Italian clothing superstores **La Rinascente** (on Piazza della Repubblica), **Coin** (on Via dei Calzaiuoli) or one of the numerous **Benetton** outfits in town (*see listings*).

Paperback Exchange
Via Fiesolana 31r (24 78 154/fax 24 78 856/
papex@dada.it). **Open** 9am-1pm, 3.30-7.30pm, Tue-Sat;
also open Mon mid-Mar to mid-Nov. **Credit** AmEx, DC,
EC, MC, V.
Used paperback fiction, and an imaginative selection of new
English novels and non-fiction, particularly art, art history,
literature and Italian culture. Founded in 1979, it has long
been a point of reference for anglophones in Florence, and
has a very useful notice board.

Seeber
Via Tornabuoni 70r (21 56 97). **Open** 9.30am-7.30pm
Mon-Sat. **Credit** AmEx, DC, EC, MC, V.
A good selection of Italian and foreign language books –
travel, food, art, fiction.

Setticlavio
*Piazza San Marco 10r (28 70 17). Bus to Piazza San
Marco.* **Open** 3.30-7.30pm Mon; 9am-1pm, 3.30-7.30pm,
Tue-Sat. **Credit** EC, MC, V.
A well stocked shop with over 30,000 titles available.

Il Viaggio
Borgo degli Albizi 41r (24 04 89). Bus 14, 23.
Open 3.30-7.30pm Mon; 9.30-1pm, 3.30-7.30pm, Tue-Sat;
summer also open 2.30-6pm last Sun of the month, closed
Sat afternoon. **Credit** AmEX, MC, V.
Lots of English guides to Italy and elsewhere, and a good
selection of walking maps, and English and Italian
travel literature.

Ceramics

Sbigoli Terrecotte
Via San Egidio 4r (24 79 713). Bus B. **Open** 3.30-7.30pm
Mon; 9am-1pm, 3.30-7.30pm, Tue-Sat. **Credit** AmEx, DC,
EC, MC, V.
Traditional and contemporary Tuscan ceramics and terra-
cotta. Everything is hand-made, some of it on the premises.

Il Tegame
Piazza Salvemini 7 (24 80 568). Bus B. **Open** 3.30-
7.30pm Mon; 9.30am-1pm, 3.30-7.30pm, Tue-Sat.
Credit AmEx, MC, V.
Ceramics, glassware and wood in a nicely cluttered shop.

Clothes

There are very little interesting, affordable clothes
to be found in Florence, which is why the small
designer shops and market stalls of London and
New York are always full of innovative-fashion-
hungry Italians. If you go to the city wearing
unusual clothes, don't be surprised to be stopped
in the street – you may even get an offer to buy the
clothes off your back. *See also boxes* **Via
Tornabuoni** *and* **Thread Zone**.

Echo
Via Oriuolo 37 (23 81 149). **Open** 3.30-7.30pm Mon;
9.30am-1pm, 3.30-7.30pm,Tue-Sat. **Credit** DC, EC, MC, V.
Seventies-style long knitted and crocheted droopy dresses,
diaphanous scarves and chiffon over-dresses. All in subtle
smoky colours (*see also box* **Thread Zone**).

Stroll
Via Romana 78r (22 91 44). Bus B, C to Via Romana.
Open 4-8pm Mon; 10.30am-1pm, 4-8pm, Tue-Sat.
Credit EC, MC, V.

An Aladdin's Cave stuffed full of designer end-of-lines. You
may be lucky enough to root out Max Mara, Byblos, Gigli,
Kookai, Maska and much more at reasonable prices.

Food & wine

As you might expect, there is no shortage of places
to stock up on Tuscan produce. Just be sure to
bring an extra suitcase.

General

Alessandro Nannini
Borgo San Lorenzo 7r (21 26 80). **Open** 8am-8pm Tue-
Sun. **Credit** AmEx, DC, EC, MC, V.
Owned by a former Formula One racing driver, who bought
a coffee factory in the Val di Pesa. As well as a coffee shop
(*see chapter* **Cafés & Bars**) you can buy its own blends of
coffee, bags of Nannini *cantuccini*, and ex-pat treats like
Twining's teas and Scottish shortbread.

Bottega della Frutta
Via della Spada 58r (23 98 590). **Open** 7.30am-7.30pm
Mon, Tue, Thur-Sat; 7.30am-1.30pm Wed.
No credit cards.
Fabulous fruit and veg shop, with carefully sourced produce
from all over Italy.

La Dolciaria
Via de' Ginori 24r (21 46 46). **Open** 9am-1pm, 4-7.30pm,
Mon-Sat. **Credit** DC, EC, MC, V.
Foods to quash ex-pat homesickness. Tiptree jams,
Twining's and Taylor's teas, Gold Blend, Quality Street and
Jacobs' Cream Crackers. Lots of sweet Italian goodies as well.

Procacci
Via Tornabuoni 64r (21 26 56). **Open** 8am-1pm, 4.30-
7.45pm, Mon, Tue, Thur-Sat; 8am-1pm Wed. **No credit
cards**.
The place to buy truffles. They are brought in every morning at around 10am during the white truffle season (mid
October to December). Also a quaint stand-up bar where genteel old ladies and gents stop by for a glass of prosecco and
a delicate sandwich smeared with a special truffle paté.

I Sapori del Chianti
Via de' Servi 10 (23 82 071). **Open** 9.30am-7.30pm
daily. **Credit** AmEx, DC, EC, V.
Food and drink from Chianti. Lots of wines, grappas in fancy
bottles, olive oils, *cantuccini, cavallucci* and *ossi di morto* biscuits, salami from the Falorni shop in Greve, and jars of
pestos, posh condiments and vegetables preserved in extra
virgin olive oil.

Stenio del Panta
Via Sant'Antonino 49r (21 68 89). **Open** 7am-1pm,
5-7.30pm, Tue-Sat. **No credit cards**
Founded early this century, Stenio is a deli close to the central market that is famous for its preserved fish (salt cod,
which soaks in a large stone sink, high quality canned tuna,
herring, Spanish sardines, and marinated anchovies). They
also sell hams, salamis and cheeses, along with olives, salted capers and artichokes in oil. Ask them to construct a sandwich (of country bread, focaccia or schiacciata) around the
fillings of your choice.

Sugar Blues
*Via dei Serragli 57r (26 83 78). Bus 11, 36, 37. Via
XXVII Aprile 46/48r (48 36 66). Bus to Piazza San
Marco.* **Open** 9am-1.30pm, 4-7.30pm, Mon-Sat.
No credit cards.
Pricey organically grown vegetables, grains, pulses, breads
and cakes plus natural cosmetics and beauty products.

*Meaty treats and cheese to please at **Stenio del Panta**. See p135.*

Bakeries

La Bottega del Arte Bianca
Borgo San Jacopo 13r (28 21 40). **Open** 8am-8pm Mon-Sat. **No credit cards**.
Upmarket modern bakery well-positioned for buying food for a Boboli Gardens picnic. There are dozens of varieties of bread, and savoury nibbles like miniature pizzas and vol au vents. Also brownies and muffins made by the American Gladys Glover bakery.

Il Fornaio
Via Guicciardini 6r (21 98 54)/Via Faenza 39r (21 53 14). **Open** 7.30am-7.30pm Mon, Tue, Thur-Sat. *Via Palmieri 24r (24 80 336).* **Open** 7.30am-2pm, 4.30-7.30pm Mon, Tue, Thur-Sat; 7.30am-2pm Wed. **No credit cards**.
Among the best selection of breads in town – Arab bread, multigrain loaves, polenta bread, olive bread, a wide selection of pizza and focaccias (by the slice) sandwiches, biscuits and cakes.

Forno Top
Via della Spada 23r (21 24 61). **Open** 7.30am-1pm, 5-7.30pm, Mon, Tue, Thur-Sat; 7.30am-1pm Wed. **No credit cards**.
Excellent bakery: try the takeaway pizza, the *schiacciata*, and the *castagnaccio* (a crisp cake made of chestnut flour and pine nuts).

Ethnic

Asia Masaia
Piazza Santa Maria Novella 22r (28 18 00). **Open** 9.30am-1.30pm, 3.30-8pm, daily. **Credit** V.
Florence's best source of foods from Asia, with all you need to cook an Indian or Thai meal. The stock ranges from mango chutney to Thai fish sauce, dried squid and prawns. They also sell woks, saki, Singha beer, henna and incense.

Vivimarket
Via del Melarancio 17r (29 49 11). **Open** 9am-1pm, 3.30-7.30pm, Mon-Sat. **Credit** V.
Not only Chinese foods, but Japanese, Mexican and North African specialities as well. Somewhere to come to satisfy those ex-pat urges for tortilla chips and jalapeños, miso soup or tofu.

Pasta

Bianchi
Via dell'Albero 1r (28 22 46). **Open** 9am-1pm, 4.30-7.30pm, Mon, Tue, Thur-Sat; 9am-1pm Wed. **No credit cards**.
Melting ravioli stuffed with spinach, ricotta and a hint of nutmeg, and potato gnocchi are among the delights on offer in this modest shop.

La Bolognese
Via de' Serragli 24 (28 23 18). Bus 11, 36, 37. **Open** 7am-1pm, 4.30-7.30pm, Mon, Tue, Thur-Sat; 7am-1pm Wed. **No credit cards**.
The fabulous fresh pasta here includes *ravioli di zucca gialla* (with pumpkin), plus versions stuffed with potato, porcini or truffles (in season), as well as torellini with smoked salmon, gnocchi and black squid ink pasta.

Pasticcerias

Most pasticcerias incorporate a bar, so are good for breakfast and snacks, but all cakes, biscuits and savouries can also be taken away (say "*per portare via*" if you want to take it away).

Cennini
Borgo San Jacopo 51r (29 49 30). **Open** 7.30am-7.30pm Tue-Sun. **No credit cards**.
A good place for a morning coffee and brioche. Small, homely, and they don't charge you to sit down. A good selection

of pastries and cakes to take away: at Easter, the homemade *colomba* (a sweet, yeasty, dove-shaped cake with candied fruit) is excellent, as is the *panettone* at Christmas.

Dolci e Dolcezze
Piazza Beccaria 8r (23 45 458). Bus 31, 32, B. **Open** 8.30am-8.30pm Mon-Sat; 8.30am-1pm, 4-8.30pm, Sun. **No credit cards.**
Probably Florence's finest pasticceria, best known for the delectable flourless chocolate cake.
Branch: *Via del Corso 41r (28 25 78).* **Open** 9.30am-7.30pm Tue-Sun.

Fabiani
Via Gelsomino 39r (23 20 017). Bus 36, 37. **Open** 6am-9pm Tue-Sun. **No credit cards.**
Strategically placed on the road out of Florence to Siena, this pasticceria has a fabulous selection of melt-in-the-mouth, buttery pastries with which to start your day as you head off for a day trip. On your way back, try the *bomboloni caldi* (hot doughnuts filled with either chocolate cream, crème patissière or jam, freshly made at around 4pm), and check yourself into the nearest cardiac clinic.

Robiglio
Via dei Servi 112r (21 45 01). **Open** 7.30am-7.30pm Mon-Sat. *Via Tosinghi 11r (21 50 13).* **Open** 8am-7.30pm Mon-Sat. **No credit cards.**
An old fashioned pasticceria with superb pastries. Try their *cioccolato caldo*, hot chocolate thick enough to stand a spoon upright in it.

Rosticcerias

These are a wonderful invention. Basically take-away joints, they offer anything you could possibly need for a ready cooked full meal, from crostini to pasta to roast meats (spit-roasted chickens are a favourite), vegetables and desserts. There's even a basic selection of wines.

Rosticceria Alisio
Via de' Serragli 75r (22 51 92). **Open** 7am-2pm, 5-9pm, Tue-Sun. **No credit cards.**
Free home delivery within central Florence.

Rosticceria Le Due Strade
Via Senese 161/163 (20 47 594). Bus 36, 37. **Open** 9am-2pm, 5-7pm, Tue-Sun. **No credit cards.**
Useful as a stop-off on your way into or out of town.

Rosticceria Giuliano
Via de' Neri 174r (23 82 723). Bus 23. **Open** 8am-3pm, 5-9pm, Tue-Sat; 8am-3pm Sun. **No credit cards.**
Relatively central place between Piazza della Signoria and Santa Croce, selling a huge selection of roasted meats and other savoury goodies.

Wine

Antico Noè
Volta di San Pietro 6r (23 40 838). Bus B. **Open** 11am-8.30pm Mon-Sat. **No credit cards.**
Tiny enoteca and drinking place squeezed under the seedy arch of San Pietro, with its winos, junkies and falafal shops. Predictable range of Tuscan reds at fairly good prices. There is an inexpensive trattoria next door (*open lunch & dinner Mon-Sat*).

Enoteca Murgia
Via dei Banchi 55/57r (21 56 86). **Open** 3.30-7.30pm Mon; 9am-1pm, 3.30-7.30pm, Tue-Sat. **Credit** AmEx, V.
Long established enoteca with a fine selection of olive oils,

limoncellos and grappas as well as wines. Service is extremely courteous, and you will be guided towards the best wines and oils for your money.

Le Volpi e L'Uva
Piazza de' Rossi 1 (23 98 132). **Open** 10am-8pm Mon-Sat. **Credit** AmEx, DC, EC, V.
Modern, forward-looking enoteca that is strong on new producers. It also has staff that take great pleasure in recommending a wine that is *just* what you want. There's always the chance to try ten or so wines by the glass at the little bar.

Household goods

Bartolini
Via de' Servi 30r (21 18 95). **Open** 9am-1pm, 3.30-7.30pm, Tue-Sat. **Credit** A, V.
Huge kitchenware shop. Everything from Alessi and Le Creuset to woks and mincers.

Giraffa
Via Ginori 20r (28 36 52). **Open** 9am-1pm, 3.30-7.30pm, Tue-Sat; 3.30-7.30pm Mon. **Credit** AmEx, DC, EC, MC, V.
Good square of presents for the home – brightly coloured ruched silk lamps, Italian and Moroccan ceramics, candles, candelabra and heavy glazed earthenware.

La Ménagère
Via Ginori 4r-8r (21 38 75). **Open** 3.30-7.30pm Mon; 9am-1pm, 3.30-7.30pm, Tue-Sat. **Credit** AmEx, EC, MC, V.
Kitchen shop whose stock ranges from a huge selection of Starck's designs for Alessi to ceramic roasting dishes in the form of a gaudy duck.

Open House
Via Barbadori 40r (21 20 94). **Open** 10am-1pm, 2.30-7.30pm, Tue-Sat. **Credit** AmEx, EC, MC, V.
A dream of a kitchen/household shop for anyone interested in contemporary design. It stocks Italian and northern European ceramics, glassware, aluminium goods and ingenious gadgetry... at a price.

Jewellery

Altri Mondi
Via degli Alfani 92r (no phone). Bus to Piazza San Marco. **Open** 3.30-7.30pm Mon; 9.30am-1.30pm, 3.30-7.30pm, Tue-Sat. **Credit** A, V.
Indian and their own contemporary designs in silver and semi-precious stones.

Il Gatto Bianco
Borgo SS Apostoli 12 (28 29 89). **Open** 3.30-7.30pm Mon; 9.30am-1pm, 3.30-7.30pm, Tue-Sat. **Credit** AmEx, DC, EC, MC, V.
Interesting and original contemporary designs are crafted in the shop using silver, gold, and other metals, precious and semi-precious stones. Prices start from L80,000.

Mercerie Ginori
Via Ginori 34r (28 72 37). **Open** 3.30-7.30pm Mon; 10am-7.30pm Tue-Sat. **No credit cards.**
Vibrant glass and mock tortoiseshell jewellery, along with some antique pieces.

Mercerie Samba
Via Santa Elisabetta 10r (21 51 93). **Open** 3.30-7.30pm Mon; 9am-12.30pm, 3.30-7.30pm, Tue-Sat. **No credit cards.**

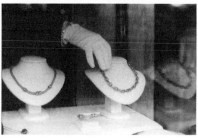

Jewel-snatcher?

Buttons, buttons and more buttons, in every colour, shape and size you could possibly imagine.

Messico e Nuvole

Via Palmieri 27r (24 26 77). Bus B. **Open** 3.30-7.30pm Mon; 9.30am-1pm, 3.30-7.30pm, Tue-Sat. **Credit** EC, MC, V.
The Italo-Mexican couple who run this shop have stocked it with a wonderful selection of ethnic goodies, specialising in colourful Mexican and Native American jewellery, ceramics, mosaics, ornamental pipes and tribal headdresses.

Parsifal

Via della Spada 28r (28 86 10). **Open** 10am-2pm, 3.30-7.30pm, Mon-Sat. **Credit** AmEx, DC, EC, MC, V.
Striking contemporary jewellery – including some wacky cut-outs – in silver plate and aluminium. Also some more classical designs.

Particolari

Via de' Cerchi 13r (21 53 41). **Open** 3-7.30pm Mon; 9.30am-1.30pm, 3-7.30pm, Tue-Sat. **Credit** AmEx, DC, EC, MC, V.
Perennially popular shop known for its intricate earring designs in gilded bronze, gold and silver plate. From around L25,000.

Pepita Studio

Borgo degli Albizi 23r (24 45 38). Bus B. **Open** 4-7.45pm Mon; 10am-1pm, 4-7.45pm, Tue-Sun. **Credit** AmEx, MC, V (for purchases over L30,000 only).
Amusing plexiglass, wood and glass jewellery, all designed by Pepita.

Seven Stars

Borgo degli Albizi 45r (23 40 556). Bus B. **Open** 3.30-7.30pm Mon; 10am-7.30pm Tue-Sat. **Credit** AmEx, DC, EC, MC, V.
Conventional, and some innovative contemporary designs, mostly in silver. Most pieces are Italian. From L40,000.
Branch: *Via Cavour 27r (28 75 25). Bus 11, 17.* **Open** 3.30-7.30pm Mon; 9.30am-1pm, 3.30-7.30pm, Tue-Sat.

Leather & shoes

Antica Cuoieria

Via del Corso 48r (23 81 653). **Open** 3.30-8pm Mon; 9.30am-7.30pm Tue-Sat. **Credit** AmEx, DC, EC, MC, V.
Classic brogues, boots and loafers for men and women, some of them hand-made.

"Birkenstock"

Via della Vigna Nuova 87r (23 96 560). Bus C. **Open** 3.30-7.30pm Mon; 9am-1pm, 3.30-7.30pm, Tue-Sat. **Credit** AmEx, DC, MC, V.

Not its official name: this is actually a nameless orthopoedic shoemakers that happens to be one of the few places in Florence to sell Birkenstock shoes, sandals and inner soles.

Bisonte

Via del Parione 31r (21 57 22). Bus C. **Open** 3-7.30pm Mon; 9.30am-7pm Tue-Sat. **Credit** AmEx, DC, EC, JCB, MC, V.
Now an internationally famous name, prices are sky high for the beautifully made chunky bags, briefcases, wallets, etc, but they are made to last.

Brovelli

Borgo San Frediano 11r (21 38 40). Bus 6, C. **Open** 3.30-7.30pm Mon; 9am-1pm, 3.30-7.30pm, Tue-Sat. **Credit** AmEx, DC, EC, MC, V.
Pleasant little shop in a funky part of Oltrarno. Luggage for sale and bag repairs.

Eusebio

Via del Corso 5r (29 29 17). **Open** 3-8pm Mon; 10am-1pm, 3-8pm, Tue-Sat. **No credit cards.**
Budget shoe shop where you can often find funky styles among the cheap and nasty dross.

Francesco da Firenze

Via di Santo Spirito 62r (21 24 28). Bus 11, 36, 37. **Open** 8.30am-1pm, 3-7.30pm, Mon-Sat. **Credit** AmEx, DC, EC, MC, V.
Hand-made shoes in thick, supple leather by a craftsman who also makes shoes and sandals for Hobbs. Amazingly, prices are about what you would pay for a pair of decent mass-produced shoes. Expect to shell out about L180,000 for a pair of ankle boots.

Furla

Via Tosinghi 5r (28 14 16). **Open** 9.30am-7.30pm Mon-Sat; 11am-7pm Sun. **Credit** AmEx, DC, EC, JCB, MC, V.
Well-made bags, purses, belts and jewellery that pick up quickly on new trends.

Madova

Via Guicciardini 1r (23 96 526). **Open** 9am-7pm Mon-Sat. **Credit** AmEx, MC, V.
A shrine to leather gloves, in every shade imaginable.

Laudato

Via Santa Monica 17r (29 22 29). Bus 11, B. **Open** 4-7.30pm Mon; 9.30am-1pm, 4-7.30pm, Tue-Sat. **Credit** EC, MC, V.
Reasonably priced leather sandals and bags; mostly hand-made.

Maraolo

Via de' Giucciardini 15r (23 98 722). **Open** 9.30am-1.30pm, 3.30-7.30pm, Mon-Sat; 10.30am-5.30pm Sun in summer; closed Mon in winter. **Credit** AmEx, DC, EC, MC, V.
Better than average selection of classic and contemporary styles at fair prices.

Markets

Cascine

Parco dell Cascine, Viale Lincoln. Bus 1, 9, 12. **Open** 8am-1pm Tue.
A much better bet than the Mercato Centrale, as few tourists venture out here. Over 300 stalls selling everything from live chickens to shoes. Lots of cheap and tacky new clothes but it's also one of the few sources of second-hand clothes in the city. Prices are often considerably lower than in the US and UK, as wearing second-hand clothes still has a stigma in Italy. The best stalls will inevitably have the biggest crowds.

Mercato Centrale
Piazza del Mercato Centrale and adjacent streets. **Open** *clothes, etc* 8am-7pm daily; *food* 7am-2pm Mon-Fri; open Sat afternoons in winter.
Fruit, vegetables, meat, fish and deli items in the 19th-century covered market, and clothes, gloves, bags, Botticelli T-shirts, souvenirs and accessories in the sprawl of stalls outside. Quality varies massively, and finding a bargain is unlikely, given the constant supply of gullible foreigners. If you find anything you really like, haggle seriously.

Mercato del Porcellino
Loggia Mercato Nuova. **Open** 9am-7pm Mon-Sat.
The 16th-century loggia (*see chapter* **Florence by Area**) is now devoted to tourist tat of the 'Straw Market' – plaster copies of Michelangelo's *David*, mass-produced leather goods, cheap jewellery and the like. Also known as the Mercato Nuovo.

Mercato di Sant' Ambrogio
Piazza Ghiberti. Bus B. **Open** 7am-2pm Mon-Sat.
Florence's foremost and cheapest produce market, far more bustling than the Mercato Centrale. Fish, meat, cheese, salamis, hams, and all manner of fruit and veg in a decaying 19th-century building.

Piazza dei Ciompi
Piazza dei Ciompi. Bus B. **Open** 9am-7pm Mon-Sat.
Also known as the Mercato delle Pulci, this is a good flea market with plenty of genuine household and wardrobe throw-outs as well as cheap hippy trail tat, and antique/bric-a-brac stalls during the week.

Paper, posters, pens

Cartoleria Ecologica La Tartaruga
Borgo Albizi 60r (23 40 845). **Open** 1.30-7.30pm Mon; 9am-7.30pm Tue-Sat. **Credit** MC, V.
Unusual stationary made from re-cycled paper, and lovely wooden toys.

A Cozzi
Via del Parione 35r (29 49 68). Bus B. **Open** 9am-1pm, 3-7pm Mon-Fri. **Credit** AmEx, EC, MC, V.
Bookbinders with a reasonable choice of books with marbled paper covers.

Fabbrica di Cornici
Via de' Servi 22r (21 69 84). **Open** 3.30-7.30pm Mon; 8.30am-12.30pm, 3.30-7.30pm, Tue-Sat. **Credit** MC, V.
Founded in 1889, this firm used to make frames for the Macchiaioli school of artists. They still make handcrafted frames, and also have a range of architectural posters.

Giulio Giannini e Figlio
Piazza Pitti 36r (21 26 21). **Open** 9am-7.30pm Mon-Sat. **Credit** AmEx, JCB, V.
Founded in 1856, this book-binding and paper-making company is still run by members of the Giannini family from the workshop upstairs. Also on sale are leather desk accessories, marbled paper-covered address books, notebooks and diaries, and unusual greetings cards.

L'Indice Scrive
Via della Vigna Nuova 76r (21 51 65). Bus C.
Open 3.30-7.30pm Mon; 9.30am-1pm, 3-7.30pm, Tue-Sat. **Credit** AmEx, DC, EC, JCB, MC, V.
Good selection of pens and other writing accessories.

Pineider
Piazza della Signoria 13r (28 46 55). **Open** 3.30-7.30pm Mon; 10am-7.30pm Tue-Sat. **Credit** AmEx, DC, EC, JCB, MC, V.
In 1774 Francesco Pineider opened a stationery shop on this

Officina Profumo Farmaceutica di Santa Maria Novella
Via della Scala 16 (21 62 76). **Open** 3.30-7.30pm Mon; 9am-1pm, 3.30-7.30pm, Tue-Sat.
Credit AmEx, DC, EC, MC, V.
This ancient pharmacy, now housed in a 13th-century frescoed chapel, was founded in the 16th century by the Dominican friars of Santa Maria Novella, who grew medicinal herbs, prepared medicines and ointments for their hospital, and distilled herbs and flowers to make perfumes and elixirs. The company is now run by the descendants of one of the friars, and many products concocted by the friars are still produced – including an aromatic vinegar for treating fainting ladies, and the Acqua di Santa Maria Novella, formerly known as antihysterical water, for its calming properties. For those who do not suffer from fainting fits, hysterics or other hypochondria, products range from shampoos, perfumes and moisturisers to a potion for bleeding gums. Distillations of hundreds of species of flowers and herbs are also sold, and staff can advise on remedies for all kinds of ailments.

site. Unfortunately the original interior was destroyed in the 1966 flood, though the shop was admirably redesigned using walnut, brass and enamelled copper. Pineider is famous for its hand-made paper and refined letterheads.

S. Agostino
Via San Agostino 21r (21 96 27). Bus to Piazza Santo Spirito. **Open** 9am-1pm, 3-7pm, Mon-Fri. **Credit** AmEx, EC, MC, V.
The daughters of **Cozzi** (*see above*) have set up their own business which, like their father's, works with leather and their own paper. One daughter specialises in paper restoration.

Il Torchio
Via dei Bardi 17 (23 42 862). Bus C.
Open 9am-1pm, 3.30-7.30pm, Mon-Fri; 9am-1pm Sat.
Credit AmEx, EC, MC, V.
A wonderful selection of hand-made papers in traditional and contemporary designs. It's a real working shop, with book-binding happening on the huge central table. There's a good range of books, boxes, stationery and albums at reasonable prices.

Zecchi
Via dello Studio 19r (12 14 70). **Open** 8.30am-12.30pm, 3.30-7.30pm, Mon-Fri; 8.30am-12.30pm Sat.
Credit AmEx, DC, EC, MC, V.
Heaven on earth for artists, this fascinating shop is worth visiting even if you are not interested in buying the high quality art supplies on sale.

Perfumes, cosmetics, erboristerie

Erboristeria Aux Herbes Sauvages
Via dei Cimatori 2r (21 75 70). **Open** 9.30am-1pm, 4.30-7.30pm, Tue-Sat. **Credit** MC, V.
A herbalist in the historic centre that makes its own tisanes, essential oils and other herbal infusions. They are also the only people in Florence to stock Daniel Ryman organic essential oils.

Farmacia del Cinghiale
Piazza del Mercato Nuovo 4r (21 21 28). **Open** 9am-1pm, 3.30-7.30pm, Mon-Fri; Sat according to rota.
Credit AmEx, MC, V.
The Cinghiale was founded in the 18th century by a herbalist named Guadagni. Upstairs was a laboratory where sci-

entists conducted experiments and, downstairs, cures were sold to the public. Apparently Cinghiale was once famous throught the city for its cornplasters and glycerine suppositories. Nowadays it has its own line of natural cosmetics.

Farmacia Franchi
Via de' Ginori 65r (21 05 65). **Open** 9am-1pm, 4-8pm, Mon-Fri; Sat according to rota. **Credit** MC, V.
Although it occupies the site of a 14th-century pharmacy, Franchi's current interior is early 20th-century, although them wrought iron sign in the window is original. The pharmacy nowadays specialisies in herbal remedies and homeopathy.

Farmacia Molteni
Via Calzaiuoli 7r (21 54 72). **Open** 24 hours daily. **Credit** AmEx, EC, MC, V.
A lavishly carved and gilded 18th-century pharmacy on the historic centre's main drag.

Nectar
Via de' Banchi 9r (28 47 00). **Open** 10am-7.30pm Mon-Sat. **Credit** MC, V.
Body Shop clone selling fruit, nut and plant scented soaps, shampoos and other unguents.

Profumeria Aline
Piazza San Giovanni 26r (21 28 64). **Open** Mon-Sat 9am-7.30pm. **Credit** AmEx, DC, EC, JCB, MC, V.
Upmarket *profumeria* stocking international cosmetic names like Clinique and Clarins.

Sigillo
Via Porta Rossa 23r (28 77 32). **Open** 3.30-7.30pm Mon; 10am-1pm, 3.30-7.30pm, Tue-Sat. **Credit** AmEx, DC, EC, MC, V.
The only source in town of Neal's Yard oils, unguents and soaps plus Côte Bastide bath oils and Hard Candy nail polish.

Top sounds at **Rock Bottom.**

Disco Emporium
Via dell Studio 11r (29 51 01). **Open** 3.30-7.30pm Mon; 9am-1pm, 3.30-7.30pm, Tue-Sat. **Credit** EC, MC, V.
Hidden in a side street behind the Duomo, this misleadingly named classical record shop specialises in historic opera recordings.

KAOS
Via della Scala 65r (28 26 43). **Open** 3.30pm-7.30pm Mon; 10am-7.30pm Tue-Sat. **Credit** AmEx, MC, V.
The hippest record shop in town, stocking a great range of UK and US imports – it's particularly strong on drum 'n' bass and jungle – along with lots of '70s vinyl. Much used by DJs.

Rock Bottom
Via degli Alfani 43r (24 52 20). **Open** 10am-7.30pm Tue-Sat. **Credit** AmEx, DC, MC, V.
Eclectic second hand CD and record store with a strong world music section (sounds from Cambodia, Ladakh and the Yemen on last visit), and sections devoted to medieval, avant garde and experimental, as well as a more predictable selection of metal, grunge and '60s classics.

Toys, gifts, crafts

Animalmania
Via il Prato 38r (21 30 65). **Open** 3-8pm Mon; 10am-8pm Tue-Sat. **Credit** AmEx, DC, EC, MC, V.
Impress your animal maniac at this unusual pet shop which sells, tarantulas, snakes and lizards.

Città del Sole
Borgo Ognissanti 37r (21 93 45). Bus B, C. **Open** 3.30-7.30pm Mon; 9am-1pm, 3.30-7.30pm, Tue-Sat. **Credit** AmEx, DC, EC, MC, V.
Well-made children's toys along with a good range of board games, puzzles and books. Look out for beautiful tangrams.

La Cooperativa dei Ragazzi
Via San Gallo 27r (28 75 00). **Open** 3.30-7.30pm Mon; 9am-1pm, 3.30-7.30pm, Tue-Sat. **Credit** V.
A great toy shop with a large selection of books and an even better selection of toys.

Disney Store
Via Calzaiuoli 69r (29 16 33). **Open** 10am-8pm Mon-Sat; 11am-8pm Sun. **Credit** AmEx, EC, MC, V.
Clothes, toys, plastic, Disney, more Disney and nothing but Disney....

Fornasetti
Borgo degli Albizi 70r (23 47 398). Bus 14, 23. **Open** 3.30-7.30pm Mon; 10am-1pm, 3.30-7.30pm, Tue-Sat. **Credit** A, AmEx, V.
A shop devoted to Fornasetti. Espresso cup and saucers from L300,000, Colosseum coffee jugs for L360,000, and a chair embellished with a stylised sun for three and a half million.

Marchi
Borgo degli Albizi 69-71r (23 40 415). Bus 14, 23. **Open** 3.30-7.30pm Mon; 9.30-1pm, 3.30-7.30pm, Tue-Sat. **No credit cards.**
Guatamalan textiles, Indian bedspreads, Nepalese lamps and all manner of jewellery, clothes, toys and nick-nacks.

Mineral Shop
Via de' Servi 120r (21 82 81). **Open** 3.30-7.30pm Mon; 9.30am-1pm, 3.30-7.30pm, Tue-Sat. **Credit** AmEx, DC, EC, MC, V.
Fossils, chunks of minerals, and conventional jewellery made of semi-precious stones.

Services

Where to go to get your goods shipped, specs fixed, letters faxed and locks picked.

Apartment & villa rentals

Florence & Abroad
Via San Zanobi 58 (48 70 04). Bus to Piazza Independenza. **Open** 10am-12.30pm, 3-6.30pm, Mon-Fri. **No credit cards.**
The English-speaking staff in this agency will do their best to find you an apartment on a short- or long-term basis. Expect to pay L3-4,000,000 per month on a holiday let, or upwards of L1,500,000 plus deposits on a longer term basis for a flat in the centre of town.

Milligan and Milligan Rentals
Via degli Alfani 68 (26 82 56/fax 26 82 60). Bus 31, 32. **Open** 9am-noon, 1-4pm, Mon-Fri. **No credit cards.**
This office is staffed by native English speakers, and specialises in student-type accommodation in and around Florence.

Palazzo Antellesi
Piazza Santa Croce (24 44 56/fax 23 45 552). Bus 23. Office **open** 9am-noon, 3-7pm, Mon-Fri. **No credit cards.**
This wonderful palazzo houses 13 beautifully furnished apartments catering for two to six people. Prices (quoted only in dollars) range from about $1,500 per week or $3,300 per month for one bedroom to $2,800 per week or $5,230 per month for three bedrooms. English is spoken.

Car & bike hire
Car hire

The main branches of the major car hire companies are conveniently situated near the station around Via Borgognissanti (Bus C or a short walk from Santa Maria Novella station). It is worth shopping around for the best rates, but prices given below are an indication of what you should expect to pay although they may vary according to season. Opening times are also liable to change between winter and summer.

Avis
Via Borgognissanti 128r (21 36 29). Bus C. **Open** 8am-7pm Mon-Fri; 8am-1pm, 3-6pm, Sat; 8am-1pm Sun. **Credit** AmEx, DC, MC, V.
The cheapest grade B car will cost around L180,000 for a (three-day) weekend and L485,000 for the week.
Branches: Peretola Airport *(31 55 88).* **Open** 8am-10pm daily. Pisa Airport *(050 42 028).* **Open** 8am-10.30pm Mon-Fri; 8am-8pm Sat, Sun.

Europcar
Via Borgognissanti 53/55 (23 60 072/23 60 073). Bus C. **Open** 8am-1pm, 2-7pm, Mon-Fri; 8am-1pm Sat; 8.30am-12.30pm Sun. **Credit** AmEx, DC, MC, V.
A Fiat Punto will cost from about L180,000 for the weekend and L595,000 for the week.

Branches: Peretola Airport *(31 86 09).* **Open** 9am-6pm, 8-10.45pm, daily. Pisa Airport *(050 41 017).* **Open** 7.30am-10.30pm daily.

Maggiore-Budget
Via Maso Finiguerra 31r (29 45 78/21 02 38). Bus C. **Open** 8am-12.30pm, 2.30-7pm, Mon-Sat; 8.30am-12.30pm Sun. **Credit** AmEx, DC, MC, V.
The cheapest car here will cost around L290,000 for the weekend and L550,000 per week.
Branches: Peretola Airport *(31 12 56).* **Open** 9am-6pm daily. Pisa Airport *(050 42 574).* **Open** 8am-7pm daily.

Car & driver hire

If you really want to do it in style, go for a chauffeur-driven car.

Autonoleggio Noci-Molli
Via Cristofori 10b (35 14 23/fax 35 55 62). **Open** 8am-7pm Mon-Fri (office hours). **Credit** AmEx, V (There is a 19 per cent surcharge for card payments.)
Prices start from a minimum of L200,000 for a car and multi-lingual driver for three hours in Florence. A six-hour day costs L350,000, and if you want to go further afield, a day out in Chianti (8 hours) will cost L450,000. Of course, they will pick you up and deliver you back to your door.

Scooter & cycle hire

To hire a scooter or moped (*motorino*) you need a credit card, an identity document and/or a cash deposit for the hire company. People under the age of 18 are required to wear a helmet when riding bikes up to 50cc. Cycle shops will normally ask you to leave an identity document rather than a deposit.

Alinari
Via Guelfa 85r (28 05 00). Bus 1. **Open** 9am-1pm, 3-7.30pm, Mon-Sat. **Credit** MC, V.

Motorent
Via San Zanobi 9r (49 01 13). Bus to Piazza Independenza. **Open** 8.30am-12.30pm, 2.30-7pm, daily. **Credit** AmEx, MC, V.
Hiring a bike costs L3,500 per hour, L20,000 per day, and L100,000 for a week. For a moped, prices are from L10,000 per hour, L50,000 per day and L250,000 for a week. These rates include a full tank of petrol.

Dry cleaners & laundrettes

It is worth shopping around for dry cleaners (*tintorie*) in Florence as some are far cheaper than others. Most laundrettes are not self-service; they will do your washing for you, charging by the kilo.

In a whirl at **Wash & Dry**.

Lucy & Rita
Via della Chiesa 19r (22 45 36). Bus 11, 36, 37.
Open 8am-1pm, 2.30-7.30pm, Mon-Fri.
No credit cards.
Near Piazza Santo Spirito, this small shop does not have the cheapest prices in Florence (L4,000 for a jumper or shirt, L7,000 for a pair of trousers, L18,000 for a suit), but they do a beautiful job of cleaning (dry or wet) and ironing.

Serena
Via della Scala 30r (21 81 83). Bus to Santa Maria Novella station. **Open** 8.30am-8pm Mon-Fri.
No credit cards.
In Piazza Santa Maria Novella, this cleaners charges L5,000 to wash and iron a shirt, L17,000 to dry clean a suit.

Wash & Dry
Via Nazionale 129r/Via dei Servi 105r/Via della Scala 52/54r/Via dei Serragli 87r (29 15 04/freephone 167 23 11 72). **Open** 8am-10pm daily; *last wash* 9pm.
No credit cards.
This new chain of self-service laundrettes offers machines which wash and dry in 50 minutes. Charges are L6,000 for 8 kilos, L12,000 for 18 kilos and L6,000 for a dry.

Delivery food

Just about the only food you can have delivered to your door in Florence is pizza or Chinese.

Il Panda
Via Fra' Bartolomeo 58r (57 38 76). **Open** 10.30am-2.30pm, 5.30-10.30pm, daily. Delivery orders accepted noon-2pm, 7-10.30pm, daily. **No credit cards.**
This Chinese takeaway also brings food to your door; complete meals from L8,500-L11,000 per head, rice dishes from L4,000, fish and chicken dishes from L6,000. L5,000 extra for delivery.

Pronto Pizza
(71 67 67/71 67 68). **Open** 6.30-11pm daily.
No credit cards.
Pizzas here cost from L6,000 for a plain Margherita to L15,000 for a creation with just about everything on top. Delivery is free (and should take no longer than 30 minutes), and there is no minimum order.

Runner Pizza
(33 33 33). **Open** noon-2pm, 6-10pm, Sun-Fri; 6-10pm Sat.
No credit cards.
The price of a pizza ranges from L8,000-L10,000, and this includes a 'free' drink or ice cream. Delivery costs L2,000 if you only order one pizza; it is free if you order more.

Faxing & photocopying

Faxes can be sent from specialist fax shops, some stationers (*cartolerie*) and some *tabacchi*. The same places will make photocopies, but it is often much cheaper to go to one of the many photocopying centres around the University area (in Via degli Alfani/Via San Gallo) where prices can be half those in a *cartoleria*. For e-mail and courier services, *see chapters* **Students** *and* **Business**.

Bumble Bee
Via Santa Monaca 23 (28 90 23/fax 28 89 25/e-mail bumble@dada.it). Bus B to Santo Spirito.
Open noon-8pm Mon-Fri; 10am-2pm Sat.
Florence's only English-run computer communications centre. Here you can use word processing faciltities, send and receive faxes and e-mail (L5,000 per hour to send, L2,000 per message to receive), surf the internet (L10,000 per hour plus the phone call) and print from floppy disks.

Centro AZ
Via degli Alfani 20r (24 77 855). Bus 31, 32. **Open** 9am-1pm, 3-7pm, Mon-Fri; 9am-12.30pm Sat. **No credit cards.**
A large range of copying services and a fax service. Faxes carry a standard charge of L3,000 plus the cost of the call.

Copisteria Elletra
Via San Gallo 68r (47 38 09). Bus 11, 17. **Open** 8.30am-1.30pm, 2-7.30pm, Mon-Fri; 9am-12.30pm Sat. **Credit** AmEx, MC, V.
Another well-equipped copying shop. Faxes from here cost L7,000 per page to the UK and L9,500 per page to the US.

Print and Service
Piazza Ghiberti 9r (23 45 344). Bus to San Ambrogio.
Open 9am-7pm Mon-Fri; 9am-1pm Sat. **Credit** AmEx, DC, EC, MC, V.
Faxes cost L5,000 plus the price of the call; e-mail is charged at L18,000 per hour to send, and L1,000 per page to receive.

Florists

Flower stalls are at most of Florence's markets .

Calvanelli
Via della Vigna Nuova 24 (21 37 42). Bus C. **Open** 7am-1pm, 3.30-7.30pm, Mon, Tue, Thur-Sat; 7am-1pm Wed.
No credit cards.
There is no charge for delivery within the city.

Galli
Via Guicciardini 11 (29 47 42). Bus B, C.
Open 7.30am-7.30pm Mon-Sat; some Sun mornings.
No credit cards.
Delivery in Florence costs from L5,000 on top of the price of the flowers.

Giovanni
Piazza San Giovanni 7 (21 50 08). Bus 11, 17.
Open 7am-1.15pm, 3.15-7.30pm, Mon, Tue, Thur-Sat; 7am-1.15pm Wed. **Credit** V.
For delivery within the *centro storico*, a bunch of flowers will cost from L25,000.

Health & beauty

Hairdressers

Hairdressers are closed on Mondays in Florence.

De Style

Via Cavour 170Ar (57 82 95). Bus 1, 11. **Open** 9am-6pm Tue-Sat. **Credit** AmEx, V.
This lively salon leans towards the young and trendy, but caters for all ages. A wash and cut costs L38,000, and a blow dry L22,000. English is spoken.

Mario's

Via della Vigna Nuova 22r (29 48 13). Bus C. **Open** *Hairdresser* 9am-6pm Tue-Sat; *Beauty Salon* 9am-7pm Tue-Sat; *Profumeria* 3.30-7.30pm Mon; 9am-7.30 Tue-Sat. **Credit** AmEx, DC, EC, JCB, MC, V.
This shop on chic Via della Vigna Nuova combines a *profumeria* (selling perfumes, cosmetics and other beauty products), a beauty parlour on the ground floor and a hairdressing salon upstairs. Some staff speak English in this popular haunt of the well-heeled Signoras about town. Prices for a haircut begin at L40,000, but drying is extra at about L30,000. Downstairs, a full leg wax costs L45,000, a facial from L50,000 and a full body massage from L35,000.

Stefano Pavi

Via dei Serragli 17 (28 76 36). Bus 11. **Open** 9am-8pm Tue-Sat. **Credit** DC, EC, MC, V.
This predominantly men's hairdressers, in an old palazzo just south of the Arno, offers a lot more than a hair cut; the whole works are available from sauna and turkish baths, through a small gym to courses in relaxation therapy. A men's wash and cut starts from L50,000.

Health centres

Acquabel

Piazza Pier Vettori 12 (22 94 34). Bus 6. **Open** 10am-8.30pm Mon-Fri; 10am-3pm Sat. **Credit** AmEx, EC, MC, V.
A wide range of beauty treatments is on offer here plus a gym, sauna, turkish bath, jacuzzi and hairdresser. Prices for a facial begin at L76,000, a haircut and dry will cost from L50,000, and membership for the day, which gives you use of the gym, sauna, jacuzzi and turkish bath, costs L36,000.

Hito Estetica

Via de' Ginori 21 (28 44 24). Bus 11, 17. **Open** 9am-8pm Tue-Sat; 1-8pm Mon. **Credit** AmEx, MC, V.
Based in elegant, old Palazzo Tolomei Biffi, Hito specializes in treatments using only natural products, including Iurvetic techniques on face and body. Prices start from L35,000 for a facial and L35,000 for a leg wax.

Istituto Freni

Via Pasquale Villari 6B (67 66 86). **Open** 9am-1pm, 3-7pm, Mon-Fri; 9am-1pm Sat. **No credit cards.**
If your feet give out after all those museums, come to the Istituto for foot treatments ranging from massage to more gruesome remedies. The centre also offers other beauty treatments; facials cost from L80,000, leg waxes from L60,000.

Locksmiths

Avoid the 24-hour emergency locksmiths listed under *'Fabro'* in the local Yellow Pages as their charges are abusive. To get back into a flat, call the fire brigade; into a car, call the **ACI**, the *Automobile club d'Italia* (*see chapter* **Essential Information**).

SOS Casa

(43 40 30/43 44 45). **Open** 8am-8pm daily, including public hols. **No credit cards.**
Ridiculously expensive, but useful for any kind of household emergency, SOS Casa's prices start with a call-out charge of L30,000 on weekdays and L40,000 on weekends. Add to this L40,000 per hour and the cost of any materials used, and you have a hefty bill, but it's reassuring to know they are there. Plumbers, locksmiths, carpenters, electricians are all on call.

Mobile phone hire

Aglietti & Sieni

Viale Lavanini 28 (47 37 47). Bus 8. **Open** 9am-1pm, 3-7.30pm, Mon-Fri; 9am-1pm Sat.
No credit cards.
It costs L90,000 to hire a mobile phone for a week and L300,000 for a month. Payment must be made in advance and a deposit of L300,000 is required.

Porta Rossa Telefonia

Via Porta Rossa 14 (28 49 11). **Open** 9.15am-1pm, 3.30-7.30pm, Tue-Sat; 3.30-7.30pm Mon. **Credit** AmEx, DC, EC, MC, V.
This is a smaller shop than the above, and has fewer telephones available for hire, but its central location is an advantage, and staff are helpful. Rent for a day is L13,000, L83,000 for a week and L260,000 for a month. A deposit of L400,000 is required.

Opticians

Photographic and optical lenses go together in Italy, and many photographic shops sell glasses just as many opticians sell basic photographic equipment.

Pisacchi

Via Condotta 22/24r (21 45 42).
Open 4-8pm Mon; 9am-1pm, 4-8pm, Tue-Sat.
Credit AmEx, DC, EC, MC, V.
This shop carries out eye tests and is a contact lens specialist.

Sbisa

Piazza Signoria 10r (21 13 39). **Open** 9am-7.30pm Tue-Sat; 3.30-7.30pm Mon. **Credit** AmEx, DC, EC, MC, V.
Armani, Gucci, Ralph Lauren, Valentino, Versace; this shop has them all plus good range of photographic and other optical equipment.

Photography

Bongi

Via Por Santa Maria 82/84r (23 98 811).
Open 9am-1pm, 3.30-7.30pm, Tue-Sat.
Credit AmEx, DC, EC, MC, V.
One of the biggest and best-equipped shops in the centre of the city. It also carries a wide range of second-hand photographic equipment.

Foto Levi

Vicolo dell'Oro 12/14r (29 40 02). **Open** 9am-1pm, 3.30-7.30pm, Mon-Fri; 9am-1pm Sat. **Credit** AmEx, DC, EC, MC, V.
Tucked away behind the Ponte Vecchio (by the Alitalia office), this tiny shop is a useful central place to have your film developed. Ready in 20 minutes, a 24 exposure colour film will cost L18,000. Levi also sells a range of glasses and, of course, photographic film.

Foto Ottica Fontani
Viale Strozzi 18/20A (47 09 81). Bus 1, 13. **Open** 3.30-7.30pm Mon; 9am-1pm, 3.30pm-7.30pm, Tue-Sat.
No credit cards.
This family-run shop prints over 3,000 films per day and is a mecca for all photography enthusiasts. Prices for developing film are by far the cheapest in Florence (L9,000 for 24 colour exposures), and your pictures will be ready in a day. They also stock lenses by Armani, Byblos and Ralph Lauren.

Picture framers

Leonardo Romanelli
Via Santo Spirito 16r (28 47 94). **Open** 9am-1pm, 3-8pm, Mon-Sat. **No credit cards.**
Picture framing is generally cheap in Italy and the friendly Leonardo Romanelli offers an excellent range of frames and top quality workmanship. A small frame costs L20,000.

Repairers

Guido
Via Santa Monaca 9 (no phone). Bus 11. **Open** 7am-12.30pm, 3-6.30pm, Mon-Fri. **No credit cards.**
Guido lived in Australia for 25 years, and is delighted to speak English to anybody who takes their museum-weary shoes to him for any kind of repair.

Pelletterie Brovelli
Borgo San Frediano 11r (21 38 40). Bus 6, 11, C. **Open** 9am-1pm, 3.30-7.30pm, Tue-Sat; 3.30-7.30pm Sat. **Credit** AmEx, DC, EC, MC, V.
Repairs to all leather goods (except shoes). They also sell bags, suitcases, umbrellas, gloves, etc.

Anna Maria Sernesi
Via dei Serragli 82 (no phone). Bus 11. **Open** 9am-12.30pm, 3.30pm-7pm, Mon-Fri. **No credit cards.**
If you eat too much pasta and bust the zip on your trousers, take them to this miniscule workshop. Alterations and repairs are undertaken on all garments, including leather.

Time Out
Via dei Bardi 70r (21 31 11). **Open** 9.30am-1.30pm, 3.30-7.30pm, Tue-Sat; 3.30-7.30pm Mon. **Credit** AmEx, DC, EC, JCB, MC, V.
Just south of the Ponte Vecchio, this well-named shop specialises in antique watches, both buying, selling, and mending them with original parts.

Walter's Silver and Gold
Borgo dei Greci 11Cr (23 96 678). Bus 23. **Open** 9am-6pm daily. **Credit** AmEx, DC, EC, MC, V.
English-speaking Walter does all types of jewellery repair.

Shipping

Gondrand
Via Baldanzese 198 (88 26 376). Bus 28, C. **Open** 8.30am-12.30pm, 2.30-6.30pm, Mon-Fri. **No credit cards.**
Gondrand is a long way out of town, but provides reliable international or local shipping and moving. Offices throughout Italy, storage facilities and free estimates. English spoken.

Ticket agencies

When booking tickets over the phone, make sure that the arrangements for the collection or delivery of the tickets are specified clearly.

Box Office
Via Faenza 139r (21 08 04). Bus to Santa Maria Novella station. **Open** 10am-7.30pm Tue-Sat; 3.30-7.30pm Mon.
No credit cards.
Tickets for concerts, theatre and exhibitions in Florence, Italy and abroad. There are 20 branches in Tuscany. Go in person: the phone will be busy.
Branch: *Chiasso de Soldanieri 8r (21 08 04).*
Open 9am-8pm Tue-Sat. **No credit cards**
Located in a unisex hairdressers – book your tickets and get a hairdo (L60,000) at the same time. If you book more than five tickets, they will be delivered free. No phone bookings.

Travel agencies

CTS (Student Travel Centre)
Via dei Ginori 25r (28 95 70). Bus 1. **Open** 9.30am-1.30pm, 2.30-6pm, Mon-Fri; 9.30am-12.30pm Sat.
No credit cards.
The official student travel service offers discounted air, coach and train tickets to all destinations. Although some discounts are only available for students, you do not need to be one to take out the obligatory membership (L43,000 for non-students, L15,000 for students).

Eyre & Humbert
Corso Italia 5r (23 82 251). Bus C. **Open** 9am-1pm, 3-7pm, Mon-Fri; 9am-12.30pm Sat. **Credit** EC, MC, V.
One of the two oldest travel agencies in Florence, this friendly office deals with the usual range of travel services including train tickets. It is located opposite the Teatro Comunale, on the west side of the city.

Intertravel
Via Lamberti 39r (21 79 36). **Open** 9am-6.30pm Mon-Fri; 9am-1pm Sat. **Credit** AmEx, EC, MC, V.
A busy and efficient travel agency offering a full range of travel services, a currency exchange and a DHL service.

Lazzi Express
Piazza Adua/Piazza Stazione (21 51 55). Bus to Santa Maria Novella station. **Open** 9am-6.30pm Mon-Fri; 9am-2pm, 3-7pm, Sat. **No credit cards.**
Lazzi has information and tickets for coach services within Italy, and for the Euroline services to European cities.

Nouvelles Frontieres
Piazza N. Sauro 17r (21 47 33). Bus 11. **Open** 9am-1pm, 2.30-6.30pm, Mon-Fri; 9am-1pm Sat. **No credit cards.**
Some of the cheapest air tickets available in Florence, both charter and scheduled services, and you don't need membership. They also have a wide range of long haul destinations and package holidays, and are agents for the Corsica/Sardinia ferry line, which serves Elba and Capraia.

Video rental

New GMG Videocentre Club
Viale Mazzini 14r (23 45 987). Bus 13. **Open** 4-8pm Mon; 9am-1pm, 4-8pm, Tue-Sat. **No credit cards.**
A little way from the centre, this is the best-stocked shop for English-language videos in town with over 1,000 titles, both new and old, and plenty for children. A year's membership costs L50,000, and you then pay L4,000 per video per night. Non-members pay L6,000 per video.

Punto Video
Via San Antonino 7r (28 48 13). **Open** 9am-8pm Mon-Sat. **No credit cards.**
Between the station and the central market, this shop has over 500 English titles in stock. Membership is free, and videos cost L5,000 per night.

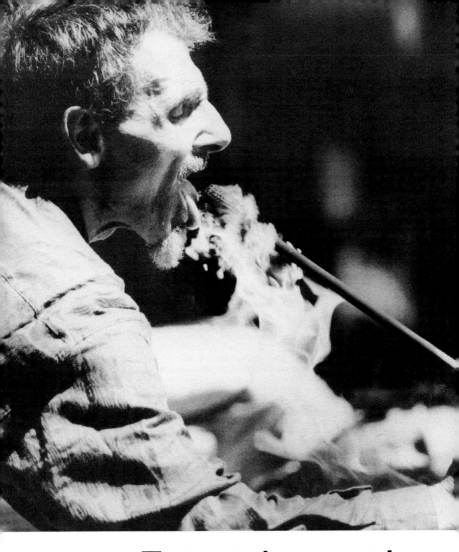

Entertainment in Florence

Dance & Theatre

The arts in Tuscany are more than just art: some of Italy's finest and most interesting dance and theatre projects are based in the region.

For a small city, there are a surprising number of opportunities to see **dance** in Florence – from classical ballet to contemporary dance, from renowned visiting companies such as the Kirov, Tokyo or Martha Graham to little-known, small-scale productions. Like all the arts, dance suffers from lack of funds, with state money going only to well-established companies, while smaller projects fight a continual battle against diminishing resources. In spite of this, there are plenty of people with enough energy and dedication to keep things going, and the result is a healthy calendar of dance events during the year.

Summer, with its outdoor arts seasons and festivals, is a good time to catch such events, but they are not always well publicised, particularly the smaller productions, so keep an eye on the billboards, or ask at the tourist offices.

Italian **theatre** is one of the most evolved in Europe, with a long and distinguished history, and Tuscany has a particularly fine theatrical tradition. Every little town had its theatre (there are still around 300 in the region) and many date back as far as the 15th and 16th centuries. Some of the most interesting surviving buildings are in Montalcino, San Casciano, Santa Croce sul'Arno, Siena, Lucca and Pisa.

Today, Florence and Tuscany are still rich in theatrical activity and you can see anything from the great Italian works of Goldoni and Pirandello to foreign classics (mostly in Italian, of course) to mainstream contemporary and fringe productions. Once again, there's a chronic lack of funding for smaller initiatives, but individual enthusiasm and hard graft guarantee a profusion of interesting small-scale projects.

Dance companies

Maggio Danza

Corso Italia 16 (21 11 58/21 35 35/fax 27 79 410/e-mail teatro.comunale@infogroup.it). **Open** *box office* 11am-5.30pm Tue-Fri; 9am-1pm Sat; and one hour before all shows for tickets for that performance. **Credit** AmEx, DC, EC, MC, V.

Maggio Danza is the resident company at the Teatro Comunale. Founded in 1967, and undergoing some years of inconsistent standards, it was under director Evgheni Polyakov (in the late '70s/early '80s and late '80s/early '90s) that the company was brought up to scratch. The work of the current director, American avant-garde choreographer Karole Armitage, has provoked much controversy. Most of the Maggio Danza productions are staged as part of the Teatro Comunale's programme, but they have recently started touring. Maggio Danza's repertoire ranges from classical ballet to ambitious contemporary productions. The season runs from October to December, and from May to July, with several productions being staged within the Maggio Musicale Fiorentino festival at either the Teatro Comunale or Teatro della Pergola. At the end of June, there is an open-air evening of dance in Piazza Signoria (admission free). In July, the Boboli Gardens provide a fine setting for productions, and the company also takes part in the Estate Fiesolana at the Roman Amphitheatre in Fiesole (*see chapter* **Music: Classical & Opera**).

Balletto di Toscana

Via Claudio Monteverdi 3A (35 15 30).

This small, full-time company (14 dancers, all Italian) was founded by Cristina Bozzolini in 1986, although the associated ballet school goes back to 1970. State funding is supplemented by private contributions, and the company has a full schedule of productions throughout the year in Tuscany, the rest of Italy and abroad. Both classical and contemporary works are included in the repertoire.

Florence Dance Center

Borgo della Stella 23r (28 92 76).
Open 9am-10pm Mon-Fri.

This dance centre, near Piazza del Carmine, acts as dance school, performance and exhibition space and organiser of dozens of dance events throughout the year – most importantly, the Florence Dance Festival in July and August (*see below*). Its energetic and forward-thinking directors, Marga Nativa and American choreographer Keith Ferrone, are the driving force behind the centre, which is an important reference point for dance in Tuscany and Italy.

Dance venues & festivals

Danza Primavera

Teatro SMS di Grassina, Piazza Umberto 1, Grassina (64 44 81/63 90 356). Bus 31.
Held annually in Grassina, near Florence between mid-April and June, this dance festival involves mostly young Italian dancers and also organises workshops.

Estate Fiesolana

Teatro Romano, Via Portigiani 1, Fiesole (21 98 53). Bus 7.
Dance has always played an important part in this festival just outside Florence, and its open-air setting in the Roman amphitheatre makes it worth the trip up the hill. Maggio Danza and Balletto di Toscana make regular appearances, as do visiting companies and choreographers such as Bob Wilson.

Florence Dance Festival

Borga della Stella 23r, Florence (28 92 76/fax 21 78 10).
Date July.
This festival of international contemporary dance (implying contemporary interpretation rather than repertoire), brainchild of Marga Nativa and the Florence Dance Center, takes place annually in Piazza SS Annunziata. For about three weeks in

July, a stage is erected in the Piazza with seating for 1,000. Around eight productions are staged, ranging from classical ballet to jazz dance, with Italian and international soloists and companies taking part. There is also a choreography competition aimed at young exponents of contemporary and jazz dance.

Teatro Verdi

Via Ghibellina 99 (21 23 20). **Open** box office 10am-noon, 4-7pm, daily. **No credit cards.**
Teatro Verdi, opened in 1854, hosts a splendid variety of events – dance, music, theatre, operetta, grand opera – throughout the year. Visiting companies making recent appearances have included the Kirov Ballet, Lindsay Kemp and Balletto Toscano.

La Versiliana

Viale Morin 16 (0584 23 938). **Open** box office 10am-1pm, 5-11pm, from 1 July. **No credit cards.**
Season of music, operetta, prose and dance based in Marina di Pietrasanta. The main venue is the Teatro della Versiliana, an open-air theatre in the pleasant setting of a pine wood. Dance companies are usually inportant names.

Theatres in & around Florence

The Tuscan theatre season is short, running approximately from September to April.

Il Fabbricone

Via Targetti 10, Prato (0574 60 85 01). **Open** box office 10am-noon, 4-7pm, Tues-Sat. **No credit cards.**
It was in the '70s that this fabric factory was first used as a theatre, and it's since gained a reputation for good quality experimental repertoire.

Teatro Le Laudi

Via Leonardo da Vinci 2r (57 28 31). **Open** half an hour before performances. **No credit cards.**
Works by writers from Kafka to Tennessee Williams to Goldoni.

Teatro della Limonaia

Via Gramsci 426, Sesto Fiorentino (44 08 52). **Open** *for telephone bookings only* 10am-6.30pm Mon-Fri. **No credit cards.**
A tiny, delightful space created from an old lemonary which could be in New York rather than staid Florence. Shows are mainly alternative. Look out for the original language **Intercity Festival** (*see below*).

Teatro Metastasio

Via Cairoli 59, Prato (0574 60 85 01). **Open** box office 10am-noon, 4-7pm, Tue-Sat. **No credit cards.**
This 16th/17th-century 'Teatro Al'Italiano', with its pink and gold decor and 680 seats, is one of the best places to see prose works, both classical and contemporary, in Tuscany; inaugurated in Italy. The season runs from October to May, and all the great Italian actors and directors work have worked here.

Teatro della Pergola

Via della Pergola 12/32 (24 79 651). **Open** box office 9.30am-1pm, 3.45-6.45pm, Tue-Sat; 9.45am-noon Sun. **No credit cards.**
The gorgeous, intimate 17th-century Teatro della Pergola is Florence's official *Teatro della Prosa*. From October to April you can see the great Italian classics such as Goldoni, but the programme also offers Italian translations of the likes of Shakespeare, Neil Simon, Beckett, Molière and Ivan Turgenev.

Teatro Puccini

Piazza Puccini (36 20 67). **Open** box office *(during season)* 4-7.30pm Mon-Fri; 10am-1pm, 4-7.30pm Sat. **No credit cards.**

Serious and not-so-serious theatre (light opera, musicals, one-man variety shows, etc) is on offer at this large, fascist-style building.

Teatro di Rifredi

Via Vittorio Emanuele 303 (42 20 361). **Open** *Sept-Apr* 4-7pm Mon-Fri. **No credit cards.**
A mixed bag of a schedule, including classics from the likes of Pirandello as well as more contemporary works.

Teatro Verdi

See above for details.
Some prose works, classical and more contemporary, is always included in the varied programme at this theatre.

Fringe companies

Small, fringe companies to look out for include:

L'Arca Azzura

Borgo degli Albizi 15 (23 40 430).
Founded in 1983 by playwright and director Ugo Chiti, this company identifies strongly with Tuscany, its traditions and language and appears regularly in Florence and other theatres and festivals in the area. It is the driving force behind the **Teatro delle Regioni** festival (*see below*).

Compania di Krypton

Teatro Studio di Scandicci, Via Donizetti 58, Florence (box office & info 75 73 48/info 75 18 53).
Founded in 1982 when their lighting, stage, sound techniques were very much avant-garde, this company works with a variety of material and experiments with video, projections, lasers, multi-vision, microphones and other special effects.

Pupi e Fressedde

Teatro Manzoni, Via Gramsci 127, Pistoia (0573 99 161).
A young company with an eclectic repertoire that works with many schools projects.

Teatro del' Carretto

Piazza del Giglio 13, Lucca (0583 48 684).
A dynamic company, founded in 1983 and based in Lucca. Their work is full of surprises – music, machines, sound effects, masks, incredible mobility and an overall dream-like quality.

Theatre festivals

Intercity Festival

Teatro della Limonaia, Via Gramsci 426, Sesto Fiorentino (44 08 52). **Date** Sep, Oct.
This 'Intercity festival from town to town' is one of the few places in Florence to hear contemporary theatre in original language, and it celebrated its tenth anniversary in 1997. Each year, a different city is chosen (Madrid, Lisbon, Moscow, Budapest have all featured in the past) and playwrights, actors and theatre companies from the country concerned are invited to Florence to participate. London was the chosen city in both 1996 and '97, and guests included Steven Berkoff, Sarah Kane, Claire Dowie and Tony Harrison. Video shows, exhibitions, lectures and workshops are also on offer. Principal venues are Teatro della Limonaia, Teatro Studio di Scandicci and Teatro Fabbricone in Prato.

Teatro delle Regioni

(21 98 51/23 40 429). **Date** 3/4 days in May.
This short festival explores the concept of regional theatre and plays written for the festival work with the vernacular and dialects of the regions concerned. Very Italian.

Film

The picture postcard landscapes of Tuscany may be favourites with foreign film-makers, but you'll be pushed to find a cinema showing such flicks in their original language.

Tuscany is experiencing something of a cinema renaissance. A spate of Anglo-Hollywood films have exploited its abundance of ready-made sets, keeping village policemen busy holding back literally two or three onlookers, and lining the pockets of plastic vine leaf suppliers (the real ones have an annoying tendency to wither in the off season).

It all started with *Room With A View*: for a couple of summers after its release in 1985, the Merchant-Ivory film of EM Forster's novel filled the *pensioni* of Florence with wannabe Edwardian Romantics; she with the lacy dress, he with the linen jacket and panama hat. Since then we have had *Much Ado About Nothing*, in which Kenneth Branagh chose to ignore the bard's references to 'Messina' and plumped for postcard Chiantishire instead; Jane Campion's *Portrait of a Lady*, which was partly set in and around Lucca; and, most recently, *The English Patient*, which had Ralph Fiennes dying in an abandoned convent on the outskirts of Pienza (though other scenes were shot around Viareggio and Lucca). And now – strange but true – Mel Gibson is making a film based around Siena's annual Palio horse-race.

But it isn't just cypress-struck foreigners who have been fomenting the boom. Local directors have been flocking to Tuscany in droves. Bernardo Bertolucci's 1996 hit *Stealing Beauty* – a will-she-won't-she-lose-that-cherry yarn set in deepest Chianti – can hardly be said to have shown foreign audiences an unknown corner of the region. But a couple of new films may be more enlightening, if they find an overseas distributor: Francesca Archibugi's *Il Vento* (The Wind) is set in the marble-quarrying villages around Carrara, while Paolo Virzì's *Ovo Sodo* (Hard Boiled Egg) takes place in his home town, the industrial port of Livorno.

Most Italians, however, associate Tuscany not with earnest arthouse fare, but with downmarket comedy. The box-office sensation of the 1996-97 season was *Il Ciclone*, a romantic comedy about the arrival of a troupe of flamenco dancers in a sleepy Tuscan town, directed by former stand-up comedian Leonardo Pieraccioni. The film grossed over $40 million nationally – more than Jurassic Park, more than Disney, more even than Roberto Benigni's *Il*

*The palatial **Odeon**.*

Mostro, the previous Italian record holder. The funny thing is that Benigni too is a Tuscan actor-director who cut his teeth on the cabaret circuit. Known abroad mainly for his work with Jim Jarmusch, portraying a bemused Italian tourist in *Down By Law*, and a raving taxi driver in sunglasses in *Night on Earth*, he is a national hero at home, famous both for his over-schmaltzy comic features and for his occasional 'shocking' TV appearances, during which he can be guaranteed to call at least one sexual organ by its common-or-garden name – neither of them particularly Tuscan characteristics, it must be said. But Benigni proved his toscanitè in a now legendary TV reading of Dante's *Inferno*.

Moviegoing in Florence

Very few cinemas in the city show foreign films with their original soundtracks (*versione originale*). The majority only offer English-language films one night a week, usually on Mondays. Another option for English speakers are the various cineclubs which offer more varied programmes including independent and documentary films.

If you do speak Italian you can take advantage of the cheaper matinee shows (before 6.30pm) at many first-run cinemas on weekdays (L7,000 as opposed to the standard price of L12,000).

You should be prepared for long queues on Friday and Saturday nights. If you don't arrive at least 40 minutes before the start of the film don't be surprised if you end up sitting on the floor or standing at the back. When the '*posto in piedi*' light is on, the tickets being sold are standing room only – though irritatingly they cost the same as regular tickets.

For showtimes check the listing in Florence's daily newspaper, *La Nazione*. For information on festivals and other special events, the monthly *Firenze Spettacolo* is a good source. Sometimes special film events in English will be listed in the English-language monthly *Events*.

Although there are numerous first-run cinemas throughout Florence and its nearby suburbs, very few offer foreign films with their original soundtrack. Italians appear to have an aversion to subtitling. Dubbing is big business in Italy, shooting to fame the actors who dub the voices of Hollywood stars like Tom Cruise and Robert DeNiro. However, *versione originale* (VO) films are slowly gaining popularity and can be seen in some of the following cinemas.

Astra Cinehall

Via Cerretani 54r (29 47 70). **Open** *box office* 3.30pm, last show 10.45pm, daily. **Tickets** L7,000 Mon-Fri until 6.30pm, otherwise L12,000. **No credit cards**.
Located just two blocks from the Duomo, this small cinema has only one screen but is very popular thanks to its central location. Italian-language only.
Air-conditioning.

Astra Due Cinehall

Piazza Beccaria (23 43 666). Bus 14, 23 to Piazza Beccaria. **Open** *box office* 3.15pm, last show 10.45pm, daily. **Tickets** L7,000 Mon-Fri until 6.30 pm, otherwise L12,000. **No credit cards**.
This cinema shows mostly first-run films in Italian but every now and then you can catch a picture in VO.
Air-conditioning.

Cinema Astro

Piazza San Simone near Piazza Santa Croce (no phone). Bus 14 to Teatro Verdi. **Open** *box office* 7pm, last show 10pm, Tue-Sun. **Tickets** L8,000; L6,000 Wed for students. **No credit cards**.
The Astro is the only cinema in Florence which exclusively shows English-language films six days a week. Even bet-

ter, most films are relatively recent releases, making the cinema something of a cultural lifeline for Anglophone ex-pats.

Goldoni

Via Serragli 109 (22 24 37). Bus 36, 37 to Porta Romana. **Open** *box office* 3.30pm, last show 10.45pm, daily. **Closed** June, July.
No credit cards.
This cinema, near Porta Romana, was one of the first to show English-language films. It now also runs some French films on its regular VO night every Monday. Understandably popular with Florence's many foreign students, it's advisable to go to an early show if you want to beat the crowds.

Odeon Original Sound

Via Sassetti 1 (21 40 68). **Open** *box office* 3.30pm, last show 10.45pm, daily. **Closed** 25 June-1 Sept.
No credit cards.
English-language films are shown every Monday in this cinema near Piazza della Repubblica.
Air-conditioning.

The various film clubs in Florence offer another alternative for avid moviegoers. They are relatively inexpensive to join, especially for students, and often offer discounts for the first-run cinemas. Most of these film societies have discussions following screenings or presentations by local filmmakers.

CineCitta

Via Pisana 576 (73 24 510). Bus 26 towards Scandicci. **Shows** 8.30pm Fri-Sun. **Tickets** L5,000 plus L9,000 membership. **No credit cards**.
This film club is run by the Casa del Popolo Fratelli Taddei (community centre). Films range from current Hollywood action pictures to special festivals of obscure Italian classics. In the past these events have included films by Pupi Avati and Alessandro Benevenuti.

Istituto Francese

Piazza Ognissanti 2 (23 98 902). **Tickets** L6,000; free with a *tessera Istituto Francese* membership card.
No credit cards.
Sponsored by the French government to promote French culture, the Istituto (unsurprisingly) shows mainly French films. However, it sponsors a number of festivals and events throughout the year which often include films by French, Italian, American and English directors.

Libreria Del Cinema Crawford

Via Guelfa 1r (21 64 16). **Open** 9.30am-1.30pm, 3.30-7.30pm, Mon-Sat. **Credit** V.
This is the only bookstore in Tuscany which specializes in cinema, film memorabilia and rare books. The store sells movie posters, videos of both Italian and foreign films, Italian film magazines and books. It also organises conferences and exhibitions on film-related topics, and sponsors screenings. A great place to find out about upcoming film events in and around Florence.

Stensen Forum/LunediClub

Viale Don Minzoni 25a (57 65 51). Bus 1, 7. **Shows** 9.15pm Mon. **Tickets** L5,000, plus L2,000 annual membership. **No credit cards**.
Both Italian and foreign films are the staple of this film club. You must become a member of the group by purchasing an annual membership (*abbonamento*). Along with film screenings, the group sponsors lectures, debates and presentations by filmmakers.

Cinema al fresco.

Festivals & summer programmes

Currently two major international film festivals occur annually in Florence. The **Festival dei Popoli** takes place during the first two weeks of December, with films shown in various clubs and cinemas throughout Florence. The festival's theme changes from year to year but always centres around a current social issue, showing both narrative and documentary film. The other major festival also takes place during the first two weeks of December. **Under Florence** shows independent film and videos by Italians as well as foreigners, and awards a prize to an outstanding Tuscan each year. Films are shown at various locations around the city. For information on both, contact **Cinema Alfieri Atelier**, Via dell'Ulivo 6 (*24 07 20*).

Like many other Italian cities, Florence closes most of its cinemas during June, July and August. Instead of sitting inside during the warm summer evenings, Florentines go to watch films *all'aperto* (outside). The following three

function every summer, but it is always worth keeping an eye out for other *cinema all'aperto* starting up.

Arena di Marte

Palazzetto dello Sport di Firenze, Viale Paoli (67 88 41). *Bus 10, 20, 34.* **Dates** mid June-late Aug. **Shows** 9pm, 11pm, daily. **Tickets** L8,000. **No credit cards.**
The Cooperativa Atelier organises two outdoor cinema seasons in Florence: Arena di Marte and Raggio Verde. There are two screens at the Arena di Marte, both with two shows nightly.

Chiar di Luna

Via Monte Uliveto 1 (23 37 042). Bus 12, 13.
Dates June-Sept. **Shows** 9.30pm daily. **Tickets** L10,000. **No credit cards.**
Recent commercial releases every night, at a site off Viale Raffaele Sanzio, between Ponte Vittoria and Porta Romana.

Raggio Verde

Palacongressi Firenze, Viale Strozzi (26 02 609). Bus 1, 10. **Dates** late June-early Sept. **Shows** 9.30pm & 11pm daily. **Tickets** L8,000. **No credit cards.**
If you don't want to leave the city centre then the arena here is another option for filmwatching under the moonlight. Two different films are shown nightly. Located near Santa Maria Novella train station.

Music: Classical & Opera

Despite a lack of public funding, the city is a vibrant centre of music in Tuscany.

Florence's musical scene is lively, although how innovative it is, is open to debate. One problem is, of course, money. In Italy, state funding only goes to established organisations such as the state opera houses (the **Teatro Comunale** in Florence, for example). Regional funding is destined for more local projects, but these are the same every year, and there is little left for more modest enterprises. The standard of productions, particularly opera and concerts, put on by the main beneficiaries of this money is generally very high, but can that justify lack of funding for smaller, often more innovative, musical initiatives? It is almost impossible for emerging talent to attract investment.

The Florentine opera and concert-going public are very conservative. They will pack the theatre night after night for a bog-standard production of *Turandot* or *Rigoletto*, but only a handful will turn up to hear anything new. Take the spectacular (and spectacularly expensive) production of contemporary composer Silvano Bussotti's *L'Ispirazione* some years ago; it played to practically empty houses.

Opera-going in Italy is an active experience. Apart from first nights (when you go to see and be seen in your latest Armani or Versace number), appreciation is vocal, both positive and negative. The action can be held up for several minutes after an aria which has been particularly well (or badly) sung. Many a poor tenor whose top notes don't quite hit the Pavarotti standard has suffered the humiliation of cat calls and whistles, and the Teatro Comunale still has an unofficial claque which attends every concert and opera and leads the audience vocals.

If you're interested in smaller, more unusual events, watch out for posters around town, and buy the local papers and events magazines (*see* chapter **Media**). The various tourist boards are usually well supplied with information, and there is a useful publication called *Eventi di Toscana* which lists events in Tuscany by the month. And even if the standard of some performances is not high, then the settings in cloisters, churches, castles and villas often compensates.

Principal institutions

Teatro Comunale
Corso Italia 16 (21 11 58/21 35 35/fax 27 79 410/e-mail teatro.comunale@infogroup.it). **Open** *box office* 11am-5.30pm Tue-Fri; 9am-1pm Sat; and one hour before all shows for tickets for that performance. **Credit** AmEx, DC, EC, MC, V.

Florence's municipal theatre is its principal musical institution; a fact which balances a year-round programme of international quality against the shameful lack of public funding for other smaller enterprises. Built in 1882 and extensively renovated in 1957, it is architecturally unexciting, both inside and out, and has suffered in the past from severe acoustical problems. The best seats in the house, in terms of acoustics, are in the second gallery. The theatre is home to a full symphony orchestra (L'Orchestra del Maggio Musicale Fiorentino), chorus, ballet company (Maggio Danza) and the legions of stage, wardrobe and domestic staff that keep a full-time opera house on its feet. It's had its ups and downs; at one time, it was not at all unusual for a first night to be cancelled due to the staff going on strike. However, having gone through a period of relative calm under the guidance of Zubin Mehta (principal conductor since 1985), and with the increasing presence of young members of the orchestra and chorus, the theatre is back on the international stage, and operatic and symphonic productions are, on the whole, of a high standard. Recent guests have included Semyon Bychkov, Carlo Maria Giulini, Riccardo Muti, Seiji Ozawa, Sir Georg Solti, Andrew Davis and Myung-Whun Chung. On the operatic front, the principals may not be La Scala superstars, but are often interesting performers. On the production side, David Hockney, Derek Jarman, Franco Zeffirelli, Jonathan Miller and Graham Vick have all worked here. The orchestra and, recently, the chorus tour regularly, and in 1998 will perform Puccini's *Turandot* in Beijing, in the Forbidden City, produced by Zhang Yimou of *Red Lantern* fame.

The theatre's performing year is divided into three parts. From January until March the concert season offers a new programme each week with performances on Friday and Saturday evenings and Sunday afternoons. October to December sees the opera and ballet season with, normally, four operatic productions, a couple of ballets (including something suitably festive around Christmas), and the odd concert.

The highlight comes in May and June with the Maggio Musicale Fiorentino festival. Founded in 1933, it is the oldest festival in Italy and, with Salzburg and Bayreuth, one of the oldest in Europe. It offers a mixture of concerts – some by visiting international orchestras, ballet and opera companies. Programmes here are usually more interesting than some of the standard fare on offer during the rest of the year, and generally have a theme. The main venue is the Teatro Comunale itself, but **Teatro Verdi** and the exquisite 18th-century **Teatro della Pergola** are also used (*see below*).

Graham Vick's production of Lucia di Lammermoor *at the* **Teatro Comunale**. *See p151.*

Teatro della Pergola

Via della Pergola 12/32 (24 79 651). **Open** *box office*
9.30am-1pm, 3.45-6.45pm, Tue-Sat; 9.45am-noon Sun.
No credit cards.
Inaugurated in 1656, the Pergola is generally acknowledged
to be the oldest theatre in Italy. An intimate venue, it is a glorious example of its kind, and is ideally suited to chamber
music and small-scale opera such as Mozart.

The Amici della Musica season of chamber music concerts, 90 per cent of which are held at the Teatro della
Pergola, offers concerts by world class performers, and the
odd local group. Again, like the Teatro Comunale, pro-
gramming is not thrilling, and certain fields of music are
neglected. There is very little contemporary repertoire on
offer here, and early music is given only a low priority.
However, if you want to hear some of the world's great string
quartets (Borodin, Emerson, Tokyo, Alban Berg) and recital-
ists in the exquisite surroundings of this 18th-century jewel,
you'll not be disappointed. Concerts are usually held on
Saturday and Sunday at either 4pm or 9pm, and the season
runs from October to April (no telephone bookings are
taken). Be prepared for distractions from the rest of the audience. A large part of the boxes are often filled with elderly,
fur-coated ladies who are more interested in the social
aspects of concert-going, and tend to chat through performances and constantly unwrap sweets.

Teatro Verdi

Via Ghibellina 99 (21 23 20). **Open** *box office* 10am-
noon, 4-7pm, daily. **No credit cards**.
Opened in 1854 as an opera house, Teatro Verdi these days
is a rather scruffy looking building from the outside and now
hosts a huge variety of productions. From Bruce Springsteen
to the Philadelphia Orchestra, from the *Rocky Horror Show*
to *The Nutcracker*, from *The Merry Widow* to Lindsay Kemp;
they've all been presented in the 1,500-seat, red and gold
auditorium. Opera, ballet, prose, chamber music operetta,
rock, jazz; there's something for everyone.

Scuola Musica di Fiesole

*Villa La Torraccia, San Domenico (59 97 25). Bus 7, and
and a ten-minute walk.* **Open** 8.30am-8.30pm daily.
Tickets L10,000; reductions for students and OAPs.
No credit cards.
An impressive 16th-century villa in extensive grounds is the
setting for the Music School at Fiesole. Piero Farulli, viola
player of the legendary Quartetto Italiano, and renowned
teacher, is the life blood of the school, and influence behind
the Concerti per gli Amici concert series which takes place
in the 200-seat auditorium at the villa. Between January and
June, and September and December, chamber music concerts
are held roughly every two weeks. Performers are mostly
Italian, many of them ex-students or teachers at the school,
(although international names also crop up), and it's well
worth making the trip to San Domenico (just below Fiesole)
for an alternative to some of the rather stale repertoire and
standard names on offer in town.

Orchestra Regionale Toscana

*Via dei Benci 20 (24 27 67/e-mail www.dada.it/ort-
ort@dada.it).* **Open** *ticket office* see **Teatro Verdi**.
The Orchestra Regionale Toscana, known locally as the
ORT, is a young, energetic, 40-strong chamber orchestra
which was founded in 1980. Its remit was to take classical
musical into the hitherto musical desert of Tuscany outside
Florence. Their season runs from December to May with two
or three concerts a month being played in Florence, and
between 35 and 40 concerts in other Tuscan towns including Pisa, Livorno, Lucca, Siena and Pistoia. For many years,
the ORT's principal Florentine venue was the church of
Santo Stefano, but the Ufizzi bomb of 1993 changed this, and
most concerts are now played in the Teatro Verdi (*see chapter* **Dance and Theatre**). Many international names appear
among soloists and conductors, and the orchestra's repertoire covers everything from Baroque to contemporary
music, with particular emphasis being given to the 19th and
20th centuries.

Accademia Bartolomeo Cristofori

Via Camaldoli 7 (22 16 46). Bus B. **Open** 3-6pm Mon-Fri.

Opened in 1990 and named after the 18th century Florentine 'inventor' of the pianoforte, this institution is based in an unassuming street at the heart of San Frediano. It houses a fine collection of early keyboard instruments, and runs a workshop for restoration and repair. Concerts and seminars, usually concerned with some aspect of early keyboard technique or repertoire, are held regularly in the small, beautifully constructed concert hall next door.

Annual events in Florence

Dec/Jan **Christmas concerts** on Florence's antique organs (*28 08 81*).

1 Jan **New Year concert** by the Scuola di Musica di Fiesole (*59 571*).

June-Oct **Concerts** during the opening of Villas and Gardens, and the evening openings of museums (*28 08 81*).

Oct **Vittorio Gui Conducting Competition** at the Teatro Comunale (*24 06 72*).

Annual events in Tuscany

Estate Fiesolana

(21 98 51/e-mail estate.fiesolana@fts.toscana.it). Bus 7. **Dates** early July, Aug. **No credit cards.**

This festival of music, dance and theatre is based at the Roman Amphitheatre in Fiesole.
http://www.fts.toscana.it

Puccini Opera Festival

Torre del Lago (0584 35 93 22/fax 35 02 77). **Dates** end July-mid Aug.

Puccini's villa on the shore of Lago di Massaciuccoli provides an atmospheric setting for the staging of two or three of the Maestro's operas every year. The stage is erected on the beach, and the 3,150 seats are placed in such a way as to provide the audience with the lake as backdrop to the stage. Don't forget your mosquito repellent. Five performances of each opera are given, and there are usually international soloists involved (although the orchestra often leaves a lot to be desired). Tickets, priced from L45-L120,000, are on sale all year from the above number, or from some travel agencies, and the booking services listed below. To get here by public transport, take the train to Viareggio and bus to Torre del Lago which stops 150m from the auditorium.

Barga Opera Festival

Opera Barga, Via Fornacetta 11, Barga (0583 72 36 01/72 32 50/e-mail operabarga@lunet.lu.it). **Dates** mid-July-mid Aug. **Tickets** L10-20,000. **No credit cards.**

The most intense activity is during the first two weeks of this festival, which combines instrumental and vocal courses with a concert series involving both teachers and students. There is usually an operatic production, and 1998 will see the re-opening of the late 18th-century Teatro dei Differenti in Barga (*see chapter* **Provinces of Lucca and Massa-Carrara**), recently restored and a central venue of the festival. For information, call the above numbers or the tourist office in Barga (*0583 72 34 99*).
http://www.operabargalunet.lu.it

Estate Musicale Chigiana

Accademia Chigiana, Via di Città 89, Siena (0577 46 152). **Dates** July, Aug.

The courses and concerts (both chamber music and larger-scale productions) run by this musical academy take place in and around Siena – venues include the spectacular abbeys

of San Galgano and Sant'Antimo. The Settimana Musicale Senese (a week of music, usually during July) in Siena is the most important period of the festival. Details of tickets and programmes are available from the above number.

Metastasio Classica

Teatro Metastasio, Via B Cairoli 59, Prato (0574 60 85 01). **Open** *box office* 10am-noon, 4-7pm, Tue-Sat. **Dates** Dec-Apr.

Chamber music, recitals and orchestral concerts at the famous theatre in Prato.

As well as the above listings of the principal festivals and seasons in Tuscany, look out for:

Camaiore, Lucca (*0584 96 22 33*). Organ Festival (June).

Impruneta, Florence (*055 29 08 32*). International choral competition concerts held on Saturdays (Sats in June).

Monterchi Concert series held in the garden of the museum of the Madonna del Parto (June).

San Miniato, Pisa (*0571 42 745*). Concerts in castles and villas (June).

Tavernelle Val di Pesa, Florence (*055 80 76 525*). Concerts at the superb monastery of Badia in Passignano (Spring/early Summer).

Vaglia, near Florence) (*055 29 08 32*). Concerts in the grounds of Villa Demidoff (June).

Minor musical associations

Many smaller musical organizations put on worthwhile events. Look out for posters.

Agimus

Via della Piazzola 7r (58 09 96/fax 58 03 01).

An association of young musicians in Florence that organises concerts throughout the year. Most interesting is the Festival Estaste which is held in July and August in the courtyard of Palazzo Pitti with concerts, recitals and opera.

Florence Symphonietta

Via Santa Riparata 40 (847 78 05).

A young, active organisation that puts on concerts – anything from a guitar/violin duo to full chamber orchestra – in and around Florence.

L'Homme Armè

Via San Romano 56, Settignano, Florence (tel/fax 69 77 19).

A fine, small, semi-professional chamber choir which performs repertoire ranging from Medieval to Baroque. There is a summer and an autumn season of three concerts each.

Orchestra da Camera Fiorentina

(78 33 74).

This young Florentine chamber orchestra plays a season of mostly Baroque and Classical concerts between February and the end of September with a break in August.

Tickets

For the main ticket agencies in Florence, *see chapter* **Services**. Many hotels and travel agents book tickets for the main venues. Tickets for productions at the Teatro Comunale are sometimes hard to find as a large proportion of these seats are sold to season ticket holders. However, tickets are put on sale individually and, contrary to popular belief, you may well be lucky.

Music: Roots, Rock & Jazz

Kurt is dead. Long live the Cobain clones.

Florence is a conservative city. Those few of its inhabitants who choose to rebel, certainly have plenty to rebel against, but what might be only an insignificant sub-culture in many cities, is given considerably more weight here by the huge numbers of students in Florence.

Music is naturally central to that rebellion, and among the angry young things of Florence there is a huge enthusiasm for rock, indie and roots. Taking American and English youth culture as its role model, the scene is populated with replicas of Jimi Hendrix, Kurt Cobain and Keith of Prodigy fame, as immaculate in their own way as their Armani clad big brothers, incongruously slouching around the medieval streets with a well studied Generation X apathy.

Tenax is the major live music venue catering to the hunger for the hip. Its superb programmes draw in international artists as varied as Tricky, Incognito, John Spencer Blues Explosion and the Gypsy Kings, as well as Italian stars like Articolo 31 and Neffa (both Italian mafia rap), and Agricantus, a southern-based world music group. Tenax also holds disco nights with themes, competitions for amateur Italian bands, dance-shows and contemporary art happenings.

The *centri sociali*, basically squatted venues such as **CPA Fi-Sud** and **CSA Metamorfosi**, are also important alternative venues. The resident Dub band in CPA Fi-Sud packs in the crowds and Giacalone, a band member, also works for a local radio station playing out classic ska, dub and reggae. **Palasport** at the Campo di Marte (box office: Via Faenza 139r, tel 21 08 04) is a big mainstream venue that hosts international acts such as John McLaughlin and The Cure.

As the summer begins, there is ample opportunity to bask in the sun and appreciate good music and beer at the various Tuscan festivals. **Arezzo Wave** boasts a fine schedule of local and international artists. The main jazz event of the summer is **Umbria Jazz** across the border in the laidback town of Perugia, another fabulous outdoor event encouraging a range of cultural activities and highlighting world famous artists. In late summer there's **Pistoia Blues**.

The Auditorium Flog

Via M Mercati 24b (49 04 37). Bus 8, 14, 20, 28. **Open** depends on event, call for details. **No credit cards**.
A classic student venue with a diverse selection of live music and disco nights and a large stage with decent lighting and acoustics. Flog is very much a cheaper version of Tenax and is usually packed out with cool students and rather less cool drongos. Entrance is normally free, although you can pay up to L15,000 for a special night or live concert. It is pretty dingy and dark inside with a large main room and long bar, without concessions for poverty stricken students – L8,000 for beer, L12,000 for spirits. Look out for their monthly flyers detailing nights of funk, rock and trip hop with cult classic films being shown above the pulsing crowds. If local underground bands interest you this is the place to go. Dance events, blaxploitation and roots music to gothic cyber punk and industrial techno all get a look in.

Be Bop

Via Dei Servi (no phone). **Open** 6pm-1am daily, but erratic. **No credit cards.**
This is a rather stylish jazz and blues bar decorated in fetching Art Nouveau style. Bow-tied barmen efficiently serve a selection of fine German beers and quality cocktails averaging L10,000 – the caipirinha is a literal knock out. On Monday nights the resident band covers rock and reggae standards while jazz and bluesmen also do their thang on occasions. Be Bop resembles an English beer garden with a roof, lots of wooden furniture and no specific dancing area. The crowd of mainly student and musos packs the place out on Mondays – usually a quiet night for the rest of Florence.

Jazz Café

Via Nuova de Caccini 3 (247 97 00). **Open** 9.30pm-1.30am Tue-Fri; 9.30pm-2.30am Sat. **Admission** L10,000 annual membership. **No credit cards.**
An intercom and viewing screen confronts anyone attempting to enter the Jazz Café. If you look sufficiently beatniky, you will be allowed to descend into the pretty underground bar with brick-vaulted ceilings. There's always live jazz on Friday and Saturday nights, when you will be bathed in sultry, smoky fusion or exhilarated by modern experimental. On Tuesday there is a free jamming session where any musician (usually a mix of quality musos and eager students) is welcome to stand up and claim his/her five minutes of fame. The atmosphere is relaxed and informal, attracting an older crowd with excellent cocktails – the mandarin punch is delicious – and photos of jazz greats on the walls. When there is no live music a screen shows concerts by masters such as Dizzy Galespie through to Keith Jarrett.

Rock Café

Borgo Degli Albizi 66r (24 46 62). **Open** 11pm-late Mon-Sat. **No credit cards.**
On entering the Rock Café, you may be surprised to find that no-one here looks remotely like they are into Rock. However, the vibrations from the dance floor may cause some invol-

untary pogo-ing. The temperature on the downstairs dance floor, complete with flashing strobe lights and pulsating bodies, can reach tropical levels with the humidity turning poseurs to prats as their Police sunglasses get fogged up and their make-up melts. You can sometimes hear the odd acid jazz and techno number amid the Bon Jovi and AC/DC. All three of the bars are well-stocked with multitudinous beers and spirits – a minimum of L10,000 must be spent. The mix of the usual trendy Italians, American army cadets and English sex, sun and fun followers co-exist happily. Not for the thrash metal fan or the music snob, but a fair place to get the feel of truly being on holiday.

Spazio Uno

Via Del Sole (no phone). **Open** 9.30pm-2am daily, but erratic. **No credit cards.**
A small live-music venue with the slightly grotty air of a student bar, plus an area for dancing. Local rock and jazz bands play regularly and, on Wednesday nights, crowds of students and travellers in the know pile in for cocktails – not marvellous quality but strong and astoundingly cheap at L3,000. There's a very relaxed party atmosphere with drunken punters getting down and making free with the drum kit. The decor is enhanced by psychedelic projections onto a screen, symbolising the mental state of the drinkers.

Tenax

Via Pratese 46 (30 81 60/fax 30 71 01/info 0336 68 28 98). Bus 29, 30. **Open** 9pm-4am Tue-Sun.
No credit cards.
Tenax is one of the most famous gig venues in Florence with a packed and diverse weekly schedule of popular international bands on tour and local and national Italian celebs and amateurs. Located on the periphery of Florence (and therefore free of the noise level laws that inhibit most central clubs), the pumping bass is cranked up to a level where you feel it through your body rather than via your ears. The spacious club boasts an enormous raised platform dance floor, and ante-chambers, filled with computer games, pool tables and bars, stretching as far as the eye can see. Upstairs are more bars, sofas and café-type seating areas with balconies to view the revellers below. Tenax follows every gig with a disco, often packing out the dance floor with a lot more fervour than the band did. The club music mixes '80s classics by The Cure, Depeche Mode and the Thompson Twins with, somewhat bizarrely, a dusting of the Dream Warriors, A Tribe Called Quest and R Kelly. The crowd is often a strange mix of the left over giggers who could have attended anything from The Brand New Heavies to Motorhead, and cheesy girls with lacy bra-tops, lycra minis and Robert Smith hair, but the atmosphere is generally care-free and amiable. All drinks are L12,000 or L15,000, even if you only want a Perrier, so be sure to go with a fat wallet. Look out for flyers in bars and shops with the forthcoming month's schedule. You may be pleasantly surprised to find your favourite band playing and tickets are cheap.
http://www.dada.it/tenax

Centri Sociali

The *centri sociali autogestiti* are a widespread and distinctive feature of contemporary Italy; no major city is without at least one. These mega-squats are usually located in abandoned buildings and attract a mixed crowd of lefty intellectuals in tweed jackets, pierced punks with dirty dreadlocks and club victims with super-fluorescent plastic clothes and light bulbs in their hair (all of whom, strangely, seem to own at least one dog). They act as unofficial social and arts centres, putting on gigs, exhibitions, films and sometimes offering courses and counselling. The atmosphere is normally relaxed and friendly, although it can be a little rough. Florence's three *centri sociali* have similar political views yet, for reasons best known to themselves, they avoid any interaction or co-operation with each other.

CSA Indiano

Piazzale delle Cascine, Parco delle Cascine (no phone). Bus 30. **No credit cards.**
The Indiano is the city's oldest *centro sociale*. Occupied for more than ten years, it always had the reputation of being more scruffy and less politically involved than the other *centri*. Its founders wanted to have a good time and give exposure to top punk and hardcore bands (particularly from the US). After a couple of years, however, the police closed it down and designated the building as the new HQ for the mounted *carabinieri*, who patrol the nearby Cascine park. However, the city administration abandoned the project and the building, and the squatters moved back in. So, freshly repainted and renamed, it started all over again. The Indiano organises concerts and raves, but also occasional political demonstrations in support of political prisoners around the world.
This year they've scheduled some excellent dance nights on Fridays and Saturdays, with music that includes techno, drum 'n' bass and jungle. Gigs by Italian and foreign bands provide entertainment on other nights. Entrance is very cheap – from L5-8000 depending on the event – as are food and drink. The *centro*, located at the one end of the Cascine park, is easily accessible by car. By bus, take the number 30 from the train station – the driver will know where to drop you off – then walk another 100m in the direction of Vivai Fiorentini.

CPA Fi-Sud (Centro Popolare Autogestito Firenze Sud)

Viale Giannotti 79 (no phone). Bus 31, 32.
No credit cards.
Located in the southern part of Florence, this nine-year-old *centro* is the biggest and most active of the three. Its 1,000-capacity concert hall, known as 'the spaceship', is the largest alternative concert venue in the city. The *centro* also runs a vast range of other activities including a small library, various theatre and film clubs and a photography group. The most interesting project here is the provision of shelters for homeless non-EC citizens. Currently there are around 20 Africans living here. Every Wednesday there is the public assembly where all the *centro*'s various groups meet. Concerts and parties are usually at weekends, but check out the flyers around the city for precise details. Again the prices are low: L5,000 for entrance and about the same for drinks.

CSA Ex-Emerson

Via Niccolò da Tolentino (no phone). Bus 14B.
No credit cards.
Florence's third *centro sociale* is the most politically engaged – maintaining its connections with the *Autonomia Operaia*, the Italian protest movement of the 1970s – and remaining convinced that most of the world's troubles are down to conspiracies by the corporations and conservative governments. Ex-Emerson was particularly active two or three years ago but operates a more low-key operation now (they don't put up flyers like the other *centri*). Every Monday is movie night, with a good selection of old and little known films, while a photography course takes place every Wednesday (the *centro* has a well equipped dark room). Gigs are held every Friday and Saturday from about 8pm – usually by little known Italian bands.

Nightlife

Great Auntie Florence goes early to bed? Don't you believe it – this is one swinging old dear.

> The opening times and closing days of bars and clubs in Florence are notoriously vague and erratic, and change without warning. Phones that are actually answered are a rarity, so be prepared to take a chance.

Florentines rarely eat before 9pm, although they may sip a leisurely aperitif in a bar beforehand. Consequently, bars, pubs and clubs don't ever get going until around 11pm. The only Italians you are likely to find out drinking before this time are desperate carabinieri youths, who have a 11pm curfew. When the natives do finally flock in, don't be surprised if many of them make one drink last most of the night. Italians see booze more as a gentle social lubrication than the shortcut to oblivion favoured by northern Europeans. Most venues are laid out to ensure maximum pose factor for its clientele. Dancing is regarded by the majority of Florentine club-goers as just another way of getting noticed.

Clubs rarely stick to set nights for specific musical styles, preferring to chuck a bit of everything onto the turntables. Most clubs will have a card system of paying that can seem confusing, but is in fact fairly simple. If you're not asked for an entrance fee, you will be handed a small card which must be given in at the bar when buying drinks, and using the cloakroom. It will be stamped, returned to you and requested at the till when you leave. It can be a shock to the system having to pay for six pints and a pina colada all at once, but the bouncers are famously unrelenting when it comes to blagging your way out.

Bars

The African Bar

Via Verracini 10r (35 16 61). Bus 17, 22, 29, 30, 35 (ask to be let off at the Esselunga supermarket on Via Toselli). **Open** 9.30pm-2am daily.
No credit cards.
Off the beaten track but well worth tracking down. Plush red velvet sofas and armchairs, and candle-lit tables evoke a '70s cocktail lounge, while the music drifting through the room ranges from the haunting sounds of Mozambique to reggae and Otis Redding. Punters can make requests from the proprietor Midi's extensive, eclectic record collection. Drinks are all priced at L10,000, and at least one is obligatory on entry, but with exotic cocktails, and measures of Baileys of near half-bottle proportions, the clientele of business types and couples have no complaints. The African Bar is open all day and serves a sublime mix of African and Italian food.

The Art Bar

Via Del Moro 4r (28 76 61). **Open** 6pm-1am daily.
No credit cards.
A wonderfully cosy bar doling out high quality cocktails adorned with cascades of fruit. The pina colada, made with fresh coconut, is the best in Florence. During happy hour (6-9.30pm) all drinks – usually L10 000 – are half price so you can get sloshed for little dosh. The cocktail menu only lists a selection of the potions the barman will knock up for you – so why not test out his skills with your latest invention. The place is small and gets packed early with sophisticated Florentines who barely start their drinks before leaving – it has been known for people to cruise with an extra long straw to suck up the leftovers.

Cactus

Via Ponte Alle Mosse (35 97 83). **Open** 8.30pm-1am daily, but erratic. **No credit cards.**
The well waxed and worshipped bodies of Harley and Ducati machines outside give a clue to Cactus's clientele. Indeed the Florentine taste for Americana finds full expression in this Western theme bar. A good selection of whiskies, liqueurs and imported bottled beers are stocked, although you can only get one Italian beer on tap. Prices are average at L7,000 for beers and L10,000 for mixers and cocktails. The pool table at the far end is surrounded by leathery, bearded dudes in crumpled trousers. Music is loud and varied, with rock vying (surprisingly) with progressive jazz, dance and jungle. The walls are splattered with badly translated American expressions and signposts to well-known cowboy counties. Can be rough on occasions.

Café Pasco

Via Galliani 12r (35 06 06). Bus 17, 23. **Open** 8.30pm-approx 1am Mon-Sat.
No credit cards.
If you are heading for Café Pasco make sure your clothes have got an elasticated waist or, better still, wear a kaftan as this is a Utopia for cocktail fiends, cake fetishists and food fanatics. A mind-numbing number of liqueurs, spirits and other drinks are offered alongside a fine selection of ice-creams, cakes and sandwiches. The zombie cocktail is deadly and the martini comes shaken not shhhhtirred complete with an olive – strangely hard to acquire for your martini in most bars. The decor is reminiscent of a 1930s lido, with cool blue mosaics climbing the wall and a soft languid light. The crowd is quiet and the space well utilised to create an intimate atmosphere. One of the major advantages of this place is that, being out of the centre, it is not competing with those ridiculous central piazza prices, yet the quality is splendiferous. L10,000 for a cocktail and L7,000 for cakes and ice-creams.

Caracao

Via Ginori 10r (21 14 27). **Open** 5.30pm-1.30am Tue-Sun, usually closed Mon. **No credit cards.**
This entirely convincing replica of a South American bar should not be missed. A huge wooden bar adorned with every imaginable type of cocktail and staffed by the most professional of barmen is the honey pot around which the punters buzz. The cheapest and most exciting time to go is happy hour from 7pm to 10pm, during which all the cocktails are L5,000 and salty tortilla chips and spicy salsa make perfect

Central Park, *probably the trendiest club in Florence. See page 159.*

partners for the brain-blowing margaritas. Seating is minimal, consisting of a handful of barstools, so you may find yourself hanging from a coat hook if you stand too near the wall, but it's well worth the discomfort. The cackle of American students and predatory growlings of love-hungry Italian Casanovas create a hum of revelry and high spirits; you will float out of this bar beaming.

Gap Café
Via dei Pucci 5 (28 20 93). **Open** 7pm-1am Mon-Sat.
No credit cards.
With the tantalising allure of discount drinks, a central location and late-night opening, this bar draws in a huge crowd of revellers on a budget-seeking tourist. The decor is bare yet stylish, but beware of the crashed-out adolescent Art History students wobbling and vomiting after one huge tequila too many. If you are lusting for sophistication and long drinks steer clear. L5,000 for cocktails and spirits at happy hour (7-11pm).

Genesi
Piazza Duomo 21 (28 70 47). **Open** 9pm-2am Tue-Sun.
No credit cards.
Lurking in the shadow of the Duomo, Genesi is a civilized joint patronised by the more discerning tourist. An immense ceramic snake frames the bar, looking out onto an interior with a table layout designed to give murmuring young couples a bit of privacy. Smooth jazz chords drift from a corner occupied by trad combos most nights of the week. Prices are what you would expect for a central bar: L12,000 a cocktail. As you often find in Italy, barmen are capable of small miracles; the *affogato* – ice-cream doused in creamy coffee – is a delight.

Papillon
Piazza del Duomo 1 (71 46 35). **Open** approx 3pm-1am daily, but erratic. **No credit cards.**
Papillon is studiedly chic. The heavily styled '80s decor suits the Fly guys and girls who frequent it in their Versace togs, 6-inch platforms and overpowering *eau de toilette*. A mirrored-wall can be horribly distracting for those who thought

they weren't vain, while a beautiful semi-circular bar at the far end of the room ensures the staff a full view of your preening. Upstairs is curiously named Tea Room, an exact replica of downstairs entirely lacking any trace of tea room quaintness. However, considering the location, the drinks are fairly priced at L12,000 for a cocktail.

The Rex Café
Via Fiesolana 25r (24 80 331). **Open** 5pm-2am daily.
No credit cards.
Gaudi-esque mosaics decorate the central bar, Art Nouveau wrought iron lamps shed a soft light, film noir prints hang from the ceiling, and a luscious red ante-chamber creates a secluded space for intimate gatherings. Friendly, efficient, multi-lingual bar staff serve up excellent, exquisitely presented tapas until around 10pm. The crowd is diverse and Rex is large enough to accommodate discreet business symposiums and pre-club hedonists. The sounds are in keeping with the visual aesthetics. During the week, a mixture of trip hop, salsa and the occasional club classic can be heard. At weekends some of Florence's most enlightened DJs grace the decks. The Rex is primarily a cocktail bar; most concoctions are around L10,000; wine is about L5,000 a glass. You can sling your gins until 2am so a moderate pace is advisable.

La Torre
Lungarno Cellini 65r (68 06 43). **Open** 8.30am-5am daily. **No credit cards.**
For drinks, food and cigarettes in the wee hours, La Torre is virtually the only place in Florence to go. Situated in the San Niccolò district, and easily identified by the medieval tower next to it, this bar/restaurant is a heavenly place to while away the early morning hours after a hardcore club session. The first thing to greet you as you walk in the door is the enticing aroma of fried garlic – indeed there's fine fare on offer here, such as *spaghetti al vongole*, *crostini* and a variety of tapas. Expressionist oil paintings decorate the warm red and yellow walls, creating a relaxing atmosphere. The usual cocktails, beers and wine are available at the bar

(L7-L12,000) and are all served in elegant glasses. The clientele tends to be stylish, as is the soundtrack of jazz, dub and drum 'n' bass that provides a nice subtle background to animated chat.

Zoe's
Via Dei Renai 13r (24 31 11). **Open** 8am-1am Mon-Sat; 5pm-1am Sun. **Credit** AmEx, V.
Friendly staff are a feature of this vibrantly decorated, elegant bar. During happy hour (5-10pm) they ensure that the bar and tables are well provided with crisps, popcorn and local morsels such as foccasia stuffed with salamis and cheeses. Try the Zoe's cocktail – a lethal mix of vodka, gin and cointreau blended with fresh strawberries, sugar and crushed ice. The place is always throbbing with a loud crowd of cocktail gluggers and at L6,000 a go during happy hour you can see why.

Pubs

Chequers
Via della Scala 7r (28 75 88). **Open** 6.30pm-1.30am Sun-Thur; 6.30pm-2.30am Fri, Sat. **Credit** V.
A popular pub near the local national service barracks – beware the eagle-eyed, freshly shorn, acne-afflicted guys in packs; they are desperately on the pull. The English-speaking bar staff are very friendly and the place is so huge that there's no particular vibe or dress code; you can create your micro-climate in a distant corner. It's basically a regular watering-hole catering for the masses with wooden chairs and tables, and off-white wall-paper. There's a happy hour between 8 and 10pm when drinks are half price. Theme parties are a rather frequent occurence. Music is of the in-yer-face indie-rock variety – Nirvana, Faith No More, Doors et al. If you are travelling alone this is the place to make a bee-line for as you will be able to hook up with travellers of all different nationalities, though women may find those spotty sex-starved soldiers too persistent for comfort.

Fiddler's Elbow
Piazza Santa Maria Novella (no phone). **Open** approx 11am-1am daily.
Always crammed with a mix of young foreign students searching for adventure, and a bouncy crowd of hungry local and military youths. This is one of the worst bars in Florence but, thanks to its central location, it is also almost certainly the busiest. The decor is drab, dark and dingy but then the clientele are not there to lounge – the Fiddler's is the pub equivalent of a fast-food joint: you go in, you pull and you leave (or go home and squeeze your spots depending on your luck). Consequently the place is a huge pain for women travelling without heavy duty protection as the guys are predatory and work in packs. Then again there is usually a supply of flatter-hungry bimbos to be sopped up once they realise you're not interested. The bar staff seem incapable of speaking Italian, making the Fiddler's Elbow a good pastiche of one of the worst or London-Irish dives.

Kikuya
Via Benci 43r (234 48 79). **Open** 7pm-1.30am Wed-Mon. **Credit** V.
Kikuya specialises in powerful, fairly cheap and extremely large cocktails. A smaller venue would be hard to find but, as with the majority of pubs in Florence, you won't have a problem finding a seat if you arrive before 8pm. The large, well-lit bar has a few tables and chairs scattered around it, and there's a side room with a fair amount of seating space and full table service. Unlike most pubs, Kikuya features live bands – usually Italian and acoustic – who play so close to drinkers that you can almost reach out and have a twang yourself. There is also a TV screen in the main seating area showing live sport and the occasional bikini-watch if a bloke gets his hands on the zapper. Happy hour runs from 7-10pm (cocktails are only L5,000 and sandwiches are half-price).

The B-52 cocktail is guaranteed to constrict your windpipe for several minutes – but who ever said that getting out of your head was painless.

The Lion's Fountain
Borgo degli Albizi 34r (23 44 412). **Open** 4pm-2am daily. **No credit cards**.
Another of Florence's many Irish pubs, but this place's atmosphere and homey decor are a cut above the rest. The music is the barman's own choice (generally familiar classics, '80s pop and traditional pub ballads such as *American Pie*). Food is generally good – sandwiches, salads and port cake are served until the early hours. Two TVs show local and foreign sporting events for the beer-swillers. They pull a fair pint of Guinness and the atmosphere is open and friendly to all. You can even get cocktails here.

The Old Stove
Via Pellicceria 24r (28 46 40). **Open** noon-2.30am daily. **No credit cards**.
Coat your hair with gel, put on your most puffy puffer jacket and head to the Old Stove, the most typically Italian Irish pub in the city. This cramped den is all tables and chairs and very little bar, with full table service from narky waitresses serving watery cider, and the inevitable *Pulp Fiction* soundtrack blaring from the speakers just to make sure you don't start to feel too comfortable. Be prepared to be singed by gesticulating cigarette smokers, ignored by overworked waitresses and to break a leg slipping on the floor of the toilet after 9pm on a Saturday. The Guinness is not bad.

Robin Hood Tavern
Via dell'Oriuolo (24 46 79). **Open** 5pm-1am daily. **No credit cards**.
This pub has the air of a gone-to-seed seaside boozer. Nevertheless, it's one of the larger pubs in Florence and is always crammed with travellers and Italian Anglophiles – usually students and Indie kids – making it a very rowdy place. Barely drinkable Guinness is on tap and a mediocre selection of beers and spirits will set you back L7,000 for a pint and L10,000 for a short. If you are feeling extra stingy you could pay L3,000 for a glass of revolting Chianti. Decoration is drab and dank with beer barrels, dart-boards and smutty postcards doing little to cheer. The owner, an ex-biker from Birmingham, blasts out heavy duty Rock.

Il Tripper Tre
Borgo Ognissanti (31 03 26). **Open** 8pm-2am, usually closed Mon. **No credit cards**.
This is a smallish rockers' bar plastered in pop-rock memorabilia – look out for the Elvis pendulous pelvis clock. The music is deafening and the beer selection is limited, with only Harp, Kilkenny and Guinness on tap, but the latter isn't bad, and not too pricey at an average L7,000 for a pint and L8,000 for spirits. Grungy, friendly Italian students make up the bulk of the clientele. Not the place to go if you're looking for adventure, but if beer, fags and howling Kurt Cobain is your thing then swing your dreds down to this small, friendly, smoky bar.

Clubs

Cabiria Café
Piazza Santo Spirito 4r (21 57 32). **Open** 8am-1.30am Mon, Wed-Thur; 8am-2.30am Fri-Sun. **No credit cards**.
This mega-trendy dive doubles up as a daytime café and always manages to keep a cosy, exclusive air whether it's 2am or 2pm. The main congregating area is unfortunately in the micro corridor alongside the bar where long hair will be dipped from drink to drink walking towards the toilet at the other end of the room. The loo is a work of art in itself, plastered in 'adult' cartoons of women with 1½ cm waists, 2m legs and gravity defying E cups. At the end of the bar is a wide screen projector, always tuned in to the local TV channel TMC2 (somewhat pointlessly, as they never have the

sound on). However, if you want to be rid of a persistent admirer, you can always fixate zombie-like on Tom and Jerry and may eventually get the message. The main seating area in the back room is beautiful yet functional with greeny blue walls, stunning chandeliers, nailed-down chairs and tables, a huge 'bar at the Folie Bergères' mirror and the occasional sandbag. The DJs start up around 9pm and play an eclectic selection of sounds, including trip hop, reggae and jazz.

Central Park
Parco Delle Cascine (no phone). **Open** from about midnight till late. **No credit cards**.
Probably the trendiest club in Florence – this is the place to see serious local clubbers inspired by the freshest music. The resident DJs also work at the funkiest record shop in Florence, KAOS on Via della Scala, and therefore have access to all the latest jungle, hip hop and trip hop sounds. The decor is sombre and dark. Semicircular booths surround an ample dance floor. Don't miss Saturday night – a progressive selection of jungle and drum 'n' bass is played out on a wicked sound system by the hardcore jungle DJs. Special events with live PA and psychedelic local artists' installations drag the crowds in. There is the common card system of paying at the till before you leave for the minimum sum of L15,000 including a drink, but it's no rip-off here. Condoms are dispensed in the toilets although unfortunately the deafening bass will probably shag you out before you get the chance to use them.

Full-Up
Via della Vigna Vecchia 25r (29 30 06). **Open** 11pm-4am Tue-Sat; closed June-Sept. **No credit cards**.
Boob tubes, open-necked shirts, hairy chests and huge cleavages are in abundance in this mirrored-walled, disco-lit club. There are also plenty of comfy snogging sofas, but lads-on-the-pull will probably find that most girls here are too busy looking at their own reflections to give them a second glance. The music tends to be an unbearable mixture of Euro-cheese and dated house, although prices are reasonable at L12,000 for a mixer and L15,000 for a cocktail. Admission is free before midnight, L10,000 after.

Lido
Lungarno Pecori Giraldi 1 (23 42 726). Bus 8, 23.
Open 11pm-3am Tue-Sun. **No credit cards**.
One of the prettiest bar/clubs in Florence by virtue of its view of the Arno. Entrance is by way of what seems to be a ramp leading up to a fire exit. Inside, Lido's not huge but the glass windows and garden extend down to the river bank, while awkwardly-placed chairs spill onto the central dance floor. There is no entry fee, and therefore no obligatory bevying, although drink prices are reasonable, ranging from L3,000 for cheap wine to L10,000 for spirits and mixers. A diverse weekly music schedule rotates DJs specialising in hip hop, trip hop, jungle and drum 'n' bass. Keep a lookout for DJ Pise who organises all the events, makes collectable flyers and specialises in Incredibly Strange Music. The crowd can be strange too, and sometimes look at odds with the music, but if you drink enough wine and whirl yourself into a disco daze you won't notice them – this isn't a meat market so at least you wont get slimed on. Enjoy the ambience but slap on plenty of mosquito cream.

Maracana Discosamba Ristorante
Via Faenza 4 (21 02 98). **Open** 11.30pm-4am Tue-Sun.
No credit cards.
This latino club is surprisingly classy, but don't expect to see the 'suits' downing jugs of Sangria and loosening their ties on the dance floor – most Italians would never dream of dancing so hard that they sweat. The club is a huge octagon with a central dance-floor equipped with poser platforms. The DJ is positioned in a raised box and balconies assure a perfect view of cleavages and bald patches. The huge bar runs along one wall and stocks an impressive range of spirits, beers and wine, all costing around L10,000. Music is chiefly samba and salsa, with the Gypsy Kings (inevitably) and Macarena (unfortunately) prominent. Admission is between L15,000 and L30,000.

Maramao
Via dei Macci 79r (24 43 41). **Open** 6pm-2am Tue-Sun.
Credit AmEx, DC, EC, MC, V.
Be sure you have on your sleekest shade of black, your blankest expression and your split ends tucked away or you

In the Mood in **The Mood 1**. *See page 160.*

will be sure to suffer severely by comparison with the coif-feured clientele you will encounter in this discobar. Maramao has a sharp, linear decor with metallic fixtures under electric blue lighting. A ramp leads up to the dance floor, bar and a balcony which overlooks the controlled and self-consciously sober hip-swingers. The DJ, imprisoned in a self-contained attic 12ft above the floor, plays an excellent mix of the most up-to-date dance with Latin American sam-ples and happy house. Admission is free and drinks aver-age out at around L10,000, so getting drunk won't break the bank, and there is table service if you can't stand up. Look out for the photographs of Maramao's revellers on the walls alongside the ramp – they are 'um, well... ur...' says Mark, our *Time Out* photographer.

Meccanò

Viale degli Olmi 1 (33 13 71). Bus 1, 9, 12, 17, 26, 27, C. **Open** *restaurant* 9.30-11.30pm Tue-Sat; *club* 11pm-4am. **Admission** L30,000 (including first drink). **Credit** AmEx, DC , EC, MC, V.

Florence's most famous club is a massive maze of a place with a Saturday Night Malarial Fever atmosphere. The rare and, to some, offensive spectacle of go-go dancers on pedestals (displaying more enthusiasm and flesh than tal-ent) can be found on the main dance floor, but they're the lucky ones who get some breathing space. The dance area is always so packed you will find that the only dance move available to you is the gangster rapper head nod. However, you're more likely to hear Euro-house and dated rave than the sounds of Tupac and Dr Dre. There are three bars and lounge areas. Drinks are fairly expensive, starting at L10,000. The crowd is mixed, which in Italy means shop assistants in cool threads, next to accountants in cool threads. Girls be forewarned, if you follow the less-is-more style in clothes you may find yourself in some bother on exit as Meccanò is situated in the Cascine park, famous for hookers, hustlers and pimps. The extra money on a taxi would be well spent.

The Mood 1

Corso Tintori 4 (no phone). **Open** approx 10pm till late Tue-Sat. **No credit cards.**

Despite its English name, this is very much a Florentine nightspot. In common with several other clubs in Florence it is situated underground, transformed from a wine cellar into a genuinely sophisticated subterranean dancing expe-rience. The Mood 1 styles itself a 'house' club, but the music is as diverse as the punters it attracts. Tuesday night's eclec-tic selections of drum 'n' bass and Thursday's mix of hip hop, soul and swing are particularly popular with students. The crowd really gets stomping when a party is organised – usually once a week. Expect the odd celebrity DJ. When the relentless pounding bass gets too much, relax in the chill-out room or lounge at the bar, sipping cocktails. Admission is just L15,000.

Pegasos

Via Palazzuolo 82r (21 34 31). **Open** approx 10.30pm till late. **No credit cards.**

Strictly speaking, Pegasos is a private club, but anyone can join. Simply ring the doorbell and on entering the staff will take your name, slap it on a card and away you go. Shane MacGowan doppelgangers be forewarned – a split second vetting system is in play. Once inside, however, you can ponce till daybreak (6am) with a hyper-trendy (yet curi-ously friendly) crowd. Candle-lit tables and low lighting creates an intimate atmosphere. Psychedelic projections onto the turquoise walls send out oceanic vibes to the blissed-out crowd whilst DJ Francesco spins ambient licks, pumping dance with rumblings of intelligent drum 'n' bass. If you are in need of re-hydration, hot shoe shuffle to the bar where beer sets you back L7,000, wine L5,000 and spir-its and cocktails L10,000. Admission is free. See if you can spot your parents in the panoramic black and white of Woodstock behind the bar.

Pongo

Via Verdi 59r (no phone). **Open** approx 10pm till late. **No credit cards.**

In the shadows of Santa Croce, the jungle jugular pulsates with the most vital nutrients for vampiric breakbeat junkies. Audio Logic 100% – pure jungle and drum 'n' bass – at Pongo on a Tuesday night must not be missed. A handful of the best drum 'n' bass and jungle fiends lash the crowds with steaming London trax. DJ Peedoo, a staunch drum 'n' bass disciple punishes the sound system with Ed Rush, Maldini and compulsory Alex Reece and Bukem to keep the pace rac-ing. DJs Lovecalò and Simone Fabbroni continue the crusade playing out Goldie, Doc Scott and Peshay to an eager crowd. The interior is stark and the bar flows along the length of the chill-out room. Climb the ramp to access the tribal gath-ering. A minimalistic dance floor and flickering vision, enforced by strobe lighting create unavoidable encounters with clubbers and columns. A cryptic admission system exists. Entry is free, but granite faced sentinels dispense black calling cards to be exchanged for white exit cards with your obligatory L10,000 drink. No drink, no exit, so teetotal clubbers out there beware.

Space Electronic

Via Palazzuolo 37 (29 30 82). **Open** 10pm-2am daily; closed Mon in winter. **Credit** AmEx, MC, V.

This vast venue (claiming to be the largest in Europe) with mirrored walls and dark, smoky interior is the quintessen-tial cheesy continental discotheque. The columns on the lower floor are supported by grotesque plastic devils sym-bolising, unintentionally, one assumes, the fearful reality of this clubbers' hell; a modern day inferno with several of the seven deadly sins happening before your eyes, although dreary insipidness is the most offensive sin on show here. The unsuspecting tourists that have been tempted in do not deserve the extreme tortures and lusty tongues of the des-perate Romeos who drunkenly thrust their pelvises spas-modically in the hope of contact with something. Surprisingly, however, decent music and a good dancey vibe can be found on the lower of the two dance floors; Thursday is a revelation, with chilled hip hop and swing. Beware Saturday night, though: it's a cattle market with BSE regu-lations blatantly flouted. Admission is L25,000.

Yab

Via Sassetti 5r (21 51 60). **Open** 8pm-4am Wed-Mon. **Credit** AmEx, DC, V.

If anyone tells you that this is the place to be, be assured that they are either horribly deluded, lying through their teeth or insane. This preening, poncy excuse for a club is nothing but a sad, dreary relic of the worst type of '80s disco, attempt-ing to appear modern and swish to the try-hard regulars and unsuspecting tourists. Most of this huge place is taken up by a dance floor covered by squares which light up Michael Jackson 'Billie Jean' style, surrounded by wall-to-wall bars on raised platforms. There is seating space which usually displays 'reserved' cards, always empty but covered in used glasses which the dickie-bowed waiters frantically clear away in anticipation of the never-to-arrive VIPs. The music is a horrendous mix of never-cool dance tracks and fairly good dance tracks ruined by no-talent DJs. However, you won't see the crowd complaining since dancing is the last thing on anyone's mind in Yab. This is strictly a cattle-mar-ket – the tighter the jeans, lower the top, and harsher the make-up, the greater the chance of pulling – and the compe-tition is fierce. Watch out for the sly and sneaky card sys-tem (and bouncers) employed here. A card is handed to you on entry which must be handed in at the till before exiting with a minimum of L30,000 spent. The only indication of this rip-off scheme is a miniscule sign by the entrance, usually with a fatheaded bouncer conveniently placed directly in front of it obscuring your view. If you find yourself trapped in this nightmare of a club, the best advice is to order the stiffest of drinks available, pay up and then run for your life.

Sport & Fitness

Where to practise your breast stroke, golf strokes and oar strokes.

Sporting goods shops

Galleria dello Sport
Via Ricasole 25/33r (21 14 86). **Open** 9am-7.30pm Mon-Fri; 9am-1pm, 3.30-7.30pm, Sat.
Of the centrally located sporting goods stores, the Galleria offers the widest selection of standard gym attire and athletic shoes.

Olimpia Sport
Via Lamberti 12r (28 76 72). **Open** 9.30am-7.30pm Mon-Fri; 9.30-1pm, 3.30-7.30pm, Sat.
Reliable supplier of sporty equipment and clothing.

Canoeing

If you want to canoe on the Arno, you'll need to join one of the clubs below.

Societa Canottieri Comunali
Lungarno Ferrucci 6 (68 12 151/68 12 549).
Open 8.30am-9pm daily. **Membership** L180,000 plus L470,000 annual fee or L40,000 per month.
Free lessons and training are given to new members. There's are also a gym. Bring a passport-size photo when applying for membership (available 4-7pm Mon, Wed, Fri).

Societa Canottieri Firenze
Lungarno Luisa de' Medici (28 21 30/21 10 93).
Open 8am-8pm daily. **Membership** L100,000 (1 month).
This rowing society enjoys a prime location on the bank of the Arno under the Uffizi. There are also gym facilities, a tank and showers. Again, bring a passport-size photo when applying for membership.

Football

Florentines are football fanatics, despite the fact that the local Serie A team, **Fiorentina**, are perennial under-achievers. Fiorentina play at the **Stadio Artemio Franchi** (*57 26 25/57 88 58*). The season runs from August to May. Games are played on Sundays and begin at 2.30/3pm. Tickets range from around L30,000 (for seats on 'le curve', where the rowdier fans sit) to L200,000, depending on the team that Fiorentina is playing.

Golf

Centro Golf Ugolino
Via Chiantigiana 3, Impruneta (23 01 009). **Open** 9am-6.30pm daily. **Rates** *18 holes* L95,000 Mon-Fri; L110,000 Sat, Sun. *9 holes* L70,000 Mon-Fri; L80,000 Sat, Sun.
This course in Impruneta, south of Florence, is the nearest to the city. Tournaments are often played on the weekends, at which time the course is not open to the public. Phone for the week's schedule and to make reservations.

Angst-ridden times on the football pitch.

Gyms

Indoor Club
Via Bardazzi 15 (43 02 75/43 07 03). **Open** 10.30am-10pm Mon-Sat. **Membership** L100,000 annual fee plus L390,000 for every two months (minimum two-month membership).
The gym has an indoor pool, full weight facilities and aerobics classes.

Palestra Ricciardi
Borgo Pinti 75 (47 84 44/24 78 462). **Open** 9am-10pm Mon-Sat. **Membership** L110,000 (1 month); L230,000 (3 months); L410,000 (6 months); L730,000 (1 year).
This is the largest, most central and modern of Florence's gyms; it is consequently also the most expensive. It offers plenty of Nautilus and free weights, bicycles, aerobics and strength-training classes.

Palestra Women Club
Via Corelli 83 (43 02 02). **Open** 10am-10pm Mon-Fri. **Membership** L100,000 (1 month).
Women-only private gym.

Top Club
Via Masaccio 101 (57 47 86). **Open** 10am-10pm Mon-Fri; Sat 10am-6pm. **Membership** L100,000 (1 month); L210,000 (3 months).
Top Club is small but has character. There is a room of Nautilus weights, one of free weights and one with a few stationary bikes, also used for aerobics classes and stretching.

Horse riding

Maneggio Marinella
Via Di Macia 21, Travalli Calenzana (88 78 066).
Open 9am-1pm, 3.30-7.30pm, Mon-Fri.
Rides are normally organised for Saturday and Sunday, and cost L20,000 per person per hour. You should phone during the week to reserve a spot. They can also arrange lessons and special/group trips on request.

Skating

There are no ice-skating rinks in Florence.

Pista Patinaggio
Via di Soffiano 11 (70 25 91). **Open** hours vary Sat, Sun (phone for details).
There's a monthly fee of L70,000, offering unlimited access to this roller skating rink in the Oltrarno.

Sport clubs/unions

Centro Universitario Sportivo (CUS)
Via delle Rovere 2 (42 50 336/45 46 70). **Open** 9am-6pm daily Mon-Fri. **Membership** L10,000.
Membership of this students-only sports complex – the university sports club – is a bargain (bring your student ID card and a photo). Facilities and equipment offered include basketball courts, football (teams and competitions can be organised), tennis and weight-training. Membership is available 9am-1pm, 3-6pm, daily.

Complesso Affrico
Viale Fanti 20 (61 06 81). **Open** 8am-7pm Mon-Fri.
This public sports facility has tennis courts, basketball courts and football fields. Membership (L120,000 per year) entitles you to reduced rates for court and equipment rental (eg tennis courts cost L14,000 per slot for members, L16,000 for non-members). The complex employs tennis coaches (and can arrange playing partners with similar levels of ability) and organises mens' basketball and football teams. Membership is available 8am-noon, 4-7pm, daily.

Complesso Assi Gigliorosso
Viale Michelangelo 64 (68 12 686). **Open** *playing grounds* 8am-dusk Mon-Sat; 8am-noon Sun.
Membership L400,000 (annual) or monthly (*see below*).
The Assi complex houses fields for athletics, basketball and

volleyball as well as a gym. Monthly memberships are available to students and foreigners only, and cost L50,000 (for access to the running track) or L80,000 (for access to all facilities). Membership is available 9am-1pm, 3-6pm, Mon-Fri.

Swimming pools

Amici del Nuoto
Via del Romito 38b (48 39 51). **Open** *pool* noon-9pm Mon-Sat.
Membership fees are L90,000 per month, which entitle you to use the pool two times per week.

Fiorentina Nuoto, Via di Ripoli 72 *(68 77 58. Open 9am-1pm, 3-7pm, Mon-Fri)*, has extensive information on swimming teams, competitions, and swimming lessons. Its main pools are:

Piscina Bellariva
Lungarno Colombo 6 (67 75 41). **Open** 8-11pm Tue, Thur; 9.30am-1.30pm Sat, Sun. **Admission** L9,500; *under14s* L6,000.

Piscina Marcellino
Via Chiantigiana (65 30 00 00). **Open** 10am-9pm Mon-Sat. **Membership** L80,000 per month (unlimited access).

Piscine Pavoniere
Via Catena 2 (35 26 07). **Open** *summer* phone for details.

Walking & jogging

Most joggers head for the **Giardino dei Semplici**, **Bobolino** or **Forte Belvedere** (*see chapter* **Florence By Area**). If you are interested in taking part in organised events, or running with groups, contact the following:

Organizzazione Firenze Marathon
Casella Postale 597, 50100 Firenze (tel/fax 57 28 85).
Contact for details of Florence's December marathon.

Associazione Atletica Leggera
Via Matteotti 15 (57 14 01). **Open** 9am-1pm, 3.30-6.30pm, Mon-Fri.
Well-informed and helpful organisation who can supply information on local running clubs and races.

Calcio in costume

One of the most spectacular, colourful and violent events of the Florentine year is the celebrated **Calcio in costume** or **Calcio storico**. Strapping representatives of the city's four ancient quarters – Santa Croce, Santa Maria Novella, Santo Spirito and San Giovanni, clad respectively in blue, red, white and green costumes, parade through the city before settling ancient rivalries in Piazza Santa Croce. The game is a no-holds-barred version of football, the origins of which may be as old as the city itself. Calcio was certainly going strong in the 15th century and, although the tradition fell into disuse at the end of the 18th century, it was revived in 1930. The game is played over one hour by two teams of 27 men, with the only rule being that you have to get the ball over your opponent's end line to score. Four matches are played annually, usually in June (*see chapter* **Florence By Season**). It is, unsurprisingly, a pretty violent affair. For more information contact: Calcio Storico Fiorentina, Piazza di Parte Guelfa 1r (*2398302/http://www.globeit.com/globeit/caf/home.html*).

Florence in Focus

MODERN PAINTERS

Major British and American writers contribute to the U.K.'s most controversial art magazine:

- ■ JULIAN BARNES

- ■ WILLIAM BOYD

- ■ A.S.BYATT

- ■ PATRICK HERON

- ■ HILTON KRAMER

- ■ JED PERL

- ■ JOHN RICHARDSON

- ■ PETER SCHJELDAHL

- ■ RICHARD WOLLHEIM

Autumn issue out 14 September will include a wealth of features on The Venice Biennale

Business

It is possible to make deals without oiling wheels in Italy – here are a few useful starting points.

Auditors & accountants

Arthur Anderson & Co
Viale Matteotti 25 (58 27 43/fax 57 44 39). **Open** 9am-1pm, 2-6pm, Mon-Thur; 9am-1pm, 2-5pm Fri.

Coopers & Lybrand
Viale Matteotti 25 (58 07 47/fax 58 71 63). **Open** 9am-1pm, 2-6.30pm, Mon-Fri.

Deloitte & Touche
Via Cavour 64 (23 96 385/fax 28 21 47). **Open** 9am-1pm, 2-6pm, Mon-Fri.

KPMG Peat Marwick Consultants
Corso Italia 2 (21 33 91/fax 21 58 24). **Open** 9am-1pm, 2-6pm, Mon-Fri.

Price Waterhouse & Associates
Via Bonifacio Lupi 11 (47 17 47/fax 47 07 79). **Open** 8am-1pm, 2.30-6.30pm, Mon-Fri.

Banks

Most banks are open from 8.30am-1.20pm, 2.30-3.30pm, Mon-Fri; closed on Sat, public holidays. Banks close early on the days preceding national holidays (around 11am). Below are listed the main branches.

Banca Commerciale Italiana
Via dei Tornabuoni 16 (27 851/fax 21 99 76).

Banca Mercantile Italiana
Piazza Davanzati 3 & Piazza Strozzi 10r (27 651/fax 27 65 207).

Banca Toscana
Via del Corso 6 (43 911/fax 43 79 036).

Cassa di Risparmio di Firenze
Via Bufalini 4-6 (26 121/fax 26 12 907).

Deutsche Bank
Via Strozzi 16r (27 061/fax 21 88 03).

Monte dei Paschi di Siena
Via de Pecori 6-8 (49 711/fax 49 71 239).

Business centres, receptions & conference organisers

Castello di Vincigliata
Via di Vincigliata 13 Fiesole (59 95 56).
This historic castle, located in the hills near Fiesole, is used primarily for weddings and social receptions. It has beautiful gardens and commanding views of the surrounding area. Up to 150 people can be accommodated, and there are full catering and translation services available. It costs L1,500,000 to rent a room for a half-day.

Centro Affari Firenze (& Palazzo degli Affari)
Via Cennini 5 (27 731/fax 27 73 433).
This complex organises local and international business meetings and conferences. It can accommodate up to 1,800 people and offer catering and translation services.

Centro Internazionale Congressi Firenze
Piazza Adua 1 (26 025/fax 21 18 30).
A centre specialising in international meetings; it can accommodate parties from five to 1,000.

Convivium
Via de Sanctis 12-18r (66 68 78/fax 67 99 91).
Convivium owns a variety of locales – mostly villas – in Tuscany which they rent out for conventions and banquets. The buildings, surroundings and services are of the highest quality; and the prices charged match. Depending on the occasion and services required, villa rental typically costs several million lire per day.

Palazzo Budini Guttai
Piazza SS Annunziata 1 (21 08 32/fax 21 20 80).
This 15th-century palazzo is now used to hold business meetings and conferences for up to 40 people. A standard room costs L400,000 (plus IVA, value added tax) per half-day, and catering can be arranged. There are no translation services.

Business information

Camera di Commercio, Industria, Artigianato e Agricoltura (Chamber of Commerce)
Piazza Giudici 3 (27 951/fax 27 95 259).

Consulates

The nearest consulates for Australia and New Zealand are in Rome.

British Consulate
Lungarno Corsini 2 (28 41 33/fax 21 91 12). **Open** 9.30am-12.30pm, 2.30-4.30pm, Mon-Fri.

United States Consulate
Lungarno Vespucci 38 (23 98 276/fax 28 40 88). **Open** 9am-1pm Mon-Fri.

Couriers

Bartolini
Via Ponte all'Asse 12, Sesto Fiorentino (30 950/fax 37 55 78). **Open** 8.30am-noon, 2-6pm, Mon-Fri.
Bartolini offers an express service in Italy and to the rest of Europe (excluding Scandinavia). To send a 5kg package

50-horse power **Pony Express**.

from Florence to Rome costs L55,000; from Florence to the UK is L70,000 and takes three days. Prices include pick-up.

DHL

Toll-free 1678 29 069.
Letters (up to 150g) cost L58,000 to the UK, L56,000 to the US (guaranteed delivery within 48 hours). A 5kg package is L180,000 to the UK, L204,000 to the US (guaranteed delivery within 2-3 days). Free same-day pick-up is offered if you phone before 3pm.

Federal Express

Toll-free 1678 33 040. **Open** 8am-7pm Mon-Fri.
Letters (up to 500g) cost L50,400 (plus IVA) to the UK, L50,000 to the US. A 5kg package is L152,900 (plus IVA) to the UK, L183,000 to the US. Next-day service is guaranteed for all deliveries placed before 4pm (except on Friday). Free pick-up.

Menicalli

Via della Fonderia 79 (22 94 80/fax 22 95 85).
Italy-wide courier service with guaranteed delivery within 24 hours. Standard letters cost L30,000 plus IVA.

Pony Express

Via Corelli 27 (43 87/toll-free 167 01 11 00).
Open 8.30am-7.30pm Mon-Fri.
Pony Express guarantees delivery in Florence within one hour and within 24 hours for other destinations in Italy and the rest of the world. A letter within Florence costs L10,000, and L36,000 to elsewhere in Italy. Packages up to 1kg are L75,000 to the UK and L80,000 to the US. Free pick-up is offered only in the morning.

UPS

Toll-free 1678 22 055.
Letters (up to 500g) are L73,000 to the UK, L59,000 to the US (guaranteed delivery by 10.30am the next day). A 5kg package costs L189,200 to the UK, L216,000 to the US (guaranteed delivery within two days). Free same-day pick-up is offered if you phone before 1pm.

Freight forwarders

Danzas

Via Provinciale Lucchese 181/77, Sesto Fiorentino (23 861/fax 34 10 51). **Open** 8.30am-12.30pm, 2.30-7pm, Mon-Fri.
Danzas charges L200,000 to forward a 5kg package to the US or the UK. There is a pick-up charge of L20,000.

Interpreters & translators

Centro Comit

Viale Lavagnini 54 (49 65 67/fax 49 94 96). **Open** 9am-1pm, 3-7pm, Mon-Fri.
Translators and interpreters.

Emyservice

Lungarno Soderini 1 (21 92 28/fax 21 89 92).
Open 9.30am-1.30pm, 3-7pm, Mon-Fri.
Emyservice claims to offer a full written and spoken translations in "all" languages. Prices vary depending on the service requested; phone for further details.

Interpreti di Conferenza

Via Faenza 109 (23 98 748). **Open** 9am-1pm Mon-Fri.
Specialises in providing interpreters for business meetings.

Limousines

Euronoleggio

Via Torcicoda 99/9 (tel/fax 78 39 96/cellular phone 0336 32 02 72). **Open** 9am-1pm, 3-7pm, Mon-Fri; cellular number always available.
A limousine or minivan (holding up to eight people) plus driver costs L200-300,000 for eight hours, plus petrol and driver expenses.

Europedrive

Via Bisenzio 35/37 (42 22 839/fax 42 22 893).
Open *phone service* 7am-1am daily.
A limousine (or minivan) and personal driver is L280,000 for six hours (typically three hours in the morning and three hours in the afternoon; it costs an additional L30,000 to have six consecutive hours), and includes 100km worth of petrol. Hourly rates are L40,000 8am-8pm; L50,000 from 8pm.

Photocopying centres

See chapter **Services: Faxing & Photocopying**.

Postal & packing services

David

Via del Pollaiolo 83 (70 50 72/fax 73 98 794).
Open 9am-1pm, 3-7pm, Mon-Fri.
This firm is concerned chiefly with large (ie commercial) moves and industrial packing. At-home (or office) pick-up is guaranteed. As prices vary widely depending on size, weight and fragility of the items being shipped, it is best to phone them for the most accurate prices quotes.

Oli-Ca

Borgo SS Apostoli 27r (23 96 917). **Open** 9am-1pm, 3.30-7.30pm, Mon-Fri; 9am-1pm Sat.
Not only does Oli-Ca sell Florentine paper and boxes and accessories of all sizes, but they also offer full packing services. For the full preparation (ie all materials and labour included) of a box measuring 70 x 40 x 25cm, the cost is L15,000. They do not have a mailing service; the main post office is two blocks away.

Children

Places for splashing, dashing, playing and straying.

A city brimming with heavyweight art galleries, churches and museums does not, on first consideration, appear the ideal place to take children. However, Florence has plenty of child-friendly attractions, as well as the exciting atmosphere of a happening cosmopolitan city. Much of Florence may be preserved in aspic, but the incursions of the modern world provide a welcome cultural frisson: next to the Ponte Vecchio, a McDonalds; next to the Duomo, an internet café.

Games & toys

For internet centres, *see chapter* **Students.**

Blues Brothers
Via Alamanni 37/a/b/c (21 63 14). **Open** 3.30-8pm Mon; 10.30am-8pm Tue-Sat. **No credit cards.**
Role-playing games and miniature figures for sale, plus lots of space to play.

Look no hands.

Fantasy Inn
Via San Gallo 97r (47 59 73). **Open** 3.30-7.30pm Mon; 9.30am-1.30pm, 3.30-7.30pm, Tue-Sat. **No credit cards.**
Magic cards, T-shirts and posters for sale plus a games room.

Ludoteca Centrale
Piazza SS Annunziata 13 (24 80 477). **Open** 9am-1pm, Mon, Tue, Thur, Fri; 3-7pm Sat.
Free recreation centre with books and toys to borrow; play rooms, library and comfy sofas to fall into.

Next Generation
Via San Gallo 113Br (48 31 65). **Open** 4.20pm-midnight daily **Admission** L5,000 membership card.
No credit cards.
The place to play Laser Warriors, a shoot-em-up game for up to 20 people (only for children aged 14 and over). L10,000 a game (30 per cent discount on Mondays). Note that you need to obtain a membership card the day before you want to play.

Stratagemma Roleplaying & Co
Via dei Servi 15r (21 59 12). **Open** 3.30-7.30pm Mon; 9am-7.30pm Tue-Sat. **Credit** AmEx, V.
Specialises in role-playing games such as Dungeons & Dragons and Magic, with a large games room. Also sells T-shirts, books, gadgets and posters on fantasy themes.

Puppet shows

Sala Vanni
Piazza del Carmine (69 76 62).
Excellent puppet shows are often held here in the Oltrarno from October to March.

Book shops & libraries

In addition to the places listed below, **After Dark** stocks a good selection of comics and **Paperback Exchange** has an excellent children's section plus stuffed toys to amuse the little ones while you browse (*see chapter* **Shopping: Books**).

After Dark
Via de' Ginori 47r (29 42 03). **Open** 10am-2pm, 3.30-6.30pm Mon-Sat. **Credit** AmEx, DC, MC, V.
Sells a huge range of English and American magazines, comics and books.

Biblioteca dei Ragazzi Santa Croce
Via Tripoli 34 (24 78 551). **Open** 9am-1.30pm Mon, Wed, Fri; 2.30-5.30pm Tue, Thur.
Anyone can borrow or browse the books, compact discs, video cassettes and magazines in this peaceful library for children from 2 to 16.

Children's Lending Library
St James' American Church, Via Bernardo Rucellai 9 (for info call Kathy Procissi 57 75 27 or Mary Diamond 71 47 79). **Open** 10-11.30am, 4-6pm, Wed; 11.30am-1pm Sun.
A friendly library with a good range of books, videos and games in English.

Casting a patrician eye in the **Boboli Gardens**.

Tempi Futuri
Via de' Pilastri 20/22r (24 29 46). **Open** 3.30-7.30pm
Mon; 9.30am-1pm, 3.30-7.30pm, Tue-Sat.
No credit cards.
Good stockist of comic books.

Parks & gardens

Boboli Gardens
Pitti Palace.
Full of labyrinths, grottoes, fountains, statues and hidden
spots, the Boboli offers plenty of diversions for children –
and magnificent views of the city. The Vasca di Nettuno is
a favourite place to take small children to play with pebbles,
and feed pigeons, ducks and fish. Owls and herons can sometimes be spotted in the park.

Le Cascine
Bus 17, C.
Florence's largest park – site of regular fairs, fun fairs and markets – is at its most animated on Sundays. Here you can rent
rollerblades and go swimming. Swings and slides and games
dot the park and there are snacks, balloons and toys for sale.

Giardini d'Azeglio
Piazza d'Azeglio.
With swings, slides and games, this shady park is peaceful
during the day, but becomes very animated around 4.30pm
when school's out, with football games, a small used toys
market and other activities.

Giardino di Borgo Allegri
Borgo Allegri.
This former parking lot in a district near Santa Croce has
been transformed by local senior citizens into a charming
garden full of flowers, with games for small children.

Country excursions

If you are without transport, the easiest and quickest way to get out into the fabulous Tuscan countryside for walks and picnics is to take either the
number 7 bus to Fiesole or the 10 to Settignano (a
15-minute ride from Santa Maria Novella station).
There are numerous walks around these two towns.

Another interesting possiblity is to go on one-
day bike rides organised by **I Bike Italy** (*23 42
371 or 0368 45 91 23*).

For other activities in the country, such as bal-
looning and organised hikes, *see chapter*
Specialist Holidays.

Food

Visiting a bakery can be fun. Besides bread, there
is always a great variety of salty or sweet things
to eat. Florentine mothers give finger size pieces
of *schiacciata all'olio* (white pizza with salt and
olive oil) to their babies to chew on (often bakers
will offer a slice to your child the second you walk
in the shop). The taste for *schiacciata* clearly
remains, since big square pieces of it are bought
by children before school, for breakfast, stuffed
with a little ham or mortadella or for *merenda*, a
term which covers any kind of eating which is not
an official meal. Every time of year has its speciality – in September during the grape harvest
you have *schiacciata all'uva* (sweet white pizza
with grapes) and *castagnaccio* (a heavy, strongly
flavoured flat cake made with chestnut flour with
pine nuts and raisins); for Christmas, *panettone* (a
blown-up version of Christmas cake); during carnival you have *schiacciata alla Fiorentina* (flat yellow cake with icing sugar sprinkled on top) and
cenci 'rags' (sweet, deep-fried strips of light pastry
doused with icing sugar); for Easter a '*colomba*'
dove-shaped sponge cake with almonds.

All very culturally interesting, but kids are
always happy to see a...

McDonalds
Santa Maria Novella Station (29 20 40). **Open** 8am-
midnight daily.
There's are branches within and outside the station. By the
time this guide is published a new branch will have opened
in a wonderful site by the Arno close to the Ponte Vecchio.

Mr Jimmy's American Bakery
Via delle Brache 12-14r (29 26 64). **Open** 10am-6.30pm
Mon-Fri; 11am-1pm, 3.30-6.30pm, Sat.
For those who carve a brownie or chocolate chip cookie.

Pit Stop
Via F Corridoni 30r (42 21 437). Bus 14, 28.
Open 7.30pm-1am daily. **No credit cards**.
An amazing 128 different first courses and 90 different kinds
of pizzas.

Pizza Taxi
North Florence (43 43 43); South Florence (23 44 444).
Open 4-10.30pm daily. **No credit cards**.
Choose a pizza, a drink and a film on video, all for L12,500.

Festivities

The Tuscan year is packed with festivals, many
of which are particularly enjoyable for children.
During carnival times in February, you'll see children running around in fancy dress in the piazzas
and especially on the Lungarno Amerigo Vespucci

(from Piazza Goldoni to the American Consulate) especially on Sundays. For other festivals and events during the year, *see chapter* **By Season**.

La Rificolona

Every September children make paper lanterns with a candle in the centre or buy them in the local stationary shops (which almost always double as toy shops, selling masks, tricks and confetti during carnival time). They then meet in the evening either in Piazza SS Annunziata or along the river (posters give details of the dates and whereabouts of the gatherings). After dark, with their lanterns lit and bobbing up and down on long bamboo poles, the children parade about singing. The tradition is that the boys use peashooters to blow paper darts into the lanterns carried by the little girls so set them on fire. You often see a delighted little boy and wailing little girl holding a burning lantern at the end of a pole with everyone around laughing.

Befana

In the past, it was on the Befana (Epiphany), not at Christmas, that children in Italy got their presents. On the eve of the 6th of January a poor old tattered woman (the *befana*), riding a broom or a donkey and carrying a sack full of toys, fills children's stockings with toys, fruit and sweets (or a piece of coal, if they have been naughty). Today, Christmas is the major celebration but there is a lingering affection for the Befana (there was uproar when it was cancelled as a public holiday a few years ago; the holiday was rapidly restored). On the eve of the Befana children leave biscuits and milk for the poor old lady and a little hay for her donkey near the fireplace where they have hung their stockings. Bars sell ready-made stockings full of sweets and chocolate, and you can also buy black candy coal.

Water fun

Le Pavoniere

Viale Catena (33 39 79). Bus 17. **Open** *end May-Sept* 10am-6pm daily. **Admission** L9,000. **No credit cards.**
Peaceful swimming pool in the centre of the Cascine park surrounded by shady trees. Not for very small children unless they know how to swim. A bar sells sandwiches and ice cream.

Piscina di Bellariva

Lungarno Colombo (67 75 21). Bus 34. **Open** *May-Sept* 10am-6pm Mon, Wed, Fri-Sun; 10am-6pm, 8.30-11pm, Tue, Thur; *Oct-Apr* 8.30-11pm Tue, Thur; 9.30am-12.30pm Sat, Sun. **Admission** L9,500. **No credit cards.**
A great place for small children. Safe wading pools, grassy lawns, trees and a bigger pool for older kids and adults.

Best museums for kids

For details, *see chapter* **Museums**.
Museo Antropologia e Etnologia
Museo Archeologico
Museo di Geologie e Paleontologie
La Specola
Museo Stibbert
Museo di Storia della Scienza

Piscina Costoli

Viale Paoli, Campo di Marte (67 80 12). Bus 10, 17, 20. **Open** *June-early Sept* 10am-6pm daily. **Admission** L9,000. **No credit cards.**
A huge swirling water slide makes this pool a big hit with older kids.

Rowing on the Arno

Ponte San Niccolò (next to tourist bus park).
From May to September the Lido rents little rowing boats for L20,000 an hour.

Out of town

The best way to escape the Florentine smog is by car, although buses and trains run to most major destinations.

Giardino Zoologico 'Città di Pistoia'

Via Pieve a Celle 160, Pistoia (0573 91 12 19). **Open** 9am-7pm daily. **Admission** L13,000; *3-9s* L9,000; *under-3s* free. **No credit cards.**
Florence no longer has a zoo; this is the nearest. There's also a restaurant. Note that there is no entrance after 6pm.

A big hit with children are the various hot springs; open year round. *See also chapter* **Livorno, Grosseto and the Coast.**

Bagni Vignoni

This small town, 20 minutes from Siena by car, has an ancient hot pool in its centre, although swimming in it is no longer allowed. To enjoy the spa waters, go to the modern outdoor swimming pool at the **Hotel Posta Marcucci** *(0577 88 71 12)* which has wonderful views out over the surrounding countryside.
Open 9am-1pm, 2-6pm, daily. Those who have an all-day ticket may remain on the premises during the one-hour lunch break during which no swimming is allowed.
Admission L18,000 for the day, L12,000 for the afternoon. **No credit cards.**

Calidario

(0565 85 15 04). **Open** 8.30am-midnight daily. **Admission** L20,000; *2-10s* L10,000; *under 2s* free. **No credit cards.**
One of the best organised hot springs, with wonderfully clear water. The immense swimming pool (open until midnight, for parents who fancy a splash themselves while the kids sleep) has a slide plus a restaurant, pizzeria and disco in the evening.

Saturnia

Just outside the village there is an abandoned mill and a river of hot sulphurous water. The waterfalls and steaming pools can be enjoyed by anyone at anytime (free).

Babysitting

Check the notice boards of the **American Church** (*see above*), **British Institute** (*see chapter* **Students**), **Paperback Exchange** (*see chapter* **Shopping**) and **Ludoteca Centrale** (*see above*).

Canadian Island

Via Gioberti 15 (67 75 67/67 73 21/fax 67 73 21). Bus 3, 6, 34. **Open** 3-6.30pm Mon-Fri; 9.30am-1pm Sat. **Admission** L40,000 per afternoon. **No credit cards.**
You can leave your children here for a few hours to play or do handicrafts in an English-speaking environment while mixing with Italian children who are learning English. English-speaking summer camps are also organised; call the above number for details.

Gay

Florentines Leonardo da Vinci, Botticelli, Cellini and Michelangelo had more to declare than their artistic genius....

In 1795, under Grand Duke Ferdinando III, Tuscany became one of the first states in Europe to repeal anti-homosexual laws. In fact, these laws had been largely ignored for centuries, apart from the imposition of paltry fines by the so-called *Uffiziali di Notte* (Night Guardians). Apparently, in the 1400s, about half of the city's youths had been fined by the Uffiziali. The city has long been a tolerant place, home to gay artists of the calibre of Leonardo da Vinci, Botticelli, Benvenuto Cellini and Michelangelo Buonarotti, as well as prominent Medicis, who were said to have filled up the Palazzo Pitti with their curly-haired darlings (*see chapter* **History: Medici Who's Who**). Not surprisingly, in the era of the Grand Tourists, Tuscany became extremely popular with homosexuals from all over Europe, especially Britain and Germany.

Today, Florence remains one of the most gay-friendly cities in Italy, though Italian fondness of *buon gusto*, good taste, dictates that you never forget the rules of discretion when cruising in the open. To get the listings of the latest gay and lesbian events in town, you should get a copy of *Quir*, Florence's own bi-monthly gay magazine, either from **ArciGay/Lesbica** (*see below*) or from one of the newsstands in the centre of town. It's also worth scanning the gay info on the internet, particularly at the excellent site http://www.dada.it/caffe/gay.

Gay Organisations

ArciGay/Lesbica
Via del Leone 5/11r (tel/fax 39 87 72/counselling 28 81 26).
There are regular meetings at 9.30pm on Mondays plus a young gay group 4-7pm on Saturdays. Free HIV testing on Wednesday afternoons.

Consulenza Legale
(28 85 02/21 30 92).
Free legal services for gay people, courtesy of ArciGay.

Clubs

Satanassa
Via Pandolfini 26r (24 33 56). Bus 14A, B, C.
Open 10pm-4am Tue-Sun. **Admission** free, but minimum drinks charge L12,000. **Credit** AmEx, V.
Located near Santa Croce, this gay disco has a cocktail bar on the upper level, plus a dark room and a video room, and the disco proper on the lower level. The music is trendy by Italian standards and there are live shows on Saturdays.

Tabasco
Piazza Santa Cecilia 3r (21 30 00). Bus 23, B, C. **Open** 10pm-3am Sun-Thur; 10pm-6am Fri, Sat. **Admission** free, but minimum drinks charge L12,000. **Credit** AmEx, V.
Opened in the '70s, this was Italy's first gay bar and, arguably, her best-known. It is run by the same lad who owns **Satanassa** and **Florence Baths**. Besides the disco and a bar, there is also a dark room, a video room, and video games. The place is usually filled with a young crowd at the weekends, although it's not always easy to get beyond the bouncers. A bit hard to find, it's located at the far side of a tiny dead-end alley on Via Vacchereccia, just off Piazza della Signoria.

Bars

BarH
Via San Zanobi 54r (47 65 57). **Open** 9pm-1am Wed-Mon. **No credit cards.**
A bit off the beaten track, BarH is located halfway between Accademia delle Belle Arti and Piazza Indipendenza. It's a wonderful place to drop by for a drink and to get info from the desk run by the extremely helpful staff of ArciGay/Lesbica, who also publish a short but very useful gay guide to Florence and Tuscany, appropriately called *Il giglio fucsia* (The Pink Lily).

Crisco
Via Sant'Egidio 43r (24 80 580). Bus 12, 14, 15, 23, A, B, C. **Open** 10pm-4am Mon, Wed, Thur, Sun; 10pm-6am Fri, Sat. **No credit cards.**
Strictly men and members-only (although free temporary membership is available on the door), Crisco is bar plus dark room plus video room. It now puts on 'Gay Tea Afternoons' at weekends. Definitely worth a visit.

Piccolo Café
Borgo Santa Croce 23r (24 17 04). Bus 14, A, B, C.
Open 5pm-1am daily. **No credit cards.**
Run by two very friendly lads, Beppe and Antonio, neither of whom are gay, this art café has become very popular with gays and lesbians of all ages. The Piccolo is an excellent venue for gay and lesbian artists of all kinds: every 15 days or so Beppe and Antonio host shows of photography, painting, sculpture, etc. They also organise sports tournaments.

Restaurants

The following, although not exclusively gay, are gay-friendly. That said, as long as you are fairly discreet, you should have no problems in most restaurants (*see chapter* **Restaurants**).

Gauguin
Via degli Alfani 24r (23 40 616). **Open** 8-11pm Mon-Sat. **Average** L30,000. **Credit** AmEx, EC, MC, V.
A gay-owned vegetarian restaurant serving Mediterranean cuisine. It gets busy at weekends so its best to book.

Transsexual car sales.

Mastro Ciliegia

Via Matteo Palmieri 34r (29 33 72). **Open** 12am-2.30pm, 8pm-midnight, Tue-Sun. **Average** L35,000.
Credit AmEx, V.

This pizzeria-trattoria-rosticceria is conveniently located near Satanassa Disco Bar and is a favourite stopover for gorgeous Florentines on their way to the disco. It's also very reasonably priced, leaving you with plenty of extra cash to spend on drinks in the small hours – pizza and a beer will cost you as little as L15,000. If you speak Italian, have a chat with the old lady running the place: she is very gay-friendly, though she will tell you candidly that *'i clienti son clienti'*, as long as they pay.

Hotels

Florence boasts a few gay-friendly hotels, although it has to be said that the tag itself doesn't mean that much. In some places, the management will tell you that 'gay-friendly' simply means that the hotel staff won't crack up with laughter at the thought of two men or two women sharing a double bed together (but, then again, where in Italy would they?); in others, they openly say that most of their staff are gay and would be glad to give you a crash course in *Firenze gaia*.

Hotel Derby

Via Nazionale 35 (21 93 08). **Rates** *single* L60-100,000; *double* L100-150,000. **Credit** AmEx, DC, EC, MC, V.
Located near the main train station, Santa Maria Novella, this two-star hotel has a pleasant terrace where breakfast is served. Mixed patronage.

Hotel Morandi alla Crocetta

Via Laura 50 (23 44 747). *Bus 6, 31, 32.* **Rates** (breakfast extra) *single* L110,000; *double* L190,000.
Credit AmEx, DC, EC, MC, V.
Very small, cosy three-star hotel. Not terribly central, but across the street from the Museo Archeologico and very popular with gays.

Hotel Wanda

Via Ghibellina 51 (24 21 06). *Bus 14.* **Rates** (breakfast extra) *double* L140,000. **Credit** DC, EC, MC, V.
The Hotel Wanda is run by a very efficient young woman who has realised that gay and lesbian tourism offer an excellent market niche. It is possible to lodge in this two-star hotel, a few minutes' walk from the Duomo, for as little as L30,000 per person (bread and breakfast in multiple rooms). Gay and lesbian couples get a ten per cent discount.

Sauna

Florence Baths

Via Guelfa 93r (21 60 50). *Bus 10, 18, 19.*
Open *winter* 2pm-1am daily; *summer* 3pm-1am daily.
Admission L20/25,000. **Credit** AmEx, V.
The only gay sauna in Florence also has a steam room, Jacuzzi, video room, snack bar and the so-called 'relax rooms' offering privacy and seclusion. The location, near the main train station, is within walking distance of most major sites.

Beaches

There are plenty of beaches in Tuscany where nudists are tolerated. Nudism is not illegal in Italy but, depending on the whim of the local authorities, it is sometimes discouraged by the police. The rule of thumb is to keep away from beaches over-crowded with frightfully nice, middle-class families with noisy children. You may want to try some of the following beaches out for yourself; however, be extra careful in the *pinetas* as the cruising scene can be fairly heavy.

La Lecciona
Sandy beach about 3km south of Viareggio (Lucca), on Viale dei Tigli, about half a kilometre past Bar La Lecciona. The nearby *pineta* is used for daytime cruising. Stop off in Viareggio on your way back to gorge on sumptuous fish antipasti alongside local dockworkers at **La Darsena** (*see* chapter **Tuscan Restaurant Tour**).

Romigliano
Six kilometres south of San Vincenzo (Livorno), sandy beach and daytime cruising in the *pineta* along the Strada della Principessa.

Sassoscritto
Gay and lesbian beach with fine cliffs about 1km south of Livorno on Via Aurelia. Can be reached by bus from the city centre; get off at Il Romito, near the Sassoscritto restaurant.

Florence underground

For many people the lure of Florence does not stop at (or even include) the artistic treasures of churches, museums and art galleries. Even the fabled city on the Arno, glorious birthplace of the Renaissance, has a deeper and darker side. When the museums close their doors and the trattorias close their kitchens, Florence's 'other' emerges. Like so many other cities Florence has its share of urban blight, drugs, AIDS and prostitution. The sex industry in Florence exists on the streets and in the discos but what makes it unusual is that it is not only involved in the traffic of women, but the traffic of men as well. Just after 11pm, you will begin to notice the lovely 'women' materialising in certain sections of the city, particularly the areas by the train station and the Parco delle Cascine. Stroll down to Via delle Belle Donne ('street of the beautiful women'), and you might see a number of these 'ladies' clothed only in their *pellicce* (furs). On the streets that used to be lined with the *case chiuse* (brothels), men can still satisfy their carnal desires; and large number of mainly married men and foreigners do just that.

Serving a somewhat more elite clientele is the infamous transvestite who works out of her Mercedes, always parked at the Piazza Ognissanti, just outside the ritzy Excelsior hotel. The locals refer to her as 'Quella Famosa', the famous one. When clients are in short supply, she can usually be spotted chatting with the *carabinieri*.

It's a common rite of passage and one of the oldest traditions among adolescent Florentine boys to take the '*puttana tour*' or the tour of the prostitutes along the boulevard in the Parco delle Cascine. The Cascine is the territory of the *travestiti* and *transsessuali*, of which there are over 15,000 in Italy. On the streets of Florence there are two transvestites for every female prostitute, which is perhaps what draws the lines of cars on Saturday nights.

Prostitution is both male and female, ambiguous, androgynous, atypical. Perhaps it is this very ambiguity which makes the transvestites so sought after. After the influx of the Brazilian *viados* in the 1970s there have been clearly marked territories for each of the various groups of transvestites and transsexuals, with Italians and foreigners sticking to separate zones, and the women leaving the centre of the city altogether.

When daylight hits and the parade of transvestites has gone inside, it is time for the few ageing icons of the traditional, time-honoured world of prostitution world to start work. The women who spend their days sitting in wooden chairs on the corner of Via della Scala, dressed in their bustiers and leather pants, with graying hair and exhausted bodies, are an improbable neighbourhood watch. They keep a sharp eye on their patch as they wait for prospective clients, and are authorities on all the comings and goings of their *vicini* (neighbours).

While Florence is considered to be a quintessential Italian city deeply steeped in tradition, Florentine society has in fact always been extremely open. Tuscany is renowned for its left-wing, progressive politics and willingness to accept new ideas. And in this place, so often referred to as a museum city, nobody seems to feel that men who dress up like women are anything but ordinary. Florentines appear to respect and tolerate what many would consider 'unnatural' given the strong Catholic values of Italian society. Perhaps it's a form of rebellion against Catholicism that sends so many men to seek sex on the streets. Or maybe it's the ambivalence that Italian men feel towards their often overbearing *mamma* which makes the extreme femininity of the transvestites so alluring or androgyny of the transsexuals so tempting. For whatever reason, both Italian men and foreigners continue to frequent the Florence underground, and the industry is booming.

Media

Your guide to the Tuscan movers and shakers.

Newspapers

The once modest local newsstand has now become a sort of media-supermarket packed to the gills with the videos, computer courses, perfumes, sunglasses, toys, CDs and CD-Roms which newspapers and magazines offer free with purchase, in the hope of increasing sales. Actual newspaper sales, however, remain low throughout the country: only one in ten Italians reads a daily paper.

Chianti News
A monthly in German, Italian and English geared to tourists and foreign residents living or travelling in Chianti. Lots of useful addresses and info on local villages and events. Free from bookshops, hotels, etc.

Fuori Binario
Florence's *Big Issue*, sold on the streets by the homeless.

Il Manifesto
Small left-wing paper with a page dedicated to Florence and Tuscany.

La Nazione
The most popular Tuscan daily newspaper. Detailed coverage of local and provincial news.

La Repubblica
The most liberal Italian newspaper. The Tuscan edition includes about 20 pages of local news.
http://www.repubblica.it/

La Stampa
Owned by the Agnelli family. A dry, right wing read.
http://www.lastampa.it/

Il Tirreno
Livorno newspaper focussing on life along the coast.

L'Unità
The newspaper of the left-wing PDS. There is a Tuscan insert, *Il Mattino*, which includes detailed local news and useful information such as public transport timetables.

Il Vernacoliere
Satirical monthly published in Livorno whose victims are usually TV stars and politicians – and the Pisans (*see chapters* Pisa *and* The Tuscans).

Classified ads

La Pulce comes out every Monday, Wednesday and Friday; *Secondamano*, weekly, and *Portobello* on Monday and Friday. Here you can find ads for anything and everything, from puppies to houses to rent by the sea. Some ads are in English.

Foreign titles

Most newsstands in the centre of town have foreign titles but you'll find the widest range under the arcades in Piazza della Repubblica and at Santa Maria Novella train station.

The Cecchi Gori Story

Though the Cecchi Goris are the most prominent Florentine dynasty of modern times, they are not quite 20th-century Medicis. Mario, the patriarch, founded the empire when he set up Massima film with Dino De Laurentiis in 1953. Over the next 40 years, Cecchi Gori was the king of Italian low- to middlebrow comedy, producing classics of the genre (Dino Risi's *Il Sorpasso*, 1962) as well as frankly forgettable titles like *My Wife is a Witch* and *Seven Kilos in Seven Days*.

His son Vittorio never faced much of a career dilemma: he started helping daddy at age 14, and over the next 25 years combined his cinematic duties with some serious water-skiing and a series of flirtations that kept Italy's gossip press busy. Finally, in 1983, he met Yugoslav dental hygienist turned B-movie actress Rita Rusic on the set of *Attilla Scourge Of God* – a film so bad it soon achieved cult status. They were married the same year. Rita has taken over the film production side of the Cecchi Gori empire, with startling results – last year's *Il Ciclone*, a romantic comedy set in rural Tuscany, broke all previous box-office records, grossing a massive $40 million. Vittorio looks after the TV side of things – he owns the two national 'Telemontecarlo' channels – as well as holding down a seat in the Italian Senate and following the fortunes of Fiorentina football club, of which he is chairman. The rest of his energies are spent duelling with arch-enemy Silvio Berlusconi, of whom he once remarked: "One of Berlusconi's men wrote that I'm not as tall as *il Cavaliere*. It's true: I don't wear high heels".

Magazines

Events in Florence and Tuscany
English mag focusing on celebs, stars and aristos. Also articles on gastronomy and news, plus classified ads and services.

Firenze Oggi/Florence Today
Freebie found in most hotels. A useful, reasonably accurate, but far from comprehensive listings mag with information on events, restaurants, bars, etc. In English and Italian.

Firenze Spettacolo
Patchy listings mag with an English-language insert called *Florencescope*.

Firenze Toscana/Firenze Noi/Firenze Qui
Three similar glossies with photos of the Tuscan countryside, holiday itineraries, gastronomy and curiosities. In Italian.

Florence Concierge Information
Free of charge, found at tourist offices, this lists events, useful information, timetables, etc. In English

Vivapiazza
Consumer-oriented magazine with information on ecology as well as cultural events, fairs and markets. In Italian.

Florence & Tuscany Online

In Italy Online
http://www.initaly.com/
A monthly e-zine, *In Italy* contains useful info about where to stay, eat and enjoy yourself in Tuscany. Included are quirky details about museums and festivals, a calendar of outdoor markets and details of offbeat destinations for walking and driving tours, plus a host of useful links. You can e-mail **initaly@initaly.com** with any queries you may have. On-line hotel reservations available. In English.

Welcome to Italy
http://www.emmeti.it/
Information is accessible by place, itinerary or geographical location, the latter being the easiest. Over 1,000 places to stay (on-line reservations available), restaurants, local events, shopping, plus articles on fashion, food and drink. There are also interesting facts about olive oil (queries to **museum@graffiti2000.com**), as well as links to related sites. In English, Italian, German and Japanese.

Firenze Online
http://www.fionline.it/
Tourist info, music, shops, services and media events. Centring on events in Florence, this colourful site specialises in arts and entertainment, with information about what's going on at theatres, art galleries and museums, plus information on places to stay. There is a special section on how to go about finding a job in Italy. E-mail **info@fionline.it** for further information. In English and Italian.

Italian Tourist Web Guide
http://www.masternet.it/itwg/itwg.htm
Hotels, resorts, restaurants, camping sites, on-line reservations, art, history, plus info about the sea-side and trekking in the mountains. There are links to listed hotel home pages, so you can see what you're getting for your money as images of rooms download. Also listed are some vital facts about travelling within Italy. Any queries to **itwg@masternet.it**. In English and Italian.

Italian Wines on the Web
http://ourworld.compuserve.com/homepages/marcolc/toscana.htm
Italian Wines goes through the history of winemaking in the region, from the time of the Etruscans to the present day. The site gives the lowdown on varieties of grape, types of soil and the processes involved in creating a good vintage, through to the temperature wine should be served at. Plenty of facts on Chiantis and Super Tuscans such as Sassicaia and Tignanello. In English.

Italian Internet Winery
http://www.ulysses.it/
Not as detailed as the Italian Wines on the Web site, but these pages are interesting nonetheless, and have the advantage of listing local wineries from whom wine can be ordered via e-mail. More information from **info@ulysses.it/**. In English.

Television

Despite 30-plus terrestrial channels, there is not a lot to keep you glued to the box. The myriad local stations tend to broadcast little but fortune tellers and demonstrations of household electrical goods. The nationally broadcasted **Mediaset** channels put out all the familiar American series dubbed into Italian and riddled with ads. RAI channels are the least interrupted, but there's still a stodgy diet of quiz shows and high-kicking, bikini-clad bimbettes.

Sky and CNN news in **English** are broadcast in the early hours of the morning by TVL and TMC. The French channel, Antenne 2, is accessible in Tuscany. TMC2 is Italy's version of MTV.

Radio in Florence

Controradio
93.6 MHz
A radio station dedicated to social issues which broadcasts jazz, rock, indie, avant garde music. On Saturday and Sunday from 10am an American DJ broadcasts in English.

Nova Radio
101.5 MHz FM
No ads. Run by volunteers and committed to social issues, it independently broadcasts jazz, soul, blues, reggae, World music, Hip Hop, Rap, ethnic music, alternative rock, etc.

Radio Diffusione Firenze
102.7 MHz FM
Mainstream pop music.

Radio Montebeni
108.5 MHz
Classical music only.

Students

Art addicts, connoisseurs of the classics and lovers of the Italian language are drawn to study in the city on the Arno.

For centuries Florence has been a crossroads for students, aesthetes and *bon viveurs* from all over the world. The city's attractions (including its wonderful climate) have enticed many foreign (and particularly American) academic programmes to Tuscany. The region is home to more than 20 American university programmes, countless language schools and art courses and, consequently, English is heard on the streets and in restaurants, bars and cafés almost as frequently as Italian. Here's how to get a seat on the Tuscan academic gravy train for yourself.

Finding a course

For information about courses in Florence, the first stop should be in your college or university's study abroad office or advisor. In the US the best information sources on study possibilities are the **Institute of International Education**, the **Italian Consulate**, **CIEE** and the internet.

Associazione Scuole di Italiano come Seconda Lingua (ASISL)

c/o Scuola Palazzo Malvisi, Via Fiorentina 36, 47021 Bagno di Romagna (0543 91 11 70/fax 0543 91 13 48).
ASISL quality-controls 14 schools in Florence, two in Siena, one in Arezzo and one in Pisa. All ASISL schools are also examination centres for the Certificazione di Conoscenza della Lingua Italiana of the Universita' per Stranieri ('University for Foreigners') in Siena. ASISL's HQ changes every two years; for 1997-98 they are at the above address.

Council of International Educational Exchange (CIEE)

205 E 42nd Street, New York, NY 10017, USA (212 666 4177/fax 212 822 2699).
Write for information on study and work outside the US.

Institute of International Education

809 UN Plaza, New York, NY 10017-3580, USA (212 883 8200).
For those who can visit in person, there is a library packed with helpful information on the ground floor.

Italian Consulate

690 Park Avenue, New York, NY 10021, USA (212 737 9100).
Contact the Consul General for info on Italy and visas.

Promozione Turistica, Turismo sociale e Sport Servizio

Via di Novili 26 (43 82 111/fax 43 83 064).
Open 9am-1pm Mon-Fri.
The body to contact for information on non-ASISL classes available throughout Tuscany. Publishes helpful booklets.

Universities in Florence & Tuscany

If you are interested in studying alongside Florentine undergraduates, contact the nearest Italian consulate by the end of August of the year in which you'd like to study, and request an appliaction to do a *corso singolo*, or one-year of study in the University of Florence. The consulate might provide you with a scholarship but, if not, the fees for taking up to five classes and exams are approximately L1,100,000. In order to follow a complete course of study, you also need to contact the consulate, but must already have studied at university level for at least two years. Contact the department in which you would like to study, and they will then give specific instructions on the requisite paperwork and examination. Students are usually expected to pass an Italian language exam held in September, plus an exam specific to their chosen department. The date for this application is due in the middle of May, but it's always best to request information well in advance.

Exchange programmes for students within the EC exist (Erasmus scholarships), but you must arrange these through your home university.

Georgetown University

Villa Le Balze, Via Vecchia Fiesolana 26 (59 208/fax 59 95 84). For application and information contact: *Michelle Siemeitowski, Director of Programs, Box 571006, Villa Le Balze, School of Summer and Continuing Education, Washington, DC 20057-1006, USA (202 687 5624/fax 687 8954).*
Georgetown hosts semester- or year-long programmes for undergraduates, usually college juniors. There's also the opportunity for Georgetown students to study directly at the University of Florence.

Middlebury College

Via Verdi 12 (tel/fax 24 57 90). For application and information contact: *Roberto Veguez, Middlebury College, Language Schools, Middlebury, Vermont 05753, USA (802 443 5000/fax 802 443 2075).*
Semester or year-long programme for undergraduates, taught entirely in Italian. Students stay in apartments or with families. There is also a graduate programme in language and culture.

New York University

Villa La Pietra, Via Bolognese 120 (50 071/fax 47 27 25). For application and information contact: *NYU, Center for International Study, 269 Mercer Street, 8th Floor, Room 811a (212 998 8720 or 3805/fax 212 995 4833).*
Undergraduate year-abroad programmes are held in one of

the gorgeous Renaissance villas that were bequeathed to NYU by Sir Harold Acton in his will. American and Italian scholars hold courses for the students.

Rutgers University

Chaisso del Buco 14 (21 37 44). For application and information contact: *Director of International Studies, Seth Gopin, Study Abroad Office, Milledoler Hall, Room 205, Rutgers Univserity, New Brunswick, NJ 08903, USA (908 932 7787/fax 908 932 8659).*
Small American programme which enrolls its undergraduates directly in the Univerisity of Florence under the rubric of the Rutgers' Dante programme. Offers a spring semester called the Medici programme consisting of art, language, culture and history classes (taught in English).

Sarah Lawrence in Florence

Palazzo Spinelli, Borgo Santa Croce 10 (24 09 04/fax 24 80 044). For application and information contact: *Sarah Lawrence Office of International Programs, Westlands, Bronxville, NY 10708, USA (914 395 2305/fax 914 395 2666).*
Small, intensive, year-long programme taught by Italian professors. For students already versed in Italian, the programme offers an opportunity to study at the University of Florence. Students stay with families in single rooms.

Syracuse University

Villa Rossa, Piazza Savonarola 15 (57 13 76/fax 50 00 531). For application and information contact: *Syracuse University, DIPA, 119 Euclid Avenue, Syracuse, NY 13244-4170, USA (315 443 3471/fax 315 443 4593/toll-free phone in US 1 800 235 3472).*
The largest American undergraduate year-abroad programme in Florence. Courses are taught in English, but language classes are part of the curriculum. There are two graduate programmes: masters in art history and architecture.

Universita' di Firenze: Centro di Cultura per Stranieri

Via Vittorio Emanuele 64 (47 21 39/fax 47 16 20).
Contact the *centro* for info about directly enrolling at the University of Florence, or to participate in the university's courses designed for foreigners. All classes are in Italian.

Universita' di Firenze: Centro per Studenti Stranieri

Via La Pire 4 (27 57 229/university info 27 571).
Contact this office (hidden in a courtyard) for general information and advice.

Universita' per Stranieri, Siena

Sede Amministrativa, Via Pantanito 45, 53100 Siena (0577 24 01 11/fax 0577 28 10 30).
Sede Didattica e Segreteria Studenti, Piazzetta Grassi 2, 53100 Siena (0577 49 260/fax 0577 28 10 30).
The 'University for Foreigners', the hub of all international student academic activity in Tuscany, is based within Siena's medieval walls. The main courses are in Italian language, but there are also options in art, art history and Italian culture.

Universitario Europeo

Via Dei Roccettini, 9, 500016 San Domenico di Fiesole (46 85 373/fax 46 85 444/e-mail applyres@datacomm.iue.it).
This highly prestigious and unique university was set up by the EU to promote European integration. Doctoral programmes in Economics, History, Law, and Political and Social Sciences generally last 3 years. Classes are mainly conducted in English and French. Students come from both within and without the EU; if you aren't awarded a grant, tuition will cost you L20 million a year, but many of the students are on individual government scholarships.
http://www.iue.it/

Studying archaeology

Budding archaeologists who want to participate in one of the many digs in Tuscany should contact the **Soprintendente Archeologo** in Florence. All Tuscan sites are coordinated from the same address. Students must specify a Tuscan city and, if possible, commune in which they want to work. The Soprintendente will pass on the student's request to the professor in charge of the relevant area. It is then the professor's responsibility to respond to the student's request. Note: if you dream of becoming Tuscany's Heinrich Schliemann, be prepared to persevere; otherwise your letter could become drawer-lining.

Soprintendenza Archeologia della Toscana

Soprintendente Archeologo, Via della Pergola 65 (23 575/fax 24 22 13).

Archeological Institute of America

656 Beacon Street, Boston, MA 02215-2010, USA (617 353 9361/fax 617 353 6550).
Eleven dollars will buy you a newsletter called *Archeological Fieldwork Opportunities Bulletin*, which lists archaeological digs throughout the world.

Studying art

The artist in search of Florentine inspiration need only walk through the Uffizi, around Fiesole or up to San Miniato to become enthused with the will to create. In addition, however, there are academic programmes to offer structure for the practitioners of most artistic disciplines.

Florence Academy of Art

Via delle Casine 21r (24 54 44/fax 23 43 701).
This school is hidden behind unpromising garage-like doors on a winding street near Santa Croce. The academy dedicates itself to the 'training of the professional realist painter' and offers an intensive three-year programme (taught in English). Summer classes are also available.

Istituto per l'Arte e il Restauro

Palazzo Spinelli, Borgo Santa Croce 10 (24 60 01/fax 24 07 09/e-mail ps~info@spinelli.it).
Reputedly the finest Italian art restoration school. Courses are either one- or two-year and cover restoration, design, painting and printmaking, antique trade and market values, and commercial and editorial graphics. Classes are held in Italian, but language courses are available.

Oro e Colore: Laboratorio Scuola, restauro di opere dorate e dipinte

Via della Chiesa 25 (tel/fax 22 90 40).
Month-long classes in art restoration, gold-leaf restoration, wood intaglio and other techniques. The number of students is limited and classes are in Italian. The secretary is available by phone (9am-1pm, 3-7pm, Mon to Fri).

Studio Art Center International (SACI)

Via San Gallo 30 (48 61 64/fax 48 62 30). Institute of International Education, 809 UN Plaza, New York, NY 10017-3580, USA (toll-free phone in US 1 800 344 9186/fax 212 984 5325).
SACI runs courses taught in English. Undergraduate and

graduate programmes for credit, and summer study. Contact the Institute of International Education in New York, or the address in Florence.

Universita' Internazionale dell'Arte
Via Forbici 26 (57 02 16).
Yearly, half-yearly and shorter courses offered in art, art restoration, museum studies and archaeology. Classes are taught in Italian. Write to the secretary for details.

Studying fashion

Fashion Institute of Technology
Villa Strozzi, Via Pisana 77 (70 02 96/fax 70 02 87). International Fashion Design Program in Florence and New York, State University of New York, USA. For application and information contact: *Mr Armoni, Fashion Institute of Technology, 7th Avenue at 27th Street, Room A605, New York, NY 10001, USA (212 760 7601/fax 212 594 9413).*
FIT offers semester- and year-long courses in international fashion design.

Studying language & culture

Schools specialising in Italian language and culture abound in Florence. Mostly summer attractions, the classes offered are usually intensive (a month or two in duration) and provide a good grounding for a short-term Tuscan stay.

ABC Centro di Lingua e Cultura Italiana
Via de' Rustici 7 (21 20 01/fax 21 21 12/e-mail arca@fi.pisoft.it).
Language teaching at six levels, plus the *perfezionamento* grade. ABC also holds classes in cooking, culture and art, and offers special courses to help prepare for the September language entrance exam for the University of Florence.

British Institute
Piazza Strozzi 2 (28 40 31/fax 28 70 71) or Lungarno Guicciardini 9 (28 40 32).
Offers two-week and month-long courses in history of art, Italian language, drawing and cooking, all taught by Italian nationals. This is the only British institution of its kind in Florence. Its resources include a vast library and information on events and contacts.

Koinè
Via de' Pandolfini 27 (21 38 81/fax 21 69 49).
Six levels of language instruction, and also cooking classes.

Lorenzo de' Medici Institute of Italian Studies
Via dell'Alloro 14r (28 71 43/fax 23 98 920).
One-month courses in language, cooking and art history.

Scuola Leonardo da Vinci
Via Brunelleschi 4 (29 44 20/fax 29 48 20/e-mail scuolaleonardo@trident.nettuno.it).
Offers classes in language, art history, painting and wine.

Scuola Machiavelli
Piazza S Spirito 4 (23 96 966/fax 28 08 00).
Smaller than some of the other language schools, and therefore more able to gear courses to personal requirements, this teachers' co-operative offers Italian language teaching at all levels and classes in Italian culture. It also organises courses with local craftsmen and artisans, many of whom have workshops in the area. Pottery, fresco, mosaic, trompe l'oeil and book-binding are among the skills on offer.

Student information

Student Point
Viale Gramsci 9a (24 31 40). Bus 80. **Open** 2.30-6.30pm Mon, Wed, Fri.
This office offers help and advice to foreign students who are in Florence for study purposes. Staff, who obviously speak a range of foreign languages, will assist with accommodation, finding a language school, getting a *permesso di soggiorno*, finding a doctor and so on. They will also do their best to send you to the right place to tune into the Florence 'scene'.

Paperwork

EC citizens don't need a visa, but upon arrival might be asked to acquire a *permesso di soggiorno* ('permission to stay'). Citizens of Canada, the United States, New Zealand, Australia and South Africa who are staying in Italy for more than three months should obtain a visa from the Italian consulate at home prior to departure, as well as the *permesso di soggiorno*, which is available in the Italian city where you will be staying. For details of how to obtain the *permesso, see chapter* **Essential Information: Bureaucracy.**

American Express
Via Dante Alighieri 22r, POB 617, 50125 Florence (50 981). **Open** 9am-5.30pm daily.
Receives and holds letters for cardholders (no packages, and non-cardholders must pay a small fee).

Finding an apartment

It's not an easy task, and almost impossible to arrange from abroad. The simplest solution is to have your academic programme house you with a family or in a flat with other students. Exchange students, and those who arrive independently of a programme might be faced with the challenge alone.

If staying for more than one month, arranging to take a one-month language or art course at one of the many small institutes would most likely provide a room and a base of operation for a month, during which time you can explore the city in search of longer-term housing.

La Pulce ('the flea'), a biweekly newspaper, lists reasonably priced rooms to let, although you may find that many places advertised have already been taken before the paper's publication.

Better luck in an apartment-search might be found by scouring bulletin boards (*see below*). The university area around San Marco, and Via degli Alfani near Piazza Brunelleschi in particular, is littered with ads for roommates: *'posto letto'* (sharing a room with someone else) and *'camera singola in appartamento'* (single room in flat with others). If you have a number where you can be reached (getting a mobile phone is not a bad idea), you can post an ad on bulletin boards. Anglophones, and other potential roommates, check the bulletin boards in the **Paperback Exchange** (*see below*) and the following places.

CTS Travel
Via de Ginori 25r (28 95 70/fax 29 21 50).

Mr Jimmy's
Via San Niccolò 47 (29 26 64). **Open** 10am-7pm Mon-Sat.

Accommodation agencies

Using an agency is an expensive alternative, but one particularly useful for large groups of people looking for an empty apartment, or for individuals after a studio or one-bedroom flat. Check in the yellow pages (the *'pagine gialle'*) under *'agenzie immobiliari'*. When you find a flat, a fee (usually around ten per cent of one year's rent) is paid to the agency plus one month's deposit and a month's rent in advance. Monthly rents vary according to location (the *centro storico* is the priciest; areas like Rifredi, Scandicci and San Jacopino are more affordable), size and quality, and many are required to be paid *in contanti* (in cash). A studio, or *monolocale*, in the centre of Florence, should cost around L1,200,000, while a room in an apartment with others could cost as little as L500,000. Cheapest of all is sharing a room, costing around L200-300,000 per month. Most apartments come furnished. Always ask if *'le spese sono incluse?'* (if utilities are included in the rent) – gas and electricity are sometimes paid by the landlord, but are usually the renter's responsibility.

Computers & the internet

If you are bringing your computer along for your Florentine sojourn, you will find many options for services that offer internet access. Examples include *dadanet* and *mclink*. Some American services offer nodes for use in Florence. CompuServe and America Online members, for instance, can log on in Florence, although for higher rates than normal. An alternative is to use the computing and internet facilities available at the places below.

Bumble Bee
Via Santa Monaca 23 (28 90 23/fax 28 89 25/e-mail bumble@dada.it). Bus B to Santo Spirito. **Open** noon-8pm Mon-Fri; 10am-2pm Sat. **No credit cards.**
Florence's only English-run computer communications centre. Here you can use word processing faciltities, send and receive faxes and e-mail (L5,000 per hour to send, L2,000 per message to receive), surf the internet (L10,000 per hour plus the phone call) and print from floppy disks.

CIMA
Borgo degli Albizzi 37r (24 77 245). **Open** 9.30am-7.30pm Mon, Wed, Fri; 9.30am-7.30pm, 9.30pm-1am, Tue, Thur, Sat; also last Sun of month. **Credit** AmEx, DC, EC, MC, V.
A membership to have an electronic mailbox here for six months is L35,000, for 12 months L50,000. Use of the computers costs L10,000 for one hour, L28,500 for three hours and L45,000 for five hours. In addition to offering internet access, CIMA is a savvy hangout that attracts an avant garde crowd and hosts literary events.

Internet Train
Via dell'Oriuolo 25/r (tel/fax 23 45 322/e-mail info@fionline.it. **Open** 10am-7.30pm Mon-Fri; 10am-2pm Sat. **Credit** AmEx, MC, V.
Located down the block from the Duomo, there are 10 PCs at customers' disposal here. The *abbonamenti*, or membership fees, are L15,000 for one month, L50,000 for six months or L100,000 for one year. To send e-mail you must buy a L10,000 card for one hour's useage (including five minutes free time you log on). A larger, second branch (with 40 PCs) opened in Via Guelfa in September 1997.
http://www.fionline.it

PC Self Service
Via San Gallo 4r (21 11 03). **Open** 10am-7.30pm Mon-Fri; 10am-2pm Sat. **No credit cards.**
Computers at your disposal as well as internet connections and e-mail services.

Libraries & bookshops

Public libraries in Florence can exhaust even the most enthusiastic scholar; long queues, endless paperwork, and the non-availability of books make foreign libraries and the purchase of books more attractive prospects. *See also chapter* **Shopping**.

Biblioteca Nazionale
Piazza Cavallegeri 1 (24 91 91). **Open** 9am-7pm Mon-Fri; 9am-1pm Sat.
You'll need a letter of presentation here, plus a lot of patience; ordering one book can take hours, if not days.

Bookcart
The bookcart parked under the Loggia del Pesce in the market of Piazza Ciompi is open from around 9am-7pm. Books include art, Florentine history and an impressive collection of *fumetti* (cartoons and comics).

British Institute Library
Lungarno Guicciardini 9 (28 40 32). **Open** 9.45am-1pm, 3-6.30pm, Mon-Fri.
Requires a membership fee, but offers a reading room that overlooks the Arno and a good literature and history library.

Feltrinelli International
Via Cavour 12/20r (21 95 24). **Open** 9am-7.30pm Mon-Sat. **Credit** AmEx, DC, EC, MC, V.
Chic shop near the Duomo; offers books in many languages.

Kunsthistorisches Institut in Florenz
Via G Giusti 44 (24 79 161/fax 24 43 94). **Open** 9am-6pm Mon, Wed, Fri; 9am-7pm Tue, Thur.
One of the largest collections of art history books in Florence is held by this German institute. As usual, a letter of presentation is necessary to borrow books.

Paperback Exchange
Via Fiesolana 31r (24 78 154/fax 24 78 856). **Open** 9am-1pm, 3.30-7.30pm, Mon-Sat. **Closed** Mon; mid-Nov to mid-Mar. **Credit** AmEx, DC, EC, MC, V.
An extensive selection of books in English (both new and second-hand) and a useful bulletin board. Bring in an old book and get credit towards another used book. The staff are a great help and always ready to chat.

Villa I Tatti, Harvard University
Via di Vincigliata 26 (60 32 51/fax 60 33 83). **Open** 9am-6pm Mon-Fri.
Graduate students with letters of presentation from a professor take bus 10 and trek uphill to gain access to Harvard's Florentine villa and library.

Women

Prepare to be ogled.

As you might guess from the number of idealised Madonnas gracing the walls of its galleries and churches, Tuscany has a long tradition of worshipping the images of women. This still holds true today, and while most Italian women expect to be looked at and admired, it can be somewhat daunting for a newcomer. Unfortunately, Italian men on the pull tend to concentrate their energies on pale-skinned, blonde-haired foreign women – cashing in on the Latin lover image and hoping that they won't need to work as hard to get them into bed. Fortunately however, the Italian male ego is frail, and most will wither before you if eyed with contempt. Oddly, you may be much less hassled if alone than in a group – the canny lads favour the latter as the chance of scoring clearly increases with the number of potential targets. If you want to avoid the boys on the make stay clear of tourist spots at night, and avoid looking like a tourist: leave your shorts and rucksack behind, and dress as you would on a hot day in the city at home.

Women's groups

Il Giardino dei Cigliegi
Piazza dei Ciompi 11 (first floor) (24 36 490). Bus C.
Open 4-7pm Mon-Thur.
This organisation sponsors debates, seminars and other events on women's issues.

Laboratorio Immagine Donna
Via San Gallo 32 (47 46 80).
Organises an international film festival each year of films written and directed by women.

Il Teatro delle Donne
Piazza dei Ciompi 11 (2nd floor) (23 47 572). Bus C.
Open 9am-4pm Mon-Fri.
A woman's group which produces plays written by women, sponsors discussions on women's theatre and puts on performances in conjunction with other theatres in the area.

Bookstores &archives

Archivio di Studi di Storia delle Donne
Biblioteca Communale Centrale, Via San Egidio 21 (26 16 512). Bus 14, 23. **Open** 9am-7pm Mon-Fri; 9am-1pm Sat.
The central library holds a large collection of research, books and articles relating to the history of women.

Libreria Delle Donne
Via Fiesolana 2B (24 03 84). Bus C. **Open** 3.30-7.30pm Mon; 9am-1pm, 3.30-7.30pm, Tue-Sat.
This is not only a bookshop but a place to hear lectures,

Grope-free zone.

research women's issues and participate in activities regarding women. Although the shop is not exclusively dedicated to gay women, there is an extensive selection of lesbian literature. It is also possible to order copies of any book in English.

Health services & help lines

The pharmacy located inside Santa Maria Novella train station is open 24 hours a day (*21 67 61*). Tampons (*assorbenti esterni*) and condoms (*preservativi*) can be purchased in pharmacies and supermarkets. Abortion is legal in Italy and is performed in hospitals, but the private clinics listed below can give consultation and references.

Artemisia Centro Donne Contro La Violenza Catia Franci
Via del Mezzetta 1 (helpline 60 23 11). **Open** 10am-6pm Mon-Fri.
This crisis centre can provide a medical examination as well as counselling for women who have been sexually assaulted.

It also runs a home for women who are victims of domestic violence and sexual assault. The helpline is staffed during office hours.

Progetto Donna – Assessorato Pubblica Istruzione

Clinica Ostetrica, Ospedale di Careggi, Viale Morgagni (42 77 493). Bus 14. **Open** 24 hours daily.

Women who are victims of sexual assault should come here for medical attention. Legal services and psychological counselling are available 9am-1pm, 3-5pm, Mon-Fri (*28 47 52*) at Viale Santa Maria Maggiore 1, Careggi.

Santa Chiara

Piazza Independenza 11 (49 63 12/47 52 39). Bus 10, 25, 31, 32. **Open** 8am-7pm daily, by appointment.

This private clinic offers gynaecological exams and general physicals. Call for an appointment.

Lesbian Florence & Tuscany

Gay and lesbian groups have made great strides in gaining acceptance in Italian society. The situation has improved hugely in the last ten years but there is still a long way to go. It is still nearly impossible to live as an openly lesbian woman in most small towns of Tuscany, but Florence is another story. Many of the clubs which were once for gay men only have opened their doors to lesbians. Lesbian groups in Florence are well organised and are actively promoting acceptance for gay women all over Italy.

The best source for current events geared especially to gay women is the *Libreria delle Donne* (*see above*). It has a bulletin board announcing local events in Florence and throughout Tuscany, including weekend excursions, festivals, etc. You can also check out *Quir* magazine, available free from most major bookstores in Florence and at the Tourist Information Centre in Lucca. There are a fair number of spots for women only, but these tend to frequently change. Check with **ArciLesbica** for the most up-to-date information on lesbian haunts. You should also take a look at the extensive gay info available on the web at http://www.dada.it/caffe/gay.

Lesbian organizations

ArciLesbica

Via San Zanobi 54 (47 65 57). Bus 1, 12.

ArciLesbica is one of the most important lesbian organisations in Italy and has affiliates in most major cities, including Florence and Pisa. It runs support groups, conversation groups for foreigners and sponsors numerous events for lesbian women. Membership costs L20,000 per year. At the time of going to press ArciLesbica was in the process of moving to the address above and opening times were not yet available; phone for details.

Branch: Via Calafai 3, Pisa (*050 57 75 40*).

L'Amando(r)la Associazione Lesbica Separatista

(0360 31 10 58/61 57 90).

Separatist women's group. Meetings are on Wednesdays at 9pm, but call first as times and locations of meetings vary.

Consultorio per la Salute delle Persone Omosessuali

Via del Leone 5 (28 81 26). Bus B. **Open** 4-8pm Mon-Sat.

Medical and gynaecological exams, counselling and support groups available for gays and lesbians. Free, anonymous AIDS tests available between 3.30pm and 5.30pm every Wednesday.

Books & magazines

Quir, published monthly by ArciGay/Lesbica, is also available in an English edition. There is a section advertising special events and new women-only venues. Available at the **Paperback Exchange**, **Libreria delle Donne**, and **Feltrinelli International** (*see above* and *chapter* **Shopping: Books**) Paperback Exchange is one of a number of English bookstores in Florence. It has a large selection of books on gay and lesbian studies. Copies of *Quir* can be picked up here and it's a good source for current events geared towards gays and lesbians. You can also buy a copy of the 'Mappa Gay-Lesbica', the gap map of Tuscany, which is published by ArciGay/Lesbica. It costs L5,000 but is free if you go to the Arci Centre.

Discos, clubs & bars

055 Revolution

Via G Verdi 57 (24 40 04). Bus 14. **Open** 11pm-3am Sun. **No credit cards**.

'Eterea Night', held every Sunday, is an exclusively gay and lesbian affair.

Caffè Pasco

Via G Galliano 12 (35 06 06). Bus 17. **Open** 7am-1am Mon-Sat. **No credit cards**.

Monday nights are reserved for women only. The atmosphere is cosy and chummy, and food and drinks are excellent.

Frau Marleen

Viale Europa, Torre Del Lago, Lucca (0584 34 22 82). **Open** 11pm-4am Thu, Sun. **No credit cards**.

Gay and lesbian nights are held here every Thursday and Sunday.

GAO Bar

Via Viccolo delle Croce Rossa 7, Pisa (050 57 64 20). **Open** 10pm-1am Tue-Sun. **No credit cards**.

Located near the railway station, this coffeehouse and snack bar (run by the Arci association) attracts a studenty crowd. Good spot to find out about gay and lesbian events happening in Pisa.

Piccolo Café

Borgo Santa Croce 27 (24 17 04). Bus B, 13. **Open** 5pm-1am daily. **No credit cards**.

Every Tuesday and Thursday evening is gay and lesbian night, sponsored in conjunction with ArciGay/Lesbica. Its name is fitting as it's a tiny place, so be sure to get there early if you want a table.

Beaches

Tuscany has several beaches that are popular gay and lesbian haunts. (*See chapter* **Gay**.)

Tuscany

Introduction

You will be relieved to know that there is far, far more to Tuscany than hill towns preserved in aspic, the rolling countryside of Chianti, the Leaning Tower of Pisa and interminable Renaissance canvases. In the north of the region, gentle, undulating hills give way to rugged mountains thickly forested with pines and chestnuts. There are spectacular mountain drives, particularly in the Alpi Apuane, source of Carrara marble. The east, around the city of Arezzo, is also richly forested, and at its best when ignited with the colours of autumn – also the optimum time for collecting mushrooms, chestnuts and truffles. The south, made up of the provinces of Livorno and Grosseto, is rarely visited by tourists, although Italian families flock to its beaches. Inland, however, there are Etruscan sites, hot springs and hill towns, rarely visited and all the better for it. There are also two fantastic unspoilt natural enclaves, the Monti dell'Uccellina natural park and Monte Argentario, and islands, like Giglio and Capraia, of far more appeal than the more touristy Elba. Tuscany also has an industrial belt, stretching from Florence via the towns of Pistoia and Prato to Pisa and the coast. If you are starting from Florence, pretty countryside is close at hand: Chianti starts on its doorstep, and to the north is the lovely region of the Mugello.

Public transport in Tuscany

As long as you have time and patience, it is quite possible to see a good deal of Tuscany on public transport. There are still little local **trains** (called *diretto* or *locale*) which stop at old-fashioned stations belonging to tiny villages; to track these down and plan routes you need to buy a comprehensive train timetable, available at most large stations.

The Tuscan **bus** network is cheeringly comprehensive, although in more remote villages, buses are timed to coincide with the school day, leaving early in the morning and returning at lunchtime – which means you either have to limit yourself to a morning in a certain place, or commit yourself to over-nighting. It is not difficult to hitch in the countryside, as long as you are reasonably neatly dressed (no self-respecting Italian would want to be associated with a scruffy passenger). There is no national bus network in Italy, and even within Tuscany there are several bus companies. The following are the main local companies, but *see also chapter* **Getting Around**.

CAP *Via Nazionale 13, Florence (055 21 46 27).* Northern Tuscany.
CAT *Via Fiume 2, Florence (055 28 34 00).* Southern and central Tuscany.
CLAP *Piazza Stazione 15, Florence (055 28 37 34).* Northern Tuscany.
Nardini *Via Roma 7, Barga (0583 73 050).* Garfagnana.
RAMA *Via Topazio 12, Grosseto (0564 45 67 45).* Grosseto and the Maremma.
TRA-IN *Piazza San Domenico, Siena (0577 22 12 21).* Siena province.

Highlights of Tuscany

Abbeys & monasteries
Camàldoli (*see p248*)
Monte Oliveto Maggiore (*see p209*)
San Galgano (*see p214*)
Sant'Antimo (*see p214*)

Art & architecture
Arezzo (*see p250*)
Carmignano (*see p193*)
Lucca (*see p234*)
Monterchi (*see p248*)
Pienza (*see p212*)
Pisa (*see p200*)
Pistoia (*see p196*)
Prato (*see p197*)

San Gimignano (*see p215*)
Sansepolcro (*see p249*)
Siena (*see p219*)

Beaches
Isola del Giglio (*see p261*)
Monte Argentario (*see p261*)
Viareggio & the Versilia (*see p227*)

Etruscan Tuscany
Chiusi (*see p212*)
Sovana (*see p265*)
Volterra (*see p199*)

Hill towns
Barga (*see p230*)

Capalbio (*see p259*)
Lucignano (*see p245*)
Montalcino (*see p213*)
Montepulciano (*see p211*)
Monteriggioni (*see p215*)
Pitigliano (*see p265*)

Springs & spas
Bagni di Lucca (*see p230*)
Bagno Vignoni (*see p212*)
Saturnia (*see p264*)

Unknown Tuscany
Fivizzano (*see p233*)
Foiano della Chiana (*see p245*)
Gropina (*see p245*)
Loro Ciuffena (*see p245*)

Massa Marittima (*see p263*)
Val di Lima (*see p230*)
Val d'Orcia (*see p213*)

Walking
Chianti (*see p216*)
Monti dell'Uccellina Parco Naturale (*see p262*)
Orbetello (*see p261*)
Orecchiella Parco Naturale (*see p232*)

Wine
Chianti (*see p216*)
Montalcino (see p213)
Montepulciano (*see p211*)

Loving it, hating it

The Gushing

"[It is] the most beautiful city I ever saw."
Mary Shelley *on Florence.*

"I felt, upon entering this world of refinement, as if I could have taken up my abode in it for ever."
William Beckford *on arriving in Florence.*

"Florence is beautiful, as I said before, and must say again and again, most beautiful."
Elizabeth Barrett Browning *on Florence.*

"[I was] astonish'd at the profusion of fine things."
David Garrick *on Florence's cultural riches.*

"Let us look back on Florence while we may, and when its shinging dome is seen no more, go travelling through cheerful Tuscany, with a bright remembrance of it; for Italy will be the fairer for the recollection."
Charles Dickens *on leaving Florence.*

"...overflowing with everything that makes for ease, for plenty, for beauty, for interest and good example."
Henry James *on Lucca.*

"You cannot imagine how pretty the country is... millions of little hills planted with trees, and tipped with villas or convents."
Horace Walpole *on the country between Florence and Siena.*

"It was for this country that I was predestined."
Matthew Arnold *on Tuscany.*

The Grudging

"Florence is like a town that has survived itself. It is distinguished by the remains of early and rude grandeur; it is left where it was three hundred years ago."
William Hazlitt.

"...the Newgate-like palaces were rightly hateful to me; the old shop and market-streets rightly pleasant; the inside of the Duomo a horror, the outside a Chinese puzzle."
John Ruskin *on Florentine buildings.*

"...a fine old city, that strikes you with the same veneration you would feel at the sight of an ancient temple, which bears the marks of decay, without being absolutely dilapidated."
Tobias Smollett *on Pisa.*

"When a man sees the prodigious pains and expense that our forefathers have been at in these barbarous buildings, one cannot but fancy to himself what miracles of architecture they would have left us, had they only been instructed in the right way."
Joseph Addison *on Siena's Gothic buildings.*

The Groaning

"It is popular to admire the Arno... It would be a very plausible river if they would pump some water into it. They call it a river, and they honestly think it is a river, do these dark and bloody Florentines. They even help out the delusion by building bridges over it. I do not see why they are too good to wade."
Mark Twain.

"Florence is the most tormenting and harassing place to lounge or meditate in that I have ever entered... everybody is idle, and therefore they are always in the way."
John Ruskin.

"I would defy even a Scottish highlander to find means of subsistence in so rude a soil."
William Beckford *on the country between Bologna and Florence.*

"[It is] like an overgrown actor at one of our minor theatres, without his clothes: the head is too big for the body, and it has a helpless expression of distress."
William Hazlitt *on Michelangelo's* David.

"...a masterpiece of ridiculous taste and elaborate absurdity... In every corner of the place some glittering chapel or other offends and astonishes you."
William Beckford *on Siena cathedral.*

"...a large and disagreeable city, almost without inhabitants."
Percy B Shelley *on Pisa.*

"I would rather be condemned for life to the galleys than [be] ... exposed to the intolerable caprices and dangerous resentment of an Italian virago."
Tobias Smollett *on Tuscan women.*

A Tuscan Restaurant Tour

You know what to expect... or do you?

The stone farmhouse on a hill overlooking hills striped with vineyards and polka-dotted with olive trees; the wooden tables under the grape-slung trellis, where sun-wrinkled peasants mingle with the cast of *Stealing Beauty*; the carafe of the estate's own Chianti; the bottle of young green olive oil; the freshly baked bread, the hand-made pasta, and the salad plucked an hour ago from the kitchen garden....

Astonishingly enough, there are a few (a very few) places like this – though you may have to make do with German financiers and precious Londoners as dinner mates. For the main part, though, you should forget anything you've ever heard about it being impossible to eat a bad meal in Italy, and banish dreams of stumbling by

chance every lunchtime over an Ur-River Café or Chez Panisse. The fact is that the vast majority of Tuscany's restaurants are mediocre.

Tuscan cuisine (*see chapter* **Food in Tuscany**) is, to put it politely, basic – dominated by beans, bread, tomatoes and olive oil. Dishes such as *pappa al pomodoro*, a mushy bread and tomato soup, can be scrumptious if the tomatoes are intense and ripe, the basil fresh, and the olive oil luscious and fruity, but unutterably boring if the ingredients are indifferent. The same goes for such dishes as *fettunta con fagioli*, toast with white beans, *ribollita*, bread, bean and cabbage soup, and *panzanella*, bread and tomato salad, all of them with nowhere for poor ingredients to hide.

So why are the standards in its restaurants so poor? Largely because Tuscan restaurants not only have a captive audience, but a captive audience of middle class Northern Europeans and Americans among whom it is currently fashionable to idealise the cooking of southern European peasants. With critical faculties befuddled by Tuscan hills and several glasses of Chianti, theyn either don't notice, or refuse to admit, that the food they are eating is dull. Consequently the restaurants don't have to try very hard. Also, surprisingly, many Tuscans appear to have rather low standards where food is concerned: perhaps because the vast majority of them are now disconnected from the land, and have as little idea as any city dweller how a freshly plucked tomato or just dug-up potato tastes.

Tuscan restaurants vary hugely in style, ranging from excruciatingly pretentious places like the much-lauded **Gambero Rosso** in San Vincenzo, a place worth going to only if you crave humiliation from strict waitresses with cement perms and the charm of traffic wardens, to exuberant places like **La Pievina**, where the ebullient middle-aged waitress-cooks get tipsier with every visit to the kitchen, and end up flirting with upright burghers from München.

There's a positive new trend in Tuscany for young foodies – some of them without formal chef training – to leave their jobs as professionals in the city, and to set up country restaurants, often in houses left to them by grandparents. Their restau-

rants tend to be tasteful and relaxed, the food carefully sourced, and the recipes inspired by, but not shackled to, tradition. Good examples are **La Maiola** near Bagni du Lucca, **La Martinatica** in Pietrasanta, and **Osteria alla Piazza** near Castellina in Chianti.

Finally a word on prices. Restaurants in Tuscany are considerably cheaper than in London or New York. You can still eat an entire meal, including wine for L35,000. For restaurants in Tuscan cities, *see chapters* **Arezzo**, **Lucca**, **Pisa**, **Siena** and **Florence: Restaurants**.

Around Siena & Chianti

L'Angolo

Via Galilei 20, Località Acquviva, Montepulciano (0578 76 72 16). **Open** lunch & dinner Tue-Sun. **Average** L30,000. **Credit** AmEx, DC, EC, MC, V.

Set in the middle of a housing estate at the end of an unfinished road, and looking at first glance like the sort of place you'd come to get your bike repaired, L'Angolo is about as far removed from the Tuscan dream restaurant as you could imagine. The interior is all varnished pine, and photos of Caribbean beaches and family weddings. The food, however is great. Bruschetta come with lots of fruity olive oil, pasta is home-made, and in the late autumn, there are loads of dishes laced with generous amounts of white truffle, including a light crisp pizza (that comes with an entire truffle to shave) and an incredible *panna cotta*.

Arnolfo

Piazza Santa Caterina 2 (0577 92 05 49). **Open** lunch & dinner Wed-Mon. **Average** L85,000. **Credit** AmEx, DC, EC, MC, V.

It is often the case in Tuscany that restaurants that local foodies love are too pretentious for modern American or northern European tastes. You may find Arnolfo to be such a place but, on the other hand, the food is in the main excellent, and

the waiting staff very attentive. You can eat either à la carte, or select one of the fixed menus. The summer fish menu is highly recommended, and partners well with a fresh, spicy Vernaccia di San Gimignano from small grower Fontaleone.

You can sit outside in summer, although sadly there is no view, and conversation may at times be drowned by local lads on Vespas. All the breads are baked on the premises throughout the night, and brought out as they are ready: indeed the owner-chef, Gaetano Trovato, was recently in Japan teaching the Japanese how to make bread. The fish menu includes a terrine of super-fresh turbot (*rombo*), featherlight ravioli with clams and courgette flowers, and a *fantasia di pesce* – a mixture of fish in a saffron broth. *Dentice* (dentex) with black olives and tomato is a triumph.

Da Antonio

Piazza Marconi, Castelnuovo Berardenga (0577 35 53 21). **Open** *Mar-Oct* lunch & dinner Tue-Sun; *Nov-Feb* dinner Tue-Sun. **Average** L50,000 (lunch); L80,000 (dinner). **Credit** EC, MC, V.

Antonio Farina is from the Versilia, the stretch of the Tuscan coast around Viareggio. About five years ago he decided to open a restaurant devoted to fish in the heart of carnivorous Chianti. He has two fishing boats on the coast, and has fresh catches brought in twice a week. The menu changes according to the fish available, and everyone eats the same, for the fixed price of L80,000. There are always several *antipasti* – perhaps prawns cooked inside courgette flowers, a plate of swiftly fried microscopic *bianchini* (like whitebait only smaller) served with plenty of lemon, a light salad of *farro* (spelt); white fish, tomato, basil and capers, or scampi cooked with balsamic vinegar. Then there'll be a pasta dish, say *tagliolini* with a sauce of tomato and *scoglie*, or spaghetti with a mixture of crustaceans, including lobster. The 'main' course is usually some grilled fish and a salad; and finally a sorbet, or other light pudding. The lunch menu is a shorter, simpler affair.

Dorandò

Vicolo dell'Oro 2, San Gimignano (0577 94 18 62). **Open** lunch & dinner Tue-Sun. **Average** L60,000 excluding wine. **Credit** AmEx, DC, EC, MC, V.

Dorandò specialises in reinventing historic recipes, based on the foods of Etruscan, Medieval and Renaissance Tuscany. It's a relaxed, stylish place, with a young, enthusiastic staff, and the menu describes the history of each dish as well as listing the ingredients in detail, so for once you know exactly what you are getting. *Cibreo* is a chicken liver pâté so rich that Catherine de' Medici nearly died of eating too much. Fortunately the portions at Dorandò are chloresterol-wise. Fish lovers should opt for the oddly delicious *sorra marinata con rucola e dolici*, a dish with Etruscan roots, made of salted white tuna meat steeped in a marinade that includes cloves, juniper berries and thyme. It is served dressed with the ground down marinade. One of the finest *primi* is *pici all'Etrusca*, skinny hand-rolled pasta tubes, served with a tingling mint-leaf pesto. Follow up with *faraona al ginepro*, guinea hen spicily seasoned as it would have been in medieval times, or *baccalà con patate*, a dish designed for fasting days when no meat could be eaten, made of well-soaked salt cod mashed with potato. The most unusual dessert is *lattaiolo*, a coriander-flavoured caramel custard, a favourite during the Renaissance.

Locanda dell'Amorosa

Località Amorosa, Sinalunga (0577 67 94 97). **Open** dinner Tue; lunch & dinner Wed-Sun. **Average** L70,000. **Credit** AmEx, DC, EC, MC, V.

As befits its name, the Locanda dell'Amorosa is precisely as romantic as a Tuscan restaurant should be. It is housed, along with an equally enchanting hotel, in a cluster of honey stone medieval buildings – including a chapel – that formed the heart of an estate. The restaurant occupies the former stables, but really you want to eat outside here, on an elegant terrace overlooking sunflower fields. Service is attentive, but unobtrusive. There are two fixed menus, one (3-course) for L65,000, the other (7-course) for L95,000, but you can also pick and choose. If you are not particularly hungry you can have one *antipasto*, one *primo*, one *secondo* and a salad bewteen two, each course divided into half portions.

The menu changes every season, but look out for a salad of raw porcini, rocket and crumbled parmesan, and the *insalata di alici e razza con olive nere e pomodoro fresco*, a delicate salad of fresh anchovy, skate, black olives and tomatoes. Skip traditional Tuscan dishes like *ribollita* – you'll eat better ones for a third of the price elsewhere – and plump instead for one of the more refined *primi*: a light risotto of courgettes and courgette flowers, perhaps, or a musky dish of gnocchi with *porcini* mushrooms and truffle oil. If you like fish absolutely fresh and barely cooked, try the *scottata di pesci*, a selection of different fish dressed with onion, herbs, oil and lemon. Otherwise there is a good selection of grilled meats – including a young Chianina steak to share between two – and some rather more complex roasts, like guinea fowl breast stuffed with figs. Desserts are not a house speciality, but there is a good range of local cheeses. The light, fresh estate white wine is perfect for summer al fresco dining.

Osteria alla Piazza

La Piazza, near Castellina in Chianti (0577 73 35 80). **Open** lunch & dinner Tue-Sun. **Average** L60,000. **Credit** MC, V.

Founded by Giovanni Lecchini, a former engineer, in his grandparents' rose-covered farmhouse, Osteria alla Piazza is an elegant, but relaxed place, where you can eat outside in summer overlooking the rolling Chianti hills. Food is innovative, but never pretentious. Fresh top quality ingredients are used with great effect in *spaghetti piccanti con pomodoro e rucola* (perfectly *al dente* spaghetti in a tongue-singeing chilli and tomato sauce, topped with cubes of juicy raw tomato and fresh chopped rocket) and *farfalle con pesto e pomodoro fresco* (farfalle with an intense fresh pesto topped with a pile of fresh tomato). *Tagliata* – thin strips of flash-fried steak – is a Piazza speciality, and comes combined with various vegetables – like *funghi porcini* or asparagus. These dishes can be over-salted, so to be on the safe side request them *senza sale* (without salt) or *con poco sale* (with little salt).

La Pievina

Via Lauretina 9, La Pievina, Nr Asciano (0577 71 83 68). **Open** *July-Sept* dinner Wed-Sun; *Oct-June* lunch & dinner Wed-Sun. **Average** L60,000. **No credit cards.**

They wear red and white ruffled pinnies and matching mobcaps; their cheeks get more wine-flushed with every visit to the kitchen; and all three of them gaze longingly at male diners, giving their favourites parting gifts of pink and yellow sponge cake wrapped in a napkin marked with a scarlet lipstick kiss. All three are over 50.

The ladies' restaurant is cluttered with all manner of rustic paraphernalia, and although there are seats outside, to eat there would be to miss all the fun. There is a set meal every day, alternating between fish and meat. Almost before you have had a chance to sit down, there will be a bottle of chilled local white wine, a basket of fresh crusty bread and a bowl of peanuts before you. Then the *antipasti* – all *ten* of them – start coming, little plates of delicious fishy goodies, such as sardines marinated in rosemary and sage, cockles with *ragù*, smoked mackerel with black pepper and lime, and perfect seafood crostini, the seafood mixed with a touch of chilli and sweet, luscious tomato.

Best of the several *primi* are *pici* (hand-rolled tubes of pasta) in a strangely palatable sauce of fish, offal and chilli, and a saffrony seafood risotto. To follow are grilled fish of the day, and, if the ladies like you, a branch of a tree hung with prawns. Finally you'll be pressed to eat your way through six desserts, and to sample the dozen or so different *grappas*.

Sciame

Via Ricasoli 9, Montalcino (0577 84 80 17). **Open** lunch & dinner Tue-Sun. **Average** L35,000. **No credit cards.**

Sciame's clinically white plaster walls and green-stained pine furniture may not look very Tuscan but, in fact, this is a trattoria so popular with the locals that if you don't book, you'll probably have to wait. As is to be expected in Montalcino, there is a great selection of Rosso and Brunello di Montalcinos, and plenty of advice on hand to help you choose one to suit. Food is simple, local and high quality: the *affettato misto*, for example, is a plate of locally cured meats and salamis. *Primi* include a *zuppa di fagioli*, bean soup that is probably the best in Tuscany – rich, russety, and long-slow-cooked, served with a small red onion to be slivered on top, a flask of fruity olive oil, and grated parmesan. Other good *primi* include home-made potato gnocchi with gorgonzola or mushrooms, and *maccheroni con sugo di cinghiale*, home-made egg pasta in a winey wild boar sauce. For *secondo*, there's a *scottiglia*, a mixture of meats (chicken, pork, rabbit, sometimes wild boar) braised in a herby, chilli-kissed sauce and served on slices of toast. To accompany, have a dish of roast potatoes, yellow peppers and carrots. Best bet for pudding is a plate of *ossi di morto* (literally, bones of the dead); actually light brittle biscuits made of egg white, almonds and sugar, accompanied by a glass of local *vin santo*.

Trattoria del Montagliari

4km outside Greve in Chianti, on the road to Panzano in Chianti (055 85 21 84). **Open** lunch & dinner Tue-Sun. **Average** L50,000. **Credit** MC, V.

This rough stone *casa colonica* is on an estate that produces its own wine, olive oil, balsamic vinegar, conserves and bottled sauces. In winter you eat inside by an open wood fire; in summer on an idyllic terrace fringed with acacia trees and wild roses overlooking the gently undulating Montagliari vineyards. The food is excellent, and most of the ingredients are local. Try *panzanese di pecorino di Chianti*, fresh (under 12 days old) velvety pecorino, with tomatoes and basil, or *crostini di milza*, toast spread with a delicious dark, spicy pâté made of spleen by local butcher Cecchino. In autumn they do a mean *zuppa di funghi porcini*, in spring *penne strascicate al sugo di pecora* (large penne served with a sauce of juicy, flavoursome spring lamb with a hint of chilli). The lamb round here is great (if it's local it will say *nostrale* on the menu) and roast in the wood oven to succulent, melting, rosemary-suffused perfection in *agnellino al forno*. Puddings are also superb, especially the *torta di mele*, a buttery apple pie, best eaten with a glass of Montagliari *vin santo*. If you like the Montagliari wine – a classic Chianti fusion of heady fruit and sweaty vinyl, and a light summery slightly *pétillant* white – it's on sale at the tiny estate shop.

Villa Miranda
Località Villa, Radda in Chianti (0577 73 80 21).
Open lunch & dinner daily. **Average** L55,000.
Credit EC, MC, V.

An 18th-century coaching inn, with accommodation (in converted farm buildings with swimming pool) as well as a restaurant. The *padrona* is Donna Miranda, a huge headscarved Tuscan mamma who oversees all, from grilling *bistecca alla fiorentina* on the massive wood-stove to reprimanding aged local pensioners, in to watch football on TV and have a little company, should they become too rude to the tourists. At lunch time there is a set menu (three courses for L25,000). You may as well stick with Villa Miranda's own wines; they started life in the vineyards behind the house – a light, summery white, and a range of reds including the aptly titled Super Miranda, a powerful plummy pungent red that goes just fine with a *bistecca alla fiorentina*.

Antipasti are good, especially the *bruschetta al pomodoro* in summer when tomatoes are sweet. For *primi*, Miranda cooks up a dense, rich chilli-spiked *zuppa di farro* (spelt soup) and a light *ravioli al burro e salvia* (ravioli with sage butter), while queen of the *secondi* is the *bistecca alla fiorentina*, which comes charred, woodsmoky, impregnated with herbs and very rare. Best choice for pudding is a plate of homemade almond biscuits (*biscotti*) with a glass of *vin santo* to dunk them in.

Around Florence & Pisa

Da Delfina
Via della Chiesa 1, Località Artimino, near Carmignano (055 87 18 074). **Open** lunch & dinner Tue-Sat (sometimes closed Tue lunch); lunch Sun.
Average L60,000. **No credit cards.**

Occupying a *casa colonica* and overlooking the multi-chimneyed Medici Villa of Artimino, Da Delfina is an elegant place, whose style and quality belie the reasonable prices. The menu changes with the seasons, but care and imagination is lavished on all dishes from the simplest *crostini* (where the liver pâté has just the right flavour and texture), to a refined *sfomato di ortiche*, a pale green mousse of wild leaves that comes lukewarm with a purée of pumpkin. The *ribollita* here is the authentic stuff – thick, tasty, filling winter food, but the most outstanding of the *primi* is *gnocchi alla parietaria*, featherlight gnocchi mingled with melted butter and a unique local herb.

Da Delfina chooses its meat carefully. Go for *scottadito*, succulent wood-grilled spring lamb chops, or tender, herby wood-roasted *capretto* (goat kid). Salads come with freshly torn mint leaves. Puddings vary from day to day. One to attempt to replicate at home is creamy yogurt, mixed with *panna cotta*, crushed amaretti biscuits, honey and liqueur, topped with cherries, rasperries and tiny wild strawberries. Always call ahead to book.

Enoteca Giovanni
Via Garibaldi 25, Montecatini Terme (0572 71 695).
Open lunch & dinner Tue-Sun. **Average** L75,000.
Credit AmEx, DC, EC, MC, V.

A relaxed restaurant popular with local businessmen and foodies, that started out as a wine shop, but is now decked out in flowery wallpaper and pastel napery. The food is creative but never daftly so, and both the innovative dishes and those that take their cue from local tradtion are superb. Good *antipasti* to try are *fiori di zucci ripieni*, courgette flowers

stuffed with potato, basil and garlic and baked with parmesan, and a salad of succulent tuna and crisp young asparagus in a balsamic dressing. As for pasta, there's a lovely *tagliolini* with prawns and rocket, and they smother skinny yellow *pennette* with a pungent, garlicky sauce of *funghi porcini*. For a light secondo try *carpaccio* with rocket and parmesan, or a fillet of John Dory (*sanpietro*) with courgette flowers. Locally inspired desserts include *castagnaccio*, a crisp cake of chestnut flour, pine nuts and rosemary.

Around Arezzo

Locanda al Castello di Sorci
Via San Lorenzo, San Lorenzo, near Anghiari (0575 78 90 66). **Open** lunch & dinner Tue-Sun.
Set meal including limitless wine L30,000.
Credit AmEx, EC, MC, V.

A Tuscan down-home sort of place, occupying a two-storey heftily beamed outbuilding on the estate of the 15th-century Castello di Sorci. You arrive, join the fast-moving queue of off-duty locals, and are instructed to go to a specific room, where you are allocated a table. Then nothing happens for a while, until a girl carrying a tray of unlabelled bottles appears, and plonks one on every table. She then comes back, first with jugs of water, then with plates of *crostini* and cured meats: perhaps not the best you've ever eaten, but then there's plenty of good stuff to save room for. Every day you get a plate of hand-made eggy tagliatelle with a tasty lamb *ragù*, plus a second authentically peasanty dish that changes every day; Tuesday is *tagliolini con fagioli* (thin pasta ribbons with beans), Wednesday *quadrucci con ceci* (squares of pasta with chickpeas), Thursday is *gnocchi*, Friday *ribollita*, Saturday *farro* and *risotto con funghi*, and Sunday polenta or *risotto con funghi*. The main course is a plate of grilled free-range chicken, lamb and rabbit; the pudding usually a substantial slice of sponge cake with a bottle of *vin santo*. Coffee is served downstairs at the bar.

Around Lucca & the North

La Ceragetta
Via Ceragetta 5, Capanne di Careggine, near Isola Santa (0583 66 70 65). **Open** lunch & dinner Tue-Sun.
Average L27,000. **No credit cards.**

An ersatz Alpine chalet with artex walls high up in pine-wooded mountains, where the wine is unlimited and Italian families wind up singing *Yellow Submarine* and *Volare*, is probably as far removed from the collective northern European dream of Tuscany as lederhosen and bratwurst. But La Ceregetta exists, with a vengeance, and you can be sure that if there is anyone there with a Notting Hill or TriBeCa address, it will be you. A full meal with absolutely everything from your third bottle of wine to your fifth grappa included, costs L27,000. The proceedings begin with a glass of *prosecco*, closely followed by a bottle of basic white wine, and a plate of *antipasti*, including *crostini* topped with piping hot mushrooms. There are usually three *primi*, best of which is the risotto – if you're lucky a richly flavoured mushroom one. After the *primi* comes a glass of *limoncello*, a strong lemon liqueur, then a plate of mixed grilled meat (delicious rabbit) and a mixed salad. Puddings tend to be aimed at kids rather than adults, but look out for fresh *pecorino* served with honey.

La Darsena
Via Virgilio 172 (0584 39 27 85). **Open** lunch Mon; lunch & dinner Tue-Sat. **Average** L35,000 (lunch); L45,000 (dinner). **No credit cards.**

A fantastic little fish trattoria tucked away in the little grid of streets behind Viareggio's docks known as the Cantieri. It is owned and run by Giulio, who used to own a posh restaurant in Croydon, and is a wonderfully animated, totally

Where do you find
out what's happening
in London ?

http://www.timeout.co.uk

Time Out

Your weekly guide
to the most exciting
city in the world

unpretentious place, especially at noon when the local boat-workers come by for lunch. Kick off with the selection of hot *antipasti*, including crisp, piping hot deep-fried *bianchini* (minute white-bait type fish); anchovies marinated in oil, lemon and onion; *inzimino*, a stew of squid and spinach; pink, tender octopus dressed with lemon and parsley; and mussels delectably stuffed with a mixture of minced veal, breadcrumbs, parsley and parmesan, served with a garlicky tomato sauce. At this stage you'll be asked if you want to "go on to the end", which means continue with a selection of cold antipasti. Unless you have the appetite of a docker it would be wise to desist and save room for a pasta course. Try *spaghetti allo scoglio* (spaghetti with rockfish – baby squid, tiny prawns etc) either *in bianco* (with wine, oil, parsley and garlic) or *al pomodoro*, with a tomato sauce; rock fish also come as a delicious risotto. For *secondi* there's a great *fritto misto*, light crispy deep-fried prawns, squid and baby flat fish; *rombo* baked with potato, tomato and black olives; *gamberoni in guazzetto*, prawns in a soupy garlicky tomato sauce served with toast to sop it up; and *misto alla griglia*, a selection of freshly grilled fish.

Il Giardinetto

Via Roma 151, Fivizzano (0585 92 060). **Open** *July-Sept* lunch & dinner daily; *Nov-June* lunch & dinner Tue-Sun; closed Oct. **Average** L35,000. **Credit** V.

Il Giardinetto is a hotel with restaurant that belongs to a bygone age. At lunchtime the hotel's permanent guests – genteel old ladies in hats and gentlemen in immaculate suits – gather in the dining room overlooking a romantic garden with overgrown terracotta urns and a statue of Venus. Food, served by the ageing hotel owner, with the help of a trolley, is cooked in the sort of kitchen your granny would have if she were Italian, and though it's not uniformly fantastic, there are enough good dishes for a satisfying meal. Start with a local white, a refreshing fizzy Santerenzio, and follow with a bowl of substantial minestrone, drizzled with olive oil and served with brown and white bread. Continue with the best of the *secondi*, a truly tasty slice of rabbit stuffed with bacon and egg. Save room for the hotels two stunning desserts, a creamy *semifreddo* of crushed amaretti and cream, and a lovely light ice cream with blackcurrents.

La Maiola

Località Maiola di Sotto, Bagni di Lucca (0583 86 296). **Open** dinner Mon, Wed-Sat; lunch Sun and by appointment. **Average** L40,000. **Credit** AmEx, DC, EC, MC, V.

Probably the best country restaurant in Tuscany, La Maiola was opened up a few years ago by a former computer engineer, Enrico Franceschi, in his grandparents' old house, high in the wooded hills above Bagni di Lucca. A true connoisseur, who cares more about the quality of the food he serves than making a profit, Enrico employs a relative to drive around Tuscany and Emilia Romagna searching for the best prosciuttos, salamis, oils, wines and cheeses. Food, cooked by Enrico's wife Simonetta, is the kind of fare Lucchese families would have traditionally eaten on special occasions. There are three set menus, all of them superb value. Before you have even chosen your wine, an *amuse gueule* is brought to the table, with a glass of the lemony house aperitif. Then the *antipasti* start arriving, *crostini* with grilled courgettes and sweet *peperonata*; crispy slices of polenta, slices of succulent prosciutto, peppery salami and a platter of baby river trout, which you eat whole. *Primi* include a light *zuppa di farro*, home-made pasta with a pungent rabbit sauce, and delicate ravioli with *ragù*. Then comes a plate of *tagliata* (strips of steak) with fresh green peppercorns and a scrumptious Lucchese dish, *coniglio con le olive*, rabbit stuffed with juicy black olives. Accompanying this are the vegetables of the day. Desserts are also home-made; among them a delicious almond cake, *torta di almenda*, that goes perfectly with a *vin santo*.

La Martinatica

Via Martinatica 20, Pietrasanta (0584 79 25 34). **Open** lunch & dinner Wed-Mon. **Average** L65,000. **Credit** AmEx, DC, EC, MC, V.

La Martinatica is housed in an old olive mill, and through glass laid into the floor you can still see the water wheel that operated the olive press. Run by a mother and son team, Mirella and Riccardo, there are set fish and meat menus every day. The fish menu is truly superb – kicking off with a light *antipasto*, maybe a fish pâté or thin slices of mellowly smoked swordfish. For *primi*, Riccardo makes various fish stuffed ravioli with a pasta so thin that it is virtually translucent. Another must if it is on the menu is *spaghetti al nero con gamberetti*, squid ink spaghetti with utterly fresh prawns, slivers of chilli and garlic. The main fish courses are skilfully simple – boiled lobster accompanied by a heap of Tuscan white beans (a surprisingly good combination), or mussels and clams in a garlicky, winey broth served over slices of toast. Desserts are home-made. One to look out for is *budino di ricotta e limone con salsa di fragola*, a delectably refreshing mousse of ricotta and lemon with a fresh strawberry coulis.

Specialist Holidays

Fly, bike, walk, cook or paint your way around Tuscany.

Walking, cycling & touring

The Alternative Travel Group
69-71 Banbury Road, Oxford OX2 6PE (01865 31 56 78/fax 31 56 96). **Dates** Spring & Autumn. **Prices from** £1,060 for 8 days all inclusive.
Offers an excellent range of escorted walking and cycling trips in groups of no more than 16 with experienced guides. They also arrange customised trips for independent minded travellers, organising 'a la carte' schedules.

Chianti Rooster Tours
For information contact Dario Castagno (mobile 0337 70 69 58/fax 0577 32 25 34). **Dates** all year.
Tours and excursions of small groups of people to places off the beaten track in and around Chianti.

Club Alpino Italiano (CAI)
Via Studio 5 (fax 055 23 98 580). **Open** 5-7.30pm Mon-Fri.
CAI organizes hiking trips through Tuscany and Italy, and are responsible for marking all national hiking and walking trails. They also produce good walking maps.

Cycling for Softies
2-4 Birch Polygon, Manchester M14 (0161 248 8282/ fax 0161 248 51 40). **Dates** May to October.
Prices from £699 for 8 nights excluding flights.
You make your own way through the rolling hills of Chianti, staying in carefully chosen family-owned hotels. Bicycles and an information pack with route maps and a regional booklet are provided and your luggage is transported between hotels.

Ramblers Holidays
Box 43, Welwyn Garden City, Herts AL8 6PQ (01707 33 11 33/fax 01707 33 32 76/e-mail ramhols@dial.pipx.com). **Dates** Spring & Autumn
Prices from £422 for 1 week half board including flights.
Centre-based walking and sightseeing holidays staying in Florence, Siena or San Marcello.

Veni Vidi Bici
All tours leave from Parcheggio Parterre, Piazza della Libertà, Florence (mobile 0333 89 55 586/fax 055 68 50 64 for information & reservations).
This programme, started by a group of students and outdoor enthusiasts in 1996, offers a variety of bike tours around Florence and throughout Tuscany. The trips are often organised around themes (eg Medici villas, the Chianti Trail, etc) and last from a day to a week. Customised itineraries can also be arranged for groups of more than nine people. All trips depart from the Parcheggio de Parterre, Piazza della Libertà. Prices (including bike, insurance and meals – and accommodation for weekend and week-long trips) are L55,000 for one day, L150,000 for a weekend (Saturday morning to Sunday evening) and around L400,000 for week-long excursions. Throughout the summer (rainy days excepted) there are bike tours of Florence for L25,000.

Waymark
44 Windsor Road, Slough (01753 516 477/fax 01753 517016). **Dates** Spring & Autumn. **Prices from** £725 for 2 weeks half board.
Centre-based walks from San Gimignano and 'three stop' walking tours staying in different hotels while your baggage is transferred.

Art history

Prospect Art Tours
454-458 Chiswick High Road, London W4 (0181 995 2151/fax 0181 742 1969). **Dates** Spring & Autumn.
Prices from £850 per week all inclusive.
Offers music and art history holidays complete with concert tickets, museums and specialist guides in Florence and Lucca.

Specialtours
81a Elizabeth Street, London SW1 9PG (0171 730 2297). **Dates** Spring and Autumn. **Prices from** £1,200 per week all inclusive.
Specialist one-off tours visiting museums and gardens with lectures by art historians. Details available every September.

Cooking schools

Italian Cookery Weeks Ltd.
5 Cullingworth Road, London NW1 (0181 208 0112).
Dates May to September. **Prices from** £1,055 per week including flights.
Excellent food and wine with daily tuition in cookery by cook Susanna Gelmetti, and occasional trips and excursions.

La Bottega Del 30
Via S. Caterina, Villa a Sesta, Siena (tel/fax 0577 35 92 26). **Dates** All year. **Prices from** L2,500,000 for two people per week excluding travel.
A hands-on course in Chianti cooking run by Helene Stoquelet who after ten years in her successful restaurant has decided to share her secrets. The price includes room and board and five half day cooking lessons, side trips and evening meals out.

Tasting Places
136B Lancaster Road, London W11 (0171 229 7020/fax 0171 229 4383). **Dates** Spring & Autumn.
Prices from £925 per week excluding flights.
High quality courses run by an organisation headed by London chef Alastair Little. Teachers include Alastair Little, Thane Price, Antony Worrall Thompson, Elizabeth Luard and Sophie Grigson.

Villa Delia

Via del Bosco 9, Ripoli di Lari, Pisa (0587 68 43 22/fax 0587 68 43 31). Reservations made through Umberto Management Ltd. 1380 Hornby Street, Vancouver, BC V6Z 1W5 (604 669 3732/fax 604669 9723/e-mail klloyd@helix.net/Internet: http://www.umberto.com). **Dates** April to October. **Price from** Can$3,150 per person excluding flights.

Set in a rustic 16th century villa, the package consists of 9 nights accommodation, food, morning cooking classes instructed by regional chefs, lead by resident chef Marietta Menghi, and afternoon excursions to local markets, cultural centres and wine tastings. Non-package rates are also available, enquire direct.

Painting courses

Simply Tuscany

598 Chiswick High Road, London W4 5RT (0181 995 9323/fax 0181 995 3346). **Dates** May to September. **Prices from** £865 a week excluding flights.

One and two week watercolour holidays led by landscape artist Sandra Pepys with day trips to Lucca and Florence.

Verrochio Art Centre

Via San Michele 16, Casole d'Elsa, 5303151 Italy. Bookings through Rose Konstam, 37 Eaton Mews, Handbridge, Chester, CH4 7EJ (tel/fax 01244 676 585). **Dates** May-October. **Prices from** £570 for two week course full board excluding flights.

A family-run operation offering specialist painting and sculpture courses with tuition and studio space, in a hill top village.

Hot-air ballooning

Chianti Balloon Club

Constantine Tourneau, Il Porto, Piranella 53010 Siena (0577 36 32 32/fax 0577 36 31 52). **Dates** April to September depending on weather conditions. **Price** L400,000 per person.

Flights over Chianti from a village 10km outside Siena and a champagne breakfast on landing.

Discovery Club

Robert Ethrington, Via de Goti 17, Rapolano Terme. 53040 Siena (0577 725517/fax 0577 725519). **Dates** April to September depending on weather conditions. **Price** L250,000 per person.

Well-organised company offering a choice of take off sites: Rapolano Terme, Montepulciano and Monte Oliveto. Prices include a champagne breakfast.

Language schools

See also chapter **Students**.

British Institute of Florence

Palazzo Lanfredini, Lungarno Giucciardini 9, Florence (055 28 40 33/fax 055 28 70 71). **Dates** August. **Prices from** £275 for one week language course excluding travel and accommodation. Family discounts. Courses in Italian language, opera and art history with optional excursions. Accommodation in an old seminary for £13 per day with breakfast.

Centro Fiorenza

Via S. Spirito 14, Florence (055 23 98 274/fax 055 28 71 48/e-mail fiorenza@mbox.vol.it). **Dates** Spring and Autumn. **Prices from** £345 for two week course excluding accomodation.

Intensive Language courses as well as courses in History of Art and Tuscan cuisine on the island of Elba. Home-stay, flats or hotels arranged.

Centro Linguistico Italiano Dante Alighieri

Via de' Bardi 12, Firenze, Italy (055 23 42 984/ fax 055 23 42 766/e-mail dante_fi@saatel.it/ web site: http://www.hyperborea.com/dante-alighieri). **Dates** all year. **Prices from** £325 for 2 week language and culture course.

Specialised language and cultural courses ranging from 2 weeks to 9 months. Accommodation with a family from L750,000 a month.

Cooperativa "Il Sasso"

Via del Voltaia nel Corso 74, Montepulciano (0578 75 83 11/fax 0570 75 75 47). **Dates** all year. **Prices from** L520,000 for 2 week course.

Run two- or four-week language courses for all levels. You can also take courses in history of art or mosaics. Rooms in a hotel, flat, or with a family can be arranged.

Italian Cultural Institute

39 Belgrave Square, London SW1 8NX (0171 235 1461/ 0171 823 18870).

Good source of information for language courses in Italy.

Scuola Leonardo da Vinci

Via Brunelleschi 4, Florence (055 28 02 03/fax 055 294820/e-mail scuolaleonardo@trident.nettuno.it/web site: http://www.trident.nettuno.it/mall/leonardo). **Dates** all year round. **Price** L740,000 for four weeks.

Schools in Florence, Siena and Rome and also offers courses in history of art, Italian cuisine, wines, drawing & etching. Accommodation arranged.

Farming holidays

WWOOF

19 Bradford Road, Lewis, Sussex, BN7 1RB (no phone). Or contact Elisa Grandis, Caslare Acquachiara, Via Vallicorati 11, Guardistallo Pisa.

If you really want to gain an intimate knowledge of rural Tuscany, WWOOF, an acronym for Willing Workers on Organic Farms, organises working holidays on organic farms, especially at the times of the grape and olive harvests. Generally, food and board are provided in exchange for about four hours work a day, with the rest of the day free to explore. Conditions vary considerably from farm to farm and you should check out working conditions before you go. Living conditions are sometimes fairly primitive and you should go prepared to turn your hand to just about anything. To receive a list of participating farms you need to become a member, after which you will receive a regular newsletter.

Around Florence & Pisa

Beyond the industrial sprawl of the Arno valley there are attractions, both man-made and natural, worth seeking out.

This is a huge area, stretching from the border with Emilia-Romagna in the north to Volterra in the south, but the attractions are thinly spread. Tuscany's industrial belt slices right through the middle, clogging the Arno valley from Florence via Pisa to the coast, and spreading up and around the sizeable cities of Pistoia and Prato. Industrial rings notwithstanding, both Prato and Pistoia are well worth a visit, both of them with great cathedrals and the engagingly watchable sort of streetlife over-touristed Florence lacks.

Driving along the heavily choked roads of the Arno valley is not a pleasant experience, though you can strike off up into the gentle foothills of Monte Albano to potter around Medici villas, or head up higher to the little town of Vinci, birthplace of Leonardo. The best area for relaxed, take-it-as-it-comes pottering, is however the Mugello, watered by the river Sieve, sheltered by the thickly wooded slopes of the Apennines, and butting into Emilia-Romagna. As the attractions are so sparse, and the area is not condusive to touring, this gazzetteer is organised alphabetically.

Carmignano

In the south of the newly created province of Prato is a little town that can boast one absolute wonder and at least two delightful surprises. The best way to appreciate the former is to start with the latter. So head for the main square and the **Bar Ristorante Roberto** (*055 87 12 375. Open lunch daily; dinner by reservation*) whose mundane exterior belies what's to be had within. Adjacent to the bar is a small, modest-looking dining-room with just seven tables and plastic beading on the walls. This is where the indomitable Fedora will ply you with delicious homely food (pasta with an excellent *ragù*, gently stewed lamb, salted cod cooked with wild leeks, onions, fresh tomatoes and Swiss chard), wine and a coffee for an incredible L15,000. This no-nonsense 70-year-old widow has just won the contract for cooking the local school lunches as well, so the place is never closed. Will the next generation have their Fedoras? You can turn over such thoughts as

The latest news.

you sample more of the excellent Carmignano wine at villa-farms such as **Capezzana** (*055 87 06 091. Open 8.30am-12.30pm, 2.30-6.30pm, Mon-Fri*), **Bacchereto** (*055 87 17 191. Open 4-7pm Tue, Thur*), **Il Poggiolo** (*055 87 11 242. Open 8am-noon, 2-5pm Mon-Fri; 8am-noon Sat*) or **Castelvecchio** (*055 87 05 451. Open 9am-1pm, 2-6pm, Mon-Fri; 9am-12.30pm Sat*). The latter two are in Carmignano itself. The wine is an elegant, balanced red made from a blend of Sangiovese, Cabernet and Canaiolo grapes.

Thus prepared for spiritual enlightenment, you should make your way up the main street to the 13th-century church of **San Michele** (always open), to see Pontormo's stupendously graceful *Visitation*, painted around 1528-30.

Certaldo Alto

With its sturdy walls and crenellated fortifications, the medieval historic nucleus of Certaldo peeps over the Valdelsa in a glow of warm pink brick. Although the settlement actually dates back to Etruscan times, its main claim to fame is the fact Giovanni Boccaccio (1313-75) – author of the *Decameron* – was born and died here. The **Casa del Boccaccio** (*0571 66 49 35*) is now open to the public, though it is of little intrinsic interest. By contrast, the frescoed rooms of the **Palazzo del Vicario** (*0571 66 12 19. Open 8am-8pm*

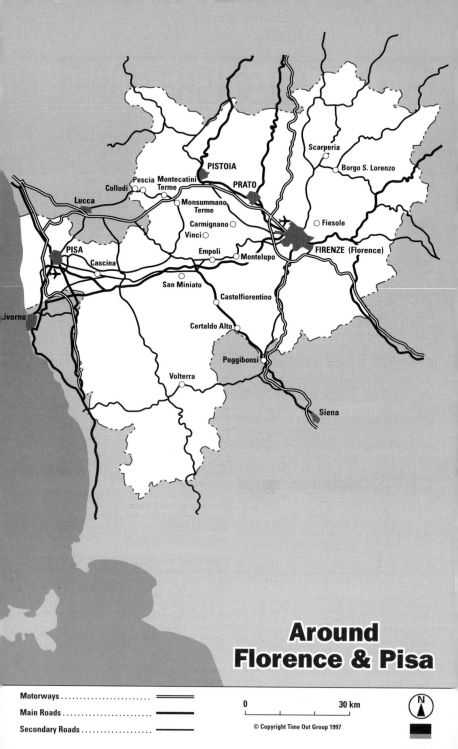

Around Florence & Pisa

Motorways ....
Main Roads ....
Secondary Roads ....

0   30 km

© Copyright Time Out Group 1997

Scarperia
Borgo S. Lorenzo
PISTOIA
Pescia Montecatini
Collodi   Terme
Lucca
PRATO
Monsummano
Terme
Carmignano
Vinci
Fiesole
FIRENZE (Florence)
Empoli
Montelupo
PISA
Cascina
San Miniato
Castelfiorentino
Livorno
Certaldo Alto
Poggibonsi
Volterra
Siena

daily. Admission L5,000) are well worth a visit. Moreover, alongside the Palazzo is the most charming little hotel with beautiful views and an exceptional restaurant. The **Osteria del Vicario,** Via Rivellino 3 (*0571 66 82 28. Open lunch & dinner Thur-Tue. Rates double L95,000*) has five double rooms, as well as a small dining-room and a wisteria-clad portico where gourmets will enjoy some inventive dishes devised by Enzo Pette, who takes his culinary calling very seriously.

Collodi

Something for the children that most parents can cope with too: **Pinocchio Park** (*0572 42 93 42. Open 8.30am-sunset daily. Admission L11,000; 3-14-year-olds L6,000*). It was established in 1956 to celebrate the locally-born author of that most appealing of children's stories. Remarkably kitsch-free, it features specially designed works by a number of outstanding artists, including a major sculpture by Emilio Greco, mosaics by Venturino Venturi, a restaurant designed by Giovanni Michelucci in 1963, and a sort of Pinocchian adventure path punctuated by 21 bronze sculptures by Pietro Gonzaga. Once the children have had their fill, the parents should be allowed to enjoy the magnificent historic gardens of **Villa Garzoni,** (*0572 42 95 90. Open 8.30am-7pm daily. Admission L10,000*) perched above the village. The residence dates from 1633, and it is thought that the gardens were initially designed by its owner, the marquis Romano di Alessandro Garzoni. By 1652 they were already outlined in their present form, though they took over 170 years to complete: a superb example of 18th-century Tuscan taste and culture that can stand up to comparison with the gardens at Versailles, Fontainebleau, Potsdam, etc.

Fiesole

Without Fiesole, there would never have been a Florence. For this stubborn Etruscan hill-town proved so difficult for the Romans to subdue, that they ended up setting up camp in the river valley below. Eventually the Romans did manage to take Fiesole, and it became one of the most important towns in Etruria, a role it hung on to until the 12th-century when Florence finally vanquished it in battle.

Fiesole, however, soon found a new role as a refined suburb where aristocrats could escape the heat and hoi polloi of Florence. In the 14th century, it was to the villas of Fiesole that Boccaccio sent his courtly raconteurs to escape the plague and tell the stories of the *Decameron*; and half a milennium later, it was again to Fiesole that EM Forster had his corsetted Edwardians picnic and Lucy have her first kiss in *Room with a View*. Nowadays, just 20 minutes by bus from Florence,

Fiesole can get uncomfortably packed in high summer, but is well worth a visit in spring or autumn.

The main square, Piazza Mino, named after the artist Mino da Fiesole, is lined with cafes and restaurants and dominated by the immense honey-stone campanile of the 11th-century **Duomo**. Inside, the columns are topped with capitals dating from Fiesole's period under Roman occupation. There are more relics of Roman Fiesole down the hill: a theatre which is still used for plays in summer, and the **Museo Faesulanum** (*open 9am-6pm Wed-Mon*), a replica Roman temple with finds from Bronze Age and Etruscan and Roman Fiesole. Close by are a complex of partially restored Roman baths, and remains of Etruscan walls.

Head down Via San Francesco to see the church of **Sant'Alessandro**, founded in the 5th or 6th century over Roman and Etruscan temples. There are fabulous views from the terrace outside, and vibrant onion marble columns within. **San Franceso**, further down the hill, has a collection of souvenirs from China brought back by missionary monks.

There are some nice walks around Fiesole, but the best is down the steep, twisting Via Vecchia Fiesolana to the Dominican monastery of **San Domenico**, where Fra Angelico was once a monk. The church still retains a delicate *Madonna and Angels* by him.

For lunch, it is wise to avoid the tourist traps in town and head out to the hamlet of Maiano, 3km away past the Villa San Michele hotel. **Le Cave da Maiano**, Via delle Cave 16 (*055 59 95 04. Open lunch & dinner. Closed lunch Mon*), is a rustic place with views from its terrace over a lush ravine, serving homely dishes such as polenta topped with garlicky *porcini*, *pappa al pomodoro*, and *riso allo spazzocamino*, a truly peasanty dish of rice, beans and *cavolo nero*, and wood-roast pigeon, chicken or steak. For pudding have home-made *cantuccini* with *vin santo*, or, in season, fresh fig flan.

Montecatini Terme

Montecatini Terme is a spa town founded in the 18th-century, that now has something of the sleazy

The sterile elegance of **Montecatini Terme.**

undertow of a casino town. It also suffers from horrendous traffic jams, a situation that has been made all the worse by the recent opening of a hypermarket. It does, however, retain a certain, if sterile, elegance, and it is worth a considerable detour and post-prandial traffic jams to eat at **Enoteca Giovanni**, Via Garibaldi 25 (*0572 71 695. Open lunch & dinner; closed Mon*). Try *insalata tiepida di gamberetti e clamari*, a juicy warm salad of shrimp and squid, or *tagliolini con gamberetti e rucola*, fine ribbons of pasta with prawns and rocket, or *pennette* with porcini (*see chapter* **A Tuscan Restaurant Tour**).

Monsummano Terme

Despite its proximity to Montecatini, Monsummano is a pleasant, if unthrilling, town with two major spa hotels. If you can take the time (and have the money), go for the four-star **Grotta Giusti Hotel** which has its own treatment centre (*0572 51 165/fax 0572 51 269. Open 1 Mar-30 Nov; Spa 0572 51 008/fax 0572 51 007. Open 24 Mar-1 Nov. Rates doubles from L210,000; singles from L130,000*). It is located in a fine, well-appointed villa in an ample park overlooking the town. Aches, pains and disorders of all sorts are eased and, even if you don't have any, there's nothing like wallowing in hot mud, steaming in Turkish baths and having various parts of your anatomy massaged to enhance your view of life.

Montelupo

The people of Montelupo have been making glazed pottery since medieval times. In 1973 the old public laundry in the Castello district was dismantled to reveal a two-metre-wide well that over the centuries had been filled with ceramic rejects and shards, many of which are now on show in the excellent **Museo della Ceramica** (*0571 51 352. Open 9am-noon, 2.30-7pm, Tue-Sun*). This institution also comprises an archaeological section and is currently supervising excavations at a large Roman villa in the vicinity where baths and three pottery kilns have so far come to light. The locals have never forsaken their original vocation and their products are on show and sale in the old cinema building and surrounding stalls every third Sunday of the month. The town also hosts a flower festival the first Sunday in April, an antiques market in May and a 'Festa Internazionale della Ceramica' during the last week of June.

Pescia

Straddling the river Pescia and surrounded by mountains, Pescia is the main town of the Valdinièvole. Although once it made silk and paper, its main source of income these days is the

Pistoia's **Baptistery**: *good enough to lick.*

cultivation of citrus fruits, indoor plants and cut flowers. The local olive oil is also good, and should be liberally added to a steaming plate of *fagioli di Sorana*, a special type of bean, smaller than the usual Tuscan variety, that has been awarded its own DOC stamp of quality. For this and other gastronomic pleasures such as the local *farinata* (polenta mixed with beans, cabbage, and potatoes) repair to **Da Sandrino** at Ponte di Castevecchio (*0572 40 70 14. Open lunch Mon; lunch & dinner Wed-Sun*). In town, by day try the pastries at the **Pasticceria Svizzera** (Ruga Orlandi 74); and by night sample wines and savoury snacks at the **Enoteca Wine Club** (Via Amendola 19).

Pistoia

If Prato is Florence's sparky little sister, Pistoia is its country aunt; a relaxed, old-fashioned place, where the pace is slow and life is still in tune with the countryside – despite the fact that its Breda factory produces most of Italy's buses and railway carriages. Encircled by walls dating back to the 14th century, the quiet, easy-going historic centre contains a number of fine Romanesque and Gothic buildings, leading in towards its elegant colonnaded cathedral.

Everything closes down for three hours or so around lunchtime, and since you can't beat them, you might as well join them, with a glass of wine and a plate of local goodies. These include the savoury *biroldo*, a sort of spicy boiled sausage, then *migliaccio* which is a pancake made with pig's blood, pine-nuts, raisins and sugar, and *confetti*, small, spiky white sweetmeats. You can find the latter at **Corsini** in Piazza San Francesco and Bertinotti in Viale Ardua. You should also try the excellent bread baked in traditional wood-burning ovens at the **Forno della Paura** in Via N Sauro. Crafts still practised in the area include lace-making and the production of copperware.

Things to see

The **Duomo** has an imposingly simple Romanesque interior and a campanile with exotic tiger-striped arcades on top. Squatting just opposite is the octagonal, 14th-century, green-and-white-striped **Baptistery**. The **Museo Civico** (*0573 37 12 96. Open 9am-1pm, 3-7pm Tue-Sun; 9am-12.30pm public hols*) behind the Duomo has fine 14th-century paintings well displayed on the ground floor and some fairly dreadful late Mannerist works two floors above. In the middle is a section on one of Pistoia's foremost scions, Giovanni Michelucci (1891-1990), architect of Florence's Santa Maria Novella station. **Palazzo Tau** (*0573 32 204. Open 9am-1pm, 3-7pm, Tue-Sun; 9am-12.30pm public hols*) houses the Centro di Documentazione e Fondazione (*0573 30 285*) devoted to the other Pistoian of renown, the sculptor **Marino Marini** (1901-80). The **Ospedale del Ceppo** is justly famous for its splendid della Robbia polychrome ceramic frieze (1526-29). The parish church of **Sant'Andrea** features a magnificent carved stone pulpit (1298-1301) by Giovanni Pisano.

Where to stay

Hotel Leon Bianco *Via Panciatichi 2 (tel/fax 0573 26 675/26 676).* **Rates** *single* L100,000; *double* L150,000. **Credit** AmEx, DC, EC, MC, V.
Centrally located, pleasant hotel.

Hotel Piccolo Ritz *Via A Vannucci 67 (0573 26775/fax 27 798).* **Rates** *single* L85,000; *double* L120,000. **Credit** EC, MC, V.
Conveniently close to the station but otherwise an unremarkable hotel.

Villa Vannini *Villa di Piteccio (0573 42 031/fax 26 331).* **Rates** *double* L140,000. **Credit** EC, MC, V.
You'll find a country house atmosphere and great food at the comfortable and slightly eccentric Villa Vannini. Great value.

Where to eat

Lo Storno *Via del Lastrone 8 (0573 26 193).*
Open lunch Mon-Wed; lunch & dinner Thur-Sat. **Average** L25,000. **No credit cards.**
A traditional osteria serving dishes such as tripe, spelt and bean soup and salted cod with leeks.

La BotteGaia *Via del Lastrone 4 (no phone).*
Open 10.30am-2.30pm, 5.30pm-1am, Tue-Sat.
Average L10,000. **No credit cards.**
No more than a cellar with a few tables where Elio will tempt you with well-selected wines, home-made flans, local cheeses and similar lighter sustenance.

Tarabaralla *Via del Lastroneno 13 (0573 97 68 91).*
Open 6.30am-2.30pm, 4-9.30pm, Tue-Sat; 4-9.30pm Sun.
No credit cards.
Superb takeaway pizza from L6,000.

Events

Arts & Crafts show and market of local products held in the ex-Breda factory (May/June); **Pistoia Blues** music festival (July); **Giostra dell'Orso** procession and jousting tournament in traditional costume (25 July).

Prato

Poor old Prato suffers badly from the little sister syndrome: nearby Florence is so much more famous and beautiful that few visitors pay much attention to an industrial sibling with a population devoted to the manufacture of worsted cloths. Yet unassuming Prato has a lot to say for herself. Speed through the unprepossessing outskirts and make for the attractive walled city centre surrounding the pale swallow-tailed Ghibelline bastions of the 13th-century Emperor's Castle (*see chapter* **History: Tuscany in the Middle Ages**), built by Frederick II, to protect his pro-imperial representative from the locals.

Like its big sister, Prato was a dynamic trading centre back in the Middle Ages. Accountancy was virtually invented here by one Francesco di Marco Datini, whose meticulous accounts and sheafs of private letters eventually gave Iris Origo enough material to write *The Merchant of Prato*, a book

Prato shopping

Why not turn Prato's industrial heritage to your advantage? You can buy fine fabrics at keen prices at the following factory outlets: **Lanificio Cangioli** for suit lengths, Via del Bisenzio a San Martino 6 (*0574 46 86 46*); **Enrico Pecci di A Pecci** for combed and carded cloths, Via di Pantano 16E, Capalle (*055 89 890*); **Gruppo Osvaldo Bruni** for knitwear, Via Galcianese 67/69 (*0574 60 75 91*); **Maglieria Artigiana** for cashmere knitwear, Via del Mandorlo 19/21 (*0574 55 03 84*); **Ottomila** for cashmere and woollen knitwear, Via Friuli Venezia Giulia 20/22, Macrolotto (*0574 62 06 32*). If you fancy having shirts made to measure using fine cottons, linens and silks from the north of Italy, go to **Baldini**, Via del Pellegrino 6 (*0574 38 464*). You'll need a fitting the first time, and your order will be dispatched to you within 20 days.

After all this racing round, hole up for a reviving drink or light lunch at the pleasantly spacious, unhurried **Caffè Pasticceria Giulebbe**, Via Piave 24 (*0574 60 53 70*). Make sure you take away some Prato almond biscuits, known locally as *Mattonelle*, from **Biscottificio Mattei**, Via Ricasoli (*0574 25 756*), and a range of goodies from **Gastronomia Barni**, Via Ferrucci 24 (*0574 33 835*), **Pastificio Forno Branchetti**, Via del Serraglio 6 (*0574 30 171*), and **Forno Loggetti**, Via Matteotti 11 (*0574 25 267. Open mornings only*).

about his life in 14th-century Prato. Twentieth-century Prato is a vibrant, forward-looking place, with a lively theatre scene, and one of Italy's most active centres for contemporary art. It also hosts numerous concert cycles, temporary exhibitions, trade shows and a multi-faceted annual event revolving around cartoon and comic art. To find out more, call on the well-run (and polyglot) **Tourist Information Office**, Via Cairoli 48, just behind the church of Santa Maria delle Carceri (*0574 24 112. Open 9am-1pm, 2.30-6.30pm, Mon-Sat*).

Things to see

The **Duomo** is an amazing Romanesque-Gothic building in pinkish brick with half-finished green and white marble striped façade. On one corner, canopied by what looks like a Chinese parasol, is a 15th-century pulpit designed by Michelozzo and carved with reliefs of dancing children and cherubs by Donatello (now replaced by casts). The overall effect is one of strangely harmonious asymmetry. Inside there are frescoes by Paolo Uccello and Filippo Lippi: the latter was responsible for the *Lives of Saints John the Baptist and Stephen* in the choir, and apprently used his nun-lover Lucrezia Buti as a model for Salome at Herod's Banquet. The **Museo dell'Opera del Duomo** (*0574 29 339. Open 9.30am-12.30pm, 3-6.30pm Mon, Wed-Fri; public hols 9.30am-12.30pm*) is located in part of the Palazzo Vescovile to the left of the Duomo. Exhibits include Donatello's original bas-reliefs of dancing putti, a fresco attributed to Paolo Uccello and works by both Filippo and Filippino Lippi. The **Palazzo Pretorio** is now home to the **Galleria Comunale** (*0574 61 63 02. Open 9.30am-12.30pm, 3-6.30pm, Mon, Wed-Fri; public hols 9.30am-12.30pm*). It features della Robbia polychrome terracottas, a tabernacle by Filippino Lippi, miraculously restored after the ravages of war, a fine *tondo* by Signorelli and Filippo Lippi's *Madonna del Ceppo* (1453) with its realistic portrayal of the Prato merchant Datini, whose activities were so vividly described by Iris Origo. **Palazzo Datini** is the pre-Renaissance residence of Datini (1330-1410), the banker who is said to have initiated Prato's mercantile fortunes (*see above*). Located in the Convent of San Domenico, the **Museo di Pittura Murale** (*No phone. Open 9am-noon Wed-Sun*) houses 14th- and 15th-century frescoes found in and around Prato. The church of **Santa Maria delle Carceri**, just opposite the Tourist Information Office, is a masterpiece of early Renaissance architecture designed by Giuliano da Sangallo. Prato has a magnificent collection of textiles dating from the 5th century to the present; the **Textile Museum** in which they are to be displayed in the Palazzo Comunale is nearing completion. The **Museo d'Arte Contemporaneo Luigi Pecci** (*0574 57 06 20. Open 10am-7pm Wed-Mon*), with its ample exhibition space, is located in the outskirts, near the autostrada exit Prato Est.

Where to stay

Art Hotel Museo *Viale della Repubblica 289 (0574 57 87/fax 57 88 80)*. **Rates** *single* L200,000; *double* L250,000. **Credit** AmEx, DC, V.
Stylish but not exactly charming hotel, out near the Luigi Pecci Museum.

Hotel Flora *Via Cairoli 31 (0574 33 521/fax 0574 40 289)*. **Rates** *single* L75-140,000; *double* L105-198,000. **Credit** AmEx, DC, EC, MC, V.
Centrally located, pleasantly old-fashioned hotel.

Hotel Giardino *Via Magnolfi 4 (0574 26 189/fax 60 65 91)*. **Rates** *single* L115,000; *double* L160,000. **Credit** AmEx, DC, EC, MC, V.
Agreeable establishment just behind the Duomo.

Villa Rucellai *Via di Canneto 16 (0574 46 03 92)*. **Rates** *double* from L120,000. **No credit cards**.
Wonderful old villa with a medieval tower that has been home to the Rucellai family for generations. Simple, but full of character and, with its hillside setting, a great getaway from industrial Prato.

Where to eat

Il Baghino *Via Accademia 9 (0574 27 920)*. **Open** lunch & dinner Tue-Sat; lunch Sun, Mon. **Average** L45,000. **Credit** AmEx, DC, EC, MC, V.
Tuscan cuisine with local specialities like stuffed celery.

La Cucina di Paola *Via Banchelli 16 (0574 24 353)*. **Open** lunch & dinner Tue-Sun. **Average** L50,000. **No credit cards**.
Top notch local fare.

Il Piraña *Via Valentini 110 (0574 25 746)*. **Open** lunch & dinner Mon-Fri; dinner Sat, Sun. **Average** L75,000. **Credit** AmEx, DC, EC, MC, V.
Excellent fish, but pricey.

Events

Prato Estate (July/Aug) Concerts, films, open-air shows all over the city; **Musica d'Autunno** (Oct/Nov) Concert series; start of **Metastasio** and **Fabbricone Theatre** seasons (Nov).

San Miniato

Snaking along the crest of a lofty hill, with views back to Fiesole and on to the coast, this town was able to dominate both the Pisa-Florence road and the Via Francigena, which brought pilgrims from the north to Rome. In the 12th and 13th centuries it was fortified and became one of Tuscany's foremost imperial centres, but succumbed to Florence in the mid-1300s. Unfortunately the interiors of both the 13th-century **Duomo** and the slightly later church of **San Domenico** were subjected to some heavy-handed Baroque 'improvements', making the main reasons for visiting consumerist

The spacious **Loggiati di San Domenico** are used for an antiques and collectibles fair on the first Sunday of each month, an organic foods market on the second, and an arts and crafts market on the third. The surrounding area is rich in truffles, and November weekends are devoted to tasting them. Good food and wine are to be found in the family-run **Antro di Bacco**, Via IV Novembre 3/5 (*0571 43 319. Open lunch & dinner Mon, Tue, Thur-Sat; lunch Wed*). Likewise just outside town at **Il Convio** (*0571 40 81 14. Open lunch & dinner Thur-Tue*).

Scarperia

This pleasant little town in the rolling Mugello countryside was founded in 1306 as northernmost military outpost of the Florentine Republic. Because of its strategic location, it enjoyed considerable prosperity until the 18th century, when the main road over the Apennines to Bologna was opened further west. Despite its successive decline, one tradition deriving from its military past has survived: that of knife grinding and cutlery. Today the workshops of Scarperia still make the traditional bone-handled pocket knives that older country folk in Italy use for their husbandry and at the table. Each region has developed a special shape of its own, and you can watch the knives being skilfully pieced together by hand at the **Conaz** factory at Via Giordani 2 (*055 84 61 97*), just outside the walled historic nucleus of the town. Scarperia hosts an international knife exhibition and market during the first half of September.

Back in the spacious central square is the **Palazzo dei Vicari**, built in the 13th century on designs by Arnolfo di Cambio. Distinctly reminiscent of the Palazzo Vecchio in Florence, it was the residence of the republican governors whose coats of arms now decorate the façade. Inside there are frescoes dating back to the 14th-16th centuries, including a *Madonna and Child with Saints* by the School of Ghirlandaio.

For Mugello cuisine, try **Il Torrione** in the main street, Via Roma 78/80 (*055 84 30 263. Open lunch & dinner; closed Mon*), or **Villa il Palagio** (*055 84 63 76. Open lunch & dinner; closed Mon*), just outside the walls in Viale Dante. The locals swear by a restaurant right beside the Autostrada A1 exit for Barberino di Mugello: **Cosimo de' Medici** (*055 84 20 370. Open lunch & dinner; closed Mon*), where the cuisine (and name) apparently make up for the unprepossessing location. Another great place, much favoured by locals, is **Il Paiolo**, Via Cornocchio 1 (*055 84 20 733. Open lunch & dinner; closed Tue*) which specialises in grilled meats – you won't find a bigger *bistecca* outside Texas.

Vinci

As the birthplace of Leonardo, this little town attracts a constant stream of visitors. Towering over the modest urban development is the Castello dei Guidi, which houses an interesting **Museo Leonardiano** (*0571 56 055. Open winter 9.30am-6pm daily; summer 9.30am-7pm daily*) featuring models of machines and instruments devised by the Renaissance polymath. The place is usually teeming with children who can also indulge their precocious shopping instincts at the various souvenir stores. Yet miraculously the place has not been ruined and is worth a visit. To refuel flagging energies, try **La Torretta**, Via della Torre 19 (*0571 56 100. Open lunch & dinner; closed Mon*), **Leonardo**, Via La Querciola 43 (*0571 56 79 16. Open lunch & dinner; closed Wed*), or **Il Frantoio** at Sant'Ansano (*0571 58 40 95. Open dinner Mon, Tue; lunch & dinner Wed-Sun*), which specialises in unusual pizzas.

Volterra

Although Volterra is only 30km from the coast to the west and San Gimignano to the east, you drive though such rolling expanses of unspoilt countryside to get there that the town itself feels like an island in the midst of an unchanging agricultural sea. And a treasure island, to boot. It was one of the foremost centres of Etruscan culture during the 5th century BC, then became a Roman municipality, achieved independence as a free Commune in 1193, and ended up as a recalcitrant part of the Florentine dominions in the early 16th century. Enclosed within well-preserved medieval walls, its somewhat severe palaces now contain some superb collections of art and archaeology. Since Etruscan times the people of Volterra have specialised in the production of fine translucent artefacts in alabaster, which is quarried in the vicinity. There are still plenty of workshops where you can watch skilled craftsmen at work, usually without masks despite the white powdery dust that fills the air.

Things to see

The central **Piazza dei Priori**, one of the finest medieval squares in Italy, is dominated by the crenellated **Palazzo dei Priori**, built between 1208 and 1254, and now the City Hall. Behind the palazzo stands the 12th-13th-century **Duomo**. The **Pinacoteca e Museo Civico** (*0588 87 580. Open mid Mar-early Nov 9am-7pm daily; early Nov-mid Mar 9am-2pm daily. Admission L12,000, includes Museos Etrusco and Diocesano*) features some fine medieval painted wooden sculptures, works by Signorelli and Ghirlandaio, and an almost surreal *Deposition* painted with amazing chromatic audacity by Rosso Fiorentino in 1521. In the **Museo Diocesano d'Arte Sacra** (*0588 86 290. Open mid Mar-early Nov 9am-1pm, 3-6pm, daily; early Nov-mid Mar 9am-1pm daily*) is another important work by Rosso Fiorentino, the *Madonna Enthroned with Saints John the Baptist and John the Evangelist* (1521). The **Museo Etrusco** (*0588 86 347. Open as Pinacoteca above*) is a collection so rich that it deserves at least half a day's attention. Note the figurative detail of the figures depicted on the lids of the funerary urns. You'll see the same physical types among many of the local people (*see chapter* **History: DH Lawrence & The Etruscans**). The **Roman Theatre**, which you can reach by going down Via Guarnacci until you reach the medieval Porta Fiorentina then turning left down Viale Francesco Ferrucci, dates back to the early imperial period (1st century BC), and first came to light during excavations in the 1950s.

Where to stay

Hotel San Lino *Via San Lino 26 (0588 85 250/fax 0588 80 620).* **Rates** *single* L120,000; *double* L180,000. **Credit** AmEx, DC, EC, MC, V.

Hotel Sole *Via dei Cappuccini 10 (0588 84 000/fax 0588 87 491).* **Rates** *double* L110,000. **Credit** AmEx, EC, MC, V.

Where to eat

Da Badò *Borgo San Lazzaro 9 (0588 86 477).* **Open** lunch & dinner Thur-Tue. **Average** L30,000. **No credit cards.**
Go for the game (wild boar, rabbit, etc) and, when in season, the dishes made with local wild mushrooms.

Trattoria del Sacco Fiorentino *Piazza XX Settembre (0588 88 537).* **Open** lunch & dinner Sat-Thur. **Average** L30,000. **Credit** AmEx, DC, EC, MC, V.
Handy for lunch after visiting the Etruscan Museum. Try the green gnocchi and pasta dishes with veg sauces.

Pisa

There's more to Pisa than magnificent medieval monuments and teetering towers.

If you have only one hour to spend in Pisa, you will probably leave the city with the impression that it is no more than a dreary backdrop for the legions of tourists tramping around the **Campo dei Miracoli** (Field of Miracles) amid crowds of street vendors selling Leaning Tower night-lights. Despite housing some of Italy's finest universities and institutions of art, to most of the world Pisa means just one thing: the **Torre Pendente** (the Leaning Tower or, literally, 'dangling tower'), which draws millions of visitors a year to the city. Linger awhile, however, and you'll be pleased to discover that there's a little more to the town than the tower.

A couple of minutes walk from the Field of Miracles is the splendid Piazza dei Cavalieri, surrounded on all sides by some of Giorgio Vasari's finest architectural creations. Elsewhere, look out for Pisa's Romanesque trademarks – delicate marble arcades (filled or open) and alternating strips of coloured marble. The arcaded shopping strip of Borgo Stretto, the popular markets Vettovaglie (food) and Antiquariano (junk and antiques) and Corso Italia are prime spots for a taste of Pisan life. Check out as well the excellent theatrical and musical productions at Teatro Verdi, or the social scene in the the pubs, bars and *osterie* studding the alleys around the theatre. If you get culture fatigue, head for the nearby coast, with its sandy beaches and brash resorts.

Better a death in the family than a Pisan at the door

Pisa's origins are murky. It may originally have been a Greek colony or Etruscan settlement, but little is known for sure until the 1st century BC when the Romans moved in. During the middle ages the opportunistic and adventurous Pisans built up a merchant fleet that traded extensively with North Africa and the East, bringing back wealth and ideas which made Pisa one of Italy's most important maritime republics between the 11th and 13th centuries (her rivals were Amalfi, Genova and Venice). The silting up of its harbour and rapacity of rival cities gradually extinguished the Pisan flame – it fell to Genova in 1284, Milan in 1396 and finally to Florence in 1406.

Pisa may have lost its independence nearly 600 years ago, but Pisan pride remains as strong as ever. An age-old rivalry, fuelled by centuries of commercial and political competition still exists between Pisa and its conqueror, Florence. A common Florentine proverb goes: *'Meglio un morto in casa che un Pisano al'uscio!'* (Better a death in the family than a Pisan at the door!) to which a Pisan proverb responds: *'E che Dio ti contenta!'* ('And may God grant your wish!'). Famous Florentines like Dante and Machiavelli were not shy either about broadcasting their dislike for Pisa. Bitchy Dante at his pettiest exhorts the nearby islands of Gorgona and Capraia to clog up the Arno and wash Pisa away (*Inferno*, Canto XXXIII).

Nor do Livorno and Pisa get on. You may spot charming graffiti scrawled on the odd Pisan wall saying *'Livorno merda'* (Livorno shit) and *'viola merda'* ('purple shit', referring to the colour of football team Fiorentina's shirts). The scurrilous Livornese magazine *Il Vernacoliere* is full of anti-Pisa banter; one recent issue reported that a Pisan had recently been cloned; next time, it commented, they'll try it on humans.

The phone code for Pisa is **050**

Campo dei Miracoli

Unwisely constructed on marshy reclaimed land, all four of the major buildings on the Field of Miracles are somewhat out of kilter; although none by as much as the Tower. The three buildings – Duomo, Baptistry and Leaning Tower – do, however, look stupendous, rising gleaming white and intricate from a field of improbably emerald green. Today, a caravan of kitsch-vendors besieges the swarming masses of tour groups and school parties, all gazing glassy-eyed upwards at the gravity-defying tower.

Tickets

Ticket offices are in the southeast corner of the Piazza (sharing a room with the entrance to the Museo dell'Opera del Duomo, a gift shop and a satellite of the tourist information office) in the entrance to the Museo delle Sinopie, the Baptistery and in the entrance to the Camposanto. For information call *56 05 47*. Ticket options are as follows:

L17,000 (all sights); L15,000 ticket (any four sights); L12,000 (Museo del Duomo, Cathedral and Baptistery); L10,000 (any two sights); L2,000 (Cathedral).

Opening times

Jan, Feb, Nov, Dec Cathedral 10am-12.45pm; Baptistery 9am-4.20pm; Campo Santo 9am-12.40pm, 3-4.45pm;

Hallucinations on the **Campo dei Miracoli**.

The **Bapistery**: *a wedding cake in stone.*

Museo delle Sinopie 9am-12.40pm, 3pm-4.40pm; Museo del Duomo 9am-4.20pm. All are open daily.

Mar, Oct Cathedral 10am-1pm, 3-5.40pm, Mon-Sat; 1-5.40pm Sun. All other monuments are open 9am-5.40pm daily.

Apr-Sept All monuments are open 8am-7.20pm daily, except for the Cathedral which is open 10am-1pm, 3-7.40pm, Mon-Sat; 1-7.20 pm Sun. To see the church on Sunday mornings, you'll have to do the pious thing and go to mass.

Bus number 1 runs from from the train station to the Piazza del Duomo; the walk takes around 20 minutes.

Cathedral

Pisa's cathedral is one of the earliest and finest examples of Pisan Romanesque architecture. Begun in 1063 by one Buscheto, the blindingly white marble and delicate four-tiered arcaded façade must have provided the inspiration for many a wedding cake designer. The façade, fittingly for the then cosmopolitan Pisa, incorporates Moorish mosaics and glass within the arcades (further examples of which can be more closely inspected in the Museo del Duomo). Buscheto's tomb is set in the wall on the left side of the façade. Touching the brass doors (by the school of Giambologna, 1602) is said to make wishes come true.

The main entrance is around the other side of the building facing the Leaning Tower. The **Portale di San Ranieri** features bronze doors by **Bonanno da Pisa** (1180) depicting scenes from the life of Christ. Maritime reliefs and palm trees along the bottom panels attest to the scope of the seafaring Pisans' travels; they really did know what palm trees looked like.

Inside, the cathedral smells as if it has been coated in varnish and looks as if it's still recovering from a devastating fire in 1595. **Giovanni Pisano**'s superb Gothic **pulpit** (1302-

11) was all but incinerated in the fire and lay forgotten and dismembered in crates until the 1920s when someone decided to put it together again. Faith, Hope and Charity support the centre, while the outer pillars represent Christ and the cardinal virtues of the Church. The 16th-century censer suspended nearby is often said (listen to the tour-guides) to have triggered Galileo's discovery of the principles of pendular motion. In fact it was cast six years after the discovery – in 1587. Crane your neck to admire the Islamic-inspired dome, decorated by a vibrant fresco of the *Assumption* by Orazio and Giralomo Riminaldi (1631). Behind the altar is a mosaic by **Cimabue** of Saint John (1302).

Baptistery

The starkness of the marble baptistery (constructed 1153-1400) may be a bit of a surprise after the elaborate decoration of the cathedral. Most of the Baptistery's precious artwork has been shuffled off for safekeeping to the Museo del Duomo, leaving bleak, blank walls in the sternly measured interior. **Nicola Pisano**'s **pulpit** of 1260 was the first of the clan's productions, setting the style for the rest, and depicts the Nativity, Adoration of the Magi, Presentation in the Temple, Crucifixion and the Last Judgement. Before you leave, ask one of the guards to sing. The acoustics are incredible, the echoes turning the voice of a soloist into what sounds like an ethereal chorus of angels.

Leaning Tower

Located in the southeast corner of the Campo dei Miracoli, the tower has been infamous from day one. Leaning almost as soon as it was erected (initially in the opposite direction), it is a seven-tiered campanile (although the bells haven't been rung since 1993 for fear of accentuating the tilt still further). The building was begun in 1173 or 1174 and the top level, housing the seven bells, was added in 1350. It stands at 54.5m high, and leans a further 1.2mm every year; it's currently skewed about 4.5m off centre. In 1989, the last year the tower was open to the public, more than one million visitors scrambled up the 293 steps. Now, out of fear that the whole thing will collapse, the area around the tower is fenced off, so snappers will have to be satisfied by the look-I'm-holding-up-the-tower shot. The best views of the campanile are from the courtyard of the Museo del Duomo, and by night when lit by spotlights – despite the hype, it's still a wonderfully romantic place. Incidentally, if you want to annoy a Pisan, start arguing that the tower was actually built to lean from the outset as a calculated tourist stunt.

Campo Santo

The 'Holy Field' centres on a patch of dirt that, according to legend, was carried from the Holy Land to Pisa on the backs of Crusaders in the 13th century. Lining the Gothic cloisters around the green field are the gravestones of Pisans thought special enough to be buried in holy soil. On the West wall hang two massive lengths of chain that used to be strung across the entrance to the Pisan port to keep out enemy ships. Stolen by Genova, and passed on to Florence, one bit of chain was only returned to Pisa in 1848 by Florence, and the other returned by Genova in 1860.

In 1944, an Allied bomb landed on the Campo, destroying many of the frescoes and sculptures, including a reportedly fabulous cycle by Benozzo Gozzoli. A few, however, did survive, including a *Triumph of Death*, and a *Last Judgement and Hell*, hammering home the transitoriness of wordly pleasures. The former work is attributed to the Florentine artist Bonamico Buffalmacco. If you've read the 8th day of Giovanni Boccaccio's *Decameron* (1350) you'll catch the irony: Boccaccio characterises Buffalmacco as a light-hearted prankster and buffoon. Look for the particularly vivid corner of *Inferno* (Hell) where demons fork humans into a big green monster's mouth.

Museo dell'Opera del Duomo

This museum, in the shadow of the Tower, contains works from the Baptistery, the Campo Santo and the Cathedral. Highlights from the downstairs rooms include a lanky polychrome wooden *Christ on the Cross* by Borgognone (12th century), vibrant, concentric mosaics from the Cathedral parapet and a clutch of works by Giovanni Pisano, notably his ivory *Madonna and Crucifix* and *Madonna and Child*. Walk out into the tranquil courtyard for a crowd-free view of the Tower. Upstairs, there's a mixed bag of paintings, *intarsia* (intricately inlaid wood), costumes and assorted relics. The 16th-century intarsia (inlaid wood) shows a painstaking attention to perspective and geometrical design. The ticket office, tourist information desk and bookshop for the entire Campo dei Miracoli are in the lobby.

Museo delle Sinopie

The bombings of 1944 and subsequent restorations uncovered *sinopie*, the reddish-brown preliminary sketches, from beneath the frescoes in the Campo Santo. Such designs were meant to be hidden forever after the artist covered over the orginal '*arriccio*' (dry plaster on which the sketches were made) with a lime-rich plaster called *grassello*. The museum has two floors of 14th- and 15th-century sinopias by Buffalmacco, Traini (a Pisan), Gaddi, Bonaiuiti, Antonio Veneziano and Spinello Aretino. The sketches seem on the point of floating away, like delicate shadows on a screen. On the first floor is an enormous Christ holding the Circle of Creation, with nine layers of angels, the Zodiac, stars, moon, fire and air concentrically surrounding the centre of the world, divided into Asia, Europe and Africa.

Other sights

The city of Pisa straddles the river Arno, enclosed within what remains of its medieval walls. Between the Piazza della Stazione and the Arno, the Mezzogiorno (south) part of the city contains few sights. The main focus for visitors is north of the river in the area known as Tramontana, especially around the Campo dei Miracoli. Once you've

Appreciating the Arno.

had your fill of its monuments, head out to see what else Pisa has to offer. Most of the following places are blissfully free of the tourist crush around the Leaning Tower.

Piazza dei Cavalieri

Pisa's second most important piazza is home to the **Palazzo dei Cavalieri**, seat of one of Italy's most esteemed universities, the **Scuola Normale Superiore**, established by Napoleon in 1810 (his mum was of Pisan descent). The piazza itself has long been a focal point of the city. The Romans used the square as their forum, and Cosimo I Medici based his religious/military order of the Knights (*Cavalieri*) of Santo Stefano here in the 16th century. Vasari designed most of the piazza's buildings, as well as decorating the façade of the university. He commenced work on the **Chiesa dei Cavalieri**, dedicated to Santo Stefano, in 1565, and left the façade for Don Giovanni de' Medici to finish. The church's campanile, also designed by Vasari, was erected in 1570-72.

Facing the church, the **Palazzo della Conventuale** is another of Vasari's designs, erected as home to the Knights of Santo Stefano. The neighbouring **Palazzo del Consiglio dell'Ordine** and **Palazzo Gherardescha** are also Vasari creations. The Palazzo Gherardescha occupies the site of a medieval prison: in 1288 Count Ugolino della Gherardesca and three of his male heirs were condemned to starve to death there for engaging in covert negotiations with the hated Florentines. It took Ugolino nine months to die in prison (during which time he allegedly snacked on his own kids). Dante, horrified by his plight (and cannibalism) seizes another chance to knock the Pisans by depicting the Count gnawing on someone's head for eternity in Hell (Canto XXXI-II, *Inferno*).

You will see the Maltese Cross everywhere in this piazza but nowhere else in Pisa. This is because Cosimo wanted to hammer home the parallel between his new Knights of Santo Stefano and the famous crusading Knights of Malta. Elsewhere you are more likely to spot the Pisan cross, with two balls resting on each point. When the Medici moved in, they emblazoned their *palle* (*see box* **Florence by Area: More Balls Than Most**) everywhere to show the Pisans who was boss.

Santa Maria della Spina

Lungarno Gambacorti.

This gorgeous, tiny Gothic church on the bank of the Arno was, at the time of publication, closed for restoration and swaddled in a chrysalis of scaffolding. Originally an oratory, the church took its present form in 1323. It gets its name from the fact that it used to be the proud owner of what was claimed to be a thorn from Christ's crown, brought back by Crusaders.

San Nicola

Via Santa Maria (24 677). **Open** 8.30am-noon, 3-7pm, Mon-Sat; 5-7pm Sun.

Dating from 1150, this church is dedicated to one of Pisa's patron saints, San Nicola da Tolentino. In the fourth chapel is a painting showing the saint protecting Pisa from the plague, sometime around 1400. The campanile, built on typically unstable Pisan ground, consequently leans. An arcade joins the church to the **Palazzo Reale**. It was from the tower of this Palazzo, called the **Verga d'Oro** ('the rod of gold') that **Galileo Galilei** let Grand Duke Cosimo II look through his telescope to see the satellites of Jupiter.

Museo Nazionale di San Matteo

Piazza San Matteo in Soarta, Lungarno Mediceo (54 18 65). **Open** 9am-7pm Tue-Sat; 9am-1pm Sun, public hols. **Admission** L8,000.

The 12th-13th-century building once housed the convent of the Sisters of San Matteo. It now contains a collection of Pisan and Islamic medieval ceramics and paintings by

Pisan festivals and celebrations

Pisa's most attention-grabbing festivity is the **Gioco del Ponte**, which occurs annually on the last Sunday in June, and attracts a crowd of over 100,000 people. The event is basically a hyped-up tug of war on the Ponte di Mezzo. Pisans north of the Arno (the Tramontana) compete against their southern rivals (the Mezzogiorno), re-enacting a competition that dates to the Middle Ages. In centuries past, victory went to the gang which threw more of its competitors into the river. Today the winners don't have to lob anyone off a bridge, they just have to wear Renaissance costumes and heave a 7-ton *carrello* (a 'carriage') along a 50m strip with all their might. Six teams from each side take turns to try to push their opponents backwards.

On the evening of 16 June every year Pisa is bathed in candlelight. The **Luminaria** sees candles outline the roofs along the Arno, as well as the porticoes of the leaning tower. On the following day, devoted to San Ranieri, Pisa hosts a **Regatta** which celebrates the city's former maritime glories with a parade and boat displays by representatives from the ancient quarters of the city: the neighbourhoods of Santa Maria, San Franceso, San Martino and Sant'Antonio.

Another Regatta occurs every four years in Pisa (the next will be in the year 2000). This is a boat race in which Pisa competes with boats from the other three historic maritime republics of Italy, (Amalfi, Venice and Genova, which also take turns to host the Regatta).

Just to be different, Pisans celebrate *capodanno*, or **New Year**, on **25 March** in the Cathedral to commemorate the approximate date of the zodiacal new year when the Sun passes into Aries, as well as to celebrate the Annunication (when the angel dropped in on Mary, ie exactly nine months before Christmas and Jesus' birth). If you happen to show up at the Duomo on the feast of the Annunciation, March 25th, you'll be lucky enough to see a religious manifestation with high-up church officials taking part, but that's about it as far as New Year pomp and circumstance goes in Pisa proper.

Masaccio and **Fra Angelico**, a *Madonna and Child with Saints* by Domenico **Ghirlandaio** and a bust by **Donatello**. There's authentic **Gioco del Ponte** gear here too; admire the garb worn by medieval Pisans when they locked heads on the Ponte di Mezzo (*see box* **Pisan Festivals**).

Orto Botanico
Via L Ghini 5 (55 13 45). **Open** 8am-1pm Mon-Fri.
Admission free.
Step out from the fray of the Field of Miracles into an oasis. Founded by Luca Ghini in 1543, then replanted in different parts of the city, the oldest University botanic garden in Europe found its permanent home on this site in 1595. It was originally used to study the medicinal values of plants. Look out for the 200-year-old myrtle bush the size of a tree and a clump of papyrus reeds in the arboretum. Groups of ten people or more must make an appointment.

Restaurants

When eating in Pisa you'll encounter much that is generically Tuscan. Lucca and Pisa quarrel over who can claim *necci* (chestnut flour pancake) or *bordatino* (bean soup with cabbage and flour) for her own. Pisa does claim the *cecina*, a crisp pizza made of crushed chickpeas. Pisa is also famous for its sauteed baby eels, *cee alla Pisana*. (*cee* comes from *ciechi*, or blind ones). *Trippa alla Pisana* is tripe with a pesto-like sauce of parsley, walnuts, basil and almonds; *pappardelle alla Pisana*, is pappardelle with a sauce of goose or duck liver, porcini, wine and tomatos. For *dolce* try the typical *torta co' bischeri* which is a dense conglomeration of rice, chocolate, pine nuts, egg and grapes. Local wines include Montescudaio, in red and white guises, Chianti delle Colline Pisane and Bianco di San Torpe'.

Expensive

Cagliostro
Via del Castelletto 26/30 (tel/fax 050 57 54 13/e-mail cagliostro@ita.flashnet.it). **Open** 12.15-1.30pm, 7.45-11.45pm, Mon, Wed-Sat; 12.15-1.30pm, 7.45pm-12.15am, Fri, Sat. **Average** L25,000 (lunch); L45,000 (dinner).
Credit AmEx, DC, EC, MC, V.
This intriguing enoteca/restaurant/bar, off Via Ulisse Dini near Piazza dei Cavalieri, is named after the famous Sicilian Count who masqueraded as an alchemist and doctor in France and Italy during the 18th century. The art exhibits that hang in the cavernous interior alternate, but the twisting lighting fixtures, wave-like bar and wrought-iron furniture are permanent. The atmosphere is funky, artsy yet hyper-elegant, and it's a delight to eat in the garden during the warmer months. An extensive wine list complements the eclectic menu which draws on recipes from all over Italy. First-courses like *pappardelle al ragù di anatra* (pappardelle in duck sauce) cost around L14,000, while *baccalà* Pisan-style is an intriguing *secondi* (L16-22,000). Ever-present on the menu are *sformati* – vegetable and cheese dishes. *See also below* **Nightlife** *and* **Shopping**.
http://www.nsm.it/notti.italiane/

Il Ristoro del Vecchio Macelli
Via Volturno 49 (050 20 424). **Open** 1-3 pm, 8-10pm, Mon, Tue, Thur-Sat; 8-10pm Sun; closed 10-24 Aug. **Average** L50,000. **Credit** AmEx, DC, EC, MC, V.
Much loved by Pisan sophisticates, this refined restaurant is notable for the quality of its ingredients and standards of presentation. The Vanni family will construct your meal

around your preference: *di terra* (meat) or *di mare* (seafood). You may not want to dwell too long on the fact that the building is a restored 15th century slaughter-house. The site was previously occupied by the church of Santa Chiara and the crypt lies hidden beneath the kitchen. Call ahead to reserve.

Moderate

Cliff
Via Repubblica Pisana 4, Lungomare, Marina di Pisa (36 830/fax 36 901). **Open** noon-3pm, 6pm-midnight, Thur-Tue; open daily in summer. **Average** L35,000.
Credit AmEx, DC, MC, V.
Facing the sea, this restaurant has an attractive covered outdoor dining area where a variety of seafood, meat dishes, pizzas and pastas can be sampled (*menu turistico* L25,000). The bar inside attracts a drinking-only crowd at weekends, when the place stays open later than usual.

La Mescita
Via Cavalca 2 (54 42 94). **Open** 8-10.30pm Tue-Sun; closed Aug. **Average** L35,000. **No credit cards**.
Run by Marco Griffo, a talented young chef committed to using fine simple ingredients, La Mescita is a pretty, tranquil restaurant at the heart of the vibrant Vettovaglie market, you'll find this trattoria on the right after leaving the Loggia. The wine list is huge. *Primi* are generally L10,000, *secondi* are around L15,000. The *sformati* of cheese and vegetables are delicious. A pleasant atmosphere, with soft music and indoor greenery, is enhanced by impeccable, if rather slow, service.

Pizzeria Trattoria Toscana
Via Santa Maria 163 (56 18 76). **Open** 11am-11pm Thur-Tue. **Average** L20,000. **Credit** AmEx, DC, EC, MC, V.
If trekking around the Campo dei Miracoli has sapped all your energy and you cannot gather yourself to move far, you will be forced to pick your way through a circus-like restaurant agglomeration of tents and neon signs. The food here is fine, if as generic as its name. *Pizze* L6-12,000, *primi* L7-12,000, *menu turistico* L18-30,000.

Lo Spuntino
Vicolo dei Tinti 26 (58 02 40). **Open** noon-3pm, 6pm-midnight, Sat-Thur. **Average** L20,000. **Credit** MC, V.
Crossing over Ponte di Mezzo, and walking in the direction of the Piazza del Duomo, take the second right off Via Guglielmo Oberdan and turn down the alley beneath the neon sign of a minskirted woman porting a pizza. Any of the 18 types of pizza will cost from L8-12,000, as will the antipasti, *primi* and *secondi*. It's compact but comfortable inside with some outdoor seating. It is pretty toursity, but the food is good enough to compensate. Desserts, crepes, and other light dishes give this little restaurant its name ('*lo spuntino*' means 'snack'). The *menu turistico* is L12,000.

Il Vecchio Dado
Lungarno Piccardi 23, near Ponte di Mezzo (58 09 00). **Open** 12.30-3pm, 7.30-11.30pm, Thur-Tue.
Average L35,000. **Credit** AmEx, DC, MC.
A warm atmosphere and a river view are two of the attractions of this typically Tuscan pizzeria in a popular spot next to the Royal Victoria Hotel. There's a huge range of pizzas, pastas, *contorni*, meat and seafood dishes. Pisa is not known for pizzas, but here they're pretty good. Reservations advisable or you may find yourself standing.

Cheap

La Nando Pizzeria
Corso Italia 103 (27 242). **Open** 10.30am-2.30pm, 4-10pm, Mon-Sat. **Average** L11,000. **No credit cards**.

You'll be drawn in from the street by the enticing smells. Pizzas around L7,000 or around L2,000 for a slice, plus dishes of the day. The *ceci* is truly tasty. There's no table-service – sit yourself at a table in the back, or perch on a bar seat and people-watch through the window.

Numero Undici

Via Cavalca 11, Market Vettovaglie (no phone).
Open noon-3pm, 6-10pm, Mon-Fri; 6-10pm Sat.
Average L7,000. **No credit cards.**
A tiny place in the heart of the market, serving wine and snacks. Sit at one of the four fruity-coloured tables inside and contemplate the board-walk-like ceiling, or seat yourself under a huge umbrella outside amid the market's fruitcarts. There's a comfy D-I-Y feel to the green walls and wine-box lined foodbar. The sandwiches on foccaccia bread are excellent. *Foccaccina* cost L3-7,000, or a hot dish of the day is around L5,000. No table service.

Bars, cafés & gelaterias

Bar Duomo

Via Santa Maria 114 (28 294). **Open** 7am-7pm Fri-Wed.
No credit cards.
Join the crowd at one of Pisa's busiest bars if you feel like sipping a *prosecco* at a table facing the Campo dei Miracoli. An espresso will cost you L1,400 standing or L3,000 with your feet up.

Bar La Loggia

Piazza Vittorio Emmanuele II 11 (46 326). **Open** 7am-1am Tue-Sun. **Credit** AmEx, EC, MC, V.
Art Deco-ish hangout across from Caffè Gambrinus, and close to the train station. Sit outside in warm weather and nibble on crepes, gelati or hot dishes and snacks.

Caffè Gambrinus

Corner of Via C Battisti & Piazza Vittorio Emmanuele II (59 86 57). **Open** 7am-1am Sun-Fri. **No credit cards.**
Prissy, flouncy decor, but very comfy – a good place to wait for your train.

Happy Drinker Pub

Via Del Poschi 7 (57 85 55). **Open** 7pm-1am Wed-Mon.
No credit cards.
Just off Borgo Stretto, look for the yellow sign hanging over the little tunnel-like street that marks the entrance of this jolly drinking joint. Beers costs around L7,000 a pint, and there's also bottled Guinness and a good selection of sandwiches and snacks. Upbeat British '80s music keeps the Anglophile Italian crowd happy.

Lo Sfizzio

Borgo Stretto 54 (58 02 81). **Open** 7.30am-1am Mon-Sat.
Credit AmEx, DC, EC, MC, V.
Sitting at the end of the loggia of Borgo Stretto, this sizeable café offers cocktails and gelati. Although the name means 'little vice', it's actually a thoroughly wholesome place.

Lo Spaventapasseri

Via La Nunziatina 10 (44 067). **Open** 9.30am-1am Tue-Sat; 4pm-1am Sun. **No credit cards.**
Look for the sign with a scarecrow (*spaventapasseri*). Two rooms in back have table-space and blaring music. Gelati and yogurt start at L3,000. Young patrons during the day leave notes for each other on the bulletin board.

Nightlife

Pisa has its lively nightspots but don't expect London or Barcelona; Pisans don't party 'til dawn. In the summer months, especially June, the strip

Getting fruity at **Numero Undici.**

along Marina di Pisa offers outdoor musical entertainment and various cultural activities, as well as a sprinkling of nightclubs. However, Pisan youth tends to head out to Viareggio for dancing, and occasionally even as far as Bologna.

Bean an Tì

Via Antonio Ceci 56 (23 062). **Open** 6pm-midnight Mon-Sat. **No credit cards.**
Gaelic for 'woman of the house', this Irish pub is, perhaps surprisingly, styled after traditional rustic Tuscan watering-holes, joining the two drinking cultures under one roof. Appropriately, it attracts a mix of Italians and English-speakers.

Big Ben

Via Palestro 11 (58 11 58). **Open** 6pm-1am daily.
No credit cards.
Down the street from Teatro Verdi, and across from the Synagogue, Big Ben offers standard pub beverages in a kitschy but comfortable den. Look for the miniature Big Ben in the window, the coloured glass scenes of London life and Jack the Ripper posters. The Anglophile Italian crowd who drink here will be delighted to practise their English on you. L7,000 for a pint of Guinness.

Cagliostro

Via del Castelletto 26/30 (tel/fax 57 54 13). **Open** *bar* 7.45pm-1am Wed-Mon. **Credit** AmEx, DC, EC, MC, V.
Off Via Ulisse Dini near Piazza dei Cavalieri, Cagliostro is a delightful sensory experience. In the evening this enoteca/restaurant opens its doors to the drinking crowd. Every Monday after 9.30pm you can take part in a lively debate hosted here called Caffè Parlant. Sample a plate of three cheeses (L7-10,000) to accompany one of the 25 rums or 25 whiskies. From 7.45-9.30pm cocktails cost L5,000 (non-alcoholic ones are L4,000). Only wines under L40,000 a bottle are available by the glass. *See also above* **Restaurants** *and below* **Shopping.**

Corobrillo

Via delle belle Torre 20 (59 89 55). **Open** 10.30pm-2am daily; closed July, Aug.

In a street parallel to Via Palestro (close to the river), this is the only karaoke spot in town. Ignore the 'members only' sign, but if you want to be a regular you have to pay L10,000 for a *tessera* (membership card). Around L5,000 for a drink at the bar, L7-10,000 if you're sitting.

Millibar

Via Palestro 39 (58 00 21). **Open** 6.30pm-1am daily; closed July, Aug. **No credit cards.**

In the winter months live 'pop rock' music resounds in this bright, neony place across from Teatro Verdi. Serves sandwiches and drinks.

Pappafico

Via Litoreana 14, Marina di Pisa (35 52 814 or 35 037/e-mail pappafico@infomark.it). **Open** 11.30pm-3.30am Tue, Thur-Sun; open daily June-early Sept. **Credit** V.

The place to go to dance in the Pisa area. Latino or basic disco music packs the punters into the Davy Jones' lockerlike interior. Food too.

Teatro Verdi

Via Palestro 40 (94 11 11/fax 94 11 58). **Open** *ticket office* 9am-noon Tue, Thur, Sat; 5.30-7.30pm Mon, Wed, Fri. **Credit** V.

Come here to enjoy an evening of dance, drama or music. Students and the under-18s qualify for discounts. Be punctual when attending the events: latecomers are not allowed to enter. Classical music is the most usual fare for the intellectual crowd here.

Cinema Club: Arsenale

Vicolo Scaramucci 4 (50 26 40). **Admission** L10,000 annual membership; L5,000 for a ticket to a showing of English-language film. **No credit cards.**

Film and literary activities in English.

Accommodation

The quality and price of accommodation in Pisa varies considerably. Rates are normally higher during the peak season (approximately April to June, September and October); by law, room prices should be displayed near the front desk of all hotels. Always reserve during high season, and well in advance for the Luminaria, Regatta and Gioco del Ponte (*see box below* **Pisan Festivals**).

Expensive

Grand Hotel Duomo

Via Santa Maria 94 (56 18 94/fax 56 04 18). **Rates** *single* L200,000; *double* L280,000; *suite* L330,000. **Credit** AmEx, DC, EC, MC, V.

In the midst of the Duomo-kitsch jungle, look up to find the bubble-lettered sign above the entrance. This should hint at what's in store. Inside you'll find plush green carpets, a business atmosphere and a huge complex of air-conditioned rooms (suites include a living-room area). Call in advance if you want to use the garage. A service charge of eight per cent is added and prices climb if you want full or half-board.

Royal Victoria

Lungarno Pacinotti 12 (94 01 11/fax 94 01 80). **Rates** *single* L100-125,000; *double* L130-155,000. **Credit** AmEx, DC, EC, MC, V.

This classic, elegant hotel has been run by the Piegaja fam-

ily since 1839. The building, parts of which are over 1,000 years old, has been carefully preserved, and the wide corridors have frescoed ceilings. Many rooms face onto the Arno, making this hotel an excellent choice for viewing the festivities in June (*see box below* **Pisan Festivals**); river breezes compensate for lack of air-conditioning in the warmer months. The hotel installed TVs in every room with reluctance, previously preferring that hotel patrons relax by reading the complimentary books they distribute. Book well in advance.

Moderate

Albergo Amalfitana

Via Roma 44 (29 00 00). **Rates** *double* L90,000. **Credit** V.

Don't be discouraged by the cheesy illuminated 'hotel' sign that hangs above the entrance. The rooms within are clean, modern and equipped with air-conditioning and TV. Reserve at least ten days in advance. Bar downstairs.

Albergo Bologna

Via Mazzini 57 (50 21 20). **Rates** *single* L68,000; *double* L95,000; *triple* L125,000; *quad* L155,000. **Credit** AmEx, DC, EC, MC, V.

No air-conditioning but rooms are spacious and there's private car parking in this centrally located hotel. The bar and lounge is a great place to stretch out.

Cheaper

Albergo Galileo

Via Santa Maria 12 (40 621). **Rates** *single* L38,000; *double* L50,000. **No credit cards.**

In Pisa it's illegal to use Galileo Galilei's full name for commercial purposes, so this dreary *pensione* gets away with half of it. The corridors and public areas are littered with loose tiles and charity shop furniture. Five out the nine rooms, however, are capped with massive, vibrant 17th-century frescoes. Ask for the huge rooms nine or ten. Reserve well in advance.

Albergo Gronchi

Piazza Arcivescovo 1 (56 18 23). **Rates** *single without bath* L32,000; *double* L50,000. **No credit cards.**

Pleasant and clean, and ideal if you have dreamed of parking yourself for the night under the tower. Midnight curfew. Always reserve in advance.

Very cheap

Campeggio Torre Pendente

Viale delle Cascine 86 (56 06 65). **Rates** *'caravan' room* L40,000 (one or two people); *bungalow* L50-90,000 (up to 5 people); *tent* L8,000 plus L9,500 per person. **Open** mid-Mar-Sept. **No credit cards.**

To reach this camp site take bus number five and ask for the *'campeggio'*, or take the 15-minute walk from Piazza Manin. Staff have a tendency to gruffness. Midnight curfew.

Camping Internazionale

Via Litoranea in Marina di Pisa (36 553). **Rates** L8,000 per person. **Open** 15 Apr-Oct. **Credit** MC, V.

With a private beach, bar and pizzeria, campers never have to leave this upbeat campsite unless they choose to. No reservations are taken, but the staff claims that there's always a spot to pitch. Take ACIT bus from Piazza della Stazione to Marina di Pisa/Tirrenia and ask for the *'campeggio'*.

Casa della Giovane

Via F Corridoni 29 (43 061). **Rates** *double/triple* L20,000 per person. **No credit cards.**

As this boarding house caters mostly to students, the place is usually packed in term-time – July to September is usually the best time to find a room. 10pm curfew. Close to the station.

Centro Turistico Madonna dell'Acqua
Via Pietrasanta 15 (89 06 22). **Rates** *single* L20,000; *double* L30,000. **No credit cards**.
The only hostel in Pisa. Take bus number 3 from the Piazza della Stazione. If you're feeling especially penitent you can even attend Sunday mass in the little church of the Madonna dell'Acqua nearby. You should call between 6pm and 11pm to reserve a room.

Shopping

Pisa's main shopping street is the stretch of Corso Italia, that runs from Piazza Vittorio Emmanuele (where the train station is) up towards the river. Corso Italia is also the prime location for the Pisan early evening *passeggiata*. Here you'll find all you need, from bars to bookshops to jewellers. Cross the Ponte di Mezzo to find the loggia of Borgo Stretto; the small streets branching off provide the other main shopping area. Where Borgo Stretto meets the Ponte di Mezzo you'll find the **Mercatino Antiquario** the second weekend of every month. The **Mercato Vettovaglie** is a cornucopia of fruit and vegetables. If you're into kitsch, don't miss the line-up of vendors at the Campo Santo. And don't pay more than L2,000 for a miniature tower! ·

The Bookshop
Via Rigattieri 39 (59 86 87). **Open** 9.30am-1pm, 3.30-7.30pm, Mon-Sat. **No credit cards**.
At the foot of Borgo Stretto you'll find the only English-language bookstore in Pisa, and one of the few in Tuscany. This is a well-stocked store with around 5,000 titles, mainly in English but also in Spanish, German, and French. The extremely helpful staff will order any books that aren't in stock. The shop is an offshoot of the British School next door (*57 34 44*) where courses include classes in Italian and English.

Cagliostro
Via del Castelletto 26/30 (57 54 13). **Open** 12.15-1.30pm, 7.45-11.45pm, Mon, Wed-Sat; 12.15-1.30pm, 7.45pm-12.15am, Fri, Sat. **Credit** AmEx, DC, EC, MC, V.
The enoteca of this restaurant/bar stocks an extensive selection of Italian wines. Try a bottle from the mammoth list, or sample a whisky or rum with a plate of cheese. *See also above* **Restaurants** *and* **Nightlife**.

Casigligliani
Corso Italia 86 (42 564). **Open** 9am-1pm, 4pm-8pm, Tue-Sun. **Credit** AmEx, V.
Funky Italian housewares.

Pasticceria Salza
Borgo Stretto 46 (58 01 44). **Open** 7.45am-8.30pm Tue-Sun. **No credit cards**.
Purportedly the best pasticceria in Pisa, you can sample the goodies sitting at the tables outside under the arcade of the Borgo Stretto.

Pizzicheria Gastronomia a Cesqui
Piazze delle Vettovaglie 31 (no phone). **Open** 7am-1.30pm, 4-8pm, Mon, Tue, Thur-Sat; 7am-1.30pm Wed. **No credit cards**.
In the middle of the market. Part the beaded curtains and stock up on cheeses, pastas, wines and takeaway hot snacks.

Day trips from Pisa

Heading out of Pisa towards the beach you will come across the 11th-century church of **San Pier in Grado**, which boasts to be the spot where

Taking it easy on **Piazza dei Cavalieri**. *See page 203.*

Saint Peter first set foot off the boat from Antioch. This area used to sit on Pisa's river port, but the Arno changed directions and left the church of Saint Peter stranded. Vibrant 14th-century frescoes depict the lives of Peter and Paul, and sit above 24 columns of the Ionic, Corinthian, Composite, Sirian and 'leaves of water' varieties. An excavation in the rear of the church reveals a pillar from the 1st century, attesting to the church's age. Otherwise, the interior mirrors the exterior in its austerity.

In **Marina di Pisa**, you might want to dine by the sea looking out to the island of Gorgona (used as a prison) at the restaurants **Cliff**, or **Pappafico**. If you continue along the coast in the direction of Livorno, you will reach **Tirrenia**. This contains private beaches, an American military base, a zoo and the flashy resort **Hotel Continental** which sits directly on the beach.

The huge park of **San Rossare**, Via Aurelia Nord (*52 52 11. Info office open 8am-2pm Mon-Fri*), offers nature lovers a reprieve from crowded museums, dusty cities and crowded beaches. Guided walks, bicycle tours, horse treks and jaunts in horse-driven carriages are available

San Miniato, sitting on the main route connecting northwest Europe to Rome, hosts a kite-flying event for children on the first Sunday after Easter, fireworks for the festival of San Giovanni on June 23, a drama festival in July, an international festival of puppet theatre (also in July) and an annual national white truffle fair as one of the events of 'San Miniato November'. Contact the tourist office on Piazza del Popolo (*0571 42 745. Open 10am-1.30pm, 3-7pm, daily; June-Sept 3.45-7.45pm daily*) for more information on accommodation and events.

Grand Hotel Continental

Largo Belveder 26, Tirrenia (37 031/fax 37 283).
Rates *single* L161,000; *double* L235,000. **Credit** AmEx, DC, EC, MC, V.
The Grand Hotel Continental is a well equipped hotel, justly reknowned for its 200 luxury rooms. It also boasts an Olympic-sized swimming pool, tennis courts, beach access, parking and TV in every room. Open year-round; reserve well in advance for summer.

Useful information

Tourist information

Azienda Promozione Turistica (APT) *Via Benedetto Croce 26 (40 096 or 40 202/fax 40 903).* **Open** 9am-1pm, Mon-Fri .
Tourist Information Offices: *Piazza della Stazione 11 (42 291).* **Open** 8am-2pm Tue, Wed, Fri; 8am-5pm Mon, Thur. *Piazza del Duomo (56 04 64).* **Open** 9am-8pm daily.

Transport

Airport Galileo Galilei airport (*50 07 07*). **Open** 11am-5pm Mon-Sat; 11am-2pm Sun.
Appropriately named after Pisa's famously outspoken star-gazer, the airport is extremely convenient for both Pisa and Florence. Frequently departing trains, as well as bus number 7, will bring you from the airport to Pisa Centrale, and drop you off in Piazza della Stazione in Pisa proper (four minutes, L1,000). International, domestic and charter flights all arrive here, making arrival in Pisa a good choice even for those proceeding directly to Florence.

Bus station CPT *Piazza Sant'Antonio (23 384).* For services to Livorno and Volterra. Lazzi *Piazza Emmanuele 11 (46 288).* **Open** 7.30am-7pm Mon-Sat; 9am-1pm Sun. For buses to Lucca, Pistoia, Prato and Florence. Bus tickets within the city cost L1,300.

Car hire Avis (*42 028*), **Budget** (*45 490*), **Eurodollar** (*46 209*), **Hertz** (*49 187*), **Maggiore** (*42 574*). All have offices in Pisa airport.

Railway station Pisa Centrale *Piazza della Stazione (28 117; train info 1478 88 088).* Ticket office **open** 7am-9pm daily. From the main train station board a train for Rome (L27,000, 3 hours Intercity, 4 hours otherwise), Genoa (L15,000, 2 hours) Lucca (25 minutes), Livorno (L2,000, 15 minutes), or one of the frequent trains for Florence via Empoli (L7,200, one hour). Some trains also stop at Pisa Aeroporto and San Rossore (the latter is closer to the Campo dei Miracoli).

Taxis
Radio Taxi (*54 16 00*); Piazza Stazione (*41 252*); Piazza Duomo (*56 18 78*); Piazza Garibaldi (*58 00 00*).

Emergency services

Ambulance *Via San Frediano 6 (58 11 11), Via Bargagna (94 15 11), Via Pietrasanta 161A (83 55 44).*

Carabinieri (112).
Via Guido da Pisa (54 25 41).

Police (113).
Questura *Via Mario Lalli (58 35 11).*
Polizia Stradale (Road Police) *Via M Canevari (58 05 88).*
Vigili Urbani (Local Police) *Via del Moro 1 (50 14 44 or 50 26 26).*

Post Office *Piazza Vittorio Emmanuele II 8 (24 297).* **Open** 8.15am-7pm Mon-Fri; 8.15am-noon Sat, public hols.

Hospital Santa Chiara *Via Roma 67 (59 21 11).*

Markets

Vettovaglie Market
Piazza Vettovaglie houses a food and dry-goods market every day (except Sundays) from early morning until around 1pm. Turn off of Borgo Stretto onto Via delle Collone, and you will find the market stretching from under the piazza arches.

Mercatino Antiquario
On the second weekend of every month (except July and August), this market fills the piazza and nearby streets by the Ponte di Mezzo. Full of assorted furniture, books, jewellery and general bric-a-brac.

Chianti & Siena Province

Welcome to Tuscan cliché-land.

South of Florence is where the Tuscany we dream about begins. The steep wooded valleys of the Garfagnana, the beach umbrellas of Versilia and sunflowers of the Casentino are all undeniably part of the region, but they don't really nuzzle their way into collective consciousness like that lone cypress on the ridge of a hill, or that walled village surrounded by vines. This is familiar second-home terriotry – and yet there are surprises. Even Chianti – a name which conjures up red-faced stockbrokers on sunlit terraces – can take the breath away with its wildness. And it would be wrong to lump all those hill towns together: each has its own variation on Tuscan cuisine, its own subtly different dialect and its own annual excuse to dress up in medieval costumes and get drunk.

Southeast of Siena

Monte Oliveto Maggiore & the Crete Senesi

The view is stunning whichever way you come; up the wooded ridge from Buonconvento or – the most dramatic option – down through the eroded bluffs of the *Crete* (bare hills and ravines weirdly eroded by heavy rain) from Asciano. A bend in the road, and you see it: surrounded by cypresses, the compact brick cluster of Italy's most visited Benedictine monastery makes it look like a fortified early Renaissance conference centre – and in a way, it was. Founded in 1313 by Bernardo (formerly Giovanni) Tolomei, a scion of one of Siena's richest families, the monastery began life as a solitary hermitage in an area so arid it was referred to as a *deserto*. But Bernardo soon drew a large following, and the Olivetan order was recognised by the Pope in 1344. Over the next two centuries the monastery reached the height of its political influence: for miles around, the land and the people who worked it were owned by Monte Oliveto. The wealth of the order was channelled into the embellishment of its buildings and the assembly of a remarkable library; the complex became a meeting-point for artists and scholars from around the

world. The most tangible result of this energy is the Saint Benedict fresco cycle in the main cloister, painted by Giovanni Antonio Bazzi, better known as **Il Sodoma**, between 1505-8, with the exception of nine earlier panels by Luca Signorelli. Sodoma was a colourful character with a taste for exotic pets and young boys (if Vasari and his nickname are to be believed), and he went to town on these, often bizarre, scenes from the Saint's life (a typical example: "How Benedict Got A Billhook That Had Fallen In The Lake To Jump Back Into Its Handle"). The monastery church was given a Baroque makeover, but it preserves some fine intarsia choir stalls from 1503-5.

In true Benedictine style, you can buy restorative liqueurs in the monastery shop and keep body and soul together at **La Torre** (*0577 70 70 22. Open lunch & dinner; closed Tue. Average L35,000*), a surprisingly good restaurant by the main gate. The hostel (*0577 70 70 17*) is open only to bona fide spiritual retreaters.

The Medieval feud of **Asciano** lies at the heart of the Crete Senesi – which, with its white clay hills, and deep gullies looks just like stylised quattrocento drapery. Asciano is a pleasant enough town, with a impressive Romanesque church (the **Collegiata di Sant'Agata**) and, next door, a worthwhile **Museo di Arte Sacra** (admission on request at the Collegiata) – it hosts a small but classy collection of works by Sienese artists of the 14th and 15th centuries, including a fine *Saint Michael* by Ambrogio Lorenzetti (one of only six works which are undoubtedly his). Just outside Asciano is the eccentric **La Pievina** restaurant (*see chapter* **A Tuscan Restaurant Tour**).

Public transport around here is patchy to say the least; one daily bus leaves Siena for Asciano and Chiusure, leaving you with a 2km-walk to Monte Oliveto and no bus back until the following morning. A better option is to take the train from Siena (get off at Asciano-Monte Oliveto, not Asciano – even if you want to visit the town itself). From here it is a vigorous 9km-march along a pretty minor road to Monte Oliveto: by far the best way to approach the monastery (to pick up the minor

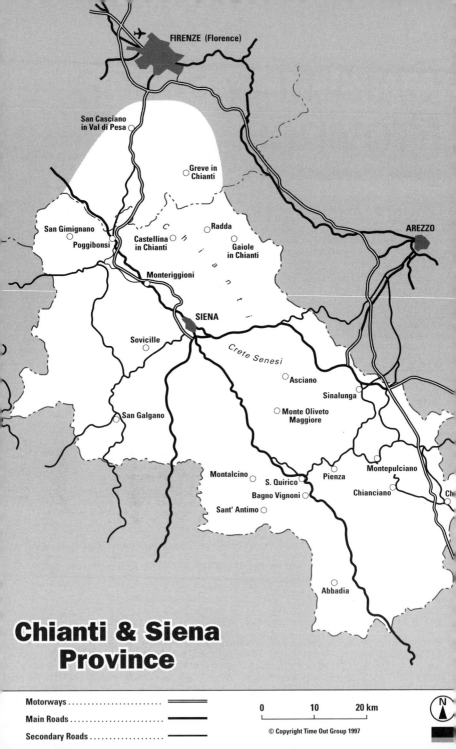

FIRENZE (Florence)

San Casciano
in Val di Pesa

Greve in
Chianti

San Gimignano

Radda

Poggibonsi

Castellina
in Chianti

Gaiole
in Chianti

AREZZO

C h i a n t i

Monteriggioni

SIENA

Sovicille

Crete Senesi

San Galgano

Asciano

Sinalunga

Monte Oliveto
Maggiore

Montalcino

S. Quirico

Pienza

Montepulciano

Bagno Vignoni

Chianciano

Ch

Sant' Antimo

Abbadia

Chianti & Siena
Province

Motorways ....

Main Roads ....

Secondary Roads ....

0   10   20 km

© Copyright Time Out Group 1997

N

road, head back along the Siena road and strike left when the houses run out). Currently there is a useful morning train from Siena at 8.14am (it's a half-hour journey), with feasible return options from Asciano at 4.21pm and 5.40pm, leaving plenty of time for lunch.

Montepulciano

The view from the Pienza road explains why many think of this as the quintessential Tuscan town. Above, the walled hilltop cluster of houses and palazzi, High Renaissance statements trapped in a tight medieval groundplan, based on a disorienting, DNA-like spiral of streets. Down below, in glorious isolation at the end of an avenue of cypresses, the honey-coloured vision of San Biagio, one of the most perfect of all Tuscan churches. Montepulciano stands as a symbol for the two opposite forces that determined the Italian Renaissance: physical hassles and/or pleasures versus soaring intellectual aspirations.

The dualism continues right through into what makes this a great place to visit: Montepulciano keeps body and soul together, twinning its artistic pulls with a noble red wine (Vino Nobile di Montepulciano). Most of the things to see here are the legacy of the town's boom years in the century or so following 1511, when it came under the influence of Florence. Architects like Antonio da Sangallo the Elder and Vignola were bought in to rework the Medieval fabric of the place and put up some lasting monuments: Sangallo was especially active, rebuilding the town walls and taking on a few stately town residences before excelling himself down at San Biagio.

Things to see

The central Piazza Grande, the town's highest point, is where most of the sights huddle. Don't let the rough brick façade of the **Duomo** put you off: the interior is a treasure trove. The magnificent humanist Argazzi tomb (1428) by Michelozzo di Bartolomeo has been spread democratically around the church; there is also a fine Gothic tryptich of the *Assumption* by Taddeo di Bartolo over the altar (1401) and, towards the top of the left nave, an exquisite *Madonna and Child* (cradling a goldfinch) by Sano di Pietro (or Simone Martini, depending on who you believe). Also in the square are Sangallo's **Palazzo Tarugi**, with loggia, the 13th-century **Palazzo Comunale**, which deliberately echoes the Palazzo Vecchio in Florence, and the **Palazzo Contucci** across the square, another Sangallo creation which offers the added pull of a wine shop on the ground floor, where a consortium of local producers offer their wares at reasonable prices.

On the way back down to the main Porta al Prato, you can take in the 16th-century **Palazzo Cervini** – now a bank – with its wave-pattern frieze, and two nearby churches: **Sant'Agostino**, another work by Michelozzo, and **Santa Lucia**, with a good Signorelli *Madonna* to the right of the altar. Whatever else you see, the pilgrimage church of **San Biagio**, a 20-minute walk from Porta al Prato (or take a short cut from the Porta dei Grassi to the west) is a must. Designed by Antonio da Sangallo the Elder and built between 1518 and 1545, this Bramante-influenced study in proportion is a

jewel of the High Renaissance. Come at sunset when the honey-coloured travertine is resplendent. Across the lawn stands the graceful **Canonica** with its double-arched façade, also by Sangallo.

Where to stay

Il Borghetto *Borgo Buio 7 (0578 75 75 35/fax 75 73 54)*. **Rates** *single* L100,000; *double* L130,000.
Credit AmEx, DC, EC, MC, V.
In a narrow lane off the Corso, this tiny hotel in a pair of adjacent Medieval houses does big breakfasts (extra cost) with home-made cakes and has a pretty garden around the back.

Il Marzocco *Piazza Savonarola 18 (0578 75 72 62/fax 757530)*. **Rates** (breakfast extra) *single* L70,000; *double* L105,000. **Credit** AmEx, DC, V.
On the Corso, in a 16th-century palazzo opposite the church of San Bernardo, Il Marzocco has spacious rooms with antique furniture; angle for one of the first-floor doubles with terrace.

Where to eat

See also chapter **A Tuscan Restaurant Tour**.

Diva e Maceo *Via di Gracciano nel Corso 92 (0578 716951)*. **Open** lunch & dinner; closed first 3 weeks July. **Average** L35,000. **No credit cards.**
Solid, if dull, regional cooking, good wine (they also own the enoteca next door), decent prices: three reasons why booking ahead here is a good idea. Try the *pici* (fat, hand-rolled spaghetti) or the *tagliatelle al sugo d'anatra* (in duck sauce). Local meat and game feature prominently, and all the desserts are home-made.

Rosticceria di Voltaia *Via Voltaia nel Corso 86 (0578 75 75 82)*. **Open** lunch & dinner Tue-Sun. **Average** L20,000. **Credit** EC, MC, V.
If you're after a quick plate of pasta, this friendly place will come up with the goods – though beware of the house red, which doesn't appear to be from around these parts. They are only six tables.

La Grotta San Biagio *(0578 757607)*. **Open** lunch & dinner Thur-Tue. **Average** L55,000. **Credit** AmEx, DC, EC, MC, V.
Next door to San Biagio, this decidedly upmarket joint, fronted by a wine bar, occupies the rooms Sangallo lived in while working on the church. It offers a vaguely francophile reading of local specialities including *pollo al Vino Nobile*. Tables outside in summer.

Bars & enotecas

Don't miss the **Antico Caffè Poliziano** *(0578 75 86 15. Open 7am-1am daily)* halfway up the Corso: its recently refurbished Art Nouveau elegance strikes an oddly decadent note in such a stern town. The coffee, cakes and sandwiches are all good, though the downstairs restaurant is a tad overpriced. If you're thinking of buying wine, the **Enoteca Oinochoè** at Via Voltaia nel Corso 82 *(0578 75 75 24. Open 9am-7.30pm Mon-Sat)* has a good selection, and you can also leaf through piles of antique prints (the owner's other line). Otherwise you can trawl the outlets of the individual wineries: among the best are **Avignonesi**, Via Gracciano nel Corso 91 *(0578 75 78 72. Open 9am-1.30pm, 2.30-7.30pm, daily)* and **Poliziano** – 10km out of town at Montepulciano Stazione, Via Fontago 11 *(0578 73 81 71. Open 8.30am-noon, 2.30-6pm, Mon-Fri)*. *See also chapter* **Wine**.

Festivals

In July or August the town hosts the **Cantiere Internazionale d'Arte**, a modern music festival/workshop presided over by German composer Hans Werner Henze, which has expanded over the years to take in experimental theatre and dance. The **Bruscello** festival (14-16 Aug) is a modern street-theatre version of the Medieval mystery play tradition; while the **Bravio delle Botti** on the last Sunday in August provides the good townspeople with an excuse to dress up, throw flags, roll barrels through the streets and drink a lot of wine. Ring the **tourist office** in Via Ricci for the latest information (*0578 75 73 41. Open 10am-noon, 4-6pm, daily*).

Pienza

It doesn't look like 'the ideal city of the Renaissance': it looks like a sleepy village with delusions of grandeur and a nice line in potted geraniums. But that's the whole point of Pienza: it was a one-horse town before native son Eneo Silvio Piccolomini, elected Pope Pius II in 1458, gave Bernardo Rossellino *carte blanche* to build a rational, humanist new town here in 1459.

When both the Pope and his architect died five years later, Pienza went back to being a one-horse town – with one hell of a main square. It's remarkable how much was achieved in such a short time. Stand in the centre of Piazza Pio II and gyrate slowly: everything you see was either put up or restructured between 1459 and 1462 – the cathedral, the Palazzo Vescovile, the Palazzo Comunale and the Palazzo Piccolomini itself. As such, this is a unique opportunity to experience what Milton Keynes might have looked like if it had been built in the 15th-century Florentine style. And the fact that all the sights are within two minutes of each other makes Pienza an ideal half-day destination, easily reachable from Siena and Montepulciano by TRA-IN bus. The adventurous can even try hoofing it from Montepulciano: for details, see *Walking and Eating in Tuscany and Umbria* by James Lasdun and Pia Davis (Penguin, 1997), which includes a number of walks in the area.

For fans of *The English Patient*, the abandoned convent where the Italian part of the film was set is just a few kilometres north of here, at **Sant' Anna in Camprena**. The frescoes by Sodoma which Juliet Binoche dangled on a rope to see can be viewed from ground level, if you manage it squeeze in between the film crews – it's a very popular location.

Things to see

The **Duomo** has been battling subsidence at its apse end ever since it was built – hence the cracks, and the sinking feeling you get as you walk down the nave. Rossellino built it over the site of the Romanesque chapel of Santa Maria, following the Pope's brief to create a luminous monument to the new-found confidence and intellectual syncretism of the Humanist age. The side chapels have some good early Renaissance altarpieces by Vechietta and others, and there is a fine font by Rossellino in the crypt.

Other Sienese works and papal paraphanalia can be found in the **Museo della Cattedrale**, Via Casello 1 (*No phone. Open winter 10am-1pm, 3-5pm, daily; summer 10am-1pm, 4-6pm, Wed-Sun; closed Tue. Admission L2,500*). Next door, the Palazzo Vescovile was given its present appearance by Rodrigo Borgia – one of a number of cardinals who Pius II roped in on the Pienza new-town project.

The plum, of course, was reserved for the Pope himself: the **Palazzo Piccolomini** (*0578 74 85 03. Open Oct-June 10am-*

12.30pm, 3-6pm, daily; July-Sept 10am-1pm, 4-7pm, Tue-Sun. Admission L5,000), on your right facing the Duomo.

It was inspired by the rational measures of Leon Battista Alberti's Palazzo Rucellai in Florence, which Rossellino had just finished working on. Inside, a strictly-martialled guided tour takes you to Pius II's private apartments – but the real treat is the hanging garden, which perches symmetrically between the graceful inner façade of the palace and the expanse of Tuscany beyond: the view stretches across to Monte Amiata, Radicofani with its tower, and Monte Cetona to the left – described by Piccolomini as "the portal of the winter sun".

Where to eat

Latte di Luna *Via San Carlo 2/4 (0578 74 86 06).* **Open** lunch & dinner Mon, Wed-Sun. **Average** L45,000. **Credit** EC, MC, V.
Creative regional cooking – *pici, tagliolini al tartufo, anatra alle olive* (duck with olives) – in a central lane just inside the Porta al Giglio. Book ahead for one of the tables outside, where you can dine to the dulcet tones of a minah bird.

Sette di Vino *Piazza di Spagna 1 (0578 74 90 92).* **Open** 9am-11pm Mon, Tue, Thur-Sun. **Average** L20,000. **No credit cards.**
A good place for a snack or light meal, with tables outside in a pretty square just off the Corso. Filled rolls, good vegetable platters, and *pecorino di Pienza* – the famed local sheep's milk cheese – in a variety of forms, including one matured in ashes (*stagionata sotto le ceneri*).

Chiusi

A transport hub on the Rome-Florence rail line: change here for trains to Siena (a slow but pretty route) and Lago Trasimeno, and buses to Montepulciano, Pienza and Perugia. For Etruscan enthusiasts, Chiusi is a destination in its own right; it has the best collection of Etruscan tombs outside of the Tuscany-Lazio coastal hinterland. In town, the **Museo Archeologico Nazionale** at Via Porsenna 93 (*0578 20 177. Open 9am-2pm Mon-Sat; 9am-1pm Sun. Admission L4,000*) has a worthy but rarely inspiring collection of artefacts. From here guided tours leave more or less hourly for the tombs, which are set in pretty farmland between the town and the small, reed-fringed Lago di Chiusi. Underneath the bell-tower of the Duomo, founded in the 6th century, is a curious Roman Piscina – a sort of underground cistern.

If you're caught here at mealtimes, head for **La Solita Zuppa** in Via Porsenna 21 (*0578 21 006. Open lunch & dinner; closed Tue. Average L35,000*), a cosy spot with an overbearingly friendly hostess and a great line in Tuscan soups.

Bagno Vignoni & the Val d'Orcia

Bagno Vignoni has to be seen to be believed. This tiny hamlet just south of San Quirico d'Orcia on the Siena-Rome road would be just another farming community were it not for its remarkable main square. Here, overlooked on three sides by a ragged collection of houses and flanked on the fourth by a low Renaissance loggia, is a pool.

Where we might expect parked cars, there is only an expanse of warm water, at its hottest (51°C) at the end where the thermal spring rises. For centuries people came here to soothe their aches and pains in unhygenic bliss, but these days the pool is off-limits. Featured in a memorable scene from Tarkovsky's *Nostalgia*, it has been the making of the village, which is now peppered with herbalists, craft shops and cafés – one of them run by Erin Pizzey (of battered-wife-refuge fame).

Bagno Vignoni has been well and truly discovered in recent years, which means that booking rooms and restaurant tables – especially at weekends – is essential. The best place to eat is the **Antico Osteria del Leone** (*0577 88 73 00. Open lunch & dinner; closed Mon. Average L40,000*) which does classic regional cuisine – including an excellent *zuppa di cereali* (vegetable, pulse and cereal soup) – at surprisingly reasonable prices. For lunchtime or early evening snacks, the **Bottega di Cacio**, Piazza del Moretto (*0577 88 74 77. Open 10.30am-7.30pm daily*), offers filled rolls with pecorino cheese or salami and good local wine.

The village's two hotels make for a difficult choice: **Le Terme** (*0577 88 71 50. Rates single L75,000; double L120,000; though you may be obliged to take half-board, especially at weekends*) has the view of the square, while the modern **Posta Marcucci** (*0577 88 71 12; double L194,000; you may have to take half-board, at L133-145,000 per person*) down the road has the thermal open-air swimming-pool – open all year round, and hot enough to enjoy even when there's snow on the surrounding hills. Resolve the dilemma by putting up at Le Terme and taking towel and costume along to the Posta Marcucci: half-day entrance to the pool (after 2.30pm) costs L12,000 (bring a swimming cap). Alternatively, have a free dip down below the village, where the water (a bit tepid by this stage) cascades into a basin which is just deep enough to splash around in.

The **Val d'Orcia** west of Bagno Vignoni is a beautiful, wild place, with fortified villages like **Ripa d'Orcia** (where the castle has been turned into a hotel – *0577 89 73 76. Rates double L150,000*) perching above the river gorge. The latter can be reached at the end of a spectacular 1-hour walk: for details see Lasdun & Davis' *Walking and Eating in Tuscany and Umbria* (Penguin, 1997).

For more artistic thrills, head north to **San Quirico d'Orcia**, where the **Collegiata** awaits. This is one of the most graceful Romanesque churches in Tuscany, adorned by three portals with carvings of lionesses, sea-serpents and strange beasts; behind the altar is a beautiful set of intarsia choirstalls. There is a helpful tourist office across the way (*0577 89 72 11. Open Mar-Oct 10am-1pm, 3.30-6.30pm; closed Mon*). To the

right of the central Piazza della Libertà is the **Horti Leonini**, a walled Renaissance garden which hosts regular sculpture exhibitions. Bagno Vignoni is connected to San Quirico and Buonvconvento by occasional RAMA buses (*0564 96 64 33*); San Quirico itself is a stop on the more frequent TRA-IN Siena-Montepulciano route.

Montalcino

Lofty, windswept and proud, Montalcino was the last outpost of the Sienese Republic: a group of exiles held out here against the Florentines for two years after the fall of Siena in 1557. In recognition of its stand, the town is granted the honour of leading the procession at Siena's Palio (*see chapter* **Siena**). Today, Montalcino is a placid and prosperous walled enclave, known above all for its wine, the sturdy red Brunello di Montalcino (*see chapter* **Wine**), which consistent quality and astute marketing have turned into Italy's most highly prized and highly priced DOCGs (super-DOC). Brunello ages in oak for a massive four years – if you want something younger and less solemn, go for the year-old Rosso di Montalcino, which in the hands of top producers is extremely capable of great things.

What to see

The 14th-century **Rocca** is the best place to start: this is a castle and a half, all towers and ramparts – great for playing at Guelphs and Ghibellines, though the piped Vivaldi which greets you as you walk in is not quite the right soundtrack. At the foot of the main tower is an enoteca which offers a good selection of Brunellos and Rossos as well as olive-paste tartini and other snacklets. Above you can climb to the ramparts (*0577 84 92 11. Open 9am-1pm, 2.30-8pm, Tue-Sun. Admission L3,500; ticket from the enoteca*) which offer a marvelous view: to the east and north, a parched landscape that eventually gives way to the Crete around Monte Oliveto; to the south and west, trees and vines – and the local football pitch. Piazza del Popolo is the focus of town life; around the corner is the **tourist office** (*0577 84 93 31. Open 10am-1pm, 3-7pm, Tue-Sun*); here too is the tall, shield-studded Palazzo Comunale and a graceful 15th-century loggia with a double row of arches.

In the square, the **Fiaschetteria Italiana** – a café/winebar with a well-stocked cellar out the back – is a good place to sit and watch the tourists go by. Of the town's churches, **Sant'Agostino** is the most rewarding (if you can get in) with a good 15th-century rose window and Sienese trecento frescoes. Montalcino's three museums are currently closed while their meagre collections are combined into a single civic museum – due to open in Via Ricasoli some time in the autumn of 1997.

Where to stay

There are very few accommodation options in town. The tourist office in Piazza del Popolo can put you on to private rooms.

Affitacamere Anna *Via Saloni 23 (0577 84 86 66). Rates single L60,000; double L90,000.* **No credit cards.** Just down the road from Il Giglio, this place is under the same management, but has slightly cheaper rooms.

Fattoria dei Barbi *(0577 84 94 21)*. *(See also below* **Restaurants***)*. **Rates** *on application*. **Credit** EC, MC, V.
One of the best options for those with transport is the *agriturismo* on offer here.

Il Giglio *Via Saloni 5 (0577 84 81 67)*. **Rates** *single* L70,000; *double* L100,000). **Credit** EC, MC, V.
Hard up against the town walls, this is the best of the few options in town: most of the 12 pretty frescoed rooms have spectacular views.

Where to eat

Most of the real action here is out of town. Also, *see chapter* **A Tuscan Restaurant Tour.**

Fattoria/Taverna dei Barbi *8km SE of Montalcino, off the Sant'Antimo road (0577 84 93 57)*. **Open** lunch Tue; lunch & dinner Thur-Mon. **Average** L45,000. **Credit** EC, MC, V.
As well as operating one of Montalcino's best wineries, local powerhouse Donatella Cinelli offers *agriturismo* accommodation *(see above)* and has time left over to administer a literary prize and head Italy's wine tourism association. The restaurant, in a converted barn, uses the farm's own produce in its regional dishes; the soups and grilled meat are good, and in winter a roaring fire welcomes guests.

Poggio Antico *in the hamlet of the same name, 4km SW of Montalcino on the Grosseto road (0577 84 92 00)*. **Open** lunch & dinner Tue-Sat; lunch Sun. **Average** L70,000. **Credit** EC, MC, V.
Grossly pretentious place which you are bound to hear recommended as the best restaurant in the area. The food is good, but not of a standard that makes it worth putting up with the over-fastidious service: a polite request to have your bottle of wine left on the table, rather than secreted over the other side of the room, receives the sort of response you might expect if you had asked to piss in the wine bucket.

Sant'Antimo

No, there's nothing quite like it. Especially if you turn up around vespers in summer (6.30pm) when the low sun highlights the soft creamy yellow travertine of the church, caught in the dip of a green valley. If the beauty of the building and its setting weren't enough, there is the music as well: inside, at this hour, a group of alarmingly tall young monks gather to intone Gregorian plainsong, their white habits glowing in the light filtering through windows of onyx. When the monks aren't there, their recorded voices ring out just the same – and you can even buy a copy of the CD.

The **Abbey of Sant'Antimo**, 10km south of Montalcino, certainly existed in 812; the locals like to think it was founded by Charlemagne. For three centuries it was a powerful Benedictine monastery, but in the 13th century it began to decline and, in 1462, the last monks were evicted by papal decree (Pius II needed them for the glorification of Pienza). The abbey stayed empty until 1979, when a group of enterprising French Premonstratensian monks, enchanted by the beauty and the acoustics of the place, started fixing up some of the buildings in the monastery precinct; in 1992 they moved in permanently. There are now eight brothers (most in their twenties or thirties) who spend four or five hours a day singing plainsong (as the cool young abbot says, "If I'd wanted to strum a guitar I'd have joined the Franciscans"). Inside the church, don't miss the carved onyx capitals, one of which shows Daniel in the lion's den, and the apse with its rosette of tiny chapels; outside, too, there are some fine details, including a curious bas-relief of a winged bull with a female head.

In the adjacent village of **Castelnuovo dell'Abate** there's a decent trattoria, the **Osteria Bassomondo** *(0577 83 56 19. Open lunch & dinner Tue-Sun. Average L35,000)*, which also produces its own wine. This is where you pick up or get off the bus to Montalcino (four a day, one on Sundays). Otherwise, it's a splendid 3-hour walk.

West of Siena

San Galgano

Swords in stones and roofless abbeys are not things we normally associate with Tuscany – and the flat expanse of woodland this Gothic building looms out of is another Celtic touch. The secondary road (No. 73) between Siena and Massa Marittima takes you through a wild, sparsely-populated corner of the region – the valley of the Merse and its tributary the Farma offer one of Tuscany's most intact and unusual ecosystems, where Mediterranean species like the cork-oak rub shoulders with beech trees, normally only found at much higher altitudes. The fauna includes foxes, badgers, kingfishers and numerous birds of prey. Around three TRA-IN buses a day cover the Siena-Massa route; ask to be put off at '*il bivio per San Galgano*'.

San Galgano was a centre of Cistercian power in the 13th and 14th centuries; its wordly monks acted as arbiters in local disputes and farmed out their services as lawyers, doctors and architects (many worked on the building of Siena's cathedral). Built between 1224 and 1288 on a Latin cross plan, the abbey church is like an open-top primer of the classic French Gothic style. It was abandoned in the 16th century and slowly fell to pieces. By the beginning of the last century, roofless and towerless, it was being used as a barn. But the dereliction only adds to the magic of the site; after rain, a perfect mirror-image of the church and the sky is reflected from the puddles in the nave.

On a hillock above is the **Cappella di Montesiepi**, a curious circular Romanesque chapel built on the site of Saint Galgano's hut. Galgano was a local knight who saw the error of his warlike ways and became a Cistercian hermit. When he struck his sword against a stone to signify his renunciation of war, it was swallowed up – and there it remains. X-ray analysis has shown that there is indeed a fair length of iron inside the rock (though the authoritative TCI guide observes tersely that "the sword you see today is modern"). Inside the chapel are some badly faded frescoes by Ambrogio Lorenzetti, and a striped cotto-and-travertine beehive dome.

Monteriggioni

Dante compared the town's 14 towers to giants immersed up to their navels in an infernal pit; not the first association that springs to mind, it must be said. But the walls are undeniably impressive: built in 1213-19 and reinforced half a century later, they were put up when Monteriggioni became a Sienese garrison town, facing the Florentine threat to the north. Once inside, you realise that it was all a bluff: this sleepy village is hard put to fill up the space inside the walls, and only manages it by throwing in a kitchen-garden or ten. But it's a pleasant place to while away an hour or two, with a little Romanesque-Gothic church and some sweet Medieval cottages, a number of which now house craft shops. It also has a good restaurant, **Il Pozzo** (*0577 30 41 27. Open lunch & dinner Tue-Sat; lunch Sun. Average L55,000*), which does copybook versions of all those standard regional dishes – though it is slightly over-priced.

With a car, the nearby hamlet of **Abbadia Isola** is worth a look for what remains of a Medieval Cistercian abbey: the church at the back of the courtyard (now occupied by cars and kids on bicycles) has a good altarpiece by Sano di Pietro.

San Gimignano

San Gimignano is too pretty for its own good. From far off it is unmistakable, a postcard hilltown bristling with towers. Inside, the photo opportunities continue: almost every house you see along the two main streets, Via San Giovanni and Via San Matteo, dates from between 1200 and 1400, making this Tuscany's most perfectly preserved Medieval town. In the centre, two remarkable adjoining squares contain a wealth of monuments including the remarkable **Collegiata**, whose walls are covered with trecento frescoes.

But all this beauty comes at a price. Because it is so small – it takes around a quarter of an hour to walk the length of the town – San Gimignano does not have Florence or Siena's ability to absorb and ignore the tourist influx. On summer weekends, indeed, it sometimes seems to have capitulated entirely, with the tour groups so thick on the ground that there are pedestrian bottlenecks at the narrowest points. The locals – all 7,000 of them – are mostly involved in servicing this invasion, and although the *sangimignanesi* are at heart noble, poetic souls, this may not be immediately apparent to the tourist who is charged in a bar for a glass of tap water (an unheard-of practice), nor does the

sign outside the alimentari advertising 'Sexy Pasta' help to get the message across.

Come out of season, come during the week, at the very least stay overnight so that you can experience *la città delle torri* in the early morning, when it is at its most magical. Stray off the main drag; stick to brick-paved backstreets with views over vernaccia-clad hillsides, where the village atmosphere of the place comes through most strongly. Or else stay in a friend's villa out of town, like Tony Blair, whose visit in the summer of 1996 has since been blown up to epic proportions by the local press.

What to see

It makes sense to invest in a combined museum ticket (*biglietto cumulativo*), which gives you access to all five of the paying sights administered by the town council: the **Museo Civico**, the **Torre Grossa**, the **Cappella di Santa Fina**, the **Museo Etrusco/Museo di Arte Sacra**, and the **Collezione Ornitologica**. Although the latter two are not must-sees, the first three definitely are, and you still save money. The ticket costs L16,000, or L12,000 for each member of a family group with kid(s) between 6 and 18. You can buy it from whichever museum you start from.

Buses (from Siena via Poggibonsi) and tourist coaches disgorge at Piazzale Martiri di Monte Maggio, a leafy square just outside the Porta San Giovanni (1262), the most impressive of the town gates. From here the Via San Giovanni, lined by 13th-century palazzi hosting 20th-century food and souvenir emporia and wine shops (one inside an abandoned church), leads up into the centre of town. If you're looking for a hotel room in high season, stop inside the gate at the **Cooperativa Hotels Promotion** (*see below*), otherwise continue up into Piazza della Cisterna, a picturesque jumble of towers and townhouses with a 13th-century well in the middle. Ignore the heavily advertised **Museo della Tortura** at the Via del Castello end – an overpriced and exploitative private venture – and continue up into Piazza Duomo, the town's cultural and political hub.

The plain Romanesque façade of the cathedral or **Collegiata** (*0577 94 03 16. Open 9.30am-12.30pm, 3-5.30pm, daily*) stands in stark contrast to the glorious interior. Almost every inch of wall-space is frescoed, animating the Bible in two separate cycles for the benefit of the largely illiterate 14th-century congregation. Those on the left (painted by Bartolo di Fredi in around 1367) illustrate scenes from the Old Testament: note the details, such as the cool tom-tom player in the *Temptation of Job* panel. On the right is Barna di Siena's (or just possibly Lippo Memmi's) New Testament cycle – artistically more forward-looking, they actually pre-date Bartolo's by some 20 years. At the end of this wall is the **Cappella di Santa Fina** (*Phone & hours as Collegiata. Admission L3,000, or with combined ticket*) a collaborative masterpiece from the 1470s designed by Giuliano and Benedetto da Maiano with scenes from the life of pious local girl Santa Fina courtesy of Domenico Ghirlandaio.

The **Museo Civico** in the Piazza del Popolo (*0577 94 03 40. Open Mar-Oct 9.30am-7.30pm, daily; Nov-Feb 9.30am-1.30pm, 2.30-4.30pm, Tue-Sun*) has one or two artistic jewels and also gives access to the **Torre Grande** – at 164m, the tallest of the town's towers, and also the only one you can go up. In the museum, Lippo Memmi's *Maestà* (1317) in the Sala di Dante is a magnificent work, with its serried ranks of gilded saints and angels. There are some good 14th- and 15th-century altarpieces and, in a room at the top of the stairs, a delightful series of frescoes of married life from the 1320s, a Boccaccio-esque subject almost unique in the visual arts of this period. The slog to the top of the tower (not for the infirm or unfit: it ends with a near-vertical ladder) is well worth it for the breathtaking view over the rooftops and the rolling Tuscan countryside, which looks almost flat from this height. Be warned that it can be chilly up here.

The combined **Museo Etrusco/Museo di Arte Sacra** has a motley and uninspired collection, only really worth a look if you have the combined ticket. The same goes for the stuffed birds of the **Ornithological Collection** a couple of blocks to the west, though the setting – a deconsecrated chapel – adds a certain *je ne sais quoi* to these dusty grebes and spoonbills. The Florentine **Rocca** above has been laid out as a public garden, with a children's play area.

From Piazza Duomo, the Via San Matteo, with some of the best of the town's palazzi, continues the route of the Via Francigena – the old pilgrim road to Rome – north to the Porta San Matteo. Hang a right just before the gate to get to **Sant'Agostino** (*0577 94 03 83. Open Apr-Sept 7am-noon, 3-7pm, daily; Oct-Mar 7am-noon, 3-6pm, daily*), a barn-like 13th-century monastery church which contains San Gimignano's remaining artistic plum: the *Life of Saint Augustine* fresco cycle behind the main altar (bring plenty of change to light it up). Painted in the 1460s by Benozzo Gozzoli, these lively, colourful scenes are of interest more as a record of contemporary Tuscan life than as a saintly narrative. The church has some other good works, and gives access to a pretty quattrocento cloister.

Where to stay

San Gimignano has virtually cut out the bottom end of the hotel market in the attempt to attract the right sort of tourist: all four of the hotels inside the walls are three-star operations. But what it does have is a network of private rooms, most of which are clean and charming, some of which offer near-hotel facilities. The **Cooperativa Hotels Promotion** (*0577 94 08 09. Open 9.30am-1pm, 3-7pm, Mon-Sat; 3-7pm Sun*) just inside the Porta San Giovanni, at Via San Giovanni 125, will put you in touch with available hotel rooms; they also have three cheaper sets of rooms above restaurants on their books. The **Tourist Office** in Piazza del Duomo has a list of *affitacamere* (private rooms), *appartamenti* and *agriturismo* ventures in the surrounding countryside; you can either phone these directly or book via **Mundi Travel** at Via San Matteo 74 (*0577 94 08 27. Open 9.30am-12.30pm, 3.30-7.30pm, Mon-Sat*).

L'Antico Pozzo *Via San Matteo 11 (0577 94 20 14).*
Rates *single* L125,000; *double* L180-240,000.
Credit AmEx, EC, MC, V.
The highest prices and the most impeccable design sense of the San Gimignano hotels.

La Cisterna *Piazza della Cisterna 24 (0577 94 03 28).*
Rates *single* L108,000; *double with panoramic balcony* L181,000. **Credit** AmEx, DC, EC, MC, V.
Located in a 14th-century palazzo, this is the best choice for those looking for peace and quiet – providing you can get one of the rooms around the back (the others face onto the square).

Le Vecchie Mura *Via Piandornella 15 (0577 94 02 70).* **Rates** *double* L70,000. **No credit cards.**
For budget travellers, the two double rooms above this restaurant are recommended, with beautiful views east over the hills. The owner also has a self-contained flat with garden and parking in another part of town.

Where to eat

For coffee and cakes, steer clear of the bars in the two main squares; **Lucia e Maria** in Via San Matteo 55 is a better option, especially for a late breakfast. The **Gelateria di Piazza** in Piazza della Cisterna 4 modestly claims that it serves "the best ice-cream in the world". It doesn't, but it's certainly the best in town; try the dolce amaro flavour, a calorie-controlled mix of chocolate, coffee, nuts and cream. Also *see chapter* **A Tuscan Restaurant Tour**.

Enoteca Gustavo *Via San Matteo 29 (0577 94 00 57).* **Open** 8.30am-8.15pm Sat-Thur. **Credit** AmEx, DC, EC, MC, V.
If you want a quick snack washed down with a glass of Vernaccia di San Gimignano – one of the few Italian whites that improves with age – stop here. There are four small tables out back, overlooked by a framed photo of El Che, where you can eat *bruschette* of various kinds, *cacio e pere* (Pienza cheese and pears), a good selection of *sott'oli* (vegetables pickled in oil) and other local goodies. Alternatively, pick up a bottle of wine here, get the alimentari next door to make you some filled rolls, and head up to the Rocca.

Dorandò *Vicolo dell'Oro 2 (0577 94 18 62).*
Open *summer* lunch & dinner daily; *winter* lunch & dinner Tue-Sun. **Average** L70,000. **Credit** AmEx, DC, EC, MC, V.
A calm, serene restaurant with a young staff that serves food based on research into Etruscan, Medieval and Renaissance food. Some good dishes to try include *pici* with a mint pesto and guinea hen with juniper.

Osteria delle Catene *Via Mainardi 18 (0577 94 19 66).* **Open** lunch & dinner Thur-Tue. **Average** L45,000. **Credit** AmEx, DC, EC, MC, V.
The only joint in town not to fall into either of the above traps. Don't let the minimalist surroundings put you off – this is tasty regional cooking with an alternative slant: among the starters, the *pipe ai broccoli* (curiously translated as 'pasta with blockheads') are excellent, as is the leek and saffron soup; rabbit, boar and *nana col cavolo nero* (duck with red cabbage) liven up the main course. The wine list offers a good selection of local and national labels at very reasonable mark-ups.

Festivals

Carnival is a good time to visit: colourful processions in the streets and carnival floats on the four Sundays before Shrove Tuesday give the locals the upper hand for once. On the third weekend of June, the **Feria delle Messi** is a re-evocation of a Medieval guild fair. In July there is generally a series of concerts and other events, billed as the **Festival Internazionale**: for details ring the tourist office (*0577 94 00*).

Chianti

Chianti is the ultimate expatriate dreamscape. Lazy lunches on vine-trellissed patios outside rustic villas, washed down with the most celebrated of local products: it's a deep-rooted fantasy, and one which has given rise to a full-scale industry. There is a greater concentration of high-class holiday lets, upmarket *agriturismo* operations and packaged walking tours (complete with rucksack transport, cellar visits and gourmet lunch stops) in this small rural enclave between Florence and Siena than anywhere else in Italy. An enterprising German has even set up a 'See Chianti by hot-air balloon' service (*see chapter* **Specialist Holidays**).

Every stockbroker's dream home in Chianti.

And the fantasy has also brought hordes of rich foreigners – mainly British and German – who are desperate to retire into it: hence the region's by-name, 'Chiantishire'. The phenomenon was examined – and encouraged – by John Mortimer, in his comedy of manners novel *Summer's Lease*, and again by Bernardo Bertolucci in his 1996 film *Stealing Beauty*.

The odd thing is, it's all true. In Chianti, every corner brings another perfectly-framed postcard into view. Some of this has to do with the sensitive, small-scale agricultural exploitation of the area, which has been going on ever since these hills were first settled by the Etruscans. Vines came to dominate the scene in the first half of the 19th century thanks to the efforts of local landowner Baron Bettino Ricasoli, who was alert to the growing market for fine wines. The search for quality meant that plots were kept small, but lovingly maintained: the *mezzadri* or sharecroppers who leased the land from the Baron were required to build a new dry-stone terrace for the vines every single year.

However, despite its Big Red vocation, Chianti is by no means overrun by vines: most of the area is wooded, especially towards the east, where the Monti dei Chianti rise to a height of almost 900m, providing some fine walking. Even in the agricul-tural heartland, the south-facing vineyards tend to be carved out of the surrounding oak forests, which shelter porcupines, foxes and wild boar; and the whole area is covered in wild flowers in the spring and early summer.

The influx of foreigners and money has created work for builders, gardeners and cleaners, but done little to improve the lot of the average village artisan or agricultural labourer – though it has certainly helped the look of the place, salvaging farmhouses which would otherwise have fallen apart. Famous vineyards are bought up as investments by Milanese pharmaceutical companies, holiday homes are brokered by firms based in London and Munich, and few of the profits ever find their way back into the local economy. This is one of the reasons why the town councils of this earthly paradise have long been strongholds of the Italian left.

What to see

In order to really appreciate the area, you need your own transport, as buses are sporadic at the best of times. This does not need to be of the four-wheeled variety, though: criss-crossed by a network of minor roads (shown as white on most maps), these hills are perfect walking and cycling territory. Backbone of the region is the old N222 Florence-Siena road (now superseded by a two-lane *superstrada* that skirts the western edge of the region), which passes through the towns of Greve and Castellina. From the latter another scenic B-road branches off east to Radda and Gaiole, above which is the 11th-century Benedictine abbey of Badia a Coltibuono. The other main centres are San Casciano in Val di Pesa – less than 20km south of Florence, and the only town of any size in the Chianti Classico area – and Castelnuovo Berardenga to the south.

There are any number of isolated chapels, vine-locked castles and picture-postcard villages within the enclave: the following is a necessarily selective list of highlights.

Around San Casciano in Val di Pesa

This town has one of the area's most worthwhile churches, the 14th-century Gothic **Santa Maria del Prato**, just inside the only surviving town gate. Inside is a painted crucifix attributed to Simone Martini. Five kilometres northwest of here on the Cerbaia road (turn left at the hamlet of Talente) is the pretty Romanesque chapel of **San Giovanni** in Sugana, with a good sculpted font.

North of San Casciano is the village of **Sant' Andrea in Percussina** (*see chapter* **Florence: Restaurants**), where Machiavelli lived while writing his 'how to make enemies and execute people' manual *The Prince*, in between furious card games with the local gravedigger, miller and baker down at the osteria. His house is now the **Antica Fattoria Machiavelli**, one of the best of the wineries in this neck of Chianti.

Around Greve in Chianti

A businesslike town focussing on a huge main piazza surrounded by a picturesque assembly of traditional buildings housing a couple of hotels, the excellent Falorni butchers, and a very good bookshop. Greve is devoted to the ruby nectar, and one of the best of the many wine shops is the **Enoteca del Gallo Nero** at Piazzetta Santa Croce 3. The minor road west of here is full of interest: **Montefioralle** is a tiny fortified village long held as a feud by the Vespucci family – as in Amerigo, the 16th-century merchant and explorer who gave his name to America. (Curiously, another Stateside pioneer, Giovanni da Verrazzano, also hailed from around these parts, as the statue in Greve's main square testifies.) The church of Santo Stefano has some good 13th-century paintings.

Another 5km to the west, past the castle of Montefili, is the 11th-century **Badia a Passignano** abbey, once a centre of the wealthy Vallombrosan order, set amidst olive groves with some good 16th-century frescoes in the adjacent church.

Around Radda in Chianti

Radda was capital of the 14th-century League of Chianti, a chain of Florentine defensive bulwarks against Siena, which also included Castellina and Gaiole. Its central position and relatively intact medieval fabric makes it one of the best bases for exploring the region. The village of **Volpaia** to the north is worth a look, as is the magnificent estate of **San Polo in Rosso** to the south, a castle perched in photogenic glory at the end of a white road.

Around Gaiole in Chianti

This small, workaday town is set on the edge of one of the wildest parts of the region. North of here, up towards the ridge of the Monti dei Chianti, is the **Badia a Coltibuono**, another Vallombrosan abbey in a marvellous setting, amid high fir and cedar forests; it is the starting point for some good waymarked footpaths. Like most other historic buildings around these parts, it now hosts a winery, with the bonus of a restaurant (*see below*).

South of Gaiole, past the impressive fortified farm of Meleto is one of Chianti's best known castles, and one of the few that are visitable: the **Castello di Brolio**. Centre of the estate of the same name (which also includes the isolated farmhouse where the film *Stealing Beauty* was shot; a Swiss banker now rents it and does not appreciate sightseers), it is in fact largely a 19th-century reading of what a real castle should look like – the original was wrecked by Aragonese troops in 1478 and finally destroyed by the Sienese 50 years later. It was rebuilt after 1860 by Baron Ricasoli, the man responsible for pushing the Chianti wine industry into the major league. Inside there is a good 14th-century chapel; you can also visit the Baron's ponderous apartments (*0577 74 90 66*).

Around Castellina in Chianti

Though not as immediately attractive as Greve, Castellina is another good base. The 14th/15th-century town centre is dominated by an imposing Rocca (now the local council headquarters). North of here, just off the road to Panzano, is the pretty Romanesque **Pieve di San Leolino**.

Where to stay

Castellina Colle Etrusco Salivolpi *Via Fiorentina 89 (0577 74 04 84)*. **Rates** *double* L140,000. **Credit** AmEx, EC, MC, V.
One of the best medium-range option in the area, in a restored farmhouse with attached pool; it's also handy for the Albergaccio restaurant (*see below*).

Greve Del Chianti *Piazza Matteotti (055 85 37 63)*. **Rates** *single* L120,000; *double* L150,000. **Credit** EC, MC, V.
Centrally located, medium range hotel.

Greve Giovanni da Verrazzano *Piazza Matteotti (055 85 31 89)*. **Rates** *single* L100,000; *double* L120,000. **Credit** AmEx, DC, EC, MC, V.
The other main hotel in Greve.

Parco Naturale di San Michele Villa San Michele *(055 85 10 34)*. **Rates** *double* L90,000. **No credit cards**.
This upmarket hostel in the middle of a natural park offers a fine base for exploring the highest part of the Chianti hills, east of Greve and Radda.

Radda Giovannino *Via Roma 8 (0577 73 80 56)*. **Rates** *single* L50,000; *double* L80,000. **No credit cards**.
Rents out private rooms – a good choice (one of the only choices, in fact) for budget travellers.

Radda Relais Vescine *(0577 74 11 44)*. **Rates** *single* L180,000; *double* L260,000. **Credit** AmEx, EC, MC, V.
At the other end of the scale to Giovannino, this village, 5km west on the Castellina road, has been entirely converted into a high-class hotel, with restaurant, pool and tennis courts.

Where to eat

See also chapter **A Tuscan Restaurant Tour**.

Badia a Coltibuono Abbey restaurant *(0577 74 90 31)*. **Open** lunch & dinner daily. **Average** L50,000. **Credit** EC, MC, V.
The restaurant at the abbey has a setting to die for – and the food's not bad either, with the emphasis on mushrooms, soups and local game.

Cerbaia La Tenda Rossa *Piazza del Monumento 9/14 (055 82 61 32)*. **Open** lunch & dinner Mon, Tue, Fri-Sun; dinner Thur. **Average** L100,000. **Credit** AmEx, DC, EC, MC, V.
This village, northwest of San Casciano, is home to one of Tuscany's most highly rated restaurants: a dream dinner here will set you back around L100,000 a head.

Castellina Albergaccio *Via Fiorentina 35 (0577 74 10 42)*. **Open** lunch & dinner Mon-Sat. **Average** L60,000. **No cardit cards**.
Albergaccio is the fiefdom of angry young chef Francesco Cacciatori, who is, it must be said, a genius. For first-timers, the *sapori toscani* fixed-price menu is recommended.

Greve Bottega del Moro *Piazza Trieste 14r (055 85 37 53)*. **Open** lunch & dinner Thur-Tue. **Average** L35,000. **No credit cards**.
Trad Tuscan cooking is supplemented by some off-the-wall surprises like bulghur wheat and artichoke ratatouille.

Radda Al Chiasso dei Portici *Chiasso dei Portici 1 (0577 73 87 74)*. **Open** lunch & dinner Wed-Mon. **Average** L35,000. **Credit** AmEx, DC, EC, MC, V.
A good cheap option with tables outside in a small courtyard.

Siena

The most singular of Tuscan cities.

You can only hope to understand Siena by trying to understand the Sienese. If a new child comes to school in the city, virtually the first question they'll be asked is *"Di che contrada sei?"*, what *contrada* are you from? For the essence of being Sienese is belonging to a *contrada* (*see box*), one of 17 districts in the city that have represented each citizen's civic rights, duties and aspirations since medieval times. And you only belong to a *contra-*

> The telephone code for Siena is **0577**

da if you are born in it. So, by definition, no-one – Italian or otherwise – can be an adoptive Sienese no matter how long he/she lives within the city's walls or abides by its historic customs and present-day precepts. Outsiders are treated with respect,

Useful information

Tourist information

Centro Servizi Informazioni Turistiche Siena (APT) *Piazza del Campo 56 (28 05 51/fax 27 06 76).* **Open** 8.30am-7.30pm Mon-Sat (more restricted in winter).

Guides The APT has a list of individual guides.

Telephones Most public phones take Telecom Italia phone cards as well as coins; there's a Telephone Service in Via dei Termini 40.

Transport

Railway Station *Piazza Fratelli Rosselli (28 01 15).* The station is at the bottom of the hill on the east side of the city. There's a regular bus service linking it with the city centre and other districts: bus no. 1 will take you up to La Lizza and San Domenico (from where the regional buses leave); no. 2 runs to La Lizza; no. 3 to San Domenico and beyond to Pian dei Mantellini. Siena is basically a branch line. You can get direct to Florence in an hour and a half, but must change in Empoli for Pisa. In the other direction you head slowly for Grosseto on the coast, passing through some fabulous countryside on the way.

Buses The outer city lines leave from Piazza San Domenico (*20 42 45*) and serve a much wider geographical area than the trains. If you're not sure you want to run to the expense of hiring a car, check the bus destinations first. You'll be surprised how many villages and towns they link. Note that it's quicker to get to Florence by bus than by train: one hour if you get the *rapido* that goes straight down the superstrada with no detours.

Bicycle Hire – DF Bike *Via Massetana Romana 54 (27 19 05).*

Car Hire *with driver* **Balzana Autonoleggi** *Via P Fracassi 2 (28 50 13);* **Giamello Giorgio** *Via Guido da Siena 7 (50 381); coaches & minibuses* **Sena Srl** *Via Montanini 92 (28 32 03); self-drive* **Hertz** *c/o Albergo Lea, Viale XXIV Maggio 10 (45 085);* **Avis** *Via Simone Martini 36 (27 03 05).*

Motorcycle Hire – Automotocicli Perozzi *Via del Romitorio 5 (22 31 57).*

Markets & festivals

Markets
Siena has the most fantastic **general market** that covers a huge area from Piazza La Lizza to the Fortezza every Wednesday morning and accounts for a great deal of absenteeism in public offices. It starts at 8am and ends at 1pm, but you need to be there early for the best finds: lambswool sweaters for L20,000 (central back end of La Lizza), prototype designer clothes, odd lengths of quality curtain materials (about the 4th stall down on entering La Lizza). Staples of unbeatable quality are pure linen jacquard woven tableware from Russia (L20,000 for a tablecloth for 12 – about the 6th stall down on entering La Lizza) and some excellent curtain and upholstery materials (half way down La Lizza take the path down to the left and carry on along the lower level keeping to the left until you reach it).

Every two years an **Antiques Show & Market** is held between February and March in the Magazzini del Sale at Palazzo Pubblico.

Festivals
The **Chigiana** also puts on a classical concert season (Oct-Mar).
The **Palio** (*see box*) takes place every year on 2 July and 16 August.
Accademia Chigiana (*46 152*) is an important summer music school which organises an excellent concert cycle (July).
Siena Jazz (*27 14 01*) is a major summer event (end July-early Aug).
Teatro dei Rinnovati (*29 22 65*) runs a lively theatre season (Nov-late Mar).
The **Settimana dei Vini** takes place in the Fortezza Medicea (Enoteca) (1st half of June).

Emergency services

Ambulance Misericordia (*22 21 99*); public assistance (*28 01 10*) Night-time and holiday medical emergency service.
Hospital (*58 64 66/58 61 11*).
Carabinieri (*112*).
Municipal Police (*29 25 50/29 25 58*).
Police Headquarters (*20 11 11*).

View from the **Torre della Mangia** *(p224).*

east. When the Sienese were defeated at Colle di Val d'Elsa in 1269, the political and social balance of the city was in for radical change. The Guelph party, allied to Florence, took over the government, thus paving the way for the rise of merchants and 'middling' people, at the expense of the earlier Ghibelline aristocracy (*see chapter* **History: Guelph v Ghibelline**).

The Governo dei Nove, as it was called, remained in power from 1287 to 1355, bringing with it stability and prosperity. Siena's merchants and bankers excelled throughout Europe; while back at home magnificently audacious buildings like the Palazzo Pubblico, Torre della Mangia and the Cathedral, along with the paintings of Duccio di Buoninsegna, Simone Martini and the Lorenzettis all spoke for the climate of prosperity and confidence.

The golden age of Siena came to a brusque end towards the middle of the 14th century. First there was famine, and then, in 1348, the black plague killed three fifths of the population. Troubled times were to follow, with popular uprisings and internal struggles that resulted in a number of short-lived lordships: first that of Gian Galeazzo Visconti, Duke of Milan, followed by that of Pandolfo Petrucci il Magnifico. In 1531, the city was occupied by the Spanish in the name of the Emperor Charles V, and when the Sienese rose up against these foreign governors, Cosimo I de' Medici saw that the time was ripe for extending the Florentine dominions south. He besieged Siena, and the city capitulated in April 1555. Two years later the proud Sienese Republic was no more.

Siena did not prosper under the Medicis. However, what the city did discover was its vocation for spectacular public events. The foremost of these, the Palio horse race, took root between the end of the 1500s and the beginning of the 1600s, when it acquired its present-day form as a twice-yearly (2 July and 16 August) show of colour, speed and passion (*see box*). The fortunes of Siena finally began to look up under the Lorraine Duchy in the late 18th century. 1849 saw the opening of the railway line to Poggibonsi and Empoli, and by 1861 the tracks had been extended south to connect the city up with Chiusi, and hence with Rome. If those links brought Siena new prospects and a revival of self-confidence in the 19th century, the fact that they have grown little since then is surely what makes the city such a haven of coherence today.

but will never be welcomed into the bosom of the city. This means that Siena will never be a melting-pot, an urban centre that admits of conflict and can nurture innovation. But by the same token, it's a uniquely coherent, cohesive city with a history that still means something very real to its inhabitants. As a result, it's remarkably crime-free and confident – some, including a few Sienese, might even say complacent. While cities the world over groan and convulse, Siena remains a work of art.

Some history

According to legend, Siena was founded by Senius and Aschius, who fled from Rome after the death of their father Remus, taking with them the symbol of the she-wolf suckling the twins. The tale is totally unfounded, but like most legends, points to a basic truth: Siena is indeed of Roman origin. However, it wasn't until the Middle Ages, when it was linked to France and Rome by the great new Via Francigena, that it acquired any real importance.

Once firmly on the map, Siena soon grew to be an important administrative and commercial centre. During the first half of the 12th century, its municipal institutions gained in strength and did their best to supplant the Bishops in governing the city. This bid for independence gained momentum in the following centuries, when the Sienese not only tried to quell the feudal lords of the surrounding territories, but also struggled with Florence for regional hegemony. However, by 1145 the Florentines had acquired Poggibonsi, to the north of Siena, and Montepulciano to the south-

Sights

Note that you can save some money by buying a combined ticket for L9,500 that includes the Libreria Piccolomini, Museo dell'Opera Metropolitana, Battistero di San Giovanni and Oratorio di San Bernardino.

Churches

Duomo

Piazza del Duomo (47 321). **Open** *1 Jan-15 Mar* 7.30am-1.30pm, 2.30-5pm, daily; *16 Mar-31 Oct* 9am-7.30pm daily; *1 Nov-31 Dec* 7.30am-1.30pm, 2.30-5pm, daily. **Admission** free.

This is one of Italy's finest examples of the way Romanesque architecture could be reconciled with the new Gothic style. It was built on the site of an earlier church between the end of the 12th and the beginning of the 13th century, and during the next 150 years was enlarged and embellished in a flurry of grandiosity that was supposed to culminate in a truly vast Duomo Nuovo. What is now Piazza Jacopo della Quercia (on the left of the Cathedral) was to be the main nave, while the existing body of the building was to become the transept. A number of structural failures and the terrible plague of 1348 put paid to these aspirations.

Yet even in its more modest state, the Duomo is an impressive achievement. The black and white marble facing was begun in 1226, and some 30 years later work began on the dome, one of the oldest in Italy.

With its three vast aisles and zebra-striped marble, the Cathedral interior is truly magnificent. It also has polychrome marble floors, parts of which are covered up for protection. Most impressive are the 13 scenes in inlaid marble beneath the dome, the work of the Sienese Mannerist **Domenico Beccafumi** (1521-24) and his pupil, which are only uncovered on special feast days. In the apse there is a splendid inlaid and carved wooden choir (14th-16th century), and above this a circular stained glass window, one of Italy's earliest, made in 1288 to designs by **Duccio di Buoninsegna**.

In the left transept is a pulpit carved by **Nicola Pisano** (1265-68) with the help of his son Giovanni and pupil, Arnolfo di Cambio. At the far end of the left aisle there is a door leading through to the **Libreria Piccolomini** (*Open 2 Jan-15 Mar 10am-1pm, 2.30-5pm, daily; 16 Mar-31 Oct 9am-7.30pm; 1 Nov-31 Dec 10am-1pm, 2.30-5pm, daily. Admission L2,000; L1,500 concessions*), built in 1492 to house the library of Aeneas Sylvius Piccolomini, the Renaissance Humanist who became Pope Pius II (*see p212* **Pienza**). It was constructed at the behest of his nephew (later Pope Pius III), and decorated between 1502 and 1509 by **Pinturicchio** with lively scenes from Pius II's life. Pius had worked as a diplomat before becoming Pope – look out for the scene in which he meets James II of Scotland.

Battistero di San Giovanni

Piazza San Giovanni (28 29 92). **Open** *2 Jan-15 Mar, Nov, Dec* 10am-1pm, 2.30-5pm, daily; *16 Mar-30 Sept* 9am-7.30pm daily; *Oct* 9am-6pm daily.
Admission L3,000; L2,000 for parties of over 15.

Squeezed under the Duomo's apse, is the oddly rectangular Baptistery (most are octagonal). It was frescoed by various Renaissance artists, including **Vecchietta**, but the focal point is the magnificent **Font** (1417), one of the masterpieces of the early Renaissance in Tuscany, traditionally attributed to **Jacopo della Quercia**. It features magnificent bronze bas-reliefs by della Quercia himself, by **Donatello** and **Ghiberti** and rather more modest ones by Turino di Sano and Giovanni di Turino.

Basilica di San Francesco

Piazza San Francesco (28 90 81). **Open** 8am-noon, 3pm-5pm, daily. **Admission** free.

The Franciscans generally built churches with spacious, unencumbered interiors that would enhance rather than obscure their devotions. With its single nave and transept divided into a series of high-vaulted chapels, this church is no exception. Founded around the year 1228 and enlarged a century later, it was frescoed by Taddeo di Bartolo, Sassetta, Perugino and possibly even Raphael. Sadly, these were destroyed in a fire in 1655. The mock gothic facade is an early 20th century addition.The church still houses some admirable works of art, including the original portal by Francesco di Giorgio, which has been placed against the left-hand wall. In the first chapel of the left transept is a fresco of the *Crucifixion* by **Pietro Lorenzetti**, and in the third chapel a *St Louis of Anjou before Boniface VIII* and the *Martyrdom of the Franciscans* by his brother **Ambrogio** (both artists died in the Black Death of 1348).

Oratorio di San Bernardino

Piazza San Francesco (42 020). **Open** *1 Apr-31 Oct* 10.30am-1.30pm, 3-5.30pm, daily. **Admission** L2,000; L1,500 for parties of 15 or over.

To the right of San Francesco, this oratory was built in the 15th century on the site where St Bernard used to pray. On the first floor is a magnificent fresco cycle painted between 1496 and 1518 by **Beccafumi** and **Sodoma**, along with their lesser contemporary, **Pacchia**. Note, especially in Beccafumi, the use of reds and greens, the gentle curvilinear rhythms of the figures and the dream-like atmosphere of the background skies: prime ingredients of early Sienese Mannerism.

Basilica di San Domenico

Piazza San Domenico (28 08 93). **Open** 7am-1pm, 3pm-6.30pm, daily. **Admission** free.

This soaring brick edifice was one of the earliest Dominican monasteries in Tuscany. Building began in 1227 on a site near the city outskirts, where the friars could address the common people and hopefully curb their tendency towards heretical egalitarian beliefs and behaviour. History has not treated it kindly: fires, military occupations and earthquakes have all done their bit over the centuries, and what you see today is largely the fruit of mid-20th-century restoration. However, various things of interest have survived intact. Half way down the nave on the right is the recently restored chapel of *St Catherine* with frescoes by **Sodoma** (1526), and at the end of the nave a *Madonna Enthroned* attributed to **Pietro Lorenzetti**. Just beyond this is a work that bears witness to the universal spirit of the Renaissance: the *Adoration of the Shepherds* painted around 1475-80 by **Francesco di Giorgio**, who was not only a great architect and sculptor but also a fine painter.

Museums

Note that opening times of Sienese museums and galleries vary from year to year.

Museo Civico

Piazza Pubblico, Piazza del Campo (29 22 30). **Open** *7 Jan-29 Feb, Nov-24 Dec* 9.30am-1.30pm daily; *Mar, Oct, 27 Dec-5 Jan* 9.30am-6pm Mon-Sat; 9.30am-1.30pm Sun; *Apr, Sept* 9.30am-6.30pm Mon-Sat; 9.30am-1.30pm Sun; *May, June* 9am-7pm Mon-Sat; 9am-1.30pm Sun; *July, Aug* 9am-7.30pm Mon-Sat; 9am-1.30pm Sun. **Admission** L8,000; L4,000 concessions; L6,000 groups of 15 or over.

Access to the museum is via the courtyard of Palazzo Pubblico and up a modern iron staircase. The first four rooms of the picture gallery display paintings by artists both local and otherwise of the 16th to 18th centuries. Don't spend too long here, and waste no time on the **Sala del Risorgimento** with its gushing 19th-century frescoes. Instead, head straight for the **Sala del Concistorio** whose frescoed vaults were painted by **Domenico Beccafumi** between 1529 and 1535. Note also the elegant Renaissance marble portal sculpted by **Bernardo Rossellino** (architect of Pienza) in 1446.

From here, wander through the ante-chapel with its early 15th-century frescoes by **Taddeo di Bartolo**, and on the other side you'll find yourself in the **Sala del Mappamondo**, which houses one of Siena's foremost jewels: the fresco of the *Maestà* painted by **Simone Martini** in

1315. Recent restoration has drawn attention to the fact that the faces of the main figures (the Madonna and Child and the Saints beside her) are re-paints. While he was engaged on this job, Martini went to Assisi, where he saw what Giotto had accomplished a little earlier. On his return to Siena he couldn't resist chiselling out the faces he'd already painted and replacing them with new versions that spoke for the lesson he'd learnt in Assisi. The fresco on the right-hand wall illustrating the *Equestrian Portrait of Guidoriccio da Fogliano* was once attributed to Simone Martini, but is thought by some historians to be a 16th century fake.

In the adjacent **Sala della Pace** (also known as the **Sala dei Nove**) there is another stupendous fresco cycle: **Ambrogio Lorenzetti**'s *Effects of Good Government in the City and in the Country* (1338-40), commissioned by the Government 'dei Nove' ('of the nine'), whose self-satisfied political manifesto it embodies. On the opposite wall is the flip side – *Bad Government and its Effects* – replete with all sorts of nasty goings on. Ironically, a few years after the frescoes were finished, Siena was decimated by the Black Death (Lorenzetti and his family were among the victims) and a tyrannical government came to power. Beyond this room is the **Sala dei Pilastri**, which contains the museum's earliest works, including the late 13th-century *Maestà* by **Guido da Siena**, the earliest flowering of Sienese painting.

Pinacoteca Nazionale

Palazzo Buonsignori, Via San Pietro 29 (28 11 61). **Open** 8.30am-1.30pm Mon; 9am-7pm Tue-Sat; 8am-1pm Sun. **Admission** L8,000.

This is one of Italy's foremost art collections, especially the fine Sienese Trecento and Quattrocento *fondi d'oro*, or paintings with gilded backgrounds. The 2nd floor is devoted to Sienese masters of the 12th to 15th cen-

The Palio

To the outside observer, the Palio is simply a horse-race which takes place twice a year in the middle of Siena, in honour of the town's patron saint and protectress, the Virgin Mary. To the Sienese, this is the focal point of the entire year, an event of social, emotional, historical and cultural significance that is impossible to exaggerate.

The perimeter of the beautiful, shell-shaped Piazza del Campo is covered with the local bright yellow earth (as in Raw Sienna). Tall external walls are set up, ominously padded with mattresses, behind which steep wooden seats are constructed for fee-paying spectators – many of them wealthy tourists. The Sienese themselves, up to 30,000 of them, prefer to stand, tightly contained in the middle of the square, along with a few gutsy low-budget travellers. The aerial view of the Piazza appears divided into sections of electrifying hues as the supporters of each *contrada* (district of the city) stick together, dressed in their teams' colours, waving flags and singing in a frenzy of excitement.

The proceedings start at about five o'clock at the end of a hot summer's day. Groups of men in heavy, velvet medieval costumes emerge from a huge 12th-century palazzo entrance. They parade around the piazza, dexterously spinning and tossing flags to the accompaniment of rhythmic drumming. While tourists clap enthusiastically, the Sienese are prey to mounting tension. At the end of five hours, wilted visitors slouch in their chairs, exhausted, while the Sienese seem immune to their long exposure under the baking sun. There is a final manic rush of *contradaioli* through the last open gate to see the start of the race.

Eight out of the city's 17 *contrade* are drawn by lot to participate in the Palio. Their horses are also chosen by lot, and are ridden into the Campo bare-back. They approach two parallel ropes which mark the starting point. A chaotic period of jostling, shoving and even biting takes place between jockeys and horses. Eventually a degree of order is restored. A gun-shot sounds, the crowd erupts, and the horses charge three times around the square. The race, for which the Sienese have been preparing and waiting for all year, is over in less than 90 seconds. The first horse over the line (with or without its jockey) wins the Palio, and a rectangular banner decorated with the image of the Virgin Mary for its *contrada*.

The reactions of the *contradaioli*, depending on their allegiance, range from weeping, shrieking and tearing out of the hair, to rapturous kissing and embracing. The anguish of the second-placed *contrada* is enough to make the winners their sworn enemies throughout the coming year. The winning *contradaioli*, some still in their medieval dress, only abate their tears to suck dummies, locally considered symbols of re-birth. Later, banquets, dancing and wine transform the streets of Siena into nightly bacchanals. The winning *contrada* basks in its glory all year long, setting the city's dynamics until the next July.

The Palio establishes a sense of identity which binds the Sienese together to the outside world as much as it drives them apart within the town. Its impact extends far beyond the actual race and provides the social and moral foundations on which the Sienese, young and old, male and female, build their lives. This is a horse race apart – there is no official betting, the pride and honour of the winning *contrade* is enough of a reward.

Tickets L250-400,000 (balconies).
Date 2 July & 16 Aug.

turies: **Margarito d'Arezzo, Guido da Siena, Duccio di Buoninsegna, Simone Martini,** the **Lorenzettis** and **Sano di Pietro**. Gold leaf could create some impressive lighting effects: see, for instance, the *Madonna and Child* attributed to Duccio di Buoninsegna or to the young Simone Martini (Room 6). And for glittering embellishments in precious reds and blues (the latter made from costly lapis lazuli) as well as gold; note how **Ambrogio Lorenzetti's** *Piccola Maestà* (Room 7) is as finely worked and detailed as a miniature. Compare these with the *Madonna dell'Umiltà* (Room 13) painted over a century later by **Giovanni di Paolo**, an artist who stuck to the ornate International Gothic style while his contemporaries largely opted for Renaissance clarity and perspective. The background landscape and the surrounding trees contribute to the overall dream-like, mystical quality of the painting. Also, don't miss the late 14th-century works of **Bartolo di Fredi** and his pupil **Taddeo di Bartolo** in rooms 9 to 11.

The first floor features some magnificent works by the Sienese Mannerist school of the early 1500s, particularly those of **Sodoma** and **Beccafumi**. Note the curiously harmonious use of acerbic greens and pungent pinks and yellows in Beccafumi's *Nativity of the Madonna* (Room 31). The one large room on the third floor is devoted to the **Spannocchi Collection**: works by north Italian and European artists of the 16th and 17th centuries.

Spedale di Santa Maria della Scala

Piazza del Duomo (58 64 10). **Open** *7 Jan-31 Mar* 10.30am-4.30pm Mon-Fri; 10.30am-5.30pm Sat, Sun; *Apr, Sept* 10.30am-5.30pm daily; *May, June* 10am-6pm daily; *July, Aug* 10am-6.30pm daily; *Oct* 10.30am-4.30pm daily; *2 Nov-5 Jan* 10.30am-4.30pm Mon-Fri; 10.30am-5.30pm Sat, Sun. **Admission** L8,000; L4,000 concessions; L4,000 for groups of 15 or over.

This institution was founded between the 9th and the 11th century as a hospital for pilgrims (the Via Francigena was the main north-south pilgrim route) and the Sienese. Between 1440 and 1444 it was embellished with frescoes by **Domenico di Bartolo, Priamo della Quercia** and **Vecchietta**, and as time went by it acquired donations in the shape of vast tracts of land which led it to play an important role in the agricultural development of the surrounding area. The last remaining sections of Siena hospital moved out from these ancient premises only quite recently, and restoration is currently under way to turn the whole complex into a major arts centre that should include restoration workshops, permanent and temporary exhibition space and a range of other facilities. Progress is slow, depending as it does on the availability of funds. For the moment the **Museo Archeologico** (*Open 9am-2pm Mon-Sat; 9am-1pm Sun; closed 2nd & 4th Sun of the month. Admission L4,000*) is housed here, and there are several rooms devoted to temporary exhibitions.

Museo dell'Opera Metropolitana

Piazza del Duomo (28 30 48). **Open** *2 Jan-15 Mar, Nov, Dec* 9am-1.30pm; *16 Mar-30 Sept* 9am-7.30pm; *Oct* 9am-6pm. **Admission** L6,000; L5,000 groups of more than 15. The museum occupies the projected, but never completed, nave of the Duomo, and displays works taken from the cathedral. On the ground floor is a large hall divided into two by a vast 15th-century wrought iron gate. Along the walls you can enjoy a far better view of **Giovanni Pisano's** ten magnificent marble statues (1284-96) than you would if they were still in their original location on the façade of the cathedral. Of great interest in the centre of the room are the tondo with a *Madonna and Child* by **Donatello** and the wonderfully sculptural bas-relief of the *Madonna and Child with St Anthony Abbot and Cardinal Antonio Casini* by **Jacopo della Quercia**, commissioned in 1437 and probably not quite completed when the artist died in 1438. On the first floor is the **Sala Duccio** with the famous *Maestà* painted (on both sides) by **Duccio di Buoninsegna** between 1308

and 1311 for the Great Altar of the Duomo, an earlier *Madonna and Child* by the same artist, and the triptych with the *Nativity of the Virgin* by **Pietro Lorenzetti** showing some wonderfully elegant 14th-century interiors. Outstanding among the largely Sienese paintings on the 2nd floor are the *Madonna and Child* by **Sano di Pietro,** the four Saints that once belonged to a polyptych by **Ambrogio Lorenzetti** and several works by the great Sienese Mannerist painter of the early 1500s, **Domenico Beccafumi**.

Monuments

Siena's most immediate and imposing monuments are perhaps the immense walls that still embrace the city and the gates through which all visitors must pass to reach the centre. Here are some highlights from within the walls.

Piazza del Campo

The beautiful, shell-shaped heart of Siena has been the city's main public space since the Middle Ages. In fact, in 1262 the Republic of Siena devoted 19 statutes to regulating how it should be used and, in 1297, established that all the houses overlooking the Campo should have mullion windows with two lights. The brick paving in nine sections that lead the eye down to Palazzo Pubblico is a design that dates back to 1347. It is around the perimeter of the Campo that the Palio horse races takes place on 2 July and 16 August each year (*see box*).

Le Contrade

The *contrade* are municipal districts that were formed between the end of the 12th and the beginning of the 13th century, when the Siena Commune chose to decentralize a number of its administrative functions. At the head of each institution was a *sindaco*, or mayor, who answered directly to the central governor (the *Podestà*) and was flanked by councillors elected by the people. General maintenance, tax-collecting and keeping public order thus became the privilege and duty of what were originally 42 contrade. Between the 15th and the 16th century, the *contrade* were reduced in number to 23, and as their political and administrative raison d'être diminished, they focused their energies on the organisation of the public games that had long been popular in the city. By 1675, six of them had disappeared, leaving the Aquila (eagle), Bruco (caterpillar), Lupa (she-wolf), Onda (dolphin), Valdimonte (ram), Nicchio (shell), Leocorno (unicorn), Giraffa (girafe), Drago (dragon), Oca (goose), Selva (forest), Civetta (owl), Tartuca (tortoise), Chiocciola (snail), Pantera (panther), Torre (tower), Istrice (porcupine). These are the competitors in the annual Palio horse race that has enflamed the hearts of the Sienese since the year 1310.

The **Fonte Gaia**, designed by Jacopo della Quercia in 1419, sits in the centre of the upper side of the Campo. This rectangular basin was placed here as a terminus for the 25km of subterranean galleries and wells that brought water from the countryside northeast of the city to its centre. In 1858, the marble panels of the structure were replaced by copies. The originals are currently located in the loggia of Palazzo Pubblico.

Palazzo Pubblico
Piazza del Campo.
This fine example of Gothic civic architecture was begun at the end of the 13th century, at about the same time as Palazzo Vecchio in Florence. As the seat of city government, it stands for the culmination of a long process of emancipation from feudal and ecclesiastical power. In architectural terms, it represents the moment of transition from the fortress to the urban palace.
The 88-metre tall **Torre del Mangia** (*Open 7 Jan-29 Feb, 2 Nov-24 Dec 10am-3.30pm daily; Mar, 27 Dec-5 Jan 10am-4pm; Apr, Oct 10am-5pm; May, June, Sept 10am-6pm; July, Aug 10am-7.30pm. Admission L5,000*) was begun in 1325 and completed in 1348. Until 1379, a certain Giovanni di Duccio, nicknamed 'il Mangia', used to climb up the bell tower to strike the hour.

Fonte Branda
Via di Fontebranda.
It's a steep walk down from Via di Città to this monumental 12th-century spring, still tinkling with water and usually invitingly cool and quiet. In its day, Fonte Branda not only supplied half the city with water, but also provided the necessary power for numerous flour mills as well as an essential raw material for cloth dyers and leather tanners.

Palazzo Salimbeni
Piazza Salimbeni.
The square itself was designed at the end of the 19th century by **Giuseppe Partini**, one of the main exponents of Sienese Gothic revival. He also restored, and to some extent remodelled, the façade of 13th-century Palazzo Salimbeni, headquarters of the Monte dei Paschi bank, and in 1880 provided the neo-Renaissance façade for the Palazzo Spannocchi (on the right) that Giuliano da Maiano had designed for Pope Pius II's Treasurer in 1470.

Restaurants

If you get up at dawn on a winter morning and drive out of Siena, you're bound to come across small convoys of battered cars heading out for a morning's shooting. In September and October it's pheasant and hare they're after, around Christmas, the main quarry is the wild boar that inhabit the surrounding woodlands. They end up as *pappardelle alla lepre* (pasta ribbons with hare sauce), *pici al ragù di cinghiale* (skinny rolls of pasta with wild boar sauce) or *cinghiale in umido* (gently brazed wild boar).

Expensive

Al Marsili
Via del Castoro 3 (47 154/fax 47 338). **Open** lunch & dinner Tue-Sun. **Average** L50,000. **Credit** AmEx, DC, EC, MC, V.
Reliably good nosh, especially the *crostini di fegato e milza* (lightly toasted bread topped with a spicy liver and spleen mince); *pici* with *ragù*; and *faraona alla Medici* (guinea fowl cooked with pine nuts, almonds and plums).

Antica Trattoria Botteganova
Strada Chiantigiana 29 (28 42 30/fax 27 15 19). **Open** lunch & dinner Tue-Sun. **Average** *tasting menu* L65,000 incl wine; *fish menu* L70,000. **Credit** AmEx, DC, EC, MC, V.
Less than a kilometre down the road from Porta Ovile, this pleasant trattoria changes its excellent *menu degustazioni* according to the season.

Cane e Gatto
Via Pagliaresi 6 (28 75 45). **Open** dinner Mon-Wed, Fri-Sun. **Average** *menu degustazione* L60-65,000. **Credit** AmEx, DC, EC, MC, V.
With Sonia in the kitchen and Paolo out front with the customers, this is a slightly precious little restaurant near Porta Romana. The food, however, is good, focussing on a *menu degustazione* that consists of several *antipasto*, a soup, a risotto, two fresh pasta dishes, two meat courses with different vegetables and two desserts. Those who can't quite face the whole works may simply pick and choose. Excellent wines accompany each course.

Moderate

Castelvecchio
Via Castelvecchio 65 (49 586). **Open** lunch & dinner Wed-Mon. **Average** L35-40,000. **Credit** AmEx, DC, EC, MC, V.
In a pleasant little restaurant located in what were once the stables of one of Siena's oldest palazzi, Mauro conjures up new dishes using traditional ingredients, while Simone takes care of customers and wine. At least two vegetarian *primi* and *secondi* every day, and, unusually for Italy, a major vegetarian focus on Wednesdays.

Fori Porta
Via Tolomei 1 (22 28 22). **Open** lunch & dinner Thur-Tue. **Average** L40,000. **Credit** AmEx, DC, EC, MC, V.

Nannini

Nannini is a household name for Sienese of all ages; not only because the family has been producing traditional Sienese sweetmeats (most famously *panforte*, a spicy cake made with nuts, candied fruit and honey) for two generations, but also because Gianna Nannini, granddaughter of the original *pasticceri*, has made a major name for herself as a pop singer. To sample their goodies, sit under the awnings of the **Bar Pasticceria Posta** in Piazza Matteotti 32 (*28 32 82. Open 7am-8pm daily*) for an ice-cream or an aperitif, or stop off at the smaller **Bar Gelateria in Monte** in Piazza Salimbeni 95/99 (*28 10 94. Open 7.30am-8.30pm daily*) on your way down to Piazza del Campo, or get a more substantial bite to eat and a drink or a coffee at the **Bar Pasticceria Conca d'Oro** in Banchi di Sopra 24 (*41 591. Open 7.30am-8.30pm Mon; 7.30am-midnight Tue-Sun*). To be truthful, the produce as such is not exceptional, but the Sienese don't seem to notice. Nannini is one of their institutions, and therefore to be revered.

Just outside Porta Romana, this is a real gem of a trattoria. The menu reflects the changing seasons. Go for *coniglio Fori Porta* (rabbit cooked with bay leaves and dressed with a light saffron sauce).

Guidoriccio

Via G Duprè 2 (44 350). **Open** lunch & dinner Mon-Sat. **Average** L35,000. **Credit** AmEx, DC, EC, MC, V.
Traditional Tuscan fare with an accent on truffles (*tartufi*) and wild mushrooms (especially *porcini*).

L'Osteria

Via de' Rossi 79/81 (28 75 92). **Open** lunch & dinner Mon-Sat. **Average** L35,000. **Credit** AmEx, EC, MC, V.
An informal place popular with students where you eat simple, well-cooked Tuscan food at wooden tables with rough paper placemats. Grilled vegetables are available as an alternative to meat courses. It's worth reserving a table.

Cheap

Il Grattacielo

Via de' Pontani 8 (28 93 26). **Open** 8am-2pm, 5-8pm Mon-Sat. **Average** L18-20,000. **Credit** AmEx, DC, EC, MC, V.
If you don't manage to get one of the very few tables you can stand up near the bar and down a few glasses of wine (on tap) and a slice of roast pork or *prosciutto* with bread. Other simple dishes available, but avoid the lunchtime rush.

Osteria del Ficomezzo

Via dei Termini 71 (22 23 84). **Open** lunch & dinner Mon-Sat. **Average** L15-40,000. **Credit** AmEx, DC, EC, MC, V.
Pleasant first floor eatery overlooking Piazza del Campo, ideal for a quick, inexpensive lunch or a more relaxing and indulgent evening visit.

Osteria Il Tamburino

Via Stalloreggi 11 (28 03 06). **Open** lunch & dinner Mon-Sat; lunch Sun. **Average** L25-30,000. **Credit** EC, MC, V.
Small, no-nonsense eating place, located conveniently near the Duomo. Homely cuisine, including good gnocchi.

Bars, cafés & gelaterias

Bar dell'Orso

Loc. Colonna di Monteriggioni 17 (30 50 74). **Open** Apr-Sept 6.30am-11.30pm daily; *Oct-Mar* 6.30am-11.30pm Thur-Tue. **Credit** AmEx, EC, MC, V.
Located about 12 minutes north up the Cassia towards Monteriggioni, this busy haunt is much more than a bar: it's a haven for the hungry at practically any time of the day or night. Antonella, who once worked at Cibreo in Florence, has selected the finest cold cuts and cheeses to be had anywhere, there's an excellent choice of wines, and they serve Illy coffee, the best in Italy. You can munch a sandwich that's a meal in itself under the portico or at one of the tables inside, where you'll also find the daily papers.

La Costarella

Via di Città 33 (28 80 76). **Open** 8.30am-midnight Wed-Mon. **No credit cards.**
If you've hoofed it up the steep hill from Fontebranda (and even if you haven't), consider this your prize: excellent ice-cream, including home-made versions of the *cornetti*, now normally found only in industrial versions. And this is not all. You can sit at a table on the mezzanine floor at the back of this gelateria bar and drink your coffee overlooking Piazza del Campo: the whole view, minus the other tourists.

L'Enoteca Italica

Fortezza Medicea (28 84 97). **Open** noon-8pm Mon; noon-1am Tue-Sat. **Credit** AmEx, EC, V.
In the massive vaulted viscera of the Fortress constructed by Cosimo de' Medici in 1561 is Italy's only national Wine Cellar. A public company, the Enoteca comprises 850 different wines from all over the country, 300 from Tuscany. By making a prior booking, groups can indulge in an organised tasting session (with small eats to absorb the alcohol). Otherwise simply go there and follow your nose.

L'Enoteca I Terzi

Via dei Termini 7 (44 329). **Open** 11am-4.30pm, 6.30pm-1am, Mon-Sat. **Credit** AmEx, DC, EC, MC, V.
Michele and Marcello set up this wine cellar in December 1995 in a carefully renovated brick-vaulted building in the historic heart of Siena. The selection is predominantly Tuscan, but also includes wines from other regions and countries. Simple fare, in the shape of cold meats, crostini, cheese and bread, is available to accompany the imbibing.

Fonte Gaia

21/23 Piazza del Campo (28 16 28). **Open** 8.30am-midnight daily. **Credit** AmEx, DC, EC, MC, V.
If the madding crowd doesn't disconcert you, then sit here at one of the 32 tables out on the square for a slow cappuccino and watch the world go by against one of Europe's finest architectural backdrops. Piazza del Campo has a wonderfully muted acoustic, creating a sort of veil between you and what goes on beyond. There's an upstairs room for similar views on rainy days. Sandwiches and *primi piatti* also available.

L'Officina

Piazza del Sale 3 (28 63 01). **Open** 6pm-3am daily. **No credit cards.**
This is a bar (the locals would call it a 'pub'), with seating inside for 80 and outside for 40, patronised by students, foreigners and young Sienese professionals. Its special feature is a stage with a large video screen where they show motorbike videos, cartoons, concerts.... Live music is also often on tap.

Tea Room

Via Porta Giustizia 11 (22 27 53). **Open** 9.30pm-3am Mon-Sat. **No credit cards.**
A lot of thought has gone into creating this venue for night-owls: a wonderfully motley collection of tables, a fireplace to sit beside in the winter, all sorts of details in the furnishing that you wouldn't expect outside a private house. Francesco, who set up Tea Room in 1991, organises live music (mostly jazz) two evenings a week in the summer and concerts most Saturdays. He also offers a fine wine list, a good selection of cocktails, beers and grappas and a choice of 50 different teas and infusions as well as delectable home-made tarts and flans.

Accommodation

Siena offers hotels for all pockets and tastes. However, demand is fairly consistent throughout the year, so book in advance.

Expensive

Certosa di Maggiano

Via di Certosa 82 (28 81 80/fax 28 81 89). **Rates** *single* L450,000; *double* L500-1,300,000. **Credit** AmEx, DC, EC, MC, V.
Located just outside Siena on the south side, this thoroughly classy 4-star establishment in a beautifully converted monastery has all the advantages of a country residence (including gardens, a pool and tennis courts) while remain-

ing within a stone's throw of the city. Don't be surprised if the staff make you feel you're privileged to be staying here.

Jolly Hotel Excelsior
Piazza La Lizza 1 (28 84 48/fax 41 272). **Rates** *single* L195-250,000; *double* L275-400,000. **Credit** AmEx, DC, EC, MC, V.
Also a 4-star hotel, yet everything that the Certosa di Maggiano isn't: brash, hideously decorated in the worst of '70s taste, but friendly and central.

Moderate

Antica Torre
Via Fieravecchia 7 (tel/fax 22 22 55). **Rates** (breakfast L10,000) *single* L95-115,000; *double* L120-160,000. **Credit** AmEx, EC, MC, V.
This delightful little hotel near Porta Romana is a gift at the price. Pleasant management, just eight rooms and guaranteed peace. Make sure you book.

Pensione Palazzo Ravizza
Pian dei Mantellini 34 (28 04 62/fax 22 15 97). **Rates** *double without bathroom* L100-180,000; *double with bathroom* L120-215,000. **Credit** AmEx, EC, MC, V.
Thirty recently refurbished rooms with fine views over Siena, beautiful gardens and an excellent in-house restaurant are just three reasons why this place is such good value. The location is to the left of Piazza delle Due Porte as you head away from the centre. As you set out in the morning, pop into the nearby Chiesa del Carmine to admire *St Michael Driving out the Rebel Angels*, a masterpiece by the Sienese Mannerist painter Domenico Beccafumi (1486-1551).

Santa Caterina
Via ES Piccolomini 7 (22 11 05/fax 27 10 87). **Rates** (breakfast L15,000) *single* L130-150,000; *double* L170-200,000. **Credit** AmEx, DC, EC, MC, V.
Just outside the walls beyond Porta Romana, a friendly, unpretentious hotel run by Christian (Irish) and Ingrid (German). The 19 rooms are perfectly pleasant, although those on the road-side can be rather noisy. Nice garden.

Cheap

Alex
Via G Gigli 5 (28 23 38). **Rates** *double* L100-138,000. **Credit** V.
Comfortable, small, family-run hotel located just outside Porta Pispini. The place has a friendly atmosphere and features amazing bathrooms, plonked like portacabins in the middle of the bedrooms. Breakfast included.

Lea
Viale XXIV Maggio 10 (28 32 07). **Rates** *single without bathroom* L50-65,000; *double* L95-105,000. **No credit cards**.
Slightly down-at-heel, but well located and quiet, with good views of the Duomo.

Piccolo Hotel Il Palio
Piazza del Sale 19 (28 11 31/fax 28 11 42). **Rates** (breakfast L8,000) *single* L60-120,000; *double* L75-150,000. **No credit cards**.
Conveniently located just up the road from the railway station, a stone's throw from the central square La Lizza. A bit noisy on the street-side.

Shopping

Siena's main street is Via di Città, which branches into two just above Il Campo: Banchi di Sotto heads downwards, and Banchi di Sopra climbs

gradually up to Piazza della Posta. All are lined with fine shops, but what makes Banchi di Sopra so special is that it is also the focus of the late-morning and early-evening passeggiata.

Atelier Fotografico N. 107
Via di Città 107 (28 54 98). **Open** 9.10am-1pm, 3.40-7.30pm, Mon-Fri; 9.10am-1pm Sat. **Credit** DC, EC, MC, V.
Usual photographic services, plus the unusual: they will also carefully develop and print black and white film by hand.

L'Enoteca di San Domenico
Via del Paradiso 56 (27 11 81). **Open** 9am-8pm daily. **Credit** AmEx, DC, EC, MC, V.
Discerning and obliging Francesco Bonfio has selected some truly fine wines, spirits, speciality foods and typical sweetmeats. Most are Tuscan. He is happy to arrange delivery.

Ghini
Via dei Montanini 45/47 (46 323). **Open** *21 June-15 Sept* 9.30am-1pm, 4-8pm, Mon-Fri; 9.30am-1pm Sat. *16 Sept-20 June* 3.30-7.30pm Mon; 9.30am-1pm, 3.30-7.30pm, Tue-Sat. **Credit** AmEx, DC, EC, MC, V.
A smart but friendly outfitters for women and men. Classic Italian good taste with an emphasis on cut and quality fabrics. Worth a visit anyway, but especially if you're looking for something that will still look good a few years hence.

Libreria Feltrinelli
Via Banchi di Sopra 64/66 & 52 (44 009/fax 27 02 75). **Open** 9am-7.30pm Mon-Sat. **Credit** AmEx, DC, EC, MC, V.
This is part of a nationwide chain of quality bookstores (*see also chapter* **Florence: Shopping**). No. 64/66 has an academic slant; no. 52, is strong on art, architecture, Tuscanography, languages and foreign paperbacks.

Libreria Senese
Via di Città 62/64/66 (28 08 45/fax 28 03 53). **Open** 9am-8pm Mon-Sat. **Credit** AmEx, DC, EC, MC, V.
A family-run general bookshop with plenty on local art and history, including publications in English. This is the place to come if you're feeling a bit frazzled, are short of time and could do with some advice.

Morbidi
Via Banchi di Sopra 75 (28 02 68). **Open** 8.15am-1.15pm, 5-8pm, Mon-Fri; 8.15am-1.15pm Sat. **No credit cards**.
Sienese gastronomy at its best. A wide range of products, many of them made by the Morbidi family: ravioli, tortellini, gnocchi, savoury mousses, pâtés, superb cheeses from the Salcis dairies at Monteriggioni, typical Tuscan cold meats including fennel-spiked *finocchiona*, *prosciutto crudo* and *capocollo (see chapter* **Tuscan Food***)*.

La Nuova Pasticceria di Iasevoli
Via Duprè 37 (41 319). **Open** closed Sunday afternoon and Mondays, open 8am to 12.30pm, 5pm to 7.30pm. **No credit cards**.
Typical Sienese baked confectionary such as *cantuccini, pan dei santi* (bread with raisins and walnuts: an All Saints' Day speciality made between 30 September and 5 November), *cavallucci* (bread-like dry buns spiced with aniseed), *panforte* and *ricciarelli* (soft almond biscuits). First class ingredients used to their best effect.

Ricci Ottica
Via Banchi di Sopra 34 (28 08 59). **Open** *15 June-15 Sept* 9.30am-1pm, 3-7.30pm, Mon-Fri; 9.30am-1pm Sat. *16 Sept-14 June* 3-7.30pm Mon; 9.30am-1pm, 3-7.30pm, Tue-Sat. **Credit** AmEx, DC, EC, MC, V.
The best array of spec frames (and shades) to be found anywhere in the city. Armani, Alain Mikli, Genny, Iceberg, Robert la Roche. A quality job from lenses to final spectacle. What's more, they speak English.

Massa-Carrara & Lucca Provinces

Marbles, mountains and Macarena.

The two northernmost provinces of Tuscany are a world apart from the rest of the region. Soft, vine-cloaked hills are here exchanged for rugged pine- and chestnut-covered mountains; those to the west, around Carrara, are the source of the purest, whitest marble in Italy. Compared to the rest of Tuscany, this is a poor area, its countryside severly depopulated: the largest town in the Lunigiana, the northernmost tip, has a population of just 11,000. Garfagnanans are know in Tuscany as good chefs, and it's more than likely that if your local sandwich shop or pizzeria back home is run by Italians, they will come from the Garfagnana. Those who make their fortunes often return; indeed, there's a smart suburb of the hilltown of Barga where the main street is locally known as the Via degli Americani.

Among the region's main pleasures are superb mountain drives and good hiking, expecially in the Orecchiella natural park. For Tuscans, the Riviera della Versilia is a major draw, yet this endless stretch of deckchairs and concrete between Viareggio and Marina di Carrara is not everyone's idea of the ideal seaside experience. The main town of Viareggio is, however, worth a stop for its fine fish restaurants, and the riotous fun of its carnival.

Accommodation is not particularly plentiful, and, although there are few visitors, in mid August you may have problems finding a room. In addition to the restaurants listed below, *see chapter* **A Tuscan Restaurant Tour**.

Viareggio & the Versilia

Viareggio is the largest and most rewarding town on the **Riviera della Versilia** – an unbroken swathe of sand, bathing establishments and traffic that stretches north from here to the border with Liguria. Further up, historic towns like **Pietrasanta** and **Massa**, which nestle at the foot of the imposing Alpi Apuane, have their seaside satellites, each of which is championed by the families that go back there year after year (the bland **Forte dei Marmi** even has a reputation as a haunt of writers and intellectuals).

But only **Viareggio** would make those not locked into a second home want to stop for more than a swim. It has done the seaside thing for long enough to be laid back about the whole business (Italy's first 'marine hospices' were set up here in the 1860s), and with its palm trees, elegant Art Nouveau villas and mega-discos, it's equally at home accommodating Florentine dowagers (complete with poodles) as spotty adolescents on the make. The town doesn't have a real centre – just a grid-plan of streets between the station and the seafront promenade, bordered to the north and south by two shady parks.

However, Viareggio's self-assurance does not always come cheap; in high season especially, hotels will generally insist on full board, and it is virtually impossible to find a stretch of beach that is not stitched up by some L15,000-a-throw *stabilmento balneare* (umbrella and lounger outfit). Out of season can be a good time to visit, especially if you come at *carnevale* time in February, when the town hosts Italy's most spectacular procession (on four consecutive Sundays: three before and one after Shrove Tuesday). The huge floats are sublimely Dante-esque affairs that often lampoon prominent politicians and media personalities.

Six kilometres south of town, just outside **Torre del Lago Puccini** (bus from Piazza d'Azeglio), Puccini fans might want to take a look at the composer's villa (*0584 34 14 45. Open 9am-noon, 3.30-6pm, daily. Admission L5,000*) on the reed-fringed shores of **Lago di Massaciuccoli**. The shallow lagoon is an important reserve for aquatic birds (which the composer delighted in shooting when stuck for an aria).

What to see

Hangar-Carnevale *top (inland) end of Via Marco Polo.* **Open** *Mar-Oct* 8am-noon, 2-5pm, Mon-Fri; 8am-noon Sat. **Admission** free.
This huge aircraft hangar is where the previous year's carnival floats, or *carri*, are stored, and where work on the following year's models takes place. The designers of the papier maché works of art command handsome sums.

Where to stay

Viareggio has over a hundred hotels, and in high season it's usually a question of taking the first available bed. Good streets to trawl for budget options are Via Vespucci, Via

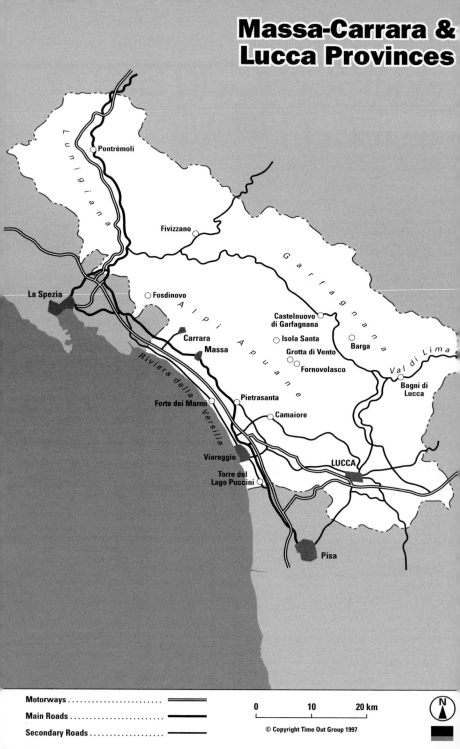

*Houses along the river Lima in the laidback spa town of **Bagni di Lucca**. See page 230.*

*The **Ponte delle Maddalena** over the river Serchio near Borgo a Mozzano. See page 230.*

Leonardo da Vinci and Via IV Novembre, which run down to the sea from the station. If you come out of season or book ahead, the following are worth a try:

Garden *Via Ugo Foscolo 70 (0584 44 025).* **Rates** *single* L125,000; *double* L180,000. **Credit** AmEx, DC, EC, MC, V.
A three-star hotel in a gloriously eclectic Liberty-style building.

Hotel Plaza et de Russie *Piazza d'Azeglio 1 (0584 44 449).* **Rates** *single* L180,000; *double* L280-350,000. **Credit** AmEx, DC, EC, MC, V.
For real *fin de siècle* luxury, try this recently refurbished 19th-century pile complete with Murano chandeliers and panoramic roof-garden.

Where to eat

La Darsena *Via Virgilio 172 (0584 39 27 85).* **Open** lunch Mon; lunch & dinner Tue-Sat. **Average** L35,000 (lunch); L45,000 (dinner). **No credit cards.**
Near the port, this restaurant offers classic seafood cooking at reasonable prices, particularly at lunchtime when the majority of customers are shipyard workers. The huge selection of *antipasti*, such as mussels stuffed with minced veal, is superb. The atmosphere is more refined in the evening. (*See also chapter* **A Tuscan Restaurant Tour**.)

Dino *Via Battisti 35/7 (0584 96 20 53).* **Open** noon-2.30pm, 4-11pm, Fri-Wed. **Average** L10,000. **No credit cards.**
A good all-purpose joint halfway between the station and the seafront that combines sit-down trattoria service with takeaway pizza, focaccia and *cecina* (chickpea flan).

Gelateria Mario *Via Petrolini 1 (0584 96 13 49).* **Open** 11am-midnight Tue-Sun. **No credit cards.**
The best ice-cream in town: try their *funghetto*, a mushroom-shaped creation with a *gianduia* cap and a frozen cream stem.

Romano
Via Mazzini 122 (0584 31 382). **Open** lunch & dinner Tue-Sun. **Average** L90,000. **Credit** AmEx, DC, EC, MC, V.
One of the best places to try excellent fresh fish.

The Garfagnana

Bagni di Lucca

One of the pleasantest places to base yourself in the Garfagnana is Bagni di Lucca, a pretty little spa town meandering up the narrow verdant lower reaches of the Val di Lima. The therapeutic qualities of its saline and sulphurous waters had been known since the 12th century, but it was in the early 19th century that it really came into its own. Napoleon's sister, Elisa Bonaparte Bacciochi, Grand Duchess of Tuscany, had a summer house here (now the Hotel Roma), and in her wake followed most of the literary alumni of 19th-century Europe: including Shelley, Byron, Browning (who recommended it as a holiday spot to Tennyson) and Heine (who, befuddled by the cult of the picturesque, thought the mountains far more agreeable than the "bizarre and Gothic" ranges of Germany). Once Napoleon had fallen, his sister's place at Bagni was taken by Grand Duke Carlo Ludovico, under whose reign Europe's first licensed casino – and birthplace of roulette – opened in 1837. Two years later, Bagni's less raffish Brits were able to pray for the souls of their gambling brethren at a neo-Gothic church built by Giuseppe Pardini.

If you want to take a spa bath go to the **Terme di Bagni di Lucca** nearby in Bagni Caldi (*0583 87 221. Open 8am-1pm Mon-Sat; also Sun in summer. Prices from L20,000*). The best place to stay is the **Hotel Roma**, Via Umberto I 110 (*0583 87 278. Rates double L70,000*). The former villa of Elisa Bachiocci, it's a marvellously old-fashioned place (Toscanini and Puccini both stayed) with lots of ancient permanent residents, and a pretty garden at the back. For eating, don't miss **La Maiola** (*see chapter* **A Tuscan Restaurant Tour**). In late July and early August Bagni hosts an opera festival, which gives recent graduates a chance to work under the direction of big name professionals.

Eight kilometres south of Bagni, spanning the Serchio near to Borgo a Mozzano, is the exaggeratedly arched **Ponte delle Maddalena** (sometimes known as the Ponte del Diavola, 'Devil's Bridge'). It was built in the 11th century by (according to local legend) Beelzebub himself in return for the soul of the first person to cross it. The canny locals sent over a dog.

Val di Lima

The Val di Lima is one of the wilder outposts of Tuscany, its roads – some of them unmade – passing through remote stone hamlets in dramatic mountain settings like **Pieve di Controne**, named for an ancient church with odd, pagan-looking geometric symbols on its façade. From Montefegatesi a rough road leads to the spectacular **Orrido di Botri**, a gorge at the foot of the almost 2,000m-high **Alpe Tre Potenze**, and on to San Cassiano, named for its 13th-century Pisan style church. Beyond, at Scesta, the minor road joins the S12.

Barga

Barga is a walled and gated hilltown of little Renaissance palaces and tangled, arched streets, dominated by an 11th-century cathedral. Modern development has been channelled into its industrial suburb, Fornaci di Barga, down on the main road, and Giardino di Barga above, full of showy villas built by emigrants who returned having made their fortunes running the sandwich shops of the UK and US.

The old town is as peaceful as it ever was. The cathedral – built of a pale local stone known as albarese di Barga – stands high on a terrace with views over the town's roofs to rich green hills. The most striking feature of the interior is the pulpit, carved by Como sculptor Guido Bigarelli in the 13th century, standing on pillars supported by lions and a dwarf, the latter a symbol of crushed paganism. Around the pulpit are animated biblical scenes.

Carrara marble

Students of sculpture, hurry along. To attend the **Accademia Statale di Belle Arti di Carrara** costs a mere L300,000 a year in fees, a room in the students' hostel is L100,000 a month, and the marble, unless you want something huge, comes free. The same marble that the Romans were mining 2,000 years again. The same marble as used by Michelangelo.

It's cheaper to live in Carrara than Serravezza or Pietrasanta, the two villages further south where artists of all nations hang out. The town is filled with empty studios – the Civic Council being unsure whether it wants sculptors, with their concomitant noise and dust, in the town or not.

Carrara is a hard-working place. Ten or 15 citizens have made millions out of the marble, but you would hardly know it, as they are up in the mountains with a paper hat on their heads at six in the morning. Miners are often like that. A handshake as hard as their very own rock, and no mucking about in a business discussion.

Do their factories sully the environment unacceptably? It is easy to see when they do, as the river Carrione, running through the centre of town, turns white. A total of 85 firms along its banks have been indicted for dumping. Some people would like to see the whole stretch of river turned into a river park, *parco fluviale*, and all secretly long to see the Carrione alive with fish. The problem is slurry from the cutting machines. Although powdered marble can be used in plaster and cement, no use has been found for certain granites that are also mined.

The firms undertake extraordinary tasks.

Supposing someone asked you to clothe the centre of Abu Dhabi in marble? Or how about the largest mosque in the world? Three marble staircases 30 feet wide? A herd of marble cows, life-size, for a Texan millionaire? The more complex the job, the better for the town. Cutting marble into slices and shipping them can be of benefit to one firm, but the staircases will keep three or four workshops in business for a year. Or six months. They work unbelievably quickly.

All the same, an air of crisis lies in the background. Until recently, Carrara sliced marble for everyone. Brazilian blocks would be shipped in, sliced, and shipped back to Brazil. Now, a lot of fancy machines have been sold abroad and new quarries have been opened in Asia and South America. The quarries behind the town are beginning to sell blocks, rather than cut cladding. Very profitable for he who owns the hole in the mountain whence it came, but no good for anyone else. So, at the moment, half a dozen firms make huge sums by selling blocks, while others find their order books for finished tiles diminishing every year.

In the same way, at the artistic level, one or two sculptors land commissions of mind-boggling grandeur and the rest hang on, to meet in the evenings at the local bar, where they speak of the job that got away in the same tones with which fishermen speak of trout in the Carrione.

Accademia Statale di Belle Arti di Carrara
(0585 71 658/72 252).
Giovani Industriali di Massa Carrara
Il Presidente Dott Carlo Telara, Via Carriona 263, Carrara 54033 (*fax 0585 50 198*).

There's nowhere to stay or eat in the old town – most of the restaurants and hotels are in the rather unattractive suburb of **Albiano**, just outside town.

Castelnuovo di Garfagnana & the Parco Naturale dell'Orecchiella

The main town of the Garfagnana is a busy place, with a nasty traffic junction at its centre. Despite being perched on the brink of the river Serchio and dominated by a 14th-century castle, it's not a beguiling place. Whatever you do, however, be sure to stop for a snack at the typical osteria, **Vecchio Mulino**, Via Vittorio Emanuele 12 (*0583 62 196. Open 7.30am-8pm; closed Sun. Average 10,000 for plate of cheese and glass of good wine*). Run by brother and sister Andrea and Cinzia Bertucci, it is basically a wine bar serving top notch cured meats, salamis, savoury snacks and cheeses from all over Italy and Europe.

Vecchio Mulino could also be your source for a matchless picnic, to be eaten on a hike in the Orecchiella natural park, just north of Castelnuovo. There are lots of mountain paths – marked on a map you can pick up from the visitors' centre at Orecchiella.

The Alpi Apuane

Fornovolasco & the Grotta del Vento

It's a fabulous drive through the Alpi Apuane, along roads carved out of the sides of ear-poppingly high crags above head-spinningly deep gorges. Stop at **Fornovolasco**, a tiny, semi-abandoned village crumbling by the side of a fast-flowing stream. **Rifugio La Buca** (*0583 72 20 13. Open lunch & dinner daily; closed Fri Nov-Mar. Average L25,000*), the unpromising looking ersatz alpine chalet by the stream, is a down-home place that serves a great tagliatelle with wild mushrooms and grilled brown river trout. The Rifugio also has simple rooms (*Rates single in multi-bed room L20,000; double L50,000*). Beyond Fornovolasco the road continues up to the **Grotta del Vento** (Cave of the Wind), packed, as good caves should be, with stalactites, abysses and subterranean lakes.

Via Isola Santa to Carrara

A fantastically scenic road runs from Castelnuovo through the Alpi Apuane to the coast. The first stretch is through the sombre, thickly forested Turrite Secca valley, where you could stretch your legs at Isola Santa, a miniscule village on a deep green lake where medieval outcasts once holed up. Close by are two restaurants, **Da Giacco**, on the main road, where Italian families tuck into meat and mushrooms grilled on an antique barbecue, and **La Ceregetta** (*see chapter* **A Tuscan Restaurant Tour**). As you continue, the scenery becomes more and more spectacular, with great white marble peaks, sheer forested hills and, as you get close to Carrara, milk-white marble mines carved into the hillsides.

Massa & Carrara

The two towns for which the region is named are modern, heavily trafficked, ringed with industry, and seem to form one conurbation. Marble capital Carrara, however, does have a pleasant old centre, up on a hill, centering on Piazza Alberica. Between Late July and October a sculpture festival is held here – sculptors are each given a block of marble in the centre of the piazza then told to get on with it. Not far away is the 11th-century Duomo with a typically Pisan façade, save for its intricate rose window, a 14th-century addition.

Two kilometres outside town on the road to Marina Carrara is the **Museo Civico di Marmo**, Via XX Settembre (*No phone. May-Sept 8.30am-12.30pm, 3-6pm, Mon-Fri*) a good run-through the history of marble and methods of production. *See also box.*

Pietrasanta

Pietrasanta is a sweet old town, set just back from the coast, but a world away from the regimented beach umbrellas and razzamatazz of the Versilia resorts. Until very recently, there was a vibrant artistic community here, mostly of sculptors, attracted by the area's excellent raw materials and the reputation of local craftsmanship. The bronze foundries are among the best in the world and the marble studios offer unmatched facilities. Not for nothing did Henry Moore come here to have his bronzes cast, choose his lumps of stone and have them roughed out by local craftsmen. If you want to find out about the work of local artists call **COS-MAVE** (*0585 79 12 97*).

The town used to be geared to the artistic community; prices were low and the ambience was laid back. However, Pietrasanta has become increasingly popular with very un-alternative Italian holidaymakers who have pushed prices up, and driven many of the artists away. Although the atmosphere is still easy-going, the town has a split personality and has lost some of its appeal, but the central Piazza del Duomo, whose 13th-century cathedral has a rose window carved from a single piece of marble as its *pièce de resistance*, is still a pleasant spot. Up the hill is the old citadel, the Rocca Arrighina, a 14th-century Castruccio Castracani construction.

For refreshment, try an *aperitivo* (a 'Bersagliere' white wine with a dash of Campari is the local poison) and lunchtime sandwich at **Bar Iris** (*0338 83 66 464. Closed Sat*), where the *panini* are particularly good, **Bar Michelangelo** (*0584 70 061. Closed Tue*) on the opposite side of the Piazza or the elegant **Bar Teatro** (*0584 72 050. Closed Sun*). For a meal, the **Gatto Nero** (*0584 70 135.Open lunch & dinner daily. Average L35,000*) in Piazza Carducci, just outside the town walls, serves interestingly prepared local food. An alternative is the **Pizzeria Betty** (*0584 71 247. Open from 8am-11pm; closed Mon*) in Piazza Duomo where you can eat in or take away delicious pizza by the slice or whole. If you want to stay in Pietrasanta, **Hotel Palagi** (*0584 70 249. Rates single L95,000; double L150,000*) is near the station. In the summer, sculpture exhibitions are mounted in Piazza Duomo or in the Sant' Agostino cloister of the **Museo dei Bozzetti** (*0584 79 11 22. Open July & Aug 6-8pm, 9pm-midnight Tue-Sun*).

The Lunigiana

Fivizzano

Fivizzano is a fine old town built around a medieval square named Piazza Medicea after the guys who whipped it from the Malaspina of Massa (who owned all the Carrara marble mines) in the 16th century and ringed the town with walls. In the centre of the square is a fountain donated by the Medici, and nearby are a couple of Florentine-style palaces. There's a refreshingly old-fashioned atmosphere to Fivizzano, almost totally untouched by tourism. If you fancy staying here, join the retired military types and ageing contessas at the wonderfully eccentric **Hotel Il Giardinetto**, Via Roma 151 (*0585 92 060. Rates single L35,000; double L60,000. Restaurant open lunch & dinner Tue-Sun; daily July-Sept. Average L35,000*). See *also chapter* **A Tuscan Restaurant Tour**.

Just to the northeast of Fivizzano is the delightfully named **Castello di Verrucula Bosi**, occupied by various feudal families over the years. It was rebuilt in the 14th century by the Malaspina after macho warlord Castruccio Castracani (*see chapter* **Lucca**) all but destroyed it.

Fosdinovo

Fosdinovo is a fortified medieval village close to the border with Liguria, dominated by a **castle** whose walls of rock rise sheer from a grassy cypress-spiked spur. Built by the Malaspina, its date is uncertain, but Dante is believed to have visited in 1306, and to have slept in a minute room with a Pietà and Malaspina crusader frescoed on its wall. The **castle** (*0187 68 891. Open for guided tours 10am, 11am, noon, 4pm, 5pm, 6pm Wed-Mon. Admission L6,000; children L3,000*) houses an eclectic little museum of arms and armour, ceramics and folksy bric-a-brac.

Pontrémoli

Pontrémoli, the biggest town of the Lunigiana – though it has fewer than 11,000 inhabitants stands at the confluence of the Magra and Verde rivers, among the chestnut-rich foothills of the Apennines. The loveliest quarter is the medieval warren north of the 14th-century Torre del Campanone, built by Castruccio Castracani to keep the rival factions of the town in check, and now serving as a campanile for the incongruously Baroque duomo.

The main reason to visit is to see the weird collection of prehistoric stele in the **Museo del Comune** housed in the austere 14th-century Castello di Pignaro. Dating from between 3000 and 200 BC, the earliest (3000-2000BC) are rectangular blocks with a rough curve for a head, a U for a face, no shoulders, and arms barely discernible from the body; steles from the second stage (2000-800BC) have spade-shaped heads, dot eyes and nose, and a smile; the latest (800-200BC) have more detailed features and are usually shown carrying a weapon in each hand. One theory is that the heads symbolised heaven, the arms and weapons the earth and the lower part, buried in the ground, the underworld. It has also been pointed out that Virgil described the Gauls who invaded Lazio as carrying two weapons.

There are a couple of good places to eat in Pontrémoli. **Locanda Bacciottini**, Via Ricci Armani 4 (*0187 83 01 20. Open July-end Sept lunch & dinner daily; Oct-June lunch & dinner Tue-Sat; lunch Sun. Average L40,000*) is the sort of place where time seems to have frozen. Try the home-made antipasti, *testaroli*, a local pasta served with pesto, roast meats, wild mushrooms and *necci*, chestnut flour pancakes stuffed with ricotta and drizzled with honey. The other is the equally old-fashioned **Bussè**, Piazza Duomo 31 (*0187 83 13 71. Open lunch Mon-Thur; lunch & dinner Sat, Sun. Average L45,000*). Antipasti include local salamis and *torte di erbe*, a kind of quiche made of wild greens and herbs, *testaroli* and *tortelloni di ricotta; secondi* are mostly meats (including good rabbit); for pud, have *spongata*, a sweet pastry stuffed with dried fruit and chocolate. Wines are all local. Accommodation is available at the **Hotel Napoleon**, Piazza Italia 2b (*0187 83 05 44. Rates single L70,000; double L120,000*).

Lucca

With a turbulent past and a somnolent present, Lucca is one of Tuscany's most fascinating, satisfying yet least known cities.

If ever a place were more than a sum of its parts, it's Lucca. There are fine buildings, but nothing to compare with Pisa's Campo dei Miracoli; it has some decent art, but only a pale shadow of Florence's riches; the city is undeniably attractive, yet Siena is, in truth, more spectacular. So what's the draw?

Defined, protected and insulated by its marvellous 16th-17th-century walls, Lucca is a time capsule – as sane, civilised and well ordered a city as you could wish for. There's a perpetual Sunday air to the place, and no pleasure is as great as simply strolling its quiet streets and elegant squares, gazing into Art Nouveau shopfronts on Via Fillungo, sipping a cappuccino and people-watching on lively Piazza San Michele, soaking up the atmosphere in Piazza dell'Anfiteatro, which retains the shape of the city's original Roman amphitheatre.

Lucca is a state of mind. A rather conservative state of mind perhaps (other Italians joke about how Lucca's walls mirror the minds around the minds of its inhabitants), but this is all to the benefit of the visitor. Despite the city being easily accessible from the other major Tuscan centres, only a fraction of the tourist buses that hurtle between Florence and Pisa bother to make the short detour to Lucca. The result is a place where tourism is no novelty but is perfectly controlled; the Lucchese like their peace and know how to keep it. Accommodation is scarce, so relatively few visitors stay overnight; cars are a rarity within the walls, so visitors have the luxury of being able to wander the streets with only the worry of being mown down by a demon cyclist (bikes being, uniquely in Italy, the favoured mode of transportation). A classic case of less is more.

Of course, there are memorable sights that shouldn't be missed – the stupendous façade of San Michele, the cathedral, mosaic-clad San Frediano, the view from the Torre Guinigi, the walls, Piazza dell'Anfiteatro – but this is a city to be absorbed rather than gawped at, to be ambled around rather than rushed through. If you allow less than a full day to visit, you will not fully appreciate Lucca.

Some history

The city's origins are ancient and somewhat obscure, but there was probably a Ligurian and then an Etruscan town on the site. By Roman

The phone code for Lucca is **0583**

times, it was certainly an important settlement, far outshining upstart Florence. In 56BC Caesar, Pompey and Crassus met at Lucca to form the first triumvirate. After Rome toppled and fell, Lucca recovered remarkably quickly, becoming the capital of the Lombards' Tuscia and then of the Frankish Margravate of Tuscany in the 9th century. When the Margravate collapsed 300 years later, independent Lucca entered its period of greatest prosperity as a wealthy silk-producing town – most of its fine Romanesque churches date from the self-confident 12th and 13th centuries. Yet the growing power of neighbouring cities, particularly Pisa and Florence, and the destructive Guelph/Ghibelline conflict (*see chapter* **History: Tuscany in the Middle Ages**) threatened to

The wedding cake façade of **San Michele**.

crush Lucca. In the early 14th century the spirited adventurer Castruccio Castracani (*see box*) earned the city a brief respite, but thereafter a slow process of decline set in. Remarkably, though, Lucca retained its independent status until 1805. A period of revitalising rule followed under Napoleon's sister, and then his widow, and then a spell under the house of Lorraine, before the city joined the united Italy in 1860.

Lucca's relative latter-day obscurity has much to do with its current low-key charm and wonderful state of preservation. The quiet pursuit of wealth is the primary concern of today's Lucchese, and the city still fully lives up to Hilaire Belloc's description as, "the neatest, the regularest, the exactest, the most fly-in-amber little town in the world, with its uncrowded streets, its absurd fortifications, and its contented silent houses – all like a family at ease and at rest under its high sun".

Sights

Churches

Cattedrale di San Martino

Piazza San Martino (95 70 68). **Open** *summer* 7am-6.30pm daily; *winter* 7am-5pm daily. **Admission** (Tomb of Ilaria del Carretto) L3,000.

The façade of Lucca's cathedral is a marvel of assymetry. Dating from the early 13th century, it abuts the 11th century campanile (the top two stages of which were added 200 years later). In order to accommodate the campanile, its architects had to miss out a couple of arches of the colonnaded arcades and make the third arch of the porch considerably smaller than the other two. None of this detracts from the charm of **Guido da Como**'s three-tier collonades with their individual stripey, swirling and carved columns or from the magnificent 12th- and 13th-century sculptures. The fine reliefs over the left doorway of the *Deposition* and *Adoration* of the Magi are probably early works by **Nicola Pisano**. The statue of St Martin, dividing his cloak with his sword to share with a beggar, is a copy – the original is inside the cathedral.

The rather gloomy interior is a mecca for fans of **Matteo Civitali** (*see box*). His most famous work is the octagonal marble *tempietto* on the left side of the nave, home to the highly venerated **Volto Santo** image of the crucified Christ. Legend has it that this captivatingly mournful wooden carving was started by Nicodemus and finished by an angel; it miraculously floated across to Italy and found itself in Lucca in the 8th century. It had a particularly keen following in medieval England – King William Rufus used to swear by it, *per vultum sanctum di Lucca*. Every year on 13 September, the Volto Santo is dressed up in various golden garments (very uncomfortable it looks in them too) and paraded around the town.

Wrestling with the Volto Santo for the honours of top attraction is the tomb of **Ilaria del Carretto**. This marble sarcophagus (currently in the Sacristy while its usual home in the left transept is being restored) is the earliest known work and masterpiece of Sienese sculptor **Jacopo della Quercia**. Ilaria, second wife of Lucchese bossman Paolo Guinigi, died in 1405, and lies in an attitude of sublime peace on tasselled cushions while her faithful dog crouches at her feet looking devotedly up at his mistress. Considering Lucca's relative paucity of great art, San Martino's other treasures include works by a more than respectable handful of big names, including the late 16th-century *Altar of Liberty*

by Giambologna, a *Last Supper* by Tintoretto, a *Madonna and Saints* altarpiece by Ghirlandaio (in the Sacristy) and a *Madonna and Child* by Fra Bartolomeo.

San Cristoforo

Via Fillungo.

A deconsecrated 13th-century church that is now part exhibition hall and part war memorial – the names of Lucca's war dead are inscribed on the walls.

San Francesco

Via della Quarquonia.

This barn-like church was largely rebuilt in the 14th century (although the upper part of the façade wasn't completed until 1930). Inside are some good 15th-century frescoes and the tombs of **Castruccio Castracani** *(see box)* and the Lucchese composer **Luigi Boccherini** (1743-1805). But you'll have to take all that on trust as the church is currently closed for that ominously open-ended Italian process of "long-term restoration".

San Frediano

Piazza San Frediano. **Open** 7.30am-noon, 3-6pm, daily; 9am-1pm, 3-6pm, public hols.

The glittering 13th-century mosaic façade of San Frediano is unique among Lucchese churches. Possibly the work of **Berlinghiero Berlinghieri**, it depicts Jesus enthroned in heaven over a gaggle of gesticulating apostles. The church itself was constructed in the early 12th century in honour of the Irish monk (also known as Frigidianus) who came to Italy on a pilgrimage and liked it so much he decided to stay. In 566, Frediano was elected bishop of Lucca and was responsible for an important reorganisation of the church in the city – as well as (allegedly) miraculously diverting the River Serchio to save Lucca from floods. On the right as you enter the spacious interior is an extraordinary mid-12th-century font in the form of a mini-tempietto, sculpted with biblical stories, over a fountain. Other gems in San Frediano include an altarpiece and tomb slabs by **Jacopo della Quercia** in the *Cappella Trenta* (fourth chapel on the right), a polychrome wooden figure by **Matteo Civitali** and a lunette by **Andrea della Robbia** behind the font. Best of all are the early 16th-century frescoes by **Amico Aspertini** in the second chapel on the left, detailing incidents from the lives of St Augustine and St Frediano, as well as the arrival of the Volto Santo in Lucca.

San Giovanni e Reparata

Via del Duomo. **Open** *June-Sept* 10am-6pm Tue-Sun; *Oct-May* 10am-1pm, 3-6pm, Tue-Sun. **Admission** L5,000 or L7,000 (with Museo della Cattedrale); L2,000 for excavations.

Lucca's original cathedral of San Giovanni dates from the 12th century, although there has been a church on the site since at least the 5th century. Extensive interior renovations and excavations have revealed fascinating traces from several periods of building, including a 1st-century Roman house, a paleo-Christian church of the 4th-5th century, 6th-7th century Lombard tombs, a 9th-century crypt and a 12th-century baptistry and baptismal font. It's worth paying the extra to explore the spooky excavations which stretch below the church, particularly if you can do so alone. Look out for the brick kilns used during the construction of the present church. Above ground, the splendid 14th-century baptistry roof and frescoes attributed to Giuliano di Simone are worth a look.

Santa Maria Corteorlandini

Piazza Giovanni Leonardi.

After the plain, grey interiors of so many of Lucca's churches, the Baroque explosion of Santa Maria Corteorlandini couldn't be a greater contrast. The apse and south side of the 12th-century church survive but the rest is a 17th-century reconstruction with masses of coloured marble, gold and trompe l'oeil frescoes. The purpose of all this splendour being, as the leaflet available in the church helpfully explains, to bring "...to a full fruition the manifold allusive potentialities linked to the iconographic language which becomes a transcription of the mystery in readable page and as original catechesis of that may not be said". So now you know.

Santa Maria Forisportam

Piazza Santa Maria Forisportam.
The name of this 12th-century church refers to when it stood just outside the town walls. To many people, it isn't Lucca's most thrilling ecclesiastical monument, but for **John Ruskin** its simple, harmonious proportions and quality of workmanship were a revelation. He considered Santa Maria Forisportam as the starting point for his study of architecture – "...for the first time I now saw what medieval builders were and what they meant." Inside, the church has that grey, damp, breezeblock-look that makes so many of Lucca's churches disconcertingly gloomy after their light, playful façades. If you visit at the right time of year, however, you can enjoy an ingenious nativity scene which slowly changes from night to day at the flick of a switch.

San Michele in Foro

Piazza San Frediano. **Open** 7.30am-12.30pm, 3-6pm, daily.
Built between the 12th and 14th centuries, San Michele's multi-tiered, arcaded façade is a masterpiece of the Lucchese take on Pisan Romanesque, and one of the town's most memorable sights. There's an uplifting playfulness and lightness of touch in the diverse columns; some geometrically patterned, some swirling spirals, some resembling totem poles carved with writhing beasts. Not all are different (as is commonly claimed) – see if you can spot the duplicates. It's also fun identifying the animals gambolling along the spandrels

The sprouting **Torre Guinigi**. *See page 238.*

over the arches, and also the anachronistic heads above some columns (Garibaldi, Cavour et al) which were added during a 19th-century renovation. The top two levels, crowned by a rather stiff Saint Michael vanquishing the dragon, front only air; funds for a higher nave having dried up in the 14th century. The plain grey, underground-car-park-like interior comes as a shock. To the right as you enter is a weathered *Madonna and Child* by Civitali that once stood outside on the right-hand corner of the church (the statue outside is a copy). The most notable painting is **Filippino Lippi**'s fine *Saints Helena, Jerome, Sebastian and Roch* in the right transept. The church stands on the site of the old Roman forum, hence its full name.

San Paolino

Via San Paolino.
Just down the road from his house, the young **Puccini** often tinkled the ivories of the organ in San Paolino. This sombre, early 16th-century church is dedicated to Lucca's patron saint and (supposed) first bishop, believed to have been sent from Antioch to Lucca by the apostle Peter in AD65. However, it's likely that this St Paulinus (probably fictional) has been confused with the same name; his remains are kept in a tiny sarcophagus behind the altar. Look out for an unusual 14th-century painting, *The Burial of St Paulinus*, in the right chapel, attributed to **Angelo Puccinelli**; a 15th-century Florentine *Coronation of the Virgin* over a view of Lucca in the left chapel; and a splendid 13th-century French stone statue of the *Virgin and Child*.

San Pietro Somaldi

Piazza San Pietro Somaldi.
Named after its original 8th-century builder, Sumuald, the church was reconstructed from the 12th to the 14th centuries. The relief around the door is by **Guido da Como** and studio (1203) and the façade's two layers of delicate arcading and columns date from 1248. On the left wall as you enter is perhaps the most arresting painting in the plain interior – *Saints Anthony Abbot, Bartholomew, Francis, Domenic and Andrew*, attributed to **Raffaellino del Garbo**.

Santa Trinità

Via Santa Croce.
The most notable features of this little church is **Matteo Civitali**'s drop-dead gorgeous, droopy-eyed *Madonna della Tosse* ('Madonna of the Cough' – invoke her to bring relief), and the delightful resident nun who will happily rabbit on to you for hours, even when you make it clear you don't speak Italian.

Museums

Casa Natale di Giacomo Puccini

Corte San Lorenzo 9, off Via di Poggio (58 40 28).
Open *15 Mar-30 June, 1 Sept-15 Nov*, 10am-1pm, 3-6pm, Tue-Sun; *July, Aug* 10am-1pm, 3-7pm, Tue-Sun; *16 Nov-31 Dec* 10am-1pm Tue-Sun; closed *1 Jan-14 Mar* except for pre-booked groups of 15 or more (call *34 16 12*).
Admission L5,000; L3,000 under-10s.
The birthplace of Lucca's most famous son has been converted into a delightful museum. Puccini was the last of a dynasty of composer/musicians who dominated the Lucchese musical scene for 150 years. He lived in this spacious flat with his extended family from his birth in 1858 until he left to further his musical studies in Milan. The museum displays a choice selection of Pucciniabilia (and plays Giacomo's greatest hits as background music) including his overcoat, the original manuscripts of his *Mass for Four Voices* and *Symphonie Caprice*, the piano on which he knocked out *Turandot* in 1924 and the lavish costume worn for the Metropolitan Opera's 1926 production of the opera by soprano Maria Jeritza. An English guide is available

Useful information

Tourist information

Azienda di Promozione Turistica (APT) *Vecchia Porta San Donato, Piazzale Giuseppe Verdi (tel/fax 41 96 89).* **Open** 9am-7pm daily. *Piazza Guidiccioni 2 (49 12 05/6).* **Open** 10am-noon Mon-Sat.

Guides To arrange your own personal guide to Lucca call one of the following guide companies: **Idea** *(49 05 30),* **La Giunchiglia** *(34 16 12)* or **Turis-Lucca** *(34 24 04).*

Wine Tours The Colline Lucchesi and Montecarlo wine regions around Lucca may be little known outside Italy but they produce some remarkably good wines. Most can be visited if telephoned in advance. A leaflet, *Le Vie del Vino in Lucchesia,* is available at the tourist office which lists many of the makers and gives phone numbers.

Lost Property *c/o Commune di Lucca, Ufficio Economato, Via C Battisti 10 (44 23 88).*

Telephones *Telecom Italia, Via Cenami 19 (between Piazza San Giusto and Via Fillungo).* Several public phones plus a machine to buy phone cards.

Transport

Airport *Tassignano (93 60 62).*

Bicycle Hire – Barbetti, *Via Anfiteatro 23 (95 44 44).* **Poli Antonio,** *Piazza Santa Maria 42 (49 37 87).* The largest concentration of bike hire shops is in Piazza Santa Maria by the northern gate. Standard hire rate is L4,000 per hour, L20,000 per day; L10,000 per hour for a tandem.

Bus Station *Piazzale Guiseppe Verdi.* CLAP buses to towns in Lucca province *(58 78 97).* LAZZI buses to Florence, Pistoia, Pisa, Prato, Abetone, Bagni di Lucca, Montecatini and Viareggio *(58 48 76).* At least one bus an hour leaves Florence for Lucca (first: 5.58am, last: 8.15pm) and from Lucca to Florence (first: 6.25am, last: 7.45pm). Journey takes from an hour and three quarters to two and a quarter hours.

Car Hire – Pittore (Eurodollar), *Piazza Santa Maria 34 (47 960/44 11 05).*

Parking *within the town walls* blue line: pay for maximum of 3 hours; white line: free for maximum of 1½ hours; yellow line: free for residents or with hotel permission.

Railway Station *Piazza Ricasoli (47 013).* The station is two minutes' walk from the southern gate, Porta San Pietro. Trains from Florence to Viareggio stop at Lucca (as well as Prato and Pistoia). The 78-km (50-mile) journey takes about an hour and 15 minutes, with trains leaving almost every hour from 7.40am to 10.10pm, usually at around 20 minutes to the hour.

Taxis *Piazza Napoleone (49 26 91); Railway Station (49 49 89).*

Markets & festivals

Markets Every Wednesday and Saturday a **general market** (selling clothes, food, flowers and household goods) stretches the length of Via dei Bacchettoni by the eastern wall. On the third weekend of every month a major **antiques market** fills the Piazza San Martino and surrounding streets. A **craft market,** *arti e mestieri,* sets up in the Piazza San Giusto on the last weekend of the month.

Festivals
Stagione Teatrale at Teatro del Giglio (Jan-Mar).
Santa Zita Flower Show and Market (4 days end Apr) in Piazza Anfiteatro and Piazza San Frediano.
Villas in Bloom Festival (last 10 days of May) – garden festival at Villas Mansi, Torrigiani, Bruguier, Reale, Grabau and Oliva.
Palio di San Paolino (12 July - or is it a Sat?);
Luminara di Santa Croce (13 Sept) – procession of the Volto Santo.
Settembre Lucchese (Sept, Oct) – cultural, religious and sporting events.
International Film Festival *(0584 68 75 330)* (Sept, Oct).
Stagione Lirica at Teatro del Giglio (Sept, Oct).
Natale Anfiteatro (Dec) – market of regional products and specialities.

Emergency services

Ambulance *(49 233/49 49 02/47 713).*
Carabinieri *(112).*
Police *(113).*
Fire Brigade *(115).*
"Campo di Marte" Hospital, *Via dell'Ospedale (97 01).*

---

although there are no translations of the various articles and letters on display.

Museo della Cattedrale

Via Arcivescovado (49 05 30). **Open** *Apr-Oct* 9.30am-6pm daily; *Nov-Apr* 10am-1pm, 3pm-6pm, daily. **Admission** L5,000 or L7,000 (including San Giovanni).
A fine conversion has created this light, airy, brick-and-beam museum of treasures from the cathedral. The strikingly presented exhibits are something of a mixed bag – a bishop's gown here, a carpet there – but there are gems worth seeking out, such as the figure of *John the Evangelist* by **Jacopo della Quercia,** a *Madonna and Child with Saints* (featuring a hand-jiving Jesus) by **Vincenzo Frediani** and an exquisite 13th-century Limoges casket showing three knights hacking at St Thomas Becket.

Museo Nazionale di Palazzo Mansi

Via Galli Tassi 43 (55 570). **Open** 9am-7pm Tue-Sat; 9am-2pm Sun, public hols. **Admission** L8,000; free for EC citizens under 18 and over 60.

A motley collection of Italian paintings are displayed in this 16th-17th-century palazzo. Highlights (and there aren't, in truth, that many) are a very dark *St Sebastian* by **Luca Giordano,** three (remarkably similar) battle scenes by **Salvator Rosa** and a Medici gallery which includes Cosimo I in armour by **Agnolo Tori** and the bastard (in both senses of the word) Alessandro de' Medici, looking misleadingly butter-wouldn't-melt-ish. There are also a couple of evocative portraits of **Puccini.** The lavishly decorated rooms are a sight in the themselves, particularly the frescoed *Salone del Ballo,* and a bridal suite that adds several new dimensions to the term Baroque excess.

Museo Nazionale di Villa Guinigi

Via della Quarquonia (49 60 33). **Open** 9am-7pm Tue-Sat; 9am-1.30pm Sun. **Admission** L4,000; free to EC citizens over 60.
Built by Paolo Guinigi at the height of his power in 1418, this hefty villa contains a varied collection of architectural finds, art and sculpture from the Lucca region. The ground

The serene, statue-filled garden of the **Palazzo Pfanner**.

floor is largely devoted to Bronze Age, Etruscan and Roman knick-knacks, including reconstructed Ligurian tombs. The high, beamed ceilings of the upstairs rooms provide a fine setting for most of the museum's paintings. Among the most notable works are several 13th-century painted crucifixes, a lovely **Matteo Civitali** *Annunciation* and two splendid **Fra Bartolomeo**s. Don't miss **Ambrogio** and **Nicolao Pucci**'s superb 16th-century intarsia panels showing views over Lucca.

Monuments

Ramparts

Lucca's 16th-17th-century ramparts are one of the town's great glories and a stroll (or bike ride) around at least part of their 4-km (2.5-mile) circumference is a must. When they were completed in 1650, these walls – 12-m high, 30-m wide at the base, and punctuated by 11 mighty bastions – represented the state-of-the-art in terms of military fortifications. Ironically, they were never tested – apart from when they saved Lucca from flood water in 1812. Not long after, the Duchess Maria Luisa earned the eternal affection of the city by declaring the walls a public park, planting them with splendid avenues of plane, holm-oak, chestnut and lime trees. Today, they are Lucca's playground; the domain of cyclists, roller-bladers, pram-pushers, romancing couples and doddering OAPs. The grassy bastions are the sites for picnics, impromptu football games and children's playgrounds.

The only spot for refreshment along the walls is the **Antico Caffè della Mura** in Piazzale Vittorio Emanuele (*see below* **Bars, Cafés & Gelaterias**). If you fancy a peek at the inside of one of the bastions, phone ahead to the **Centro Internazionale per lo Studio delle Cerchia Urbane (CISCU)** (*46 257*).

Torre Guinigi

Via Sant'Andrea (48 524). **Open** *Nov-Feb* 10am-4.30pm daily; *Mar-Sept* 9am-7.30pm daily; *Oct* 10am-6pm daily. **Admission** L4,500; L3,000 concessions.

No visitor to Lucca should pass up the chance to climb one of the city's most distinctive landmarks. Part of the 14th-century palazzo of the powerful Guinigi family, the Torre Guinigi, with its tower-top garden planted with seven scrubby holm-oaks, offers fabulous views over the city and to the hills beyond. There's not much room at the top, so try to visit at a quiet time.

Parks & gardens

Giardino Botanico

Via del Giardino Botanico (44 21 60). **Open** *Apr-Oct* 9am-1pm Tue-Sat; 9am-1pm, 2.30-6.30pm, Sun; *Nov-Mar* 9pm-1am Tue-Sat. **Admission** L5,000; children L3,500.

Tucked under the southeastern wall, the botanical gardens are planted with a cross-section of Tuscan flora and are a delightful, shady spot for a stroll.

Palazzo Pfanner

Via degli Asili 33 (48 524). **Open** *1 Mar-31 Oct* 10am-6pm daily; *1 Nov-28 Feb* by appointment. **Admission** L2,000; childen under 8 free.

The 17th-century palazzo is currently being restored but you can still admire its wonderful galleried external staircase and visit the small but perfectly formed, statue-filled, 18th-century garden. There are also good views into the garden from the ramparts.

Villa Bottini

Via Elisa (49 41 36). **Open** *gardens* 9am-1pm daily. **Admission** free.

There's not much to look at in the gardens of this 17th-century villa, but as one of the very few public green spaces within the walls, it's a good spot to rest after a hard morning church spotting. The house itself hosts exhibitions and lectures (normally free entry) and is worth a look for its ceiling frescoes.

Restaurants

Lucchese specialities to look out for include: *zuppa di magro* (thin soup without meat), *farro* (*see box*), dishes made with chestnut flour (*farina di castagne*), *agnello con olive* (lamb with olives), river trout (*trote*) from the Garfagnana, truffles and *buccellato* (a usually ring-shaped sweet bread, flavoured with aniseed and raisins, and topped with sugar syrup). The Lucchese trace the origins of the latter back to the Romans, who called the bread issued to their soldiers *bucellatum*.

Expensive

La Buca di Sant'Antonio
Via della Cervia 3 (55 881). **Open** 11am-11pm Tue-Sat; 11am-3pm Sun. **Average** L50,000. **Credit** AmEx, DC, EC, MC, V.
Booking is essential at this justly famed restaurant. There's been a hostelry on the site for more than 200 years, and La Buca's menus is an agreeable mix of the classic and the contemporary. Look out for signature dishes such as the rich *papardelle alla lepre* (with hare), the memorable spit-roasted kid (*capretto*) and *minestra di farro alle garfagnana* (vegetable soup with *farro* from the Garfagnana – *see box*). The *menu turistico* is excellent value at L30,000.

La Mora
Via Sesto di Moriano 1748, Sesto di Moriano (40 64 02). **Open** noon-2.30pm, 7.30-10pm, Thur-Tue. **Average** L60,000. **Credit** AmEx, DC, EC, MC, V.
Sauro Brunicardi's superb restaurant, located in an old posthouse to the north of Lucca, is one of the region's finest. The cooking centres on Lucchese specialities – you'll find no finer *minestra di farro* anywhere. Eating al fresco in fine weather is a delight.

Puccini
Corte San Lorenzo 1/2, off Piazza Cittadella (31 61 16). **Open** 12.30-4.30pm, 7pm-1am Mon, Thur-Sun; 7pm-1am Wed. **Average** L60,000. **Credit** AmEx, DC, EC, MC, V.
Seafood is not easy to find on restaurant menus in Lucca, but this upmarket newcomer has already established a reputation for top notch and imaginative fish cooking. Pale yellow walls hung with prints, wooden floors and a pleasantly unstuffy atmosphere are the setting for dishes such as *ravioli di mare* (L18,000) and scallops in white wine (L16,000). Outdoor dining is an attraction in the summer.

Moderate

Canuleia
Via Canuleia 14 (47 470). **Open** noon-3pm, 8-10.30pm, Mon-Sat. **Average** L35,000. **Credit** AmEx, DC, EC, MC, V.
Booking is usually imperative at this very popular, unpretentious trattoria. The discreet, frosted glass façade fronts a cool, brick-and-tile interior where diners tuck into hearty Tuscan dishes. *Antipasti* cost L5,000, *primi* are L5-7,000, *secondi* are L14-18,000, *dolce* are L5,000.

Da Giulio in Pelleria
Via della Conce 47 (55 948). **Open** noon-3pm, 7.15-11pm, Tue-Sat. **Average** L30,000. **Credit** AmEx, DC, EC, MC, V.
Huge trattoria near the west gate that's probably grown a little too big for its own good – service can be brusque, and it's firmly on the tourist trail. However, Da Giulio still knocks out reliable, earthy Tuscan dishes at keen prices. Pastas are excellent, particularly the *ravelli* – a variation on ravioli stuffed with meat and herbs. Straightforward *secondi* include the literally named and translated *pollo alla mattone* ("chicken roasted under the pressure of a brick").

Da Leo
Via Tegrimi 1 (49 22 36). **Open** noon-2.30pm, 7.30-10.30pm, Mon-Sat. **Average** L28,000. **No credit cards.**

Castruccio Castracani

Lucca was a town of major regional importance from the 8th to the 11th centuries as the capital of the Frankish Margravate of Tuscany. However, when the Margravate broke up, the growth of independent cities such as Florence, Siena and Pisa threatened Lucca's own independence. In 1314 the Pisans seized Lucca. Things looked black for the city, until, galloping over the horizon in true 7th Cavalry fashion, came Castruccio Castracani. This little known but ambitious noble from the Garfagnana had spent most of his life in exile, partly in England. Quite how he managed to stage such an extraordinary turnaround is still not known, but within a year he had kicked out and subdued the Pisans and inaugurated what was to be seen as Lucca's (short-lived) golden age. From 1316 he ruled Lucca and set out to conquer most of western Tuscany. In 1325 he crushed the Florentines at Altopascio and went on to besiege Florence.

In all likelihood the city would have fallen had it not been for Castruccio's sudden death in 1328, probably from malaria.

The little Lucchese empire did not survive long. Inter-noble squabbling gave the Pisans the chance to get their own back, and Lucca had to suffer 70 years of Pisan oppression before buying her independence back from the Emperor Charles IV in 1399. The memory of Pisan domination was so bitter that the Lucchese tore down the fortress that Castruccio had built in 1324 to designs by Giotto, but from where the Pisans had governed. The Palazzo Ducale now stands on the site.

Castruccio was just the sort of canny, take-no-shit warlord that Macchiavelli thought Italy needed more of a century later, and the Florentine honoured him with an entertaining (and largely fictitious) biography, *La Vita da Castruccio Castracani di Lucca*.

Farro

As everyone knows, all the ancient Roman plebs needed to keep them happy was bread and circuses. More likely than not, the bread they nibbled upon would have been made from *farro*. The popularity of this variety of soft wheat (known as spelt or emmer in English) has declined over the centuries as hard wheats have become more favoured. The Lucchese still love it, however, and make bread with *farro* (*pane di farro*), usually grown in the valley known as the Garfagnana, north of Lucca. The most famous manifestation of *farro* (which can be found on the menu of virtually every trattoria in the city) is the hearty wheat and vegetable soup, often simply known by the name of its main ingredient.

If you crave a trad trattoria, you'll do no better in Lucca than this frenetic, friendly place. Peer into the kitchen while you wait to be seated in the barn-like restaurant with its high, beamed ceiling and miscellany of pictures scattered over the walls. The handwritten menu lists such warming dishes as the Lucchese speciality *farro* (*see box*) and *tortellini in brodo*, plus simple *secondi* – roast pork, fried chicken, trout in white wine et al. Tarts, *tiramisù* and gelati are the desserts. The air of barely controlled chaos is maintained by one of the Buralli brothers – a seriously unhinged Tuscan version of Russ Abbott.

Cheap

Da Guido
Via Cesare Battisti 28 (47 219). **Open** noon-2.30pm, 7.30-10pm, Mon-Sat. **Average** L18,000. **Credit** AmEx.
The weathered brothers Bernardo and Leo Barsotti preside over one of Lucca's most basic but best loved trattorias. A TV flickers in the corner, crusty locals shoot the breeze at the bar and the kitchen serves up plain but filling dishes like boiled chicken, roast rabbit and excellent home-made *tortelli*. *Primi* are from L4,000, *secondi* L7,000, *dolce* L3,000.

Gli Orti di Via Elisa
Via Elisa 17 (49 12 41). **Open** noon-3pm, 7-11pm, Fri-Tue. **Credit** AmEx, MC, V.
No-nonsense, good value trattoria/pizzeria run by the son of the owner of the rather more upmarket La Buca. Pastas and pizzas cost around L8,000 and there's a good self-service salad bar. Handy if you're in the relative culinary desert of the eastern part of Lucca.

Locanda Buatino
Borgo Gianotti 508 (34 32 07). **Open** 8am-midnight Mon-Sat. **Average** L25,000. **No credit cards**.
Originally serving the needs of traders at the local agricultural market, this ancient *locanda* just outside the northern gate is a gem. Owner Giuseppe Ferrua took it over five years ago and has managed to make the Buatino all things to all people, attracting an admirably mixed clientele. The food is no-nonsense rustic Tuscan (although there are occasional foreign food nights, such as when the Sri Lankan kitchen staff cook their native specialities) and superb value: L19,000

for three courses with wine and coffee in the evening. Grizzled old timers play cards by the bar while youngsters admire the art exhibited on the walls or chill to the (excellent) jazz in the back room on Monday nights. A winner. (*See also below* **Accommodation**).

Takeaway pizza

Da Felice
Via Buia 12. **Open** noon-2pm, 5pm-1am, Tue-Sun. **No credit cards**.
You'll find no better pizza in Lucca – thin, crisp bases, good tomato sauce, fine mozzarella. Most people opt for slices of margarita, sold at the bargain price of L1,800 per *etto* (100g), and wolf it down off small metal trays while perched on stools around the tiny frontage.

La Sbragia
Via Fillungo 144/146 (49 26 41). **Open** noon-2pm, 5pm-1am, Tue-Sun. **No credit cards**.
Buzzing pizzeria on the main shopping street – so popular that a ticket numbering system operates at the busiest times. You can take pizza away or eat in the small, brick-vaulted room next door (which incorporates part of an ancient pillar in its decor). A ham pizza costs L8,000, mushroom is L6,000. Twenty per cent is added to prices if you choose to eat in.

Bars, cafés & gelatarias

Lucca's not big on bars – many are of the overly-bright, quick-espresso-standing-up type. Few stay open late, and if you're here for the nightlife, you're going to be disappointed. As for **dancing**, the only option within the walls is **Dom Chischotte** in the Palazzo Bernardini; it's a combination piano bar-disco-karaoke parlour, largely frequented by unhip Pisans. Lucchese youth heads for the sweaty and swinging out-of-town discos, particularly **BP** (c/o Casina Rossa, Via Sarzamese, 4km towards Viareggio) and **Alma Bamba** (c/o Piatleta Rosso, Via Romana, 4km towards Porcari).

Antico Caffè della Mura
Piazzale Vittorio Emanuele 2 (47 962). **Open** 9.30am-3.30pm, 6pm-midnight, Wed-Mon. **Credit** AmEx, DC, EC, MC, V.
With a wall-top terrace, this is the only place to eat and drink along the ramparts. Quite pricey, but has the advantage of a late-opening bar during the summer.

Bar San Michele
Piazza San Michele 1 (55 387). **Open** 7.30am-8pm Mon-Sat. **No credit cards**.
The best place to sip a cappuccino and soak up the morning sun on Lucca's liveliest square.

Caffè di Simo
Via Fillungo 58 (49 62 34). **Open** 7.30am-8pm Tue-Sun. **No credit cards**.
Although it's the one café in Lucca that all tourists head for, da Simo is a beauty. Lots of dark wood, curved glass and shiny metal. The bar and pastry counter face each other at the front with tables at the back and a few on the Piazza Guiccardini behind. The atmosphere justifies the expense.

Casali
Via Roma 1 (49 26 87). **Open** *summer* 7am-11pm Thur-Tue; *winter* 7am-8.30pm Thur-Tue. **Credit** EC, MC, V.
Handily placed bar/gelateria on a corner of Piazza San

Michele. Best in the afternoon when it catches the sun and you can enjoy your gelati sitting outside at one of the tables on the piazza.

Gelateria Veneta
Via Veneto 74 & Chiasso Barletti 23.
The best ice-cream in town. This family gelateria uses only fresh ingredients and can call on more than 150 years of experience.

Guido Cimino
Piazza dell'Anfiteatro. **Open** noon-3pm, 6pm-midnight, Mon-Sat. **No credit cards**.
A beacon in the darkness. It may seem faint praise to dub Guido Cimino the coolest bar in Lucca, but this cracking place could hold its own with the best that London or Madrid have to offer. Three narrow rooms daubed in vibrant oranges, reds and blues, with patches of brickwork, and even a bit of old amphitheatre, showing through. Good music, a hip crowd and the best bar snacks in town (parmesan and warm bread, fresh capers, pistachios).

Accommodation

Expensive

Locanda L'Elisa
Via Nuova per Pisa (37 97 37/fax 37 90 19/e-mail elisa@lunet.it). **Rates** *single* L250-280,000; *double* L370-530,000. **Credit** AmEx, DC, EC, MC, V.
This wonderful, if heart-stoppingly expensive, villa is 3½km (2 miles) outside Lucca on N12 to Pisa. It was spruced up by an official working for Elisa Baciocchi, Napoleon's sister, who became Lucca's ruler in 1805. Its many attractions include rooms decorated with 18th-century furniture, carpets and fabrics, a conservatory restaurant and a large swimming pool.

Moderate

La Luna
Corte Compagni 12 (49 36 34/fax 49 00 21).
Rates *single* L90-125,000; *double* L125-180,000.
Credit AmEx, DC, EC, MC, V.
A great location – off the main shopping street, Via Fillungo, and seconds from the wonderful Piazza dell'Anfiteatro. This 3-star hotel has some excellent, spacious rooms (some in the annexe have frescoed ceilings), chummy staff and the rare bonus of a private car park.

Rex
Piazza Ricasoli 19 (95 54 43/fax 95 43 48). **Rates** *single* L90-110,000; *double* L130-150,000. **Credit** AmEx, DC, EC, MC, V.
Unexciting but reliable modern hotel just outside the walls by the railway station. Rooms are air-conditioned and have fridge-bars, cable and satellite TV.

Universo
Piazza del Giglio 1 (49 36 78/fax 49 36 78). **Rates** *single* L98-195,000; *double* L136-260,000. **Credit** AmEx, DC, EC, MC, V.
Traditionally *the* place to stay in Lucca, this ancient, slightly crumbling hostelry with ancient, slightly crumbling staff put up John Ruskin on the trip when he decided that

Matteo Civitali

Lucca, it has to be admitted, is something of an artistic minnow – particularly when compared to the good-sized salmon of Siena and the blue whale of Florence in the 14th and 15th centuries. However, the city did produce one great artist, or, rather, sculptor: Matteo Civitali (1435-1511). You will be forgiven for not recognising the name. Civitali is one of the least known, studied or acclaimed artistic figures in Renaissance Tuscany, yet his work has a remarkable assuredness, a lightness of touch and an individual note (which only occasionally descends into sentimentality) that mark him out as a major artist.

Civitali was born, lived and died in Lucca, and part of the reason for his obscurity is that the majority of his work never left the city. Little is known about his life beyond that he was apparently self-taught and only turned to sculpting professionally in his thirties, giving up his day job as a barber. His seated statue sits in the loggia of the Palazzo Pretorio (which he may have designed), gazing out over Piazza San Michele, and there is a 19th-century painting of Civitali presenting various of his designs, including the tempietto, to assorted Lucchese worthies in the Museo Nazionale di Palazzo Mansi.

Where to see Civitali's works:

Lucca
San Martino: Inlaid pavement in nave; pulpit; tempietto (1484); statue of St Sebastian on outside of tempietto; tombs of Pietro da Noceto (1472) and Domenico Bertini (1479); altar of St Regalus; two angels flanking the tabernacle in the chapel of the Holy Sacrament; two stoups (1498).
San Frediano: Altar; polychrome wooden Virgin Annunciate.
San Michele: Madonna on right-hand side of façade (original inside).
San Romano: Tomb of St Romanus (1490).
Santa Trinita: Madonna della Tosse.
Museo Nazionale di Villa Guinigi: Various sculptures.
Borgo a Mozzano
Wooden St Bernardine in church.
Camaiore
Virgin Annunciate (attributed) in Museo di Arte Sacra.
Lammari
Tabernacle in church (Civitali's last work).
Pescia
Virgin (attributed) in Santi Stefano e Niccolao.
Pisa
Marble lectern and candelabra in cathedral; architectural fragments in Museo dell'Opera del Duomo.
San Pellegrino in Alpe
Various sculptures in church.
Villa Collemandina
Two altars in church.

medieval architecture wasn't a load of crap after all. It's a little past its sell by date now (don't expect plugs to fit or the bar to be open when you need it), but still has a raffish charm – and great views from almost every room.

Cheaper

Diana

Via del Molinetto 11 (49 22 02/fax 47 795). **Rates** *single* 40-50,000; *double* L90-98,000. **Credit** AmEx, EC, MC, V.
A good budget option within the walls, located ten minutes' walk from the railway station and only seconds away from the cathedral. Rooms are good-sized and nicely decorated.

Piccolo Hotel Puccini

Via di Poggio 9 (55 421/fax 53 487). **Rates** *single* L75-88,000; *double* L100-123,000. **Credit** AmEx, DC, EC, MC, V.
Round the corner from young Giacomo's birthplace, and filled with Puccini memorabilia, this delightful hotel is the premier choice in its price bracket. Rooms are floor-lickingly clean – ask for the corner room (number 54) for views over the cute and cosy Piazza Cittadella in one direction and a glimpse of the magical façade of San Michele in the other. Staff are conspicuously friendly and helpful.

Very cheap

Cinzia

Via della Dogana 9 (49 13 23). **Rates** *single* L31,000; *double* L45,000. **No credit cards**.
Vines twist picturesquely round the doorway of this bargain hotel within the walls, but rooms are very basic and the immediate neighbourhood is the nearest Lucca comes to tatty. However, Cinzia is near to the Porta San Pietro and the railway station, and only a minute from the cathedral.

Locanda Buatino

Borgo Giannotti 508 (34 32 07). **Rates** *single* L30-45,000; *double* L50-75,000. **No credit cards**.
Outside the walls, but only a few minutes walk from the northern gate, the five rooms over one of Lucca's liveliest restaurants are simply furnished but with more taste than most hotels twice the price. The young English-speaking owner, Giuseppe, is charming and helpful. Superb value for money (*see also above* **Restaurants**).

"Il Serchio" Youth Hostel

Via del Brennero 673, Salicchi, 2km north of Lucca (34 18 11). **Open** 10 Mar-4 June, 1 Sept-10 Oct. From 1 Jan-29 Feb and 5 June-31 July only for groups who have pre-booked on 0586 86 25 17. **Rates** L14,000. **No credit cards**.
Take the number 6 bus from Piazzale Verdi or the railway station to reach this functional youth hostel. There is a small garden which is sometimes used for camping, but be sure to phone ahead as space is very limited. Otherwise, the nearest campsite is in Pisa, 20 kilometres (12 miles) away.

Shopping

Lucca's main shopping artery is pedestrianised Via Fillungo, lined by upmarket shops with often ornate façades.

La Bottega di Mamma Ro'

Piazza Anfiteatro 4 (49 26 07). **Open** 9am-3.30pm, 4-8pm, Tue-Sat; 4-8pm Mon. **No credit cards**.
Typically upmarket and desirable home- and kitchenware. Bright, chunky crockery, two-inch-thick wooden chopping boards, sunflower tablecloths, candles and candleholders.

*The intoxicating **Panificio Amedeo Giusti**.*

Cacioteca

Via Fillungo 242 (49 63 46). **Open** 7am-1.30pm, 3-8.30pm, Mon, Tue, Thur-Sat; 7am-1.30pm Wed. **Credit** EC, MC, V.
Cheese specialist at the northern end of Via Fillungo. Look out for the fine *raschera stagionato piccante, caciocavallo stagionato* and the literally-named *pecorino con barile* ("in a barrel"). La Cacioteca also sells hams, oils and local delicacies.

DelicoTezze di Isola Roberto

Via San Giorgio 5 (49 26 33). **Open** 8am-1pm, 4.30-8pm, Mon, Tue, Thur-Sat; 8am-1pm Wed. **Credit** AmEx, DC, EC, MC, V.
Excellent deli with a particularly enticing selection of pastas such as red pepper flavoured *strangozzi* and outsize, patriotic red, white and green *conchiglioni*. Also good for olive oils, hams, wine, porcini and cheeses. Look out for regular Saturday cheese tastings.

Panificio Amedeo Giusti

Via San Lucia 18/20 (49 62 85). **Open** 8am-1pm, 4.45-7.45pm, Mon, Tue, Thur-Sat; 8am-1pm Wed. **No credit cards**.
You'll smell Lucca's best bakery before you see it. The aroma of fresh baked foccaccia – both sweet and savoury varieties – cut from huge metre-plus loaves, is intoxicating. The torte, such as honey, and ricotta, are equally good.

Vini Liquori Vanni

Piazza San Salvatore 7 (Piazza Misericordia) (49 19 02). **Open** 4.30-8pm Mon; 9am-1pm, 4.30-8pm, Tue-Sat. **Credit** AmEx, DC, EC, MC, V.
This centrally located *enoteca* with extensive cellars is an excellent place to sample some of the local wines from the Colline Lucchesi and Montecarlo regions around Lucca. Names to look out for include Tenuta da Valgiano, Michi, Maiochi and Buonamico.

Arezzo Province

The best of eastern Tuscany.

The province of Arezzo, in the far east of Tuscany, is a verdant, fertile, richly forested area, far more northern in feel than the neighbouring province of Siena. It is perhaps at its best in autumn, when the forests are not only brilliantly coloured, but abound with mushrooms, truffles and sweet chestnuts. The region also produces what is widely reckoned to be the leanest, tenderest and most flavoursome beef in Italy: from a much prized breed of cows known as *Chianina* after the Valdichiana valley in which they graze.

Capital of the Valdichiana is Cortona, a fine old town with an enthusiastic arts scene – it hosts part of Umbria Jazz festival – and an unobtrusive quota of tourism. The river Arno has its source up in the mountains of the Casentino, and the lush upper Arno valley is home to such pretty towns as Poppi, and the monasteries of La Verna and Camáldoli: the latter surrounded by some of the most gorgeous woodland in Tuscany. Over the mountains is the upper Tiber valley, with the town of Anghiari, the two Piero towns and Caprese Michelangelo, named for its most important son. Finally, in the west of the province, close to the border with Siena, are two delightful hill-towns, Monte San Savino and Lucignano.

The tourist office in Arezzo (*0575 37 76 78*) can supply information on the province. For details of outdoor activities within the region *see chapter* **Specialist Holidays**.

West of Arezzo

Castelfranco di Sopra

Just outside this little town, laid out by Arnolfo di Cambio as a military base for Florence in the 12th century, there's an 11th-century abbey, the **Badia di San Salvatore a Soffena**, which has recently been restored. Ring the bell of the adjacent farmhouse and an old crone (or her sons) will show you the early 14th-century frescoes. Excavations in situ have brought to light a burial site and at present there are boxes of bones piled up in the rooms around the cloister. The dentally-challenged caretaker has the keys, and marvels with evident envy at the number of skulls still in possession of their teeth.

Typical landscape in Arezzo Province.

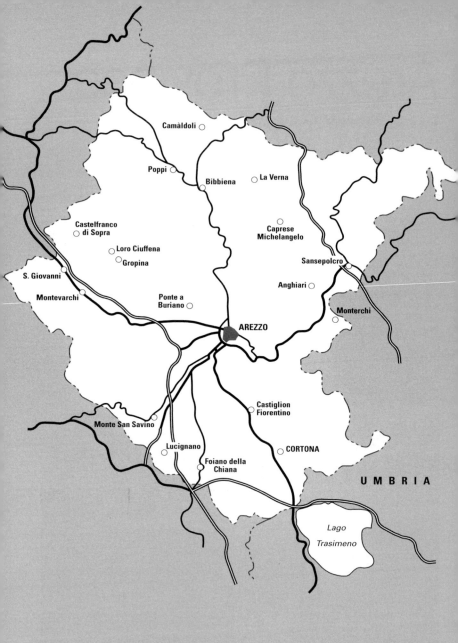

Camàldoli ○

Poppi ○

Bibbiena ○

○ La Verna

Castelfranco
di Sopra ○

○ Caprese
Michelangelo

○ Loro Ciuffena

○ Gropina

Sansepolcro ○

S. Giovanni ○

Montevarchi ○

Ponte a
Buriano ○

Anghiari ○

Monterchi ○

AREZZO

Castiglion
Fiorentino ○

Monte San Savino ○

Lucignano
○

Foiano della
Chiana ○

○ **CORTONA**

U M B R I A

Lago
Trasimeno

Arezzo Province

Motorways ....
Main Roads ....
Secondary Roads ....

0   10   20 km

© Copyright Time Out Group 1997

N

Gropina

Make a detour to see this unspoilt hamlet just off the road leading from Loro Ciuffenna to Arezzo. The Romanesque parish **church** is a beautiful example of architectural simplicity and curious carved detail. The knotted columns of the pulpit are repeated on the outside of the apse (you'll find the same motif flanking the portal of the Collegiate Church in San Quirico d'Orcia: *see chapter* **Siena and Chianti**).

Loro Ciuffena

High in the Upper Arno Valley, this medieval town straddles the Ciuffenna stream whose waters abound in trout. Over the bridge leading to the historical urban nucleus and half way down the gorge is a traditional flour mill still at work. You'll find effectively displayed figurative and abstract sculptures and drawings by **Venturino Venturi** in the **Museum of Contemporary Art**, beside the Municipio in Piazza Matteotti. For contrast, wander through the narrow sloping streets below the main road. As the name suggests, **Anarkali Bazar** in Via del Fondaccio mainly sells Eastern crafts products. However, since the owner's father is Pietro Spediti, one of the last great ironsmiths in the local tradition, you can also find beautifully wrought lamps and candlesticks. Just round the corner in Via Nanni is the **Osteria da Pippo** (*055 91 72 770. Closed Wed*) offering traditional Tuscan food. Otherwise food and lodging are available at the **Locanda La Torre** (*055 91 72 032*), just inside the town gates.

Close to Penna Alta, midway between Loro Ciuffenna and Terranuova Braccolini, **Il Canto di Maggio** (*055 97 05 147. Open dinner Thur-Sat; lunch & dinner Sun*) is a fine restaurant set in a restored farmhouse with a delightful garden. Specialities include *ravioli d'ortica* (stuffed with nettles) and pigeon *agrodolce* (sweet and sour sauce with grapes).

South of Arezzo

Castiglion Fiorentino

This pleasant walled medieval Apennine town surrounded by olive groves dates back to Etruscan times: beneath the 12th-century church of **Sant' Angelo**, the nearby walls and the Cassero tower, **Etruscan remains** have come to light, including decorative elements from the roofing of an Etruscan temple built in the 5th century BC. Many of these finds are now displayed in the excavated crypt of the church of Sant' Angelo, whose upper floors house the **Pinacoteca** (*Open 10am-12.30pm, 4-6.30pm; closed Mon*) with some fine paintings by Giotto's godson and follower Taddeo

Gaddi and 15th-century artist Bartolomeo della Gatta. In the same quarter, restoration of the imposing **Palazzo Pretorio** is also nearing completion. Walk down from here to the Piazza del Municipio, and enjoy the view from the elegant Renaissance **loggia** designed by Vasari, then turn right down Via San Michele. Here at number 42, you'll find the **Panetteria Meloni**, renowned for its bakery products. A few more turns and you'll reach Via Roma (no. 39/41), where potter **Capitini Matteo** creates and displays his traditional highly decorated glazed ware. At the other end of town, beside the 13th-century church of San Francesco, **da Muzzicone** at Piazza San Francesco 7 (*0575 65 84 03. Closed Tue*) serves good food.

Foiano della Chiana

Most people speed past Foiano en route for Arezzo, yet the original walled centre is not without charm. The **Collegiate Church of San Martino** contains a *Coronation of the Virgin* by Signorelli and a splendid polychrome *Madonna of the Girdle* by Andrea della Robbia, who also created the *Ascension* in the church of **San Domenico** on the other side of town. Apart from during religious functions, these churches are normally closed (they've been subject to theft), but the arch priest is happy to open them for you. In the town centre, what was once a Medici hunting lodge now houses municipal offices and the most extraordinary collection of early 20th-century photographic plates: the **Fototeca Furio del Furia**, a mine of information concerning pre-modern rural life in this part of Italy, although only a fraction of the archive is on show. The most important Foianese event is the **Carnival**, one of the oldest and most colourful in central Italy on the three Sundays leading up to Lent.

Lucignano

This little town is a gem: pinkish in hue, it looks out over the Valdichiana from the safety of its curious elliptical urban structure. The **Museo Civico** (*Open 9.30am-1pm, 3-6.30pm, Tue-Sun*) contains Sienese paintings of the 1300s and 1400s, including a *Madonna and Child* by Signorelli, and the walls of the Romanesque church of **San Francesco** are embellished with frescoes by Bartolo di Fredi and Taddeo di Bartolo. **Hotel/Restaurant Totò** (Piazza del Tribunale 6 *0575 83 67 63. Doubles L90,000; singles L70,000*) is located in a converted monastery. Totò indulges his passion for Tuscan country flavours in the fine restaurant (*Open lunch & dinner; closed Tue. Average L30,000*), gathering herbs, mushrooms and wild fruits, and incorporating them in dishes such as *scarselle di borragine* – a type of crepe filled with melted pecorino, borage and nutmeg.

Cortona

Overlooking the Valdichiana from the sheer Apennine hillside, Cortona is one of the beautiful historic cities of central Italy. It has found a latter-day *raison d'être* in discerning tourism, international conferences and overseas study programmes for foreign (largely American) universities. This means that the non-Cortonese practically outnumber the natives in the historic urban centre and the scenic enclaves of the surrounding countryside. However, such transformations have also injected the city with considerable cultural enterprise: it hosts excellent art exhibitions, important seminars, an annual antiques fair and, despite being a Tuscan town, plays an active role in the **Umbria Jazz** festival.

Cortona can trace its origins back to at least the 7th or 8th century BC, when it was an Etruscan stronghold. Following various vicissitudes under the Romans and Goths, it became a flourishing free commune in the 11th century AD before falling under the rule of Florence in the early 1400s. Its characteristic architecture is a happy mixture of medieval *palazzi* and Renaissance façades flanking narrow paved streets that climb up towards the Medici fortress dominating the surrounding country.

The birthplace of artists of the calibre of **Luca Signorelli** (c1445-1523), **Pietro da Cortona** (1596-1669) and the Futurist **Gino Severini** (1883-1966), Cortona once looked to a variegated crafts tradition for its income. This has now largely died out and has been replaced by new or non-indigenous artisans such as **Umberto Rossi** who fashions exquisite, virtuoso wooden objects (Via Guelfa 28) and the potter **Giulio Lucarini** whose glazed wares can be found at Via Nazionale 54 (the bar a few doors down at number 64 has pastries made in its own kitchens across the way, and is a great place for breakfast).

Things to see

Piazza della Repubblica is where the main streets meet. Its flight of steps leads up to the 13th-century **Palazzo Comunale** replete with crenellated clock tower. The grandiose **Palazzo Casali** in Piazza Signorelli houses the **Museo dell'Accademia Etrusca** (*Open 10am-1pm, 4-7pm Tue-Sun*), with collections of Etruscan, Roman and Egyptian artefacts, including a 18th-century fake Etruscan fresco that fooled historians for generations, and a **Pinacoteca** with works by Pinturicchio and Signorelli. Overlooking the town, the church of **San Nicolò** contains an altarpiece made from a standard painted on both sides by

Signorelli for the Company of St Nicholas. Just inside the city walls, the **Museo Diocesano** (*Open 9.30am-1pm, 3.30-7pm, Tue-Sun*) houses works by Signorelli, Lorenzetti and Sassetti as well as a breathtaking *Annunciation* and other paintings by Fra Angelico. On leaving Cortona en route for Camucia, stop at the elegant Renaissance church of the **Madonna delle Grazie al Calcinaio**, built between 1485 and 1513 on designs by the great Sienese polymath and architect Francesco di Giorgio Martini, who was invited to work here by Signorelli.

Where to stay

Il Falconiere Relais *San Martino a Bocena, just outside Cortona on Arezzo road (0575 61 26 79/fax 61 29 27).* **Rates** *single* L180,000; *double* L280,000; *suite* L450,000. **Credit** AmEx, MC, V.
Superior establishment with a good if pricey restaurant.

Hotel Italia *Via Ghibellina 7 (0575 63 02 54/fax 63 05 64).* **Rates** *single* L65-75,000; *double* L100-110,000. **Credit** EC, MC, V.
Reasonable family-run establishment.

Hotel Sabrina *Via Roma 37 (0575 63 03 97/fax 60 46 27).* **Rates** *single* L60-70,000; *double* L80-100,000. **Credit** EC, MC, V.
Charming little hotel for B&B.

Hotel San Luca *Piazza Garibaldi 1 (0575 63 04 60/fax 63 01 05).* **Rates** (breakfast extra) *single* L75,000; *double* L120,000. **Credit** AmEx, DC, EC, MC, V.
Average hotel; often taken over by American study groups.

Hotel San Michele *Via Guelfa 15 (0575 60 43 48/fax 63 01 47).* **Rates** *single* L110,00; *double* L150,000.
Credit AmEx, DC, EC, MC, V.
Well-appointed accommodation in a tastefully restored Renaissance palace in the town centre.

Where to eat

Agrisalotto *Santa Caterina, towards Camucia (0575 61 74 17).* **Open** dinner Wed-Sun. **Average** L55,000 incl wine. **Credit** AmEx.
Plenty of home farm produce, simply but skilfully cooked.

Preludio *Via Guelfa 11 (0575 63 01 04).* **Open** lunch & dinner daily; closed lunch Nov-Apr. **Average** L40,000. **Credit** AmEx, EC, MC, V.
Typical Tuscan fare at reasonable prices.

Tonino *Piazza Garibaldi 1 (0575 63 05 00/fax 60 44 57).* **Open** lunch & dinner daily. **Average** L40,000. **Credit** AmEx, DC, EC, MC, V.
Cheek by jowl with the Hotel San Luca, this place serves classic cuisine and has a view over the valley.

Trattoria Dardano *Via Dardano 24 (0575 60 19 44).* **Open** lunch & dinner Thur-Tue. **Average** L30,000.
Family-style cooking at fair prices popular with locals.

Events

Copperware Fair (end Apr); Cortona section of **Umbria Jazz** (late July); **Antique Furniture Fair** (late Aug-early Sept).

Monte San Savino

Much of the prosperity and architectural impact of this hill-top town dates back to the late 1400s and 1500s, when the **Di Monte** family rose to power and influence (Giovanni Maria Di Monte became Pope Julius III in 1550). The Di Monte residence, now the **Palazzo Comunale**, was designed by Antonio da Sangallo the Elder in 1515-17 and best reveals its true Renaissance elegance when viewed from the hanging gardens that project out over the landscape on the far side of the building. Just opposite, on the road side, is the **Loggia dei Mercanti**, also commissioned by the Di Monte family. Built in 1518-20, it is believed to be the work of another of the town's illustrious offspring: the sculptor and architect **Andrea Sansovino**. The town is still bustling with activity. Apart from the potters specialising in pierced and engraved ware at the **Ceramiche Artistiche Lapucci** (Corso Sangallo 10), Monte San Savino also hosts some important exhibitions. It is also the venue for an open-air film festival in the summer, the **Festival Musicale Savinese** in August (master-classes and recitals) and the earthier **Sagra della Porchetta** (Roast Suckling Pig feast), usually the first weekend of September.

If you want to stay, the best value is the **Verniana**, 7km out of town, beyond well-signposted Gargonza. Rooms are simple, but clean, and there is a swimming pool in the garden. For luxury, admittedly of a rather sterile kind, head for the medieval **Castello di Gargonza** (*0575 84 70 21/fax 84 70 54/e-mail gargonza@teta.it*), now a tad too perfectly restored as a hotel and restaurant. Expect to pay L160-250,000 for a double room. The restaurant is nothing special.

North and East of Arezzo

Anghiari

This honey-coloured stone town, of Roman origin and medieval and Renaissance development, clings proudly to the side of a steep hill facing Sansepolcro, still surrounded by its medieval walls. It – or rather its environs – should have been the subject of a painting by Leonardo (in Florence's Palazzo Vecchio, *see chapter* **Museums**), the *Battle of Anghiari*, celebrating a Florentine victory over Milan in 1440, but unfortunately the artist only completed the cartoons.

Anghiari, and the upper Tiber valley in which it stands, have long been known for their wood crafts, a tradition celebrated at the snappily-titled **Museo delle Arti e Tradizioni Popolari dell'Alta Valle del Tevere** (*Open 9am-7pm Mon-Sat; 9am-1pm Sun, public hols*) in Palazzo

Rustic dining: **Locanda Castello di Sorci**.

Taglieschi. As well as toys and furniture, there is a magnificent polychrome wooden sculpture of the Madonna by Jacopo della Quercia. The craft tradition continues today in the admirable **Istituto Statale d'Arte**, housed in a former monastery in the ancient centre, which trains youngsters from all over the region in the restoration of wooden artefacts, particularly antique furniture. One of the foremost products of this school is **Mastro Santi**, who specialises in carving and marquetry in his workshop (Via Nova 8), on the north side of town. Anghiari is also home to some of the finest traditional weaving to be found in Italy: **Busatti** (Via Mazzini 14) produces and sells towels, table cloths, upholstery and curtain materials woven on proto-industrial jacquard looms using naturally dyed linen, wool, hemp and cotton yarns. There's an annual crafts market in late April or early May, featuring local products.

If you want to base yourself in the area, you could rent a farmhouse on the nearby **Castello di Sorci Estate** (*0575 78 90 66*). Otherwise there is a very reasonably priced modern hotel with a covered swimming pool on the edge of town: **Oliver**, Via della Battaglia 14 (*0575 78 99 33/fax 78 99 44*). Castello di Sorci also offers the area's most fun eating experience, in its **Locanda Castello di Sorci** (*0575 78 90 66. Open lunch & dinner Tue-Sun. Average L30,000*), an earthy inn, hugely popular with Italian families, with a

Piero's Madonna del Parto *in* **Monterchi**.

daily changing fixed menu of home-made pasta, grain and pulse soups, and country staples such as fried rabbit and stewed lamb. To get there, take the Arezzo road and, after about 2km, follow signs off to the right. *See also chapter* **A Tuscan Restaurant Tour**.

Camáldoli

Founded in 1012 by Romualdo, a Benedictine monk who thought the Order's life style too cushy, the Camáldolite monks are an ecologically-minded bunch of vegetarians who grow all their own food and plant 5,000 trees in the surrounding forest every year. They have also done a far better job at preserving the spiritual atmosphere of their mission than have their Franciscan 'brothers' at La Verna (*see below*). In fact the explanatory leaflet (in Italian) available at Camáldoli is a rare example of clarity and quiet intelligence. The monastery itself comprises a baroque church containing two paintings by Vasari (a *Madonna and Saints* and a *Nativity*), who was summoned to work here by the monks in 1534. At the famous **Pharmacy** with its carved walnut cupboards dating back to 1543, you can buy toiletries, soaps and liqueurs made by the monks. This, however, is but the monastery's public face: a 3km walk through beautiful forest brings you to the tranquil **Hermitage** (Eremo) where the monks live, Carthusian-style, in silence, in individual cells, each with its own vegetable garden and chapel. If you want to stay in the wonderfully peaceful forest, try **Il Rustichello**, Via Corniolo 14 (*0575 55 60 20. Doubles L90,000; singles L65,000*).

Caprese Michelangelo

Pilgrims, both cultural and gastronomic, will enjoy the short drive up the hillside north of Anghiari to Caprese Michelangelo, where **Michelangelo** was born. There's actually nothing of the great artist's output to be seen there, but the views are splendid and an old man of military mien will show you where the Buonarroti family lived (now the **Museo Michelangiolesco**) and put you through

your sculptural paces with the help of photographs hung from the walls. For lunch, try one of the eight restaurants that serve a population of only 1,500. In the hamlet of **Fonte della Galletta** above the village is a family-run trattoria of the same name (*0575 793925. Open lunch and dinner, Fri-Sun in winter, daily in summer*) serving a great *insalata di funghi* (with wild mushrooms) and *minestra di farro con i funghi* (spelt and mushroom soup) along with pasta with locally-foraged truffles, excellent game and luscious desserts.

La Verna

Tucked up among the forests of the Casentino at an altitude of 1,129m, this monastery was founded in 1214 by St Francis, who received the stigmata here ten years later. It's now a large conventual complex comprising a basilica, two churches, a chapel and various souvenir shops. Despite the beauty of the surroundings, the whole place smacks slightly of Disneyland. Convoys of chewing, munching, drinking school children don't help. Avoid coming here at weekends, when the tourist buses practically have to queue up for parking space.

Monterchi

Perched on a hilltop half way between Sansepolcro and Arezzo, Monterchi's main claim to fame is the Piero della Francesca fresco of the extraordinary *Madonna del Parto*, showing two subdued angels pulling back the door of a tent to reveal a pallid, pregnant Madonna. Recently restored, it is on view in an exhibition space made out of what used to be the local school (*Open 9am-1pm, 2-6pm, Mon-Sun. Admission L5,000*). One of this small town's sturdy bastions has recently been excavated to accommodate **Al Travato**, a pleasant tavern selling good food and wine. Local products, both gastronomic and otherwise, can also be found at the **Bottega del Pozzo Vecchio** at Via dell'Ospedale 13. Each year on the fourth Sunday of September people flock to the **Sagra della polenta con le salsicce e i fegatelli**, a popular binge featuring polenta, sausages and pig's liver.

Poppi

Attributed in part to Arnolfo di Cambio (architect of the Palazzo Vecchio in Florence), the cheerfully turretted **Castello dei Conti Guidi** that dominates this pleasant porticoed town is now used for temporary art exhibitions and as a library for Poppi's extensive archives. Many of the rooms are decorated with magnificent early frescoes, including a complete cycle with Stories from the Gospel painted in the early 1300s by Giotto's main follower, Taddeo Gaddi.

Sansepolcro

Close to the borders with Umbria and the Marche, Sansepolcro is sheltered by the Luna mountains and refreshed by the Tiber as it flows down from its Apennine source. Although many of the town's 16,000 inhabitants now live in the outskirts, the walled historic centre is a bustling place as yet unadulterated by tourism. Sansepolcro was the birthplace of supreme Renaissance artist, **Piero della Francesca** (c1416-92), and his pupil, mathematician, **Luca Pacioli** (1445-1517), whose treatise on geometry was illustrated by Leonardo da Vinci. Piero's paintings are in the **Museo Civico** (*Open 9.30am-1pm, 2.30-6pm, daily*): the *Resurrection*, with a solemn Christ stepping from his tomb while soldiers sleep, and the *Madonna della Misericordia*, showing a giant Madonna sheltering under her huge cloak the members of the confraternity that commissioned the painting.

Sansepolcro's 14th-century **Duomo** is also worth a visit, with an *Ascension* by Raphael's teacher, Perugino (currently being restored *in situ*) and a fresco by Bartolomeo della Gatta. Piero's home, the **Casa di Piero della Francesca** (*not open to the public*), is an elegant Renaissance residence, built, in all likelihood, to his own designs. It is now the headquarters of the Piero della Francesca Foundation.

There are latter-day applications of Renaissance perspective at the **Taberna Artis** of **Paolo Giovannini**, whose family has long specialised in trompe l'oeil painting (Via Aggiunti 82). Other traditional crafts practised locally include goldsmithery, wrought ironwork and embroidery. However, it's the food industry that has long accounted for Sansepolcro's evident prosperity: the first Buitoni pasta factory was set up here in 1827: there are even rumours of a pasta museum. There are sausages and pork cuts preserved in oil at the **Salumeria Aldo Martini** (Via XX Settembre 95), excellent bread at the **Panificio La Spiga** (Via Santa Caterina 72/76) and the products of award-winning ice-cream-maker **Palmiro Ghignoni** just outside the city walls.

If you want to stay, the **Albergo Fiorentino**, Via Luca Pacioli 60 (*0575 74 03 50/fax 74 03 70*), is a friendly family-run hotel on the upper floors of a centrally located palazzo. Restaurant **Ventura**, Via Aggiunti 30 (*0575 74 25 60. Open lunch & dinner Sun-Fri. Average L60,000*), serves home-made tagliatelle, ravioli, bean soup, sauces with wild mushrooms (mostly ceps) or truffles found locally, and excellent grilled meats. Another good restaurant is **Trattoria Al Coccio** , Via Aggiunti 83 (*0575 74 14 68. Open lunch & dinner. Closed Wed*), serving home-made ravioli and fresh *panzanella*. Every year Sansepolcro hosts a crossbow competition in traditional costume, the **Palio della Balestra** (second Sun in September).

Mona Lisa

Chances are you've never noticed the bridge behind the Mona Lisa's left shoulder. Most of us are held by that enigmatic smile, and if we notice the background at all, it is to dismiss it as a fantasy landscape that somehow contrasts with its wildness and jaggedness with the serene poise of La Gioconda herself.

And on the whole, the critics have tended to agree. In his classic *The Renaissance*, Walter Pater referred to the background as 'that cirque of fantastic rocks'. Writing a hundred years later, Kenneth Clark concurs: 'From his earliest work', he claims in his biography of the artist, 'Leonardo had felt that the only possible background to a picture was a range of fantastic mountain peaks'.

Carlo Starnazzi, a 46-year-old schoolteacher and part-time palaeontologist from Arezzo, claims to have discovered the exact point from which the landscape behind the Mona Lisa was painted. Leonardo, he says, was recreating the view from the top of Quarata castle, 70m above the level of the river and 2.2km as the crow flies from that faintly sketched bridge, which is called Ponte a Buriano. The river we see in the painting is, therefore, not some Alpine fantasy but Leonardo's beloved Arno, about 10km from Arezzo, just upstream from its confluence with its tributary, the Chiana. This, says Starnazzi, is the white meander which disappears behind the sitter's left shoulder – not a road, as most people seem to believe.

The commercial opportunities are obvious: with a fixed camera and a chair, the owners of the castle could make a fortune out of the tourists queuing up to have their photographs taken against the Mona Lisa backdrop. There's just one problem: Quarata castle fell down a few centuries ago, and from the mound that is left, you can't even see the river, which is hidden behind a stand of trees. But at least the bridge is still there. Ponte a Buriano, a graceful seven-arched structure built between 1240 and 1277, is the oldest bridge over the Arno, pre-dating the Ponte Vecchio in Florence by almost 100 years. And now that the Mona Lisa connection has been suggested, the locals are determined to make the most of their new-found tourist potential. Already a do-it-yourself reproduction of Leonardo's famous portrait has gone up next to the bridge, with the words 'Ponte a Buriano – a bridge to Paris' underneath.

Arezzo

Most that glitters is gold in ancient Arezzo, but this wealthy, sleepy town is slowly waking up to the potential of its attractions and dusting down its artistic and architectural treasures.

Arezzo has been cleaning up a number of its finest buildings over the past few years and, outside each newly plastered and pointed façade, has installed a descriptive placard (in Italian) under the heading *Arezzo nascosta*: Hidden Arezzo. It's a title that sums up the city to perfection. There's so much more to it than meets the eye. Not only art, but also wealth. Whereas 40 years ago it was still basically a market town backed by a rural economy, today it is the world's foremost centre for industrially produced gold jewellery. Ask a jeweller in Timbuktu about Piero della Francesca and he may look at you blankly; mention Arezzo and he'll get out a gaggle of gold chains of the sort churned out daily by the kilometre in the factories (workshops, the locals like to call them – they're still self-confessed *contadini* at heart) sprawled across the outskirts of the city.

The Aretini are renowned for driving a hard bargain without wasting too much time on niceties. Hardly surprisingly, they are masters of

> The phone code for Arezzo is **0575**

an art that often goes hand in hand with goldsmithery: tax evasion. As a result, there are more Ferraris in the Arezzo area than in any other part of Italy. You won't see them, however. Their crafty owners bumble around in dented Fiats during the week and only take the Testa Rossa out of the garage for a Sunday spin or a late-night foray to one of the dubious Valdichiana nightclubs.

Yet things in Arezzo have been changing over the past few years. The second and third generation of *orafi* (goldsmiths) are better educated than their forebears, are used to having money and the time it buys, and are thus more inclined to focus attention on their home town and its potential attractions. Moreover, Arezzo's monthly antiques market draws hordes of dealers and customers from all over Italy and beyond. So the local author-

Detail from Piero della Francesca's Legend of the True Cross, in **San Francesco**.

ities have been promoting a major restoration programme involving various palazzi, two magnificent museums, the Piero della Francesca fresco cycle – due to be unveiled in the year 2000 – and the hitherto unkempt Fortezza Medicea that will provide a pleasantly airy crown to the city when completed. Arezzo now also has its own Arts Faculty (an offshoot of the University of Siena), and this has not only encouraged bookshops and cinemas to awaken from their torpor, but has also provided eager patrons for cafés and night haunts. So old places are getting a face-lift under new management, and new ones are gradually opening to cater to discerning tourists as well as affluent locals. Only gradually, however: the city still lacks a really good hotel, though a couple have recently been adequately revamped. To judge by the current trend, it's just a matter of time....

Some history

In the 3,000 years of its development, Arezzo has gained much from its fortunate geographical position. Located half way down the Italian peninsula on a double hilltop backed by thickly wooded mountains, the site attracted an early prehistoric settlement and, later, the Etruscans who founded a city there in the 7th century BC. It soon became a cultural and commercial crossroads for the inhabitants of the four fertile valleys of the Tiber, the Chiana, the Arno and the Casentino. Under the Romans, Arezzo provided a strategic base for imperial expansion towards the north. The city walls were enlarged, the amphitheatre, baths and aqueduct were built, and by the middle of the 1st century BC reddish-brown pottery manufactured in Arezzo was being exported to the furthermost reaches of the Roman Empire. The Lombard occupation of Tuscany around 570-75 AD brought considerable destruction to the city followed by a long period of decline. By the end of the 11th century, the Church had acquired great tracts of land and enormous power. The cathedral itself as well as numerous churches and monasteries were built as an expression of this authority, and Arezzo could boast a famous school directed by a musical genius of the calibre of Guido d'Arezzo (*see box*). Yet the population stalled at 10-15,000 inhabitants and was not to grow until around 1200, when the balance of power changed as a mercantile economy began to develop and a number of aristocratic families emerged to contest the bishops' wealth and influence.

A new vernacular literature flourished in 13th-century Arezzo, public buildings were erected (including the Palazzo del Comune, begun in 1232) and artists were called in from afar to decorate them. Cultural ferment reached its peak under the enlightened rule of Bishop Guido Tarlati (1312-28) and was followed by a bleak period in which the city lost its autonomy and was taken over by

Florence. Despite the presence in the city of Renaissance masters such as Piero, and the architects Bernardo Rossellino and Sangallo the Elder, Arezzo did not prosper under the Medicis or the Lorraines. Their dominion lasted from 1434 to 1859, during which time the population dwindled and society grew increasingly rural and conservative. Granted, during the 16th century the city produced some outstanding intellectuals such as the poet Pietro Aretino and Giorgio Vasari (*see box*), the official Medici architect. Yet they tended to operate within the broader context of Tuscan, and therefore Florentine, creative enterprise. Arezzo slept on, and it was only after the last war when mechanised agriculture and the demise share-crop farming left rural communities without an income that the people of Arezzo discovered their new industrial vocation.

Sights

Churches

Duomo

Piazza Duomo (23 991).
Open 7am-12.30pm, 3-6.30pm, daily.
Built on the site of an early Christian church devoted to St Peter Martyr, the Cathedral was the fruit of a papal decree of 1203 establishing that the Bishop's See and principal place of worship should be transferred from their original location outside the city to within the walls. Since St Peter's church was deemed too modest for this elevated new role, a major building programme was begun in 1278, but only lasted 12 years. The project got under way again under Bishop Guido Tarlati (1312-28), was again abandoned, and was finally completed between 1471 and 1510. During the next 300 years the interiors were improved, by destroying all but one of the original chapels and the frescoes that decorated them. In 1535 Vasari designed the disproportionately large organ loft in the left-hand aisle, the campanile was built in fits and starts between 1857 and 1860, and the façade was only added in 1900-14.

Despite such vicissitudes, the interior is impressive. The soaring ogival-vaulted nave and two aisles lead the eye towards magnificent stained glass mullioned windows that are largely the work of **Guillaume de Marcillat** (1519-24). Moreover, in the aisle to the left, beside the door leading to the sacristy, there is a quietly majestic fresco of Mary Magdalen painted around 1459 by **Piero della Francesca**. Just beside this is a finely sculpted funerary monument to Guido Tarlati, who died in 1327. It is the work of two Sienese artists, Agostino di Giovanni and Agnolo di Ventura.

San Francesco

Piazza San Francesco (20 630). **Open** 8.30am-noon, 2-6.30pm, daily.
Renowned the world over for the fresco cycle (c. 1453-64) by Piero della Francesca, one of the consummate masterpieces of the Quattrocento, the centrally located church of San Francesco has happily survived many a dire fate. It was begun in the second half of the 1200s at the behest of the Franciscan friars who had reached Arezzo several decades earlier, and was finished towards the end of the Trecento. During the 15th and 16th centuries, the interiors were embellished with shrines, chapels and frescoes (including the Piero ones) commissioned by the families of the wealthiest Arezzo merchants. Then in 1556 a fire broke out during a theatrical event held in the church. The flames

The sandstone arcades of **Santa Maria della Pieve.**

were extinguished before they could damage the art and architecture, but 28 people died on the spot, and a further 58 over the next few days. During the next two centuries the Gothic chapels and shrines were demolished and the walls whitewashed. The church was deconsecrated during the Napoleonic occupation (1818) and was turned into a theatre. There was worse in store: later in the century it was used as a military barracks.

Most visitors to the church come to see the famous **Piero della Francesca** fresco cycle illustrating **The Legend of the True Cross** on the walls of the choir. The theme is a slightly arcane one, telling the story of the cross on which Christ was crucified, both as an actual wooden object and as a symbol. To complicate understanding even further, Piero chose not to tell the story chronologically, but to arrange his scenes so that they echoed one another: an Old Testament battle is juxtaposed with the battle in which Constantine defeated Maxentius, while the Queen of Sheba has an identical face to St Helena, the mother of Constantine, who excavated the relics of the cross on a visit to the Holy Land.

By the late 1980s it was clear that the fresco required attention. A meticulous scientific analysis of the structural and atmospheric ills of the underlying architecture kept experts busy for several years and was followed by painstaking conservative restoration of both the building and the frescoes (meaning that what's lost cannot be replaced, but further damage can be avoided by removing the causes). During this long, drawn-out process, certain sections of the frescoes remained on view until mid-1997, when they were curtained off for the final stages of what has proved to be a major undertaking. If all goes according to plan, they should be unveiled in the year 2000.

The church has much to offer, even with Piero's magnum opus concealed from sight. In the last chapel on the right before the altar, and in the Guasconi and Tarlati chapels respectively on the right and the left behind the altar, there are frescoes painted by Spinello Aretino at the end of the 1300s. The Tarlati chapel also houses an early *Annunciation* by Luca Signorelli. The fine stained glass rose window in

the façade is the work of Guillaume de Marcillat (1524), creator of the stained glass in the Cathedral.

Santa Maria della Pieve

Corso Italia (22 629). **Open** 8am-1pm, 3-6.30pm, daily.
This magnificent example of Romanesque architecture was built over a paleo-Christian church erected where there was once a Roman temple. In its early days as a parish church it acted as a point of reference for the people of Arezzo in their struggle against the bishop residing outside the city walls. The sandstone structure as we now see it dates back to the mid-12th to 13th centuries and features an astounding façade composed of five wide arches on the ground floor surmounted by three orders of increasingly serried loggias, placed one above the other so that the vertical thrust of the columns gains momentum and culminates in the bell-tower, where the arch motif is repeated. The simplicity of the monumental interiors sets off the red and gold splendour of the polyptych above the main altar, painted at the behest of bishop Guido Tarlati by **Piero Lorenzetti** in 1320-24. In the *Annunciation* above the central panel, note the way the artist has represented the Virgin Mary against a background of earthly architectural perspective that contrasts with the golden purity surrounding the other saintly figures.

San Domenico

Piazza San Domenico (22 906). **Open** 7am-1pm, 3.30-6pm, Mon-Sat; 8am-1pm, 3.30pm-6pm, Sun, public hols.
The Dominicans first came to Arezzo in the early 13th century and began building a church for themselves in 1275. The construction was completed during the course of the 1300s and was embellished with frescoes, shrines and chapels commissioned by the city's foremost aristocratic families. The walls of the single aisle were originally decorated all over with frescoes, though only fragments of these remain. The main chapel can boast a work of art of extraordinary importance: a **Crucifix** by **Cimabue**, painted around 1260-70, when the artist was still a young man. Note the Byzantine influence in the portrayal and bodily stance.

SS Annunziata

Via Garibaldi 185 (26 774).
Open 8am-noon, 3.30-7pm, daily.
According to popular credence, a pilgrim returning home from Loreto to La Spezia in February 1490 got caught in a terrible storm and popped into this oratory to pray to the Madonna (rather than shelter from the rain). While kneeling there he saw tears well from the eyes of the statue of the Madonna now kept above the main altar, and as he marvelled an obliging angel descended to re-light a lamp that had blown out. Miracles well handled can be a source of revenue, so the Company of SS Annunziata immediately decided to build a church on the spot. The artist who drew up the original plans was Bartolomeo della Gatta, whose model was Francesco di Giorgio's church of Santa Maria delle Grazie al Calcinaio, just outside Cortona (*see chapter* **Arezzo Province**). However, he died before the job was completed and his place was taken by **Antonio da Sangallo**, then engaged on designs for the Fortress in Arezzo (*see below*). Sangallo was familiar with Bramante's innovative architecture, and was able to add the beautiful atrium to the original design. Inside the church itself there is another fine stained glass window by Guillaume de Marcillat: the *Assumption of the Madonna* in the apse.

Santa Maria delle Grazie

Via Santa Maria (20 620). **Open** 7.30am-noon, 4-7pm, daily.
Located outside the city walls on the south side, the famous loggia fronting this church is considered the foremost architectural masterpiece of the Renaissance in Arezzo. It is part of a building complex erected between 1428 and 1520 comprising the portico that surrounded the square, the convent, the church of Santa Maria delle Grazie and the chapel of San Bernardino da Siena. The reason for building in this particular spot is a splendid illustration of how faith and superstition are practically interchangeable terms. Since prehistoric times the people of Arezzo had worshipped the miraculous waters of a spring known as the Fonte Tecta, devoted to Apollo in Etrusco-Roman times and still revered for its healing qualities in the early 15th century. Saint Bernardino of Siena preached in Arezzo in 1425 and again in 1428, and on both occasions inveighed against the false beliefs of the Aretini. Not content with words, one Sunday after Easter 1428 he invited the faithful to follow him. Armed with a wooden cross, he led them to the spring, which soon succumbed to his superior powers. In its place an oratory was built and embellished with a fresco by the Aretino painter Parri di Spinello portraying the *Madonna della Misericordia* (1428-31), still visible inside the church.

Museums

Casa Vasari

Via XX Settembre 55 (30 03 01). **Open** 9am-7pm daily. **Admission** free.
Indefatigable painter, architect and historian, Vasari (*see box below*) bought himself a brand new house in his home town in what was then the Borgo di San Vito. Between 1540 and 1548, he and his assistants devoted due attention to finishing and decorating it, though in the end he only actually lived here for a short period. Perceiving that there was greater scope for his ambitions at the Medici court, in 1554 he moved to Florence. His Arezzo residence was purchased by the State in 1911, was restored in 1955 and again in 1977, and is now a museum that preserves its private house atmosphere. To visit, you have to ring on the door bell and wait for the caretaker to come down from his dwelling on the upper floor. You will be ushered in and allowed to wander through the highly ornate rooms on the *piano nobile* and out into the small hanging gardens. What you see will probably explain why Vasari is now best remembered as a historian. However, as a whole the house provides many an interesting insight into Mannerist taste in Tuscany.

Guido d'Arezzo

Guido d'Arezzo, also known as Guido Monaco in view of his calling, was a Benedictine monk and musical theorist who was born around 990. He received his early training at Pomposa, near Ferrara, which was then an important centre of culture and research with a splendid library. It was here that he first started working on a revolutionary method for transcribing musical sounds into systematic graphic form. The monks, who had hitherto simply learnt what they sang by heart, did not appreciate such tiring innovations and made life so difficult for Guido that in 1025 he moved to Arezzo, where he created a famous School of plainchant at the Cathedral, then located outside the city walls on the mount known as La Pionta. Over the next ten years he contributed milestones to the development of musical science, establishing rhythmical rules (the *Regole ritmiche*), defining antiphony (the *Antifonario*) and addressing the problem of the use of the musical staff (in the *Prologo*). We owe to him the diatonic scale, the doh-re-mi of our school choirs and childhood piano lessons, and the fact that we can buy sheet music and take an active part in the most elusive and sublime of arts

Museo Archeologico Mecenate

Via Margaritone 10 (20 882). **Open** 9am-2pm Mon-Sat; 9am-1.30pm Sun, public hols; closed 2nd & 3rd Sundays of month. **Admission** L8,000; free for under-18s and over-60s.
Named for Maecenas, a high-living Roman from Arezzo who became advisor to Emperor Augustus, this is an interesting collection of artefacts well displayed in a singularly suitable location: an ex-Olivetan Monastery built during the 15th-16th centuries on a site that curves around one side of the Roman amphitheatre. In one of the first rooms on the ground floor you'll see some highly expressive 2nd-1st century BC heads that must surely have been familiar to the 20th-century sculptor Marino Marini (*see chapter* **Florence: Museums**). The collections comprise fine Etruscan funerary objects, including urns, jewellery, votive figures and pottery, as well as fragments of Roman mosaic floors and bronze statuettes. But pride of place goes to the magnificent examples of highly refined coral-red pottery made in the Arezzo workshops between the 1st century BC and the 1st century AD.

Museo del Duomo/Diocescano d'Arte Sacra

Piazzetta dietro il Duomo (23 991). **Open** 10am-noon Thur-Sat. **Admission** L5,000.
With its upper floor location and restricted opening hours, this collection is hardly visitor-friendly. The powers that be are now looking round for a more suitable venue within the vicinity of the cathedral, for which many of the assembled artefacts were originally created. They include a 12th-century polychrome wooden Crucifix and three frescoes by Spinello Aretino as well as a terracotta bas-relief attributed to Bernardo Rossellino.

The backside of **Santa Maria.**

Fondling backsides in **Il Prato.**

Museo Statale d'Arte Medievale e Moderna

Via San Lorentino 8 (30 03 01). **Open** 9am-7pm daily. **Admission** L8,000; free for under-18s and over-60s.
The collections are housed in the elegant 15th-century Palazzo Bruni-Ciocchi, whose courtyard is said to have been designed by Bernardo Rossellino, the architect of Pienza (*see chapter* **Chianti & Siena Province**). The building is often referred to as 'la Dogana' because it was used as a customs house during the early 19th century. Happily, it has been well renovated to suit its new purpose. On the ground floor near the entrance there are Romanesque and Gothic stone carvings: bas-reliefs, ornate capitals and a number of sculptures found in or around Arezzo. The Medieval and Renaissance painting sections on the first floor are particularly strong, and include a gem-encrusted *Madonna and Child Enthroned* (c. 1270-80) by Guido da Siena as well as several works by Spinello Aretino and his followers. To the left of the main vestibule that groans under the weight of Vasari's enormous *Wedding Feast of Ahasuerus and Esther* (1548) there is a magnificent and beautifully displayed collection of 13th to 17th century glazed ceramics, most of them from central Italy.

Monuments

Anfiteatro Romano

Built during the 2nd century AD using local sandstone and travertine, the Roman Amphitheatre was located to the south of the city so that it could be easily reached by spectators from other parts of the region. Although no trace of the outer walls remains, the length of the main axis (122m) suggests that the elliptical structure was designed to accommodate from 8,000 to 10,000 people. Like the Roman baths and the aqueduct (a fascinating fragment of which can be seen at the **Archaeological Museum**, *see above*), the Amphitheatre suffered at the hands of the Germanic tribes who invaded the territories of the Roman Empire during the 5th and 6th centuries. Nearly 1,000 years later, Cosimo I, the first Medici Grand Duke (1537-74), thought nothing of using the handy blocks of stone for building the city fortifications. What remains (and there is still quite a lot of it, including the original pit or stage) has just been divested of encroaching greenery and should be available in the future for gentle collective use.

Piazza Grande

Much of the picturesque charm of this large, sloping square lies in its harmonious irregularity. Its present-day aspect is the fruit of a number of brilliant designs spanning 400 years or so. In fact the area first began to take shape in the Middle Ages, as witnessed by the rounded apse of the **Church of Santa Maria** with its three tiers of Romanesque arches projecting plumply into the square – or rather trapezoid. Next to this is the baroque **Palazzo**

del **Tribunale** and the smaller **Palazzo della Fraternità dei Laici**, a veritable compendium of architectural styles. The ground floor is distinctly Gothic, whereas the upper elevation (1434) is a tribute to Renaissance architectural ideals. The man who managed to reconcile tradition with innovation so cleverly was **Bernardo Rossellino**, who was later to pull off a similar feat on a much larger scale in Pienza. The palazzo was given its crowning glory nearly a hundred years later, when Vasari designed the clock tower replete with three chiming bells. However, Vasari's major achievement is the grandiose **Palazzo delle Logge** with the portico that once housed the city's most elegant stores and was off-limits for the *plebaglia*, or common folk. Nowadays, the portico, the square itself and all the surrounding area pullulate with bargain-hunters from all walks of life attracted by the vast antiques market held here the first Sunday of every month. The square is also used for the annual **Giostra del Saracino**, an historic jousting tournament in full costume that takes place on the first Sunday in September.

Fortezza Medicea

When the Medici took possession of Arezzo in 1531, they lost no time in improving its defences in view of the recent development of gunpowder and cannon fire. The overall project involved reducing the perimeter of the city walls, cutting down the number of access gates to four, creating seven bulwarks along the walls, and reinforcing the great fortress overlooking the town. This latter task led to a thoroughly rational, yet aesthetically pleasing, design. The new fortress was built between 1538 and 1560 on a star-shaped plan drawn up by Antonio da Sangallo the Elder. It featured three pointed projections and two heart-shaped ramparts providing a bastion that could cope with attack from any quarter. Well, almost any quarter. Local yobs have sprayed the inner walls of the ramparts with graffiti, while others have seen fit to use quiet corners as a refuse dump or toilet. However, all is apparently not lost. Some structural restoration is under way, and the surrounding gardens are being replanted. With a little cleaning up the Fortezza should prove to be a welcome island of airy quietude.

Parks & gardens

Il Prato

Tucked between the Fortezza Medicea and the Cathedral, the Prato is the only patch of green within the city walls, and even this is balding here and there. However, current replanting of trees and regrassing of... well, you wouldn't call them lawns... should reduce the dust that gets up with the slightest breeze and improve the general look of what is actually a perfectly pleasant place for reading a book or enjoying a little *dolcefarniente*.

Restaurants

The area around Arezzo abounds in wild mushrooms, especially the highly prized *porcino* (cep); moreover, the black truffle (*tartufo nero*) is also found in the vicinity. So look out for such sauces on pasta or *crostini* (toasted bread – usually an hors d'oeuvre, but good as an alternative to pasta if you want a lighter meal). Another typical first course is a soup made with *pasta e ceci*, pasta and chickpeas. As for the meat course, the local Chianina breed of cattle produces some of the best beef to be had in Italy, so steaks are particularly succulent and tasty.

Expensive

Buca di San Francesco
Via San Francesco 1 (23 271). **Open** noon-2.30pm Mon; noon-2.30pm, 7-9.30pm, Wed-Sun. **Average** L45,000. **Credit** AmEx, DC, EC, MC, V.
Founded in 1929 and furnished in Thirties medieval revival style, Arezzo's most famous restaurant has catered to illustrious patrons as varied as Harry Truman, King Gustav of Sweden, Salvador Dali and Charlie Chaplin. Do as they presumably did: go for the *zuppa di farro* (spelt soup) and the *pollo in porchetta* (chicken stuffed with herbs and salt then roasted). The owner assures us that anyone arriving with a copy of this guide will receive a free, numbered and signed print – although what of, we can't be sure.

Il Cantuccio
Via Madonna del Prato 76 (26 830). **Open** 12.30-2.20pm, 7.30-10.20pm, Thur-Tue. **Average** L45,000. **Credit** AmEx, MC, V.
Step down into Il Cantuccio's vaulted basement in the city centre for local fare from a menu that varies according to the season.

Mario
Viale Michelangelo 86 (24 310). **Open** 12.30-3pm, 7.30-10pm, Tue-Sun. **Average** L45,000. **No credit cards.**
Close to the station, Mario serves up inventive cuisine with due passion: for instance *risotto alla principessa* – a risotto made with shrimps and truffles.

Moderate

L'Agania
Via Mazzini 10 (25 381). **Open** noon-2.30pm, 7-10pm, Tue-Sun. **Average** L30,000. **Credit** AmEx, MC, V.
Just round the corner from the Antiques Market area, this place always seems a bit disorganised and is usually quite noisy, but the food's good and the atmosphere friendly. Tripe and a dish called *grifi* (stewed cheek of veal) are always available, but if this is not quite you, try the herb-stuffed roast rabbit instead.

Il Mulino
Chiassa Superiore 75 (36 18 78). **Open** noon-2pm, 7-9.30pm, Wed-Mon. **Average** L40,000. **Credit** AmEx, DC, EC, MC, V.
Head out of town in the direction of Bibbiena, and after about 10km you'll reach this excellent restaurant serving dishes such as *pappardelle al germano* – no, not Teutonic noodles, but pasta ribbons dressed with a wild duck sauce.

Il Torrino
Il Torrino 1 (36 02 64). **Open** noon-3pm, 7-10pm, daily. **Average** L40,000. **Credit** AmEx, DC, EC, MC, V.
Eight kilometres out of Arezzo on the Sansepolcro road, Il

Dog days on **Piazza Grande**.

Torrino is well worth the drive for both the food and the view. There's truffles and funghi aplenty in the right season. The *cappelli d'alpino* (ravioli made with nettles and stuffed with greens and ricotta) is highly recommended.

Cheap

Cecco
Corso Italia 215 (20 986). **Open** 12.30-2.30pm, 7.30-9.30pm, Tue-Sun. **Average** L25,000. **Credit** AmEx, DC, EC, MC, V.
Located at the station end of Arezzo's main drag, this trattoria serves traditional Tuscan cuisine and also offers a tourist menu for L16,000 which will buy you a pasta course, a meat course with veg and fruit for dessert.

Otello
Piazza Risorgimento 16 (22 648). **Open** noon-3pm, 7-10pm, Tue-Sun. **Average** L20,000.
Good pizza, but also home-made pasta and tasty trout just a stone's throw from the station.

Bars, cafés & gelaterias

For most Tuscans, a bar is a place you visit often but briefly for your morning cappuccino, a quick stand-up espresso after lunch and maybe an *aperitivo* before going home. By and large the only people who linger there for any length of time are pensioners playing cards in a smoky corner. So the word has none of the night-haunt implications it does in English. If anything these are rendered by the word 'pub', a term recently adopted for a new breed of venues serving drinks and sometimes food until late. Such places are often quite nicely designed and laid out, with little tables, marble surfaces, terrazzo floors and the ubiquitous muzak. By contrast, for a quiet chat over a decent cup of tea you should look for a Sala da Thè.

Bar Pasticceria Mignon

Via di Tolletta 16/20 (29 860). **Open** 7am-1pm, 3.30-8pm, Tue-Sun. **No credit cards**.
Exquisite cakes and pastries, home-made jams and candied fruits, and one door down a tea room where you can enjoy such sweetmeats with a decent pot of tea.

Caffè dei Costanti

Piazza San Francesco 19-20 (21 660). **Open** *Oct-May* 6.30am-8pm Tue-Sun; *June-Sept* 6.30am-midnight Tue-Sun; closed 4-18 Aug. **No credit cards**.
Situated beside the Arts Faculty and opposite the Basilica di San Francesco, this large, family-run establishment has rooms for playing cards and billiards, plenty of space for a quiet coffee or tea, a handsome bar selling home-made ice-cream and pastries, and tables out on the square where you can watch the world go by.

Caffè dell'Opera

Via Leone Leoni 72 (25 581). **Open** 9.30am-3am Tue-Sun. **Credit** V.
This place comes into its own in the evening, when some of the tables are drawn aside and people let off steam on the raised dance floor. On Wednesday, Thursday, Saturday and Sunday there's live Latin American music, and a disco on Tuesday and Friday.

Il Gelato di Guiducci

Via dei Cenci 24 (23 240). **Open** 11am-1.30pm, 2-11.30pm, daily. **No credit cards**.
A corner shop besieged from both sides by a continual flow of devotees of all the brown-beige-white ice-creams: cream, sweet rice, coffee, chocolate, hazelnut, etc. These are the specialities, though fruit flavours are also available.

Irish Pub

Via Oberdan 61 (23 313). **Open** 7.30pm-1.30am Tue-Sun; closed mid-June-Sept. **No credit cards**.
You know what to expect. Largely patronised late of an evening by 16- to 25-year-olds.

St Anton Pub

Via Garibaldi 150 (35 26 76). **Open** 7pm-1am Thur-Tue. **No credit cards**.
A long vaulted room with bays on either side: one of the new-style haunts where the kids go for a drink before setting off for an out-of-town disco (in summer usually the Dolce Verde at Castiglion Fibocchi). Pizza and other food also served.

San Gregory Pub

Via Vittorio Veneto 97 (21 81 18). **Open** 8pm-1am Tue-Sun; closed June-Sept. **No credit cards**.
Young professionals and entrepreneurs come here on Thursday and Friday evenings to catch up on chat with one ear and listen to music with the other.

Accommodation

Arezzo itself is still strangely lacking in hotels of any real charm, though there are various pleasant establishments in the countryside nearby. However, to judge by current improvements in restaurants, cafés and bars, it won't be long before some enterprising Aretino invests a little gold dust in creating some suitably attractive downtown accommodation.

Expensive

Val di Colle

Loc. Bagnoro (36 51 67). **Rates** *double L250,000.* **Credit** AmEx, MC, V.
Located 4km from the centre of town (beyond the stadium on the south side), this 14th-century country residence has

Arezzo cool.

been meticulously restored and beautifully furnished to create a gem of a small hotel. Antique furniture, paintings by Marino Marini, Vasarely and other modern masters, and beautiful linen can be found in the hotel's eight rooms. Breakfast is included in the price.

Moderate

Continentale
Piazza Guido Monaco 7 (20 251/fax 35 04 85). **Rates** (breakfast L15,000) *single L98,000; double L150,000.* **Credit** AmEx, DC, EC, MC, V.
Dull but decent, the sort of place that is likely to look worse after being 'improved'. Expect to pay around L30,000 for a meal in the surpassingly good restaurant (closed Sun and Mon).

Milano
Via Madonna del Prato 83 (26 836/fax 21 925). **Rates** *single L100,000; double L150,000.* **Credit** AmEx, DC, EC, MC, V.
Slightly characterless building containing a 27-room hotel that was revamped a couple of years ago and is now quite pleasant by downtown Arezzo hotel standards.

Villa Burali
Loc. Policiano 154 (SS 71) (97 90 45). **Rates** *L80-120,000 apartment for 2; L200-240,000 apartment for 4.* **Credit** AmEx, DC, EC, MC, V.
Located 7km from Arezzo towards Cortona, this well renovated 17th-century villa now comprises 11 mini-apartments. The place has a swimming pool in the grounds and its own restaurant (closed Mon).

Cheap

Villa Severi Youth Hostel
Via Redi (29 047). **Rates** (breakfast L2,000) *L20,000 per person.* **No credit cards.**
An agreeable old villa under new management with rooms sleeping between three and ten people. To get here, take the number 4 bus from outside the station in the direction of the Ospedale Vecchio and get out at the Ostello della Gioventù. At present they're returfing and replanting parkland just opposite; when the job's finished it should provide a pleasant patch of green, complete with sports facilities.

Shopping

Arezzo's main shopping artery is Corso Italia, the top end of which is a pedestrian precinct. As you wander along it you'll see the usual range of chic shoe and clothes shops, as well as a number of antique stores up towards the Pieve di Santa Maria. What follows is a magpie collection of specialist shops which you might not otherwise come across.

Amadeus
Via Guido Monaco 41A (37 09 34). **Open** 4-8pm Mon; 9am-1pm, 4-8pm, Tue-Sat. **Credit** V.
Myriad ties, scarves and belts. Italian designer labels as well as a slightly quirky collection of ties custom made for this shop. An ideal place for a getting a pressie for yourself or to take home.

La Boite d'Or
Piazza Risorgimento 4 (22 257). **Open** 9am-1pm Mon; 9am-1pm, 4-8pm, Tue-Sat. **Credit** V.
Don't expect to find Arezzo-made jewellery here, or in any of the better city jewellers. The locals go straight to the source (the factory) and cut out the middle man. Like most of her colleagues (Duranti in Corso Italia, to mention but one of many) what Lucilla Bianchini has done is seek out the work of a few artist-goldsmiths whose creations she sells exclusively: Gabriella Rivalta's enamelled gold necklaces and earrings, for instance. Just across the square is Max Mara, where you can look for a new outfit to go with the jewellery you've just bought.

Casa della Renna
Piazza San Michele 15 (35 67 74). **Open** 8am-1pm, 4-7.30pm, Mon-Sat. **No credit cards.**
Leather clothing off-the-peg and made-to-measure.

Imaginaria Arti Visive
Via Oberdan 31 (35 30 85). **Open** 9.30am-1pm, 4-8pm, Mon-Fri. **Credit** V.
Just off Corso Italia, this is both a bookstore and a gallery-cum-platform for cultural events: art, music, poetry, etc. It is also an information board for interesting things going on.

Libreria Pellegrini
Piazza San Francesco 7 (22 722). **Open** 9am-1pm, 4-8pm, Mon-Sat; closed *winter* 9am-1pm Mon, *summer* 4-8pm Sat. **Credit** AmEx, DC, EC, MC, V.

Giorgio Vasari

Giorgio Vasari (born in Arezzo in 1511, died in Florence in 1574) was an extraordinarily versatile man of great energy, considerable ambition and large ego. A technically expert though self-indulgently grandiose artist, he was acquainted with all the main schools of painting and liked to boast of the ease and speed with which he could execute the many commissions he received. (He once bragged to Michelangelo that he and two assistants had frescoed the 27m-long walls of the salon of the Cancelleria in Rome in just 100 days – "It looks like it," responded the master.) In his own time Vasari was also renowned for his achievements as an architect, especially once he had moved to Florence and become the official Medici architect and impresario. His designs include the Uffizi in Florence, the Palazzo delle Logge in Arezzo, the panoramic Loggia at Castiglion Fiorentino, the Palazzo dei Cavalieri in Pisa, the tomb of Michelangelo in Santa Croce in Florence and work for Pope Pius V in Rome that won him a knighthood in 1571. However, today Vasari's fame rests on his *Le Vite de' più eccellenti architetti, pittori e scultori italiani* (*The Lives of the Most Eminent Italian Architects, Painters, and Sculptors*, 1550). And if Vasari's self-conscious, vapid paintings attract little interest today, his opinions on Italy's panoply of outstanding Renaissance artists and architects remains respected and a vital source of information.

Belt up, Arezzo style.

A good general selection of books, plus a very well-stocked section on guide books (mostly in Italian) and maps. Also carries a range of books in English, including Penguin Classics and contemporary fiction.

Macelleria
Via Madonna del Prato 43 (23 728). **Open** 7.30am-1.30pm, 4.30-8pm, Mon, Tue, Thur, Fri; 7.30am-1.30pm Wed, Sat. **No credit cards**.

Apart from selling fine cuts of meat, Simonetta Maggini also makes her own sausages, salamis and other cold meats as well as preparing succulent specialities such as *anatra in porchetta* (duck stuffed with a mixture of garlic, wild fennel and salt and then roasted slowly in the oven).

Mondo Antico
Via Cavour 24/26 (21 801). **Open** 10am-12.30pm, 4-7.30pm, Mon-Fri; 10am-12.30pm Sat. **Credit** AmEx, DC, EC, MC, V.
In the road leading into Piazza San Francesco, this store sometimes has some amazing colonial furniture from the '20s and '30s – mostly from India and Indonesia.

Pasticceria de' Cenci
Via de' Cenci 17 (23 102). **Open** 8am-1pm, 4-8pm, Tue-Sat; 8am-1pm Sun. **No credit cards**.
Toothsome delights, both savoury and sweet.

Pitti
Via San Lorentino 15 (29 779). **Open** 9am-1pm, 4-7.30pm, Mon-Fri; 9am-1pm Sat. **No credit cards**.
Just opposite the Museo Statale d'Arte Medievale e Moderna, this hardware shop features an incredibly wide range of *maniglieria*, or handles for doors, drawers, cupboards, and so on in brass, steel, iron, glass, porcelain, wood, plastic, bone, and stone.

Stradivarius
Via Madonna del Prato 28 (22 010). **Open** 10am-1pm, 4-7.30pm, Mon-Fri; 10am-1pm Sat. **Credit** AmEx, DC, EC, MC, V.
Arezzo has more than its fair share of antiques stores, but this one stands out for its specialisation: linen, lace, drawn threadwork, needlework, etc.

Useful information

Tourist information
Azienda di Promozione Turistica (APT) *Piazza della Repubblica 22 (37 76 78/fax 20 839).* **Open** Oct-Mar 9am-1pm, 3-6.30pm, Mon-Sat; 9am-1pm 1st Sun of month; *Apr-Sept* 9am-1pm, 3pm-7pm, Mon-Sat; 9am-1pm Sun.
Conveniently located opposite the station; English spoken.

Guides The APT has a list of individual guides.

Telephones Most public phones take Telecom Italia phone cards as well as coins; at the beginning of Via Porta Buia there's a room with several phone booths and an operator.

Transport
Bicycle Hire – **City Bike** *Via de' Cenci 15 (24 541).*

Buses *Piazza della Repubblica.*
There are various lines heading out to rural areas from the terminal opposite the station. For info and tickets call ATAM Point in the same square *(38 26 51)*.

Car Hire – **Avis** *Piazza della Repubblica (35 42 32);* **Hertz** *Via Gobetti 35 (27 577).*

Railway Station *Piazza della Repubblica (27 353).*
The InterCity and InterRegionale trains take 40 minutes to reach Florence; local trains make more stops and the journey takes an hour (beware: IC trains require a supplement, to be bought with your ticket; you can get it on the train as well, but you have to pay a hefty surcharge. Before boarding all tickets must be punched in the square yellow boxes you'll find along the platforms).

Markets & festivals
Markets Every Saturday there's a **general market** selling clothes, food, flowers and household goods. On the first Sunday of each month and the previous Saturday the whole of the historic nucleus of Arezzo is completely taken over by the **Antiques Fair**: fine furniture, jewellery, rugs, bric-à-brac, collectibles and plenty of absolute rubbish. Exhausting but fun.

Festivals
Stagione teatrale at **Teatro Petrarca** *(23 975)* (November to March).
Stagione teatrale at **Piccolo Teatro** *(27 721)* – promotes an annual festival of one-act plays from October to December.
Arezzo Wave *(91 10 05)* – vibrant festival, with lots of indie music (early July).
Giostra del Saracino – a jousting tournament in full costume (first Sunday in September).
Concorso Polifonico Internazionale Guido d'Arezzo – international choral singing competition (late August).

Emergency services
Ambulance Croce Bianca *(22 660);* Misericordia *(24 242).*
Carabinieri *(112).*
Police *(113).*
'San Donato' Hospital *(30 57 47).*
USL (Unità Sanitaria Locale) *(30 51).*

Livorno, Grosseto & the Coast

Spectacular seaside scenery contrasts with the evocative but little visited ancient Etruscan heartland.

Far removed from the cultural honeypots of Florence, Siena et al, Grosseto, the southernmost region of Tuscany is often quite literally left off the tourist map. The same goes for the province of Livorno, a coastal strip whose beaches are popular with local Italians but little known outside the region. A brief stop in one of the ribbon resorts that service the main towns should be enough to explain why. Family holiday destinations like Marina di Grosseto and San Vincenzo are fine if you're a teenager on the make or an overwrought parent looking for enough facilities to keep a clutch of bored kids busy. But the fact that most seaside *pensioni* insist on at least half-board in the high season, and the L15,000 and up charged for a beach umbrella by the side-to-side *stabilimenti* that carve up the beachfront (often the only way to get access to the sea) make this an expensive, as well as a crowded, way to escape from the inland heat.

For those who are prepared to stray off the beaten track, however, there are two enclaves down south that are as unspoilt as anything Italy has to offer: Monte Argentario and the Monti dell'Uccellina reserve. And then there are the islands: Tuscany has more of them off its coast than any other mainland Italian region. Some are already well-known to tourists: mountainous Elba, which can seem an offshore German protectorate in summer, and Giglio, a haven for yachties and well-heeled Italian tourists. For island purists far-flung Capraia (a former penal colony, accessible by ferry from Livorno) offers the requisite sun-drenched solitude.

Inland, much of Grosetto and Livorno provinces are blissfully free of the tourist hordes who hog and clog the coastal resorts and big cultural destinations further north and east. The area close to the border with Lazio was once one of the most densely populated parts of ancient Etruria and remains rich in Etruscan ruins and relics.

The Maremma coast

Capalbio

Coming from Rome along the coastal Aurelia trunk-road or the adjacent Rome-Genova rail line,

*Beach in the **Monti dell'Uccellina** park.*

this perfectly preserved postcard village is one of the first things you see in Tuscany, clustered around its tower on a hilltop about 7km back from the coast. It has become famous as the summer HQ of Rome's rich left-wing politicos, writers and university profs, many of whom have houses in or around the village. The **Maria** restaurant at Via Comunale 3 (*0586 89 60 14. Open lunch & dinner. Closed Tue. Average L45,000*) is a good spot to try classic Maremmana food, including wild boar dishes and *acquacotta*, a traditional simple bread soup.

While the village itself is a pleasant place to wander around, what brings most people here is the long beach that stretches all the way from **Chiarone** – where there is a good campsite (*0564 89 01 01. Open May-Sept. L13,000 per day per tent; L14,500 per day per person*) – to **Ansedonia**, a former Etruscan hilltop settlement now bristling with upmarket holiday villas. To get there, catch one of the three or four daily trains from Grosseto or Rome that stop at Capalbio station, and walk the 3km down to the beach alongside the Lago di Burano lagoon (now a WWF reserve). If you time it right you will be able to eat in the **Bar della Stazione** (*0564 89 84 24. Open lunch & dinner; closed Tue. Average L40,000*), an unassuming station bar with an excellent trattoria in the back room, where you can dine to the roar of passing trains.

Livorno, Grosseto & the Coast

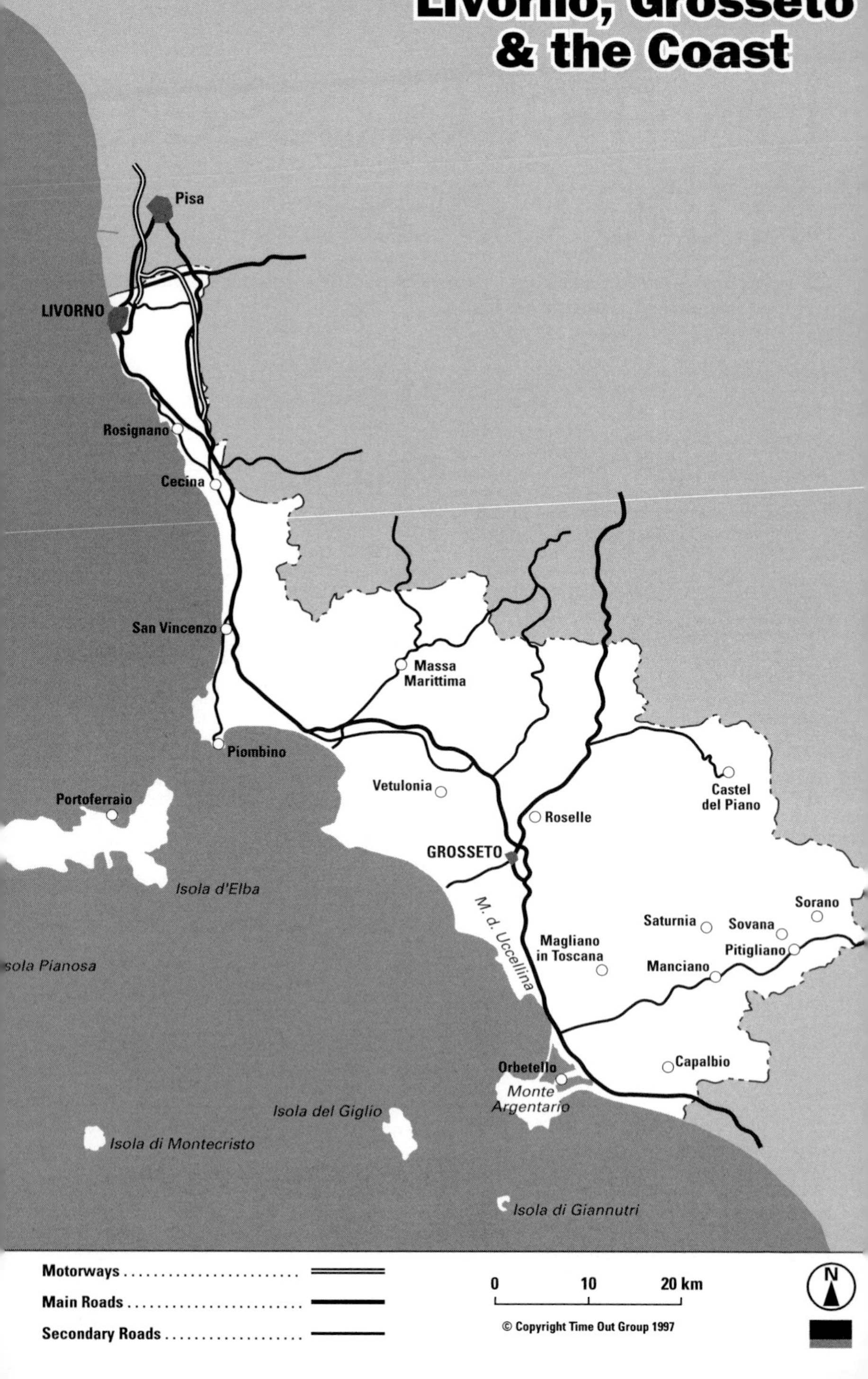

Pisa

LIVORNO

Rosignano

Cecina

San Vincenzo

Massa Marittima

Piombino

Vetulonia

Portoferraio

Castel del Piano

Roselle

GROSSETO

Isola d'Elba

Isola Pianosa

M. d. Uccellina

Saturnia

Sovana

Sorano

Magliano in Toscana

Pitigliano

Manciano

Isola del Giglio

Capalbio

Orbetello

Monte Argentario

Isola di Montecristo

Isola di Giannutri

Motorways ....

Main Roads ....

Secondary Roads ....

0   10   20 km

© Copyright Time Out Group 1997

N

Isola del Giglio

With its vine-covered terraces rising precipitously from the sea above pastel houses, and its rocky coves offering snorkelling of Cousteau-like splendour, it's hardly surprising that the island of Giglio should have been more than discovered in the last couple of decades (*tourist information 0564 80 94 00*). Come out of season – especially in Spring, when the wild flowers are out – to see it at its best and ensure a bed for the night. There are three villages: **Giglio Porto**, where the ferry docks; **Campese** on the other side, with the island's best beach and a growing number of resort hotels; and the picturesque village of **Giglio Castello** on the ridge between the two, with its medieval walls and steep narrow lanes.

Overlooking Giglio Porto, the three-star **Castello Monticello** (*0564 80 92 52. Rates half board per person L120,000*) occupies a crenellated folly. For the ultimate full-immersion sun and sea experience, try **Pardini's Hermitage** (Cala degli Alberi, near Giglio Castello *0564 80 90 34. Rates full board L205,000*), located in a secluded cove only accessible on foot or by boat (the staff will come and fetch you).

Tony's, on the northern end of the beach in Giglio Campese below the tower (*0564 80 64 52. Open Apr-end Oct 7am-1am*), can be relied on for everything "from a cappuccino to a lobster". Pizzas start at L8,000.

Orbetello

Bulging out like a knuckle in the middle of the central of the three slender isthmuses that connect Monte Argentario to the mainland, Orbetello is a pleasant, lived-in town. It has fine remnants of Spanish fortifications dating from the 16th and 17th centuries, when this was the capital of the Stato dei Presidi, a small Spanish enclave on the Tuscan coast. There is a small **Antiquarium** with some uninspiring Etruscan and Roman exhibits, and the **cathedral** has a pretty Gothic facade, but Orbetello is really more about atmosphere than sightseeing. Join the evening *struscio* (the aimless evening parade up and down the central Corso Italia) before taking in a plate of eels (fished from the lagoon) at one of the town's many good, simple trattorias such as **Il Nocchino** at Via dei Mille 64 (*0564 86 03 29. Open lunch & dinner; closed Wed. Average L35,000*). Of the town's three cheaper hotels, the **Piccolo Parigi**, Corso Italia 159 (*0564 86 72 33. Rates single L45,000; double L70,000*), is the nicest option.

From Orbetello station (3km east of town), buses leave regularly for the centre, Porto Santo Stefano and Porto Ercole (*see below*). If you get the Porto Ercole bus and ask to be put off at "il bivio per la Feniglia" you can visit the **Tombolo della Feniglia** – the southernmost isthmus, which borders the lagoon on one side (watch out for killer mosquitoes) and the sea on the other. Only walkers and cyclists are admitted to this peaceful pine forest, which is inhabited by a small colony of roe deer. Walk a couple of kilometres to the sea, and you will have a sweeping sandy beach almost to yourself. There is a campsite, the **Feniglia** (*0564 83 10 90. Office open 10.30am-1pm, 4-8pm daily. Rates L10-16,000 per day per tent; L10,000 per day person*) at the top (Argentario) end of the Tombolo. The best eating option on the beach – apart from a couple of snack bars – is the delightful **Mama Licia** (*0564 83 41 87. Open summer lunch & dinner daily; winter lunch daily. Average L50,000*) serving excellent seafood.

In the middle of the Parco dell'Uccellina, inland between Talamone and Fonteblanda, is the excellent, rustic, open-air **Ristoro Buratta** (*0564 83 56 14. Open lunch & dinner daily; closed Nov-Apr. Average L25,000*).

Just north of Orbetello, off the Aurelia is **La Parrina** (*0564 86 26 36. Open 8am-1pm, 3-7pm, Mon-Sat*). This Azienda Agricola produces its own fruit, vegetables, wine, olive oil and superb cheeses, all of which are sold at very reasonable prices at the farm shop. There are also apartments to rent.

Monte Argentario

You can trek up rocky Monte Telegrafo – all 635m of it, swim off rocky coves where (unusually for the Mediterranean) you can actually see the fish, or hang out with the yachties. A mountain rising abruptly from the sea, Monte Argentario is the Tuscan coast at its most rugged. It looks as though it should be an island, and it was until the 18th century, when the two long outer sand-spits created by the action of the tides finally reached the mainland.

Porto Santo Stefano to the north and the smaller, more exclusive **Porto Ercole** to the south are the only towns. A tortuous 'panoramic' road connects the two, with unasphalted stretches on the southern side where the best swimming coves are. Porto Santo Stefano is the jumping-off point for the island of Giglio (five ferries a day in summer operated by Torema; *0564 81 08 03*).

One of the nicest places to eat in Porto Santo Stefano is **Dal Greco** at Via del Molo 1 (*0564 81 48 85. Open lunch & dinner; closed Tue. Average L70,000*), a seafood restaurant with a terrace overlooking the quay; in Porto Ercole, **Bacco in Toscana**, Via San Paolo della Croce 6 (*0564 83 30 78. Open dinner Mon, Tue, Thur-Sat; lunch Sun. Average L50,000*) offers excellent seafood at reasonable prices. For hotels in Porto Santo Stefano, the **tourist office** in Corso Umberto (*0564 81 42 08. Open 9am-1pm, 4-6pm, Mon-Sat*) is the best starting-point. More exclusive Porto Ercole offers only the one-star **La Conchiglia**

(0564 83 31 34. Rates single L55,000; double L90,000) and the two-star **Stella Marina** (0564 83 30 55. Rates single L90,000; double L155,000) in the budget range. If you have the cash, though, splash out on the exclusive, secluded **Il Pellicano** (0564 83 38 01. Rates double L596,000), perched splendidly above the rocky coastline some 3km out of town, with its own private, rocky beach.

A more affordable out of town option is **Lo Strambotto**, an unmarked trattoria with rooms (0564 60 50 02. Rates double L60,000 or L60,000 half board per person. Restaurant open dinner Tue-Sat; lunch & dinner Sun. Average L35,000). It is reached by exiting the Aurelia at Albinia, following the road to Manciano, turning right to Cutignolo and continuing for just under 3km.

Monti dell'Uccellina

Between the fishing village of **Talamone** and the **Ombrone** river estuary lies one of the wildest and most beautiful stretches of the Tuscan coast. Rising in hog-backed swells between the sea and what used to be a malarial swamp, the **Monti dell'Uccellina** has long been a *parco naturale*, and in this case the designation is more than just a label. The park is run and regulated with military efficiency from a visitor's centre (0564 40 70 98. Open 8am-4pm daily. Admission L8-9,500. From 15 June to 30 Sept reserve can only be visited with a guide) at **Alberese**, a small village on the landward side of the hills. (While you're waiting to join a tour – or perhaps more advisably, on the way back – try a cocktail at the small kiosk bar in the main square: the Swiss barman has won several bar-tending prizes). Centuries of isolation and its present protected status make this a birdwatcher's and fauna-spotter's paradise: at dusk you stand a good chance of seeing wild boar, and perhaps even the elusive crested porcupine. Birds – either migratory or resident – include ospreys, falcons, hoopoes, kingfishers, herons and the rare Knight of Italy. The flora ranges from the mudflats and umbrella pines of the estuary to the untouched Mediterranean *macchia* of the hills, taking in gorse, wild rosemary, dwarf pines and cork oaks.

The park is divided into two areas, each with its own timetable. The outer areas, which include the Marina di Alberese beach 'resort' (ie a car park and snack bar) and the salt marshes beyond – home to long-horned Maremma cattle and a variety of wading birds – are open every day from 9am until one hour before sunset. The inner areas – which include four waymarked trails – keep the same hours, but are accessible only on Wed, Sat and Sun, by arrangement with the visitor's centre in Alberese. From here a bus (included in the entrance fee) takes eager hikers to **Pratini** in the centre of the reserve, point of departure for the four trails, the most rewarding of which is the three-hour round-trip up

to the ruined 11th-century abbey of **San Rabano**. It's worth phoning ahead to book in summer, as places on each tour are strictly limited. From Pratini you can also wander down to the beach – a sweep of white sand between a 16th-century watchtower and a distant cliff – which is the most enticing and least crowded stretch of sand on the whole Tuscan coast. The same point can be reached by trudging along the sand for an hour from Marina di Alberese.

Talamone offers the only accommodation for miles around: try the three-star **Capo d'Uomo** (0564 887077. Open Apr-Oct. Rates single L100-120,000; double L140,000).

From Grosseto to Livorno

Between two of Tuscany's least visited provincial capitals, there are some pleasant resorts and a few stretches of protected coastline, but the real pulls are either just back from the coast or just off it – on the island of **Elba** (see below). Inland, Etruscan sites like **Roselle** and **Vetulonia**, both within a 15-km radius of Grosseto, are worth a detour, as is the fine medieval town of **Massa Marittima** (see below).

Its distance from the main centres and the lack of any single cultural goldmine means that this southernmost area of Tuscany is often, quite literally, left off the tourist map of the region. But for those with their own transport, or with the necessary reserves of time and patience, the depopulated expanses of the Etruscan heartland can be as rewarding as the more familiar cypress-and-fresco territory further north.

Grosseto, the regional capital, is not really worth a stop: even before the town was ravaged by Second World War bombing raids, insensitive rebuilding had altered the original Medieval aspect of the centre, including the early 14th-century Duomo. Around the edge of town, a series of characterless housing estates offer one of Tuscany's few serious attempts at urban malaise. If you do find yourself with time to kill between trains, take a half-hour walk around the hexagonal defensive walls erected by Grand Duke Ferdinando I in 1593. The bastions which stud the six angles have been turned into picnic-friendly public gardens.

Along the coast itself, **Castiglione della Pescaia** is one of the most attractive resorts, combining the no-nonsense bustle of a fishing port with a good selection of hotels and restaurants. Exclusive **Punta Ala** is a purpose-built playground for the idle rich, complete with marina, golf course and private beaches: a modern, free-market version of the region's island prison colonies.

Between here and Livorno a series of carbon-copy family resorts, each with adjacent umbrella-pine picnic area, offer little reason to stop. If anyone recommends that you stop in San Vincenzo to eat at the **Gambero Rosso** restaurant, ignore them. That this is the best restaurant in Italy is a myth that needs exploding: the food *is* quite good, but the staff are so ludicrously pretentious and the atmosphere so brittle that eating there is simply not a pleasant experience. Still, it could be useful to recommend it to those irritating people in the villa next door who party round the pool to Macarena every night; it's at Piazza della Vittoria 13 (*0565 70 10 21. Open lunch & dinner; closed Tue. Average L100,000*).

Massa Marittima

In this wild, depopulated part of the Maremma, Massa is an unexpected enclave of art, history and civic pride. Its isolated position was one of the reasons it managed to survive as an independent city state for 110 years before being taken over by Siena in 1335; the other was its mineral wealth. Massa dominates the high southern ranges of the Colline Metallifere, a rich source of iron, copper and other minerals, which were one of the economic driving forces behind the early Renaissance. When the mines were closed in 1396, Massa's boom years were followed by half a millenium of neglect, until a small-scale return to mining and the draining of the surrounding marshes turned the tide in the middle of the 19th century. As a result, the town is preserved in amber: its centre represents one of the most uniform examples of 13th-century town planning anywhere in Tuscany.

Things to see
The **Duomo** was built in the Pisan style; it harmoniously blends Romanesque and Gothic details, despite the time lapse between its foundation in the early 13th century and the addition of the campanile in 1400. The bare stone interior is an artistic treasure-house: among the highlights are the Baptistery, with 13th-century bas-reliefs by Giroldo da Como, and the Arca di San Cerbone behind the altar, with more exquisite bas-reliefs showing scenes from the life of San Cerbone, 6th-century Bishop of Populonia. Also on the central Piazza Garibaldi, on the severe 13th-century Palazzo della Podestà, is the **Museo Civico Archeologico** (*0566 90 22 89. Open Apr-Sept 10am-12.30pm, 3.30-7pm, Tue-Sun; Oct-Mar 10am-12.30pm, 3.30-5pm*), with a small Etruscan collection and a marvelous 1330 *Maestà* by Ambrogio Lorenzetti. Up Via Moncini is the **Città Nuova** or 'new town' (ie the 13th-14th century bit rather than the 12th-13th century bit) with a fine Sienese arch.

Where to stay
Sole *Corso Libertà 43 (0566 90 19 71/fax 90 19 59).* **Rates** *single* L75,000; *double* L115,000. **Credit** AmEx, V. The three-star Sole, in a characteristic old palazzo, filled a gap when it opened a few years ago.

Cris *Via Roma 9/10 (0566 90 33 30).* **Rates** *single* L28,000; *double* L45,000. **Credit** AmEx, DC, EC, MC, V. The only other option in town is this unremarkable one-star hotel.

Where to eat
Da Tronca *Vicolo Porte 5 (0566 90 19 91).* **Open** lunch Thur-Tue. **Average** L35,000. **No credit cards.**

A lively, cheap osteria in the centre of town, of the creative regional variety: try the *tortelli di zucca gialla e crema di noci* (marrow-filled tortelli with walnut sauce).

Enoteca Grassini *Via della Libertà 1 (0566 94 01 49).* **Open** 9am-3pm, 5-10pm, Mon-Sat. **No credit cards.** You can put together a picnic, eat a filled roll at the counter or sit down for a plate of honest local fare (soups are a strong point).

Festivals
The big pull is the **Balestro del Girifalco** on the first Sunday after 22 May (the feast day of San Bernardino of Siena, who was born here). The locals certainly take this pageant seriously: the Renaissance costumes are dazzling, the *sbandieratori* (flag-throwers) faultless, and the final contest – when teams from the town's three *terzieri* attempt to shoot down a mechanical falcon with their crossbows – is a sight worth seeing.

Livorno

Livorno (nobody calls it 'Leghorn' any more) is a big working port: if you take it on its own no-nonsense terms, it can be a refreshing antidote to art-history overload, as well as a good hopping-off point for the islands of Elba, Capraia, Corsica and Sardinia.

Blanket bombing during the last war did away with most of its few historic monuments, and postwar reconstruction finished the job: Buontalenti's long, majestic Piazza Grande was cut in two and all that remains of the 16th-century Duomo is Inigo Jones's fine portico. But art and architecture was never really the main point of the place. Developed as a sea port by Cosimo I, it owed its prosperity to a far-sighted constitution proclaimed in 1593 which allowed foreigners to reside in the city regardless of nationality and religion. Livorno soon became a bustling cosmopolitan trading centre with a large Jewish community – coming mainly from Portugal and Spain – which even developed its own dialect, known as *Bagitto*.

Today it is still the **Porto Mediceo** that is the focus of city life, with fishing boats clustered under the weathered red-brick bastion of the **Fortezza Vecchia**, designed by Sangallo the Younger in 1521. From here the canals of the area known ambitiously as **Venezia Nuova** extend, tracing the pentagonal perimeter of Francesco I's late 16th-century plan for an 'ideal city'. This is a good place to wander, taking in the sights, sounds and smells of the port; here too are some of the city's famed seafood restaurants – try **Gennarino**, just east of the Duomo (*0586 88 8 093. Open lunch & dinner; closed Wed. Average L45,000*) or the excellent **La Chiave**, just across the moat from the imposing, gloomy Fortezza Nuova, Scali delle Cantine 52 (*0586 88 86 09. Open dinner Thur-Tue. Average L50,000*). Another great spot to sample typical Livornese dishes is **L'Antica Venezia**, Via dei Bagnetti 1 (*0586 88 73 53. Open lunch & dinner Tues-Sat. Average L30,000*). Try the famous *cacciucco*, a thick, rich fish soup served with toasted garlicky bread or *fritto di paranza*, deep-fried squid and little fishes. A good place for *vino* and snacks is **Enoteca DOC**, Via Goldoni 40-44 (*0586 88 75 83. Open lunch Tue-Sun. Average L30,000*).

Piombino & Elba

Piombino is where you catch the ferry to the island of Elba – and the town's ugly, moribund steelworks will hardly make you want to linger. But there is good walking across a surprisingly unspoilt headland to the tiny fishing port of **Baratti**, where you can visit the Etruscan necroplis of **Populonia** (semi-official guides wait to show you around; a L5,000 tip should do the trick).

When Napoleon turned up on the island of **Elba** in May 1814 for an enforced stay there was little here except a thriving iron ore mining industry, small-scale wine production and widespread poverty. When he did a runner ten months later, few of his schemes to improve the islanders' lot had borne fruit, and little changed until the advent of mass tourism in the 1970s, which came just as the last workable reserves of ore were drying up. The retooling has been a mixed blessing; the island is deserted in winter as only out-of-season resorts can be, while in August its resident population of around 30,000 is swollen to almost a million. Early summer or September are the best times to visit.

Portoferraio is the island's capital, main ferry port and transportation hub. It's also the focus of Napoleonic interest: the man's town residence, the **Palazzo dei Mulini**, is worth a visit for its views and Empire-style furnishings, so incongruous in this Mediterranean setting. His summer retreat, the Neoclassical **Villa Napoleonica di San Martino** (6km southwest of town, off the road for Marciana), is strictly for pilgrims.

Choosing between Elba's many seaside village resorts can be a problem, as most look pastelly and comfortable without really grabbing the attention. Some recommended spots that get the accommodation, food and clean beaches package about right are the stretch between **Enfola** on its narrow isthmus just east of Portoferraio and **Biodola** with its long sandy beach; the verdant sprawl of **Sant'Andrea** in the northwest corner; and the small-scale resorts south of **Capoliveri**, each clustered around a sandy cove. The villages in the rugged interior can be just as rewarding, especially out of season when walking is an option. Pretty **Marciana** in the west has fine medieval and Renaissance quarters; it is also the starting point for the ascent of **Monte Capanne** (1,018m), Elba's highest point.

First port of call in summer should be the tourist office in Calata Italia 26 (*0565 91 46 71. Open summer 8am-8pm daily; winter 8am-1pm, 3-6pm, Mon-Sat*), next to the bus station: they have a list of the island's hotels and will do the phoning round for you. Two more unusual options among hundreds: agriturismo at the **Monte Fabbrello** winery just outside Portoferraio (*0565 93 33 24. Rates*

4-*person apartments from L100,000 per night*) and the **Cernia** (*0565 908194. Rates half board L120,000 per person*) in Sant'Andrea, a delightful three-star hotel surrounded by a park and facing the sea with its own patch of white sand.

Magliano in Toscana

Surrounded by olive trees and kitchen gardens and ringed by impressive 15th-century brick walls, Magliano dominates the plain that stretches from here to the sea. It's a quiet, compact town and its sights needn't take up more than half an hour of your time; but one of the real attractions of the place is the evening *passeggiata* up and down the narrow main street, from the Porta San Giovanni, past the pretty patchwork church of San Giovanni Battista and a few sturdy Sienese-style noble palazzi to the opposite gate, the Porta San Martino, which opens with crenellated pomp onto a field. Come around sunset, spin out the *passeggiata* by stopping every ten metres to coo over a local bambino, and then restore your energies by sampling some of the solid Maremman specialities at **Da Sandra**, Corso Garibaldi 20 (*0564 59 21 96. Open lunch & dinner; closed Mon. Average L45,000 – book ahead for a table outside*). Wherever you eat, don't miss out on the local Morellino di Scansano red wine – it's 100 per cent Sangiovese, like many of the more self-important super-Tuscans from the Chianti area; good producers are Le Pupille and Erik Banti.

Around 2km out of town, the ruined 13th-century abbey of **San Bruzio**, a roofless octagonal pile set amidst an olive grove, is a photographer's dream. For those wanting to stick around – and with its daily bus services to Grosseto, Albenga and the coastal beaches, Magliano is not a bad base There's is a single, basic one-star hotel, **I Butteri** (*0564 58 98 24. Rates double with bath L70,000*).

Saturnia

Few come here for the village itself – a rather dour affair up on the hill with Etruscan walls and a parish hall of a museum. The interest is down below in the valley, where a lesser tributary of the Albenga has an unusual property: it's hot. A huge, Soviet-style thermal establishment diverts some of the water for its own sinister purposes, but there's plenty left over for the real attraction downstream: the **Cascatelle del Gorello**, where the soupy green stuff cascades down through a series of person-sized basins alongside a ruined watermill. Choose a pool, rip your kit off, and wallow (daubing your face with white clay scooped up from the depths is *de rigueur*). The *cascatelle* are on the road from Saturnia to Montemerano: the first sign that you're getting close is the Dantean stench of sulphur; the second the tailback of German camper vans in and out of season.

There are a couple of good restaurants in the small but perfectly-formed hamlet of Montemerano, 6km south. **Da Caino** at Via Canonica 3 *(0564 60 28 17. Open lunch & dinner; closed lunch Wed, Thur out of season. Average L80,000)* is a real temple of Tuscan cuisine, which offers a nouvelle take on local dishes and ingredients, especially game birds. The wine list is epic in extent, and the final damage is surprisingly limited: around L80,000 a head for three courses. In the same village an equally tasty low-budget option is the **Osteria Passaparola**, Via del Bivio 16 *(0564 60 28 27. Open lunch & dinner; closed Thur. Average L40,000. Rates single L50,000; double L60,000)*, which also has a few rooms.

Pitigliano, *a hilltown built on tufa.*

The Heart of Etruria

The territory covered by the Etruscan League between the 8th and the 4th centuries BC stretched from Bologna to the gates of Rome, but the area on both sides of the border between Lazio and Tuscany was the most densely settled. The classic Etruscan village was located on a tufa platform above a fast-flowing river, preferably with an adjacent hillock for use as a necropolis. **Pitigliano**, **Sovana** and **Sorano** fit the bill perfectly, and offer some of southern Tuscany's best medieval architecture into the bargain. Be warned that getting here requires a certain amount of dedication, especially for those without wheels. Pitigliano is connected by bus with Grosseto and Orbetello; for times ring **RAMA** in Grosseto *(0564 47 51 11 – this is a temporary number)* or Orbetello *(0564 85 00 00. Office open 6.30am-6.20pm Mon-Sat)*.

Perched dramatically on a narrow tufa raft, Etruscan **Pitigliano** rose to prominence in the 14th century under the Orsini family. Up until the last war it was the home of a thriving Jewish community, attracted here by increasing Medici tolerance from the 16th century onwards. This contrasted with the often harsh treatment received by Jews in the Papal States to the south. All that is left of the diaspora today is a small **Museum of Jewish History**, housed in the former synagogue in Via Zuccarelli, and a pasticceria just around the corner which still makes a local Jewish pastry called *sfratti*, literally 'the evicted'.

Modern Pitigliano is a compact, working town, best appreciated by simply wandering through the narrow lanes of the Medieval centre, with side streets offering the occasional dizzying view over the gorges below. The only real sight is the 16th-century **Palazzo Orsini** and its adjacent **aqueduct**, designed by Sangallo the Younger in such a way that its arches complete the only section of perimeter wall not formed by the houses themselves. A small museum of local history and archaeological finds is located in the palace courtyard.

For sheer atmosphere, it's hard to beat **Sovana**, a semi-abandoned village which was in the major league under the Etruscans and again between the 9th and the 12th centuries, when it became a thriving bishopric under the dominion of the wealthy Aldobrandini family. One of the clan's most famous scions, the great reforming pope Gregory VII, was born here in around 1020. With its Medici fishbone paving, the central Via di Mezzo is lined with palazzi and churches left behind by the high tide: the 13th-century **Palazzo Pretorio** (which houses a small museum of local history), the arched **Loggetta del Capitano** next door, and the exquisite, frescoed church of **Santa Maria** opposite, a Romanesque jewel which contains a unique ciborium from the 8th or 9th century. At the other end of town where the houses thin out is the **Duomo**, a Lombard-Romanesque structure with a luminous interior and a fine carved portal on the left side. Sovana also has two of the best places to sleep and eat in the area: the **Taverna Etrusca**, Piazza del Pretorio 16 *(0564 61 61 83. Restaurant open lunch & dinner; closed Mon. Average L40,000)*, and the **Scilla**, Via di Sotto 3 *(0564 61 65 31. Restaurant open lunch & dinner; closed Tue. Average L25,000)*. For food, the Taverna Etrusca has been in the ascendant for the past few years (the pasta is uniformly good, the *agnelli con capperi* , lamb with capers, reliable, and the ricotta-based desserts are outstanding).

Below the town lies the **Etruscan necropolis** area, consisting of a series of tombs cut into the tufa walls of the Fosso Calesina torrent, among which is the relatively late (2nd century BC) monumental Tomba Ildebranda, complete with pedestal and sculpted columns. You are free to wander around here; for information on the more out-of-the-way tombs, ask in the Taverna Etrusca.

To the east along a road dramatically cut into the tufa lies **Sorano**, a Medieval town which spills down the hill on a series of terraces – rather too literally, as a series of landslides have helped to depopulate the old town, which is dominated by a 15th-century **Orsini Rocca**. It's a good place for browsing around the craft shops, fostered by the local council as a way of injecting some life back into what had risked becoming a ghost town.

Vocabulary

Any attempt at speaking Italian will always be appreciated, and is often necessary; away from services like tourist offices, hotels and restaurants popular with foreigners, the level of English is not very high. When entering a shop or restaurant it's the practice to announce your presence with *'buon giorno'* or *'buona sera'*, and in the street, feel free to ask directions. People will often go out of their way to help.

Italian is spelt as it is pronounced, and vice versa. Stresses usually fall on the penultimate syllable and, if not, are indicated by accents. There are two forms of the second person, the formal **lei**, to be used with strangers, and the informal **tu**. Men and masculine nouns are accompanied by adjectives ending in 'o', women and female nouns by adjectives ending in 'a'.

PRONUNCIATION
Vowels

a – as in **a**sk
e – like **a** in **a**ge (closed e) or **e** in s**e**ll (open e)
i – like **ea** in **ea**st
o – as in h**o**tel (closed o) or in h**o**t (open o)
u – as in b**oo**t

Consonants

c before a, o or u is like the **c** in **c**at
c before an e or an i is like the **ch** in **ch**eck.
ch is like the **c** in **c**at
g before a, o or u is like the **g** in **g**et
g before an e or an i is like the **j** in **j**ig
gh is like the **g** in **g**et
gl followed by an i is like **lli** in mi**lli**on
gn is like **ny** in ca**ny**on
qu is as in **qu**ick
r is always rolled
s has two sounds, as in **s**oap or ro**s**e
sc is like the **sh** in **sh**ame
sch is like the **sc** in **sc**out
z has two sounds, like ts and dz
Double consonants are always sounded twice.

USEFUL PHRASES

hello and **goodbye** (informal) – *ciao*
good morning, good day – *buon giorno*
good afternoon, good evening – *buona sera*
I don't understand – *Non capisco/non ho capito*
do you speak English? – *parla inglese?*
please – *per favore*
thank you – *grazie*
how much does it cost/is it? – *quanto costa?/quant'è?*
when does it open? – *quando apre?*
where is... ? – *dov'è...?*
excuse me – *scusi* (polite) *scusa* (informal)
open – *aperto*; **closed** – *chiuso*
exit – *uscita*
left – *sinistra*; **right** – *destra*
car – *macchina*; **bus** – *autobus*; **train** – *treno*
bus stop – *fermata d'autobus*

ticket/s – *biglietto/i*
I would like a ticket to... – *Vorrei un biglietto per...*
postcard – *cartolina*; **stamp** – *francobollo*
glass – *bicchiere*
coffee – *caffè*; **tea** – *tè*
water – *acqua*; **wine** – *vino*; **beer** – *birra*
bedroom – *camera*
booking – *prenotazione*
Monday *lunedì*; **Tuesday** *martedì*; **Wednesday** *mercoledì*; **Thursday** *giovedì*; **Friday** *venerdì*; **Saturday** *sabato*; **Sunday** *domenica*
yesterday *ieri*; **today** *oggi*; **tomorrow** *domani*
morning *mattina*; **afternoon** *pomeriggio*; **evening** *sera*; **night** *notte*

CHATTING UP

Do you have a light? – *Hai da accendere?*
What's your name? – *Come ti chiami?*
Would you like a drink? – *Vuoi bere qualcosa?*
Where are you from? – *Di dove sei?*
What are you doing here? – *Che fai qui?*
Do you have a boy/girlfriend? – *Hai un ragazzo/una ragazza?*

BEING ALOOF

I don't smoke – *Non fumo*
I'm married – *Sono sposato/a*
I'm tired – *Sono stanco/a*
I'm going home – *Vado a casa*
I have to meet a friend – *Devo andare a incontrare un amico/una amica*

INSULTS

shit – *merda*
idiot – *stronzo*
fuck off – *vaffanculo*
dickhead – *testa di cazzo*
What the hell are you doing? – *Che cazzo fai?*

NUMBERS

0 *zero*; **1** *uno*; **2** *due*; **3** *tre*; **4** *quattro*; **5** *cinque*; **6** *sei*; **7** *sette*; **8** *otto*; **9** *nove*; **10** *dieci*; **11** *undici*; **12** *dodici*; **13** *tredici*; **14** *quattordici*; **15** *quindici*; **16** *sedici*; **17** *diciassette*; **18** *diciotto*; **19** *diciannove*; **20** *venti*; **21** *ventuno*; **22** *ventidue*; **30** *trenta*; **40** *quaranta*; **50** *cinquanta*; **60** *sessanta*; **70** *settanta*; **80** *ottanta*; **90** *novanta*; **100** *cento*.

Advertisers' Index

Please refer to the relevant sections for
addresses/telephone numbers

Index

Where there is more than one page reference, figures in bold indicate the section in the guide giving key information. Italics indicate illustrations. Unless otherwise specified, the musuems, hotels, bars, clubs, etc, listed below are in Florence.

Maps

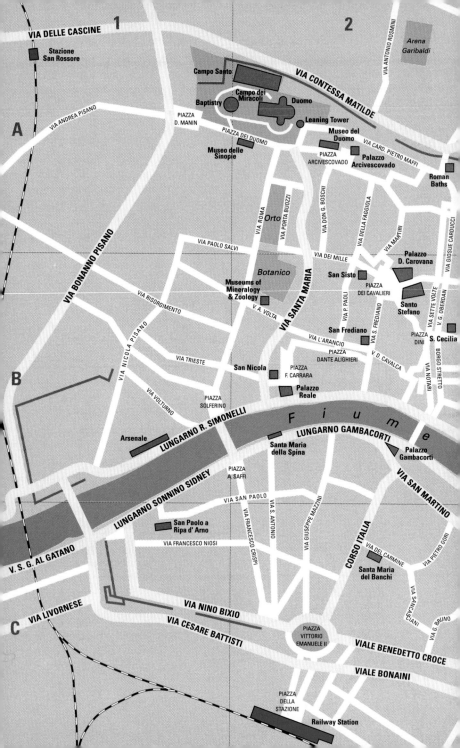

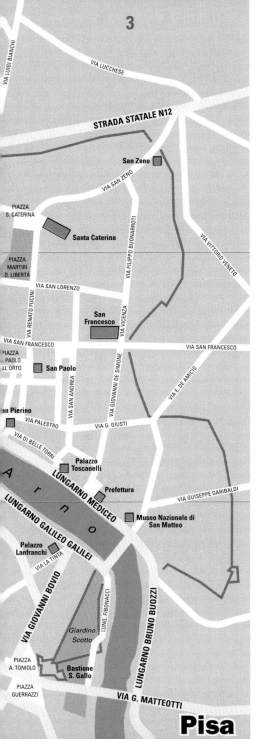

STREET INDEX

Al Gatano, Via S. G. - C1
Alighieri, Piazza Dante - B2
Arancio, Via L' - B2
Arcivescovado, Piazza - A2
Battisti, Via Cesare - C1, 2
Bianchi, Via Luigi - A3
Bixio, Via Nino - C1,2
Bonaini, Viale - C2
Bonanno Pisano, Via - A1, B1
Bovio, Via Giovanni - C3
Bruno, Via G. - C2
Buonarroti, Via Filippo - A3, B3
Buozzi, Lung. Bruno - C3
Card. Pietro Maffi, Via - A2
Carducci, Via Giosue - A2
Carmine, Via del - C2
Carrara, Piazza F. - B2
Cascine, Via delle - A1
Cavalca, Via D. - B2
Cavalieri, Piazza dei - B2
Contessa Matilde, Via - A2
Corso Italia - B2, C2
Crispi, Via Francesco - C2
Croce, Viale Benedetto - C2
De Amicis, Via E. - B3
Dini, Piazza - B2
Don G. Boschi, Via - A2
Duomo, Piazza del - A1, 2
Faggiola, Via della - A2
Fibonacci, Lung. - C3
Fucini, Via Renato - B3
Galilei, Lung. Galileo - C3
Gambacorti, Lung. - B2
Garibaldi, Via Giuseppe - B3
Giusti, Via G. - B3
Gori, Via Pietro - C2
Guerrazzi, Piazza - C3
Livornese, Via - C1
Lucchese, Via - A3
Manin, Piazza D. - A2
Martiri, Via - A2
Martiri d. Libertà, Piazza - B3
Matteotti, Via G. - C3

Mazzini, Via Giuseppe - B2, C2
Mediceo, Lung. - B3, C3
Mille, Via dei - B2
Niosi, Via Francesco - C1, 2
Notari, Via - B2
Oberdan, Via G. - B2
Paoli, Via P. - B2
Palestro, Via - B3
Pisano, Via Andrea - A1
Pisano, Via Nicola - B1
Porta Buozzi, Via - A2
Risorgimento, Via - B1
Roma, Via - A2
Rosmini, Via Antonio - A2
Saffi, Piazza A. - B2
Salvi, Via Paolo - A1
San Andrea, Via - B3
San Antonio, Via - B2, C2
San Francesco, Via - B3
San Frediano, Via - B2
San Lorenzo, Via - B3
San Martino, Via - B2
San Paolo, Via - B2
San Paolo all'Orto, Piazza - B3
San Zeno, Via - A3
Sancasciani, Via - C2
Santa Caterina, Piazza - A3
Santa Maria, Via - A2, B2
Sette Volte, Via - B2
Simone, Via Giovanni de - B3
Simonelli, Lung. R. - B1, 2
Solferino, Piazza - B1
Sonnino Sidney, Lung. - B1, C1
Stazione, Piazza della - C2
Strada Statale N12 - A3
Stretto, Borgo - B2
Tinta, Via La - C3
Toniolo, Piazza A. - C3
Torri, Via di Belle -B3
Trieste, Via - B1
Veneto, Via Vittorio - A3, B3
Vicenza, Via - B3
Vittorio Emanuele II, Piazza - C2
Volta, Via A. - B2
Volturno, Via - B1

City Wall . . . . ▬

Place of Interest and/or Entertainment . . . ▢

Parks . . . . ▢

Railway Station . . . . ▢

0   200   400 m

Pisa

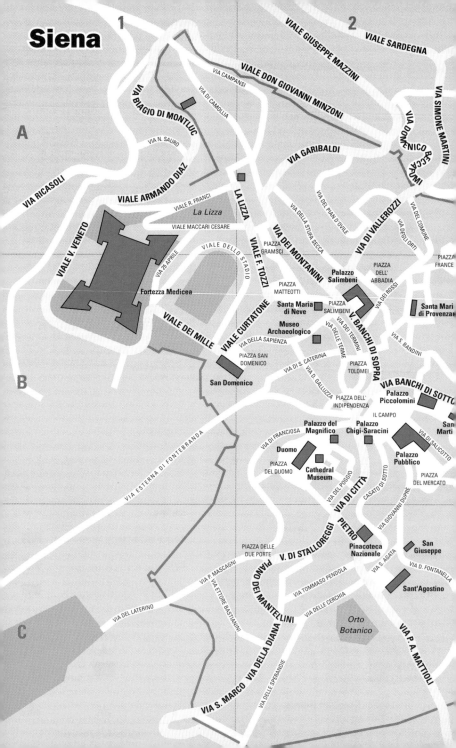

Siena

1 **2**

VIALE GIUSEPPE MAZZINI

VIALE SARDEGNA

VIA CAMPANSI

VIALE DON GIOVANNI MINZONI

VIA DI CAMOLLIA

A

VIA BIAGIO DI MONTLUC

VIA DI CAMOLLIA

VIA N. SAURO

VIA GARIBALDI

VIA SIMONE MARTINI

VIA DOMENICO BECCA...

VIA RICASOLI

VIALE ARMANDO DIAZ

VIALE R. FRANCI

LA LIZZA

VIA DEL PIAN D'OVILE

VIA DI VALLEROZZI

VIA DEL COMUNE

La Lizza

VIALE MACCARI CESARE

VIA DELLA STUFA SECCA

VIA DEGLI ORTI

VIALE V. VENETO

VIALE 25 APRILE

VIALE DELLO STADIO

VIALE F. TOZZI

PIAZZA GRAMSCI

VIA DEI MONTANINI

PIAZZA DELL' ABBADIA

PIAZZA FRANCE...

Fortezza Medicea

PIAZZA MATTEOTTI

Palazzo Salimbeni

PIAZZA SALIMBENI

VIA DEI ROSSI

Santa Maria di Provenza...

VIALE DEI MILLE

VIALE CURTATONE

Santa Maria di Neve

PIAZZA SALIMBENI

V. BANCHI DI SOPRA

VIA DEI TERMINI

VIA S. BANDINI

Museo Archaeologico

VIA DELLA SAPIENZA

VIA DELLE TERME

PIAZZA SAN DOMENICO

VIA DI S. CATERINA

PIAZZA TOLOMEI

VIA BANCHI DI SOTTO

B

San Domenico

VIA D. GALLUZZA

PIAZZA DELL' INDIPENDENZA

Palazzo Piccolomini

San Marti...

VIA ESTERNA DI FONTEBRANDA

VIA DI FRANCIOSA

Palazzo del Magnifico

Palazzo Chigi-Saracini

IL CAMPO

VIA DI SALICOTTO

Duomo

Palazzo Pubblico

PIAZZA DEL DUOMO

Cathedral Museum

VIA DEL POGGIO

VIA DI CITTA

CASATO DI SOTTO

PIAZZA DEL MERCATO

VIA GIOVANNI DUPRE

PIETRO

PIAZZA DELLE DUE PORTE

V. DI STALLOREGGI

PIANO

Pinacoteca Nazionale

San Giuseppe

VIA P. MASCAGNI

VIA ETTORE BASTIANINI

DEI MANTELLINI

VIA S. AGATA

VIA D. FONTANELLA

VIA DELLA DIANA

VIA TOMMASO PENDOLA

Sant'Agostino

VIA DEL LATERINO

VIA DELLE CERCHIA

C

VIA S. MARCO

VIA DELLE SPERANDIE

Orto Botanico

VIA P. A. MATTIOLI

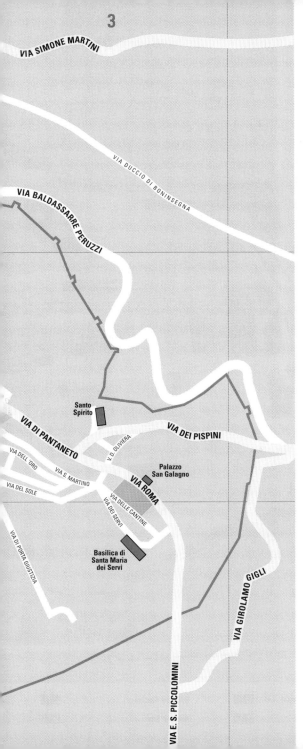

STREET INDEX

City Wall . . . .

Place of Interest . . . .

Parks . . . .

0   300 m

Lucca

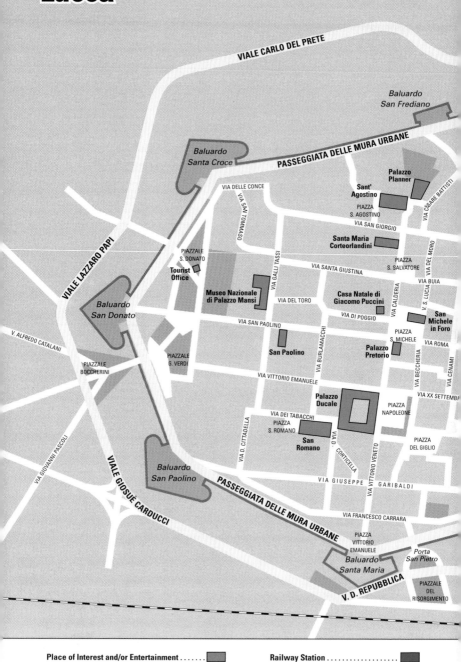

VIALE CARLO DEL PRETE

*Baluardo
San Frediano*

PASSEGGIATA DELLE MURA URBANE

*Baluardo
Santa Croce*

VIA DELLE CONCE

VIA CESARE BATTISTI

**Palazzo
Planner**

**Sant'
Agostino**

PIAZZA
S. AGOSTINO

VIA SAN TOMMASO

VIA SAN GIORGIO

**Santa Maria
Corteorlandini**

VIA DEL MORO

PIAZZALE
S. DONATO

PIAZZA
S. SALVATORE

**Tourist
Office**

VIA GALLI TASSI

VIA SANTA GIUSTINA

VIA LUCIA

VIA BUIA

VIALE LAZZARO PAPI

**Museo Nazionale
di Palazzo Mansi**

VIA DEL TORO

**Casa Natale di
Giacomo Puccini**

VIA CALDERIA

V. S. LUCIA

**San Michele
in Foro**

VIA DI POGGIO

*Baluardo
San Donato*

VIA SAN PAOLINO

VIA ROMA

PIAZZA
S. MICHELE

V. ALFREDO CATALANI

PIAZZALE
G. VERDI

San Paolino

VIA BURLAMACCHI

**Palazzo
Pretorio**

VIA BECCHERIA

VIA CENAMI

PIAZZALE
BOCCHERINI

VIA VITTORIO EMANUELE

VIA XX SETTEMBRE

**Palazzo
Ducale**

PIAZZA
NAPOLEONE

VIA DEI TABACCHI

PIAZZA
S. ROMANO

VIA D. CORTICELLA

PIAZZA
DEL GIGLIO

VIA GIOVANNI PASCOLI

VIA D. CITTADELLA

**San
Romano**

VIA GIUSEPPE GARIBALDI

VIA VITTORIO VENETO

*Baluardo
San Paolino*

PASSEGGIATA DELLE MURA URBANE

VIALE GIOSUÈ CARDUCCI

VIA FRANCESCO CARRARA

PIAZZA
VITTORIO
EMANUELE

*Porta
San Pietro*

*Baluardo
Santa Maria*

PIAZZALE
DEL
RISORGIMENTO

V. D. REPUBBLICA

Place of Interest and/or Entertainment . . . .

Parks . . . .

Railway Station . . . .

Ancient Site . . . .

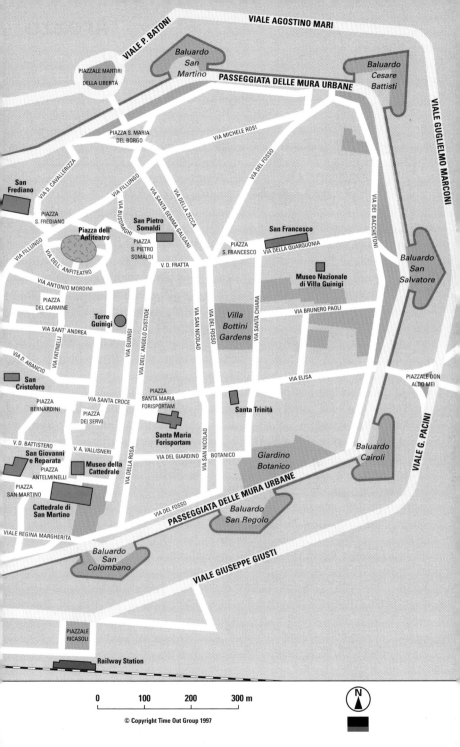

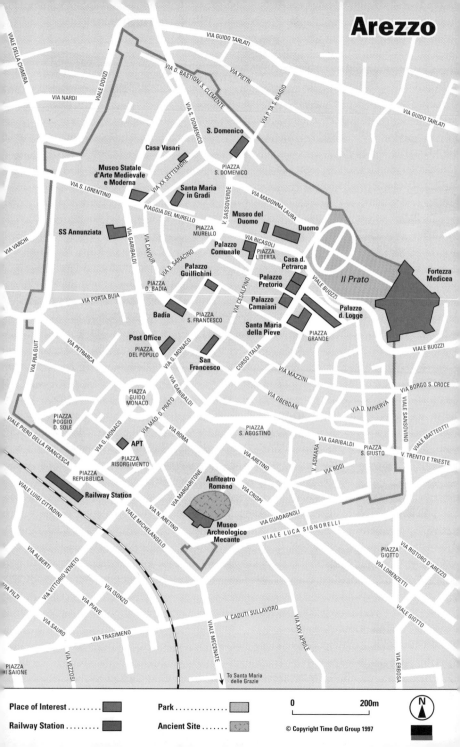

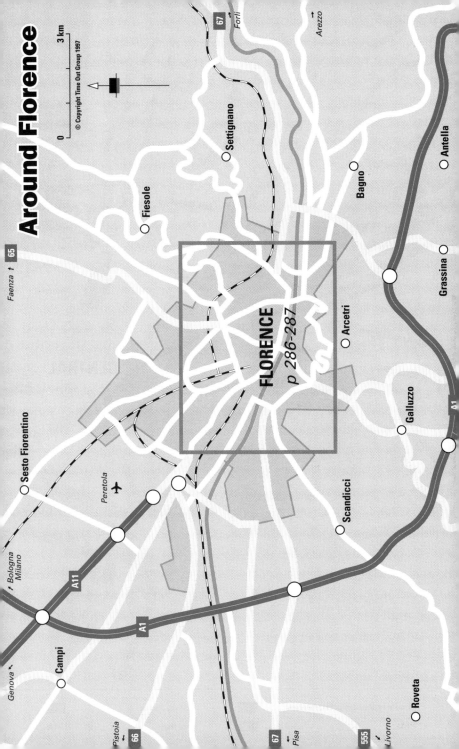

Around Florence

© Copyright Time Out Group 1997

3 km

0

Faenza ↑ **65**

67 Forlì →

↑ Arezzo

Settignano

Fiesole

Bagno

Antella

FLORENCE
p 286-287

Arcetri

Grassina

A1

Galluzzo

Sesto Fiorentino

Peretola ✈

Scandicci

Bologna
Milano ↑

A11

A1

Campi

Genova ←

Pistoia ↓ **66**

67 Pisa ↓

555

Livorno ↓

Roveta

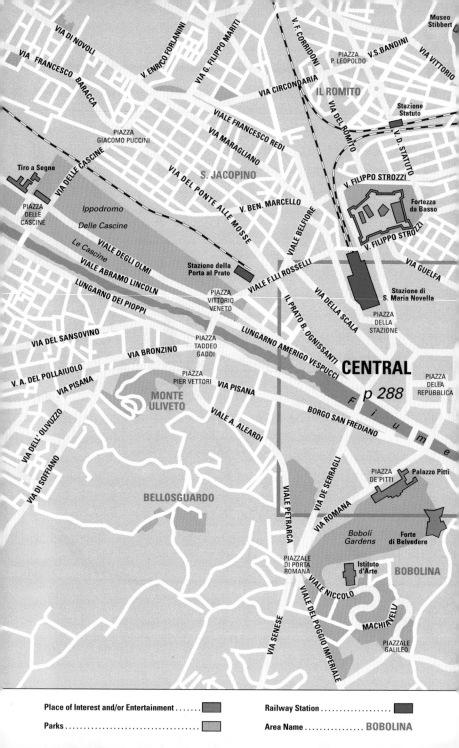

CENTRAL

p 288

Museo Stibbert

VIA DI NOVOLI

VIA FRANCESCO BARACCA

VIA ENRICO FORLANINI

V. G. FILIPPO MARITI

V. F. CORRIDONI

V. CORRIDONI

PIAZZA P. LEOPOLDO

V.S.BANDINI

VIA VITTORIO

VIA CIRCONDARIA

IL ROMITO

VIALE FRANCESCO REDI

VIA DEL ROMITO

Stazione Statuto

V. D. STATUTO

VIA MARAGLIANO

PIAZZA GIACOMO PUCCINI

Tiro a Segne

VIA DELLE CASCINE

VIA DEL PONTE ALLE MOSSE

S. JACOPINO

V. FILIPPO STROZZI

Fortezza da Basso

PIAZZA DELLE CASCINE

Ippodromo

Delle Cascine

Le Cascine

VIALE DEGLI OLMI

V. BEN. MARCELLO

VIALE BELFIORE

V. FILIPPO STROZZI

VIA GUELFA

VIALE ABRAMO LINCOLN

Stazione della Porta al Prato

VIALE F.LLI ROSSELLI

VIA DELLA SCALA

Stazione di S. Maria Novella

LUNGARNO DEI PIOPPI

PIAZZA VITTORIO VENETO

IL PRATO B. OGNISSANTI

PIAZZA DELLA STAZIONE

VIA DEL SANSOVINO

PIAZZA TADDEO GADDI

LUNGARNO AMERIGO VESPUCCI

VIA BRONZINO

PIAZZA PIER VETTORI

VIA PISANA

CENTRAL

PIAZZA DELLA REPUBBLICA

V. A. DEL POLLAIUOLO

VIA PISANA

MONTE ULIVETO

VIALE A. ALEARDI

Fiume

BORGO SAN FREDIANO

VIA DELL' OLIVUZZO

PIAZZA DE' PITTI

Palazzo Pitti

VIA DI SOFFIANO

VIALE PETRARCA

VIA DE SERRAGLI

VIA ROMANA

Boboli Gardens

Forte di Belvedere

BELLOSGUARDO

PIAZZALE DI PORTA ROMANA

Istituto d'Arte

BOBOLINA

VIALE NICCOLO

MACHIAVELLI

VIA SENESE

VIALE DEL POGGIO IMPERIALE

PIAZZALE GALILEO

Place of Interest and/or Entertainment ......

Railway Station ....

Parks ....

Area Name .... BOBOLINA

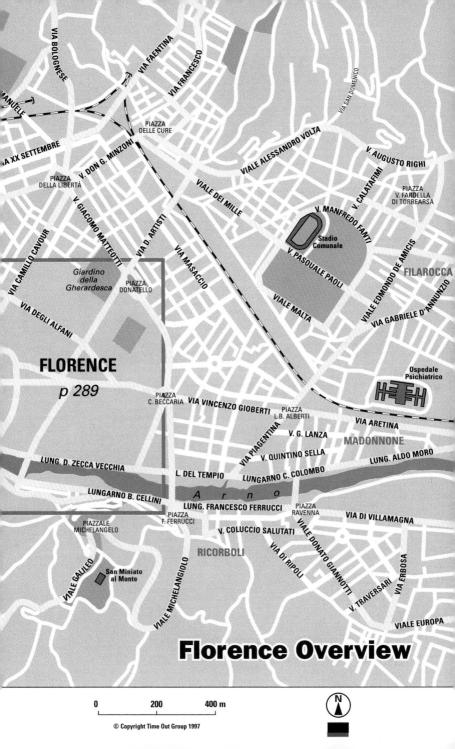

Florence Overview

VIA BOLOGNESE

VIA FAENTINA

VIA FRANCESCO

VIA SAN DOMENICO

MANUELE

PIAZZA DELLE CURE

A XX SETTEMBRE

VIALE ALESSANDRO VOLTA

V. AUGUSTO RIGHI

VIA DON G. MINZONI

PIAZZA DELLA LIBERTÀ

PIAZZA V. FARDELLA DI TORREARSA

V. CALATAFIMI

VIA GIACOMO MATTEOTTI

VIALE DEI MILLE

V. MANFREDO FANTI

Stadio Comunale

VIA CAMILLO CAVOUR

VIA D. ARTISTI

Giardino della Gherardesca

PIAZZA DONATELLO

VIA MASACCIO

V. PASQUALE PAOLI

VIALE EDMONDO DE AMICIS

FILAROCCA

VIA DEGLI ALFANI

VIALE MALTA

VIA GABRIELE D'ANNUNZIO

Ospedale Psichiatrico

FLORENCE

p 289

PIAZZA C. BECCARIA

VIA VINCENZO GIOBERTI

PIAZZA L.B. ALBERTI

VIA ARETINA

VIA PIAGENTINA

V. G. LANZA

MADONNONE

LUNG. D. ZECCA VECCHIA

V. QUINTINO SELLA

LUNG. ALDO MORO

L. DEL TEMPIO

LUNGARNO C. COLOMBO

LUNGARNO B. CELLINI

A r n o

LUNG. FRANCESCO FERRUCCI

PIAZZA RAVENNA

VIA DI VILLAMAGNA

PIAZZALE MICHELANGELO

PIAZZA F. FERRUCCI

V. COLUCCIO SALUTATI

VIALE GALILEO

San Miniato al Monte

RICORBOLI

VIALE MICHELANGIOLO

VIA DI RIPOLI

VIALE DONATO GIANNOTTI

VIA ERBOSA

V. TRAVERSARI

VIALE EUROPA

0   200   400 m

N

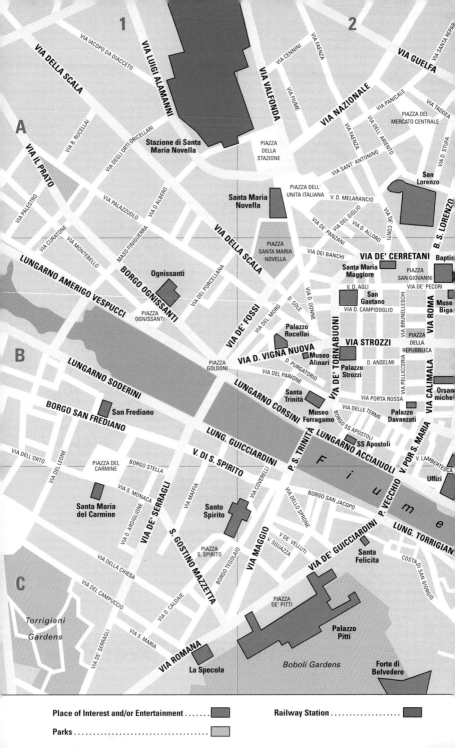

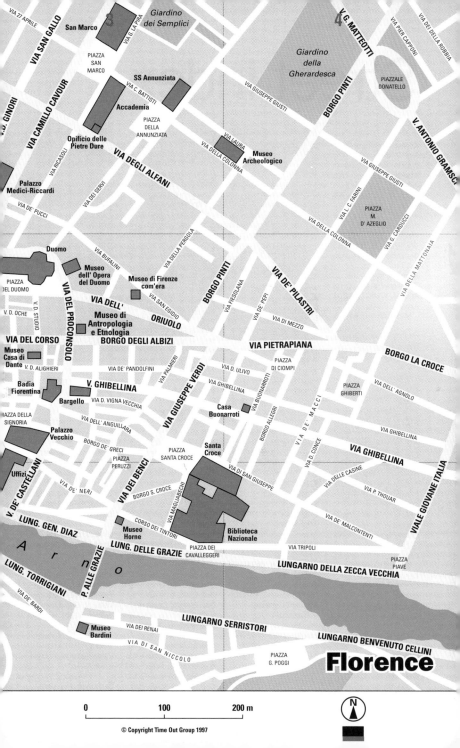

Florence

VIA 27 APRILE · VIA SAN GALLO · PIAZZA SAN MARCO · San Marco · Giardino dei Semplici · VIA G. LA PIRA · V. G. MATTEOTTI · VIA PIER CAPPONI · VIA DEI DELLA ROBBIA

Giardino della Gherardesca · BORGO PINTI · PIAZZALE DONATELLO · V. ANTONIO GRAMSCI

VIA CAMILLO CAVOUR · SS Annunziata · VIA C. BATTISTI · Accademia · PIAZZA DELLA ANNUNZIATA · VIA LAURA · VIA DELLA COLONNA · Museo Archeologico · VIA GIUSEPPE GIUSTI

V. D. GINORI · Opificio delle Pietre Dure · VIA RICASOLI · VIA DEGLI ALFANI · VIA DEI SERVI · VIA DELLA PERGOLA · VIA GIUSEPPE GIUSTI · VIA L. C. FARINI · PIAZZA M. D'AZEGLIO · VIA G. CARDUCCI · VIA DELLA MATTONAIA

Palazzo Medici-Riccardi · VIA DE' PUCCI · VIA DELLA COLONNA

Duomo · Museo dell' Opera del Duomo · Museo di Firenze com'era · VIA BUFALINI · VIA SAN EGIDIO · BORGO PINTI · VIA RESOLANA · VIA DE' PILASTRI

PIAZZA DEL DUOMO · V. D. OCHE · V. D. STUDIO · VIA DEL PROCONSOLO · VIA DELL' ORIUOLO · Museo di Antropologia e Etnologia · VIA DE' PEPI · VIA DI MEZZO

VIA DEL CORSO · BORGO DEGLI ALBIZI · VIA PIETRAPIANA · BORGO LA CROCE

Museo Casa di Dante · V. D. ALIGHIERI · VIA DE' PANDOLFINI · VIA PALMIERI · PIAZZA DI CIOMPI · PIAZZA GHIBERTI · VIA DELL' AGNOLO

Badia Fiorentina · V. GHIBELLINA · VIA D. VIGNA VECCHIA · Bargello · VIA D. ULIVO · VIA GHIBELLINA · VIA BUONARROTI · VIA GHIBELLINA

VIA GIUSEPPE VERDI · VIA DELL' ANGUILLARA · Casa Buonarroti · BORGO ALLEGRI · VIA DE' MACCI · VIA GHIBELLINA

PIAZZA DELLA SIGNORIA · Palazzo Vecchio · BORGO DE' GRECI · PIAZZA PERUZZI · PIAZZA SANTA CROCE · Santa Croce · VIA DI SAN GIUSEPPE · VIA D. CONCE · VIALE GIOVANE ITALIA

Uffizi · V. DE' CASTELLANI · VIA DE' NERI · VIA DEI BENCI · BORGO S. CROCE · VIA DELLE CASINE · VIA P. THOUAR

LUNG. GEN. DIAZ · CORSO DEI TINTORI · Museo Horne · VIA MAGLIABECHI · Biblioteca Nazionale · VIA DE' MALCONTENTI

P. ALLE GRAZIE · LUNG. DELLE GRAZIE · PIAZZA DEI CAVALLEGGERI · VIA TRIPOLI · PIAZZA PIAVE

A r n o · LUNG. TORRIGIANI · VIA DE' BARDI · LUNGARNO DELLA ZECCA VECCHIA

Museo Bardini · VIA DEI RENAI · LUNGARNO SERRISTORI · LUNGARNO BENVENUTO CELLINI

VIA DI SAN NICCOLO · PIAZZA G. POGGI

Florence

0 · 100 · 200 m

N

© Copyright Time Out Group 1997

Street Index